The Bill of Rights in the Modern State

The
Bill of Rights
in the
Modern State

Edited by

Geoffrey R. Stone
Richard A. Epstein

and

Cass R. Sunstein

The University of Chicago Press
Chicago and London

GEOFFREY R. STONE is dean of the Law School at the University
of Chicago. RICHARD A. EPSTEIN and CASS R. SUNSTEIN
are professors there.

The University of Chicago Press, Chicago 60637
The University of Chicago Press, Ltd., London
© 1992 by The University of Chicago
All rights reserved. Published 1992
Printed in the United States of America

01 00 99 98 97 96 95 94 93 92   1 2 3 4 5 6

ISBN (cloth): 0-226-77531-3
ISBN (paper): 0-226-77532-1

Library of Congress Cataloging-in-Publication Data

The Bill of Rights in the modern state / edited by Geoffrey R. Stone,
Richard A. Epstein, and Cass R. Sunstein.
   p. cm.
   Papers presented at a symposium held Oct. 25–26, 1991 at the
University of Chicago Law School.
   Includes bibliographical references and index.
   1. United States—Constitutional law—Amendments—
1st–10th—Congresses. 2. Civil rights—United States—
Congresses. 3. Welfare state—Congresses. I. Stone, Geoffrey R.
II. Epstein, Richard Allen, 1943– . III. Sunstein, Cass R.
KF4749.A2B555 1992
342.73′085—dc20
[347.30285]   92-9397
                                          CIP

ACKNOWLEDGMENT

We regard it as a privilege to acknowledge the important contribution to the success of this volume that has been made by the editors of the *University of Chicago Law Review* during the 1991–1992 academic year.

In 1987, the University of Chicago Law School received a generous grant from the Robert J. Kutak Foundation for a conference on the theme, The Bill of Rights in the Welfare State: A Bicentennial Symposium, which was held at the University of Chicago Law School on October 25–26, 1991. Once the grant was received, the three editors organized the program, invited speakers to participate in the conference, and discussed with them their topics in order to insure that the participants to each exchange joined issue on a topic of genuine importance. At the completion of the conference, the long and difficult job of editing the papers for style and content, of checking quotations and footnotes, and of preparing the entire project for publication was undertaken by the *University of Chicago Law Review* and its staff. The fruit of their labors is found in Volume 59, Number 1 of the *Law Review,* which appeared in the winter of 1992.

We would like to thank especially Dale Carpenter, the Editor-in-Chief of the *Law Review,* Donna Maus, the executive editor, and Nathan Forrestor and Kate Silbaugh, the articles editors of the *Review,* for their enlightened and ceaseless efforts in rounding out a series of drafts into the finished papers that are presented here. We should also like to thank the entire staff of the *Law Review* for undertaking and discharging so ably the many technical and often tedious tasks needed for bringing out a volume as large and comprehensive as this one is. This volume, which bears our names as editors, is as much the work of the *University of Chicago Law Review* as it is of our own labor.

Chicago, Illinois   Richard A. Epstein
May 27, 1992   Geoffrey R. Stone
                                                     Cass R. Sunstein

CONTENTS

To P.B.K. for Four Decades

Gerhard Casper†

The Supreme Court Review, founded by Phil Kurland, began publication in 1960. Phil dedicated the first two volumes to the Justices of the Supreme Court. As is so frequently the case with Phil, he was both ironic and serious when he added to the dedication the formula "May It Please the Court." Starting with the 1962 volume, first Phil and, then, his collaborators and successors expressed their affection and admiration for family members and a few friends by presenting them with "their" volume of the *Review*. In 1962, at the occasion of Justice Frankfurter's retirement from the Court, Phil inscribed that year's volume to Frankfurter, for whom Phil had clerked in 1945-46. When Dennis Hutchinson and I, in 1989, were looking for words to fit Phil, who had resigned his editorship in order to be relieved of its burdens, we had an easy

† Provost, The University of Chicago.

1

time agreeing on the very quotation Phil had chosen to capture what to him were essential qualities of Felix Frankfurter: ". . . a truly civilized man . . . confiden[t] in the strength and security derived from the inquiring mind . . . unafraid of the uncertitudes." And, if I may be permitted to travel down this road a little further, there is one other dedication that strikes me as particularly befitting Phil himself. Phil chose the text to accompany the 1987 inscription to Paul Freund: "Who embodies law's mission 'to impose a measure of order on the disorder of experience without stifling the underlying diversity, spontaneity and disarray.' " May it please Phil.

Few constitutional scholars of this century have as consistently as Phil Kurland thought about and worried about the Constitution as a complex system that cannot be reduced to one of its components. Majority rule, separation of powers between the national government and the states, separation of powers within the national government, the system of checks and balances, the Bill of Rights, and, last but not least, the independence of the judiciary, he has never viewed as separate topics that can be treated in isolation, but as the Framers' interdependent devices for the restraint of brute power, however disguised, and the minimization of force. It is therefore especially appropriate that the editors of *The University of Chicago Law Review* have decided to dedicate this particular issue to Phil Kurland on the occasion of his seventieth birthday. I know of no other conference to celebrate the bicentennial of the Bill of Rights whose contributions match those that follow in their focus on governance in the modern state.

Few constitutional scholars of this century have as consistently as Phil Kurland thought about the Constitution as posing issues about the relationship between law and reason. Phil Kurland as a scholar has therefore never been satisfied with the merely legal dimension of constitutional questions. At the University Phil is rightly seen as at home in many disciplines. He has led an intensely interdisciplinary existence because for him the law is an intellectual discipline. Again, it is therefore especially appropriate that this particular issue of the *Law Review* be dedicated to him given the conference participants' wide-ranging concern for the contributions of other fields to our understanding of the role and limits of constitutional law.

Phil came to The Law School from the Northwestern faculty in 1953, allegedly because Dean Levi had promised him that he never again would have to teach commercial law. His career at the University has been distinguished indeed and has been so recognized formally by the University through the attribute "distinguished service" in the name of the William R. Kenan, Jr. Professorship that he has occupied. A graduate of the Harvard Law School, he clerked for two of the greatest judges this country has had: one—Jerome Frank—a graduate of this school; the other, as mentioned, Felix Frankfurter. Born in Brooklyn, Phil practiced law in New York City before he turned to teaching and scholarship. His writings have been wide ranging and influential. Among his books are *Religion and the Law* (1962), *Politics, the Constitution, and the Warren Court* (1970), *Mr. Justice Frankfurter and the Constitution* (1971), *Watergate and the Constitution* (1978), and *The Founder's Constitution* (with Ralph Lerner, 1986). To his own scholarship we must add what he has contributed as editor of *The Supreme Court Review* to the work of others. Phil established a pattern of excellence in "sustained, disinterested, and competent criticism of the professional qualities of the Court's opinions" that has remained unmatched. His editorship displayed to the fullest how "unafraid of the uncertitudes" he is and what strength he derives "from the inquiring mind."

Phil's qualities of mind and judgment have been widely acknowledged. For seven years he served as chief consultant to Senator Ervin's subcommittee on separation of powers of the Senate Judiciary Committee. He is a Fellow of the American Academy of Art and Sciences and a member of the American Law Institute, a recipient of the Research Award of the Fellows of the American Bar Foundation, the Gordon J. Laing Prize of The University of Chicago Press, and the University's Llewellyn John and Harriet Manchester Quantrell Award for Excellence in Undergraduate Teaching. Phil himself, if given a chance, refers to honors he has as "second orders of chastity" and makes light of what has been well deserved.

Phil and his wife, Mary Jane Kurland, have been among the most dedicated members of the University community, in hard times as well as good times. Some of these times have been trying, and sometimes Phil has been trying, as we worried about the state of this university, and American universities in general. Charles Wegener, his colleague in the New Collegiate Division, summed it up some years ago:

> In the University Kurland enjoys a very special position not by the assiduous practice of academic politics or by occupying posts of power but by a passionate devotion to the University as an intellectual community and a most uncommon understanding of the commitments entailed by that devotion.

Mary Jane and Phil have been exemplary citizens of The University of Chicago, never self-seeking, always ready to help in the best traditions of public service. They have extended their great capacity for friendship and affection to students, colleagues, and collaborators, to old neighbors and new arrivals. They have even listened to deans, provosts, and presidents of the University vent their frustrations and disappointments in private. Those who have been the beneficiaries of their friendship cherish it.

Phil is very fond of quoting—not as a display of learnedness, but to honor those who have said it before, and, in this case, only very occasionally better. I may therefore be permitted to conclude by quoting Phil Kurland quoting, in a tribute to Felix Frankfurter, Learned Hand speaking about Louis Brandeis:

> He believed that there could be no true community save that built upon the personal acquaintance of each with each; by that alone could character and ability be rightly gauged; without that "neighborly affection" which would result no "faith" could be nourished, "charitable" or other. Only so could the latent richness which lurks in all of us come to flower.

Phil and Mary Jane have brought latent richness to flower and nourished a faith, secular and fragile as it may be. For that their "neighbors" must, and, perhaps, do indeed thank them.

In Memoriam: M.J.K.

In 1978 Phil and I dedicated the *Supreme Court Review* to our wives, Mary Jane and Regina. As our text we chose the opening lines of Bertolt Brecht's "A Song About the Good People": "The good people one knows by their becoming better as one knows them." Mary Jane Kurland died on March 7, 1992, of cancer, leaving in tears all her friends who knew how good she was. She had seen the draft of this dedication just before her final stay in the hospital. She understood that the last two paragraphs were meant for her as much as for Phil.

The Bill of Rights in the Welfare State: A Bicentennial Symposium

Geoffrey R. Stone†

The essays presented in this volume were prepared in connection with a Symposium on "The Bill of Rights in the Welfare State," which was held at The University of Chicago Law School on October 25-26, 1991. This Symposium celebrated both the Bicentennial of the Bill of Rights and the Centennial of The University of Chicago. In addition to those whose essays appear herein, we also enjoyed the participation of Vincent Blasi, Stephen Carter, Thomas Grey, Margaret Jane Radin, and Carol Rose, who served brilliantly as moderators of the five substantive debates. One might say that this Symposium assembled the most talented collection of constitutional theorists since the Framers themselves met in Constitutional Convention, or, to paraphrase John F. Kennedy's quip about Jefferson, since James Madison dined alone.

Madison was, of course, the framer, the architect of the Bill of Rights. But he himself was less than confident that his list of guarantees would make a difference. As Madison wrote to Jefferson in 1788, "experience proves the inefficacy of a Bill of Rights on those occasions when its control is most needed," offering as illustration "repeated violations of these parchment barriers . . . committed by overbearing majorities" whenever circumstances allow.

Nonetheless, when Madison presented his proposed bill to Congress, he offered two arguments for the proposition, or at least the hope, that the Bill of Rights would matter. First, Madison predicted that his list of guarantees would be treasured by the judicia-

---

† Harry Kalven, Jr., Professor of Law and Dean, The University of Chicago.

ry, that those "independent tribunals of justice would consider themselves . . . the guardians of these Rights," and that the courts would serve as "an impenetrable bulwark against every [unwarranted] assumption of power." What Edmund Burke believed about a free people, Madison believed about the courts—that they would "sniff the approach of tyranny in every tainted breeze" and that they would "be naturally led to resist every encroachment upon rights expressly stipulated for in the Constitution." Second, Madison believed that the enactment of a Bill of Rights would serve an essential educational function in a self-governing society, predicting that "the political truths declared" in the Bill of Rights would "acquire . . . the character of fundamental maxims of free government" and, as they became "incorporated with the national sentiment, [would] counteract the principles of interest and passion."

It is noteworthy that one hundred years ago there were few, if any, celebrations of the Centennial of our Bill of Rights, whereas today, we have been inundated with seemingly endless conferences, symposia, and debates celebrating its Bicentennial. This is so because, in its first hundred years, the Bill of Rights played only a minor role in our constitutional system and our national consciousness. It was not until the Supreme Court's incorporation decisions of the 1930s and 1940s, and the consequent extension of the Bill of Rights to the states, that Madison's guarantees finally emerged as a central and defining theme of our national life. Thus, in a very real sense, the Bill of Rights that we celebrate today is as much the product of the judicial doctrine of incorporation as it is of the foresight and wisdom of the Framers themselves.

This Symposium would not have taken place, and these papers would not now be available, but for the foresight, the wisdom, and the very gracious generosity of the Robert J. Kutak Foundation, which provided essential financial support. We are deeply grateful to the Foundation's inspired and enlightened philanthropy.

At the time that The University of Chicago was founded, William Rainey Harper, its first president, explained that "although many will deny that democracy has a religion," none "will deny that democracy has a philosopher—the university," he said, "is the philosopher of democracy." To fulfill this vision of our University, we offer this volume, which we hope will illumine some of the most important constitutional issues of our day.

The True Wisdom of the Bill of Rights

Philip B. Kurland†

When The University of Chicago marked its centennial at the same time that the nation's Bill of Rights was reaching its bicentennial, the Law School held a two-day commemorative symposium and dinner featuring Justice John Paul Stevens, one of the current keepers of the sacred flame: mind, I did not say Vestal Virgin. This introduction to the papers delivered during the symposium is an act of supererogation. "If it be true that 'good wine needs no bush,' 'tis true that a good play needs no epilogue."[1] And it is equally true that a good symposium needs no introduction. Just as the reader of Shakespeare's *As You Like It* can eschew the epilogue, so, too, can the reader of the symposium ignore the introduction, with which listeners to the symposium were not burdened. But having been given the opportunity to add my prejudices, cultivated over long decades, I offer a few banalities, in the hopes that some moderns will consider them truisms even if others may regard them as heresies.

As "every schoolboy knows,"[2] the American Constitution, like all Gaul, is made of three elements. The first creates the structure and authority of a republican form of government. The second provides a division of powers among the various parts of the national

---

† William R. Kenan, Jr., Distinguished Service Professor (Emeritus), New Collegiate Division, The University of Chicago, and The Law School. This introduction was prepared for *The Bill of Rights in the Welfare State: A Bicentennial Symposium*, held at The University of Chicago Law School on October 25-26, 1991.

[1] William Shakespeare, *As You Like It* (epilogue), in *The Oxford Dictionary of Quotations* 427 (Oxford, 3d ed 1979).

[2] "How haughtily he cocks his nose, To tell what every schoolboy knows." Jonathan Swift, *The Country Life*, in id at 527.

government—grossly labelled "separation of powers," which suggests monopolies but is really concerned with checks and balances, i.e., with shared powers rather than unification. And the third inhibits government power vis-à-vis the rights of individuals, rights existent and potential, patent and latent. One prime objective of each of the three parts was the liberty of the people.

It is error, although error more and more sought to be justified by academic theory, that the Constitution represents a single, cohesive theory to be found in Locke or Machiavelli or Rousseau or whomever the chosen swami may be. In fact, the Constitution was a series of pragmatic responses to a series of practical problems, as have been the Supreme Court decisions under it in the intervening centuries, however much within the perimeters of the Constitution's language.

If there had been an academic celebration of the centennial of the Bill of Rights, I expect that the "scholars" of a century ago would have been a good deal more circumspect than those of today. It was within the lifetimes of some professors not yet *emeriti* that Learned Hand observed the distinction between a Luther and an Erasmus:

> You may take Martin Luther or Erasmus for your model, but you cannot play both roles at once; you may not carry a sword beneath a scholar's gown, lead flaming causes from a cloister, Luther cannot be domesticated in a university. You cannot raise a standard against oppression, or leap into the breach to relieve injustice, and still keep an open mind to every disconcerting fact, or an open ear to the cold voice of doubt. I am satisfied that a scholar who tries to combine these parts sells his birthright for a mess of pottage; that when the final count is made, it will be found that the impairment of his powers far outweighs any possible contribution to the causes he has espoused. If he is fit to serve his calling at all, it is only because he has learned not to serve in any other, for his singleness of mind quickly evaporates in the fires of passions, however holy.[3]

You can, however, be true to scholarship and recognize that the Constitution is *not* a catalogue of rights and powers and duties. The "rights of Englishmen," some of which are stated in "the Bill of Rights," were not granted by the Constitution of 1789, just as

---

[3] Learned Hand, *On Receiving an Honorary Degree*, in Irving Dilliard, ed, *The Spirit of Liberty* 138 (Phoenix, 3d ed 1960).

the right to the writ of habeas corpus, often designated our most fundamental civil right, was not granted by the Constitution. True, some rights were specifically guaranteed by the Constitution. But from the beginning of our history, the rights guaranteed in terms by the Constitution have not been static. Some were not recognized at the "birth of the nation," in the language that we now know them, like the right to privacy and the right to freedom of religion. All were to be defined and redefined over time. The reality of our constitutional rights depended not on their identity over time, but on their continuity over time. The rule of today may be shown to have derived from the rule of yesterday, and the change is explainable by reason. Our future, like our present, is anchored in our past.

When today's constitutional rules are not dependent upon, or derived from, yesterday's, when they are not to be justified by reason but merely by fiat or personal prejudice, then the rule of law implicit in "due process" is gone. There are times when changes are made by fiat, thought to be demanded by circumstances, although not explicated by them. These instances must be few and far between, if we are to survive as a republic and a democracy. It is the Constitution that is the symbol of the uniqueness of this Nation, and the pith of that symbol—the Bill of Rights, however defined—ideally rejects the notions of arbitrary government. We pour into it, and therefore take out of it, an entire people's guide to what we need "to grow more civilized," a slow, painful, costly and always difficult choice.

In common parlance, the first Ten Amendments are "The Bill of Rights," the bicentennial of which we celebrated in December of 1991 on the two-hundredth anniversary of Virginia's ratification. But it was asserted by Hamilton in Federalist No. 84 that the entire Constitution was a Bill of Rights:

> The truth is, after all the declamations we have heard, that the Constitution is itself, in every rational sense, and to every useful purpose, A BILL OF RIGHTS. The several bills of rights in Great Britain form its Constitution, and conversely the constitution of each State is its bill of rights. And the proposed Constitution, if adopted, will be the bill of rights of the Union.[4]

---

[4] Federalist 84 (Hamilton) in Clinton Rossiter, ed, *The Federalist Papers* 510, 515 (Mentor, 1961) (emphasis in original).

In the end, the body of the Constitution did provide for trial by jury in criminal cases, did provide for trial in the vicinage, and did afford a definition of treason while limiting its sanction. Provision was made against ex post facto laws and bills of attainder; and, finally, provision was made that the mother writ of all civil liberty—habeas corpus—should "not be suspended, unless when in Cases of Rebellion or Invasion the public Safety may require it."[5]

And so the third kind of constitutional provision afforded protection for the individual against the iniquities of government—particular iniquities, to be sure, that the Americans of 1789 and their English forebears had already suffered, and for most of which they had found some specific protection through the workings of the common law.

It was about a half-century ago that the principles of the American Bill of Rights enjoyed a renaissance—perhaps "naissance" would be more apt—in this nation. In Europe and Asia it had been demonstrated that tyrants could successfully manage societies in which a person lives without rights against government, where any individual's life, liberty, and property are destructable at the whim of officials. Only in the United States and England, and to a lesser extent in France, did "freedom" have substantial roots. And these roots, like the lesser ones planted by the "War to End All Wars," had been all but extirpated by deep economic depression, by a morbid fear that "socialism" was more of a threat to freedom than the serfdom of a medieval monarchy, by the paranoia labelled by Sinclair Lewis: "It Can't Happen Here." The United States was faced with the realization that its own form of racism was no more rational than Nazism, if usually less official.

The consequence of this realization was the growth of the Bill of Rights through the incorporation of their essence against the States. I suppose it must be acknowledged that this growth began in the Hughes Court, when Benjamin Cardozo wrote the decision in *Palko v Connecticut*[6] for the Court. When the Court deals with concepts such as liberty, it is giving itself extensive authority to oversee actions of the other two national branches of government and of the states toward individuals.

Cardozo's opinion in *Palko* was articulated, it will be noted, not in terms of literary construction, but in the larger vagary of "logical imperatives":

---

[5] US Const, Art I, § 9, cl 2.
[6] 302 US 319 (1937).

So it has come about that the domain of liberty withdrawn by the Fourteenth Amendment from encroachments by the states has been enlarged by latter-day judgments to include liberty of the mind as well as liberty of action. The extension indeed, became a logical imperative when once it was recognized, as long ago it was, that liberty is something more than exemption from physical restraint, and even in the field of substantive rights and duties the legislative judgment, if oppressive and arbitrary, may be overridden by the courts.[7]

But this rejection of logic-chopping in favor of comprehension of purpose and function has long been recognized, as Holmes's familiar words in *Gompers* remind us:

[T]he provisions of the Constitution are not mathematical formulas having their essence in their form; they are organic living institutions transplanted from English soil. Their significance is vital not formal; it is to be gathered not simply by taking words and a dictionary, but by considering their origin and the line of their growth.[8]

To conclude, I suppose that what I want to say is really reducible to three observations:

First, the rights guaranteed by the Constitution in the Bill of Rights and in other places in the text require construction and do not involve merely the application of a fixed rule to a fixed fact. The significance of the facts and the function of the rule in the circumstances is dependent on the wisdom of the judgment of those charged with the adjudication. Our legal system is based on a different notion of reasoning than our sciences; it is inductive rather than deductive, which makes knowledge of the past so much more indispensable to the present and the future. This wisdom required of a Supreme Court Justice, alas, is not a subject communicable in the classroom, if communicable at all.

Second, the restraints of the Constitution are directed to the government and not to the individuals who are the governed.[9] Thus the Constitution is a different order of law. True, individual freedom is more at risk from government behavior than from the

---

[7] Id at 327.

[8] *Gompers v United States*, 233 US 604, 610 (1914).

[9] The exception is, of course, the Thirteenth Amendment, which applies to both individuals and the government: "Neither slavery nor involuntary servitude, except as a punishment for crime whereof the party shall have been duly convicted, shall exist within the United States, or any place subject to their jurisdiction." US Const, Amend XIII, § 1.

behavior of other individuals, but this in part is dependent on government fulfilling its function of protecting individuals from impositions by other individuals. A person's life, liberty, and property are at risk from both private and public force, if in different degrees, and so the judicial task must encompass protections of a nonconstitutional order as well.

Third, the "liberty" that the Bill of Rights and cognate provisions in other parts of the Constitution protect is essentially the liberty to be different. It is here that the two centennial celebrations overlap, in their commitment to diversity, in their recognition that conformity and uniformity are denials of the essence of human personality. At the opening dinner of The University of Chicago's Centennial Celebration, Milton Friedman made the point thus:

> "Why was one university so productive?"—asked economist Milton Friedman, AM, '33, one of the two U of C Nobelists who addressed the assembled diners. "In order to be a rich seedbed for new development, you do have to have a respect for diversity and a respect for innovation."[10]

Judge Learned Hand, himself born twenty years before the University, put it a little differently:

> Because once you get people believing that there is an authoritative well of wisdom to which they can turn for absolutes, you have dried up the springs on which they must in the end draw even for the things of this world. As soon as we cease to pry about at random, we shall come to rely on accredited bodies of authoritative dogma; and as soon as we come to rely upon accredited bodies of authoritative dogma, not only are the days of our Liberty over, but we have lost the password that has hitherto opened to us the gates of success as well.[11]

There never has been more uniformity of interpretation of the language of the Bill of Rights than there has been a demonstrated singlemindedness of decision by the Justices of the Supreme Court. It will be too late for the Bill of Rights to fulfill its functions if the Court begins to speak with but one voice, for then it is not likely to be a judicial voice but a political one.

---

[10] Mary Ruth Yoe, *Pomp Meets Circumstance*, U Chi Mag 26, 30 (Dec 1991).
[11] Learned Hand, *Liberty*, in Dilliard, ed, *The Spirit of Liberty* at 153 (cited in note 3).

The Bill of Rights: A Century of Progress

John Paul Stevens†

In an otherwise mundane tax opinion construing language in the Internal Revenue Code, Oliver Wendell Holmes observed that "a word . . . is the skin of a living thought."[1] As the years pass, an idea may mature, changing its shape, its power, and its complexion, even while the symbols that identify it remain constant. There is a special vitality in words like "commerce," "equality," and "liberty."

In southwestern England, the huge sarsen pillars that primitive astronomers erected and arranged at Stonehenge centuries ago convey a profound message about man's ability to reason and to create. Even though the intent of the framers of Stonehenge is shrouded in mystery and obscurity, their message is nevertheless majestic and inspiring. Only a few miles away, the highest church spire in England, the Salisbury Cathedral, stands as a symbol of the creativity, the industry, and the faith of the Christian architects and engineers of the thirteenth century. A visitor to that cathedral may view one of the four remaining copies of a famous document that was signed at Runnymede early in that century.

The message to be found in the text of the Magna Carta is neither clear nor unambiguous because its language is not plain and its style and lettering are unfamiliar. It is, nevertheless, an im-

---

† Associate Justice, Supreme Court of the United States. This Article is the text of the keynote address delivered on October 25, 1991 at *The Bill of Rights in the Welfare State: A Bicentennial Symposium*, held at The University of Chicago Law School on October 25-26, 1991. I am indebted to Nancy Marder, not only for her valuable work as a law clerk for the past year, but also for supplying the footnotes and editing the text of these remarks.

[1] *Towne v Eisner*, 245 US 418, 425 (1918).

13

portant symbol because it constitutes evidence that a once power-ful ruler, King John, promised a group of his subjects that the oc-cupant of the throne of England would thereafter obey "the law of the land."[2]

The significance of King John's promise has been anything but constant. In the two centuries after it was made, one English king after another deposed his predecessor by means that violated the law of the land. Although Henry VII was crowned after his victory at the Battle of Bosworth on August 22, 1485, he established Au-gust 21 as the date when he had become king, thus retroactively condemning his former adversaries as traitors because they had fought to defend the then-recognized occupant of the throne.[3] In the late sixteenth century, when the greatest author of all time dramatized the life of King John, he did not even mention the Magna Carta.[4] Today, at least in America, the reign of King John is remembered because of that document. In Elizabethan England, however, that great symbol had either been forgotten, or at least was not viewed with any special favor by the most popular spokes-man for the establishment.

I.

Today we focus our attention on another great symbol—a promise made 200 years ago that the newly-created federal sover-eign would obey the law in this land. That promise has surely not been forgotten, but its meaning has changed dramatically during the two centuries of its life. To emphasize the importance and the character of that change, I have entitled my remarks: *The Bill of Rights: A Century of Progress*. Because you may wonder why I re-fer to only one century, and why I refer to "progress," I shall begin with a comment on my title.

This important conference is a tribute to Chicago and to this great university. I am proud to be one of its graduates and to have taught briefly in its law school. The University of Chicago is now 100 years old. Its participation in the development of American ed-ucation—and more particularly legal education—unquestionably

---

[2] "By that instrument, the King, representing the sovereignty of the nation, pledged that 'no freeman shall be taken, or imprisoned, or be disseized of his freehold, or liberties, or free customs, or be outlawed, or exiled, or any otherwise destroyed; nor will we [not] pass upon him, nor condemn him, but by lawful judgment of his peers, or by the law of the land.'" *Hurtado v California*, 110 US 516, 542 (1884).

[3] Rosemary Horrox, *Richard III* 317, 327 (Cambridge, 1989); S. B. Chrimes, *Henry VII* 50, 63 (California, 1972); Thomas B. Costain, *The Last Plantagenets* 384 (Doubleday, 1962).

[4] William Shakespeare, *King John* (Bantam, 1988).

merits characterization as "A Century of Progress." Just two years after the founding of the University, the Midway which adjoins this campus was the location of the famous amusement park in the 1893 World's Fair where Little Egypt became famous for her erotic dancing. Forty years later, in 1933, the City of Chicago celebrated its 100th anniversary by sponsoring another enormously successful World's Fair, which also brought fame to a nude dancer named Sally Rand. Whether the First Amendment protects performances like Rand's is a question that two illustrious Chicago professors, who also wear judicial robes, recently debated in a case that I believe was correctly decided by the Court of Appeals for the Seventh Circuit[5] and incorrectly decided by a confused and fractured majority of the Supreme Court of the United States.[6]

1933 was a year in which this city—indeed the entire western world—was in the throes of a severe economic depression. Adolf Hitler came to power in 1933 and book-burning became fashionable in Nazi Germany. Chicago was then known throughout the world as the home of Al Capone, the master of organized crime who had made millions during the federal government's war on alcoholic beverages. At that time, less prosperous criminals were sometimes treated brutally by Chicago police officers seeking confessions of guilt.[7] 1933 was the year in which the city's mayor was killed in an attempt to assassinate President Roosevelt. Before the Fair opened, there were many reasons to be pessimistic about Chicago. Nevertheless, the Fair was appropriately given a name that focused on the positive and inspired Chicagoans to build for a glorious future. The Fair was named "A Century of Progress."

My selection of a title for this address reflects more than a nostalgic memory of that World's Fair. It was motivated, in part, by the fact that 1991 is a year in which an occasional echo of 1933 has sounded an alarming note. A volatile stock market, an ever-escalating deficit, and disturbing reports of mismanagement of major financial institutions remind us that in 1991—as in 1933—risk

---

[5] *Miller v Civil City of South Bend*, 904 F2d 1081, 1089 (7th Cir 1990) (en banc); (Posner concurring in the opinion and judgment of the court) (dance is expressive and therefore should be protected under the First Amendment); id at 1120 (Easterbrook dissenting) (Indiana law regulates public nudity, which is conduct, not speech, and therefore does not violate the First Amendment).

[6] *Barnes v Glen Theatre, Inc.*, 111 S Ct 2456 (1991) (statute requiring dancers to wear pasties and G-strings does not violate First Amendment). *Barnes* was a 5-4 decision, in which Chief Justice Rehnquist was joined by Justice O'Connor and Justice Kennedy. Justice Scalia and Justice Souter each filed separate opinions concurring in the judgment.

[7] See, for example, *People v LaFrana*, 4 Ill 2d 261, 265, 122 NE2d 583 (1954).

is a characteristic of a free economy. The stagnation of the Soviet economy—reminiscent of Germany in 1933—furnished the setting for the attempted coup by the KGB and the military that for a brief moment produced frightening memories of Hitler's rise to power and the ruthless behavior of his Gestapo. In Great Britain, 1991 is a year in which the re-examination of the convictions of alleged Irish terrorists has reminded us that trusted police officers sometimes fabricate confessions to obtain convictions.[8]

In this country, while dozens of universities and communities throughout the land are celebrating the bicentennial of the Bill of Rights, an extraordinarily aggressive Supreme Court has reached out to announce a host of new rules narrowing the federal Constitution's protection of individual liberties. The prosecutor's use of a coerced confession—no matter how vicious the police conduct may have been—may now constitute harmless error.[9] In a totally un-

---

[8] *Regina v McIlkenny*, 141 NLJ 456 (1991) (police fabricated confessions and relied on faulty forensic tests in case of alleged Irish Republican Army (IRA) terrorists known as the Birmingham Six). Earlier, in 1989, it also came to light that the police had fabricated interview notes to secure the conviction of other alleged IRA terrorists known as the Guildford Four. See *Regina v Richardson*, The Times (London) 33J (Oct 20, 1989).

These and similar cases have "badly shaken" the British courts, and have led the government to set up a Royal Commission to study the criminal justice system in order " 'to minimize as far as possible the likelihood of such events happening again.' " William E. Schmidt, *British Court to Review 1974 Bombing Case*, NY Times A4 (Sep 18, 1991). The ten-person commission, whose members include prominent academics, journalists, and businessmen, represent " 'a wide range of experience.' " Jonathan Ames, *Commission Line-up Welcomed*, 88 Law Society's Guardian Gazette 4 (May 22, 1991). The commission will examine "all stages of the criminal process" and will consider "the investigation and pre-trial process including the conduct of the police investigations and their supervision, the right to silence, the role of the prosecutor in obtaining evidence and deciding whether to proceed with a case and arrangements for disclosing material to the defence." Marion McKeone, *Lawyers Urge Interim Criminal Justice Reforms*, 88 Law Society's Gazette 7 (Mar 20, 1991). The goal of the commission is nothing short of reform of the criminal justice system.

[9] *Arizona v Fulminante*, 111 S Ct 1246 (1991). The Supreme Court affirmed the judgment of the Arizona Supreme Court, which had held that Fulminante's confessions were coerced and that harmless error analysis did not apply. On the one hand, three of the four members of the Court who voted to reverse concluded that no error had occurred because the confessions were not coerced; accordingly, they had no need to reach the harmless error issue. On the other hand, because it was clear to the five members of the majority who voted to affirm that the introduction of the confessions had not been harmless, there was no need for them to re-examine the settled rule that the use of a coerced confession requires automatic reversal. Only the vote of Justice Scalia, who agreed that the confessions were coerced but thought that their admission was harmless, depended on the answer to the question whether harmless error analysis applies to coerced confessions.

As a result of the Court's decision in *Fulminante*, state supreme courts must now look to their state constitutions to hold that "a coerced confession may so infect the trial process that its admission into evidence demands reversal" and that the admission of a coerced confession is not subject to harmless error analysis. *Iowa v Quintero*, 60 USLW 2165 (Iowa Ct App, Sep 17, 1991) (en banc).

necessary and unprecedented decision, the Court placed its stamp of approval on the use of victim impact evidence to facilitate the imposition of the death penalty.[10] The Court condoned the use of mandatory sentences that are manifestly and grossly disproportionate to the moral guilt of the offender.[11] It broadened the powers of the police to invade the privacy of individual citizens,[12] and even to detain them without any finding of probable cause[13] or reasonable suspicion.[14] In perhaps its most blatant exercise of lawmaking power marching under the banner of federalism, the Court completely rewrote the procedural rules governing post-conviction

---

[10] *Payne v Tennessee*, 111 S Ct 2597 (1991). Here, as in *Fulminante*, the Court reached out to address an issue that it need not have considered. In *Payne*, the Court ordered the parties to brief and argue whether *Booth v Maryland*, 482 US 496 (1987), and *South Carolina v Gathers*, 490 US 805 (1989), should be overruled. 111 S Ct 1407 (1991). As the Court's order indicates, this was an issue that was not even raised in the petition for certiorari. See Pet for Cert 3. The Court need not have revisited *Booth* and *Gathers* in any event because the Tennessee Supreme Court had held that there was no *Booth* violation, and as an alternative ground, that even if there had been a *Booth* violation, it was harmless beyond a reasonable doubt. See *State v Payne*, 791 SW2d 10, 18-19 (Tenn 1990).

[11] *Harmelin v Michigan*, 111 S Ct 2680 (1991) (upholding mandatory life sentence without possibility of parole for possession of 672 grams of cocaine). Relying on the plain language of the Eighth Amendment and a scholarly examination of historical evidence concerning the intent of the Framers, Justice Scalia argued that proportionality should not even be considered in construing the constitutional prohibition against "cruel and unusual punishments." Significantly, seven members of the Court refused to adopt an argument that was clearly at odds with the Court's prior Eighth Amendment jurisprudence. See, for example, *Weems v United States*, 217 US 349 (1910); *Gregg v Georgia*, 428 US 153 (1976); *Coker v Georgia*, 433 US 584 (1977); *Enmund v Florida*, 458 US 782 (1982); *Solem v Helm*, 463 US 277 (1983).

In *Chapman v United States*, 111 S Ct 1919 (1991), the Court construed a statute to authorize grossly disparate sentencing. The statute required a five-year minimum sentence for distributing more than one gram of a "mixture or substance containing a detectable amount of lysergic acid diethylamide (LSD)." The Court held that it is the weight of the LSD and the "carrier" containing it, and not the weight of the pure LSD, that determines eligibility for the minimum sentence. Under the Court's construction of the statute, a person distributing 1,000 doses of LSD in liquid form is subject to no minimum penalty, whereas a person handing another person a single dose on a sugar cube, which weighs about two grams, is subject to a mandatory five-year penalty. Id at 1931 n 9 (Stevens dissenting).

[12] In *California v Acevedo*, 111 S Ct 1982 (1991), the Supreme Court overruled *Arkansas v Sanders*, 442 US 753 (1979), and held that the police may search a closed container in an automobile even though they do not have a search warrant, as long as they have probable cause to believe the container contains contraband. See also *Florida v Jimeno*, 111 S Ct 1801 (1991) (consent to search car includes consent to search any closed containers found in car).

[13] *County of Riverside v McLaughlin*, 111 S Ct 1661 (1991) (Fourth Amendment permits individual to be detained for 48 hours without probable cause hearing).

[14] *California v Hodari D.*, 111 S Ct 1547 (1991) (individual was not "seized" within the meaning of the Fourth Amendment when police officer pursued and ran toward him without reasonable suspicion); *Florida v Bostick*, 111 S Ct 2382 (1991) (Fourth Amendment does not prohibit police officers from boarding bus and searching passengers, even though officers lack reasonable suspicion to conduct such a search, if passengers "consent" to search).

proceedings to foreclose judicial review of even meritorious constitutional claims in capital cases.[15] An attorney's untimely filing of a notice of appeal from a state court's refusal to grant post-conviction relief—a negligent misstep that until this year merely would have foreclosed appellate review in the state's judicial system—now bars federal review of a claim that imposition of the death sentence on the attorney's client violated the Bill of Rights.[16]

Although the Court's extraordinarily disappointing performance in 1991 can only have a sobering influence on bicentennial celebrations such as this, the work product of a single term must be viewed from a broader perspective. Even while American judges are depreciating the value of liberty, this is a time when—thanks largely to the vision of Mikhail Gorbachev, and perhaps to the symbolic power of documents like the Bill of Rights—the voices of freedom have produced the beautiful music of debate, controversy, and progress in most of Eastern Europe. Perhaps, in time, the free exchange of ideas in other parts of the world will give Americans the incentive and the courage to re-examine the reasons why our prison population—and particularly the number of inmates on death row[17]—steadily expands at an alarming rate[18] while armed conflict in the streets of our cities continues to flourish.

---

[15] *Coleman v Thompson*, 111 S Ct 2546 (1991); *Ylst v Nunnemaker*, 111 S Ct 2590 (1991); *McCleskey v Zant*, 111 S Ct 1454 (1991).

[16] *Coleman*, 111 S Ct at 2566-67.

[17] Department of Justice figures indicate that as of December 31, 1980 there were 714 prisoners under sentence of death in the United States, and as of December 31, 1989 there were 2,250 prisoners under sentence of death. US Department of Justice, Bureau of Justice Statistics, *Capital Punishment 1980* 1 (1981); US Department of Justice, Bureau of Justice Statistics, *Capital Punishment 1989* 6 (1990). In less than a decade, the total number of prisoners under sentence of death in the United States has increased by 215%. According to Bureau of Justice Statistics Director Steven Dillingham, since 1976 there have been 3,834 people sentenced to death. *40% on Death Row Are Black, New Figures Show*, NY Times A15 (Sep 30, 1991).

[18] In the 1980s, the United States' prison population doubled, whereas during the same time period in the Soviet Union, the prison population declined and in South Africa, the prison population increased by only 11%. Marc Mauer, *Americans Behind Bars: A Comparison of International Rates of Incarceration* 6 (The Sentencing Project, 1991); Ronald J. Ostrow, *U.S. Imprisons Black Men at 4 Times S. Africa's Rate*, LA Times A1 (Jan 5, 1991). The United States "now has the world's highest known rate of incarceration"; it imprisons 426 people per 100,000 population, whereas the Soviet Union imprisons 268 per 100,000 population and South Africa imprisons 333 per 100,000 population. Mauer, *Americans Behind Bars* at 3-5. In comparison, incarceration rates in Western Europe range from 35 to 120 per 100,000 population, and rates in Asia range from 21 to 140 per 100,000 population. Id. For example, the United States' incarceration rate is almost ten times that of Japan's. See id at 5.

The broader perspective from which the Supreme Court's recent decisions should be viewed is temporal as well as geographic. My topic is intended to suggest that it is appropriate to consider the significance of the Bill of Rights during an entire century and, more particularly, to determine whether that century of jurisprudence represents legitimate progress.

II.

Prior to the Civil War and the subsequent adoption of the Fourteenth Amendment, the Bill of Rights was merely a limitation on the power of the federal government.[19] Arguably, the first ten amendments were redundant because they did little more than identify some of the outer boundaries of the powers that the original Constitution conferred on the federal sovereign.[20] In the first century of its existence, the Bill of Rights was, in some respects, comparable to the Magna Carta—a relatively static symbol expressing the general idea that the federal government has an obligation to obey the law of the land.

In the second century of its life, however, the Bill of Rights became a dynamic force in the development of American law. The United States Supreme Court played a major role in that development. Its liberal—one might say "activist"—interpretation of the word "commerce" in Article I of the Constitution created the gateway to a vast expansion of the federal government's power to regulate the lives of individual citizens.[21] Increased federal regulation,

---

[19] *Barron v Baltimore*, 32 US (7 Pet) 242, 247 (1833) (holding first eight amendments inapplicable to the states); see also *Withers v Buckley*, 61 US (20 How) 84, 90-91 (1857).

[20] "I go further, and affirm that bills of rights, in the sense and to the extent in which they are contended for, are not only unnecessary in the proposed Constitution, but would even be dangerous . . . . For why declare that things shall not be done which there is no power to do? Why, for instance, should it be said that the liberty of the press shall not be restrained, when no power is given by which restrictions may be imposed?" Federalist 84 (Hamilton) in Benjamin Fletcher Wright, ed, *The Federalist Papers* 531, 535 (Harvard, 1961).

[21] See, for example, *Houston and Texas Railway v United States*, 234 US 342, 351 (1914) (power of Congress to regulate rates of interstate railroads includes power "to control . . . all matters having such a close and substantial relation to interstate traffic that the control is essential or appropriate to the security of that traffic, to the efficiency of the interstate service, and to the maintenance of conditions under which interstate commerce may be conducted upon fair terms and without molestation or hindrance"); *Wickard v Filburn*, 317 US 111, 127-28 (1942) (Congress could control farmer's production of wheat for home consumption because cumulative effect of home consumption of wheat by many farmers would affect supply and demand relations of interstate commodity market); *Heart of Atlanta Motel, Inc. v United States*, 379 US 241, 258 (1964) ("Congress may . . . prohibit racial discrimination by motels serving travelers, however 'local' their operations may appear"); *Perez v United States*, 402 US 146, 154 (1971) ("[e]xtortionate credit transactions,

as well as federal participation in criminal law enforcement, inevitably gave rise to individual claims that the federal sovereign was invading territory protected by the Bill of Rights. Of even greater significance was the Supreme Court's determination that the basic concepts described in the Bill of Rights are incorporated in the Fourteenth Amendment's guarantee that no state may deprive any person of liberty without due process of law. This construction of the Due Process Clause, or as I prefer to call it, the Liberty Clause, in the Fourteenth Amendment has transformed the Bill of Rights from a mere constraint on federal power into a source of federal authority to constrain state power.

In this century, most of the significant cases raising Bill of Rights issues have, in the final analysis, actually interpreted the word "liberty" in the Fourteenth Amendment. Indeed, the impact of that Amendment on the Bill of Rights has also led to an expansion of the meaning of the word "liberty" as it is used in the Fifth Amendment. When the Court held that the racial segregation of students in the public schools in Topeka, Kansas, violated the Equal Protection Clause,[22] simple justice indicated that the same rule should obtain in the federal enclave known as the District of Columbia. Unable to rely on the Equal Protection Clause because it applies only to state action, the Court unanimously found what is now known as the equal protection component of the Due Process Clause embedded in the word "liberty" as it is used in the Fifth Amendment.[23] Thus, through the process of judicial construction, the Bill of Rights has become a shield against invidious discrimination by the federal government as well as a shield against the misuse of state power.

The judiciary's reconstruction of the term "commerce" during this century is generally accepted as legitimate by even the most conservative critics of the Supreme Court's work product. Respected scholars have, however, questioned the legitimacy of the Court's doctrine incorporating portions of the Bill of Rights into the Liberty Clause of the Fourteenth Amendment as well as the decisions incorporating the idea of equality into the Liberty Clause

---

though purely intrastate, may in the judgment of Congress affect interstate commerce"). These cases stand in stark contrast to some of the Supreme Court's earlier cases, such as *United States v E.C. Knight Co.*, 156 US 1, 13 (1895), in which the Supreme Court "allowed but little scope to the power of Congress." *Wickard*, 317 US at 121-22.

[22] *Brown v Board of Education*, 347 US 483 (1954).

[23] *Bolling v Sharpe*, 347 US 497 (1954).

of the Fifth Amendment.[24] Because the Fifth Amendment has been a part of the Bill of Rights throughout its 200-year history, it is appropriate to say a few words about the latter criticism before discussing the broader question of incorporation.

A.

If the task of judicial construction began and ended with a grammatical and etymological analysis of legal text, or even if it were slightly expanded to include an analysis of the original intent of those who drafted and enacted that text into positive law, one would expect an impartial court to reject any claim that the word "liberty," as used in the 1791 Constitution, endorsed the revolutionary idea that all men are created equal. For the text of the Constitution in 1791, before as well as after the ratification of the Bill of Rights, expressly approved of invidious discrimination. Article IV provided positive protection for the institution of slavery[25] and Article I provided that for the purpose of apportioning congressional representatives, each slave should be counted as three-fifths of a person.[26] The interest in protecting individual freedom that animated the adoption of the Bill of Rights left these odious portions of the original Constitution untouched. The Framers had constructed a document that, like the fledgling nation itself, could be described as a house divided against itself—an institution that was half slave and half free. A Constitution that expressly tolerated the worst kind of discrimination could not simultaneously condemn all irrational discrimination.

Those who argue that the meaning of the word liberty as used in the Bill of Rights is the same today as it was in 1791 correctly point out that the draftsmen of the Equal Protection Clause of the Fourteenth Amendment proposed no parallel provision to expand the coverage of the Liberty Clause of the Fifth Amendment. Be-

---

[24] See Raoul Berger, *Activist Censures of Robert Bork*, 85 Nw U L Rev 993, 1015 (1991); John Hart Ely, *Democracy and Distrust: A Theory of Judicial Review* 32-33 (Harvard, 1980).

[25] "No Person held to Service or Labour in one State, under the Laws thereof, escaping into another, shall, in Consequence of any Law or Regulation therein, be discharged from such Service or Labour, but shall be delivered up on Claim of the Party to whom such Service or Labour may be due." US Const, Art IV, § 2, cl 3.

[26] "Representatives and direct Taxes shall be apportioned among the several States which may be included within this Union, according to their respective Numbers, which shall be determined by adding to the whole Number of free Persons, including those bound to Service for a Term of Years, and excluding Indians not taxed, three fifths of all other Persons." US Const, Art I, § 2, cl 3 (superseded by § 2 of the Fourteenth Amendment).

cause the text of the 1791 Amendment has not been changed, they assume that we should simply ignore other changes in our fundamental law 'in the process of construing that text today. The logic of that straightforward argument leads to the conclusion that the unanimous decision of the Supreme Court in *Bolling v Sharpe*[27] simply was wrong and that—as some critics suggest—the Justices had arrogantly assumed a lawmaking role to implement their own notions of wise social policy.

Notwithstanding the force of this hybrid plain language-original intent argument, the judicial recognition of the Equal Protection component of the Liberty Clause of the Fifth Amendment is so well-settled[28] that judicial opinions need not contain an explanation of the legitimacy of the rule. In a symposium such as this, however, it is appropriate to explain why the rule is firmly grounded in our law for reasons that are even stronger than the doctrine of stare decisis.

Just as the task of statutory construction requires a judge to examine the entire text of the relevant statute in order to understand the meaning of the provision in dispute, so does constitutional interpretation often involve a study of interrelated provisions. The changes in constitutional text that were effected by the adoption of the Thirteenth, Fourteenth, and Fifteenth Amendments breathed new life into the entire document. The purge of

---

[27] 347 US 497 (1954) (racial segregation in District of Columbia public schools was denial of Fifth Amendment right to due process).

[28] See, for example, *Califano v Webster*, 430 US 313, 317 (1977) (per curiam) (holding constitutional under Fifth Amendment federal social security statute treating female wage earners more favorably than male wage earners to redress "our society's longstanding disparate treatment of women"); *Califano v Goldfarb*, 430 US 199, 201 (1977) (federal statute denying survivors' benefits to female wage earner's spouse unless he can show he " 'was receiving at least one-half of his support' " from his deceased wife, but not requiring male wage earner's surviving spouse to make the same showing of dependency, violates Due Process Clause of Fifth Amendment); *United States Dept. of Agriculture v Moreno*, 413 US 528 (1973) (food stamp statute excluding any household containing individual unrelated to any other member of the household violates Due Process Clause of Fifth Amendment); *Frontiero v Richardson*, 411 US 677, 680 (1973) (holding unconstitutional under Fifth Amendment federal statutes providing that spouses of male members of the armed services were "dependents" for purposes of military benefits, but that spouses of female members were not unless they depended on their wives for more than one-half of their support); *Shapiro v Thompson*, 394 US 618, 641-42 (1969) (holding unconstitutional state and federal provisions denying welfare benefits to individuals who had resided in the administering jurisdiction less than one year); *Schneider v Rusk*, 377 US 163, 168 (1964) (holding unconstitutional a statute treating naturalized citizens as less reliable than native born citizens because "while the Fifth Amendment contains no equal protection clause, it does forbid discrimination that is 'so unjustifiable as to be violative of due process' ") (quoting *Bolling*, 347 US at 499).

the odious provisions that infected the 1791 text made it appropriate in the post-Civil War period to give the word "liberty" its ordinary meaning—indeed, a meaning that is not only acceptable to
today's judges but one that presumably would have been acceptable to an eighteenth-century jurist if the original Constitution had
not contained those odious provisions. As the Court noted in *Bolling v Sharpe*, it has not defined the word "liberty" with any great
precision, though it has often made clear that the concept encompasses more than a freedom from bodily restraint.[29] Whether the
concept is broad enough to encompass the idea of equality is a
question that is easily answered by reference to the standard articulated by Justice Holmes in his *Lochner* dissent: Is it a matter
of fundamental principle that has been so "understood by the traditions of our people and our law?"[30]

Perhaps the most articulate authority on those traditions was
a lawyer named Abraham Lincoln. He unquestionably would have
agreed with the Court's conclusion that "liberty" includes a right
to equal treatment under the law. For in his address calling for "a
new birth of freedom,"[31] he identified the direct connection between the idea of liberty that was to prevail when General Lee ordered the Confederate Army to retreat from Gettysburg on July 4,
1863, and the idea of liberty that had prevailed when the Declaration of Independence was signed on July 4, 1776. Lincoln's calculation of "four score and seven years"[32] as the interval between his
dedication at Gettysburg and the birth of the nation identifies the
Declaration of Independence, rather than the Constitution or the
Bill of Rights, as the source of his understanding of the term "liberty." The self-evident proposition enshrined in the Declaration—the proposition that all men are created equal—is not
merely an aspect of social policy that judges are free to accept or

---

[29] 347 US at 499.

[30] "I think that the word liberty in the Fourteenth Amendment is perverted when it is
held to prevent the natural outcome of a dominant opinion, unless it can be said . . . that
the statute proposed would infringe fundamental principles as they have been understood
by the traditions of our people and our law." *Lochner v New York*, 198 US 45, 76 (1905)
(Holmes dissenting).

This standard has been incorporated into subsequent cases as well. See, for example,
Snyder v Massachusetts, 291 US 97, 105 (1934) (Cardozo) (state is free to regulate its procedure "unless in so doing it offends some principle of justice so rooted in the traditions and
conscience of our people as to be ranked as fundamental"); *Moore v City of East Cleveland*,
431 US 494, 503 (1977) (plurality opinion) (the Constitution protects the family "precisely
because the institution of the family is deeply rooted in this nation's history and tradition").

[31] Abraham Lincoln, *Gettysburg Address* (Nov 19, 1863), in Henry Steele Commager,
ed, 1 *Documents of American History* 429 (Appleton-Century-Crofts, 9th ed 1958).

[32] Id at 428.

reject; it is a matter of principle that is so firmly grounded in the "traditions of our people" that it is properly viewed as a component of the liberty protected by the Fifth Amendment. The positive command expressed in the Bill of Rights that the federal sovereign must obey the law of the land unquestionably requires federal judges to respect the proposition to which the forefathers dedicated the founding of the nation itself.

B.

The text of the Liberty Clause of the Fourteenth Amendment, which provides that no state shall "deprive any person of life, liberty, or property, without due process of law,"[33] offers a different basis for criticizing the Supreme Court's decisions applying provisions of the Bill of Rights to the actions of the sovereign states.[34] As is true of the Fifth Amendment, a literal reading of that clause provides the individual with a guarantee of fair procedure before the state may deprive him of life, liberty, or property, but it does not impose any constraint on the kinds of deprivations the state may impose on its citizens. Moreover, the general requirement that there must be "due process"—which appears in both the Fifth and the Fourteenth Amendments—arguably should not encompass such specific guarantees as the right to a speedy trial, the right to counsel, or the right to compulsory process because the Sixth Amendment would be redundant if those rights were already protected by the Fifth Amendment's general guarantee of due process.[35] The Supreme Court nevertheless has concluded in a long and unbroken line of cases that the Due Process Clause of the Fourteenth Amendment does require the states not only to comply with specific procedural protections in the Bill of Rights, but also

---

[33] US Const, Amend XIV, § 1.

[34] "The words, 'due process of law,' were undoubtedly intended to convey the same meaning as the words, 'by the law of the land,' in *Magna Charta*." *Murray's Lessees v Hoboken Land and Improvement Co.*, 59 US (18 How) 272, 276 (1856). In *Davidson v New Orleans*, 96 US (6 Otto) 97, 101 (1877), the Supreme Court recognized that one was the equivalent of the other. See also Joseph Story, 3 *Commentaries on the Constitution of the United States* §§ 931-32 (Carolina Academic, 1987) (originally published, Hilliard Gray, 1833). Learned Hand reached the same conclusion: "It is my understanding that the 'Due Process Clause,' when it first appeared in Chapter III of the 28th of Edward III—about a century and a half after Magna Carta—was a substitute for, and was regarded as the equivalent of, the phrase, *per legem terrae*, which meant no more than customary legal procedure." Learned Hand, *The Bill of Rights* 35 (Harvard, 1958).

[35] This, in essence, is the argument that the Court accepted to explain its conclusion that due process of law does not require an indictment by a grand jury as a prerequisite to a prosecution for murder. See *Hurtado*, 110 US at 534-35.

to respect certain substantive guarantees. The Court's interpretation of that clause makes some state action entirely invalid regardless of the procedures the state may employ in enforcing its command.

The most striking evidence of the Court's willingness to ignore the literal meaning of constitutional text is provided by cases preventing the states from abridging the freedoms protected by the First Amendment. The text of that Amendment provides:

> Congress shall make no law respecting an establishment of religion, or prohibiting the free exercise thereof; or abridging the freedom of speech, or of the press; or the right of the people peaceably to assemble, and to petition the Government for a redress of grievances.[36]

A judge who strictly construes that text must find it difficult to understand how it limits the power of any governmental body other than the Congress of the United States. Even when the First Amendment is read in the light of the Fourteenth Amendment's command that states may not deprive anyone of liberty without due process of law, the puzzlement remains. To find the solution it is necessary to search judicial opinions.

Although the earliest opinions endorsing the proposition that the federal Constitution protects speech and associational freedom from state action were written by two of our greatest Justices—Justice Holmes and Justice Brandeis—neither of them bothered to quote any part of the text of the First Amendment to support that proposition. In his dissent in *Gitlow v New York*, Justice Holmes merely asserted: "The general principle of free speech, it seems to me, must be taken to be included in the Fourteenth Amendment, in view of the scope that has been given to the word 'liberty' as there used . . . ."[37]

Two years later, in his separate opinion in *Whitney v California*,[38] Justice Brandeis expressly endorsed the conclusion that the Due Process Clause of the Fourteenth Amendment provides sub-

---

[36] US Const, Amend I.

[37] 268 US at 652, 672 (1925) (Holmes dissenting). The majority did not disagree with this proposition. It wrote:

> For present purposes we may and do assume that freedom of speech and of the press—which are protected by the First Amendment from abridgment by Congress—are among the fundamental personal rights and "liberties" protected by the due process clause of the Fourteenth Amendment from impairment by the States.

268 US at 666.

[38] 274 US 357, 372 (1927) (Brandeis concurring).

stantive as well as procedural protection and also the proposition
that the term liberty embraces the right of free speech. I quote two
sentences from his opinion to emphasize the non-textual basis for
his conclusion:

> Despite arguments to the contrary which had seemed to me
> persuasive, it is settled that the due process clause of the
> Fourteenth Amendment applies to matters of substantive law
> as well as to matters of procedure. Thus all fundamental
> rights comprised within the term liberty are protected by the
> Federal Constitution from invasion by the States.[39]

The first two cases that Justice Brandeis cited to support that conclusion were *Meyer v Nebraska*,[40] and *Pierce v Society of Sisters*.[41]
Those, of course, are the two leading cases holding that certain
fundamental rights that are neither enumerated nor expressly
mentioned in the text of the Constitution are protected from substantive deprivation by state action. Thus, although it is familiar
learning that so-called "enumerated rights"[42]—those specifically
described in the first ten amendments to the Constitution—are incorporated in the Due Process Clause of the Fourteenth Amendment, we sometimes forget that the source of the doctrine of incorporation was the product of judicial evaluation of the fundamental
character of the rights at stake rather than an analysis of the text
of the Constitution itself.

Moreover, as the doctrine developed, the Court unequivocally
rejected the position espoused by Justice Black that the boundaries of the idea of liberty are precisely measured by the contours of
the first ten amendments. Contrary to the position Justice Black
advanced in his dissent in *Adamson v California*,[43] the Court has
neither incorporated all of the provisions of the Bill of Rights into
the Fourteenth Amendment nor retreated from the position taken

---

[39] Id at 373.

[40] 262 US 390, 400 (1923) (holding unconstitutional a state law prohibiting the teaching
of foreign languages to children because the teacher's "right thus to teach and the right of
parents to engage him so to instruct their children . . . are within the liberty of the [Four-
teenth] Amendment").

[41] 268 US 510, 534-35 (1925) (holding unconstitutional a state law that forbade parents
from sending their children to private schools because it "unreasonably interferes with the
liberty of parents and guardians to direct the upbringing and education of children under
their control").

[42] See Ronald Dworkin, *Unenumerated Rights: Whether and How* Roe *Should Be Overruled*, in this volume, 381, for the argument that the distinction between enumerated and
unenumerated rights is unstable.

[43] 332 US 46, 68 (1947) (Black dissenting).

in *Meyer* and *Pierce* that the concept of liberty includes unenumerated rights.

During the past century, while the relevant constitutional text has been as immutable as the Stonehenge monument, some of the propositions of law that the text identifies have changed significantly. Two guarantees in the Bill of Rights—one procedural and one substantive—illustrate this point.

1.

The Sixth Amendment provides that in all criminal prosecutions, the accused shall enjoy the right "to have the assistance of counsel for his defence."[44] Unlike the English common law, which perversely limited the right to misdemeanor trials, the American right to counsel has always extended to more serious crimes.[45] Whether the Amendment merely guaranteed a lawyer to the defendant who could afford to hire one or also protected the indigent is a question that the text of the Amendment did not answer. It seems clear, however, that the early practice in federal as well as state courts did not require the appointment of counsel unless the defendant made a timely request for such assistance. A series of judicial decisions in this century has defined and expanded the right.

Powell v Alabama,[46] decided in 1932, was the groundbreaking case. Special circumstances creating an intolerable risk of unfairness in a capital case convinced a majority of the Court that the absence of counsel had made the trial fundamentally unfair.[47] A

---

[44] US Const, Amend VI.

[45] *Powell v Alabama*, 287 US 45, 60-65, 69 (1932).

[46] 287 US 45.

[47] The Court concluded that given the special circumstances in the record,

the necessity of counsel was so vital and imperative that the failure of the trial court to make an effective appointment of counsel was likewise a denial of due process within the meaning of the Fourteenth Amendment. Whether this would be so in other criminal prosecutions, or under other circumstances, we need not determine. All that it is necessary now to decide, as we do decide, is that in a capital case, where the defendant is unable to employ counsel, and is incapable adequately of making his own defense because of ignorance, feeble mindedness, illiteracy, or the like, it is the duty of the court, whether requested or not, to assign counsel for him as a necessary requisite of due process of law; and that duty is not discharged by an assignment at such a time or under such circumstances as to preclude the giving of effective aid in the preparation and trial of the case. To hold otherwise would be to ignore the fundamental postulate, already adverted to, "that there are certain immutable principles of justice which inhere in the very idea of free government which no member of the Union may disregard."

Id at 71-72, citing *Holden v Hardy*, 169 US 366, 389 (1898).

few years later, in *Johnson v Zerbst*,[48] the Court construed the Sixth Amendment to deprive federal courts in all criminal proceedings of the power to take away the defendant's liberty unless he has, or has waived, the assistance of counsel; the Court rejected the Solicitor General's argument that the failure to request counsel constituted such a waiver. The rule that was applied to state criminal prosecutions during the 1940s and 1950s required counsel in all capital cases, but not in noncapital cases unless special circumstances made the particular trial unfair.[49] In 1963, in *Gideon v Wainwright*, the Court overruled earlier decisions and dispensed with the "special circumstances" requirement, at least in felony cases.[50] More recently, the Court has extended the rule to lesser offenses;[51] it has also concluded that the Constitution mandates that counsel be competent.[52] The rule of law created by the last clause of the Sixth Amendment and the Liberty Clause of the Fourteenth Amendment has unquestionably changed while the text of those amendments has remained the same.

2.

So it is with the Religion Clauses of the First Amendment. Their application to the states was the product of judicial opinions that did little more than announce an interpretation of the idea of liberty that was self-evident to the Justices. The complete explanation of this conclusion appears in *Cantwell v Connecticut*:

> We hold that the statute, as construed and applied to the appellants, deprives them of their liberty without due process of law in contravention of the Fourteenth Amendment. The fundamental concept of liberty embodied in that Amendment embraces the liberties guaranteed by the First Amendment.

---

[48] 304 US 458 (1938).

[49] See *Gideon v Wainwright*, 372 US 335, 350-51 (1963) (Harlan concurring).

[50] Id at 344-45.

[51] See *Argersinger v Hamlin*, 407 US 25, 37 (1972) ("absent a knowing and intelligent waiver, no person may be imprisoned for any offense, whether classified as petty, misdemeanor, or felony, unless he was represented by counsel at his trial") (footnote omitted).

[52] See, for example, *United States v Cronic*, 466 US 648, 656 (1984) (adversarial process protected by Sixth Amendment requires accused to have counsel acting as advocate); *Strickland v Washington*, 466 US 668, 687 (1984) (convicted defendant's claim of ineffective assistance of counsel requires showing that counsel's performance was deficient and that the deficiency prejudiced the defendant); see also *Cuyler v Sullivan*, 446 US 335, 348 (1980) (actual conflict of interest adversely affecting lawyer's performance renders assistance ineffective); *Holloway v Arkansas*, 435 US 475, 484 (1978) (Sixth Amendment right to effective assistance of counsel includes right of representation by attorney who does not owe conflicting duties to other defendants).

The First Amendment declares that Congress shall make no law respecting an establishment of religion or prohibiting the free exercise thereof. The Fourteenth Amendment has rendered the legislatures of the states as incompetent as Congress to enact such laws.[53]

History teaches us that these clauses were motivated by a concern about rivalry among Christian sects. The intolerance that characterized sixteenth- and seventeenth-century England—when royal decrees made martyrs of Edmund Campion and Thomas More, when Oliver Cromwell's puritan roundheads covered Renaissance art and literature with the austere blanket of censorship, and when English emigrants burned witches at the stake in Salem, Massachusetts—that intolerance was the product of competition among different groups sharing the same fundamental belief in the resurrection of Jesus Christ. In his *Commentaries on the Constitution*, Justice Story explained that the "real object of the [First] [A]mendment was not to countenance, much less to advance, Mahometanism, or Judaism, or infidelity, by prostrating Christianity; but to exclude all rivalry among Christian sects, and to prevent any national ecclesiastical establishment, which should give to an hierarchy the exclusive patronage of the national government."[54]

If the protection of the First Amendment were narrowly circumscribed by the specific concerns that motivated its adoption, presumably a democratic majority could discriminate against non-Christian religions, against agnostics, and against atheists. The Court, however, has unequivocally rejected that view because the principle of tolerance embodied in the First Amendment is broader than the particular history that was familiar to its authors.

> Just as the right to speak and the right to refrain from speaking are complementary components of a broader concept of individual freedom of mind, so also the individual's freedom to choose his own creed is the counterpart of his right to refrain from accepting the creed established by the majority. At one time it was thought that this right merely proscribed the preference of one Christian sect over another, but would not require equal respect for the conscience of the infidel, the atheist, or the adherent of a non-Christian faith such as Islam or Judaism. But when the underlying principle has been examined in the crucible of litigation, the Court has unambigu-

---

[53] 310 US 296, 303 (1940) (footnote omitted).
[54] Story, 3 *Commentaries on the Constitution* at § 991 (cited in note 34).

ously concluded that the individual freedom of conscience protected by the First Amendment embraces the right to select any religious faith or none at all.[55]

III.

It is the principle of tolerance that, in time, must provide the answer to the controversy that inflames so many of our most sincere and zealous citizens. Fueling that controversy is a disagreement over the point at which a seed—to use St. Thomas Aquinas's term[56]—becomes a human being. In *Stanley v Georgia*,[57] and *Griswold v Connecticut*,[58] the Court implicitly determined that a potential father, as well as a pair of potential parents, has a constitutional right to waste the seeds of potential life. In *Skinner v Oklahoma ex rel. Williamson*, the Court held that the State could not sterilize the defendant and thus deprive him of "the right to have offspring," which is a "basic liberty," because he had committed two or more felonies.[59] In the *Cruzan* case two terms ago, the Court made it clear that the Liberty Clause protects a woman's right to make basic decisions about the physical treatment of her

---

[55] *Wallace v Jaffree*, 472 US 38, 52-53 (1985) (footnote omitted).

[56] The view held by St. Thomas Aquinas is explained in a report prepared by the Congressional Research Service of the Library of Congress: "For St. Thomas, 'seed and what is not seed is determined by sensation and movement.' What is destroyed in abortion of the unformed fetus is seed, not man." Charles H. Whittier, *Catholic Teaching on Abortion: Its Origin and Later Development* (1981) (quoting *In octo libros politicorum* 7.12, attributed to St. Thomas Aquinas), reprinted in Brief of Americans United for Separation of Church and State as *Amicus Curiae* 17a, S Ct No 88-605 (Mar 30, 1989); see *Webster v Reproductive Health Services*, 492 US 490, 567-69 (1989) (Stevens concurring in part and dissenting in part); see also *Roe v Wade*, 410 US 113, 134 (1973).

[57] 394 US 557 (1969). *Stanley*'s precise holding was, of course, that the "First and Fourteenth Amendments prohibit making mere private possession of obscene material a crime." Id at 568 (footnote omitted). The Supreme Court reasoned that the Constitution protected the rights to receive ideas and to be free from unwanted governmental intrusions into one's privacy: "If the First Amendment means anything, it means that a State has no business telling a man, sitting alone in his own house, what books he may read or what films he may watch." Id at 565.

[58] 381 US 479 (1965) (holding Connecticut law prohibiting the purchase and use of contraceptives by married couples to be unconstitutional); see also *Eisenstadt v Baird*, 405 US 438 (1972) (holding Massachusetts statute prohibiting distribution of contraceptives to single persons to be unconstitutional under the Equal Protection Clause of the Fourteenth Amendment).

[59] 316 US 535, 536, 541 (1942). I recognize, of course, that the Court's opinion, written when the concept of "substantive due process" was in special disfavor, relied on an equal protection rationale. I believe this is one of several cases that is more appropriately explained as reflecting a judgment about individual liberty. See Stevens, *The Third Branch of Liberty*, 41 U Miami L Rev 277, 286, 288-89 (1986).

own body.[60] If a small tumor threatens her well-being, she has the right—a constitutionally protected right embedded in the Liberty Clause of the Fourteenth Amendment—to decide whether or not it shall be removed.[61] As a purely secular matter, if we regard a growth within her body that is no larger than an acorn as just a seed rather than a human being—as St. Thomas Aquinas did—the constitutional predicate for the decisions in *Stanley*, *Griswold*, and *Cruzan*, inexorably leads to the conclusion that the woman has a right to decide whether to waste or to preserve that seed.

That right, of course, is not absolute. Personal decisions involving the treatment of diseases, for example, must take into account the welfare of society.[62] But while the individual choice may be influenced, or even dictated, by the tenets of religious faith, the majority's decision to override such a decision must be justified by secular considerations. Many Americans are sincerely convinced that the duty to protect potential life after the moment of conception is just as imperative as it is immediately after birth, when a fetus becomes a person within the meaning of the Constitution. To the extent that such a conviction rests on religious faith rather than on physical differences between potential persons at different stages of their development, it does not provide a permissible basis for imposing the majority's will upon the individual.

The standard that should govern the judiciary in deciding whether a legislature had an adequate secular basis for interfering with an individual's decision respecting the disposition of a growth within or upon her body has been debated in a number of thought-provoking opinions.[63] Whatever standard may ultimately be ap-

---

[60] *Cruzan v Director, Missouri Dept. of Health*, 110 S Ct 2841 (1990). Justice Scalia, however, did not accept this conclusion. See id at 2861-63 (Scalia concurring).

[61] "Every human being of adult years and sound mind has a right to determine what shall be done with his own body; and a surgeon who performs an operation without his patient's consent commits an assault for which he is liable in damages." *Schloendorff v Society of New York Hospital*, 211 NY 125, 129-30, 105 NE 92, 93 (1914) (Cardozo).

[62] See *Jacobson v Massachusetts*, 197 US 11, 27-29 (1905) (balancing individual's liberty interest in declining unwanted smallpox vaccine against state's interest in preventing disease and upholding law because it was "of paramount necessity" to state's fight against epidemic).

[63] See, for example, *Thornburgh v American College of Obstetricians and Gynecologists*, 476 US 747, 795 (1986) (White dissenting) ("the state's interest, if compelling after viability, is equally compelling before viability," but "compelling" interest is not required for a right that is not fundamental); *Akron v Akron Center for Reproductive Health, Inc.*, 462 US 416, 453 (1983) (O'Connor dissenting) (regulation imposed on abortion is not unconstitutional unless it " 'unduly burdens the right to seek an abortion' " at any point in the pregnancy); *Roe v Wade*, 410 US 113, 155, 163 (1973) (Blackmun) (where fundamental rights are concerned, state regulation may be justified only by a " 'compelling state inter-

plied in answering the legal questions the abortion controversy generates, the decisional process must recognize the validity of at least three settled propositions.

First, neither a seed nor a fetus is a "person" within the meaning of the Fourteenth Amendment.[64] The meaning of that term is unquestionably a matter of federal constitutional law that state legislatures cannot modify. Responsible critics of the decision in *Roe v Wade*—those who argue that every state should have broad latitude in regulating abortion—necessarily reject any suggestion that a fetus is a person prior to birth.[65]

Second, the justification for the legislative decision not only must be secular;[66] it also must be rational.[67] Theoretically, a prohi-

---

est' " and must be "narrowly drawn to express only the legitimate state interests at stake"; the State's interest becomes "compelling" at viability); id at 170 (Stewart concurring) (right to abortion is "embraced within the personal liberty protected by the Due Process Clause of the Fourteenth Amendment" and any state interests in abridging this right must "survive the 'particularly careful scrutiny' that the Fourteenth Amendment here requires"); id at 173 (Rehnquist dissenting) ("The test traditionally applied in the area of social and economic legislation is whether or not a law such as that challenged has a rational relation to a valid state objective."); see also *Poe v Ullman*, 367 US 497, 543 (1961) (Harlan dissenting) ("[T]he full scope of the liberty guaranteed by the Due Process Clause . . . is a rational continuum which, broadly speaking, includes a freedom from all substantial arbitrary impositions and purposeless restraints . . . and which also recognizes, what a reasonable and sensitive judgment must, that certain interests require particularly careful scrutiny of the state needs asserted to justify their abridgment"); *Griswold*, 381 US at 500 (Harlan concurring) ("the proper constitutional inquiry is whether . . . [the] statute infringes the Due Process Clause of the Fourteenth Amendment because the enactment violates basic values 'implicit in the concept of ordered liberty' "); *Moore v City of East Cleveland*, 431 US 494, 501-02 (1977) (Powell writing for the plurality); id at 542 (White dissenting).

[64] *Webster*, 492 US at 568 n 13 (Stevens concurring in part and dissenting in part); *Thornburgh*, 476 US at 779 n 8 (Stevens concurring).

[65] In his dissent in *Roe v Wade*, then Justice Rehnquist wrote,

I agree with the statement of Mr. Justice Stewart in his concurring opinion that the "liberty," against deprivation of which without due process the Fourteenth Amendment protects, embraces more than the rights found in the Bill of Rights. But that liberty is not guaranteed absolutely against deprivation, only against deprivation without due process of law. The test traditionally applied in the area of social and economic legislation is whether or not a law such as that challenged has a rational relation to a valid state objective. *Williamson v Lee Optical Co.*, 348 U.S. 483, 491 (1955). The Due Process Clause of the Fourteenth Amendment undoubtedly does place a limit, albeit a broad one, on legislative power to enact laws such as this. If the Texas statute were to prohibit an abortion even where the mother's life is in jeopardy, I have little doubt that such a statute would lack a rational relation to a valid state objective under the test stated in *Williamson, supra*.

410 US at 172-73 (Rehnquist dissenting).

[66] See *Webster*, 492 US at 568-69 (Stevens concurring in part and dissenting in part); see also *Cruzan*, 110 S Ct at 2888 (Stevens dissenting) ("It is not within the province of secular government to circumscribe the liberties of the people by regulations designed wholly for the purpose of establishing a sectarian definition of life."); *Hodgson v Minnesota*, 110 S Ct 2926, 2937 (1990) ("[T]he regulation of constitutionally protected decisions . . .

bition against abortion, like a prohibition against birth control, might be justified by a general interest in increasing the population of the community or the planet. Although such a justification might make a good deal of sense after a community has been devastated by war or plague, it would surely be irrational in urban America today.

Third, the constitutional issues that the abortion controversy generates cannot be entirely divorced from the topics under consideration in this comprehensive symposium on the Bill of Rights. For the Supreme Court decisions involving so-called unenumerated rights—such as the right to marry, the right to travel, the right to exercise dominion over one's body, and the right to decide whether to bear or to beget a child—make it clear that those rights have the same source as those that are enumerated in those parts of the Bill of Rights that are enforced against the states under the incorporation doctrine.

IV.

That source is the idea of liberty. Although that idea is difficult to define, the Court has given it meaning in specific cases and controversies. On the whole, the Court's decisions interpreting and reinterpreting the idea of liberty have enlarged the concept. For example, I have no doubt that the views expressed by Justice Holmes and Justice Brandeis in their separate opinions in *Gitlow v New York*,[68] and *Whitney v California*,[69] though then unacceptable to the majority, are now part of our law. The right to marry a person of a different race,[70] or a person incarcerated in a different

---

must be predicated on legitimate state concerns other than disagreement with the choice the individual has made. . . . Otherwise, the interest in liberty protected by the Due Process Clause would be a nullity.").

[67] See *Meyer*, 262 US at 399-400 ("liberty may not be interfered with, under the guise of protecting the public interest, by legislative action which is arbitrary or without reasonable relation to some purpose within the competency of the State to effect"); *Pierce*, 268 US at 535 ("rights guaranteed by the Constitution may not be abridged by legislation which has no reasonable relation to some purpose within the competency of the State"); *Thornburgh*, 476 US at 789 (White dissenting) ("State action impinging on individual interests need only be rational to survive scrutiny under the Due Process Clause, and the determination of rationality is to be made with a heavy dose of deference to the policy choices of the legislature.").

[68] See note 37 and accompanying text.

[69] See note 38 and accompanying text.

[70] See *Loving v Virginia*, 388 US 1, 12 (1967) ("The Fourteenth Amendment requires that the freedom of choice to marry not be restricted by invidious racial discriminations.").

prison,[71] though unmentioned in the text of the Constitution, is now protected by unanimous holdings of the Supreme Court. The general trend of these decisions raises two questions that are far more important than the wisdom or lack of wisdom of any particular holding. Do they represent progress toward the constitutional goal of forming a more perfect union? If so, has that progress been attained by legitimate means?

The answer to the first question does not depend on the means by which the change has been accomplished. It would be the same if every addition to the concept of liberty that judicial decision has produced had instead been achieved by the cumbersome process of amending the text of the Constitution. If that procedure had been followed, would we have a more perfect union today than we had in 1791? Mortimer Adler has recently suggested how that question should be answered.

Although I do not endorse his suggestion that the Court should wield the power to invalidate unjust legislation even if it is not unconstitutional, he is persuasive when he argues that one's views about a just society will determine whether a change in the law represents progress. Commenting on Judge Bork's confirmation hearings, Dr. Adler wrote:

> The nominee might even have been asked whether he thought the eighteenth-century Constitution, allowing as it did for the disenfranchisement of women, blacks, and the poor who could not pay poll taxes, was or was not unjust. If he said that no objectively valid principles of justice enabled him to answer that question, he might still have been asked on what grounds the thirteenth, fourteenth, fifteenth, nineteenth, and twenty-fourth amendments were adopted in subsequent years and whether they represented progress in the direction of social justice, regression, or neither?[72]

In my judgment, no matter how one defines the "just society" or the "perfect union" mentioned in the Preamble to the Constitution, it is appropriate to characterize the amendments identified by Dr. Adler as well as the trend of decisions that I have identified above as progress.

---

[71] *Turner v Safley*, 482 US 78, 99-100 (1987) (state regulation banning marriages among inmates without supervisor's approval violates the Fourteenth Amendment).

[72] Mortimer Adler, *Robert Bork: The Lessons to Be Learned*, 84 Nw U L Rev 1121, 1123 (1990).

I am also convinced that the progress in the development of our constitutional law has been achieved by legitimate means. The risk of unwise decisions is always present, and that concern is greatest when the Court concludes that the strong presumption of validity that attaches to decisions made by the elected representatives of the majority has been overcome.[73] Moreover, just as risk is a characteristic of a free economic market, so also may every expansion of individual liberty pose some additional danger for society. But risk—even serious risk—is part of the price that must be paid for freedom.

Unlike their French counterparts, the Framers of our Constitution wisely refused to stake the fate of the nation on the will of the transient majority. With equal wisdom they made no attempt to fashion a Napoleonic Code that would provide detailed answers to the many questions that would inevitably confront future generations.[74] Instead, they used general language to construct a framework allocating decisionmaking powers among different branches of government. The provisions for the appointment and life tenure of federal judges were obviously designed to enable them to perform their professional tasks impartially, without fear of popular disapproval. Their duty to adjudicate cases and controversies obviously encompasses an obligation to interpret the text of the Constitution. As Justice Cardozo reminded us, "this power of interpretation must be lodged somewhere, and the custom of the constitution has lodged it in the judges. If they are to fulfill their function as judges, it could hardly be lodged elsewhere."[75] I firmly believe that the Framers of the Constitution expected and intended the vast open spaces in our charter of government to be filled not only by legislative enactment but also by the common-

---

[73] As Justice Powell observed in *Moore v City of East Cleveland*, "[t]here *are* risks when the judicial branch gives enhanced protection to certain substantive liberties without the guidance of the more specific provisions of the Bill of Rights." 431 US 494, 502 (1977). Even against the backdrop of *Lochner*, however, he concluded that although "history counsels caution and restraint . . . . it does not counsel abandonment . . . ." Id.

[74] Gerhard Casper has noted:

[T]he [Napoleonic] Code in many crucial provisions uses language whose level of generality is not much distinguishable from that of the Constitution. This is one reason why the code has lasted for almost 200 years. Many of its provisions are incomprehensible unless you consult the gloss put on them by French courts.

Letter from Gerhard Casper, Provost, The University of Chicago, to the author (Jan 20, 1992). In light of Casper's observation, perhaps my reference should have been to the Internal Revenue Code rather than the Napoleonic Code.

[75] Benjamin Cardozo, *The Nature of the Judicial Process* 135-36 (Yale, 1921).

law process of step-by-step adjudication[76] that was largely responsible for the development of the law at the time this nation was conceived.[77] That process has largely eliminated the use of coerced confessions in criminal trials, curtailed racial discrimination in the selection of juries, and extended First Amendment protection to artistic expression as well as to political speech.

Disagreement with a particular decision does not justify an attack on the entire decisional process. Judgments that apply principles that are embedded in the Constitution, that are supported by a candid attempt to explain the application of the principle and the relevance of prior decisions, represent appropriate developments of the law even when neither text nor history supplies the entire basis for the new decision. The work of federal judges from the days of John Marshall to the present, like the work of the English common-law judges, sometimes requires the exercise of judgment[78]—a faculty that inevitably calls into play notions of justice, fairness, and concern about the future impact of a decision. The fact that such concerns play a role in the decisional process does

---

[76] Cardozo's description of the judge's task in statutory construction is equally appropriate in describing the judge's task in constitutional interpretation:

There are gaps to be filled. There are doubts and ambiguities to be cleared. There are hardships and wrongs to be mitigated if not avoided. Interpretation is often spoken of as if it were nothing but the search and the discovery of a meaning which, however obscure and latent, had none the less a real and ascertainable pre-existence in the legislator's mind. The process is, indeed that at times, but it is often something more.

. . . .

Interpretation, thus enlarged, becomes more than the ascertainment of the meaning and intent of lawmakers whose collective will has been declared. It supplements the declaration, and fills the vacant spaces, by the same processes and methods that have built up the customary law.

Id at 14-15, 17.

[77] "Originalism was not the original interpretive doctrine of the framers nor of the framing generation. It was taken for granted that the Constitution, like other legal texts, would be interpreted by men who were learned in the law, arguing cases and writing judgments in the way lawyers and judges had done for centuries in England and its colonies." Charles Fried, *Order and Law: Arguing the Reagan Revolution—A Firsthand Account* 66 (Simon & Schuster, 1991) (footnote omitted).

For an account of the interpretive techniques used in the Framers' day, see H. Jefferson Powell, *The Original Understanding of Original Intent*, 98 Harv L Rev 885 (1985) (arguing that approaches to constitutional interpretation in the Framers' day differ from the approach now taken by those who say we should look to the Framers' intent). There has, of course, been a lively scholarly debate about Powell's view. See, for example, Raoul Berger, *"Original Intention" in Historical Perspective*, 54 Geo Wash L Rev 296 (1986) (challenging Powell's claims).

[78] Justice Harlan's advice to those engaged in the difficult task of defining due process is equally apt to those engaged in the difficult task of judging: "No formula could serve as a substitute . . . for judgment and restraint." *Poe v Ullman*, 367 US 497, 542 (1961) (Harlan dissenting).

not undermine the legitimacy of the process that, for the most part, has served the nation well for two centuries.

V.

Progress in the development of the law, to borrow again from Justice Cardozo:

> is neither a straight line nor a curve. It is a series of dots and dashes. Progress comes *per saltum*, by successive compromises between extremes, compromises often, if I may borrow Professor Cohen's phrase, between "positivism and idealism." "The notion that a jurist can dispense with any consideration as to what the law ought to be arises from the fiction that the law is a complete and closed system, and that judges and jurists are mere automata to record its will or phonographs to pronounce its provisions." Ideas of justice will no more submit to be "banished from the theory of law" than "from its administration."[79]

An important protection against the unwise use of the judicial power to interpret the Constitution has its origin in common-law jurisprudence. Judges have always attached less importance to dicta than to the portions of an opinion that are necessary to explain a judgment. The doctrine of judicial restraint, which counsels against the use of unnecessary dicta, also imposes on federal judges the obligation to avoid unnecessary or unduly expansive constitutional adjudication.[80] Justice Brandeis is the author of the leading opinion expounding this doctrine—*Ashwander v Tennessee Valley Authority*[81]—as well as some of the Court's most inspiring words about the idea of liberty. I quote three sentences from his opinion in *Whitney v California* to illustrate the latter point:

> Those who won our independence believed that the final end of the State was to make men free to develop their faculties;

---

[79] Benjamin N. Cardozo, *The Paradoxes of Legal Science* 26-27 (Columbia, 1927) (footnotes omitted).

[80] "The doctrine teaches judges to focus their attention on the issue that must be addressed in order to decide the case or controversy between the specific litigants before the Court." Stevens, *Judicial Restraint*, 22 San Diego L Rev 437, 446 (1985).

[81] 297 US 288, 346 (1936) (Brandeis concurring) ("The Court will not 'anticipate a question of constitutional law in advance of the necessity of deciding it.'") (quoting *Liverpool, New York and Philadelphia S.S. Co. v Commissioners of Emigration*, 113 US 33, 39 (1885)); see also *Burton v United States*, 196 US 283, 295 (1905) ("It is not the habit of the court to decide questions of a constitutional nature unless absolutely necessary to a decision of the case.").

and that in its government the deliberative forces should prevail over the arbitrary. They valued liberty both as an end and as a means. They believed liberty to be the secret of happiness and courage to be the secret of liberty.[82]

In response to Abraham Lincoln's call for "a new birth of freedom" in his Gettysburg Address,[83] the second century of the history of the Bill of Rights witnessed significant progressive change in the idea of liberty. Historical and textual analyses have played an important role during that century of progress, but they did not limit absolutely the Court's exercise of judgment in performing its task of interpreting the underlying meaning of a dynamic concept. Let us hope that the inability to decipher the actual intent of the architects of the Constitution—like the inability to decipher the Stonehenge text—will not prevent the exercise of sound judgment from continuing the progressive development of the idea of liberty during the third century of the life of the Bill of Rights.

---

[82] 274 US at 375 (Brandeis concurring).
[83] Quoted in Commager, ed, 1 *Documents* at 429 (cited in note 31).

EXCHANGES

PROPERTY AND THE POLITICS OF DISTRUST

Property, Speech, and the Politics of Distrust

Richard A. Epstein[†]

I. PROPERTY AND SPEECH: CONSTITUTIONAL OPPOSITES OR CONSTITUTIONAL TWINS?

My task in this article is not an enviable one: It is to persuade you that the dominant mode of thinking about property rights during the past fifty years has been a mistake of constitutional dimensions. It would be convenient if I could say that I merely favor a return to the set of doctrines that governed economic liberty and property before 1937, in the so-called *Lochner* era.[1] Yet that description would understate the difference between my views

---

[†] James Parker Hall Distinguished Service Professor of Law, The University of Chicago. This Article was prepared for *The Bill of Rights in the Welfare State: A Bicentennial Symposium*, held at The University of Chicago Law School on October 25-26, 1991, in a debate with Professor Frank I. Michelman of Harvard University, to whose work on eminent domain I continue to be heavily indebted. I should like to thank Elena Kagan, Lawrence L. Lessig, Michael W. McConnell, Daniel Shapiro, and Geoffrey R. Stone for their valuable comments on an earlier draft of this Article. I have also benefitted from the comments I received when I presented versions of this paper at a faculty seminar at the Institute of Humanities at Dartmouth College, and at a lecture at the Vermont Law School in November, 1991.

[1] The era is, of course, named after *Lochner v New York*, 198 US 45 (1905). For a leading attack on the case, see Cass R. Sunstein, Lochner's *Legacy*, 87 Colum L Rev 873 (1987). In truth, before 1937, courts routinely upheld economic regulations that deviated dramatically from common law principles, of which rent control statutes are only the most conspicuous examples. See *New York Central R.R. Co v White*, 243 US 188 (1917) (upholding the constitutionality of New York's workmen's compensation act). For a discussion of the manifest inconsistencies in those decisions supposedly protective of economic liberties, see Richard A. Epstein, *The Mistakes of 1937*, 11 Geo Mason U L Rev 5, 13-20 (Winter 1988).

and the historical evolution of the law. Some of the most restrictive decisions on property rights took place in the years before
1937, often by judges who would be described as conservative by
modern standards. I refer here by way of example to the lamenta-
ble decisions of Justice Holmes in *Block v Hirsh*,[2] and of Justice
Sutherland in *Euclid v Ambler Realty Co.*[3] The first of these upheld the power of the state to impose rent control restrictions,
"temporarily" of course;[4] and the second gave the state expansive
powers to control land use through zoning,[5] a power that has
hardly been enlarged in the ensuing sixty years of ceaseless
litigation.

I am therefore urging not a return to some lost golden era, but
the adoption of a regime for the protection of private property and
economic liberties that is far more extensive and internally coherent than the patchwork of protections afforded to these interests
under the Takings Clause before 1937. More difficult still, I believe
that all this transformation is possible even with the universal acceptance of the "welfare state"—the commitment to support people in need by casting that burden on others through the coercive
mechanism of the state—which has become a permanent part of
the basic constitutional order at both the state and federal level.
My task is made more complicated in that the defense of the present constitutional scheme is undertaken by Professor Frank
Michelman, who surely ranks among the most eloquent expositors
of the Just Compensation Clause, and as one of the most ardent
defenders of the modern legal order that I seek to undermine.[6]

In order to develop my case, I shall pursue the analysis from
an unconventional quarter: I shall look at the doctrinal structures
of First Amendment law and then indicate how they can, and
should, be carried over into the analysis and discussion of the Takings Clause. My basic conclusion is that the Takings Clause and
economic liberties should not be viewed as things alien and uncongenial to modern constitutional norms. One need only apply to pri-

---

[2] 256 US 135 (1921). I have criticized Holmes's *Block* opinion in Richard A. Epstein,
Takings: Private Property and the Power of Eminent Domain 176-77 (Harvard, 1985)
("*Takings*"); and in Richard A. Epstein, *Rent Control and the Theory of Efficient Regula-
tion*, 54 Brooklyn L Rev 741, 748-50 (1988).

[3] 272 US 365 (1926). I have also criticized Sutherland's *Euclid* opinion in Epstein, *Takings* at 131-34 (cited in note 2).

[4] *Block*, 256 US at 154.

[5] *Euclid*, 272 US at 388-90.

[6] See Frank I. Michelman, *Property, Utility, and Fairness: Comments on the Ethical
Foundations of "Just Compensation" Law*, 80 Harv L Rev 1165 (1967), an acknowledged
classic in the area.

vate property the presuppositions and techniques that have organized the law of freedom of speech. Within this framework the *sole* concession that one must make to the welfare state is to accept income redistribution funded with taxes (perhaps even progressive taxes) derived from general revenue sources. Otherwise, the edifice to protect freedom of speech carries over to private property, without losing a beat.

In comparing amendments, there is a genuine question as to which body of First Amendment law one should consult. The obvious point of departure is the body of case law developed by the United States Supreme Court. That is, of course, an incredibly complicated body of law, with many nuances that are not necessarily relevant to the present discussion.[7] More critically to this enterprise, it may well contain certain serious mistakes of both under- and over-protection of speech that can embarrass any general theory.

Some of the free speech decisions are simply wrong in principle. For example, *New York Times Co. v Sullivan*[8] protects speech more than a comprehensive theory of speech requires.[9] In the opposite direction, of course, a consistent theory also requires more extensive protection of speech than the Court now provides.[10]

Other free speech decisions, though sound in principle, incorrectly apply the principle to the case at hand. One conspicuous illustration is perhaps *United States v O'Brien*,[11] where the Supreme Court upheld the conviction of the defendant for burning his draft card, in violation of a content-neutral statute that forbade the willful destruction of draft cards for any purpose.[12] The Court announced that it followed a test of compelling state interest, which I regard as sound law.[13] But the Court then so watered down its application as to allow the weakest forms of administra-

---

[7] For one recent account, see Geoffrey R. Stone, et al, *Constitutional Law* 1011-454 (Little Brown, 2d ed 1991).

[8] 376 US 254 (1964).

[9] See Richard A. Epstein, *Was* New York Times v. Sullivan *Wrong?*, 53 U Chi L Rev 782 (1986). See also text accompanying notes 66-70.

[10] See text accompanying notes 93-95.

[11] 391 US 367 (1968).

[12] Id at 382.

[13] The relevant portion of the opinion reads:

To characterize the quality of the governmental interest which must appear, the Court has employed a variety of descriptive terms: compelling; substantial; subordinating; paramount; cogent; strong. Whatever imprecision inheres in these terms, we think it clear that a government regulation is sufficiently justified if it is within the constitutional power of the Government; if it furthers an important or substantial governmental interest; if the governmental interest is unrelated to the suppression of free expres-

tive convenience—communication with draftees, reminders of civic obligations—to count as compelling state interests.[14]

A similar debasement of the compelling state interest test is apparent in *Austin v Michigan State Chamber of Commerce*.[15] There the Court found a compelling state interest that allowed Michigan to prohibit corporations from making independent expenditures to support or oppose candidates for state elective office. The Court's inquiry on the question of state justification was, however, wholly disingenuous, for the Court contented itself with unsupported assertions that corporate contributions were "corrosive and distorting" of the overall level of political debates.[16] But there was no effort to offer any account of those rough and tumble political debates which were uncorrupted and undistorted. Nor was there the slightest recognition that different corporations might weigh in on different sides of election campaigns, or that political expenditures by corporations might be especially valuable precisely because corporations (and their out-of-state shareholders) could not vote in elections whose outcome is of major importance to them. It is difficult to see how any selective restriction on the parties entitled to engage in political speech should survive a First Amendment challenge.

I regard it, however, as mistaken to allow the covert dilutions of the compelling state interest test in either *O'Brien* or *Austin* to organize any comparison between First and Fifth Amendment law. Even after these decisions, it is possible to make sensible internal adjustments and reevaluations of First Amendment law to facilitate the appropriate comparisons.[17] Basically, the "corrections" that one must make to speech law for the analysis to be good must satisfy two conditions: First, they cannot be so numerous that they completely revise First Amendment law, and second, they must accord with the doctrine's accepted animating principles.

Finally, there is a third limitation with respect to the kinds of issues that I consider. Generally stated, both the First and Fifth

---

sion; and if the incidental restriction on alleged First Amendment freedoms is no greater than is essential to the furtherance of that interest. Id at 376-77 (footnotes omitted).

[14] Id at 378-90.

[15] 94 US 652 (1990). For trenchant criticism, see Jill E. Fisch, *Frankenstein's Monster H t Campaign Trail: An Approach to Regulation of Corporate Political Expenditures*,   V n & Mary L Rev 587 (1991).

[16] *Austin*, 494 US at 660.

[17] For an example of such reevaluation of *O'Brien*, see Dean Alfange, Jr., *Free Speech and Symbolic Conduct: The Draft-Card Burning Case*, 1968 S Ct Rev 1, 23-27, 42-46.

Amendments can apply to two distinct types of situations. In the first, the government seeks to regulate the private activities of individuals on their own property.[18] The activity could be a political meeting, or the construction of a new home. In the second, the government seeks to regulate activities on public property.[19] Thus the issue is how the government can allocate "its" own resources through contract or through grant. Typically the issue is what conditions the government may attach to its permission to use public space or to receive public funding. Sometimes the question is whether the government can condition a tax benefit upon the performance of some particular act or the making of some particular statement.[20] These latter issues are of increasing importance in modern times, and in many cases where the government acts as a contracting party, I think that the law is less protective of both speech and property than it should be.[21] Nonetheless the exclusive focus in this Article shall be on the role of government as *regulator*, not as contracting party, funding agent, or property owner.

With these caveats in mind, it is critical to understand the basic attitude that courts take toward the legislative and executive branches of government. Whatever the virtues of stirring rhetoric, it is clear that the First Amendment cannot prohibit all regulation of speech by all government at all levels. Freedom of speech is not the same as an uninhibited license to speak—to lie, to deceive, to molest, to coerce. So the fundamental postulate of distrust of government does not translate into a total ban against all government regulation of all forms of speech, but into a strong presumption that can be overridden only by establishing some compelling government interest, as the language used in *O'Brien* and *Austin* itself indicated. The key questions therefore under the First Amendment—and they are also the key questions under the Fifth

---

[18] See, for example, *Nollan v California Coastal Commission*, 483 US 825 (1987) (Commission granted a permit allowing construction of a larger house on beachfront property on the condition that the property owners grant the public an easement across their private beach).

[19] See, for example, *Lovell v City of Griffin*, 303 US 444 (1938) (permit required to distribute circulars within the city limits); *Red Lion Broadcasting Co. v FCC*, 395 US 367 (1969) (FCC requirement that each side of a public issue be presented on broadcast stations; the "fairness doctrine").

[20] See, for example, *Speiser v Randall*, 357 US 513 (1958) (veteran's tax exemption conditioned on filing of an oath that taxpayer did not advocate overthrow of the United States or California governments, nor advocate support of a hostile government during wartime).

[21] For a statement of my views, see Richard A. Epstein, *Foreword: Unconstitutional Conditions, State Power, and the Limits of Consent*, 102 Harv L Rev 4 (1988).

Amendment—are the following: First, what is the scope of the initial protection afforded by the presumption in favor of free speech? Second, how can that protection be overridden?

This inquiry, even within a strict interpretative framework, is necessarily vast. No analysis of what is meant by speech alone will determine the contours of *freedom* of speech. Instead it is necessary to detail the operations of a system of freedom, a vast undertaking that reluctant judges undertake only because they labor under the strict compulsion to decide cases. But scholars can and must be more relentless and systematic in their pursuits. The basic outlines of a system of freedom of speech must be delineated and defended. But the size of the payoff is commensurate with the difficulty of the undertaking. If we understand how this body of law works, then we will have a good road map for understanding the Takings Clause.

There are, of course, important differences between the Free Speech and Takings Clauses. The Free Speech Clause does not contain a Just Compensation Clause ("Congress may abridge freedom of speech for public use, with just compensation"),[22] and it is possible to protect freedom of speech without at all confronting what is critical about economic affairs in the welfare state: the redistribution of wealth on the basis of need. But before distinguishing property from speech, it is important to see what general view links them together. The modern insistence that speech is a fundamental liberty, while property is the creature of legislation and subject to its whims, does much to distort the proper relationship between the two sets of constitutional limitations. The Free Speech and Takings Clauses should be understood as working in harmony with each other, not in opposition. It is important therefore never to forget the essentially libertarian cast to both clauses: strong, decentralized private rights and a central government with limited powers, any exercise of which must be justified.

In this Article I shall outline the basic linkage between these two clauses in order to demonstrate that what has proved sound policy for speech should pay handsome social dividends for property and economic affairs as well. Indeed, there is good reason to believe that free speech will produce more net social benefit in a world in which property rights are more carefully protected than under the present state of affairs, where there is essentially no con-

---

[22] Compare US Const, Amend I ("Congress shall make no law . . . abridging the freedom of speech . . . ."), with US Const, Amend V ("[N]or shall private property be taken for public use without just compensation.").

stitutional protection of property and contract against prospective legislation, or, it now appears, against retroactive legislation as well.[23] In order to make this case, I shall explicate the dominant tendencies of First Amendment law through the eyes of a cautious libertarian, and then show how the parallel issues for property are usually resolved in a very different fashion.

The plan of action is therefore as follows. In Section II, I argue that the constitutional defenses of property and speech rest on the sense that government is a necessary evil. Government is necessary to preserve civil order, but its officials should not be viewed as saviors; they are self-interested persons with imperfect knowledge subject to a universal presumption of distrust.

In Section III, I identify the extensive set of issues common to freedom of speech and to the protection of private property. I show how the postulate of distrust organizes First Amendment doctrine, and how its absence explains the flaccid and unprincipled structure of the law protecting private property and economic liberties. The points of parallelism are made evident by the logical structure of the two clauses. Both clauses set initial presumptions, and not final absolutes. In both areas, therefore, the complete inquiry requires at least five stages: (1) identifying the protected private interest; (2) identifying the state actions that violate that interest; (3) justifying those state actions, if possible; (4) timing the remedy to protect the private interest; and (5) determining whether to force an exchange to curtail that interest.

Finally, in Section IV, I explain how the logical structure of the First Amendment can be carried over to deal with economic liberties, even granting the unassailable first premise of the welfare state—some form of income and wealth distribution in favor of the poor.

II. The Logic of Distrust

It is perhaps useful to begin with a point that can be lost in the more abstract discussion of constitutional theory that follows. There is, of course, both a Free Speech Clause and a Takings Clause (one that contains explicit reference to "private property"), and the extensive interpretive enterprise that follows is an effort to make sense of the two texts in the wide range of situations to which they apply. To begin, however, I do not want to concentrate

---

[23] See, for example, *Usery v Turner-Elkhorn Mining Co.*, 428 US 1 (1976) (constitutionality of retroactive taxes to fund black lung disease compensation plans).

on specific textual difficulties, but on a second aspect of constitutional interpretation of equal dignity with the first: the basic attitudes toward government that are brought to the interpretation of a particular text. Under the First Amendment that attitude clearly is, or has to be, an attitude of distrust.[24]

I do not have in mind any very narrow or technical meaning of distrust. As a matter of hornbook law, the person who receives a friend's money, which she then converts to her own use, is a person who has abused a trust. By like analogy, the person who receives public money, which she then spends for private purposes, has abused a trust as well. In each case, a person stands in a position whereby she can obtain personal gain at the expense of individuals to whom she owes a duty. In other cases, the idea of distrust has to do with favoritism: benefits are given to A that are denied to B; when their roles are reversed, some other "neutral" principle of decision is employed to make sure that A prevails again, for reasons utterly irrelevant to any public purpose. The postulate of distrust holds that persons with a public interest to protect and a political agenda to advance will be willing—across the board—to sacrifice the former in order to advance the latter.

In putting the concern in this particular fashion, the idea of distrust is a universal solvent that can be brought to bear on any political initiative. Distrust has both ancient lineage and modern application: "*Quis custodiet custodies?*" ("Who guards the guardians?") is a Latin maxim that has lost none of its vitality in its contemporary setting. By the same token, distrust is not tied to any narrow or partisan political agenda: Democrat or Republican, liberal or conservative, are equally capable of abusing the public trust. The themes of self-dealing, of waste, of corruption, which are obvious corollaries to the concern with distrust, should also resonate across the usual political lines of controversy. The point is not that all statutes and all government actions are worthy of distrust, for some genuine public interest statutes (think of the Statute of

---

[24] See, for example, Vincent Blasi, *The Checking Value in First Amendment Theory*, 1977 Am Bar Found Res J 521. In particular, Blasi notes:

> One basic value seems highly relevant to these newer claims [for First Amendment protection], yet has not been accorded a central place in our articulated theory of the First Amendment. This is the value that free speech, a free press, and free assembly can serve in checking the abuse of power by public officials.

Id at 527. I will address some of the other values later. It is sufficient to note here that the list of four values announced by Thomas I. Emerson, *The System of Freedom of Expression* 6-7 (Random House, 1970), does not contain the checking value. See text accompanying note 31.

Frauds and the standard statute of limitation) can emerge from the political process. Yet, at the very least, distrust alerts us to the constant temptation facing any public official who is entrusted with extensive power, but who is all too often subject to only limited supervision.

This theme of distrust, suitably qualified, is not only central to political theory; it is also central to any reading of our constitutional heritage. When Madison wrote that "Enlightened statesmen will not always be at the helm,"[25] it was clear that he thought that diversion of public wealth and position for private gain was the central problem that government must face. The force of his remark is only confirmed by looking at the motley collection of public officials holding high office today. Similarly, Madison's discussion of the entire structure of federalism, divided government, and the system of checks and balances at the federal level shows that the theme of distrust has worked itself into the warp and woof of our constitutional structure.

The protection of speech (which is limited to protection against actions by Congress), and the protection of property (which, if anything, is more comprehensive[26]) should be read in light of these political concerns. All too often the desire of political figures to suppress speech has to be understood as a crude effort to suppress criticism of public actors, which could lead to their *deserved* political embarrassment, removal from office, or electoral defeat. Thus the social good of free speech is found in the fundamental check it exerts on how government officials behave.[27] Harry Kalven, while no public choice theorist, was right to stress the importance of seditious libel as the central lesson of the First Amendment—the need to fear government misconduct.[28] A complex set of

---

[25] See Federalist 10 (Madison) in Clinton Rossiter, ed, *The Federalist Papers* 77, 80 (Mentor, 1961) ("It is in vain to say that enlightened statesmen will be able to adjust these clashing interests and render them all subservient to the public good. Enlightened statesmen will not always be at the helm.").

[26] Compare US Const, Amend I ("Congress shall make no law . . . abridging the freedom of speech . . . ."), with US Const, Amend V ("[N]or shall private property be taken for public use with just compensation."). The passive voice of the Fifth Amendment does not expressly limit the Fifth Amendment protection to laws passed by Congress.

[27] See Blasi, 1977 Am Bar Found Res J at 529-38 (cited in note 24), for the antecedents in Locke and Madison.

[28] See Harry Kalven, Jr., *The New York Times Case: A Note on "The Central Meaning of the First Amendment"*, 1964 S Ct Rev 191, 205 ("[A]nalysis of free-speech issues should hereafter begin with the significant issue of seditious libel and defamation of government by its critics rather than with the sterile example of a man falsely yelling fire in a crowded theatre."). Kalven may have been correct about the example, but he was wrong about the tradition. Holmes used the example of crying fire in order to show why the free-

doctrines for both content regulation and content-neutral regulation has grown up out of this fear of government misconduct.[29] This fear, while strongest for political speech,[30] surely extends to manifold other forms of artistic and literary expression as well.

A.   Distrust: A Single Rationale for Speech and Takings Law

This effort to locate a *single* concern behind the First Amendment is at variance with the common intellectual practice, which insists that there are many separate "value bases" that lie behind the interpretation of any given constitutional provision. The dominant modes of modern interpretation are far too ecumenical: They try to find a broad collection of values to justify the key constitutional provisions, and then pick that rule which best accommodates those competing values. Thus Professor Emerson's list for free speech, which has achieved the status of conventional wisdom, includes individual self-fulfillment, the pursuit of truth in the marketplace of ideas, participation in public life, and the maintenance of a stable community through interaction and exchange.[31]

I am instinctively and deeply suspicious of explanations that rely on a combination of many independent factors to generate the doctrinal structure of any area of law. The objection is formal. Two values can either cut in the same direction or in different directions. If they cut in the same direction, then it is not possible to choose between them. If they cut in different directions, then any outcome can be achieved by assigning the right weight to the preferred value. The uneasiness that many commentators have had with "balancing tests" under the First Amendment is not only because of the practical indeterminacy of such tests, but also because of their theoretical malleability: When no single variable is to be maximized, then any solution is as good as any other. We should have the same suspicion of these loose tests under the Takings

---

dom of speech was not an absolute. See *Schenck v United States*, 249 US 47, 52 (1919). But the early cases testing the limitations on speech were all concerned with seditious activities and national security. *Schenck* itself involved pamphlets urging resistance to the draft. See id at 50-51.

   [29] For exhaustive and sympathetic expositions of the basic positions, see Geoffrey R. Stone, *Content Regulation and the First Amendment*, 25 Wm & Mary L Rev 189 (1983); Geoffrey R. Stone, *Content-Neutral Restrictions*, 54 U Chi L Rev 46 (1987).

   [30] Compare Cass R. Sunstein, *Free Speech Now*, in this volume, 255, 262-63, 301 (First Amendment principally protects political speech).

   [31] Emerson, *The System of Freedom of Expression* at 6-8 (cited in note 24).

Clause, where the plastic nature of the doctrine is evident upon the slightest inspection.[32]

It is important therefore to recognize that there is weakness and not strength in the common effort to find plural bases for speech and takings law.[33] In order to show that such strategies are not appropriate, I make just two assumptions: first, that legislators and executives always have perfect knowledge, and second, that they always seek to serve the public good. On these assumptions, I argue, even if the First and Fifth Amendments were given the most stringent interpretations imaginable, every statute would be constitutional under the most stringent standards of judicial review.[34]

1. Distrust and the Takings Clause.

To demonstrate, let us begin with the Takings Clause. What kinds of economic legislation should we expect the legislature to pass if it had perfect knowledge and perfect motivation? In the first place, we should expect that each and every statute would expand the total size of the economic pie. There would be no reason for the legislature to adopt any rule that would cost the losers more than it would provide to the winners. The allocative losses involved are losses that are imposed on someone, and a legislature with perfect knowledge would know that these losses exist, and one with perfect motivation would never wish to inflict them gratuitously. Instead the legislature would adopt only those proposals that produced a net benefit for the citizenry at large. Markets would be allowed to operate where they functioned well; where they did not, they would only be restrained by the best possible system of legislation.

Thus the first consequence of this system is that each public transaction would produce a net social gain; that is, the legislature would achieve Kaldor-Hicks optimality.[35] The Takings Clause, however, is concerned not only with the size of the gain, but also

---

[32] I pursue this theme in Richard A. Epstein, *Not Deference, But Doctrine: The Eminent Domain Clause*, 1982 S Ct Rev 351.

[33] For the opposite conclusion, as applied to takings, see Stephen R. Munzer, *A Theory of Property* ch 11 (Cambridge, 1990).

[34] I have developed this argument with respect to the Takings Clause in Richard A. Epstein, *The Utilitarian Foundations of Natural Law*, 12 Harv J L & Pub Pol 713, 745-47 (1989).

[35] Under the Kaldor-Hicks standard of optimality, a transaction is judged to be efficient only if it produces a net gain, whether or not it improves the economic position of each individual party to the transaction.

with its distribution. It is designed to ensure that any allocative improvements introduced by the legislature do not suffer from attendant distributive dislocations. In other words, the Just Compensation Clause contemplates the Pareto standard of optimality,[36] not the Kaldor-Hicks standard.[37]

But if the legislature is knowledgeable and benevolent, it will also make the right *allocative* decision in every case; it will achieve Pareto optimality as well. Even if there are losers under one statute, it is likely that they will be the winners in the next, for the benevolent legislature will not favor one class of citizens over another. As the number of contexts in which legislation is passed increases, the odds that any person will be a net loser over the full set of transactions is reduced asymptotically to zero.[38] Given that the winners and losers in each case are randomly selected from the whole, it follows that there is no need for the winners to compensate the losers in any individual transaction. It also follows that the legislature will not even have to pay the administrative costs of calculating losses and gains in each case: It knows it will achieve Pareto optimality over time and across statutes, and so it can dispense with the entire process of valuation and side payments.

The motivation for the Takings Clause must come from a fear that the legislature has imperfect knowledge, imperfect motives, or both. The power to coerce is enormous, and there is the risk that it will be used to benefit those who possess it at the cost of those who suffer from it. One reason to dislike theft is that it has the tendency to move goods from high to low value uses with positive administrative costs. The same dangers inhere in legislation under a system of majority rule. The Just Compensation Clause requires payment for the taking as a means of disciplining the legislature. If the legislature can afford to pay when it takes, then the fact of compensation itself gives some reason to believe in the net social gain. The clause therefore is designed to prevent allocative losses through collective action, and that problem only arises if the legislature has imperfect knowledge or imperfect motivations. Without legislative abuse, there would be no need to insist upon compensation.

---

[36] Under the Pareto standard of optimality, a transaction is judged to be efficient if it improves, or at least does not worsen, the economic position of *each* individual party to the transaction.

[37] Thus a transaction which achieves Kaldor-Hicks optimality, but which worsens the economic position of one or more parties to the transaction, can only achieve Pareto optimality if the winners then compensate the losers.

[38] See Epstein, 12 Harv J L & Pub Pol at 746 & n 60 (cited in note 34).

On the other side of the coin, the Just Compensation Clause also eliminates the need for the judiciary to compare what the public gains from the statute with what the individual property owner loses. The danger of legislative abuse invites judicial oversight of the legislature. A compensation test thus becomes necessary in order to reduce the otherwise horrendous pressures on the judicial system to sort out which government interventions are justified and which are not. But the courts have access to little information about what kinds of transactions benefit the public, and, by definition, cannot trust any information on that score provided by the state. On the other hand, the courts *can* get tolerable measures of individual losses in a wide range of cases, or can find some structural reason in the even distribution of benefits and burdens[39] to obviate the need for direct measurement of public benefit in each case. The constitutional articulation of a just compensation standard is not equivalent to a "taking with good cause" standard. It is invoked not only to secure justice to the individual, but also to combat the untrustworthiness of government officials.

2.　Distrust and the Free Speech Clause.

The analysis of distrust under the First Amendment is similar. It is often said that the First Amendment is designed to serve other values: to encourage participation in good government; to ensure that a diversity of viewpoints are expressed; to enable personal self-realization.[40] The control of legislative abuse is thought to be only one value among many, and a late entry into the pantheon at that.

But again suppose that there were no fear of abuse, so that the legislature passed speech laws with perfect knowledge and benevolent motives. Why then the concern? The ideal legislature would be as concerned with individual self-realization as any court, and it would better know how to achieve it. If collective support for speech were necessary, the legislature would provide the proper subsidies to the proper persons in the proper amounts. It would promote the necessary diversity of opinions and provide the information necessary to facilitate good individual choices. But, if restrictions on speech were necessary to facilitate the right choices, the legislature would also provide them. Quite simply, the good

---

[39] See the discussion of disproportionate impact tests in Epstein, *Takings* at 204-09 (cited in note 2).

[40] See text accompanying note 31.

and knowledgeable legislature wants what the learned scholars of
constitutional law want. If we had no cause to distrust the legislature, then we could dispense with the costly and inconvenient apparatus of judicial review of the First Amendment, and could rely
upon Meiklejohn's good citizens to reach the right result every
time.[41] His version of the "good man" calls for a celebration of free
speech, but gives no reason why speech needs or should receive
constitutional protection.

Yet we do not take Meiklejohn's carefree attitude, and abuse
of public office is the *only* reason for political aspiration to be
transferred into constitutional protection. From virtuous legislators there is little to fear, and it is doubtful that the First Amendment will constrain them in any meaningful way. But bad legislators in power have a tendency to stay in power. Just as they will
steal, there is a risk that they will stifle criticism, rig debate, and
disseminate falsehoods to achieve their ends. It is to them, or to
their control, that the First Amendment is dedicated.

But why trust the judges, who are subject to imperfections of
their own? The answer is that there is no system of perfect control,
and judicial review is simply part of the better overall strategy to
curb abuse. The reason is that judicial review is another mechanism that provides for a division of power. With judicial review in
place, any piece of legislation has to clear an additional hurdle—which is good, because the presumption of distrust translates
into the belief that more rather than less legislation is the greater
danger. But there should be no illusion: If *all* branches of govern-

[41] See Alexander Meiklejohn, *Political Freedom: The Constitutional Powers of the People* (Harper, 1960) (originally published in 1948). As Vincent Blasi has noted, Meiklejohn's participation theory treats government as a large town meeting, composed of virtuous citizens who participate for the common good. Blasi, 1977 Am Bar Found Res J at 554-67 (cited in note 24). Meiklejohn's virtuous citizen is the antithesis of the "bad man" of whom Holmes wrote in Oliver Wendell Holmes, Jr., *The Path of the Law*, 10 Harv L Rev 457 (1897). Of Holmes, Meiklejohn said:

> As against the dogma of Mr. Holmes I would venture to assert the counterdogma that one cannot understand the basic purposes of our Constitution as a judge or a citizen should understand them, unless one sees them as a good man, a man who, in his politi-cal activities, is not merely fighting for what, under the law, he can get, but is eagerly and generously serving the common welfare.

Blasi, 1977 Am Bar Found Res J at 557 (cited in note 24) (quoting Meiklejohn, *Political Freedom* at 66).

The asserted separation between the private and public self adumbrates many of the themes prominent in the republican revival of the 1980s. See, for example, Frank I. Michelman, *Foreword: Traces of Self-Government*, 100 Harv L Rev 4 (1986); Cass R. Sunstein, *Beyond the Republican Revival*, 97 Yale L J 1539 (1988). For criticism, see also Richard A. Epstein, *Modern Republicanism—Or the Flight From Substance*, 97 Yale L J 1633 (1988).

ment have unsound beliefs or corrupt motives, then the additional division of power brought on by judicial review still will not alter any flawed outcomes achieved by the legislative process alone. The protection of private property and economic liberties fails today solely because no branch in our government—legislative or judicial—accords them the same weight that they had in the original constitutional scheme.

B. Mutual Reinforcement of Property and Speech Rights

In light of distrust, we should be very leery indeed of any proposals, such as those advanced recently by Owen Fiss,[42] that wish to reduce the protection of freedom of speech to the paltry level now afforded economic liberties. Fiss is correct to see that the basic assumptions about the behavior of government and private officials are as important to the interpretation of the First Amendment as they are to the Fifth. But he sadly underestimates the capacity for legislative abuse that lies in both these areas. The endless machinations of the Federal Communications Commission, a body which regulates both speech and property rights in the spectrum of broadcast frequencies, offer, it seems fair to say, no reason to believe that a system of extensive government regulation would improve the level of political discourse in this country.[43] A simpler strategy that would charge the government with the enforcement of property rights, by actions against interference, is far superior to endless administrative wrangles to decide which groups should receive public subsidies for what activities.

The government necessarily holds a monopoly over force. While large private organizations may develop, their net worth is not a measure of their political power, so long as they can acquire property and influence only by consent and not by coercion. In antitrust law, the size of a firm is not evidence of its market power, and the same conclusion holds for constitutional theory. Let there be many large and powerful voices: They will not speak in unison; and in any event, they will have to pay for what they wish to say.

---

[42] See Owen M. Fiss, *Free Speech and Social Structure*, 71 Iowa L Rev 1405 (1986); Owen M. Fiss, *Why the State?*, 100 Harv L Rev 781 (1987).

[43] The most influential criticism of the FCC is still R.H. Coase, *The Federal Communication Commission*, 2 J L & Econ 1 (1959). Coase's work could not have anticipated the developments of the past thirty years, during which the level of government performance has been every bit as dismal. See also Jonathan W. Emord, *Freedom, Technology, and the First Amendment* (Pacific Research Institute for Public Policy, 1991); Thomas W. Hazlett, *The Rationality of U.S. Regulation of the Broadcast Spectrum*, 33 J L & Econ 133, 133-34 (1990).

So long as there are secure property rights in the press (which there currently are not in broadcasting), then entry will be at low cost and many possible voices will be heard, checking influence with influence and power with power. The great mistake of socialism is to equate the risks of a rich market actor with those of the sole government actor. We should not repeat that mistake as a matter of modern constitutional theory.

1. Limiting factionalism through property rights.

All this is not to say that there is no danger today to our First Amendment rights. There is, but it comes from a source not usually cited. The current laws make it impossible to have well-defined property rights in anything. While possession of property may be secure against government removal, the use and disposition of virtually any asset is fair game for obstruction by the political process, whether through taxation or regulation. That political power sparks private lobbyists to petition government not only for the redress of grievances but also for partisan advantage, and legislators can demand their pound of flesh in return.[44]

Within this environment, more speech is *not* better. Freedom of speech allows factions to organize and mobilize in order to obtain wealth transfers through taxation or regulation; thus freedom of speech only reduces overall social wealth and security. The fierce battles fought by single issue political action groups of all stripes and persuasions are strong evidence of an overheated and wasteful political system in decline. It is partly for this reason that there is such a prevalent desire to control campaign expenditures, a practice which nevertheless has proved fitful and counterproductive.[45]

Yet here the right solution is not to restrict the liberty to speak or to lobby, given the additional risk of government abuse that would be created. It is rather to reduce the power of government to transfer wealth and dispense favors. Once the government cannot do the bidding of the interest groups who crowd its corridors, these groups will devote their efforts to more socially productive activities. The compression of the set of permissible government tasks will indirectly, but effectively, improve the level of

---

[44] For a brief but forceful statement, see Fred S. McChesney, *Rent Extraction and Rent Creation in the Economic Theory of Regulation*, 16 J Legal Stud 101 (1987). The contrast between McChesney and Meiklejohn is manifest.

[45] See, for example, *Buckley v Valeo*, 424 US 1 (1976). I develop this theme further in Epstein, 97 Yale L J at 1643-45 (cited in note 41).

public discourse both by changing the items on the public agenda and by redirecting the resources that are used to obtain them. In short, when viewed in isolation, expansive protection of freedom of speech is neither a good nor a bad. It becomes an unambiguous good only when paired up with a system of limited government and strong property rights.

2. Eliminating "incidental" burdens on speech through property rights.

The structure of property rights influences the patterns of speech and discourse in yet another fashion. It is accepted hornbook law that the First Amendment does not cover regulations of private property that have only an incidental effect upon speech, no matter how large that incidental effect.[46] Of course, it is understandable that the Supreme Court would adopt a rule of this sort, since it has already decided to scrap any extensive constitutional protection for property rights. It has to police the undeniable friction that takes place at the property/speech frontier. Otherwise, the Court is in danger of indirectly undoing all forms of property regulation in the name of free speech.

This danger is sufficiently great that indirect burdens may be placed on speech so long as the restriction passes nondiscrimination and intent tests. The nondiscrimination test requires that the restriction be imposed upon activities both unrelated and related to speech. The intent test requires that the government not disguise its real purpose to attack speech through the regulation in question.

The net effect of this regime is to countenance a very large reduction in the amount and quality of speech that reaches the public. I have two favorite recent examples of this problem. The first is that of the New York newspapers. Under the above two-pronged test, the government can require newspapers (whose editorial content cannot otherwise be regulated) to negotiate with unions under the National Labor Relations Act. As a result, the New York Times has been locked in extensive negotiations with its unions over work crews and job assignments for its modern New Jersey plant, which is capable of printing colored pictures.[47] Similarly, the New York Daily News has been caught in bitter union

---

[46] See Frank I. Michelman, *Liberties, Fair Values, and Constitutional Method*, 59 U Chi L Rev 91, 112 (1992).

[47] See *New York Times Reaches Agreement with Union*, Reuters Bus Rep (Dec 12, 1991).

strikes, which have resulted in violence, disrupted its service, and eventually forced the sale of the Daily News in order to escape labor negotiations.[48] The second example, which involves both religion and speech, is that of St. Bartholomew's Church in New York. Under the two-pronged test, the government can subject private organizations such as churches to zoning laws which restrict their ability to sell their property. As a result, St. Bartholomew's has been driven toward bankruptcy because it cannot sell or develop its valuable real estate, which has been declared a landmark by the city of New York.[49] In all of these cases, the courts have refused to single out the press (or religion) for special treatment, determining that the consequences of the regulations, while large, were nonetheless "incidental."[50]

But of course in real life the consequences are more than "incidental." And a stronger system of property protection would have obviated these consequences. All firms would be free to decide the workers to whom they wish to offer jobs, and all landowners would be able to develop their property, subject to the ordinary constraints of nuisance law, without having first to obtain state approval. A greater level of constitutional protection for property rights would prevent the doctrine of incidental effects from stifling constitutional protection of free speech. Indeed, a unified conception of speech and property would leave no place at all for the doctrine of incidental effects under the First Amendment, which is all to the good. That doctrine is but a concession to the reality that there are great losses that must go unredressed—it counts as a point in favor of a unified theory that it can dispense with so unsatisfactory a conception.

A system which protects private property rights, driven by a universal conception of distrust, thus improves speech in two directions. First, it undermines the incentives for unproductive factional speech by eliminating the gains from factional politics. Second, it reduces the cost of the speech that is left, by protecting speech against the incidental burdens of property regulation. And it does both without increasing the dangers of central government control.

---

[48] See David E. Pitt, *News Having Trouble Getting Paper Out*, NY Times B4 (Oct 29, 1990).

[49] See *St. Bartholomew's Church v City of New York*, 914 F2d 348 (2d Cir 1990) (upholding New York City's landmark law against Free Exercise Clause and Takings Clause challenges).

[50] Id at 355.

Constitutional law has gone badly astray in creating the massive divide between speech and property. In order to show just how badly off course it has gone, it is useful to examine the doctrinal underpinnings in both speech and takings law. In that light, my views in *Takings*[51] will not seem fanciful, idealistic, utopian or anachronistic, for they represent a point-by-point extension to the Takings Clause of much of First Amendment law. The successes of the First Amendment can, and should, point the way to the revitalization of takings law.

III. PROPERTY AND SPEECH: DOCTRINAL PARALLELS

Presently, the great divide between property and speech rests on differing conceptions of distrust in each doctrinal area. The postulate of distrust drives the law of freedom of speech and, with some exceptions, has led the Court to create a coherent and powerful intellectual structure. The opposite presumption of legislative knowledge and probity has led to a continuous judicial horror show with respect to economic liberties and private property, in which judges strain to avoid the literal meaning of constitutional provisions in order to obtain indefensible doctrinal results.

Nonetheless, the possibility of parallel construction of the Free Speech and Takings Clauses should be evident in the parallelism of the questions that arise under both of the clauses: First, what is the scope of the substantive interest to be protected? Second, what government acts violate that interest? Third, what might justify the state in violating that interest? Fourth, what is the remedy for the violation of that interest? Fifth, and perhaps surprisingly for the First Amendment, when does the just compensation principle allow the state to force an exchange?

These five questions are precisely parallel to those that arise in any private law discourse: What is the protected interest? What is the defendant's wrong? What justification can the defendant offer for the prima facie violation of the interest? What is the remedy for the private wrong? When does the libertarian principle yield to forced exchanges?[52] Essentially every substantive question in public law can be organized around these five issues. But the range of response may be so different, and parallel interests

---

[51] Epstein, *Takings* (cited in note 2).

[52] One example of a forced exchange is the case of private necessity. See *Vincent v Lake Erie Transportation Co.*, 109 Minn 456, 124 NW 221 (1910). The parallels between conditional privilege and the Just Compensation Clause were developed in Dale W. Broeder, *Torts and Just Compensation: Some Personal Reflections*, 17 Hastings L J 217 (1965).

(speech or property) subject to such divergent legal rules, that it becomes all too easy to forget that the logical structure of the inquiries in both areas is the same.

A.   Question One: The Scope of Speech and Property Rights

The first salient point in comparing speech to property rights is how much broader the coverage is that is given to freedom of speech. Coverage of speech is broader in at least two separate ways. First, it is clear that First Amendment jurisprudence correctly sweeps into its fold all forms of activities whose central mission is to communicate not only ideas and information, but also attitudes, sentiments and feelings. It goes without saying that the First Amendment covers political speech, but it covers artistic and literary expression as well. Similarly, without real tussle, the modern media—for example, fax machines, broadcasts, and electronic mail—are as strongly protected by the First Amendment as the traditional printing press. Finally, even such activities as flag burning[53] and nude dancing[54] fall within the purview of the First Amendment. There are some qualifications to the doctrine: Under current theory commercial speech tends to receive lower levels of protection than political speech, although for reasons that should be regarded as insufficient once the connections between speech and property are suitably identified.[55] And certain other forms of speech, such as fighting words and obscenity, are subject to government regulation. But rarely does the Court pretend that expressive activities are outside the sphere of First Amendment consideration altogether.

Second, constitutional scholars have strained to fit as much expressive activity as possible under the First Amendment. Thomas Emerson's influential theoretical treatment, *The System of Freedom of Expression*, quite consciously substitutes in the broader term "expression" for the narrower term "speech."[56] While the expansion of coverage makes good sense, I believe that Emerson's basic structure is wrong in one critical respect: The linguistic move from speech to expression does not remove the need to ex-

---

[53] See *Texas v Johnson*, 491 US 397 (1989).

[54] See *Barnes v Glen Theatre*, 111 S Ct 2456 (1991). See also text accompanying note 116.

[55] See, for example, *Chaplinsky v New Hampshire*, 315 US 568 (1942).

[56] Emerson, *The System of Freedom of Expression* (cited in note 24). Many have picked up the phrase "freedom of expression." See, for example, Stone, et al, *Constitutional Law* at 1011 (cited in note 7).

plain why certain forms of communication are entitled to absolute immunity from state control. The public justification for restricting speech has to be fought out in terms of the validity of claims made by the state, and not on the strength of a classificatory scheme that looks only to one side of the equation.

The third question about a constitutional right—the state justification for intruding upon the protected interest—cannot be collapsed, without serious loss of intellectual clarity, into the first question—the scope of that right. Yet that is precisely the wrong move that Emerson makes at the outset of his study when he tries to force the complex system of rules regulating communication into the single distinction between "action" and "expression," in which the former is subject to "vastly" more regulation than the latter.[57] Nevertheless, the broad coverage which Emerson affords speech is surely welcome, for the wide net breathes life into the central proposition of limited government—that all government activities should be evaluated under a presumption of distrust.

The same broad coverage is not given to private property under the Fifth Amendment, but should be. "Private property," like "freedom of speech," is a term of comprehensive import, which surely must be understood to cover more than the rights in land that were well established under the common law of estates. Just as the First Amendment protects (or should protect) the freedom of speech over the airwaves, so too should the Fifth Amendment protect any property rights that individuals acquire in the air rights, ideally through a system of first possession.[58] Similarly, the

---

[57] Emerson, *The System of Freedom of Expression* at 8 (cited in note 24). After noting the line-drawing difficulties, Emerson concluded:

> But the crucial point is that the focus of inquiry must be directed toward ascertaining what is expression, and therefore to be given the protection of expression, and what is action, and thus subject to regulation as such.

Id at 18. Earlier he had noted that,

> in order to achieve its desired goals, a society or the state is entitled to exercise control over action—whether by prohibiting or compelling it—on an entirely different and vastly more extensive basis.

Id at 8. Emerson, very much a product of the New Deal, did not perceive any serious tension between his authoritarian politics and his libertarian views on speech—an inveterate distinction that I hope to undermine, if not overturn, here.

[58] Today the government owns the airwaves, which many think allows the government to control how the spectrum is used or allocated. See *National Broadcasting Co. v United States*, 319 US 190 (1943); *Red Lion Broadcasting Co. v FCC*, 395 US 367 (1969). Historically, however, the government did not own the airwaves until after it displaced the spectrum rights originally appropriated through first possession. See Coase, 2 J L & Econ at 1-7 (cited in note 43); Emord, *Freedom, Technology, and the First Amendment* at 138-65 (cited in note 43). For a criticism of the Court's decision in *Red Lion* and *CBS, Inc. v Democratic National Committee*, 412 US 94 (1973), see Blasi, 1977 Am Bar Found Res J at 611-31

Takings Clause should protect those forms of property which in some sense are dependent not only upon natural acquisition by individuals, but also upon government recognition, most notably intellectual property—copyrights, patents, trademarks, trade secrets and the like. Likewise, the Takings Clause should protect special forms of property in traditional assets, like time-sharing plans, just as much as it protects traditional forms of property.

Moreover, the definition of property under the Takings Clause is unjustifiably narrower than under analogous private law doctrine. For example, the Takings Clause does not generally protect "good will." But tort law protects goodwill against destruction, and contract law permits private parties to transfer goodwill by legally enforceable agreement.[59] The unwillingness of the courts to recognize goodwill as an independent item of property, or at least as an element of already recognized business property, represents a true constitutional injustice.[60]

The rationale for this untoward result is conceptual and unsatisfying. It is said that the government only takes ongoing business property that it uses, and not that which it destroys. But recall Blackstone's general injunction that the purpose of compensation when government operates under its power of eminent domain is to ensure that the private holder is not left worse off by the coercive exercise of government power than he was before.[61] That objective can only be accomplished if the government must compensate for property destroyed. It surely ought not

---

(cited in note 24). Blasi stresses the power that a free press can have in checking governmental power. Id at 621. This suggests that easy access to the airwaves (no broadcast rights) will sometimes advance the checking value. Id at 625. Note too that Emerson calls for extensive social control over licensees, to the ostensible benefit of the public. See Emerson, *The System of Freedom of Expression* at 660-67 (cited in note 24). But his discussion makes no reference to Coase, and utterly ignores the difference between allocating frequencies, by protecting broadcasts against physical interference, and ordinary content regulation, which should excite serious First Amendment attention.

[59] See, for example, *Community Redevelopment Agency of Los Angeles v Abrams*, 126 Cal Rptr 473, 543 P2d 905 (1975). For criticism of the modern view, see Gideon Kanner, *When is "Property" not "Property Itself": A Critical Examination of the Bases of Denial of Compensation for Loss of Goodwill in Eminent Domain*, 6 Cal W L Rev 57 (1969).

[60] See, for example, the notorious "Poletown" case, *Poletown Neighborhood Council v City of Detroit*, 410 Mich 616, 304 NW 455 (1981). There the court's failure to take into account loss of neighborhood goodwill led the court to sustain a takeover of a neighborhood by General Motors that ignored huge elements of losses to the private owners who were dispossessed.

[61] Of the eminent domain power, such as to acquire land for a road, Blackstone asked rhetorically:

In this, and similar cases the legislature alone can, and indeed frequently does, interpose and compel the individual to acquiesce. But how does it interpose and compel?

make a legal difference if the government destroys a house before
it condemns a piece of land instead of condemning the land before
destroying the house. The goodwill associated with real property,
or even with an ongoing business, should be brought within the
scope of the Takings Clause. Unfortunately, courts today, too eager
to protect the budgets of municipal governments, allow them to
wreak destruction of valuable private assets for which any private
malefactor would have to pay.[62]

B.   Question Two: The Violation of the Right

The second part of the problem concerns not the constitutional rights that are protected, but the types of government actions that they are protected from. Although there are countless
different schemes of government action, they can best be understood as variations on a few pure types of government action. The
most obvious is dispossession—the direct takeover and operation
of private activities; others are modifications of liability rules, regulation, and taxation. The following sections compare how the
courts have treated each of these four types of government actions
when they affect property, and when they affect speech.

1.   Dispossession.

Within the area of property, there is a sharp disjunction between how the courts treat government dispossession and all other
forms of government action. Those cases where the government
takes "permanent physical possession"[63] of property are regarded
as per se takings, and the government is required to compensate
the property-owner for the taking. But with only small qualifications related to when the government compromises the property-

---

Not by absolutely stripping the subject of his property in an arbitrary manner; but by
giving him a full indemnification and equivalent for the *injury* thereby sustained.

William M. Blackstone, 1 *Commentaries* *135 (emphasis added).

[62] I have skirted here the question of whether the government should have to pay for
the destruction of goodwill when it does not take property. In my view the answer is yes. If
a store serves a neighborhood, and the government tears up the neighborhood so that the
store remains, but without customers to frequent it, the store has lost goodwill, here because
the government has forcibly interfered with an advantageous business relationship. The
state should be required to include this loss of goodwill in working its own calculus of condemnation. To ignore it would allow the government to externalize systematic harms, which
in turn would allow the government to condemn too much private land.

[63] *Loretto v Teleprompter Manhattan CATV Corp.*, 458 US 419, 426 (1982).

owner's "right to exclude,"[64] these constitute the *only* class of per se takings, for which compensation is required.

Within the area of speech, stronger protections apply. The government cannot take permanent physical possession of the New York Times printing presses, even if the government is prepared to pay compensation. The protection afforded speech against dispossession thus goes beyond that afforded property, but for reasons that are consistent with the basic logic of the Takings Clause. The reason why some takings of private property are allowed, with just compensation, is that the forcible rearrangement of property rights is understood to provide some net social benefit. But where is the net benefit when speech is suppressed? The interest in speech is typically relational—communication is of benefit to the audience as well as to the speaker—and no compensation formula easily takes that interest into account. If the government needs a printing press, it knows where to buy it; so too with raw land. On the other hand, there is the real risk that the government will condemn newspapers simply to suppress criticism. In short, prohibiting this limited class of prospective condemnations prevents hardly any socially beneficial transactions, while permitting them raises the persistent specter of government abuse. Thus the government takeover is flatly forbidden under the First Amendment.

2. Modification of liability rules.

The Court has held on a number of occasions, even before 1937,[65] that no person has any vested right in any common law rule of liability. But there has been a long line of Supreme Court cases in which the very forms of liability rules that provoke only yawns under the Takings Clause have received close attention under the Free Speech Clause. For instance, under the First Amendment, the rules of tort liability are regarded as essential subjects for mischief and abuse, and hence are given close constitutional scrutiny. The results can lead to the fortification of some common law rules of

---

[64] *Loretto* relied heavily on *Kaiser Aetna v United States*, 444 US 164, 179-80 (1979), in which the Supreme Court found a taking where the government had demanded public access to a private marina. The case was not one of dispossession, for the state did not seek to exclude the private owner from the use of the marina. But the state did compromise the right to exclude, which the Court found a fundamental stick in the bundle of property rights. To a property lawyer, the case is too easy to require extended comment. There is a taking whenever A requires B, a sole owner, to become a joint tenant with A against B's will. Otherwise A could force the joint tenancy, then partition, and through two steps take half of what B owns. Do it enough times and we have a new cottage industry of dubious worth.

[65] See, for example, *New York Central R.R. Co. v White*, 243 US 188, 198-200 (1917).

liability, but to the repudiation of others. Thus, in *New York Times v Sullivan*,[66] the Court refused to show any deference to the settled common law of defamation; instead, all of its substantive dimensions were subject to constitutional review, and in some instances revision. Thus the state cannot expand the definition of the identification requirement ("of and concerning the plaintiff") beyond the scope that it had at common law. More dramatically, the courts have found that certain critical features of common law protections for defendants have been inadequate. The strict scrutiny of liability rules, moreover, is not only directed at issues that are tangential to the overall soundness of the system, but is directed to issues that go to its heart: awarding general damages;[67] putting the burden of proof on the defendant to show truth;[68] and, most importantly, extending the privilege of "fair comment" to cover not only statements of opinion, but also false statements of fact, unless the media defendant knows them to be false or acts in reckless disregard of their truth or falsity.[69]

All these innovations should not be viewed in the same light. In some instances the Supreme Court reads the First Amendment in a sound fashion—to maintain requirements of proof that are demanded by a consistent theory of individual freedom. Placing the burden of proof on a plaintiff to prove that certain facts are false is one such innovation. But, in other instances, as with giving extensive protection to false statements of fact, the Supreme Court goes far beyond that modest office, and quickly gets itself into trouble. The major criticism of the modern law of defamation is that it affords no effective redress for public officials and public figures who have been victimized by false statements. Media defendants are allowed to shield themselves from the harmful consequences of their acts, merely by admitting that they were negligent.[70] Finally, in some cases, like the doctrine of presumed damages, the balance of equities is sufficiently close that one wonders why the court finds it

---

[66] 376 US 254 (1964).

[67] See, for example, *Gertz v Robert Welch, Inc.*, 418 US 323, 348-50 (1974) (no recovery for presumed or punitive damages).

[68] *Philadelphia Newspapers Inc. v Hepps*, 475 US 767, 776-78 (1986) (private-figure plaintiff in defamation action bears burden of showing that alleged defamatory speech is false).

[69] *New York Times*, 376 US at 279-80. For my defense of the common law baseline in this connection, see Epstein, 53 U Chi L Rev 782 (cited in note 9).

[70] See, for example, Randall P. Bezanson, Gilbert Cranberg, and John Soloski, *Libel Law and the Press: Myth and Reality* 214-18 (Free Press, 1987) (criticizing focus of defamation law on defendant's mental state and advocating separate procedures that allow adjudication of question of truth even where plaintiff cannot establish actual malice).

imperative to upset a balance of interests that seems to have worked well over time, absent an evidence of systematic abuse or untoward social consequences.

There are many errors of detail in First Amendment defamation law, virtually all of which stem from its deviation from superior common law principles. But the mistakes in application do not deny the bedrock proposition of *New York Times*: there should be constitutional scrutiny of the law of libel. That scrutiny of liability rules should carry over to the Fifth Amendment. As a matter of general theory, there are *not* two watertight compartments: one for property rights, protected by the Constitution; the other for liability rules, subject to legislative discretion and control.

To test the proposition by the extreme case, it seems clear that the total repeal of the law of trespass would constitute a complete revolution in the basic civil order. If individuals are not allowed to exclude deliberate trespassers from their ranks, then we have retreated from a system of ordered government to a system of state-sanctioned anarchy. The right to exclude under the rubric of private property has been protected in some cases.[71] But in many others, such as when factory owners seek to exclude union organizers from their land, the Supreme Court has looked upon the suspension of the common law rules of trespass not with doubt and suspicion, but with relief and welcome.[72] Similarly, in the entire area of environmental regulations, it is clear that any appeal to ideas of trespass, or nuisance, or the right to exclude carries little weight in the present constitutional order.[73]

To hold, as I argue, that legislative modifications of liability rules fall under the Takings Clause would not preclude the state from justifying its modification by appealing to the overall welfare of the community. In fact, it would facilitate a rigorous demonstration of that defense in those cases where it can be mounted. But

---

[71] See *Kaiser Aetna*, 444 US at 179-80.

[72] See *Republic Aviation Corp. v NLRB*, 324 US 793, 802-05 (1945); *Beth Israel Hospital v NLRB*, 437 US 483, 491-93 (1978). There are, of course, complications in this area, given that outside organizers may well be regarded as trespassers, even though present employees whom the employer wants to exclude are not. See *NLRB v Babcock & Wilcox Co.*, 351 US 105, 112 (1956); *Lechmere, Inc. v NLRB*, 112 S Ct 841 (1992). But now the judicial vice is to mangle the common law of trespass, instead of just disregarding it. The traditional view was clear that entry was limited to the time of its allowance, and to the purposes for which it was granted. See *The Six Carpenters' Case*, 77 Eng Rep 695, 8 Co Rep 146 (1610).

[73] See, for example, *Miller v Schoene*, 276 US 272, 280 (1928) (state act providing for the destruction of red cedar trees located within two miles of apple trees found to be constitutional, even though no compensation was given for value of standing trees or decrease in value of realty).

the converse—exclusion from constitutional scrutiny of most modifications of liability rules—can lead to the radical destabilization of the system of property rights, with (as I shall show later) long-term adverse consequences for the political and social system.

3. Regulation.

Liability rules are only one way in which the government, particularly the activist government, has altered the distribution of property holdings among the citizenry. The government has achieved the same result by imposing various schemes of regulation, such as those which were sanctioned in the early rent control and zoning cases. And the property-owner must overcome a very heavy set of burdens to obtain compensation from the state. Indeed, the Supreme Court has positively gloried in its inability to articulate clear rules to govern this area: the Court has pretended to decide each alleged regulatory taking on an ad hoc basis.[74] In fact, however, the Court has adopted a rule that is predictable, but incorrect: a virtually conclusive presumption against requiring compensation for any regulation.

In contrast, regulation is an abridgment of speech under the First Amendment in a way that it is most definitely not a taking (even a partial taking) of property under the Fifth Amendment. Where regulations of speech are imposed, the Supreme Court has an elaborate classification system designed to cull out unacceptable forms of regulation. There are divisions into high and low value speech, and into content-based and content-neutral regulations, each with its own pattern of justification.[75] But there is not the slightest suggestion anywhere in the entire body of First Amendment law that "mere" regulation of speech is outside the scope of the First Amendment. The clear perception is that the unrestrained state can stifle speech and dissent through regulation just as easily as through a direct ban. Bond or permit requirements for speakers are always closely scrutinized to see if they conceal an illegitimate effort to restrict the scope of speech generally.[76] Special scrutiny is imposed where there is the slightest hint that the restrictions are linked to the speaker's viewpoint, however distaste-

---

[74] See, for example, *Penn Central Transportation Co. v New York City*, 438 US 104, 124 (1978).

[75] See text accompanying note 29.

[76] See, for example, *Cox v New Hampshire*, 312 US 569 (1941) (conviction upheld in parade statute prosecution only because state court had held that local licensing officials could only consider time, place, and manner restrictions).

ful that viewpoint may be to the public at large.[77] The fear of
abuse of this regulatory power is the most salient explanation for
this aspect of First Amendment law.

Analytically, there is no ground for the distinction between
regulatory takings and infringements of free speech. The state has
taken the fee simple, even if it returns some portion of the land by
way of compensation. Likewise, it has taken the fee simple if it
confiscates it, but then returns it subject to new restrictions on use
and disposition. Restrictive covenants are property interests when
created by consent, and they remain so imposed by the state. What
one side—the covenantee—obtains, the other side—the covenan-
tor—loses. To treat these regulations as "mere" restrictions that
fall outside the scope of the Takings Clause is to immunize vast
areas of government behavior from judicial scrutiny in a manner
that would be incomprehensible under the First Amendment.

4. Taxation.

The last mode of government attack on private behavior is
through a system of taxation. While the formal possibility of
mounting a successful takings challenge against taxation is not explicitly denied by the Court, it is well-nigh impossible to find any
challenge that has succeeded, even before 1937.[78] As for regulations, the courts have adopted a virtually conclusive presumption
against requiring compensation for any tax.

Long ago, Justice Marshall's famous aphorism warned that the
power to tax was the power to destroy.[79] As government taxes continued to rise even before the end of the *Lochner* period, Justice
Holmes, who had so much to do with the expansion of the government power to tax, was led to say, in essence, "so what?"[80] Judges
continue to solemnly maintain that egregious taxes will fall under
the Takings Clause, but if the Supreme Court has invalidated a tax
on takings grounds in the past seventy-five years, I am not aware

---

[77] See, for example, *Thomas v Collins*, 323 US 516, 540 (1944) (invalidating Texas statute that required union organizers to obtain permit).

[78] For a typical statement, see *Magnano Co. v Hamilton*, 292 US 40, 44 (1934) (Th[e
Takings] Clause is applicable to a taxing statute such as the one here assailed only if the act
be so arbitrary as to compel the conclusion that it does not involve an exertion of the taxing
power, but constitutes, in substance and effect, the direct exertion of a different and forbidden power, as, for example, the confiscation of property.").

[79] See *McCulloch v Maryland*, 17 US 316, 431 (1819).

[80] See *Alaska Fish Co. v Smith*, 255 US 44, 48 (1921) ("Even if the tax should destroy a
business it would not be made invalid or require compensation upon that ground alone.
Those who enter upon a business take that risk.").

of it. The basic principle is evidently that the mere benefit of living in a civilized society is sufficient justification for the imposition of any tax, however indefensible its incidence or form.[81] The dangers that unsound systems of taxation can work to the operation of the economic system are not factored into the constitutional equation. But to deny that taxes are takings—when they involve the threat of seizure for those who do not voluntarily hand over property—is to use a definitional ploy to answer a question that calls for a policy response: Which forms of taxation are permissible in a democratic society, which are out of bounds, and why?

The attitude toward taxation under the First Amendment is quite different. It is recognized that taxation is yet another form of government control, which, if placed in the wrong hands or directed to the wrong means, can distort the political system. It is clear that the protection of various forms of speech against taxation does not absolutely prohibit taxation: newspapers can be taxed on their business profits like other organizations. But it has led to scrutiny of the permissible justifications for taxation, and of the permissible forms of taxation.[82]

In sum, within the law of takings, the broad class of partial takings—changes in liability rules, regulations, taxation—are all thought to trigger at most a cursory review, if they are regarded as takings at all.[83] The evasiveness of the mode of analysis is always calculated to impress upon us the need for judicial deference and legislative discretion, and thereby the justification to expand the use of government force. With the regulation of property, the pattern of judicial deference stems from the want of any deep conviction that limitations on government power are beneficial, and from the consequent unwillingness to formulate any principles that have bite.[84]

---

[81] See *Carmichael v Southern Coal Co.*, 301 US 495, 522 (1937) ("The only benefit to which the taxpayer is constitutionally entitled is that derived from his enjoyment of the privileges of living in an organized society, established and safeguarded by the devotion of taxes to public purposes.").

[82] See Section III.E.2.

[83] See, for example, *Penn Central*, in which Justice Brennan found that New York City's landmark preservation law was not a "taking" of the plaintiff's property. 438 US at 136-38. But Justice Brennan left open the possibility that, if the designation system were a taking, then government would have adequately compensated the plaintiff by awarding it transferable development rights ("TDRs"), even though the TDRs were worth only a tiny fraction of the value of the air rights of which the government had deprived the plaintiff. Id at 137. Yet under the later holding in *Kaiser Aetna*, 444 US at 180, the case would have been a taking if the government had sought to build on the plaintiff's property itself, instead of taking what is in essence a restrictive covenant on height.

[84] See, for example, Justice Brennan's statement in *Penn Central*:

There is no similar relaxed or deferential attitude within the law of speech. Commentators who care about the principle always warn that "[a] system of freedom of expression can be successful only when it rests upon the strongest possible commitment to the positive right and the narrowest possible basis for exceptions. And any such exceptions must be clear-cut, precise, and readily controlled."[85] All attacks on private speech are regarded as potentially deadly threats to the operation of the marketplace of ideas, or to full and active participation in the political process. The Court never takes the view so common in property cases that the "wisdom" of the legislation bears no relationship to its constitutionality.

C. Question Three: Justifications for Government Restrictions on Speech and Property

It is clear to limited government libertarians that liberty should not be regarded as equivalent to anarchy, either as a matter of first principle or as a matter of constitutional interpretation. The idea of anarchy is that any person is allowed to speak or do anything that he chooses, and that the sole restraint upon that conduct is private force. Within a legal system, however, the concept of liberty always means what Cardozo once termed "ordered liberty"[86]—restraints on the freedom of action that take into account the correlative duties that individual actors owe to others. That these duties exist is perfectly apparent in the world of individual actions: the right to own property and to use it as one pleases is not an authorization to kill the first person with whom one has a minor disagreement.

I believe that the system of libertarian justifications is traceable to a powerful set of utilitarian roots.[87] Restrictions on the individual's capacity to act are based on the view that all persons are better off by sacrificing their natural liberty of action than by exer-

---

While this Court has recognized that the "Fifth Amendment's guarantee . . . [is] designed to bar Government from forcing some people alone to bear public burdens which, in all fairness and justice, should be borne by the public as a whole," *Armstrong v United States*, 364 U.S. 40, 49 (1960), this Court, quite simply, has been unable to develop any "set formula" for determining when "justice and fairness" require that economic injuries caused by public action be compensated by the government, rather than remain disproportionately concentrated on a few persons.

438 US at 123-24. It is easy to fail if you do not try.

[85] Emerson, *The System of Freedom of Expression* at 10 (cited in note 24).

[86] *Palko v Connecticut*, 302 US 319, 325 (1937).

[87] I have developed this idea in Epstein, 12 Harv J L & Pub Pol 713 (cited in note 34).

cising it in a world where others use their natural powers against
them. The prohibition against the threat of force thus arises from
the mutual renunciation of the private use of force, obtained not
through voluntary agreement, but by government edict, needed to
overcome the holdout and bargaining problems that otherwise
would exist. However, for these purposes it is not important to detail the exact derivation of these utilitarian claims, for the restrictions on the use of property and freedom of action are accepted by
virtually every one, including those who conceive of a far broader
set of public justifications for the restriction of property and/or
speech.

What is equally clear under libertarian theory is that there is
no artificial divide between speech and property when the question
is whether there is any justification for limiting individual actions.
Freedom of speech implies the same limitations associated with
freedom of action, or with freedom of contract. The same concerns
with force and fraud that arise under the general libertarian theory
surface with great force in efforts to discover the appropriate limits
of both speech and property rights. For instance, the *threat* of
force will often involve the use of speech, and if not speech, then
surely those forms of expression (for example, gestures or signs)
that fall comfortably within the narrowest definitions of expression
championed under modern theory. The mere fact that the threat
and the use of force are equated under the general theory shows
that both speech and conduct are subject to the same sort of scrutiny, and for much the same reason: to improve the overall operation of the social system.

1. Justifications for restricting free speech.

   a) Preventing private force. Many First Amendment
cases deal with the government's power to punish conduct that involves the threat or use of force. The entire line of sedition cases,
from the outset of the First World War until the 1950s, were
largely devoted to a single question: When, and how, could the
government impose restrictions upon speech that posed the risk of
physical danger or disruption of public services?[88] Holmes put the
issue squarely in *Schenck* when, in conjunction with his reference
to shouting "Fire!" in a crowded theater, he noted that "[the most
stringent protection of free speech] does not protect a man from an

---

[88] For a collection of the relevant cases and materials, see Stone, et al, *Constitutional Law* at 1025-1100 (cited in note 7).

injunction against uttering words that may have all the effect of force."[89] A similar view was taken where "fighting words" threatened riot or mayhem.[90]

During the formative period of modern First Amendment jurisprudence, the police power of the state was confined to police work. No matter how much we have come to disapprove of *Schenck*, and to admire *Abrams v United States*,[91] the exceptions to the basic protection of speech were always associated with the preservation of the public order against the risk of treason or violence. The significant debates over the scope and limitation of the "clear and present danger" test were all about the narrow class of ends that government could permissibly suppress. If the speech in question threatened conduct that was not a common law offense against person, property, or national security, then its suppression was inconsistent with freedom of speech. There was no discussion about the irrelevance of the common law, or the search for novel baselines congenial to the New Deal era. There was an extensive debate over how far back to roll the carpet in order to protect against the overthrow of the government, an issue on which strong disagreement is possible.[92]

The current constitutional equilibrium on subversive speech, reached in *Brandenburg v Ohio*,[93] is consistent with the general libertarian approach:

> [T]he constitutional guarantees of free speech and free press do not permit a State to forbid or proscribe advocacy of the use of force or of law violation except where such advocacy is

---

[89] *Schenck*, 249 US 47, 52. See also note 28 (discussing Kalven's views).

[90] See, for example, *Chaplinsky v New Hampshire*, 315 US 568 (1942), in which the Court noted the "fighting words" exception to the First Amendment, and narrowly construed it to cover only those words "which by their very utterance inflict injury or tend to incite an immediate breach of the peace." Id at 572. See also *Feiner v New York*, 340 US 315 (1951), in which the Court similarly limited "fighting words" to those which posed an "immediate threat to public safety, peace or order," and sustained a conviction on those grounds alone. Id at 320, citing *Cantwell v Connecticut*, 310 US 296, 308 (1940).

[91] 250 US 616 (1919) (knowledge of probable consequences of distributing circulars sufficient to sustain conviction under Espionage Act of 1918).

[92] See *Gitlow v New York*, 268 US 652 (1925) (requires "language of direct incitement" "used with intent and purpose"); *Whitney v California*, 274 US 357 (1927) (stressing deference to the legislature, upheld conviction for membership in an organization advocating criminal syndicalism); *Dennis v United States*, 341 US 494 (1951) ("whether the gravity of the 'evil,' discounted by its improbability, justifies such invasion of free speech as is necessary to avoid the danger"); *Yates v United States*, 354 US 298 (1957) ("those to whom the advocacy is addressed must be urged to *do* something, now or in the future, rather than merely to *believe* in something").

[93] 395 US 444 (1969).

directed to inciting or producing imminent lawless action and is likely to incite or produce such action. As we said in *Noto v. United States*, 367 U.S. 290, 297-98 (1961), "the mere abstract teaching . . . of the moral propriety or even moral necessity for a resort to force and violence, is not the same as preparing a group for violent action and steeling it to such action."[94]

By the same token, it goes without saying that offensiveness does not limit the scope of First Amendment protection. The flag-burning case is the most salient illustration of political speech, designed to offend, but which nonetheless cannot be regulated because it does not pose an imminent threat of violence.[95]

The reasons for judicial protection are instructive on the theme of distrust. It is not that the harms caused by flag-burning and similar activities are not real, for they are, or that they are not substantial, for that they may be as well.[96] Instead, it is that the risks of collective reprisal are rightly regarded as so great that the government is required to stay its hand. The class of external harms that justify the police power are sharply, even artificially, limited in order to limit the scope of government action. The parallel here is to the common law conception of *damnum absque injuria* ("harm without legal injury"), which is imposed not because other persons have suffered no harm, but because the freedom of action and the social gains which that freedom brings are only possible when certain forms of harm (for example, offense, competitive loss) are not recognized by the legal system.[97]

The question of external harms does not arise, however, only in subversive advocacy cases, but in other less dramatic contexts as well. Public speech can often be noisy and offensive, and it is clear that the Court tolerates "time, place, and manner" restrictions on speech.[98] Two features about these regulations should be quickly noted. First, they are directed against conduct that the common

---

[94] Id at 447-48. Note that one could quarrel with this decision on the ground that it is too protective of speech. There may be some harms so serious in their implications that the imminence requirement should be relaxed. But for these purposes, the rule falls squarely within the libertarian tradition, and tallies closely with *Chaplinsky*.

[95] See *Texas v Johnson*, 491 US 397 (1989).

[96] "If there is a bedrock principle underlying the First Amendment, it is that the government may not prohibit the expression of an idea simply because society finds the idea itself offensive or disagreeable." *Johnson*, 491 US at 414.

[97] This point was first developed in Oliver Wendell Holmes, Jr., *Privilege, Malice, and Intent*, 8 Harv L Rev 1, 2-10 (1894).

[98] See Stone, et al, *Constitutional Law* at 1257-1337 (cited in note 7).

law ordinarily treats as nuisance, such as the use of loudspeakers or sound trucks in public places.[99] Second, the problem of selective enforcement looms large even when the regulations are content-neutral, and is taken into account when the courts review the enforcement of these "time, place, and manner" restrictions. These restrictions on speech thus require principled justification as well.

b) Preventing private fraud. Other speech restrictions are justified on the grounds that they prevent private fraud or misrepresentation. The libertarian rationale for the tort of defamation is that it constitutes the wrong of misrepresentation, directed not to the victim of the wrong, but to some third party. The *New York Times* line of cases shows how even misrepresentation cases are greeted with hostility, in large measure because of the suspicion of the abuse of government power.[100] And the same attitude of caution is shown toward state efforts to regulate the conduct, for example, of union organizers, even under circumstances where there is persuasive evidence of private fraud.[101]

Even the commercial speech cases have shown some signs of falling into the same pattern. In principle, these cases show the impossibility of maintaining the strong line between action and expression that drives Emerson's analysis of the First Amendment. A price system is best understood as a system of communication that impounds relevant information. Thus a system of price controls is best understood as an interference with the way in which the price system transfers that information.[102] Direct attacks on price controls based on takings or allied grounds have had only rare success.[103] But while the price mechanism has not been brought under the First Amendment, ordinary forms of advertisement have been, and here the libertarian potential of the First Amendment sometimes surfaces.

---

[99] See, for example, *Kovacs v Cooper*, 336 US 77 (1949).

[100] For an overview of the *New York Times* line of cases, see Stone, et al, *Constitutional Law* at 1145-71 (cited in note 7).

[101] See *Thomas v Collins*, 323 US 516 (1945) (statute requiring labor organizers to obtain a permit soliciting workers to join unions invalid under the First Amendment).

[102] For an elaboration of the point, see Daniel Shapiro, *Free Speech, Free Exchange, and Rawlsian Liberalism*, 17 Social Theory and Practice 47, 50-57 (1991).

[103] For one recent victory, see *Calfarm Insurance Co. v Deukmejian*, 258 Cal Rptr 161, 771 P2d 1247, 1252-56 (1989) (granting relief against automatic 20% rollback in insurance proposal). For one recent failure, see *State Farm v State of New Jersey*, 124 NJ 31, 590 A2d 191 (1991) (rejecting challenge to New Jersey's insurance reform legislation).

Take a case in point. In *Virginia State Board of Pharmacy v Virginia Citizens Consumer Council*,[104] the Court struck down state restrictions that barred pharmacies from advertising the price at which they sold their goods. The fanciful justifications that were offered for such regulation all had an economic cast: that advertisement would lead to a loss of the professional image among pharmacists; that able firms would be driven out of business because of their inability to compete on price, leaving a clear field to the predators to drive up the price thereafter.[105] Had this been a challenge based on the Due Process Clause, the Court indicated that these rationales, however specious, could have justified the statute.[106] But within the framework of the First Amendment, the Court immediately reverted to the libertarian analysis, and noted that the seller of a high-quality product could advertise quality in opposition to price.[107] It has been said that this decision resurrected substantive due process,[108] and so it did, but that should be regarded as one of its strongest features, not as one of its drawbacks.

2. Justifications for restrictions on property rights.

In most cases involving property or economic liberties, however, the police power, now used as a term of art, has grown so that it bears no relationship to the control of either force or fraud. Few cases of land use regulation, for example, are concerned with the control and use of force in any form. The nearest kin to trespassory force is nuisance; yet the nuisance control rationale for the police power in land use cases has been repeatedly rejected as an authoritative basis for deciding these cases.[109] Often the nuisance control rationale is rejected on conceptual grounds: that it is impossible to tell who has caused a nuisance and who has been a victim.[110] This is ironic, because the nuisance control rationale is an

---

[104] 425 US 748 (1976).

[105] Id at 764-70.

[106] Id at 769.

[107] Id at 769-70. The Court did, of course, permit regulation against advertisements that were "false or misleading in any way." Id at 771.

[108] See Thomas H. Jackson and John Calvin Jeffries, Jr., *Commercial Speech: Economic Due Process and the First Amendment*, 65 Va L Rev 1, 29-33 (1979).

[109] The process started in the 1920s with *Euclid v Ambler Realty Co.*, 272 US 365, 387-88 (1926), and *Miller v Schoene*, 276 US 272, 280 (1928), and continues today.

[110] The view has also been defended in Michelman, 80 Harv L Rev at 1196-1201 (cited in note 6); Joseph L. Sax, *Takings and the Police Power*, 74 Yale L J 36, 48-50 (1964); Joseph L. Sax, *Takings, Private Property and Public Rights*, 81 Yale L J 149, 161-69 (1971). I have criticized the view in *Takings* at 115-21 (cited in note 2).

important distinguishing principle for content-neutral cases under
the First Amendment. On the one hand, content-neutral regulation
designed to limit the use of sound trucks is routinely upheld.[111] On
the other hand, legislative characterizations of certain other conduct as "nuisances"—such as the distribution of handbills—are accorded virtually no weight at all.[112]

The difference in approach yields powerful differences in consequences. Once all specific content has drained out of the police
power language, any legitimate public function of conceivable
merit justifies government restriction on land use. The narrow account of external harms accepted under the First Amendment no
longer limits what the state may do under the Fifth Amendment.
Aesthetics, popular sentiments, and environmental objectives all
become appropriate pegs on which to hang legal justifications for
land use restrictions.[113] No explanation is given as to why the narrow account of external harms under the First Amendment is so
inappropriate here. As the ends have widened, so too the means to
achieve those ends have been broadly construed, and all the burdens of proof are set in favor of the state, so that any challenge of
land use restrictions is always an uphill battle.

Notwithstanding the many differences in the reach of the police power in speech and property cases, there does exist some con-
vergence between them, namely under the shadowy protection of
the public "morals" facet of the police power. Here the great
problems arise in mixed cases, such as those involving billboards[114]
or "adult" movie theaters,[115] where the level of regulation tolerated
by the courts is normally higher than that associated with speech
alone. In part, the rationale for these decisions is that the regulations deal not only with speech, but also with land use, where the
standards of review are clearly much lower. The outcomes are in
part defensible, especially if one could demonstrate that certain
private activities increase the risk of neighborhood violence and
disorganization. In some cases, such as the recent nude dancing decision,[116] problems of land use and free speech converge. The prin-

---

[111] See note 99 and accompanying text.

[112] See, for example, *Lovell*, 303 US 444, 451 (voiding city ordinance which put prior
restraint upon distribution of handbills and similar literature as "nuisances").

[113] See, for example, *Berman v Parker*, 348 US 26, 32-33 (1954) (holding that protection
of "spiritual" and "aesthetic" values was a legitimate exercise of municipality's police
power).

[114] See *Metromedia, Inc. v San Diego*, 453 US 490 (1981).

[115] See *Young v American Mini Theatres*, 427 US 50 (1976).

[116] *Barnes v Glen Theatre*, 111 S Ct 2456 (1991).

ciples of individual freedom collide with the "morals" facet of the police power, which sometimes operates as a supplement to, and at other times as an extension of, the state's power to prohibit various forms of violence and fraud.

These difficult cases lie at the edge of the law under any comprehensive theory, and for my purposes, at least, the location of the proper line is not the dominant concern. The so-called "morals" cases represent the easiest extension of the police power in a land use setting, and the most difficult extension of the police power in a First Amendment setting. It is the radically different responses to the easy cases that marks the difference under the two amendments. A more unified approach to the questions of speech and property would aid in the design of a more satisfactory legal response.

D. Question Four: The Choice of Remedies

The differences in judicial treatment of speech and property are also revealed in the selection of remedies against individual actors that have committed some wrong. In principle, there is a wide range of remedies available for any wrong. Some of these remedies are imposed through direct government action, as when the criminal law provides for imprisonment and fines. In addition, there is a full range of administrative and regulatory remedies designed to eliminate the harm before it begins. Injunctions can be issued against threatened harms, and most importantly a system of permits and licenses can be imposed in order to prevent these harms in the first place. Similarly, on the private side, individual plaintiffs may seek orders for damages, orders for restitution, or injunctions. In those cases where there is only a single isolated harm, the choice of remedy is relatively constrained: damages matter, injunctions do not. But with institutional defendants capable of repeat offenses, systems of social control and systems of prior restraints are feasible, and, in some circumstances—for example, driver's licenses—desirable as well.

1. Prior restraints on speech.

As with other parts of the overall system, the choice of remedies is driven in large measure by the fear of government abuse, relative to private abuse. In the First Amendment area, there is a virtual per se rule against any prior restraint of publication, no matter how harmful or defamatory the material might be. Historically, a fear of prior restraint was the first great motivating force of the free speech tradition, dating back to Milton and Blackstone.[117] In its modern form, once a restriction is identified as a prior restraint, any individual citizen is free to act in defiance of that restriction without exhausting any available administrative remedies.[118] There is no possibility that the state can postpone publication of controversial speech by making grudging administrative concessions after intolerable procedural delays.

There have been a wide variety of concerns with the licensing power, all of which work back to the common theme of distrust. It is said that licensing concentrates too much power in the hands of a small group of individuals, not only when it provides for administrative remedies, but even when it provides for judicial review of individual cases.[119] It is said that the want of clear standards only increases the risk of the improper use of discretion by political actors.[120] It is said that prior restraint keeps relevant information off the market; thus it denies the audience the right to read and comment on that information itself, and it denies the author the right to publish the material so long as he or she is prepared to pay the price.[121] It is said that the procedural protections from administrative hearings are likely to be lower than those of judicial proceedings, especially in a criminal context.[122] It is all true.

The upshot is that any form of prior restraint is struck down, even when there is an arguable ground for issuing an injunction under ordinary common law principles, as was the circumstance in the *Pentagon Papers* case.[123] Prior restraints of all forms and de-

---

[117] John Milton, *Areopagitica: A Speech for the Liberty of Unlicensed Printing, to the Parliament of England*, in George H. Sabine, ed, *Areopagitica and Of Education* (Harlan Davidson, 1951); William M. Blackstone, 4 *Commentaries* *151 ("The liberty of the press is indeed essential to the nature of a free state: but this consists in laying no *previous* restraints upon publications, and not in freedom from censure for criminal matter when published.") (emphasis in original).

[118] See *Lovell*, 303 US at 452-53 ("As the ordinance is void on its face, it was not necessary for appellant to seek a permit under it. She was entitled to contest its validity in answer to the charge against her.").

[119] *Near v Minnesota*, 283 US 697, 715 (1931) (Minnesota statute authorizing state to seek injunctions against routine publishers of malicious or defamatory information on the grounds of nuisance found unconstitutional).

[120] *City of Lakewood v Plain Dealer Publishing Co.*, 486 US 750, 769-70 (1988) (ordinance granting mayor absolute discretion in granting of applications for annual permits to place newsracks on public property found unconstitutional).

[121] See Thomas I. Emerson, *The Doctrine of Prior Restraint*, 20 L & Contemp Probs 648, 656-60 (1955).

[122] Id at 657. See also Vincent Blasi, *Toward a Theory of Prior Restraint: The Central Linkage*, 66 Minn L Rev 11, 43-47 (1981).

[123] *New York Times Co. v United States*, 403 US 713 (1971) (lifting temporary injunction against publication of information leaked to papers by Daniel Ellsworth). Among the

scriptions are routinely disallowed, save under the most extraordinary circumstances—such as where I can show you how to make a nuclear bomb cheaply. Other criminal and civil sanctions are required.

2. Prior restraints on property use.

The situation is radically different under the Takings Clause, where today it is virtually impossible for any private party to maintain a facial challenge against any form of land use regulation. Instead, the dominant rule requires that all administrative remedies first be exhausted, and that constitutional challenges be brought on an "as applied" basis.[124] The risk of government misbehavior due to local or national politics is as large here as it is with speech restrictions: there are dangers of excessive local power and bias; there are costs to outsiders (the potential buyers of the developed property) which are ignored in setting the social calculus; there is far less protection than in any judicial proceeding. There is no reason to believe that public officials who improperly thwart the distribution of leaflets will become impartial solons on economic matters. No one has that kind of a split brain, with virtue in the property hemisphere, and vice in the speech hemisphere.

Yet there is scant recognition of the evils that are endemic in this area and the social dislocations that can follow. The Supreme Court is quite content to require individual property-holders to file endless requests for variances with hostile zoning boards before considering a case at all.[125] None of the concerns with permits that dominate the First Amendment area carry over to the Takings Clause. Instead the Supreme Court has written: "[A]fter all, the very existence of a permit system implies that permission may be

---

reasons offered for the decision was that Congress had only authorized criminal sanctions against the individuals who improperly obtained or retained forbidden information, so that the decision dealt as much with separation of powers as with freedom of speech. See id at 740-48 (Marshall concurring). But at common law, a private party could normally obtain relief against a third person who acquired property with knowledge that it was not owned by the immediate seller. In principle, the analogous rule could apply to sales of information. The injunction could then be applied against persons who received stolen information in bad faith, that is, with knowledge that it had been obtained illegally.

[124] *Hodel v Virginia Surface Mining & Reclamation Ass'n, Inc.*, 452 US 264, 297 & n 40 (1981).

[125] *Williamson Planning Comm'n v Hamilton Bank*, 473 US 172, 186-88 (1985) (plaintiff seeking zoning approval had to exhaust all available administrative remedies, including petitioning the administrative agency for variances).

granted, leaving the landowner free to use the property as desired."[126] Oh?

This steadfast refusal to provide early and prompt remedies in takings cases is intimately tied to the basic propositions of takings law. The Supreme Court has noted that its own fuzzy standards of what constitutes a taking make it impossible to decide whether the government has misbehaved, and to decide what compensation, if any, to require before a matter has been brought to a close.[127] The upshot is that local governments are utterly free to ignore the interests of those whom they regulate, so long as they are willing to throw elaborate hurdles in the paths of those who would challenge their regulations. The risk of local bias and the social losses that follow from the partial or permanent development of property may well be great, but there is no way to force the issue to adjudication.

Instead of the present rules that tolerate abusive behavior and foster costly delays, the system should be redone from the ground up. The permit system should be scrapped. Neighbors and local governments should be able to sue to enjoin the completion or operation of local land uses only by showing that there is some imminent (I would settle for serious) danger of external harms. Where the future harm is uncertain, and the project goes forward, then the landowner might be required to post bond to make good the losses that its conduct might impose on strangers.

The stakes on prior restraint may not be as high for property as they are for speech, although it is hard to be dogmatic on the point without knowledge of particular circumstances. But the relevant concern is not whether a prior restraint rule causes more mischief with speech than it does with property. Instead the concern is to apply sound rules in both areas. Toward that end, the rules developed in conjunction with the First Amendment should be used to reform the impoverished law of takings. The present attitude, which allows full administrative discretion without any judicial accountability, is one of the worst blemishes of the current system.

E. Question Five: Forced Exchanges

There is one last way to test the limitations of state power under the First and Fifth Amendments. To what extent does the state have the power to single out or select the target of its regula-

---

[126] *United States v Riverside Bayview Homes, Inc.*, 474 US 121, 127 (1985). Lower courts have relied on *Riverside Bayview* to stifle challenges to rent control legislation. See, for example, *Gilbert v City of Cambridge*, 932 F2d 51, 56 (1st Cir 1991).

[127] *Williamson*, 473 US at 199–200.

tions? The general argument here is that the power to select certain practices or individuals for special government sanctions is an enormous government power that can easily fall prey to abuse. One application of this principle is that regulations do not on their face impose disproportionate burdens on similar activities. A rule that permits the state to impose sanctions on some but not on others, or even one that permits the state to impose heavier sanctions on one than on the other, is a peril against which every legal system should guard.

1. Selection bias.

a) *Free speech.* The importance of this selection bias is evident under the First Amendment, where the modern law imposes very heavy burdens on the state to use content-neutral instead of content-based regulations. Even if the content-neutral regulations are broader in their coverage than content-based regulations, the necessity of imposing burdens on friend and foe alike operates as an implicit but effective check against the abuse of government power. Thus a rule that prohibits all billboard advertisements is less dangerous than one that allows billboards for all purposes, save political campaigns, which in turn is far less dangerous than one that permits billboards to be used only by major political parties, or even by Democrats and not Republicans, or the reverse.

The key is that the total level of speech permitted is of less importance than the *mix* of speech allowed.[128] We would rather have a system in which both sides (of a two-sided issue) could speak with two units each than a system in which one side could speak with ten units of speech and the other none. The constitutional theme becomes distortion and imbalance, and content-based distinctions that go to the merits of the ideas expressed are prime examples of the problem.

b) *Takings.* The same question of political abuse and discretion can arise in connection with the regulation of property and economic liberties. As before, the power to select certain businesses or firms for regulation is easily abused by the political system. A rule that would subject margarine to heavier taxes than butter is one that gives a competitive advantage to the latter over

---

[128] See Stone, 25 Wm & Mary L Rev at 197-200 (cited in note 29).

the former.[129] A rule that bans plastic milk containers while allowing paper ones is subject to the same criticism.[130] A law that allows a zoning board selectively to designate certain parcels of land as large-lot residential land and then to designate neighboring plots of land as commercial land carries with it the same risk.[131] In takings cases, there is some language suggesting that disproportionate impact will require the state to provide compensation for the property that it has taken.[132] But the case law has easily evaded its lofty rhetorical standard, and has sanctioned facially non-neutral government regulations that are ripe for abuse.

2. Taxation.

The difference in how speech and takings law treat selection bias can be most conveniently seen if we pay attention to one particular form of government action—taxation. The taxation of newspapers, for example, could present a clear collision between the claims of free speech and the claims of government. Within a strongly libertarian world, the initial impulse is to say that institutions remain free only if they are not subject to tax at all. The usual libertarian formulation is that obligations are imposed upon parties to prevent the use of force, the commission of fraud, or the breach of promise. Taxation is premised on none of these rationales, and should therefore be illegal.

The point is not without historical precedent, for the rhetoric of free trade has on occasion been used by judges to excuse interstate commerce from all sorts of state taxation.[133] Over time, however, this "libertarian" position has been repudiated in favor of the view that state taxation of interstate commerce *cannot* be imposed on a discriminatory basis,[134] but *can* be imposed on a nondiscrimi-

---

[129] See *McCray v United States*, 195 US 27 (1904) (affirming the legislature's prerogative to tax margarine, but not butter).

[130] *Minnesota v Clover Leaf Creamery Co.*, 449 US 456 (1981) (affirming state's right to distinguish between containers for environmental purposes).

[131] See *Penn Central*, 438 US 104 (landmark designation). See also note 83.

[132] See, for example, *Armstrong v United States*, 364 US 40, 49 (1960) (The Takings Clause "was designed to bar Government from forcing some people alone to bear public burdens which, in all fairness and justice, should be borne by the public as a whole.").

[133] *Freeman v Hewit*, 329 US 249, 252 (1946) ("state is also precluded from taking any action which may fairly be deemed to have the effect of impeding the free flow of trade between states"); *Spector Motor Service v O'Connor*, 340 US 602, 610 (1951) (federal privilege of carrying on interstate commerce free from state taxation).

[134] See *Complete Auto Transit, Inc. v Brady*, 430 US 274, 287-89 (1977). For an exhaustive historical account of the subject, see Walter Hellerstein, *State Taxation of Interstate Business: Perspectives on Two Centuries of Constitutional Adjudication*, 41 Tax

natory basis. This same approach is surely correct for speech and takings law as well.

Thus First Amendment doctrine should take its cue, as indeed it has, from the cases regulating state taxation of interstate commerce. The basic principle is that the tax system works on a benefit theory of taxation, whereby the burdens associated with running a complex society are distributed *pro rata* to those institutions that benefit from its operations. The ability to pay the tax is irrelevant to the analysis. Protected by an antidiscrimination rule that covers all businesses, a newspaper that is subject to a tax has scant reason to complain, because the services provided from the taxes collected are equal or greater in value to the money surrendered to pay for them. Any nondiscriminatory system of taxation—of which flat taxes are the best candidate—should yield a net benefit to the newspaper taxed. Although the First Amendment has no explicit "just compensation" language that allows for forced exchanges beneficial to the taxed party, but imposed by the state, the eminent domain approach carries over to this situation, even if not formally acknowledged as such, in the cases.

The situation becomes more clouded when taxation is allowed to serve redistributive as well as protective ends, as in the welfare state. Then newspapers, along with all other taxed entities, could be systematically hurt by the tax, which then could be attacked on the ground that the costs imposed are an impediment to speech. This argument has been rejected, apparently without a struggle, on the ground that newspapers are not singled out for special treatment, and therefore obtain protection by anonymity: The resistance that others display to increased taxes protects newspapers against special oppression by the state, and hence against abuse. While it is quite likely that governments are willing to tax the press out of business, it is unlikely that they will set taxes to drive *all* businesses into bankruptcy. The protection afforded by the nondiscrimination rule may deviate from what is required by theories of optimal taxation, but it does afford important protection against invidious taxation by the state.

The litigated cases of taxation under the First Amendment are not concerned with the question of differential taxation rates between the press and other institutions. Instead they address the question of differential taxation among members of the press. What is instructive about this line of cases is that it develops a

Lawyer 37 (1987). For my views, see Richard A. Epstein, *Bargaining with the State* ch 9 (Princeton, forthcoming 1993).

powerful argument for the use of flat taxation across firms, which has powerful application to the general question of taxation under the eminent domain power. In *Grosjean v American Press Co.*[135] the Supreme Court struck down a license tax, equal to two percent of gross receipts, that was levied only against publications in the state whose weekly circulation was in excess of 20,000.[136] At one level, the case was easy, for there was ample information in the record that the tax assumed this form because Senator Huey Long and his state henchmen wished to attack the major papers in the state that had criticized him. But the tax was also suspect on structural grounds, because it singled out some papers for special treatment. The Court relied on both rationales to strike down the tax, avoiding the question of whether the facial discrimination within the class was sufficient to condemn the class.[137]

The structural issue was fairly raised in *Minneapolis Star & Tribune Co. v Minnesota Commissioner of Revenue*,[138] where the use tax in question was imposed on the print and ink used by all newspapers, with a $100,000 exemption per paper.[139] The Minneapolis Star attacked the tax for its discriminatory impact, noting that it bore the disproportionate brunt of the tax: only eleven out of 388 papers in the state paid any tax at all, and among that eleven, over two-thirds of the total tax ($608,634 out of $893,355) was paid by the Star alone.[140] The case raised none of the motive issues that clouded the legal question in *Grosjean*,[141] and the Court struck down the tax.

The Court noted first that general economic regulations applicable to other business—for example, the antitrust laws or the National Labor Relations Act—could unquestionably be applied to the press.[142] But the Court then noted that the special use tax on print and ink, with its special exemption, was nowhere duplicated in the Minnesota tax code.[143] The tax was a form of "special taxation" that "[could not] stand unless the burden [was] necessary to achieve an overriding governmental interest."[144] Thus the tax

---

[135] 297 US 233 (1936).
[136] Id at 240.
[137] Id at 250-51.
[138] 460 US 575 (1983).
[139] Id at 578.
[140] Id.
[141] Id at 580.
[142] Id.
[143] Id at 582.
[144] Id.

failed for two reasons: First, there was no reason to separate the press from the general system of taxation. Second, within the class of newspapers, there was no reason to impose a differential burden on the Star. The Court recognized that it was difficult to trace the economic consequences of any tax, and that, for all it knew, this tax might benefit newspapers relative to everyone else. But it found that safety necessitated that this tax conform with the others, both within the industry and across industries.[145]

In short, the state had a compelling interest in collecting revenue which justified imposing a tax, but not for imposing a tax of this form. "If the real goal of this tax is to duplicate the sales tax, it is difficult to see why the State did not achieve that goal by the obvious and effective expedient of applying the sales tax."[146] The Court was quite suspicious of the unequal distribution of the tax across members of the press. The Court's language is worth quoting in full:

> Whatever the motive of the legislature in this case, we think that recognizing a power in the State not only to single out the press but also to tailor the tax so that it singles out a few members of the press presents such a potential for abuse that no interest suggested by Minnesota can justify the scheme. It has asserted no interest other than its desire to have an "equitable" tax system. The current system, it explains, promotes equity because it places the burden on large publications that impose more social costs than do smaller publications and that are more likely to be able to bear the burden of the tax. Even if we were willing to accept the premise that large businesses are more profitable and therefore better able to bear the burden of the tax, the State's commitment to this "equity" is questionable, for the concern has not led the State to grant benefits to small businesses in general. And when the exemption selects such a narrowly defined group to bear the full burden of the tax, the tax begins to resemble more a penalty for a few of the largest newspapers than an attempt to favor struggling smaller enterprises.[147]

The point can be made more simply. Whatever revenue target the state wishes to achieve under its sales tax can be achieved by a flat tax across all firms in all industries, without any possibility of

---

[145] Id at 585.
[146] Id at 587-88.
[147] Id at 591-92 (footnotes omitted).

political abuse. Arguments in this form, however, apply not only to enterprises that fall within the scope of the First Amendment, but across the board. To give only the most notorious example, the windfall profits tax was sustained by the Supreme Court in the teeth of an explicit uniformity challenge (Alaskan north-slope oil was taxed differently), which was given the typically low standard of review that has been applied to economic matters, regardless of which clause of the Constitution they arise under.[148] But in this situation, it is difficult to figure out any sensible justification for the differential tax treatment, given that subsidies distort choices in economic markets in the same way they do in the market for speech and ideas. There are no special social costs involved in the production of oil (that is, those costs which cannot be handled by direct control of pollution), and ability to pay is irrelevant in the larger economic context as in the speech case. Similarly, it is beside the point to observe that the tax may be passed on to consumers or back to suppliers, for a flat tax surely achieves that result while sparing the court the impossible economic inquiry of tracing out the incidence of the tax burden.[149]

Point by point, then, the intellectual case against all forms of special taxation is identical in all its particulars to those developed by Justice O'Connor in *Minneapolis Star*. Unless there is some reason, of which I am unaware, why the modern preoccupations with baselines and just initial entitlements alter the results, there seems to be no reason why the arguments in *Minneapolis Star* should not be used to strike down the industry-specific special taxes that litter the present landscape.

Can the argument be carried still one step further? One way to look at the tax in *Minneapolis Star* is that it was a system of progressive taxation, in which most newspapers paid no tax, and the largest ones paid over four percent for print and ink costs in excess of $100,000. Surely the outcome in the case would have been identical if there had been a two percent tax on print and ink purchases between $100,000 and $250,000. In essence, what the Court has said is that progressive taxation on different members of the press is unconstitutional under the First Amendment because of the differential burdens that it imposes. Why does the same argument not apply with respect to a progressive tax generally? So long as the state can meet its budgets generally, then there is no

---

[148] *United States v Ptasynski*, 462 US 74 (1983).

[149] For a more extensive development of this point, see Epstein, *Takings* at 290-92 (cited in note 2).

reason why it should not adopt that form of tax which is least capable of abuse, and most amenable to judicial supervision to reach its goals.

IV. RECONCILING THE WELFARE STATE WITH ECONOMIC LIBERTIES

Now we reach the crux of the difference between private property and economic liberties on the one hand, and freedom of speech on the other. There is, as *Minneapolis Star* tells us, no case for income redistribution within the domain of speech, and indeed strong reasons to oppose it. But the same argument cannot be made with the same force with regard to income redistribution in general.

The case against income redistribution must come to grips with the common perception—the only perception that makes charitable assistance to the poor intelligible—that a dollar of income is worth more to a poor person than to a rich one. It can only overcome that perception by showing that the ostensible gains from redistribution are wholly outweighed by the manifold practical obstacles to effective redistribution, and by the unfortunate incentive effects for the creation of wealth that redistribution creates. It is very clear, notwithstanding the mythic significance that some attach to it,[150] that *Lochner* did *not* stand for the proposition that all forms of income redistribution and welfare measures were prohibited, if only because these were routinely upheld by the Court against all forms of challenges before *Lochner* was decided in 1905, and before it was overthrown after 1937.[151]

The question thus arises whether the lessons on disproportionate impact and discriminatory taxation applied with such diligence can be carried over into the welfare state, where by definition some form of income and wealth redistribution is routinely allowed, notwithstanding the explicit anti-redistributive language of the Takings Clause. I think that this reconciliation can take place, and on grounds that should be able to draw the consent of liberals and conservatives alike. The outline of the compromise, which I have

---

[150] See, for example, Sunstein, 87 Colum L Rev 873 (cited in note 1).

[151] See, for example, *Bell's Gap R.R. Co. v Pennsylvania*, 134 US 232 (1890). On the breakdown of the limitations on taxation, see Clyde E. Jacobs, *Law Writers and the Courts* (California, 1954). Note that the tax in *Pollock v Farmers' Loan & Trust Co.*, 157 US 429 (1895), was also progressive, but was not struck down on that ground. See also *New York Trust Co. v Eisner*, 256 US 345 (1921) (sustaining a progressive estate tax).

proposed before,[152] is that the state can redistribute as much as it likes from rich to poor so long as it does so through general revenue taxes. There is of course some room for redistribution even with the flat tax on income. This proposal waives all objections to progressive taxation, but insists only that the remainder of the structure protecting private property and economic liberties be respected and enforced. If the state wants to provide individuals with below market housing, then it can rent the units from private owners at market levels, relet them to poorer citizens at below market levels, and make up the difference by a tax on general revenues. The program thus places the cost of this public good (as redistribution has become) on the public at large, where in fairness and justice it belongs. The public at large has decided that the change is appropriate and thus should foot the bill for initiatives that the landowner may well have opposed. What can be done with rent control can be done with zoning, with specialized facilities for the handicapped, with subsidized health insurance for AIDS victims, and with educational vouchers for the poor. If one can make a gift transaction to the poor, it is always possible to fund it out of general revenues.

The justification for this approach has thus far been phrased in the distributive language used by Justice Black in his well known quotation from *Armstrong*.[153] But it bears repetition that the shift in financing procedure has vast implications for both democratic theory and economic efficiency. As regards the former, it encourages responsible behavior by citizens, who are no longer in the position to vote revenues for group A out of the pocket of group B. The tendency to play special interest politics will be eased by the requirement that participation entails the right to control but also entails the obligation to bear imposed obligations with one's fellow citizens. Even staunch defenders of republican virtue should prefer a responsible citizenry to the powerful one, and this reconciliation of the Takings Clause with the welfare state achieves just that end.

The efficiency argument is every bit as powerful. The nature of the programs that will be funded will differ as the method for funding those programs changes. The situation in which the voters at large can shift all the costs of running the welfare state to a tiny

---

[152] See Richard A. Epstein, *Takings: Of Maginot Lines and Constitutional Compromises,* in Ellen Frankel Paul and Howard Dickman, eds, *Liberty, Property, and the Future of Constitutional Development* 173 (SUNY, 1990).

[153] See note 132.

fraction of the population contains a built-in externality: one group decides, and another group pays. The usual economic conclusion about externalities applies: too much of the good will be demanded relative to other goods that might be purchased, a conclusion that applies even when one good is aid to the poor and the other is repaving the public streets. Correct voting procedure neutralizes some of the externalities that are otherwise implicit in the current system that invites disproportionate funding, not only of welfare payments, but of any imaginable government expenditure (whether or not pure public goods). A system that more accurately measures the public sympathy and support for various programs is surely preferable to one that so skews the inquiry that the level of production of welfare payments, relative to other goods, is excessive. The total level of goods and services should increase as well, which increases the size of the base available for redistributive purchases. Even a post-New Deal legislature, however aware of the evils of common law baselines, can only redistribute through the political process what is produced through the economic one.

Finally the proposal places a limitation on the nature and kinds of redistribution that are feasible: There is redistribution along one dimension only, from rich to poor, for it is only along that line that one can assume that a single unit of wealth means more to the recipient than it does to the donor. Gone are the days therefore of the inveterate agricultural subsidies that benefit corporate farmers at the expense of poor ghetto dwellers, and gone are the days when exclusionary zoning can keep poor people out of affluent suburbs. If redistribution of wealth from rich to poor is the goal, then a court can scrutinize the program in question to see that there is a reasonable means-end connection. The welfare state is thus reconcilable with the Bill of Rights in an imperfect but powerful way. It remains to see whether the inveterate judicial temperament keeps us chained to a jurisprudence of economic liberty that has stifled the power and initiative of this country for the last fifty years, indeed longer.

Liberties, Fair Values, and Constitutional Method

Frank I. Michelman†

Meeting a friend in a corridor, Wittgenstein said: "Tell me, why do people always say it was *natural* for men to assume that the sun went round the earth rather than that the earth was rotating?" His friend said, "Well, obviously, because it just *looks* as if the sun is going round the earth." To which the philosopher replied, "Well, what would it have looked like if it had looked as if the earth was rotating?"[1]

If judges were bringing to property-rights adjudication the same system of thought they bring to free-speech adjudication, what would our constitutional doctrine of property look like? I think the answer (for better or for worse) must be the same as the one invited by Wittgenstein's mind teaser: The doctrine would look like . . . what it looks like.

Is Professor Richard Epstein saying differently?[2] It would be surprising if he were, because insistence on the pull toward unity in constitutional thought has been a consistent mark and strength of Professor Epstein's scholarship. In *Property, Speech, and the Politics of Distrust*, Professor Epstein does say that if we would only carry over into Takings Clause analysis the "doctrinal structures," organizing "presuppositions," and "dominant tendencies" of First Amendment adjudication, we would greatly change the law of Takings.[3] But this is no claim of deep disjuncture between Takings adjudication and First Amendment adjudication as we find them conducted today. Rather, Professor Epstein looks past the

---

† Professor of Law, Harvard University. This Article was prepared for *The Bill of Rights in the Welfare State: A Bicentennial Symposium*, held at The University of Chicago Law School on October 25-26, 1991. It is heavily indebted to Ed Baker, Peggy Radin, and Fred Schauer, both for comments on a prior draft and for scholarship on which it relies. Perhaps its most extended indebtedness (acknowledged in the title and by one, lonesome citation) is to the teaching of John Rawls that the question of liberty, insofar as it has anything to do with justice, is inseparable from the question of distribution.

[1] Tom Stoppard, *Jumpers* 75 (Faber and Faber, 1972) (emphasis in original).

[2] Richard A. Epstein, *Property, Speech, and the Politics of Distrust*, in this volume, 41.

[3] Id at 42-43, 47.

surface confusions of the moment ("through the eyes," as he says, "of a cautious libertarian"[4]) to immanent, normative foundations of First Amendment law. Finding these deeper inspirations not always honored in contemporary practice, Epstein urges that their full restoration to constitutional law would return that law—including First Amendment law—to a sound condition.[5]

By Professor Epstein's standards, the state of constitutional law today is one of corruption and decline. First Amendment law is not exempt. Epstein thinks, however, that First Amendment law can be made to yield a corrective model for Takings doctrine because it is comparatively less decayed, and therefore a better initial guide to recovery and reconstruction of sound constitutional reason. Foremost among the normative impulses he finds better preserved there is distrust, "the sense that government is a necessary evil."[6] Professor Epstein, as usual, argues his case with vigor and rigor. As usual, illumination results. We see normative shapes, structures, symmetries—contestable as many of us find them—where before we had not glimpsed their possibility.

There is, though, such a thing as blinding light, the flood of incandescence that washes out of perception not just the small details but the structural fixtures of the scene before us. Part II of this Article warns against letting the light of distrust theory wash out main features of our constitutional landscape. It contends that among the fixtures of First Amendment doctrine that Professor Epstein agrees must limit any reconstructive "internal adjustment" of the doctrine[7] is one—the comparatively free pass for "incidental" restrictions of speech—that simply will not allow for canonization of distrust as *the* surpassing precept of American constitutionalism.

Section I takes more direct issue with Professor Epstein's well-known recommendations for greatly tightened judicial review of legal regulation of proprietary and economic liberties. Rather than treating contemporary constitutional law's elevation of free speech rights over property rights as a sign of decadence, I start with the thought that this practice strikes most people as making some kind of functional sense. Without claiming (or believing) that today's practice is above reproach, I describe a set of normative premises

---

[4] Id at 47.

[5] Id at 46.

[6] Id at 47.

[7] Id at 44.

that the general shape of this practice seems designed to carry out, and claim that these premises are good ones.

We begin with commonplaces. The Constitution contemplates lawmaking. It entrusts to lawmakers a range of legislative discretion. It does so, we have to presume, out of a regard for justice and welfare.[8] Presumably out of a like regard, the Constitution also establishes certain rights and otherwise limits lawmakers' discretion to make laws. The Constitution calls upon courts of law to help effectuate these rights[9] and other limits[10] on lawmaker discretion, by adjudicating claims of transgression. Yet it also calls upon the courts, in their adjudications, to support and defend the discretionary authority of lawmakers.[11]

Between discretion and limits, discretion and rights, courts are to hold the balance true.[12] But if there is a true balance, can there be more than one? Why should courts have multiple sets of scales and calipers in use: "strict" scrutiny in some cases, "loose" scrutiny in others, various "intermediate" scrutinies in still others, depending upon which rights are in question? How can our courts presume to give different protection to Fifth Amendment property rights than to First Amendment expression rights? That is our question.[13]

In this Article, I advance for consideration a loosely policy-analytic answer to this question, relying on a broadly functionalist, or consequentialist, argument. I make no claim that this kind of argument can stand by itself as a complete and sufficient response to any large question of political morality or legitimacy. Yet, I believe, most would consider such an argument an indispensable support for other forms of political justification. Suppose that we cannot discover any policy-motivated, functional reason for such a quirky-looking practice as methodically stricter judicial review under the Free Speech Clause than under the Takings Clause of

---

[8] See Sanford Levinson, *Constitutional Faith* (Princeton, 1988). The entrustment may be misguided—a question we shall be considering—but the fact of entrustment and its presumptively benign intention seem undeniable.

[9] See *Cooper v Aaron*, 358 US 1 (1958).

[10] See *Marbury v Madison*, 5 US (1 Cranch) 137 (1803).

[11] See *McCulloch v Maryland*, 17 US (4 Wheaton) 316 (1819).

[12] See id at 423.

[13] My response to the question follows some, but not all, of the leads furnished in Professor C. Edwin Baker's more elaborate response to "those . . . who claim that a principled justification has never been given for distinguishing currently protected individual liberties from currently unprotected, or minimally protected, economic or property rights." C. Edwin Baker, *Property and its Relation to Constitutionally Protected Liberty*, 134 U Pa L Rev 741, 742 (1986).

one and the same Bill of Rights. The inability to do so will tend to undermine other arguments—such as that natural law requires the quirky practice, that the Framers intended it, that hypothetical social contractors would adopt it, or even that our society's evolved wisdom and usage contain it.

If I have done my work correctly, and you do not find persuasive force in what follows, it will be because you reject certain normative assumptions I have had to build into the functionalist argument in order to make it work. In that case, my effort's value for you will have been to help make clear precisely what is questionable about a constitutional policy of " 'strict scrutiny' for speech, 'loose scrutiny' for property."

I. LIBERTIES AND INTERESTS

To value human freedom is both to interpret and to value human interest; it is to construe freedom as a human good. To value particularly defined "liberties" is to value interests more specifically distinguished—interests we may attribute to individuals whose liberties are in question, to others standing in particular relations to those individuals, or to the public at large. Consider, now, how American constitutional lawyers talk about liberty. We regularly speak not simply of liberty, but of various liberties. We speak of religious liberties, expressive liberties, economic and proprietary liberties. We thus classify liberties by function. Which label we use depends on just what it is we have in mind that a person may or may not be at liberty to do. It depends, in other words, on what sorts of interests are at stake.

Now, this way of speaking is no accident. It seems we must understand constitutional liberties as comprising certain kinds of interests, as long as we understand the Constitution as a deliberate human act. When people designedly write protections for liberties into their constitution, they must be doing so out of desire to protect corresponding interests. Why else would they do it?[14]

---

[14] To take this position is neither to overlook nor to downgrade the expressive aspect of the practice of recognizing and respecting human rights, or the centrality of this practice to moral justification of political authority. See, for example, Baker, 134 U Pa L Rev at 780-81 (cited in note 13). It is just to insist that the expressive value or moral "point" of respect for liberty would evaporate if we lacked a strong and steady sense of liberty's close connection with interest.

To take this interest-conscious view of liberty is also not necessarily to exclude from constitutional practical reason the use of "formal" conceptions of liberty that flatly rule out certain ways of collectively promoting the value of liberty for all. Compare id at 744 (observing that "[c]onstitutional interpretation inevitably is either explicitly or implicitly animated

With that for a premise, we easily reach the first, very general point of my argument: given such an interest-based classification of liberties, there may well be good reasons for agents charged with protecting the liberties to look beyond formal symmetries, and accord different forms and degrees of protection to different classes of liberties. Judges are such agents. Their protection takes the form of more-or-less censorious review of laws infringing on liberties of one or another class. There should be no great surprise in finding variation in the forms and degrees of such review, depending on which classes of liberty are in question. These variations may be an intelligent response to perceived, relevant differences among the interests corresponding to the various classes of liberties of which we speak.

A. Liberty Interests: Intrinsic Value

The interests corresponding to expressive liberties are those in people's freedom from government control over what they say and over how, when, and where they say it. The interests corresponding to economic liberties are those in people's freedom from government control over their choices and modes of productive activity and investment. The interests corresponding to proprietary liberties are those in people's freedom from government control over their retention, use, and disposition of lawfully obtained holdings of wealth.[15]

Ever since the celebrated Footnote 4,[16] theorists have considered whether stricter judicial protection for some liberties than for others can be justified by showing how the some have intrinsically deeper libertarian[17] or civic[18] value than the others. That will not

---

by value concerns"), with id at 777, 780-81 (granting the force of "pragmatic" critiques of libertarian formalism but also advocating formalistic exclusion of liberty-optimizing methods that violate individual autonomy).

[15] Baker enumerates the interests corresponding to proprietary and economic liberties as interests in the use of things, welfare-maintenance, personhood, protection against exploitation by others, allocation (facilitating acquisition and exchange), and sovereignty (power over others). Id at 744-53. For good measure, he then adds privacy, recognition and development of values, and decentralization of social power. Id at 753-54.

[16] *United States v Carolene Products Co.*, 304 US 144, 152-53 n 4 (1938).

[17] See, for example, David A.J. Richards, *Toleration and the Constitution* (Oxford, 1986); Martin H. Redish, *The Value of Free Speech*, 130 U Pa L Rev 591 (1982); Louis Henkin, *Privacy and Autonomy*, 74 Colum L Rev 1410 (1974); David A.J. Richards, *Free Speech and Obscenity Law: Toward a Moral Theory of the First Amendment*, 123 U Pa L Rev 45 (1974).

[18] See, for example, Alexander Meiklejohn, *Free Speech and its Relation to Self-Government* 1-3 (Harper & Brothers, 1948); John Hart Ely, *Democracy and Distrust: A Theory of Judicial Review* 75-98, 105-16 (Harvard, 1980).

be precisely the line of argument here. For present purposes, we can stipulate that people's freedom to say what they please is no more foundational to personal or societal fulfillment than are their proprietary securities or their freedoms of choice in productive endeavors,[19] and, further, that there is no historical American consensus that they are.[20]

B. "Negative" Liberties

We may further take it as given (for this occasion only) that American constitutional law knows only "negative" and not "positive" liberties, and knows even these negative liberties only as against the state and not as against nongovernmental agents. American constitutional lawyers regularly and sharply differentiate liberty from empowerment. We know the conceptual difference between being at liberty to speak and having the ability and resources with which to speak effectively. The prevailing view is that our Constitution by and large guarantees only the liberties, not the abilities or resources;[21] and, further, that it guarantees relief only against infringements by governments, and not by private agents.[22]

---

[19] See Frederick Schauer, *Free Speech: A Philosophical Enquiry* ch 4 (Cambridge, 1982); Stanley Ingber, *The Marketplace of Ideas: A Legitimizing Myth*, 1984 Duke L J 1, 14-15 n 67, 78-79; Robert H. Bork, *Neutral Principles and Some First Amendment Problems*, 47 Ind L J 1, 25 (1971).

[20] See generally Jennifer Nedelsky, *Private Property and the Limits of American Constitutionalism* (Chicago, 1990). From the standpoint of civic interest, proprietary "independence" was historically regarded in America as foundational to good citizenship. See, for example, Akhil Reed Amar, *Forty Acres and a Mule: A Republican Theory of Minimal Entitlements*, 13 Harv J L & Pub Pol 37, 37 (1990); Frank I. Michelman, *Possession vs. Distribution in the Constitutional Idea of Property*, 72 Iowa L Rev 1319, 1327-34 (1987). Perhaps there is one class of freedoms that have arguably occupied such a consensually preferred status in American political thought—the freedoms of conscience and religious profession.

[21] See, for example, David P. Currie, *Positive and Negative Constitutional Rights*, 53 U Chi L Rev 864 (1986) (recognizing limited exceptions to the primarily negative nature of American constitutional rights).

[22] These two limits—the negative nature of constitutional rights and the state action rule—are logically connected. See, for example, *DeShaney v Winnebago County Department of Social Services*, 489 US 189 (1989). If the Constitution guaranteed protection of my negative liberty of speech against your interference (as a private citizen), it would by the same token grant me an affirmative claim against the government to: (1) prosecute you for interfering; (2) prevent you from interfering; or (3) guarantee me the resources to prevent you from interfering myself. See Frank I. Michelman, *The Supreme Court and Litigation Access Fees: The Right to Protect One's Rights—Part I*, 1973 Duke L J 1153, 1195-96. For an example of the second alternative, see *Robins v Pruneyard Shopping Center*, 23 Cal 3d 899, 592 P2d 341 (1979), aff'd, *Pruneyard Shopping Center v Robins*, 447 US 74 (1980) (ordering property owner to refrain from denying access to persons exercising free expression rights guaranteed by California constitution).

C. Existence vs. Value of a (Negative) Liberty

Thus we readily distinguish between two types of putative constitutional entitlements. We find it natural to think that people do have constitutional entitlements to be free from certain intrusions and restraints by the state, but simultaneously that people do not have corresponding constitutional entitlements to the state's assurance of access to the means of using and enjoying this freedom. Conceptually, we have no trouble with this conjunction of having and not having. It is perfectly conceptually possible for a negative liberty against the state to exist as pure entitlement, regardless of the holder's access to the means of enjoyment. From this standpoint of pure entitlement against the state, a well-defined negative liberty has only the one dimension of existence/non-existence.[23] However—and here is a crux of my argument—matters are not so simple when we regard negative liberties from the standpoint of interests. In an interest-sensitive view, constitutionally guaranteed liberties are not simply formal entitlements, such that we either have them or we don't, and that is all there is to be said. Instead, liberties then also take on practical dimensions of magnitude and value.[24] To illustrate, imagine for a moment that proprietary liberties are absolute. Then my proprietary liberty would presumptively be worth more than that of a broke and homeless fellow citizen; there is a clear sense in which I stand to lose more than he does by a general revocation or restriction of proprietary liberties.

---

[23] If constitutional negative liberty were construed as an entitlement *in rem*—good against all agents—then distributions of legal property holdings would determine the scopes of such liberty accruing to various persons. To speak of property distribution would, then, be to speak of the distribution of negative liberty itself. See Jeremy Waldron, *Homelessness and the Issue of Freedom*, 39 UCLA L Rev 295, 302-08 (1991). However, constitutional negative liberty is construed as running only against the state. Therefore, we cannot speak of property distribution as affecting the *scope of* constitutional liberty any person has (since, under suitably general laws, rich and poor alike will have exactly identical rights to be left unmolested by the state). We can, however, still speak of property distribution as affecting the *values* of these rights to various persons.

[24] See John Rawls, *A Theory of Justice* 204 (Harvard, 1971):

[L]iberty and the worth of liberty are distinguished as follows: liberty is represented by the complete system of the liberties of equal citizenship, while the worth of liberty to persons and groups is proportional to their capacity to advance their ends within the framework the system defines.

See also Waldron, 39 UCLA L Rev at 317 (cited in note 23) ("If we value freedom . . . because of the importance of choice . . . , then that value ought to lead us to pay attention" to what choices people actually have.).

D. The Systemic Character of Liberty Under Law

A constitution is a rule of law. To speak of liberties established by a rule of law is to speak of a general scheme of liberties
for all;[25] it is to invite the question of distribution.[26] Given that the
reason for protecting liberties is regard for the corresponding interests, a constitutional scheme of liberties cannot reasonably or lawfully blind itself to the distributive relations of the liberty interests
that it cherishes and, in a sense, creates. And given further that
these liberty interests have dimensions of value, the scheme cannot
reasonably blind itself to the configurations of the values—the distributions of the values among persons—of these liberty interests.[27] It cannot disregard either the fairness of these distributions
or their social-systemic ramifications.

This is not (as you may be thinking) to admit judicial enforcement of "positive" rights through the back door. Constitutional
concern with the fair values of negative liberties-as-interests need
not involve judicially enforceable entitlements to government aid.
Such a concern may rather lead to judicial respect for government
actions designed to provide aid, or otherwise ensure the fair value
of liberty—perhaps even sometimes when such actions infringe liberties; it may be manifested in what courts will recognize as adequate justification for liberty-infringing actions.[28] Such a concern is
arguably manifest, for example, when the Supreme Court upholds
laws prohibiting political speech funded by general treasury assets
of business corporations, on the theory that government may pre-

---

[25] See Harry Kalven, Jr., *Upon Rereading Mr. Justice Black on the First Amendment*,
14 UCLA L Rev 428, 432 (1967) ("Freedom of speech is indivisible; unless we protect it for
all, we will have it for none.").

[26] See Mary Ellen Gale, *Reimagining the First Amendment: Racist Speech and Equal
Liberty*, 65 St John's L Rev 119, 154-58 (1991). See particularly id at 154 ("The idea of
equality is built into the structure of the first amendment. Free speech is guaranteed not
just to one . . . class of speakers but by simple inference to all speakers.").

[27] Compare Baker, 134 U Pa L Rev at 746 (cited in note 13):
[W]hen a community possesses the productive capacity to supply all of its members
with the resources it considers as prerequisites to meaningful life, but adopts property
rules that deny those resources to some, then . . . [t]his subordination, this denial of
the worth of those left without, is inconsistent with any social system premised on
respecting people as equals.

[28] Some recent scholarship proposes that the "government interests" allowed by courts
to justify legislative infringements of *prima facie* constitutional rights ought themselves to
be understood as manifestations of rights, or of values of equivalent import with rights.
Stephen E. Gottlieb, *Compelling Governmental Interests: An Essential But Unanalyzed
Term in Constitutional Adjudication*, 68 BU L Rev 917 (1988).

vent certain "distortions" in the political system of expressive liberty.[29]

E. Negative Liberty Interests: Scarcity and Distribution

1. Proprietary liberty.

Look, now, at constitutional proprietary liberty. It comprises the interest people have in freedom from government control over wealth; inextricably, it comprises the power that goes with wealth. The "interest" and its "value" are practically and conceptually inseparable. The interest in proprietary liberty is just the interest in maintaining proprietary value (or power).

In a capitalist order, one person's proprietary value (or power) is obviously relative to other people's.[30] A constitutional system of proprietary liberty is, therefore, incomplete without attending to the configurations of the values of various people's proprietary liberties. The question of distribution is endemic in the very idea of a constitutional scheme of proprietary liberty. Thus, it can by no means be said of laws aimed at nothing but property distributions that they are *ipso facto* antithetical to that idea.[31] Richard Epstein agrees, up to the point of exempting rich-to-poor transfers, financed by system-wide general taxes, from presumptive invalidity as uncompensated takings of property.[32] However, I mean to press the argument a good deal further.

A constitutional scheme of proprietary liberty, we said, is incomplete without attention to the distribution of wealth. Let us now add that such a scheme can hardly ignore qualitative distinctions among wealth holdings.[33] Thus, most Americans would see at least an arguable issue of justice in the question of distribution between the possessory solitudes of shorefront second-home owners and the general public's freedom of movement along the sea-

---

[29] *Austin v Michigan Chamber of Commerce*, 110 S Ct 1391, 1396-98 (1990).

[30] See, for example, Baker, 134 U Pa L Rev at 788-90 (cited in note 13).

[31] Baker similarly argues for the necessity (despite the difficulty) of distinguishing between laws that "restrict liberty" and laws that "allocate and demarcate the boundaries of decisionmaking authority" and thereby "establish[] the framework within which liberty exists." "An acceptable formal conception of liberty," says Baker, requires "a set of allocation rules." Id at 780.

[32] Epstein, in this volume, 88 (cited in note 2).

[33] See Baker, 134 U Pa L Rev at 744 (cited in note 13) ("[T]he first function of property rules is to protect use values."). Among legal theorists, Margaret Jane Radin has done the most to clarify this point. See, for example, Margaret Jane Radin, *Residential Rent Control*, 15 Phil & Pub Aff 350 (1986); Margaret Jane Radin, *Property and Personhood*, 34 Stan L Rev 957 (1982).

shore.[34] Likewise, many doubtless see issues of justice in questions of distribution between commercial landlords' profits and residential tenants' living conditions[35] (and also believe that there are circumstances in which residential renter-protection laws can effectively respond to these issues[36]). In the sight of such qualitatively discriminating, pragmatic appraisals, fairness in the constitutional scheme of proprietary liberties will sometimes call for laws whose restrictions fall unevenly on various kinds of property holdings.[37]

Such issues of proprietary justice may, moreover, be so context- and culture-dependent that they are unfit for resolution at the level of abstraction and fixity at which the text of a strongly entrenched, rarely amendable bill of rights must speak. The principle of respect for property is a core commitment of American constitutionalism, but the contours of protection have always throughout our history been wrapped in controversy.[38] Perhaps this is because the contours have always been in flux. Property—the claim to security of possession or entitlement—is significantly a matter of justified expectation, and expectation is at bottom a "cultural possession."[39] It is certainly true that our culture justifies attaching a degree of expectation to extant positive laws, but in a common-law based "culture of property," the possibility of change, of evolution, is "always understood."[40] For these or other reasons, a

---

[34] See *Nollan v California Coastal Comm'n*, 483 US 825, 847-48, 856-58, 863-64 (1987) (Brennan dissenting).

[35] Compare Margaret Jane Radin, *Diagnosing the Takings Problem*, in John H. Chapman, ed, *Compensatory Justice* (Nomos XXXIII) 248, 257 (New York, 1991) ("*Takings Problem*") ("Home-ownership carries greater moral weight in the legal system than does ownership of vacant land held for investment.").

[36] See, for example, Radin, 15 Phil & Pub Aff 350 (cited in note 33); Duncan Kennedy, *Distributive and Paternalist Motives in Contract and Tort Law, With Special Reference to Compulsory Terms and Unequal Bargaining Power*, 41 Md L Rev 563, 610-14 (1982).

[37] The distributive impacts of such restrictions would deviate from population-wide proportionality or progressivity relative to numerary net income or net worth. Thus they would fail the test adumbrated by Justice Scalia in his dissenting opinion in *Pennell v City of San Jose*, 485 US 1, 21-24 (1988), and in his prevailing opinion in *Nollan*, 483 US 825, at least as some read it. See, for example, Douglas Kmiec, *The Original Understanding of the Taking Clause Is Neither Weak nor Obtuse*, 88 Colum L Rev 1630, 1650-52 (1988).

[38] See Radin, *Takings Problem* at 248-49, 265 (cited in note 35).

[39] Margaret Jane Radin, *Evaluating Government Reasons For Changing Property Regimes* (forthcoming) ("*Regimes*"). See also Bruce A. Ackerman, *Private Property and the Constitution* 116-18 (Yale, 1977) (distinguishing between "social property" and "legal property" and emphasizing importance of the former).

[40] Radin, *Regimes* (cited in note 39). For example, in criticizing *Nollan*, 483 US 825, Radin persuasively describes (and documents) the recent "culture of private property . . . on the west coast" as evidently

> evolving toward an understanding that beaches are a special resource not treated the
> same as ordinary objects of property. . . . The cultural understanding seemed to be that

democratic constitution may well leave the precise contours of property protection, or some of them, to ongoing political hammering-out within rather broad limits.[41]

2. Economic liberty.

Very much the same is true of economic liberties, people's freedoms from government control over choices of productive endeavor or investment. These freedoms and their fair values are obviously, in practice, socially interdependent. If major corporate employers relocate their workplaces, or refuse to allow women to work on certain jobs, the displaced workers or excluded women retain their economic liberties (conceived as legal entitlements against the state), but the values of these liberties may be gravely impaired. If the government seeks to protect these values by restricting such employer actions or policies, then the values of a quite different class of economic liberties, those of actual and prospective investors in the regulated employer firms, suffer.[42] As a general matter, it seems quite likely that holding the values of economic liberties in reasonable adjustment will call for considerable regulatory control over the manner in which such liberties are exercised.[43]

---

the stereotyped private property regime, with its broad discretion of owners to control use and exclusion was, with respect to this particular resource, wrong.

Id. See also Radin, *Takings Problem* at 252 (cited in note 35) ("In some more environmentally conscious future, [decisions denying compensation for highly restrictive wetlands regulation] could come to appear easy."); Elizabeth V. Mensch, *The Colonial Origins of Liberal Property Rights*, 31 Buff L Rev 635, 646-48 (1982) (describing "voluntarist" strain in early American property law that favored direct use of resources by owners and recognized authority of communities to realign titles to correspond with personal need and desire to cultivate); Forrest McDonald, *Novus Ordo Seclorum: The Intellectual Origins of the Constitution* 13-36 (Kansas, 1985) (describing American formative-era, common-law understanding of property rights as fluid, relational, and regulable according to changing conceptions of public interest).

[41] See, for example, Michael Walzer, *Spheres of Justice: A Defense of Pluralism and Equality* 68-83 (Basic, 1983); Michael Walzer, *Philosophy and Democracy*, 9 Pol Theory 379, 391-92 (1981); Baker, 134 U Pa L Rev at 781, 783-85 (cited in note 13).

[42] No natural person's economic liberties—as distinguished from the worths of such liberties—are directly infringed by such regulations. Of course, if we attribute liberties to the corporations themselves, then those liberties are directly infringed by the regulations. Compare *Santa Clara County v Southern Pacific Railroad Co.*, 118 US 394, 396 (1886) (treating corporations as "persons" protected by the Fourteenth Amendment), with *First Nat'l Bank of Boston v Bellotti*, 435 US 765, 776 (1978) (bypassing question of "whether corporations 'have' First Amendment rights").

[43] See Baker, 134 U Pa L Rev at 790 (cited in note 13) (Given that many people spend major portions of their lives in productive activity and identify themselves with what they do, "concern for individual freedom requires that [economic] structure . . . be subject to conscious, [collective] control.").

In short, to repeat, we cannot broadly say that laws aimed at nothing but modifying property distributions or regulating the economy are inimical to the idea of a system of proprietary or economic liberty.

3. Expressive liberty.

By contrast—and here we reach an important turning point in the argument—we do find reason to say, of most laws aimed at nothing but suppressing communication, that they are inimical to the idea of a system of expressive liberty. In American constitutional thought, concerns about scarcity, distribution, and value simply have not played out in the same way for expressive liberties as they have for economic and proprietary liberties.

It may seem peculiar, but American constitutionalists have generally perceived the interests contemplated by (negative) expressive liberty as non-scarce and even, in a rather special sense, as non-competitive, as explained below. This perception arises out of a particular set of ideas about what gives communication its constitutionally estimable worth, both to individuals and to society—ideas that impart a rather special meaning to our regnant image of a marketplace of ideas.

This particular "marketplace" understanding requires that we not measure the value of my expressive liberty in terms of either the likelihood that I will speak or the likelihood that others will be moved by what I say. In fact, this understanding is powerfully inclined against any kind of comparative assessments of the values of various people's expressive liberties, as long as the negative liberties themselves are unobstructed. Insofar as it does make such assessments, the only axis of variation it recognizes is the degree to which one's communications, once launched, have a fair, competitive chance to reach others, to get through effectively to others and receive their unobstructed attention. Once equipped with such an understanding, American constitutionalists can plausibly maintain that rarely is there a need to curb anyone's expressive liberty out of a concern for the values of other people's expressive liberties; that in general everyone can talk as much as they choose, however they choose, about whatever they choose, to whomever they choose, without restricting or devaluing anyone else's freedom to communicate.

This approach is not without serious problems.[44] Nevertheless, for committed liberals, including many committed egalitarians, it contains a sufficient core of common sense to make it a reasonable starting point for a constitutional doctrine of freedom of speech. The "marketplace" approach underwrites a doctrine making highly suspect all government actions that serve no plausible goals apart from restricting expression and communication. Of course, such a presumptive rule can allow for exceptional cases in which some people's exercises of expressive freedom do adversely affect the values of other people's expressive freedoms, defining such values as the marketplace principle requires.[45] The easiest such cases to recognize are those involving conflicts of "time, place, and manner."[46]

There are other cases, such as racial hate speech, in which some people's speech arguably impairs the fair values of other people's expressive freedoms, but in which a liberally acceptable remedy is harder to fashion.[47] It does not seem obviously mistaken to

---

[44] Sensible people must admit that this is far from a fully realistic view. For a wide-ranging critique, see Ingber, 1984 Duke L J 1 (cited in note 19). First, some speech can degrade the fair value of other people's speech by simply obstructing it, as by drowning it out. Second, some speakers and messages are able to preempt or dominate the most effective channels of communication. See id at 38-40. Doing so degrades the fair value of other people's expressive liberties, measuring that value (just as "marketplace" theory demands) in terms of a fair chance to command the attention of an audience. Third, it seems hard to deny (however problematic may be the implications of admitting) that speech can degrade the fair value of other people's speech by summoning perceptions of them (quite aside from their messages) as human types unworthy of being heard or credited—that is, by exploiting cultures of oppression to induce prejudgment. See Catharine MacKinnon, *Feminism Unmodified: Discourses on Life and Law* 193-95 (Harvard, 1987); Iris Marion Young, *Justice and the Politics of Group Difference* 58-61 (Princeton, 1990); Charles R. Lawrence III, *If He Hollers Let Him Go: Regulating Racist Speech on Campus*, 1990 Duke L J 431, 468-72.

[45] See note 24.

[46] Even their apparent simplicity may be deceptive. See, for example, C. Edwin Baker, *Human Liberty and Freedom of Speech* 125-60 (Oxford, 1989) (criticizing such restrictions as neither necessary nor desirable).

[47] See, for example, Thomas C. Grey, *Civil Rights versus Civil Liberties: The Case of Discriminatory Verbal Harassment*, 8 Soc Phil & Pol 81 (1991); Lawrence, 1990 Duke L J 431 (cited in note 44). There are other arguable cases of unfair impairment by some people's speech of the value of other people's speech that a committedly liberal constitutional-legal order may have little choice but to disregard. It may happen that less meritorious arguments backed by an individual speaker's superior personal endowment of wit, chutzpah, eloquence, or charisma gain undue advantage in the speech market over more meritorious insights that a slower-witted, duller-spoken person has trouble articulating. See Ingber, 1984 Duke L J at 31 (cited in note 19) (questioning the assumption that "people can distinguish rationally between a message's substance and the distortion caused by its form or focus"). However, personal handicapping in such circumstances seems not a liberally entertainable possibility. See, for example, id at 50-55; Baker, 134 U Pa L Rev at 806-07 (cited in note 13) (explaining why "[l]egal regulation of people's use of their personal qualities to obtain

regard these as boundary cases, for which exceptions might conceivably be crafted but on which one would be ill-advised to base a general, doctrinal approach.[48]

F. Negative Liberty Interests: Interdependence and Externalities

We have seen that a constitutional scheme of liberties must rationally concern itself with how one person's exercise of liberty X affects the values of other people's liberty X. Of course, it must also rationally concern itself with how one person's exercise of liberty X affects the values of other people's liberties Y and Z. And here we discover an additional reason why expressive liberties stand on a different constitutional footing than proprietary or economic liberties.

Plainly, some people's exercises of proprietary and economic liberties can spill over to devalue other people's expressive liberties. Reasonable adjustment will often require regulation. Political campaign spending poses a problem of this kind. Few doubt that the problem is real. The existence of spending on political cam-

---

others' participation in interactions seems intuitively offensive as an overt limitation on liberty"). Again, it may happen that what an audience experiences as comparative cogency and soundness of argument is just a reflex of the comparative familiarity or conventionality of the ideas being urged. See, for example, Ingber, 1984 Duke L J at 25-36 (cited in note 19). If this is at all a frequent occurrence, then public-forum doctrines of content-neutral order-maintenance and equal access may be a recipe for ensuring that currently prevalent views and perspectives will continue to prevail regardless of their responsiveness to the interests and values of the audience. See id at 40-44. But by what standard can liberals deal out "deviance" or "dissidence" subsidies? See id at 50-55.

[48] See Gale, 65 St John's L Rev at 158-59, 168-83 (cited in note 26). It is not, however, a sufficient liberal response to the "hate speech" problem to point out that hate speech produces its degradation of the values of the expressive liberties of target-group members by transmitting derogatory "ideas" about the latter. See, for example, Charles Fried, *The New First Amendment Jurisprudence: A Threat to Liberty*, 59 U Chi L Rev 225, 245 (1992). Liberals must first decide whether verbal trashings of classes of persons do significantly prevent the intended audiences from attending to messages (claims, stories, expressions of need, arguments) that those persons utter. If the answer is yes, then some people's speech is seriously degrading the values of other people's expressive liberties (just as surely as the racially discriminating employer is seriously degrading the values of some people's economic liberties and the major polluter is seriously degrading the values of some people's proprietary liberties). Liberals must then face the question of whether the degradation is so great as to constitute as a deviation from the constitutionally contemplated system of expressive liberties. See, for example, Robert Post, *Racist Speech, Democracy, and the First Amendment*, 32 Wm & Mary L Rev 267, 312-14 (1991).

If hate speech does thus impair the fair value of expressive liberty to those who suffer the degradation, then we have a problem on our hands that no amount of imprecation can make go away. It is an especially thorny problem if it cannot be treated except by some kind and degree of restriction on expressive liberty. But see id at 317 (arguing that there are a "host of ways to address this challenge short of truncating public discourse"). Of course, being thorny does not make the problem *not* a problem, either.

paigns confirms a truth we have already established: that along with property rights come considerations of distribution and relative values of liberties that do not, in liberal contemplation, normally arise with respect to expressive liberty strictly speaking.

Of course, spillovers can run in the reverse direction, too. Exercises of expressive liberties can affect the extent and values of proprietary and economic liberties. Free public debate may lead to a rent control law or a lettuce boycott. The two cases, however, are hardly the same; the latter but not the former represents democracy in action. American constitutionalism assigns a drastically superior moral status to the political power of communicative persuasion than it does to the political power of the purse.

Just now, it seems as though a national debate may be gathering over the question of government-guaranteed, universal health care protection. Suppose that those who oppose universal health care eventually carry the day in the chambers of government, and people widely believe that this happened just because the opponents were able, by force of superior wealth, to outspend the proponents. Most Americans would find this result objectionable in principle, and the objection would be precisely to the' spillover from wealth into politics. By contrast, whatever may be objectionable about a rent control law, the objection simply cannot be that the law resulted from effective communicative persuasion in a fairly conducted debate. No one will think the law objectionable merely because free speech brought it about. If, however, the ground for objection were that disparities in wealth between supporters and opponents produced the rent-control law, then that would be a very different case.

II. The Myth of Distrust

A. Distrust As Universal Solvent

To this point, I have argued that functional differences between expressive liberties on the one hand, and proprietary and economic liberties on the other, may justify more exacting judicial scrutiny of laws restricting expression than of laws restricting proprietary and economic liberties. Here is the argument, in outline:

> (1) Liberties are interests, and as such they have dimensions of value.
> (2) A regime of law protecting liberty interests as human rights must attend to the systemic relations of their values.
> (3) Concern for such systemic relations requires restraint of expressive liberty only exceptionally.

(a) Spillovers from exercises of expressive liberty to the values of (other people's) expressive liberties are reasonably treated as exceptional.

(b) Spillovers from exercises of expressive liberty to the values of other (nonexpressive) liberties can be substantial, but there is nothing wrong with them.

(4) Concern for the systemic relations of the values of liberties often requires substantial regulatory oversight of exercises of proprietary and economic liberties.

(a) Spillovers from exercises of proprietary and economic liberties to the values of sundry liberties are not only substantial, they are often normatively problematic.

(b) The contours of the appropriate controls depend on issues of justice that are often fairly open to political debate.

(5) These functional differences between expressive liberties on the one hand, and proprietary and economic liberties on the other, can amply explain and justify a practice of exceptionally strict judicial scrutiny of laws directly infringing expressive liberties.

It is now time to acknowledge that this argument depends on certain assumptions about how lawmakers go about their business. It imagines lawmakers debating and judging, competently and in good faith, the daunting issues of values-of-liberties and systemic justice. Opposite assumptions about lawmaker motivation and competence would greatly weaken the argument, perhaps to the point of overthrowing it. If lawmakers are usually and mainly strategic self-servers, and ignorant to boot, then there is no good reason for setting them loose on these daunting issues or according them discretion to work out the issues as best they can. Conceivably, in that case, the least bad solution would be the one Professor Epstein urges: a prohibition, no less strictly enforced than the prohibition against direct restraints of expressive liberty, against laws that result in any net redistributions of wealth (saving express, population-wide, uniformly proportional or progressive taxes).[49]

---

[49] There are reasons for doubting whether Professor Epstein's is even then the least bad solution. Among them is uncertainty about why we should place greater trust in judges enforcing the prohibition, in what will often be highly contestable circumstances, than in legislatures enacting laws. There is no less injustice, and no less inefficiency, in mistakenly requiring compensation (or mistakenly frustrating government action where compensation is refused) than in the opposite mistakes. Is it so clear that judges are more trustworthy than

Suppose that were our conclusion. Distrust, then, would have swamped the counsels of what would have been constitutional prudence, supposing some modicum of lawmaker competence and good faith. Distrust would have launched a preemptive strike against constitutional practical reason. But to grant to distrust such a preemptive force in American constitutional argument is wrong.

B. Demythifying Distrust

A myth is not a falsehood; it is a warped truth. It is a truth preserved but also a truth displaced, a truth inflated and hypostatized, a reification. In recent American constitutional theory, the notion of distrust has undergone something of a mythification. To see this, all we need do is look at First Amendment doctrine—the very body of doctrine that Professor Epstein takes as containing the true model for American constitutional practice, from which he thinks judicial protection for property rights (and to a less pronounced degree, for free speech rights) has unfortunately strayed.

It is certainly true that current doctrine provides nothing like sweeping protection for proprietary and economic liberties. Neither, however, does it do so for expressive liberties. In fact, there is a very sizeable gap between current First Amendment doctrine and sweeping protection of expressive freedom against government control. The gap I have in mind is not the doctrine's allowance for exceptionally "compelling" justifications for governmental restrictions of communicative action,[50] nor is it the doctrine's refusal or dilution of protection for expressive acts classed as "not-speech" ("obscenity"[51] and, arguably, "fighting

---

legislatures in determining whether, for example, a scheme of workplace safety regulation violates any justly compensable entitlement of employer firms, or provides firms with adequate "implicit in-kind compensation"? See Richard A. Epstein, *Takings: Private Property and the Power of Eminent Domain* 195-216 (Harvard, 1985).

[50] An example of a compelling justification is preventing imminently likely "lawless acts." See *Brandenburg v Ohio*, 395 US 444 (1969). Hans Linde argues forcefully that it would be preferable to focus first on whether a given law categorically abridges freedom of speech (that is, to invalidate any law "directed in terms at expression . . . or [] association for the purpose of expression"), rather than pass directly to the question of whether the law's restrictive effects on expression are sufficiently justified by countervailing interests. See Hans A. Linde, *"Clear and Present Danger" Reexamined: Dissonance in the Brandenburg Concerto*, 22 Stan L Rev 1163, 1174-76 (1970). There can be no doubt, however, that the Supreme Court employs the latter approach in "subversive speech" cases.

[51] See, for example, *Miller v California*, 413 US 15, 23 (1973).

words"[52]) or "low-value" speech ("adult" films,[53] advertising[54]). I have in mind, rather, the protection gap resulting from the doctrine's distinction between direct and incidental governmental infringements of expressive freedom.

Current doctrine declines to treat a law (or a specific application of a law) as constitutionally suspect just because it severely burdens or impedes expressive acts. If the law plausibly serves un-forbidden ends that are themselves "unrelated to the suppression of free expression"[55]—if the law does not demonstrably aim at suppressing conduct "precisely because of its communicative attributes"[56]—then judicial protection for the "incidentally" affected free speech interest is relatively minimal.[57]

The resulting gap in protection is large. Vietnam-era criminalization of patently expressive draft-card burning gets by on pleas of administrative tidiness.[58] Exclusion from city utility poles of the political campaign material of an insurgent, low-budget city-council candidacy gets by on a plea of combatting "visual clutter."[59] (By the same reasoning, so would a total, absolute, statewide ban on billboards.[60]) Criminalization of nude dancing in indoor estab-

---

[52] See *Chaplinsky v New Hampshire*, 315 US 568, 571-72 (1942); Grey, 8 Soc Phil & Pol at 91-94 (cited in note 47).

[53] See *Young v American Mini Theatres*, 427 US 50, 70 (1976).

[54] See *Board of Trustees v Fox*, 492 US 469, 473-78 (1989).

[55] *United States v O'Brien*, 391 US 367, 377 (1968).

[56] *Barnes v Glen Theatre*, 111 S Ct 2456, 2466 (1991) (Scalia concurring). An alternative route to strict scrutiny, fashioned on the same principle, is to show that the law pursues its allegedly speech-independent aims in ways that discriminate against speech in general or against particular speech. Courts will apply strict scrutiny to laws that selectively burden speech as opposed to other activity. See *Minneapolis Star v Minnesota Comm'r of Revenue*, 460 US 575 (1983) (striking down special tax on publishing which state used to raise general revenue). Courts also apply strict scrutiny to laws that selectively burden some messages or speakers as opposed to others. See *Police Department of Chicago v Mosley*, 408 US 92 (1972) (striking down prohibition on picketing of schools except for picketing related to labor disputes involving school).

[57] If Justice Scalia has his way, it will soon be nil. See *Barnes*, 111 S Ct at 2463 (Scalia concurring) ("[A]s a general law regulating conduct and not specifically directed at expression, it is not subject to First Amendment scrutiny at all."); *Employment Division v Smith*, 110 S Ct 1595, 1598-1606 (1990) (Scalia) (holding that the First Amendment's bar against laws prohibiting the free exercise of religion does not excuse anyone "from compliance with an otherwise valid law [of general applicability] prohibiting conduct that the State is free to regulate").

[58] *O'Brien*, 391 US 367.

[59] *Members of City Council of Los Angeles v Taxpayers for Vincent*, 466 US 789, 806 (1984).

[60] The Court left this question open in *Metromedia, Inc. v City of San Diego*, 435 US 490 (1981), but that was prior to its decisions in *Taxpayers for Vincent*, 466 US 789, and *Barnes*, 111 S Ct 2456.

lishments populated by volunteer, adult customers gets by on the plea of defending public morals.[61]

If this is a doctrine born of distrust of lawmakers, the distrust is very strangely selective. Actual judicial practice distrusts government picking and choosing among things private agents can discuss or views they can express. It does not distrust government weighing—or purporting to weigh—non-speech related goals against freedom of speech. Thus, it does not distrust incumbent city officials refusing the use of utility poles for insurgent political advertising, on what might well be a pretext of aesthetic sensibility. It does not distrust the Vietnam-era Congress criminalizing draft-card burning on a transparent pretext of administrative concerns. It does not distrust a town council criminalizing nude dancing in private establishments on the excuse that it must keep you and me from prancing nude down Main Street at noon and cannot be bothered with writing a law that distinguishes the situations.[62]

Now, one may well believe (as I do) that the Supreme Court might do a much better job than it has of protecting expressive liberties while retaining this distinction between "direct" and "incidental" restrictions of expression. One may well protest the Court's near-absolute refusal to attack pretextuality,[63] to infer repressive purpose from paltriness of speech-independent purpose,[64]

---

[61] It may be that restrictions on nude dancing are defensible because the dancers ought not be regarded as volunteers, but that was not the Court's reasoning in *Barnes*. See MacKinnon, *Feminism Unmodified* at 179-83 (cited in note 44) (discussing coercion of women acting or modeling for pornography production). See also *New York v Ferber*, 458 US 747, 756-60 (1982) (justifying restriction on production and sale of child pornography as a child-protection measure). But see Margaret Jane Radin, *Market-Inalienability*, 100 Harv L Rev 1849, 1915-17 (1987) (discussing "double bind" created for women by disallowing commodification of personal sexuality).

[62] I know that this was not the official story in *Barnes*, 111 S Ct 2456, but it is a kind of story that *Barnes* and its ilk (*O'Brien*, 391 US 367; *Taxpayers for Vincent*, 466 US 789; Justice Powell's concurring opinion in *Young*, 427 US at 73; *Clark v Community for Creative Non-Violence*, 468 US 288 (1984) (no sleeping in public park)) apparently make perfectly admissible. The official story in *Barnes* is threefold: First, the town may claim (or, to be more precise, the Court may claim on the town's behalf) a general moral interest in the prevention of nudity, even among volunteers within the walls of private establishments if those establishments are also "places of public accomodation." Second, this general moral interest is quite unconnected to any concerns about communication. Third, this interest is quite sufficient to override any consequential suppression of expression. Neither the Court's analysis in *Barnes* nor that of Justice Scalia's concurrence purports to rest on the "low-value" status of dancing, or of nudity, as a form of expression.

[63] See *O'Brien*, 391 US 367. For criticism, see Frank I. Michelman, *Saving Old Glory: On Constitutional Iconography*, 42 Stan L Rev 1337, 1345 & n 28, 1353 (1990) (citing prior critics).

[64] See *O'Brien*, 391 US 367; Michelman, 42 Stan L Rev at 1345 & n 28 (cited in note 63).

to subordinate moral majoritarianism to expressive freedom,[65] or
to demand genuinely weighty, speech-independent reasons for refusing accommodations[66] and declining less restrictive alternatives.[67] Yet, whatever faults one may find with the Court's han-
dling of the direct/incidental distinction, it is hard to withstand
the inevitability of the distinction itself. The distinction is plainly
designed to preserve lawmaker discretion against the otherwise
boundless, trumping power of free expression rights.[68] It responds
to a fear that if laws were rendered highly constitutionally suspect
by their side-effects on speech, then either too many laws designed
for good and proper ends would go under, or else courts (in order
to avoid that consequence) would have to engage in too much ad
hoc "balancing" of policies and values.[69]

Clearly, there are conflicting pulls on First Amendment doctrine—a pull toward distrust, and a pull toward something like its
opposite. We can call this opposite confidence, or we can call it
resignation. Whichever, its gist remains the same: there is no future in establishing governments for purposes of looking after certain matters without trusting them to do it; establishment is entrustment.[70] This simple truth does not eradicate distrust from
constitutional thought or argument; what it does is deflate—or
demythify—distrust, and hold it to the status of a factor in (as
Frederick Schauer says) a calculus.[71]

But, you ask: If across-the-board distrust of government is not
what drives the limited-government side—the libertarian bill-of-

---

[65] See *Barnes*, 111 S Ct 2456. Compare *Poe v Ullman*, 367 US 497, 545-55 (1961)
(Harlan dissenting), in which Justice Harlan, prefiguring *Griswold v Connecticut*, 381 US
479 (1965), would have subordinated moral majoritarianism to the "fundamental" right of
marital privacy.

[66] See *Community for Creative Non-Violence*, 468 US 288.

[67] See *O'Brien*, 391 US 367. At the very least, the Court should demand justification
beyond abstract rule-formalist prudence or the nuisance to administrators or lawmakers of
having to draw lines and distinguish cases.

[68] The distinction may well be traceable to contributions from committed civil libertarians. See Thomas Scanlon, *A Theory of Freedom of Expression*, 1 Phil & Pub Aff 204, 209
(1972); Melville B. Nimmer, *The Meaning of Symbolic Speech Under the First Amendment*, 21 UCLA L Rev 29, 38-46 (1973); John Hart Ely, *Flag Desecration: A Case Study in
the Roles of Categorization and Balancing in First Amendment Analysis*, 88 Harv L Rev
1482, 1496-1502 (1975); Laurence H. Tribe, *American Constitutional Law* § 12-2 at 1496-
1502 (Foundation, 2d ed 1988).

[69] See generally John Hart Ely, *Legislative and Administrative Motivation in Constitutional Law*, 79 Yale L J 1205 (1970).

[70] This argument is advanced and examined, with characteristically engaging subtlety,
by John Dunn, *Trust and Political Agency*, in Dunn, *Interpreting Political Responsibility*
26, 26-44 (Princeton, 1990).

[71] See Frederick Schauer, *The Calculus of Distrust*, 77 Va L Rev 653 (1991).

rights side—of our constitutionalism,[72] and its support by judicial review, then what does drive it? The answer lies in substance. It lies, that is, in not imagining distrust as a universal solvent[73] indifferent to substance.[74]

American constitutionalists have, for better or for worse, always focused their attentions on the problem of the state. It is state power that our constitutional law has been concerned to establish, organize, motivate, direct, and restrain. There are certain kinds of effects that, all other things being equal, Americans have preponderantly wanted accomplished by governmental power: for example, creation, maintenance, and defense of a continentally integrated, commercial republic. At the same time, there are certain other kinds of effects that, all other things being equal, Americans have preponderantly wanted *not* accomplished by governmental power: suppression of communication, for example. Finally, there is a residual category of what we may call "contingently wanted" effects, those that Americans have expected sitting governments to pursue when and as those governments have judged it opportune to pursue them: for example, the kinds of regulatory enhancements and adjustments of the values of liberties that I sketched earlier.

When the only available rationale for a burden or restraint on expressive action depends on the speech-restrictive effect itself, then governmental power is being used—with identifiable, important exceptions—to accomplish an unwanted effect. Not so when the restrictive effect on speech is "incidental." Then the law may be accomplishing other effects that we expect our governments to pursue, including, as I have argued, certain adjustments and enhancements of the values of liberties. The calculus of distrust simply must allow some room for such adjustments. How much room is uncertain. The functionalist case for variable judicial respect of government discretion remains, in that sense, vague and perhaps uneasy. It is nevertheless a coherent case, it is rational, it is traditional, and it contains grounds for methodically differentiating how reviewing courts treat expressive, proprietary, and economic liberties.

---

[72] Some recent scholarship seeks to revive a non-libertarian, pro-popularist strain in the Bill of Rights, but not by denying that the libertarian element is also there. See generally Akhil Reed Amar, *The Bill of Rights As a Constitution*, 100 Yale L J 1131 (1991).

[73] Epstein, in this volume, 48 (cited in note 2).

[74] If "substance" encompasses the kinds of considerations I have marshalled in support of varying judicial treatments of different liberties, then distrust theory, carried to the point of swamping those considerations, is a flight from substance. Compare Richard A. Epstein, *Modern Republicanism—Or the Flight From Substance*, 97 Yale L J 1633 (1988).

C. Impossible Assimilation?

Whether Professor Epstein's alternative is likewise coherent is subject to question. The distinction between "direct" and "incidental" restrictions on expression is, after all, not a secondary detail of constitutional law. It is a crucial, organizing feature. It is a feature evidently designed to preserve the validity of a great deal of regulation whose speech-suppressive effects might otherwise render it highly constitutionally suspect. If constitutional protection of proprietary and economic liberties is truly to follow the freedom-of-speech model, must it not contain an analogously permissive, preservative feature? But what could that feature possibly be? (Someone please tell us, what is the intelligible distinction between a "direct" and an "incidental" restriction on property?[75])

A direct restriction of speech is one for which there is no plausible goal apart from restricting communication. By analogy, a direct restriction of property would be one for which there is no plausible goal apart from restricting how people use and enjoy their lawful possessions. But then to say that direct restrictions of property are strictly scrutinizable would make every bit of government regulatory action presumptively unconstitutional.[76] (Someone

---

[75] Baker has offered a possible response in the form of his proposed distinction between laws that "allocate" liberty and those that "restrict" liberty. See Baker, 134 U Pa L Rev at 785-815 (cited in note 13). Clear as this distinction may be in conception, it might prove extremely contestable in practice. On Baker's own understanding of it, it is orders of magnitude too permissive for Epstein's purposes.

[76] Professor Epstein suggests that a piece of legislation's non-redistributive nature could be demonstrated either by an explicit, special compensation payment or by a demonstration that the action carries its own implicit, in-kind compensations to those on whom it also imposes burdens. Epstein, in this volume, 51-53 (cited in note 2).

These responses, however, do not meet the objection I am raising. First, some government actions are prompted and justified by distributive considerations, in such a way that requiring compensation would defeat their purposes. Second, against what baseline of preexisting value are we to determine whether a government action is redistributive (wholly aside from any attendant compensation, explicit or implicit)? The strictest view would be that any legislatively or judicially announced deviation from positive law, or from the common law as of some fixed date, is a *prima facie* compensable taking, at least insofar as it causes a decrement in market value. Such a doctrine, I have argued, would often defeat the ends of justice. If, alternatively, we are to determine baseline values by methods sufficiently attentive to cultural evolution and expectations of legal dynamism to be consonant with justice, then it is unclear why that work is better entrusted to judges than to ordinary lawmakers.

In general, it seems that distrust-based justifications for judicial review have, to date, been remarkably inattentive to the fact that judges, too, are plausible objects of distrust. Schauer signals a welcome corrective to this silence. See Schauer, 77 Va L Rev 653 (cited in note 71). See also Robert H. Bork, *The Tempting of America: The Political Seduction of the Law* (Free Press, 1990); Ingber, 1984 Duke L J at 30 (cited in note 19) ("Members of the judiciary, responsible for upholding the values protected by the first amendment, are not

please give us an example of a regulatory goal that operates independently of curtailing anyone's use of any of their property.) The preservative side of the "direct"/"incidental" distinction would be missing.

Take a simple example. Today, it seems that sweeping anti-billboard laws are virtually exempt from First Amendment scrutiny, despite the substantial suppression of communication they effect, because they also plausibly serve aesthetic and (it is sometimes said) safety goals. Such goals are considered to be independent of any concern on the government's part about what people say or communicate to one another. Such goals, however, cannot possibly be considered independent of governmental concern about how people use their property holdings; how people use their property is exactly what such regulations are about. They are, then, direct regulations of property, although not of speech. Are they, on that account, constitutionally suspect? To say so is directly to undercut what in free speech analysis is a major premise—speech-independent considerations of public amenity or safety are not only legitimate but *redemptive* justifications for regulations that also restrict expression. Thus, the preservative side of the "direct"/"incidental" distinction would have vanished.[77] The property-restrictive effects of ordinary regulations, which in free speech analysis are their ticket to constitutional salvation, are by Professor Epstein's proposal transmuted into stigmata of constitutional sin.

In sum, the idea of having courts approach proprietary and economic rights with the same formulaic kit of analyses and "tests" that they use in free speech cases seems bound for massive

---

immune from the same processes of socialization and indoctrination that predispose the general public to certain perspectives."); Radin, *Regimes* (cited in note 39) (remarking that judges who understand their role to be that of preventing socially costly legislative rent-seeking "have yet to face the full implications of the idea that their own activities, as individuals and as government actors, should also be interpreted as rent-seeking").

[77] This trouble cannot be avoided by fiddling with the "level" of judicial scrutiny of government's justifications for laws infringing on proprietary or economic liberties—for example, by using "intermediate" rather than "strict" scrutiny, demanding that the questioned regulation "substantially" advance an "important" interest, rather than that it be "necessary" to a "compelling" interest. Any level of judicial scrutiny between quasi-automatic approval (toothless rationality review) and quasi-automatic invalidation (fatal-in-fact strict scrutiny) involves the court in what is loosely called "balancing"—that is, in judgmental second-guessing of the lawmakers' ostensible appraisals of policy and justice. So to choose such an intermediate level of judicial involvement is already, in effect, to concede that the regulation in question does truly present legitimate questions of policy and justice that someone ought conscientiously and responsibly to resolve. It is thus, again, to invite the question of why such work is better entrusted to judges than to ordinary lawmakers.

conceptual disorder. My argument has identified two sources for this disorder. The first is failing to take account of relevant differences among the ways in which various classes of liberties function in American society and what they signify. The other is overestimating the degree to which distrust of lawmakers is or logically can be thought to be the preemptively dominant theme of American constitutional thought and practice.

Religious Freedom at a Crossroads

Michael W. McConnell†

The Religion Clause jurisprudence of the Warren and Burger Courts is coming to an end—a victim, if not of its own internal contradictions, then of changes of personnel on the Court. To this we might happily say "good riddance," for a more confused and often counterproductive mode of interpreting the First Amendment would have been difficult to devise. Professor Leonard Levy observed that

> the Court has managed to unite those who stand at polar opposites on the results that the Court reaches; a strict separationist and a zealous accommodationist are likely to agree that the Supreme Court would not recognize an establishment of religion if it took life and bit the Justices.[1]

I stand at a pole opposite to Levy on most of these issues, but I agree with that assessment.

The old jurisprudence failed to distinguish between government action that promotes the free exercise of diverse faiths and government action that promotes the majority's understanding of

† Professor of Law, The University of Chicago Law School. This Article was prepared for *The Bill of Rights in the Welfare State: A Bicentennial Symposium*, held at The University of Chicago Law School on October 25-26, 1991. The author wishes to thank Albert Alschuler, Richard Epstein, Mary Ann Glendon, Abner Greene, Elena Kagan, Douglas Laycock, Larry Lessig, Ira Lupu, William Marshall, and David Smolin for helpful comments on an earlier draft, Kathleen Sullivan for stimulating discussion and debate, and the Russell Baker Fund and the Class of '49 Dean's Discretionary Fund for financial support during the preparation of this Article.
[1] Leonard Levy, *The Establishment Clause: Religion and the First Amendment* 163 (MacMillan, 1986).

proper religion—treating both with suspicion. The Court's conception of the First Amendment more closely resembled freedom *from* religion (except in its most private manifestations) than freedom *of* religion.[2] The animating principle was not pluralism and diversity, but maintenance of a scrupulous secularism in all aspects of public life touched by government. This approach successfully warded off the dangers of majoritarian religion, but it exacerbated the equal and opposite danger of majoritarian indifference or intolerance toward religion. There is reason to believe this period is coming to an end.

There is no guarantee, however, that the Rehnquist Court's approach to the Religion Clauses will be a great improvement. Initial decisions suggest that the Rehnquist Court may replace the reflexive secularism of the Warren and Burger Courts with an equally inappropriate statism. Just when the Court appears to be shedding its inordinate distrust of religion, it appears to be embracing an inordinate faith in government.

Already the new Court has adopted an interpretation of the Free Exercise Clause that permits the state to interfere with religious practices—even to make the central ceremonies of some ancient faiths illegal or impossible—without any substantial justification, so long as the regulation does not facially discriminate against religion.[3] And in a prominent case before the Court this term, the Court has been urged to modify its interpretation of the Establishment Clause to permit a clergyman to deliver a prayer at a junior high school graduation ceremony.[4] As the arguments in the invocation case illustrate, the debate over the Religion Clauses is all too often framed as if there were but two choices: more religion in public life or less; tearing down the wall of separation between church and state or building it up again. Opponents of the prayer have rallied around the Supreme Court's old Establishment Clause doctrine and have warned that any modifications would signal an erosion in our civil liberties. Defenders of the prayer contend that the government should have broader latitude to give voice to the religious sentiments of the community. Both positions, in my judg-

---

[2] Thus, Justice Blackmun could say that the term "secular liberty" encapsulates what "it is the purpose of the Establishment Clause to protect." *County of Allegheny v ACLU*, 492 US 573, 612 (1989). In a similar vein, Justice Frankfurter commented that the "essence" of the "constitutional protection of religious freedom" is "freedom from conformity to religious dogma, not freedom from conformity of law because of religious dogma." *West Virginia State Board of Education v Barnette*, 319 US 624, 653 (1943) (Frankfurter dissenting).

[3] *Employment Division v Smith*, 110 S Ct 1595, 1599-1602 (1990).

[4] *Weisman v Lee*, 908 F2d 1090 (1st Cir 1990), cert granted, 111 S Ct 1305 (1991).

ment, are wrong. We should welcome doctrinal change, but not government prayer.

This Article presents another way. In Section I, I criticize the Religion Clause jurisprudence of the Warren and Burger Courts and its influence today. In Section II, I explain why the emerging Religion Clause jurisprudence of the Rehnquist Court appears to be moving in the wrong direction. Finally, in Section III, I suggest how a proper jurisprudence of the Religion Clauses should look. My position is that the Religion Clauses do not create a secular public sphere, as was often thought in the past;[5] nor do they sanction government discretion to foster broadly acceptable civil religion in public life. Rather, the purpose of the Religion Clauses is to protect the religious lives of the people from unnecessary intrusions of government, whether promoting or hindering religion. It is to foster a regime of religious pluralism, as distinguished from both majoritarianism and secularism. It is to preserve what Madison called the "full and equal rights"[6] of religious believers and communities to define their own way of life, so long as they do not interfere with the rights of others, and to participate fully and equally with their fellow citizens in public life without being forced to shed their religious convictions and character.

I. The Old Jurisprudence and Its Influence Today

A. Inconsistency and Confusion

Any serious interpretation of the Religion Clauses must explain the relation between the two constituent parts, the Free Exercise Clause and the Establishment Clause, which are joined together in the single command: "Congress shall make no law respecting an establishment of religion, or prohibiting the free exercise thereof."[7] The Free Exercise Clause forbids Congress (and, after incorporation through the Fourteenth Amendment, *any* government) to discriminate against religion, and may require affirmative accommodation of free exercise in some contexts. The Establishment Clause, however, has been interpreted to forbid the government to aid or advance religion. In a world in which the government aids or advances many different causes and institutions,

---

[5] And as Professor Sullivan thinks today. See Kathleen M. Sullivan, *Religion and Liberal Democracy*, in this volume, 195.

[6] James Madison (speech of Jun 8, 1789), in Joseph Gales, ed, 1 *Annals of Congress* 451 (Gales & Seaton, 1834).

[7] US Const, Amend I.

this means that the government *must* discriminate against religion in the distribution of benefits. Thus the Establishment Clause is said to require what the Free Exercise Clause forbids.

The doctrinal confusion is compounded when we take into account the remainder of the First Amendment, which protects the freedoms of speech, press, petition, and assembly. The central feature of the constitutional law of speech and press is a prohibition on "content-based" discrimination,[8] except in the most compelling of circumstances. Yet the distinction between religion and nonreligious ideologies and institutions—a distinction seemingly demanded by the very text of the Religion Clauses—*is* based on the content of ideas and beliefs. The content-neutral thrust of the Free Speech Clause thus coexists uneasily with the special status of religion under the Free Exercise and Establishment Clauses.

The Court has tended to address these problems one clause at a time, building up inconsistencies often without seeming to notice them. But more remarkably yet, the Court has contrived a formula for interpreting the Establishment Clause that contains inconsistencies within a single test. The aptly named *"Lemon"* test, adopted in 1971, forbids government actions that either (1) have no secular purpose; (2) have a "primary effect" of advancing religion;[9] or (3) foster an "excessive entanglement" between government and religion.[10] In further elaborations, the Court has held that "primary effect" really means any "direct and immediate" ef-

---

[8] See Geoffrey Stone, *Content Regulation and the First Amendment*, 25 Wm & Mary L Rev 189, 196-97 (1983); Martin Redish, *The Content Distinction in First Amendment Analysis*, 34 Stan L Rev 113, 113 (1981); Laurence H. Tribe, *American Constitutional Law* § 12-2 at 789-92 (Foundation, 2d ed 1988). For a case involving interplay of free exercise, establishment, and free press concerns, see *Texas Monthly, Inc. v Bullock*, 489 US 1 (1989). See especially id at 25-26 (White concurring).

[9] The "effects" test by its language forbids government action with the "primary effect" of *either* "advancing" *or* "inhibiting" religion. *Lemon v Kurtzman*, 403 US 602, 612 (1971). But in actual practice, actions "inhibiting" religion are dealt with under the Free Exercise Clause. The only instance in which the Supreme Court has invalidated an "inhibition" of religion under the Establishment Clause was *Larson v Valente*, 456 US 228 (1982), and the reasoning in that case was based on denominational discrimination. For clarity's sake I have confined the "effects" prong of the *Lemon* test to "advancement" of religion.

If *Smith*, 109 S Ct 1595, is extended to questions of institutional autonomy, as seems likely (but see id at 1599 (citing the church property dispute cases)), litigants and lower courts are likely to invoke the Establishment Clause more often to challenge laws impinging on the ability of religious organizations to control their internal affairs and organization. See *Rayburn v General Conference of Seventh-Day Adventists*, 772 F2d 1164, 1169-71 (4th Cir 1985) (striking down application of Title VII to hiring of clergy on establishment as well as free exercise grounds). See generally Carl Esbeck, *Establishment Clause Limits on Governmental Interference with Religious Organizations*, 41 Wash & Lee L Rev 347 (1984).

[10] *Lemon*, 403 US at 613.

fect:[11] the state must be "certain" that religious organizations receiving government financial assistance for secular services to the public do not use resources purchased with those funds for the teaching or promotion of religion.[12] However, the Court has also interpreted the "entanglement" test to forbid the monitoring or surveillance of religious organizations necessary to achieve this certainty.[13] Thus, the "entanglement" prong forbids what the "effects" prong requires—leaving states no alternative but to exclude religious groups altogether. The Court has acknowledged this "Catch-22,"[14] but has not done anything to resolve the contradiction.

With doctrine in such chaos, the Warren and Burger Courts were free to reach almost any result in almost any case. Thus, as of today, it is constitutional for a state to hire a Presbyterian minister to lead the legislature in daily prayers,[15] but unconstitutional for a state to set aside a moment of silence in the schools for children to pray if they want to.[16] It is unconstitutional for a state to require employers to accommodate their employees' work schedules to their sabbath observances,[17] but constitutionally mandatory for a state to require employers to pay workers compensation when the resulting inconsistency between work and sabbath leads to discharge.[18] It is constitutional for the government to give money to religiously-affiliated organizations to teach adolescents about proper sexual behavior,[19] but not to teach them science or history.[20] It is constitutional for the government to provide religious school pupils with books,[21] but not with maps;[22] with bus rides to religious schools,[23] but not from school to a museum on a field

---

[11] *Committee for Public Educ. v Nyquist*, 413 US 756, 783-85 n 39 (1973).

[12] *Lemon*, 403 US at 619; *Grand Rapids School Dist. v Ball*, 473 US 373, 385-86 (1985).

[13] *Aguilar v Felton*, 473 US 402, 409 (1985); *Meek v Pittenger*, 421 US 349, 370 (1975); *Lemon*, 403 US at 619.

[14] *Bowen v Kendrick*, 487 US 589, 615 (1988).

[15] *Marsh v Chambers*, 463 US 783, 792-93 (1983).

[16] *Wallace v Jaffree*, 472 US 38, 56 (1985).

[17] *Estate of Thornton v Caldor, Inc.*, 472 US 703, 709-10 (1985).

[18] *Frazee v Employment Security Dept.*, 489 US 829, 834 (1989); *Hobbie v Unemployment Appeals Comm'n of Fla.*, 480 US 136, 138-40 (1987); *Sherbert v Verner*, 374 US 398, 403-4 (1963).

[19] *Kendrick*, 487 US at 611.

[20] *Lemon*, 403 US at 618-19.

[21] *Board of Education v Allen*, 392 US 236, 238 (1968).

[22] *Wolman v Walter*, 433 US 229, 249-51 (1977).

[23] *Everson v Board of Education*, 330 US 1, 17 (1947).

trip;[24] with cash to pay for state-mandated standardized tests,[25] but not to pay for safety-related maintenance.[26] It is a mess.

B. Hostility or Indifference Toward Religion

But analytical confusion was the least of the problems with the Religion Clause jurisprudence of the Warren and Burger Courts. More significant was the Court's tendency to press relentlessly in the direction of a more secular society. The Court's opinions seemed to view religion as an unreasoned, aggressive, exclusionary, and divisive force that must be confined to the private sphere. When religions stuck to the private functions of "spiritual comfort, guidance, and inspiration,"[27] the Court extended the protection of the Constitution. But the Court was ever conscious that religion "can also serve powerfully to divide societies and to exclude those whose beliefs are not in accord with particular religions."[28] The Court's more important mission was to protect democratic society from religion.[29]

This set the Religion Clauses apart from the remainder of the Bill of Rights, which protects various nongovernmental activities from the power of democratic majorities.[30] Only the Religion Clauses have been interpreted to protect democratic society from the power of the private citizen, even from the supposed power of minority religions. (Consider the parochial school aid cases, which protect the non-Catholic majority from the Catholic minority.) The explanation presumably lies not in the logic of the Bill of

[24] *Wolman*, 433 US at 252-55.

[25] *Committee for Pub. Educ. and Religious Liberty v Regan*, 444 US 646, 653-54 (1980).

[26] *Nyquist*, 413 US at 774-80.

[27] *Grand Rapids*, 473 US at 382.

[28] Id.

[29] See Justice Stevens's dissenting opinion in *Board of Education of Westside Community Schools v Mergens*, 110 S Ct 2356, 2383-93 (1990), in which he described religions as "divisive forces," id at 2391, and urged that they be excluded from public school premises on the ground that they "may exert a considerable degree of pressure *even without official school sponsorship*." Id (emphasis added). Stevens's language reflects a belief that the Establishment Clause is concerned not so much with the power of government as with the dangerous propensities of religion. By 1990, Justice Stevens was no longer speaking for a majority, but his comments indicate that the secularistic orientation of the old jurisprudence lives on.

[30] Akhil Reed Amar has recently interpreted the Bill of Rights primarily to empower popular majorities rather than to protect individual rights. See Akhil Reed Amar, *The Bill of Rights as a Constitution*, 100 Yale L J 1131, 1132 (1991). But the Court's approach to the Religion Clauses is no less peculiar under Amar's interpretation, for Amar suggests that churches should be understood as republican institutions—as vehicles for the mobilization of public opinion. Amar's view is inconsistent with the view that churches should be quarantined from public life.

Rights but in the Court's perception of religion. Before examining the details of legal doctrine, then, let us look at how the Court talks about religion.

Justice Hugo Black provides a starting point, since his opinions were so extremely influential in the early development of Establishment Clause doctrine. Black referred to the Catholics who advocated the loan of textbooks to religious schools as "powerful sectarian religious propagandists," and to their religious views as "preferences and prejudices."[31] He accused them of "looking toward complete domination and supremacy of their particular brand of religion."[32] This was a strange way to talk about people who sought equal rights for all families to direct the upbringing of their children.

The bigotry of Justice Black's language is particularly striking in light of its historical context. The reason Roman Catholics and Orthodox Jews created separate schools in the nineteenth century, while Protestants did not, was that the public schools were imbued with Protestant (and not infrequently anti-Catholic and anti-Jewish) religious and moral teaching.[33] Opposition to parochial school aid at that time was part and parcel of nativist, anti-Catholic politics.[34] The same presidential candidate whose supporters campaigned against "Rum, Romanism, and Rebellion" put his name to an almost-adopted constitutional amendment that would have banned aid to parochial schools.[35] Only in the mid-twentieth century, when overt anti-Catholicism had subsided, were legislatures in Protestant-majority states willing to consider sharing a modest portion of the resources available for education.[36] For Justice Black to portray these minorities as "looking toward complete

---

[31] *Allen*, 392 US at 251 (Black dissenting).

[32] Id.

[33] For a review of this history, see Michael W. McConnell, *Multiculturalism, Majoritarianism and Educational Choice: What Does Our Constitutional Tradition Have to Say?*, 1991 U Chi Legal F 123, 134-39; Charles L. Glenn, Jr., *The Myth of the Common School* (Massachusetts, 1988); Jonathan D. Sarna, *American Jews and Church-State Relations: The Search for "Equal Footing"* (American Jewish Committee, 1989).

[34] See generally Diane Ravitch, *The Great School Wars* (Basic, 1974).

[35] The candidate was James G. Blaine. See Allen Johnson, ed, 2 *Dictionary of American Biography* 322, 326 (Charles Scribner's Sons, 1943). On the Blaine Amendment, see Anson Phelps Stokes and Leo Pfeffer, *Church and State in the United States* 434 (Harper and Row, rev ed 1964).

[36] In New York, for example, the first enactment of parochial school aid was the provision of bus transportation, passed in 1936. See Stokes and Pfeffer, *Church and State in the United States* at 425 (cited in note 35).

122   *Michael W. McConnell*

domination and supremacy of their particular brand of religion"
was to turn reality on its head.[37]

The language in recent Supreme Court opinions is more
guarded, but continues to evince suspicion of religion. In *Grand
Rapids School District v Ball*,[38] and its companion case, *Aguilar v
Felton*,[39] for example, the Court refused to allow public school remedial teaching specialists to enter the premises of parochial
schools to provide remedial and other special assistance to educational and economically deprived schoolchildren attending those
schools.[40] Writing for the Court, Justice William Brennan explained that

> teachers in such an atmosphere may well subtly (or overtly)
> conform their instruction to the environment in which they
> teach, while students will perceive the instruction provided in
> the context of the dominantly religious message of the institu-
> tion, thus reinforcing the indoctrinating effect.[41]

The evocative words in this passage—"conform," "dominantly religious," "indoctrination"—suggest that the Justices who joined the
opinion believe that religious convictions are reached not through
thoughtful consideration and experience, but through conformity
and indoctrination. This view of religion justifies discriminating
against religious schools, because indoctrination is the antithesis of
democratic education. Moreover, the Justices seemed to view religion as not only unreasoned but insidious. The "atmosphere" of a
Catholic school has such power to influence the unsuspecting mind
that it may move even public school remedial English and math
specialists to "conform"—though their only contact with the
school is to walk down its halls.

---

[37] *Allen*, 392 US at 251. Justice Black was not the only Supreme Court Justice who
indulged anti-Catholic prejudice. In *Lemon*, Justice William O. Douglas cited with approval
an openly anti-Catholic hate tract. *Lemon*, 403 US at 635 n 20 (Douglas concurring) (quoting Loraine Boettner, *Roman Catholicism* (Presbyterian and Reformed Publishing, 1962)).
Among other illuminating statements, Boettner claimed that Hitler, Mussolini, and Stalin
learned the "secret[s] of [their] success" from the Roman Catholic Church, Boettner, *Roman Catholicism* at 363, and that "an undue proportion of the gangsters, racketeers,
thieves, and juvenile delinquents who roam our big city streets come . . . from the [Catholic]
parochial schools." Id at 370. For a further description of the book, see Douglas Laycock,
Civil Rights and Civil Liberties, 54 Chi Kent L Rev 390, 418-21 (1977).

[38] 473 US 373 (1985). Readers should be aware that the author argued this case in the
Supreme Court in support of the petitioner.

[39] 473 US 402 (1985).

[40] *Grand Rapids*, 473 US at 397; *Aguilar*, 473 US at 414.

[41] *Grand Rapids*, 473 US at 388.

This opinion stands in curious contrast to the Court's encomiums to the role of the public schools in inculcating moral values. The same Justice who wrote of "indoctrination" in the religious schools observed in another case that "local [public] school boards must be permitted 'to establish and apply their curriculum in such a way as to transmit community values.' "[42] He reasoned that " 'there is a legitimate and substantial community interest in promoting respect for authority and traditional values be they social, moral, or political.' "[43] In another opinion, the Court stated that the "inculcat[ion of] fundamental values" by public schools was "necessary to the maintenance of a democratic political system."[44] The Court seems to believe that a politically elected school board's inculcation of secular values for all schoolchildren of the jurisdiction is "necessary" for democracy. When individual parents choose an alternative set of (religious) values *for their own children*, however, this is "indoctrination" and must be viewed with suspicion.

This understanding of religion is not merely the idiosyncratic viewpoint of a transitory majority of the Court. It represents a specific and powerful philosophical position, most clearly articulated by John Dewey. Dewey, the leading philosophical influence on American secular liberalism, was a determined critic of traditional religion. He claimed that there was "nothing left worth preserving in the notions of unseen powers, controlling human destiny to which obedience, reverence and worship are due."[45] Unlike the scientific method, which is "open and public" and based on "continued and rigorous inquiry,"[46] religion is "a body of definite beliefs that need only to be taught and learned as true."[47] Religion, he said, is based on the "servile acceptance of imposed dogma."[48] This did not mean that Dewey and his followers were skeptical toward all moral teaching, or that the government should remain "neutral" toward conflicting points of view. To the contrary, Dewey contended that the public schools have an "ethical responsibility" to inculcate social values derived from scientific and democratic principles.[49]

---

[42] *Board of Education v Pico*, 457 US 853, 864 (1982) (Brennan plurality).
[43] Id (quoting Petitioner's Brief at 10) (footnote omitted).
[44] *Ambach v Norwick*, 441 US 68, 77 (1979).
[45] John Dewey, *A Common Faith* 7 (Yale, 1934).
[46] Id at 26, 39.
[47] Id at 39.
[48] Id at 5.
[49] John Dewey, *Moral Principles in Education* 7-10 (Southern Illinois, 1975). Inculcating these social values was a major theme in Dewey's work. See John Dewey, *John Dewey*

Dewey's point of view maintains a hold on mainstream thinking about religion and constitutional law, both in the academy and in the courts. Professor Kathleen Sullivan, for example, advocates the secularization of the public order on the ground that "the culture of liberal democracy" is constitutionally privileged over religious ideas. She quite frankly calls for "establishment of the secular public moral order."[50] Professor Ira Lupu argues that a vigorous protection of the free exercise of religious institutions "may undercut the project of constitutional democracy," because religions "frequently claim divine inspiration" and thus "discourage skepticism."[51] The Supreme Court's education decisions stand in this Deweyite tradition, treating religious education as "indoctrination," while sanctioning secular moral education in the public schools. Whether the Justices were aware of it or not, their opinions reflected a philosophical position avowedly hostile to traditional religion.

If the Court's education decisions sometimes reflected hostility toward religion, other decisions more often displayed indifference or incomprehension. In *Estate of Thornton v Caldor, Inc.*, for example, the Court held it unconstitutional for a state to require employers to accommodate work schedules to their employees' days of sabbath observance.[52] In a concurring opinion, Justice O'Connor explained that

---

On Education: Selected Writings 23-60, 295-310 (Modern Library, 1964); John Dewey, *The School As A Means of Developing a Social Consciousness and Social Ideals in Children*, 1 J Soc Forces 513 (1923). I do not mean to take a position here on whether Dewey's nontheistic philosophy is a "religion," a subject that is embroiled in the controversy over "secular humanism." For a thoughtful and sympathetic analysis of Dewey's "religion," see Steven C. Rockefeller, *John Dewey: Religious Faith and Democratic Humanism* (Columbia, 1991). For present purposes, the relevant point is that Dewey opposed all traditional theistic religion, supernaturalism, and metaphysical idealism, and thought that government should use education to impose an alternative secular morality.

[50] Sullivan, in this volume, 198 (cited in note 5). Sullivan's "establishment" is expressly theological in nature. She explains that the civil moral order she sees embodied in the Constitution must be understood "not as a neutral *modus vivendi*, but rather as a substantive recognition that there is more than one path to heaven and not so many as once thought to hell." Id at 200. This is not the disestablishment of religion. It is the establishment of Unitarian-Universalism.

[51] Ira C. Lupu, *Reconstructing the Establishment Clause: The Case Against Discretionary Accommodation of Religion*, 140 U Pa L Rev 555, 597 (1991). Ironically, though reasoning from a similar indictment of religion, Sullivan and Lupu reach opposite conclusions. Sullivan advocates strong protection for religious autonomy in the private sphere, but would exclude religious groups entirely from public programs. Lupu would provide no protection for religious institutional autonomy, but would allow religious groups (if they can survive government regulation intact) to participate in public programs, including education, on an equal basis.

[52] *Estate of Thornton*, 472 US at 708-10.

[a]ll employees, regardless of their religious orientation, would value the benefit which the statute bestows on sabbath observers—the right to select the day of the week in which to refrain from labor. Yet Connecticut requires private employers to confer this valued and desirable benefit only on those employees who adhere to a particular religious belief.[53]

It would come as some surprise to a devout Jew to find that he has "selected the day of the week in which to refrain from labor," since the Jewish people have been under the impression for some 3,000 years that this choice was made by God.[54] Jewish observers do not seek the right to "select the day" in which to refrain from labor, but only the right to *obey* laws over which they have no control. Sabbath observers are not "favored" over co-workers, any more than injured workers are "favored" when given disability leave. The law simply alleviates for them a conflict of loyalties not faced by their secular co-workers. Justice O'Connor's error was to reduce the dictates of religious conscience to the status of mere choice. Some people like to go sailing on Saturdays; some observe the Sabbath. How could the State consider the one "choice" more worthy of respect than the other? In Stephen Carter's apt phrase, this is to "treat religion as a hobby."[55]

In *Lyng v Northwest Indian Cemetery Protective Ass'n*, the Supreme Court considered whether the Forest Service constitutionally could construct a logging road in a National Forest through the ancient sites of worship of the Yurok, Karok, and Talowa Indians of Northern California.[56] This road, the Court conceded, would "virtually destroy" the Indians' ability "to practice their religion."[57] The Supreme Court nonetheless upheld the project without inquiring whether its purpose was "compelling"[58] or even important. The Court explained that "government simply could not operate if it were required to satisfy every citizen's religious needs and desires."[59] One might think that the government would have to give some substantial justification to destroy a reli-

---

[53] Id at 711 (O'Connor concurring).

[54] See Exodus 20:9-10 (Revised Standard Version) ("Six days you shall labor, and do all your work; but the seventh day is a Sabbath to the Lord your God"). See also Nathan A. Barack, *A History of the Sabbath* 8-16 (Jonathan David, 1965).

[55] Stephen Carter, *Evolutionism, Creationism, and Treating Religion As A Hobby*, 1987 Duke L J 977.

[56] 485 US 439, 441-42 (1988).

[57] Id at 451.

[58] See discussion of the "compelling interest" test in text accompanying notes 67-70.

[59] 485 US at 452.

gion. But the Court responded that free exercise rights "do not divest the Government of its right to use what is, after all, *its* land."[60] There is, admittedly, no evidence of hostility to religion in the opinion, only indifference—an indifference so obvious that the Court was moved to warn that "[n]othing in our opinion should be read to encourage governmental insensitivity to the religious needs of any citizens."[61] But how could the opinion be read any other way?

These decisions do not give the impression that the Justices consider religion a particularly important aspect of life. Freedom of worship may be worthwhile in the abstract, but it is outweighed by virtually any secular interest. In its attitude toward religion, the Court may typify the gulf between a largely secularized professional and academic elite and most ordinary citizens, for whom religion commonly remains a central aspect of life.[62] How many of the Justices and their clerks have had personal experience with serious religion—religion understood as more than ceremony, as the guiding principle of life?[63] How many have close friends or associates who have had such experiences? For those who have lived their lives among academics and professionals, it may be difficult to understand why believers attach so much importance to things that seem so inconsequential.

The religious symbol cases are a final example of the Court's uncomprehending attitude toward religion. According to the Court, a city may include the display of a religious symbol as part of a holiday celebration only if the religious symbol is in close proximity to secular objects, which mitigate its religious message. Thus, a plurality of the Court permitted the menorah in *County of Allegheny v ACLU* because it was next to a forty-five-foot tall Christmas tree,[64] and a majority permitted the nativity scene in *Lynch v Donnelly* because it was surrounded by a Santa Claus house, rein-

---

[60] Id at 453 (emphasis in original). One might ask from whom the government got the land, but that, evidently, is another question.

[61] Id.

[62] John Davidson Hunter, *Culture Wars* (Basic, 1991). For discussions of the differences in religious conviction between the most educated classes and other Americans, see Robert Wuthnow, *The Restructuring of American Religion* 161-64 (Princeton, 1988); George Marsden, *Are Secularists the Threat? Is Religion the Solution?*, in Richard J. Neuhaus, ed, *Unsecular America* 31, 32-33 (Eerdmans, 1986); Steven D. Smith, *The Rise and Fall of Religious Freedom in Constitutional Discourse,* 140 Pa L Rev 149, 170-77 (1991).

[63] The backgrounds of some of the recent appointees suggest a more intensive engagement with religious life. It will be interesting to see how this affects the tone and reasoning of the Court's work in this area.

[64] 492 US 573, 617-18, 634-35 (1989).

deer, candy-striped poles, a Christmas tree, carolers, cut-out figures representing such characters as a clown, an elephant, and a teddy bear, hundreds of colored lights, a banner stating "Season's Greetings," and a talking wishing well.[65] In contrast, the Court held unconstitutional the nativity scene in *Allegheny*, which was tastefully displayed with a backdrop of greenery and poinsettias, but unaccompanied by secular signs of the season.[66] Practitioners have dubbed the holdings in *Lynch* and *Allegheny* "the three-plastic animals rule."

The Court appears to have arrived at the worst of all possible outcomes. It would be better to forbid the government to have religious symbols at all than to require that they be festooned with the trappings of modern American materialism. After all, no one's religion depends on whether the government displays the symbols of the Christian and Jewish holidays. But if there are to be religious symbols, they should be treated with respect. To allow them only under the conditions approved by the Court makes everyone the loser.

The religious symbols cases are themselves the perfect symbol of the Supreme Court's attitude toward religion. The Court does not object to a little religion in our public life. But the religion must be tamed, cheapened, and secularized—just as religious schools and social welfare ministries must be secularized if they are to participate in public programs that are supposed to be open to all. Authentic religion must be shoved to the margins of public life; even there, it may be forced to submit to majoritarian regulation.

C. Legal Doctrine

The formal legal doctrines espoused by the Warren and Burger Courts reinforced their lack of sympathy for religion. This may seem not to be true of the Free Exercise Clause doctrine, under which the Warren and Burger Courts forbade the enforcement of laws burdening the exercise of religion unless necessary to achieve a compelling governmental interest. The compelling interest test is, after all, the most exacting level of constitutional scrutiny. But in the years between the test's formal appearance in 1963[67] and its formal abandonment in 1990,[68] the Supreme Court rejected all but one claim for free exercise exemption outside the field of unem-

---

[65] 465 US 668 (1984). See also *Allegheny*, 492 US at 596.
[66] *Allegheny*, 492 US at 598-600.
[67] *Sherbert*, 374 US 398.
[68] *Smith*, 110 S Ct 1595.

ployment compensation.[69] In every other case decided on the merits, the Court found either that the claimant's exercise of religion was not burdened or that the government's interest was compelling.[70] The doctrine was supportive, but its enforcement was half-hearted or worse.

In its Establishment Clause doctrine, the Court upheld the values of religious liberty in a few important cases, most notably the school prayer cases of the early 1960s.[71] But the formal Establishment Clause doctrine, the *Lemon* test, has an inherent tendency to devalue religious exercise. Each of the prongs plays a part.

The first prong requires a secular purpose for all government action.[72] This requirement is right and proper—except when purposes that the majoritarian culture considers "secular" happen to be fraught with religious significance to a minority. Then a due regard to the interests of the minority should permit the government at least to take their religious needs into account, even if the accommodation serves no "secular" purpose. Was it really an establishment of religion for the Occupational Safety and Health Administration to modify its hardhat rule out of respect for the religious dress of Sikh construction workers?[73] Was it an establishment to exempt sacramental wine from Prohibition?[74] Did these provisions have any purpose other than the protection of religion? As Justice O'Connor has commented: "It is disingenous to look for a purely secular purpose when the manifest objective of a statute is to facilitate the free exercise of religion by lifting a gov-

---

[69] The exception was *Wisconsin v Yoder*, 406 US 205 (1972).

[70] *Jimmy Swaggart Ministries v Bd. of Equalization*, 493 US 378, 391-92 (1990) (not burdened); *Bowen v Roy*, 476 US 693, 709 (1986) (not burdened); *Tony and Susan Alamo Foundation v Sec'y of Labor*, 471 US 290, 303-05 (1985) (not burdened); *Bob Jones Univ. v United States*, 461 US 574, 604 (1983) (compelling interest); *United States v Lee*, 455 US 252, 258-59 (1982) (compelling interest); *Hernandez v Comm'r of Internal Revenue*, 490 US 680, 682 (1989) (probably no burden; in any event, compelling interest).

In special contexts, including prisons, the military, and the use of government land, the Court did not even purport to apply the test. See *O'Lone v Estate of Shabazz*, 482 US 342 (1977); *Goldman v Weinberger*, 475 US 503 (1986); *Lyng v Northwest Indian Cemetery Protective Ass'n.*, 485 US 439 (1988). There were a lot of special contexts.

[71] *Abington School District v Schempp*, 374 US 203 (1963); *Engel v Vitale*, 370 US 421 (1962).

[72] *Lemon*, 403 US at 612-13.

[73] See OSHA Instruction STD 1-6.3, originally Field Information Memorandum No 75-11 (Feb 4, 1975), revoked, OSHA Notice CPL 2 (Nov 5, 1990).

[74] Volstead Act of Oct 28, 1919, ch 85, Title II, § 3, 41 Stat 305, codified at 27 USC § 16 (1988), repealed, Act of Aug 27, 1935, ch 740, Title I, § 1, 49 Stat 872.

ernment-imposed burden."[75] To the extent that *Lemon*'s purpose prong requires the government to turn a blind eye to the impact of its actions on religion, on the implicit assumption that secular effects are all that matter, it is a recipe for intolerance.

The second prong of the *Lemon* test prohibits government action which has the effect of "advancing religion," even if the effect is unintended and even if the action also advances secular interests.[76] This prohibition tends to foster discrimination against religion in two ways. First, government action often benefits (or "advances") a broad range of activities and institutions, but the effects prong implies that the benefitted class may not include religious activities or institutions. Thus, for example, if the government subsidizes child care services, the effects prong suggests that the government must exclude church-based day care centers or, in the alternative, must require church-based centers to cease religious training and exercises as a condition to receiving the money.

Second, the effects prong fails to distinguish between advancing *religion* and advancing *religious freedom*. Any advancement of religious freedom is an advancement of religion—but not vice versa. For example, giving government employees the option of taking leave on days of religious observance would "advance" religion. But it would not induce anyone to practice religion; it would only remove an impediment to religious practice and thus expand the freedom of government workers to exercise their faith.[77] On the other hand, requiring public officials to affirm a belief in God "advances" religion by privileging the theist and penalizing the atheist.[78] By failing to distinguish between these two forms of "advancement," the effects prong of the *Lemon* test interferes with benign government actions to accommodate or facilitate free religious exercise.

The third prong of the *Lemon* test prohibits "excessive entanglement" between government and religion.[79] As with the purpose and effect prongs, there is an element of wisdom in this prohibition. Other things being equal, government involvement with religion almost always has some effect on religion, and the overarching purpose of the Religion Clauses is to minimize the effect of government action on the practice of religion. However, the entanglement

---

[75] *Jaffree*, 472 US at 83 (O'Connor concurring).

[76] *Lemon*, 403 US at 612.

[77] See *Ansonia Board of Education v Philbrook*, 479 US 60 (1986).

[78] See *Torcaso v Watkins*, 367 US 488 (1961).

[79] *Lemon*, 403 US at 613.

prong overlooks the fact that the practice of religion is frequently intertwined with public life, and consequently that government and religion must interact if religion is even to survive—let alone participate in civil society on a full and equal basis. Unfortunately, these interactions cannot always proceed on a purely secular plane, since to avoid trampling on religious interests the government must be aware of what they are. In other words, a government that is not to some extent "entangled" with religion is one that is indifferent toward it.

Moreover, for more than a decade the Court embellished the entanglement prong with the notion of "political divisiveness"—the theory that the Court must strike down any supposed benefit to religion that generates political controversy even if it is otherwise consistent with the First Amendment.[80] This was a particularly pernicious doctrine, because it armed opponents of religious interests with an invincible weapon: their mere opposition became a basis for a finding of unconstitutionality. Of course, the political victories of *either* side in such controversies could be divisive; but the doctrine did not—and could not—work both ways. In effect, the doctrine blamed the religious side of any controversy for the controversy. Since the early 1980s, the Court has abandoned the notion of "political divisiveness" as an independent ground for striking down legislation, and properly so.[81]

The three prongs of the *Lemon* test, in combination, can frustrate the goals of the First Amendment. Consider *Lyng*, the case in which Native American worshippers sought to prevent the Forest Service from building a logging road through their ancient places of worship. I have already criticized the Court's unsympathetic application of Free Exercise Clause doctrine in *Lyng*.[82] Now consider the converse case. Suppose that the Forest Service had done what the Native American plaintiffs asked in *Lyng*: had allowed their religious needs to trump the secular reasons for building the log-

---

[80] See id at 622-23; *Nyquist*, 413 US at 796-97; *Aguilar*, 473 US at 416-17 (Powell concurring). For a critique of the doctrine, see Edward McGlynn Gaffney, Jr, *Political Divisiveness Along Religious Lines: The Entanglement of the Court in Sloppy History and Bad Public Policy*, 24 St Louis L J 205 (1980).

[81] See *Lynch v Donnelly*, 465 US 668, 684 (1984) ("[T]his Court has not held that political divisiveness alone can serve to invalidate otherwise impermissible conduct."); *Mueller v Allen*, 463 US 388, 403-04 n 11 (1983) (restricting political divisiveness doctrine to cases involving a "direct subsidy" to religious institutions). The last case in which political divisiveness played a significant role in the Court's decision was *Aguilar v Felton*, 473 US 402 (1985), where Justice Powell, who provided the swing vote, concurred on political divisiveness grounds. Id at 416-17.

[82] See text accompanying notes 56-61.

ging road. How would this decision have fared under the *Lemon* test?

First, consider the *purpose* of the Forest Service's decision. All the secular criteria for building the logging road were satisfied; the only reason not to build the road would be that the Indians thought the sites to be holy. This manifestly religious reason for the Forest Service's decision would violate the first prong of the *Lemon* test.[83] Second, consider the primary *effect* of the Forest Service's decision. Clearly it would advance the religion of the Yuroks, Karoks, and Talowas. The Court itself stated that it would be a "subsidy of the Indian religion" not to destroy the Native Americans' worship sites.[84] That violates the second prong of the *Lemon* test. Finally, consider whether the Forest Service's decision would *entangle* government and religion. In order to determine where to build its roads and which portions of the National Forests to open for lumbering, the Forest Service would have to employ religious and anthropological experts to determine the character of purportedly holy sites. In the event of conflicts, the Forest Service would have to decide between conflicting claims of religious significance.[85]

In short, to accommodate the Native Americans in *Lyng* would violate all three prongs of the *Lemon* test. Yet the purposes of the Religion Clauses are advanced, not frustrated, when the government administers its property in such a way as to avoid devastating injury to the religious lives of its people. If *Lemon* stands in the way, then *Lemon* is the problem.

It is the parochial school aid cases that most starkly illustrate the perverse effects of the *Lemon* test. In these cases, the Court generally has prohibited government aid to schools that teach religion.[86] But in *Pierce v Society of Sisters*, a celebrated decision, the Court held that parents have a constitutional right to send their children to private, including religious, schools.[87] The Court explained that "[t]he fundamental theory of liberty upon which all

---

[83] Compare *Epperson v Arkansas*, 393 US 97, 107 (1968) ("No suggestion has been made that Arkansas' law may be justified by considerations of state policy other than the religious views of some of its citizens.").

[84] *Lyng*, 485 US at 453.

[85] Indeed, the government conducted just such an investigation in *Lyng*—the investigation that concluded that this particular project would virtually destroy the Indians' religion. Id at 442.

[86] See *Lemon*, 403 US at 625; *Wolman*, 433 US at 255; *Nyquist*, 413 US at 769. Only relatively modest forms of aid of a secular character have been permitted. See *Allen*, 392 US at 248; *Everson*, 330 US at 18; *Regan*, 444 US at 661-62.

[87] 268 US 510, 534-35 (1925).

governments in this Union repose excludes any general power of
the State to standardize its children by forcing them to accept instruction from public teachers only."[88] Without aid to private
schools, however, the only way that parents can escape state
"standardization" is by forfeiting their entitlement to a free education for their children—that is, by paying twice: once for everyone
else's schools (through property taxes) and once for their own. By
taxing everyone, but subsidizing only those who use secular
schools, the government creates a powerful disincentive for parents
to exercise their constitutionally protected option to send their
children to parochial schools. Nondiscriminatory allocation of educational resources would restore religious parents to the neutral set
of incentives they faced before the government taxed them to support secular education. Whether nondiscriminatory funding is constitutionally required to achieve the promise of *Pierce* is a complicated question, not unlike the question whether the constitutional
right to abortion recognized in *Roe v Wade*[89] requires nondiscriminatory funding of abortion and childbirth.[90] But even if nondiscriminatory funding is not constitutionally *required*, it was one of
the greatest inversions of constitutional values in its history for the
Court to hold that nondiscriminatory funding is constitutionally
forbidden.

In her contribution to this symposium, Professor Sullivan defends the parochial school aid cases on the ground that "[a]ll religions gain from the settlement of the war of all sects against all" as
well as from the "provision of universal public education."[91] But
nowhere does she explain why giving advantages to secular viewpoints over religious viewpoints is necessary to the achievement of
civic peace.[92] The "war of all sects against all" is more plausibly

---

[88] Id at 535.

[89] 410 US 113 (1973).

[90] See Michael W. McConnell, *The Selective Funding Problem: Abortions and Religious Schools*, 104 Harv L Rev 989 (1991). The Supreme Court rejected a nondiscriminatory
funding claim in a summary decision in *Luetkemeyer v Kaufman*, 419 US 888 (1974), over a
dissent by Justice White and Chief Justice Burger. The question has never been squarely
presented in a case on the merits. The principle of nondiscrimination does not necessarily
make it unconstitutional for the government to pay for public schools but not to pay for
private schools, since the discrimination in that case would be based on the ownership of the
schools rather than their ideational content. But it would undoubtedly be unconstitutional
for the government to pay for secular private schools and not religious schools, or to maintain a public school system with a monopoly on public funds if the dominant justification
for this was to circumvent the requirement of equal treatment.

[91] Sullivan, in this volume, 221 (cited in note 5).

[92] Professor Sullivan does not claim that public schools are, could be, or should be "neutral" toward competing points of view. Id at 200-201.

averted by a universal principle of equal treatment, where none is permitted to gain an advantage through the force of government. To permit religious choices only at the cost of forfeiting an equal share in public goods is not freedom of religion. Nor does Sullivan explain how educational choice conflicts with the idea that universal education is a public good, benefitting all. Any education that satisfies objective criteria standards of educational quality generates public as well as private benefits, and should be equally entitled to public support.[93] Religious parents do not seek to be absolved from paying their fair share toward the public good of education; their objection is to being excluded from that good. In any other context, Professor Sullivan would be the first to recognize that it is unconstitutional for the government to refuse to fund an otherwise eligible activity solely because of the content of its speech.[94]

The parochial school aid decisions of the Warren and Burger Courts can be divided into two categories: those that forbade any assistance to nonpublic schools, and those that allowed assistance only upon conditions that undermined their purpose for being. In *Board of Education v Allen*, for example, the Supreme Court permitted the state to provide textbooks to parochial school students only if they used the same secular textbooks that the public schools used.[95] This holding effectively required the parochial schools to secularize their curriculum if they wished to receive assistance. The very "standardization" of education held to be unconstitutional in *Pierce* (when accomplished through the regulatory power) was held to be constitutionally required in *Allen* (when accomplished through the spending power). Even this conditional grant was too much for the dissenters, who argued that since the schools teach religious doctrine they should not receive *any* public assistance.[96] Not a single member of the Court suggested that religious freedom and diversity might be enhanced if parents could choose the philosophical orientation of their children's education without forfeiting their fair share of public educational resources.

---

[93] In this era of Afro-centric and other particularistic multi-cultural schools, it is no longer possible (if it ever was) to argue that religious schools should be excluded because they do not present a unifying common curriculum. See McConnell, 1991 U Chi Legal F 123 (cited in note 33).

[94] See Kathleen M. Sullivan, *Unconstitutional Conditions*, 102 Harv L Rev 1413 (1989).

[95] *Allen*, 392 US at 243-45.

[96] Id at 250 (Black dissenting).

Despite their differences, the two sides on the Warren and Burger Courts shared a conception that everything touched by government must be secular. One side was deeply suspicious of religion, especially Catholicism, and concluded that quarantine was the only way to stave off theocracy. The other side was willing to accept a certain role for religion in public life, so long as religious institutions sacrificed their distinctively religious character. Whichever side might prevail in a particular case—the results swung back and forth between the two—the decisions consistently favored the secular over the religious. The Justices simply did not conceive of a world in which the governmental role was confined to finance, and the content of education left to the free choices of individual families. The Court thus placed the welfare-regulatory state on a collision course with religious freedom. As the sphere of government expanded, the field of religious pluralism had to shrink.

II. THE EMERGING JURISPRUDENCE OF THE REHNQUIST COURT

The Religion Clause jurisprudence of the Warren and Burger era was thus characterized by a hostility or indifference to religion, manifested in a weak application of free exercise doctrine and an aggressive application of an establishment doctrine systematically weighted in favor of the secular and against genuine religious pluralism. Far from protecting religious freedom against the vagaries of democratic politics, the Religion Clauses during this period became an additional instrument for promoting the politically dominant ideology of secular liberalism.

The ideology of secular liberalism, while still strong among the American elite, has lost its position of unquestioned dominance. On the left, a postmodernist intellectual current has cast doubt on the idea that secular liberalism should enjoy a privileged position and has opened the possibility for treating religion as one of many competing conceptions of reality. It is no longer intellectually credible to maintain that secular liberalism is simply the "neutral" position.[97] On the right, the resurgence of conservative religious

---

[97] A major theme of feminist legal studies, critical legal studies, critical race studies, and other postmodernist jurisprudence is that the seemingly objective cultural norms of liberalism privilege a particular (white, male, capitalist, rationalistic, heterosexual, Eurocentric) point of view and should be replaced by a radically pluralistic, multi-cultural approach. See, for example, Stephen Gardbaum, *Why the Liberal State Can Promote Moral Ideals After All*, 104 Harv L Rev 1350, 1350-53 (1991); Mari Matsuda, *Voices of America: Accent, Antidiscrimination Law, and a Jurisprudence for the Last Reconstruction*, 100 Yale L J 1330, 1392-1407 (1991); Martha Minow, *The Supreme Court 1986 Term—Foreword: Justice*

movements among both Protestants and Catholics—and to a lesser extent among Jews—has made religion a more salient force in the political culture. If taken to extremes, this religious resurgence might well support measures inconsistent with the pluralist religious ideals of the First Amendment. Calls for a "Christian America" and the return of organized prayers in the schools give genuine—if often exaggerated—cause for alarm. But appropriately channelled, this shift in popular attitudes could provide a corrective for the secularist biases of the previous judicial era.

It is too early to tell how the Rehnquist Court ultimately will treat the Religion Clauses. The new Court seems prepared to repudiate the approach of the old, and in important areas—discussed in detail in Section III—has ameliorated unfortunate features of Warren and Burger Court Establishment Clause doctrine. But these improvements on establishment issues have come at a heavy price: the radical reduction of free exercise rights. Moreover, even where the results seem correct, the Rehnquist Court has failed to articulate a coherent vision of what it is attempting to accomplish. The positive developments, without exception, have involved the Court's decision *not* to overturn actions taken by the political branches. Thus, it is possible that the Court has mistaken the real vices of the old jurisprudence as ones of excessive judicial activism rather than of favoring the secular over the religious.

One of the anomalies of the Warren and Burger approach was its expansive reading of both the Free Exercise and Establishment Clauses (though in the case of free exercise this expansive reading was largely an illusion). If the government attempted to regulate a religious activity, it might be held to violate the Free Exercise Clause; if it carved out a religious exemption, this might be held an establishment. The government seemed destined to lose, no matter what policy it adopted toward religion. There was, accordingly, some legitimacy to then-Associate Justice Rehnquist's complaint that "[b]y broadly construing both Clauses, the Court has con-

---

Engendered, 101 Harv L Rev 10, 11-12 (1987). One would think that this jurisprudence would be receptive to arguments for religious pluralism, on the ground that the old jurisprudence privileges a secular worldview in the guise of "neutrality" and suppresses the various religious alternatives. For the most part, however, postmodernist legal scholarship has either ignored religion or treated it with hostility, as if it were part of the hegemonic culture to be overthrown. See Ruth Colker, *Feminism, Theology, and Abortion: Toward Love, Compassion, and Wisdom*, 77 Cal L Rev 1011, 1015 (1989) (criticizing "the hostility toward and ignorance of theology . . . in feminist theory"). Notwithstanding the general failure of postmodernists to apply their critique to issues of religion, however, their attack on liberal neutrality has fatally wounded the Religion Clause jurisprudence of the Warren and Burger Courts as an intellectual position.

stantly narrowed the channel between the Scylla and Charybdis through which any state or federal action must pass in order to survive constitutional scrutiny."[98]

The initial response of the Rehnquist Court has been to shrink the scope of both Religion Clauses and thereby to restore a significant degree of governmental discretion. This response can be seen as part of a general jurisprudential shift in favor of greater judicial restraint, which in other constitutional areas may be a welcome corrective. But judicial restraint, for its own sake, is not a faithful mode of interpreting the Religion Clauses. There is a crucial difference between the discovery of "rights" not expressly or implicitly protected by the Constitution, where the dangers of judicial legislation and the need for judicial restraint are greatest, and the enforcement of rights firmly based on the text and tradition of the Constitution.

The original theory of the First Amendment was not deferential to government in matters of religion. Daniel Carroll, one of two non-Protestant members of the First Congress, captured the spirit during the deliberations over what would become the Religion Clauses of the First Amendment. "The rights of conscience," he said, "will little bear the gentlest touch of governmental hand."[99] The Religion Clauses were born of distrust of government in matters of religion, based on experience. Those groups most vocal in demanding protection for religious freedom—the Quakers, the Presbyterians, and above all the Baptists—were precisely those groups whose practices were out of keeping with the majoritarian culture and who had borne the brunt of governmental hostility and indifference.[100] It is a mistake to read the Religion Clauses as a triumph for the forces of Enlightenment secularism. Proponents of religious freedom were the least secular and most "enthusiastic" of the sects. But it is equally mistaken to treat the Religion Clauses as acquiescing in governmental interference with religion. The advocates of the Religion Clauses valued their religious convictions too much to allow them to be subjected to governmental power. The overriding objective of the Religion Clauses was to render the new federal government irrelevant to the religious lives of the people.

---

[98] *Thomas v Review Board*, 450 US 707, 721 (1981) (Rehnquist dissenting).

[99] Speech of Daniel Carroll (Aug 15, 1789), in Gales, ed, 1 *Annals of Congress* at 757-58 (cited in note 6).

[100] Michael W. McConnell, *The Origins and Historical Understanding of Free Exercise of Religion*, 103 Harv L Rev 1409, 1437-41 (1990).

This objective has been vastly complicated by the emergence of the welfare-regulatory state. During the early days of the Republic, the reach of the federal government was strictly limited, and the matters within its jurisdiction—chiefly foreign and military affairs and commerce—had little effect on religion. Recall that Madison and the other Federalists initially argued that a Bill of Rights was not necessary because the powers of the federal government were so limited that it could pose no danger to our liberties.[101] With some exceptions, if the federal government simply took no actions directed at religion, the objectives of the Religion Clauses would be fulfilled.[102] As the powers of the federal government expanded and the coverage of the First Amendment was extended to the states, however, this ceased to be true. The government now fosters a vast sector of publicly-supported, privately-administered social welfare programs, and the allocation of resources in this sector inevitably affects religion. The government also now regulates the non-profit sphere, and these regulations similarly affect religion. Where once the government could treat religious institutions with benign neglect, the welfare-regulatory state requires a substantive policy toward religion that will preserve the conditions of religious freedom without hobbling the activist state. Unfortunately, neither the free exercise nor the establishment jurisprudence that seems to be emerging in the Rehnquist Court addresses that central problem.

A. Free Exercise

The Rehnquist Court's tendency to defer to majoritarian decisionmaking is most clearly evident in its reversal of free exercise doctrine. As noted above, the Warren and Burger Courts held governmental action invalid when it imposed a burden on the exercise of a sincerely held religious belief without compelling justification.[103] This meant that the government sometimes had to make accommodations or exceptions to laws that burdened the exercise of religion. In 1990, in *Employment Division v Smith*, the Rehnquist Court held that "the right of free exercise does not relieve an individual of the obligation to comply with a 'valid and neutral law of general applicability on the ground that the law proscribes (or

---

[101] Max Farrand, 2 *The Record of the Federal Convention of 1787* 587-88 (Yale, rev ed 1937).

[102] For examples of how the enumerated powers of Congress could affect religion, see McConnell, 103 Harv L Rev at 1478 nn 342-52 (cited in note 100).

[103] See text accompanying notes 67-70.

prescribes) conduct that his religion prescribes (or proscribes).' "[104]
If the law is "generally applicable," the government need not show
that it serves an important (let alone compelling) purpose, even if
its effect—as in *Smith* itself—is to make the practice of a religion
virtually impossible.[105] Thus *Smith* holds that the state may forbid
the central religious practice of a centuries-old religion now called
the Native American Church—the sacramental ingestion of peyote—even though there was no evidence that this practice had
deleterious consequences for the practitioners or for anyone else.[106]

I have criticized the *Smith* decision elsewhere at length,[107] and
I will not repeat those arguments. Nonetheless, a few observations
on *Smith* will illustrate why I am concerned that the Rehnquist
Court may be as mistaken in its way as were the Warren and Burger Courts. First and foremost, the *Smith* decision gives social policy, determined by the State, primacy over the rights of religious
communities to order their affairs according to their own convictions. *Smith* describes this effect as an "unavoidable consequence
of democratic government."[108] Is apprehension of illegal aliens a
policy of the government? Then the government can dragoon the
Quaker Church, which for centuries has welcomed strangers and
aliens in compliance with its reading of biblical principles, into enforcing the law against immigration.[109] Does the government favor
preservation of old buildings in their original configuration? Then
the government can determine how churches design their houses of
worship.[110] Does the government believe that homosexuality is a
legitimate lifestyle? Then the government can require a religious
university, which preaches that homosexual acts are sinful, to play
host to gay rights organizations on its campus and to support them
with its student funds.[111] Under *Smith*, the state is more powerful,
the forces of homogenization are more powerful, and the ability of

---

[104] *Smith*, 110 S Ct at 1600 (quoting *United States v Lee*, 475 US at 263 n 3).

[105] Id at 1599.

[106] Id at 1597-98, 1606.

[107] Michael W. McConnell, *Free Exercise Revisionism and the* Smith *Decision*, 57 U
Chi L Rev 1109 (1990).

[108] *Smith*, 110 S Ct at 1606.

[109] *American Friends Service Committee v Thornburgh*, 941 F2d 808, 809-10 (9th Cir
1991).

[110] See Angela C. Carmella, *Houses of Worship and Religious Liberty: Constitutional
Limits to Landmark Preservation and Architectural Review*, 36 Villanova L Rev 401
(1991).

[111] *Gay Rights Coalition v Georgetown Univ.*, 536 A2d 1 (DC App 1987) (en banc); see
Comment, Georgetown Rights Coalition v. Georgetown University: *Failure to Recognize a
Catholic University's Religious Liberty*, 32 Cath Lawyer 170 (1988).

churches to maintain their distinctive ways of life depends upon their skill at self-protection in the halls of Congress.

Second, as the *Smith* opinion candidly acknowledges, its interpretation will place "those religious practices that are not widely engaged in" at a "relative disadvantage."[112] Some religions are close to the center of prevailing culture in America. Their practices rarely, if ever, will conflict with an "otherwise valid law,"[113] because, in a democracy, the laws will reflect the beliefs and preferences of the median groups. Religious groups whose practices and beliefs are outside the mainstream are most likely to need exceptions and accommodations. If most Americans shared the Quakers' attitudes toward immigration, we would not sanction employers for employing aliens; if most residents of the District of Columbia shared the Catholic teaching on sexuality, the District would not forbid discrimination on the basis of sexual preference. Moreover, only some of the religious groups in need of exceptions and accommodations will win the ear of the legislature. Those groups whose beliefs are least foreign and least offensive to the mainstream, and those with the largest numbers and greatest visibility, will be better able to protect themselves than will the smaller, more unpopular groups. *Smith* thus not only increases the power of the state over religion, it introduces a bias in favor of mainstream over nonmainstream religions. That bias may not displease those who believe in the wisdom and virtue of majoritarian culture, but it is not consistent with the original theory of the Religion Clauses.

Third, the *Smith* Court treated the claim for a free exercise exemption as essentially a request for a special benefit. In an earlier opinion, Justice Scalia, the author of *Smith*, characterized free exercise exemptions as "intentional governmental advancement" of religion.[114] This misstates the issue. The Native American Church was not asking government for "advancement"; it was asking to be left alone. When the government criminalizes the religious ritual of a church, it "prohibits" the free exercise of religion in the most direct and literal sense of the word. If the courts cannot distinguish the failure to "prohibit" from the decision to "advance," it is no wonder that their decisions are so confused. To conceive of free exercise exemptions as requests for special benefits implicitly assumes that the state has the natural authority to regulate the church, and that choosing not to do so is a favor. That is not the

---

[112] *Smith*, 110 S Ct at 1606.
[113] Id at 1600.
[114] *Edwards v Aguillard*, 482 US 578, 617 (1987) (Scalia dissenting).

inalienable right to freedom of religion conceived by those who wrote and ratified the First Amendment.

Finally, *Smith* converts a constitutionally explicit liberty into a nondiscrimination requirement, in violation of the most straightforward interpretation of the First Amendment text. If the Constitution guaranteed the "right to own cattle," who would interpret it to allow the government to ban the ownership of all animals, so long as cattle are not "singled out"? The freedom of citizens to exercise their faith should not depend on the vagaries of democratic politics, even if expressed through laws of general applicability.

B. Establishment

The Rehnquist Court's greatest contributions to Establishment Clause doctrine have been its dismantling of some of *Lemon*'s mistakes. In *Corporation of Presiding Bishop v Amos*,[115] the Court removed the most serious doctrinal obstacles to legislative accomodations of religion. For the first time, the Court held unequivocally that the government may exempt religious organizations from a regulatory burden, even when not required to do so under the Free Exercise Clause. The Court did not abandon the *Lemon* test, but held that "it is a permissible legislative purpose to alleviate significant governmental interference with the ability of religious organizations to define and carry out their religious mission,"[116] and that the effects test is not necessarily violated by "statues that give special consideration to religious groups."[117] In *Board of Education v Mergens*,[118] the Court upheld the Equal Access Act, which requires public schools to permit religious (as well as political and philosophical) student clubs to meet on school premises on the same terms as other noncurricular clubs. The Court rejected the argument that religious activities must be excluded from any officially-sanctioned presence within a public school, on the ground that secularism can be counter to neutrality: "if a State refused to let religious groups use facilities open to others, then it would demonstrate not neutrality but hostility toward religion."[119] The degree to which this decision breaks with the old jurisprudence is shown by the fact that four of the five

---

[115] 483 US 327 (1987).
[116] Id at 335.
[117] Id at 338.
[118] 110 S Ct 2356 (1990).
[119] Id at 2371.

courts of appeals to rule on the issue had held, under *Lemon*, that it would be unconstitutional to allow student religious clubs to meet.[120] In *Bowen v Kendrick*,[121] the Court made strides toward allowing religiously affiliated organizations to participate in publicly funded educational and social welfare programs on an equal basis with secular groups. The implications of these decisions will be discussed at greater length in Section III.

Notwithstanding these encouraging decisions, the course of Establishment Clause doctrine remains very much in doubt. In none of these cases did the Court explicitly announce a change in doctrine. *Amos* was important in establishing the legitimacy of accommodation, but left the limits of the accommodation doctrine unclarified. *Mergens* is unlikely to have much application outside of its particular context. *Kendrick* entailed a rather unpersuasive manipulation of the ambiguous concepts of the *Lemon* test. It augured doctrinal change, but provided no hint of what form the change may take.[122] The Court may well adopt an affirmatively pluralistic interpretation of the Establishment Clause, as is discussed in Section III, but it might also retreat to a posture of deference to majoritarian decisionmaking. In the remainder of this Section, I will discuss the specific proposals by members of the new Court for revising the *Lemon* test.

1. Dropping the entanglement prong.

Three members of the Court have proposed modifying the *Lemon* test by eliminating the third prong, "entanglement", which some have blamed for the chaotic and inconsistent results of the Court's establishment cases.[123] Justice White has attacked and ridiculed the entanglement prong ever since his dissent in *Lemon* it-

---

[120] *Brandon v Board of Education*, 635 F2d 971 (2d Cir 1980); *Lubbock Civil Liberties Union v Lubbock Independent School Dist.*, 669 F2d 1038 (5th Cir 1982); *Nartowicz v Clayton County School Dist.*, 736 F2d 646 (11th Cir 1984); *Garnett v Renton School Dist.*, 874 F2d 608 (9th Cir 1989), cert granted, judgment vacated, and case remanded, 110 S Ct 2608 (1990), on remand, 772 F Supp 531 (W D Wash 1991). Only the lower court in *Mergens*, in the Eighth Circuit, had upheld the Act. *Mergens v Board of Education*, 876 F2d 1076, 1079-80 (8th Cir 1989).

[121] 487 US 589 (1988).

[122] On its surface, *Kendrick* appeared to confine the rigors of the *Lemon* test to elementary and secondary education. But there is no persuasive reason to single out the educational sector for special constitutional rules.

[123] See, for example, Justice O'Connor's dissent in *Aguilar*, 473 US at 430. See also Jesse Choper, *The Religion Clauses of the First Amendment: Reconciling the Conflict*, 41 U Pitt L Rev 673, 681 (1980).

self,[124] calling it "curious and mystifying," "insolubly paradoxical," "redundant," "superfluous," and without "constitutional foundation."[125] Recently Chief Justice Rehnquist and Justice O'Connor have joined him.[126] According to these Justices, state efforts to ensure that public resources are used only for nonsectarian ends should not in themselves serve to invalidate an otherwise valid statute. If a statute has neither a purpose nor an effect of advancing or endorsing religion, these Justices "would not invalidate it merely because it requires . . . some state supervision to ensure that state funds do not advance religion."[127]

Without modifying the effects prong, however, eliminating the entanglement prong could actually make matters worse. No longer would there be a constitutional obstacle to the government surveillance needed to ensure that funds are not used to "advance religion" (as that concept is misleadingly employed in the *Lemon* cases). The state could root out religious elements in the activities of all religious organizations participating in public programs. The effects prong without the entanglement prong imposes a classic unconstitutional condition: the recipient may receive benefits to which it is otherwise entitled under neutral criteria, if and only if the recipient waives its freedom of speech with respect to religion. For example, in *Lemon* itself, by agreeing to pay fifteen percent of the salaries of teachers in parochial schools, the state would have obtained not only the warrant, but the constitutional obligation, to ensure that those teachers excised any religious content from their classes, one hundred percent of the time. Only the entanglement prong of *Lemon* stood in the way. The *Lemon* Court held that the governmental interference with the operations of the parochial school which would have been necessary to enforce the secular use limitation was an unconstitutional entanglement between church and state; thus the Court denied the aid altogether.[128] In other words, the entanglement prong averted the unconstitutional condition by refusing to permit aid *even if* the school were willing to waive its freedom of speech.

Parochial school supporters universally perceived the result in *Lemon* as a disaster. But without the entanglement prong, the pro-

[124] *Lemon*, 403 US at 661-71 (White dissenting).

[125] See *Roemer v Maryland Public Works Bd.*, 426 US 736, 768-69 (1976) (White concurring) (quoting earlier opinions).

[126] *Aguilar*, 473 US at 430 (O'Connor, joined by Rehnquist, dissenting).

[127] Id.

[128] *Lemon*, 403 US at 611-25.

gram at issue in *Lemon* would have effectively destroyed religious education. Few schools could have resisted an offer of subsidies for their teachers' salaries, and the curriculum of the parochial schools would have become indistinguishable from that of the public schools. Under *Allen*, the religious schools would have received free textbooks, provided that those textbooks were strictly secular. Under *Lemon* faculty salaries would have been subsidized, provided that their classroom teaching was strictly secular. Religion would have become irrelevant to the core educational offerings of the school. The entanglement prong of the *Lemon* test, which cut religious schools off from funding, and thus from secularization, was a blessing in disguise for religious choice and diversity.

2. Dropping the purpose prong.

In a 1987 opinion joined by Chief Justice Rehnquist, Justice Scalia urged "[a]bandoning" the first prong of the *Lemon* test, the requirement of a "secular purpose."[129] He relied on two major points: (1) that it is not possible to determine legislative purpose;[130] and (2) that the Court has not clearly defined the requirement of a "secular purpose."[131] The first point is not peculiar to the Religion Clauses. Indeed, the argument about legislative purpose is one of the most important questions cutting across the fields of constitutional law. It affects everything from the Equal Protection Clause to the Commerce Clause to the Bill of Attainder Clause.[132] I shall not enter into the debate here, other than to say that it would be unprincipled to abandon the purpose prong of the *Lemon* test on these grounds if the Court intends to inquire into legislative purpose in other contexts.

Scalia's second point about the purpose prong is more telling. The Court *has* been singularly unhelpful in defining the requirement of a "secular purpose." Does it mean that the legislature may not have been motivated by "religious considerations?"[133] This definition would render all religious accommodations suspect, for

---

[129] *Edwards*, 482 US at 640 (Scalia dissenting).

[130] Id at 636-39.

[131] Id at 613-19.

[132] John Hart Ely's analysis of this issue, though more than twenty years old, is still the best general study of the question. See John Hart Ely, *Legislative and Administrative Motivation in Constitutional Law*, 79 Yale L J 1205 (1970). With reference to the Religion Clauses, Ely advocates making illicit purpose a necessary, as opposed to a sufficient, element of the constitutional claim. Id at 1314.

[133] *Lynch*, 465 US at 680.

reasons discussed above.[134] Does it forbid the legislature from making religiously-informed judgments, or basing legislation on the religiously-informed judgments of their constituents? This definition would be bizarre, for religion remains the single most important influence on the values of ordinary Americans. Are laws against stealing suspect because most Americans would identify the Ten Commandments as the source of their moral intuition against theft? Left undefined, the purpose prong is an invitation to mischief—a not-so-subtle suggestion that those whose understandings of justice are derived from religious sources are second-class citizens, forbidden to work for their principles in the public sphere. This understanding would be a sharp and unwarranted break from our political history. From the War for Independence to the abolition movement, women's suffrage, labor reform, civil rights, nuclear disarmament, and opposition to pornography, a major source of support for political change has come from explicitly religious voices.

Nonetheless, abandoning the purpose prong would be an overreaction. Legislative purpose is relevant in at least two contexts. First, one element in the Establishment Clause analysis of a statutory program is whether its benefits are available generally, to nonreligious and religious recipients alike. Purpose is a necessary backstop to facial neutrality. A law's facially neutral categories may be pretextual, especially where they produce disproportionate effects. The absence of a strong secular justification for the categorization is the best evidence that the program favors religion over nonreligion, or one religion over another.[135]

Second, a program with an effect that favors one religion may nonetheless be constitutional if there is a powerful secular justification for it. The National Holocaust Memorial in Washington contains many exhibits that pertain to the Jewish religion; but the obvious historical justification for "singling out" Judaism in this context should rescue it from any establishment challenge. Similarly (though less clearly), Congress made a large grant to the Roman Catholic Church a few years ago for the purpose of assisting illegal aliens in applying for amnesty under the Immigration Re-

---

[134] See text accompanying notes 72-75.

[135] The same is true for free exercise cases: a facially neutral rule that "happens" to bear most heavily on a particular religious practice should not be sustained without persuasive secular justification. A law outlawing all hallucinogenic drug use is nondiscriminatory; a law outlawing only peyote use would, in all likelihood, be a measure directed against the Native American Church. Under the legal framework of *Smith*, an inquiry into purpose is more necessary than ever before.

form Act.[136] Though the effect was discriminatory, the justification was strong: the target population is understandably mistrustful of government agents and the Catholic Church is uniquely positioned to reach them.

These considerations suggest that, instead of abandoning the inquiry into purpose, the Court should define the concept more carefully. But even if Justice Scalia were correct that the purpose prong should be abandoned, this modification to the *Lemon* test would be of relatively little consequence. Situations in which the legislature lacks *any* secular justification for its actions are rare, and in the vast majority of cases the Court has found the purpose prong easily satisfied. In only four cases has the Supreme Court struck down a statute because it lacked a secular purpose,[137] and in three of those cases the Court would likely have found the statutes unconstitutional on other grounds if it had not used the purpose test.[138] The purpose prong is the least significant part of the *Lemon* test, and eliminating it would do little to solve the problems created by *Lemon*.

3. Nonpreferentialism.

In several opinions in 1985, then Associate Justice Rehnquist urged that the Establishment Clause be interpreted solely to forbid "establishment of a national religion" and "preference among religious sects or denominations."[139] According to Rehnquist, "[t]he Establishment Clause did not require government neutrality between religion and irreligion nor did it prohibit the Federal Government from providing nondiscriminatory aid to religion."[140] Rehnquist, who has not mentioned this suggestion since, may have abandoned it. Although the nonpreferentialist position may lead to correct results in a large number of cases, it is theoretically unsound. Under that approach, the government could use its taxing

---

[136] The Immigration and Naturalization Service contracted with "qualified designated entities" (QDEs) to perform most of these services, paying them $15 for each application processed. Cheryl Devall, *Legal Status for Illegal Aliens Right Around Corner, U.S. Says*, Chi Trib 3 (May 3, 1987). The U.S. Catholic Conference, acting through its dioceses, was the most prominent QDE: by early 1987, the Catholic Charities of Los Angeles alone had registered 276,000 probable applicants. David Holley, *Groups in L.A. Ready to Assist Aliens Listed*, LA Times A1 (Apr 24, 1987).

[137] *Edwards*, 482 US at 585-89; *Jaffree*, 472 US at 56; *Stone v Graham*, 449 US 39, 40-41 (1980); and *Epperson*, 393 US at 106-07.

[138] *Jaffree* is the exception.

[139] *Jaffree*, 472 US at 106 (Rehnquist dissenting).

[140] Id.

and spending power to augment the position and resources of the religious sector—an effect that is no less objectionable than augmenting the secular sector under the *Lemon* test.

Rehnquist proposed the nonpreferentialist approach on the strength of certain seemingly powerful evidence of the original understanding.[141] Since that time, however, more complete historical research has refuted the nonpreferentialist argument.[142] I do not expect nonpreferentialism to figure prominently in future decisions.

Indeed, in the years since 1985, Rehnquist has joined opinions for the Court that implicitly reduce the standard of review for government actions that discriminate among religions.[143] These actions used to receive "strict scrutiny," even more difficult to satisfy than the *Lemon* test. By contrast, the *Smith* opinion observed:

> It may fairly be said that leaving accommodation to the political process will place at a relative disadvantage those religious practices that are not widely engaged in; but that unavoidable consequence of democratic government must be preferred to a system in which each conscience is a law unto itself or in which judges weigh the social importance of all laws against the centrality of all religious beliefs.[144]

---

[141] Rehnquist's dissent in *Jaffree* closely followed the historical research of Robert L. Cord, *Separation of Church and State* (Lambeth, 1982). See also Michael J. Malbin, *Religion and Politics: The Intentions of the Authors of the First Amendment* (American Enterprise Institute for Public Policy Research, 1978).

[142] See Douglas Laycock, *The Origins of the Religion Clauses of the Constitution: "Nonpreferential" Aid to Religion: A False Claim About Original Intent*, 27 Wm & Mary L Rev 875 (1986). Dean Rodney Smith has offered a rebuttal to Laycock, but his principal argument seems to be with Laycock's use of the term "nonpreferentialism" rather than with Laycock's historical analysis of Rehnquist's position. Rodney K. Smith, *Nonpreferentialism In Establishment Clause Analysis: A Response To Professor Laycock*, 65 St John's L Rev 245 (1991). Smith distinguishes among three possible forms of "nonpreferentialism," of which Smith supports one (nonpreferentialism as to matters of conscience) and Laycock supports another (nonpreferentialism between religion and nonreligion). Id at 247-48. Smith and Laycock both reject the third (nonpreferentialism among religions), which is what Laycock means by "nonpreferentialism," and which represents Justice Rehnquist's position in the *Jaffree* dissent.

[143] Under prior rulings, the Supreme Court treated discrimination among religions as the most serious of Establishment Clause offenses, subject to the highest level of scrutiny. See, for example, *Larson*, 456 US at 244 ("the clearest command of the Establishment Clause is that one religious denomination cannot be officially preferred over another"). This conclusion has voluminous support in the history of the First Amendment, and I know of no First Amendment theorist who disputes it. For a summary of the historical evidence, see McConnell, 57 U Chi L Rev at 1130-31 (cited in note 107).

[144] *Smith*, 110 S Ct at 1606.

This language indicates that the Justices who make up the working majority on the Rehnquist Court consider the principle of denominational neutrality to be less important than the need to avoid balancing tests. In *Hernandez v Commissioner*, a shocking decision that received little attention, the Internal Revenue Service had denied tax deductions to members of the Church of Scientology for certain fixed-price payments they made to participate in worship services.[145] The IRS had a formal written policy of allowing deductions for comparable practices by other religions, such as pew rent and the sale of tickets to Jewish high holy days, and the government offered no explanation for treating the Scientologists differently.[146] The Court nonetheless upheld the action, reasoning that "the IRS m[ight] be right or wrong with respect to these other faiths," and that the Court would have to wait for a more complete factual record about the other faiths before reviewing the allegation of discriminatory treatment.[147] This reasoning empties the requirement of equal treatment of any force, since the government is free to continue to treat Protestants and Jews in one way and Scientologists in another. Only Justices O'Connor and Scalia dissented in *Hernandez*; Justices Brennan and Kennedy did not participate in the decision.

Hernandez suggests that, far from making the principle of denominational neutrality the exclusive focus of Establishment Clause analysis, the Rehnquist Court is discarding or neglecting it. This trend will only exacerbate the Court's tendency toward acquiescence in governmental decisions that favor mainstream religious traditions.

4. The endorsement test.

A more prominent alternative to the *Lemon* test is the so-called "endorsement test," first proposed by Justice O'Connor in a concurring opinion[148] and sporadically embraced by opinions for the Court in subsequent cases.[149] According to Justice O'Connor, the most "direct infringement [of the Establishment Clause] is

---

[145] 490 US 680 (1989).

[146] Id at 701-03.

[147] Id at 702-03.

[148] *Lynch*, 465 US at 688 (O'Connor concurring).

[149] *Grand Rapids*, 473 US at 389-90; *Mergens*, 110 S Ct at 2371-72; *Edwards*, 482 US at 587; *Allegheny*, 492 US at 592-93.

148   *Michael W. McConnell*

government endorsement or disapproval of religion."[150] She explained that

> Endorsement sends a message to nonadherents that they are outsiders, not full members of the political community, and an accompanying message to adherents that they are insiders, favored members of the political community. Disapproval sends the opposite message.[151]

There is some appeal to the endorsement concept, principally because it focuses on how the governmental practice affects the "outsider," which I take to mean the religious minority. There is no obvious merit in government action with the sole purpose or effect of endorsing one religious belief over another, since the government is unlikely to be a valuable contributor to our understanding of spiritual truth. Notwithstanding its initial appeal, however, the endorsement test is not an attractive alternative to the *Lemon* test, for several reasons.[152]

a) The impossibility of defining "endorsement." First, the very "goal" of the endorsement test, according to Justice O'Connor, is to identify a principle that is " 'not only grounded in the history and language of the first amendment, but one that is also capable of consistent application to the relevant problems.' "[153] Yet this goal of consistency is the test's greatest failing. There is no generally-accepted conception of what "endorsement" is, and there cannot be. Whether a particular governmental action appears to endorse or disapprove religion depends on the presuppositions of the observer, and there is no "neutral" position, outside the culture, from which to make this assessment. The bare concept of "endorsement" therefore provides no guidance to legislatures or lower courts about what is an establishment of religion. It is nothing more than an application to the Religion Clauses of the principle: "I know it when I see it."[154] Consider the following examples:

---

[150] *Lynch*, 465 US at 688 (O'Connor concurring).

[151] Id.

[152] For other arguments in opposition to the endorsement test, see Steven D. Smith, *Symbols, Perceptions, and Doctrinal Illusions: Establishment Neutrality and the "No Endorsement" Test*, 86 Mich L Rev 266 (1987).

[153] *Jaffree*, 472 US at 69 (O'Connor concurring) (citation omitted).

[154] See William P. Marshall, *"We Know It When We See It": The Supreme Court and Establishment*, 59 S Cal L Rev 495 (1986).

(1) How would the parochial school aid cases fare under the endorsement test? The majority position has been that most forms of aid to religious schools are impermissible, in part because it creates an appearance of a "symbolic union" between church and state.[155] A significant segment of the population believes that the use of government funds to assist religious education is tantamount to putting priests on the payroll. On the other hand, granting funds to secular schools but not to equally qualified religious schools creates at least the *appearance* of disapproval. Parents of children attending religious schools often claim they are treated as second-class citizens, unable to receive public benefits to which they would otherwise be entitled for the sole reason that the ideological content of the education they have chosen is religious.

(2) Does tax-exempt status convey a message of endorsement of churches? The government grants tax exemptions on the theory that exempt organizations provide benefits to the public. Including churches on this list implies that they are wholesome and beneficial institutions, especially when the statute mentions "churches" explicitly. But what message would be conveyed by excluding churches from the class of tax-exempt charities?

(3) Do public schools endorse religion if they refrain from teaching evolution? The majority of the Supreme Court so held, on the ground that disbelief in evolution is a tenet of fundamentalist Christianity.[156] A fundamentalist Christian might think, however, that teaching evolution without discussing creationist objections expresses disapproval of his religious view.[157] Justice Black, in confronting this issue, concluded that leaving evolution out of the curriculum was a neutral way to avoid taking an official position on a controversial religious issue.[158]

(4) Did the government endorse religion by providing worship services to the men and women fighting the war against Iraq? Or would failure to do so have conveyed disapproval?

---

[155] *Grand Rapids*, 473 US at 389-92.

[156] *Epperson*, 393 US at 107-09.

[157] Others think so too. See Gregory Gelfand, *Of Monkeys and Men—An Atheist's Heretical View of the Constitutionality of Teaching the Disproof of a Religion in the Public Schools*, 16 J L & Educ 271 (1987).

[158] *Epperson*, 393 US at 112-13 (Black concurring).

(5) Does exemption of religious organizations or of religiously motivated individuals from a law of general applicability "endorse" religion? Opponents of religious accommodations argue that "[s]pecial treatment for religion connotes sponsorship and endorsement"[159] and that exemptions "create[] ill will and divisiveness among the American people."[160] Justice O'Connor agrees that exemptions cause resentment, but holds that this resentment is "entitled to little weight" because accommodations promote the "values" of the Free Exercise Clause.[161] Others, such as Professor Laycock, say that exemptions do not appear to endorse religion at all.[162] I know all of these people to be reasonable observers, well schooled in the values underlying the First Amendment. That does not seem to help.

For each of the above questions, it is tempting to answer "yes" to both sides of the question—the government action in question conveys endorsement, but the opposite action conveys disapproval. Any action the government takes on issues of this sort inevitably sends out messages, and it is not surprising that reasonable observers from different legal and religious perspectives respond to these messages in different ways. These examples raise some of the most important and most often litigated issues under the Establishment Clause, and the concept of endorsement does not help to resolve them.

To be sure, most of us have strong intuitions about how to resolve the foregoing examples. But those intuitions are based—or should be based—on substantive conceptions about the proper relationship between religion and government. Strict separationists will take the position that any provision of financial or other assistance to religion is an endorsement. Advocates of "facial neutrality" will take the position that any action that "singles out" religion for special treatment more favorable than that given to secular groups or ideologies is an endorsement. Accommodationists will say that benefits to religion that are either facially neutral or that accommodate the free exercise of religion are neutral in their

---

[159] William P. Marshall, *In Defense of* Smith *and Free Exercise Revisionism*, 58 U Chi L Rev 308, 320 (1991).

[160] Ellis West, *The Case Against a Right to Religion-Based Exemptions*, 4 Notre Dame J L Ethics & Pub Policy 591, 602 (1990).

[161] *Jaffree*, 472 US at 83 (O'Connor concurring).

[162] Douglas Laycock, *Formal, Substantive, and Disaggregated Neutrality Toward Religion*, 39 DePaul L Rev 993, 1003 (1990); Douglas Laycock, *The Remnants of Free Exercise*, 1990 S Ct Rev 1, 16-17.

symbolic effect, and that anything less would be an expression of disapproval. The concept of "endorsement" adds nothing to any of these analyses. Indeed, it detracts from the analysis, because it eliminates the need for the judge to explain the true basis for the judgment. A finding of "endorsement" serves only to mask reliance on untutored intuition.[163]

b) *Inconsistency with accommodation.* Second, not only is the endorsement test indeterminate, it is not evenhanded. It perpetuates some of the implicit biases of the *Lemon* test.[164] The endorsement test casts suspicion on government actions that convey a message that religion is worthy of particular protection—as any accommodation of religion necessarily does—and thus encourages indifference toward religion. There is no way to distinguish between government action that treats a religious belief as worthy of protection, and government action that treats a religious belief as intrinsically valuable. Why accommodate religion unless religion is special and important? Justice O'Connor's endorsement test is therefore in tension with her accommodationist interpretation of the Free Exercise Clause.

Justice O'Connor attempts to avoid this tension by specifying that her "reasonable observer" who is the judge of endorsement "would take into account the values underlying the Free Exercise Clause."[165] Presumably, the reasonable observer who is the judge of disapproval would similarly "take into account the values underlying" the Establishment Clause. But this attempt to reconcile accommodation to the endorsement test is circular. If our reasonable observers know the "values" underlying the Religion Clauses, and if those values are something other than endorsement and disapproval, what need have we of the endorsement test? We should look directly to the principles of the Free Exercise and Establishment Clauses and not be waylaid by issues of perception.

---

[163] Justice O'Connor has defended her endorsement test against the charge of indeterminacy. *Allegheny*, 492 US at 628-30 (O'Connor concurring). She admits that the test "may not always yield results with unanimous agreement at the margins," pointing out that this is equally true of other tests. Id at 629. But Justice O'Connor focuses her attention in this discussion solely on the religious symbols cases. My point is that the endorsement test is indeterminate in other contexts, where substantive doctrines provide reasonably clear guidance and superior results.

[164] See text accompanying notes 71-96.

[165] *Allegheny*, 492 US at 632 (O'Connor concurring).

c) *The bias against religion.* Much like the effects prong of the *Lemon* test,[166] the apparent symmetry of the endorsement test—its equal condemnation of actions that "endorse" and actions that "disapprove" religion—is spurious. No court applying the test has ever struck down a governmental action because it appeared to "disapprove" of a religion. The reason lies in the structure of the Religion Clauses. Disapproval of religion is not an "establishment" of religion because the government typically has a secular purpose for its action, and because there is no "religion" that is being "established." For example, when the New York public schools train their teenage pupils in the use of condoms, this plainly creates an appearance of "disapproval" of a tenet of the Roman Catholic Church. (Imagine the reaction if the schools instructed their students in the method of natural family planning.) But there is no "religion" of condom advocacy on the other side—nothing but a particular secular view regarding public health and sexual hygiene. To solve difficulties of this sort, attorneys for traditionalist parents have tried to portray secular ideology as the religion of "secular humanism," but this strategy has been a failure.[167] When the government prefers secular ideas to religious ideas, it does not violate the Establishment Clause, no matter how strong the "message of disapproval."

The appearance of disapproval more plausibly violates the Free Exercise Clause. But plaintiffs who assert free exercise claims based on disapproval run afoul of the requirement that they identify a specific "burden" on their practice of religion.[168] In *Mozert v Hawkins County Board of Education*, parents of children in the public schools of Hawkins County, Tennessee, contended that particular textbooks, read as a whole, denigrated their religion.[169] They asked that their children be permitted to use substitute texts.[170] The Sixth Circuit rejected this claim on the ground that

---

[166] See note 9.

[167] See *Smith v Bd. of School Comm'rs of Mobile County*, 655 F Supp 939, 960-71, 980-83 (S D Ala 1987) (summarizing and adopting testimony and argument purporting to show that the public school curriculum was infused with the tenets of the "religion" of secular humanism), rev'd, 827 F2d 684 (11th Cir 1987). For a balanced introduction to the "secular humanism" controversy, see James Davison Hunter, *Religious Freedom and the Challenge of Modern Pluralism*, in James Davison Hunter and Os Guiness, eds, *Articles of Faith, Articles of Peace* 54 (Brookings, 1990).

[168] See Ira C. Lupu, *Where Rights Begin: The Problem of Burdens on the Free Exercise of Religion*, 102 Harv L Rev 933 (1989); David C. Williams and Susan H. Williams, *Volitionalism and Religious Liberty*, 76 Cornell L Rev 769, 798-850 (1991).

[169] 827 F2d 1058 (6th Cir 1987).

[170] Id at 1060.

enforced exposure to contrary views does not violate the Free Exercise Clause.[171] "What is absent from this case," according to the Sixth Circuit, "is the critical element of compulsion to affirm or deny a religious belief or to engage or refrain from engaging in a practice forbidden or required in the exercise of a plaintiff's religion."[172] If enforced exposure to materials denigrating one's religion does not communicate a "message of disapproval," I cannot imagine what would.

This result is in obvious contrast to the nativity scene cases, in which the Court has recognized a constitutional claim against being exposed to a government message supporting another religion, even when the claimant could easily avoid the exposure. Why is compelled exposure to governmental messages denigrating one's religion constitutional, while avoidable exposure to governmental messages favorable to another religion is not?

Justice O'Connor best illustrates this asymmetry in her application of her own test. In *Lyng*, the free exercise claimants, a small Native American religious minority, complained of governmental actions that were "deeply offensive, and perhaps incompatible with their own search for spiritual fulfillment."[173] One might have expected Justice O'Connor to express concern that the government's destruction of holy sites would communicate the "message" that these members of a religious minority were "not full members of the political community." Instead, she maintained that the believers would have a free exercise claim only if they were "coerced by the Government's action into violating their religious beliefs."[174] "The First Amendment must apply to all citizens alike, and it can give to none of them a veto over public programs."[175] It is very odd that Justice O'Connor considers the "coercion" test so inadequate when the messages conveyed by public programs are *favorable* to religion, but embraces the "coercion" test when the messages are *offensive* to religion. Evidently, the government is free to disparage, but not to speak favorably of, religion.[176]

---

[171] Id at 1063-65 (emphasizing that plaintiffs' objection was to the children's "exposure" to the objectionable materials).

[172] Id at 1069.

[173] *Lyng*, 485 US at 452. See notes 56-61 and accompanying text for a fuller discussion of the facts of the case.

[174] Id at 449.

[175] Id at 452.

[176] Justice O'Connor and some commentators have attempted to make a virtue of this inconsistency, arguing that "[t]o require a showing of coercion, even indirect coercion, as an essential element of an Establishment Clause violation would make the Free Exercise Clause a redundancy." *Allegheny*, 492 US at 628 (O'Connor concurring). Accord Laycock, 27 Wm &

d) The bias among religions. The endorsement test also has an implicit bias in favor of some religions and against others. Messages affirming mainstream religion (and especially "nonsectarian" theism) are likely to be familiar and to seem inconsequential. As Justice O'Connor has interpreted her approach, if a practice is "longstanding" and "nonsectarian," it is unlikely to "convey a message of endorsement of particular religious beliefs."[177] In our culture, most "longstanding" symbols are those associated with Protestant Christianity, and those most likely to be perceived as "nonsectarian" are symbols associated with liberal Protestantism, symbols common to the Jewish and Christian faiths, or symbols incorporating vague references to an unidentified deity.[178] Even so sensitive an observer as Justice Brennan has suggested that governmental religious symbols might be permissible if they are "nondenominational" or if they represent "ceremonial deism."[179] Brennan's suggestion looks very much like endorsement of a civil religion, something serious religionists of all faiths should find deeply troubling.

e) The lack of historical support. Finally, though I will not elaborate the point here, the endorsement test has no support in the history of the Religion Clauses. The generation that adopted the First Amendment viewed some form of governmental compul-

---

Mary L Rev at 922 (cited in note 142); Sullivan, in this volume, 205 (cited in note 5). But properly understood, the two clauses are symmetrical and complementary—not redundant. The Establishment Clause is about the use of governmental power *in favor of* religion (either a particular religion or religion in general), and the Free Exercise Clause is about the use of governmental power *against* religion (either a particular religion or religion in general). There is no persuasive reason to limit one form of interference with religious liberty to coercion while expanding the other to endorsement. The effect of limiting establishment to cases involving coercion may appear to be "redundant" only because of the close relation between the Religion Clauses. Disadvantaging one religion tends to support the rest—and thus could be described as an establishment. See *Larson*, 456 US at 228. Advantaging one religion tends to disadvantage the rest—and thus could be described as a violation of free exercise. See *Hernandez*, 490 US at 680. In that sense, *either* clause could be said to be a redundancy. But this "redundancy" only points out the essential unity of the two Religion Clauses, and no more justifies an asymmetrical expansion of the Establishment Clause than it does an asymmetrical expansion of the Free Exercise Clause.

[177] *Allegheny*, 492 US at 630-31 (O'Connor concurring).

[178] The term "nonsectarian" has a long history as a euphemism for liberal Protestantism, in contradistinction to Roman Catholicism and evangelical Christianity. See McConnell, 1991 U Chi Legal F at 138 (cited in note 33).

[179] *Lynch*, 465 US at 700; 716 (Brennan dissenting). Justice Brennan has stated that "[s]hould government choose to incorporate some arguably religious element into its public ceremonies, that acknowledgement must be impartial; it must not tend to promote one faith or handicap another; and it should not sponsor religion generally over nonreligion." Id at 714. I am not sure what this means, if it means anything at all.

sion as the essence of an establishment of religion.[180] The religious freedom provision of the Virginia Declaration of Rights, long recognized as the precursor to the First Amendment, began with the statement that religion "can be directed only by reason and conviction, not by force or violence."[181] Jefferson argued against the "error" that the "operations of the mind . . . are subject to the coercion of the laws,"[182] and Madison denounced "attempts to enforce [religious obligations] by legal sanction."[183] The early practice in the Republic was replete with governmental proclamations and other actions that endorsed religion in noncoercive ways, without favoring one sect over another. Consider, for example, the resolution of the First Congress requesting the President to "recommend to the people" a day of thanksgiving and prayer;[184] or the scheduling of divine services following the inauguration of President Washington.[185] If noncoercive messages of endorsement raise a constitutional issue at all, they only do so at the fringes of the constitutional principle. The Religion Clauses were not directed against the evil of perceived messages, but of government power. Justice O'Connor's position that endorsement is the "most direct" infringement of the Establishment Clause is without support in history.

f) Suggestions for improvement. The indeterminacies of the endorsement test would not be so serious if it were recognized only as an approach to a specific problem: evaluating government action where the *only* effect on religion is symbolic. In this context, all clear tests sometimes produce wrong results, and all tests that provide tolerable results are irremediably unclear. The endorsement test is more harmful when it is applied to government action that has real, nonsymbolic consequences. There, focusing on the appearance of endorsement only distracts from attention to the real effects of the government action.

---

[180] See Michael W. McConnell, *Coercion: The Lost Element of Establishment*, 27 Wm & Mary L Rev 933 (1986).

[181] Virginia Declaration of Rights, § 16 (1776), reprinted in Philip B. Kurland and Ralph Lerner, eds, 5 *The Founders' Constitution* 70 (Chicago, 1987).

[182] Thomas Jefferson, *Notes on the State of Virginia*, Query 17 (1784), reprinted in id at 79.

[183] James Madison, *Memorial and Remonstrance Against Religious Assessments*, reprinted in *Everson*, 330 US at 70.

[184] Stokes and Pfeffer, *Church and State in the United States* at 87 (cited in note 35).

[185] Id.

Even within the context of government symbols, the endorsement test suffers because it fails to distinguish between two quite different formulations. The most common formulation of the endorsement test asks, in the abstract, whether the government's message will be perceived as endorsing or disapproving religion.[186] But another formulation is that "[t]he endorsement test . . . preclude[s] government from conveying or attempting to convey a message that religion or a particular religious belief is favored or preferred."[187] The difference between these two formulations is important whenever the government "endorses" religion along with many other institutions or ideologies. It would be one thing for Illinois to declare Mormonism the official religion of the state, thus ranking it above the others; it would be another thing for Illinois to honor the accomplishments of the Mormons by creating a public monument in Nauvoo, Illinois.[188] Such a monument would not reflect negatively on the value of other religions.

The latter formulation of the endorsement test is better. The target of the endorsement test should be favoritism or preference, not endorsement. The "equal access" controversy illustrates why. The issue was whether public high schools could constitutionally permit religious student clubs to meet on their premises on the same conditions as other extracurricular student clubs. A typical condition was that a club must "contribute to the intellectual, physical or social development of the students and [be] otherwise considered legal and constitutionally proper."[189] Under the usual formulation of the endorsement test, a school could not constitutionally allow a religious club to meet under this condition, because to do so would convey the school's official opinion that the religious club would "contribute to the intellectual, physical or social development" of the students. That is an endorsement. But under

---

[186] *Lynch*, 465 US at 687-89 (O'Connor concurring).

[187] *Jaffree*, 472 US at 70 (O'Connor concurring). The problem is that Justice O'Connor and other advocates of the endorsement test have not distinguished between these formulations; instead, they have treated them as interchangeable. Compare id at 69 with id at 70. See also *Allegheny*, 492 US at 593-94 (Blackmun) (claiming that concepts of "endorsement" and "favoritism" are the same). This lack of distinction makes application of the endorsement test, even if confined to the domain of government speech, inconsistent and potentially destructive. A consistent reformulation of the endorsement test in terms of favoritism or preference would closely resemble the position of Professor Douglas Laycock, who terms the approach "substantive neutrality." Laycock, 39 DePaul L Rev 993 (cited in note 162).

[188] Nauvoo, Illinois, once the largest and fastest-growing city in Illinois, was founded by Joseph Smith in 1840 and was the center of Mormonism in the country. Sydney Ahlstrom, *A Religious History of the American People* 506 (Yale, 1972).

[189] *Bender v Williamsport Area School Dist.*, 741 F2d 538, 544 (3d Cir 1984), vacated, 475 US 534 (1986) (italics and footnote omitted).

the "favoritism" or "preference" formulation, allowing equal access would be constitutional since it would not "prefer" religion or any particular religion over the alternatives.[190]

Moreover, a "favoritism" or "preference" test would enjoy the historical support that the pure "endorsement" test so conspicuously lacks. The supporters of constitutional protections for religious freedom were insistent that sect equality is an indispensable element of that freedom.[191] To be sure, their principal focus was on differences in material treatment, but it is no great stretch to extend the principle to lesser evils.[192] In this connection, it may be significant that the South Carolina Constitution of 1778 expressly "establishes" the religion of Protestant Christianity, but without any mention of material benefits other than the privilege of incorporation. This theory, however, provides no warrant for individuating government action that merely conveys a message favorable to religion, unless the context is one of actual favoritism or preference.

5. The coercion test.

Another candidate to replace the *Lemon* test is the "coercion test," which has been proposed by Justices Kennedy, White, and

---

[190] For a more difficult example, see Pub L 102-14, 105 Stat 44 (1991). This statute recites (among other things) that the seven Noahide Laws (principles from the Hebrew Bible treated in the Jewish tradition as binding on righteous Gentiles as well as Jews) "have been the bedrock of society from the dawn of civilization"; that "the citizens of this Nation [must not] lose sight of their responsibility to transmit these historical ethical values from our distinguished past to the generations of the future"; that "the Lubavitch movement has fostered and promoted these ethical values and principles throughout the world"; and that "Rabbi Menachem Schneerson, leader of the Lubavitch movement, is universally respected and revered."

Viewed by itself, this statute is an "endorsement" of a particular religion if ever there was one. But in the context of the hundreds of celebratory joint resolutions passed by Congress every year which "endorse" any number of individuals, groups, ideas, and things, who would say that the government has communicated a message that the Lubavitchers are "preferred" over everyone else? The statute is more like the monument in Nauvoo. I am grateful to Robert Katz for bringing this example to my attention.

[191] For a summary of the evidence, see McConnell, 57 U Chi L Rev at 1130-32 (cited in note 107).

[192] SC Const of 1778, Art XXXVIII, reprinted in Benjamin Perley Poore, ed, 2 *Federal and State Constitutions Colonial Charter, and Other Organic Laws of the United States* 16-26 (GPO, 2d ed 1878). The example is not conclusive; one suspects that the provision was understood to authorize legislation providing material benefits, as was the case in neighboring Georgia. Ga Const of 1777, Art LVI, reprinted in Poore, ed, 1 *Federal and State Constitutions* 383 (implying that the legislature has the power to require citizens to contribute to religious teachers "of their own profession").

Scalia, and Chief Justice Rehnquist,[193] and embraced by the Solicitor General in a case before the Supreme Court this Term.[194] As explained by Justice Kennedy, the Establishment Clause contains "two limiting principles: government may not coerce anyone to support or participate in any religion or its exercise; and it may not . . . give direct benefits to religion in such a degree that it in fact 'establishes a [state] religion or religious faith, or tends to do so.' "[195] This approach has the considerable virtue of returning to the historical purposes of the Establishment Clause, and it would redirect attention toward the actual effects of governmental power, rather than toward mere appearances. Perhaps more importantly, it would restore the symmetry between the Religion Clauses that was broken when the Court declared that coercion was an element of the violation of the Free Exercise Clause but not of the Establishment Clause.

One of the first articles I wrote on the Religion Clauses criticized the Court for its unexplained dicta that coercion was *not* an element of an establishment violation.[196] I therefore take some satisfaction in seeing renewed interest in coercion as an aspect of the establishment analysis. But if I had it to do over again, I would take pains to emphasize that the concept of "coercion" cannot, in itself, supply a standard for distinguishing between establishments and nonestablishments, and that it is vital to understand the concept of coercion broadly and realistically. For example, the Court is now being urged to adopt the coercion test in a case involving a public prayer at a junior high school graduation ceremony.[197] I would have thought that gathering a captive audience is a classic example of coercion; participation is hardly voluntary if the cost of avoiding the prayer is to miss one's graduation.[198] Equally seriously, it appears that the content of the prayer was subject to indirect governmental control, which is a species of coercion.[199] For the

---

[193] *Allegheny*, 492 US at 659-62 (Kennedy, joined by Rehnquist, Scalia, and White, concurring in part and dissenting in part).

[194] Brief for the United States as amicus curiae, *Lee v Weisman*, No 90-1014, 15-19.

[195] *Allegheny*, 492 US at 659 (Kennedy concurring in part and dissenting in part) (quoting *Lynch*, 465 US at 678).

[196] McConnell, 27 Wm & Mary L Rev 933 (cited in note 180).

[197] *Weisman v Lee*, 908 F2d 1090 (1st Cir 1990), cert granted, 111 S Ct 1305 (1990).

[198] In defense of the invocation, one could argue that students could avoid participating in the prayer by simply ignoring it (respectfully). This argument may be more persuasive for adults.

[199] Although the clergyman delivering the invocation composed his own prayer, the school officials presented him a copy of guidelines for public prayer prepared by the National Conference of Christians and Jews and advised him that his prayer should be "non-

Court to embrace the coercion test in this form would be a small step back toward permitting the government to indoctrinate children in the favored civil religion of nondenominational theism.[200]

But it is too soon to tell how the Rehnquist Court will interpret the coercion test, or even if it will adopt the test. At this point, I am merely warning that an emphasis on coercion *could* tend toward acquiescence in more subtle forms of governmental power. It is one thing to say that the mere annoyance from seeing the government associate itself with a message of which one disapproves does not violate one's constitutional rights. It is something else to say that government pressure to conform to majoritarian beliefs does not give rise to a constitutional claim because the fist of coercion has been replaced by the subtle pressures and influences of the welfare-regulatory state. If interpreted strictly, the coercion test would increase the power and discretion of majoritarian institutions over matters of religion.

The concept of coercion is based on the distinction between persuasion and force. If a missionary comes to my door to proselytize, I might say that his actions are impertinent or annoying, but I would not say that they were coercive. In the marketplace of ideas, the consumer is assumed to be free. A strict version of the coercion test would apply the same understanding to governmental speech. John Locke, for example, maintained that the government's latitude to use persuasion in matters of religion is no more constricted than the private citizen's:

> It may indeed be alleged, that the magistrate may make use of arguments, and thereby draw the heterodox into the way of truth, and procure their salvation. I grant it; but this is common to him with other men. In teaching, instructing, and redressing the erroneous by reason, he may certainly do what becomes any good man to do. . . . But it is one thing to persuade, another to command; one thing to press with arguments, another with penalties.[201]

---

sectarian." *Weisman v Lee*, 728 F Supp 68, 69 (D RI 1990). It is not likely that a school would select a clergyman who would depart significantly from these guidelines.

[200] A possible example of a noncoercive event is the separate baccalaureate service which some school systems sponsor. Not only can this event be genuinely noncoercive, but by allowing a number of different faiths and denominations to participate, it can avoid the pitfalls of civil religion. The analysis would be different if the school acted in such a way as to create a stigma for non-participation.

[201] John Locke, *A Letter Concerning Toleration*, in Locke, 5 *The Works of John Locke* 11 (Baldwin, 12th ed 1824). John Locke was enormously influential on the Americans' concept of religious liberty, especially on Jefferson's. See McConnell, 103 Harv L Rev at 1430-

Justice Kennedy explicitly rejects this Lockean position. He has stated that by "coercion" he does *not* mean "*direct* coercion in the classic sense of an establishment of religion that the Framers knew."[202] But having rejected the strict version of coercion, which produces results that are relatively clear but wrong, he must supply an alternative definition.

There are three ways in which Kennedy's conception of coercion seems to differ from the strict interpretation. The first is that he would include within the definition "indirect" as well as "direct" coercion.[203] ("Direct" coercion is government action that forbids or compels certain behavior; "indirect" coercion is government action that merely makes noncompliance more difficult or expensive.) It took many years for the Supreme Court to recognize that so-called "indirect" burdens on the free exercise of religion, such as denying unemployment compensation benefits for claimants who refuse to accept employment for religious reasons, are unconstitutional.[204] This development was one manifestation of the decline of the right-privilege distinction in constitutional law generally.[205] Justice Kennedy's statement that the Establishment Clause is not limited to "direct coercion" suggests that he does not intend to resurrect the right-privilege distinction under the Establishment Clause. Evidently he agrees that the doctrine of unconstitutional conditions, in some form, should continue to apply to the Establishment Clause.

---

35 (cited in note 100). In the absence of conflicting evidence, it might be reasonable to impute Locke's understanding to the Framers. But see id at 1443-49 (suggesting why the dominant understanding of religious freedom in America at the time of the adoption of the First Amendment may have been broader than Locke's).

Locke's language may lead some modern readers to think he is talking of the government official's right to speak in his private capacity (for example, a president referring to God in a speech). But in context it is plain that by "magistrate" Locke meant the government—not the government official. See John Locke, *The Second Treatise of Government* ch 18, ¶ 208, in Locke, *Two Treatises of Government* 307, 452 (Mentor, 1960).

[202] *Allegheny*, 492 US at 661 (Kennedy concurring in part and dissenting in part) (emphasis in original). Kennedy's originalist interpretation seems to unravel here. If we depart from coercion "in the classic sense of an establishment of religion that the Framers knew," why invoke the Framers' view that coercion was an element of establishment? To be complete, Kennedy's argument requires an intermediate step that translates the Framers' conception of coercion into a conception that is true to their purposes but usable today.

[203] Id.

[204] The shift came in *Sherbert v Verner*, 374 US 398 (1963) (Free Exercise Clause required South Carolina to give unemployment benefits to Seventh Day Adventists who refused to work on sabbath).

[205] See William W. Van Alstyne, *The Demise of the Right-Privilege Distinction in Constitutional Law*, 81 Harv L Rev 1439 (1968).

The second way in which Justice Kennedy's conception of coercion expands upon the classic conception is that it does not forbid all aid to religion using tax-generated resources.[206] In this respect, the milder version of the coercion test gives more latitude to government action than the strict test. This seems right. There is coercion when the government taxes a citizen and uses the money to support a religious ministry. But when the government is funding a broad array of nonprofit social welfare organizations, secular as well as religious, the courts should not conclude that funding a religious social welfare ministry on equal terms is an establishment of religion, even though the coercion of the taxpayer is identical. The concept of coercion is simply not enough to distinguish between permitted and forbidden uses of tax resources.

While ruling out the extreme "no-aid" position, however, Justice Kennedy has supplied no alternative standard. He says, unhelpfully, that the Establishment Clause does not allow the government to "give direct benefits to religion in such a degree that it in fact 'establishes a [state] religion or religious faith, or tends to do so.' "[207] This leaves unanswered under what circumstances forms of government "benefit" or "tend" to establish a state religion. Indeed, Kennedy's statement implies that this is a question of "degree," turning on the amount of the aid, rather than a question of kind, turning on the structure of incentives created by government action. That cannot be right. Tax exemptions are worth billions of dollars, and do not violate the Establishment Clause so long as they do not favor religious over nonreligious charities. Yet a $100 grant to a church for hiring the minister would almost certainly violate the Establishment Clause. Madison nipped this argument in the bud when he observed that "the same authority which can force a citizen to contribute three pence only of his property for the support of any one establishment, may force him to conform to any other establishment in all cases whatsoever."[208]

Finally, in the sharpest break from the classic conception of coercion, Justice Kennedy maintains that "[s]peech may coerce in

---

[206] See *Kendrick*, 487 US at 624 (Kennedy concurring).

[207] *Allegheny*, 492 US at 659 (Kennedy concurring in part and dissenting in part) (brackets in original) (quoting *Lynch*, 465 US at 678). Does establishment encompass "indirect" coercion but only "direct" benefits? The Supreme Court in past establishment cases has been shamelessly inconsistent in its use of the terms "direct" and "indirect." See Michael W. McConnell, *Political and Religious Disestablishment*, 1986 BYU L Rev 405, 424 n 62. I hope that Justice Kennedy does not embark on a journey back into the morass.

[208] James Madison, *Memorial and Remonstrance Against Religious Assessments*, reprinted in *Everson*, 330 US at 63, 65-66.

some circumstances."[209] He explains that "[s]ymbolic recognition or accommodation of religious faith may violate the Clause in an extreme case,"[210] and goes on to say that he would forbid symbolic government actions that "would place the government's weight behind an obvious effort to proselytize on behalf of a particular religion."[211] This conclusion may be correct, but it has no logical connection to the coercion test. Speech is a necessary part of the coercion process; but as Locke argued, pure speech is not coercive, unless it is coupled with other interferences with liberty.[212]

I agree that Locke was wrong to allow the government to promote orthodoxy through speech, but the weakness in Locke's position is not that speech is "coercive." The problem is that Locke overlooks crucial distinctions between governmental and private activity: First, that the state has far superior means by which to advocate its view of spiritual truth, which are not "in common with other men"; second, that those means are supplied by the citizens through other coercive powers including taxation, thus enabling the state, unlike the private citizen, to press its views on religion with the wherewithal of dissenters;[213] and third, that the state is limited to performing those functions authorized by the people, and there is no reason to suppose that a religiously pluralistic people—especially a religiously serious pluralistic people—would entrust the function of religious instruction to political authorities. For these reasons, Justice Kennedy is on solid ground in arguing that our government does not have free rein to proselytize.

After Kennedy has made this concession, however, scant difference remains between his coercion-proselytization test and O'Connor's endorsement test (at least if the latter is given its "favoritism" interpretation). To be sure, in *Allegheny*, the creche-menorah case, the two Justices reached somewhat different conclusions with their dueling standards.[214] But the differences in result

---

[209] *Allegheny*, 492 US at 661 (Kennedy concurring in part and dissenting in part).
[210] Id.
[211] Id.
[212] See text accompanying note 201.
[213] I do not mean to imply that government speech always has these properties. Sometimes the means used by the government are similar to the means available to all citizens and sometimes the government speaks without marginal cost that must be borne by the taxpayers. In these instances, the argument against government speech is much weaker. For example, a state university press, which is otherwise indistinguishable from many private publishers, should be treated as a private speaker for Establishment Clause purposes.
[214] *Allegheny*, 492 US at 626-27 (O'Connor concurring), 664-65 (Kennedy concurring in part and dissenting in part). Compare *Mergens*, 110 S Ct 2356, in which the two Justices also applied their competing standards but reached the same conclusion.

had nothing to do with the differences in legal standard. O'Connor and Kennedy simply perceived the symbols in different ways.

Justice Kennedy began with the proposition that the government may participate in celebrations of religious holidays by "installing or permitting festive displays"[215] of some sort. While this proposition might well be challenged on a theoretical level (indeed, academics who oppose religious holiday displays typically reject it), all nine Justices seem to take this as a starting point, disagreeing only about whether specifically religious symbols may be included. Kennedy then reasoned that

> [if] government is to participate in its citizens' celebration of a holiday that contains both a secular and a religious component, enforced recognition of only the secular aspect would . . . signal not neutrality but a pervasive intent to insulate government from all things religious.[216]

This argument, as I understand it, does not focus on the lack of coercion, but on the meaning of neutrality in the context of a mixed religious-secular holiday.

Justice Kennedy's implied baseline for evaluating the neutrality of the display is the way in which the holiday is celebrated in the private sphere, presumably untainted by governmental involvement. There, we find a mixture of religious and nonreligious elements, nativity scenes as well as Santa Clauses. Implicitly, Kennedy suggests that a wholly secular governmental display would deviate from this baseline by emphasizing secular elements and extirpating religious elements. Secularism is not neutrality.[217]

Justice O'Connor, while disapproving the nativity scene, voted to uphold the menorah. She explained that "[a] reasonable observer would . . . appreciate that the combined display is an effort to acknowledge the cultural diversity of our country and to convey tolerance of different choices in matters of religious belief or nonbelief by recognizing that the winter holiday season is celebrated in diverse ways by our citizens."[218] Her position is not incompatible with Justice Kennedy's, since both recognize that religious symbols do not always have the effect of excluding or stigmatizing nonadherents; in some contexts they can "send[] a message of pluralism and freedom to choose one's own beliefs," to use Justice

---

[215] *Allegheny*, 492 US at 663 (Kennedy concurring in part and dissenting in part).

[216] Id at 663-64.

[217] See text accompanying notes 320-27 for a further discussion of this point.

[218] *Allegheny*, 492 US at 635-36 (O'Connor concurring).

O'Connor's words.[219] A menorah on public property during the Hannukah season has much the same symbolic impact as a festival on Mexican Independence Day, a parade on St. Patrick's Day, or a solemn memorial on Martin Luther King's birthday. These displays *could* be seen as exclusionary by non-Mexicans, non-Irish, and non-African Americans, but they are not. These celebrations affirm that those whose symbols are displayed are a welcome and important part of the heritage of this pluralistic land, without implying that others are any less welcome or important.

Justice O'Connor's defense of the menorah display suggests, in common with Justice Kennedy's analysis of the nativity scene, that under some circumstances the inclusion of religious elements is actually preferable to a wholly secular display, since a secular display could not communicate the message of "tolerance of different choices in matters of religious belief."[220] Just as Kennedy implicitly took issue with the proposition that secularism is equivalent to neutrality, O'Connor implicitly recognized that secularism is not equivalent to pluralism.

If there is a difference between the Justices, it seems that O'Connor is more concerned about neutrality among different religions,[221] while Kennedy is more concerned about neutrality between religion and nonreligion. As to that difference, a combination of their perspectives would be better than either view alone. The key issue is the social function that the challenged symbol serves in the life of the community. If the function is to promote a particular view by stigmatizing or excluding nonadherents, neither Kennedy nor O'Connor would permit the symbol. If the function is simply one of celebration, and if all significant elements in the community, including other religions, are welcome to use public property for appropriate celebrations of their own, both Kennedy and O'Connor would permit it.

To be sure, the coercion test (in contrast to the endorsement test) will eliminate claims by persons whose only complaint is that the government action irritates or offends them; being irritated is not the same as being influenced ("proselytized") by government action. Thus the coercion test is slightly narrower than the endorsement test. But the coercion test would treat such claims

---

[219] Id at 634.

[220] Id at 636.

[221] See id at 627-28 (criticizing Justice Kennedy's coercion test on the ground that it "fails to take account of the numerous more subtle ways that government can show favoritism to particular beliefs").

under the Establishment Clause like claims of stigmatic injury under other provisions of the Constitution. Racial minorities who allege that they have been stigmatized by government action (but who suffer no other injury) cannot sue under the Equal Protection Clause;[222] religious individuals who allege that their faith has been denigrated by government action have no claim under the Free Exercise Clause.[223] Indeed, the general rule is that plaintiffs who suffer no personal injury "other than the psychological consequence presumably produced by observation of conduct with which one disagrees" lack standing to sue.[224] Justice O'Connor's explanation that citizens of a religious persuasion other than that endorsed by the government would perceive that they are "not full members of the political community"[225] applies with equal strength to equal protection and free exercise claims, but the Court has recognized that the costs of recognizing such claims outweigh the benefit.[226] There is no evident reason to treat establishment claims with greater solicitude.

Perhaps the most serious objection to both the coercion and the endorsement test is that they address cases of symbolic action only. Neither test provides reliable guidance for the vastly more important cases in which government action actually affects the practice of religion: cases involving government funding of social welfare and educational activities of religious and nonreligious private organizations; exceptions from generally applicable laws and other forms of accommodation of the religious needs of individuals and institutions; threats to the autonomy of religious organizations with respect to their structure, leadership, and members; discriminatory treatment of minority religions by regulators and common law courts; and so forth. The coercion test is useless in these cases, because they all involve government coercion of some sort. To the extent that the endorsement and coercion tests overemphasize the symbolic cases, they retard understanding and postpone doctrinal reform. The *Lemon* test is a serious problem, but not for reasons addressed by either of these most prominent alternatives.

---

[222] See *Allen v Wright*, 468 US 737, 755 (1984); *Moose Lodge No. 107 v Irvis*, 407 US 163, 166 (1972).

[223] The requirement of a "burden" on the practice of religion as a predicate to a free exercise claim eliminates mere complaints of psychological discomfort. See text accompanying notes 67-70.

[224] *Valley Forge College v Americans United*, 454 US 464, 485 (1982).

[225] *Lynch*, 465 US at 688 (O'Connor concurring).

[226] Interestingly, Justice O'Connor authored opinions rejecting claims of stigmatic injury in those contexts. *Allen*, 468 US 737; *Lyng*, 485 US 439.

6.	Establishment implications of *Smith*.

The Rehnquist Court, with its respect for legal formalism, is unlikely to repeat the Warren and Burger Courts' mistake of reading the Religion Clauses as inconsistent principles,[227] especially since the author of *Smith*, Justice Scalia, is the most systematic thinker on the Court. Scalia is not likely to remain content with a jurisprudence in which the Court, in his words, has "not yet come close to reconciling *Lemon* and our Free Exercise cases."[228] Since *Smith* now represents the Court's interpretation of the Free Exercise Clause, it is to be expected that the Court will soon reinterpret the Establishment Clause in a manner consistent with *Smith*. What would that be?

The most logical step would be to read both clauses as embodying a formal neutrality toward religion. Under *Smith*, the Free Exercise Clause precludes government action that is "directed at," or "singles out," religion for unfavorable treatment. The Establishment Clause analog would be to preclude government action that singles out religion for favorable treatment. This position has long been advocated by Justice Scalia's sometime University of Chicago colleague, Philip Kurland. Kurland contends that the two Religion Clauses should be "read as a single precept that government cannot utilize religion as a standard for action or inaction because these clauses prohibit classification in terms of religion either to confer a benefit or to impose a burden."[229] Until 1990, the Supreme Court had rejected this position as to both Clauses. In *Smith*, the Court adopted this position as to the Free Exercise Clause. Perhaps its extension to the Establishment Clause will be the next shoe to drop.

Logical though this move might be, it is highly unlikely. The formal neutrality position would make unconstitutional all legislation that explicitly exempts religious institutions or individuals from generally applicable burdens or obligations. Yet the theory of *Smith* is that exemptions are a form of beneficent legislation, left to the discretion of the political branches. The problem with requiring exemptions under the Free Exercise Clause is not that ex-

---

[227] See Section I.

[228] *Edwards*, 482 US at 617 (Scalia dissenting).

[229] Philip B. Kurland, *Religion and the Law* 18 (Aldine, 1962); Philip B. Kurland, *The Irrelevance of the Constitution: The Religion Clauses of the First Amendment and the Supreme Court*, 24 Vill L Rev 3, 24 (1978). This position has recently been revived by Professor Mark Tushnet. See Mark Tushnet, *"Of Church and State and the Supreme Court": Kurland Revisited*, 1989 S Ct Rev 373.

emptions violate the principle of neutrality, but that enforcement under the Constitution would give judges too much discretion: "it is horrible to contemplate that federal judges will regularly balance against the importance of general laws the significance of religious practice."[230] Noting that "a number of States have made an exception to their drug laws for sacramental peyote use,"[231] the Court commented: "to say that a nondiscriminatory religious-practice exemption is permitted, or even that it is desirable, is not to say that it is constitutionally required."[232]

Smith thus *rejects* the formal neutrality position under the Establishment Clause. This is not surprising. One of the positive developments in the Supreme Court over the past ten years has been its growing acceptance of the legitimacy of accommodation of religion. The Court has accepted special treatment of religion where it facilitates the free exercise of religion, even if it is not constitutionally compelled under the Free Exercise Clause.[233] The conservatives on the Court have been the most enthusiastic supporters of this development. It would be most peculiar if the conservative wing of the Court were to repudiate the doctrine of accommodation now that it has achieved wide acceptance.

If *Smith* does not augur adoption of the formal neutrality interpretation, what does it mean for the Establishment Clause? The answer is not obvious. Other than his suggestion to eliminate the purpose prong of the *Lemon* test, Justice Scalia has not set forth a comprehensive theory of the Establishment Clause, even in his numerous separate dissents and concurrences. But while Scalia has not offered a comprehensive theory, his opinions do show a clear pattern. In each of them, Scalia suggests a modification of the *Lemon* test that is one step more deferential to the government than the *Lemon* test requires. In *Edwards*, he proposed eliminating the purpose prong.[234] In *Kendrick*, he joined an opinion by Justice Kennedy suggesting elimination of the rule that direct government funding may not go to pervasively sectarian organizations.[235] In *Texas Monthly*, he argued that tax exemptions could be skewed in favor of religious organizations.[236] In each case, he

---

[230] *Smith*, 110 S Ct at 1606 n 5.

[231] Id at 1606.

[232] Id.

[233] See Michael W. McConnell, *Accommodation of Religion: An Update and a Response to the Critics*, (Geo Wash L Rev, forthcoming 1992).

[234] See notes 129-32 and accompanying text.

[235] *Kendrick*, 487 US at 624-25 (Kennedy concurring).

[236] *Texas Monthly*, 489 US at 29-44 (Scalia dissenting).

left in place the often unprincipled doctrinal categories of the
Lemon test, modifying them only to the extent of easing the standard.[237] This pattern suggests that Justice Scalia is more concerned about cabining the judicial role in cases involving religion
than in developing a comprehensive substantive theory.

But as discussed above, deference to majoritarian decisionmaking is out of keeping with the spirit of the Religion Clauses.
The great danger of revising Establishment Clause doctrine in
light of *Smith* is replicating *Smith*'s vices of excessive deference to
governmental decisionmaking and bias in favor of mainstream religion. These vices may be preferable to the secularist bias of the
Warren and Burger Courts, but not by much.

III. A Religion Clause Jurisprudence for a Pluralistic Nation

A jurisprudence of the Religion Clauses must begin with a
proper understanding of the ideals of the Clauses and the evils
against which they are directed. We can then formulate legal doctrine. The great mistake of the Warren and Burger Courts was to
embrace the ideal of the secular state, with its corresponding tendencies toward indifference or hostility to religion. The mistake of
the emerging jurisprudence of the Rehnquist Court is to defer to
majoritarian decisionmaking. A better understanding of the ideal
of the Religion Clauses, both normatively and historically, is that
they guarantee a pluralistic republic in which citizens are free to
exercise their religious differences without hindrance from the
state (unless necessary to important purposes of civil government),
whether that hindrance is for or against religion.

The great evil against which the Religion Clauses are directed
is government-induced homogeneity—the tendency of government
action to discourage or suppress the expression of differences in
matters of religion. As Madison explained to the First Congress,
"the people feared one sect might obtain a preeminence, or two

---

[237] The ensuing doctrinal confusion is especially conspicuous in *Kendrick*, in which Justices Scalia and Kennedy joined Chief Justice Rehnquist's opinion for a five-Justice majority. There the Court rejected a facial challenge to the Adolescent Family Life Act under the
effects and entanglement prongs of the *Lemon* test, on the ground that the religiously affiliated grant recipients had not been found to be "pervasively sectarian." *Kendrick*, 487 US at
612 (effects), 616 (entanglement). This was what distinguished *Kendrick* from cases like
Grand Rapids and *Aguilar*. But in their concurring opinion, Scalia and Kennedy argued
that the "juridical category" of "pervasively sectarian institutions" was not "well-founded."
Id at 624. Thus, they vitiated the doctrinal argument for the majority, without substituting
another.

combine together, and establish a religion to which they would compel others to conform."[238] As such authorities of the day as Thomas Jefferson and Adam Smith argued, government-enforced uniformity in religion produced both "indolence" within the church and oppression outside the church.[239] Diversity allows each religion to "flourish according to the zeal of its adherents and the appeal of its dogma,"[240] without creating the danger that any particular religion will dominate the others. At some times in our history, and even in some isolated regions of the country today, the great threat to religious pluralism has been a triumphalist majority religion. The more serious threat to religious pluralism today is a combination of indifference to the plight of religious minorities and a preference for the secular in public affairs. This translates into an unwillingness to enforce the Free Exercise Clause when it matters, and a hypertrophic view of the Establishment Clause.

When scrutinizing a law or governmental practice under the Religion Clauses, the courts should ask the following question: is the purpose or probable effect to increase religious uniformity, either by inhibiting religious practice (a Free Exercise Clause violation) or by forcing or inducing a contrary religious practice (an Establishment Clause violation), without sufficient justification? The baseline for these judgments is the hypothetical world in which individuals make decisions about religion on the basis of their own religious conscience, without the influence of government. The underlying principle is that governmental action should have the minimum possible effect on religion, consistent with achievement of the government's legitimate purposes.

Virtually everything government does has *some* effect on religion, however indirect. No doctrinal formulation can eliminate the difficult questions of judgment in determining when the government's purpose is sufficiently important, when its chosen means are sufficiently tailored, or when the effect of the action on religious practice is sufficiently minor or indirect. But we *can* be clear about the ideal toward which a jurisprudence of the Religion Clauses should be directed.

---

[238] Speech of James Madison (Aug 15, 1787), in Gales, ed, 1 *Annals of Congress* at 758 (cited in note 6).

[239] See Thomas Jefferson, *Notes on the State of Virginia*, Query 17 at 214-20 (Trenton, 1784); Adam Smith, *The Wealth of Nations* 622-44 (Ward Lock, 1838).

[240] *Zorach v Clausen*, 343 US 306, 313 (1952).

A.   A Pluralist Approach to the Free Exercise Clause

In free exercise cases, the pluralist approach would be something like the approach of the Warren and Burger Courts—albeit with more vigorous and consistent enforcement. This is not to say that the "compelling interest test" was without problems. The test was excessively abstract and failed to define its key operative concepts. It provided little guidance to legislatures or lower courts about what burdens on religious practice triggered heightened scrutiny, or about how to evaluate the governmental interest. The first requirement for scholarship in this field, should *Smith* be overturned, is the development of more precise definitions of the elusive concepts of "burden" and "compelling governmental interest."[241]

Apart from the question of generally applicable laws, at issue in *Smith*, there are two other currents of change in free exercise jurisprudence, one from the right and one from the left. From the right comes the movement to resuscitate the right-privilege distinction by limiting the Free Exercise Clause to outright "prohibitions" of religious practice. From the left comes the movement to transform the free exercise right into a right of personal autonomy or self-definition. Both should be confronted and resisted.

1.   "Prohibitions" of religious practice and conditions on government aid.

In *Lyng*, the Court emphasized that the "the crucial word in the constitutional text is 'prohibit.' "[242] From this, the Court concluded that the Free Exercise Clause does not limit how the government controls its property, even when, as in *Lyng*, the government owns holy sites indispensable for religious worship.[243] Thus the Forest Service could build a road over an American Indian holy site and "virtually destroy" the religion.[244] By the same reasoning, the Free Exercise Clause would not limit the government's exercise of other nonregulatory powers, even if the government's action or inaction made the exercise of religion difficult or impossible. The Free Exercise Clause would apply only when the govern-

---

[241] For more extended discussion of this problem, with tentative suggestions for its solution, see McConnell, 57 U Chi L Rev at 1141-49 (cited in note 107); Michael W. McConnell and Richard A. Posner, *An Economic Approach to Issues of Religious Freedom*, 56 U Chi L Rev 1, 38-54 (1989).

[242] *Lyng*, 485 US at 451.

[243] Id at 451-52.

[244] Id at 451.

ment made religious practice unlawful (and even then, under *Smith*, the Clause would not apply if the prohibition were generally applicable and not directed at religion). Presumably, the government could draft men and women into the Army and send them to distant lands, and then refuse to provide for their religious worship needs; it could incarcerate prisoners without providing chapels or chaplains. The government could require all citizens to pay taxes to support welfare or educational programs, but then condition the benefits from the programs on rules which conflict with religious principles. These would not be "prohibitions" and so would not be coerced.

Lyng thus raises the central question surrounding the enforcement of constitutional rights under a welfare state: are the conditions which the government attaches to the use and distribution of resources subject to the same constitutional limitations as direct governmental legislation? Specifically, does the word "prohibit" in the First Amendment limit the Free Exercise Clause to "negative" legislation—direct prohibitions—aimed at religion? I am not persuaded that a 1791 audience necessarily would have understood the term "prohibitions" so narrowly;[245] but even if it would have, we cannot fulfill the purposes of the Free Exercise Clause under modern conditions without adapting to the vastly expanded role that government now plays in our lives. Like every other constitutional protection, the Free Exercise Clause should be understood to be violated by unconstitutional conditions as well as by direct restraints.[246]

---

[245] See McConnell, 103 Harv L Rev at 1486-88 (cited in note 100).

[246] See Richard Epstein, *The Supreme Court, 1987 Term—Foreword: Unconstitutional Conditions, State Power, and the Limits of Consent*, 102 Harv L Rev 4 (1988); Sullivan, 102 Harv L Rev 1413 (cited in note 94); *Unconstitutional Conditions Symposium*, 26 San Diego L Rev 175 (1989).

Professor Sullivan's excellent *Unconstitutional Conditions* article places her in the forefront of the academic movement to recognize the denial of government "benefits" as a form of coercion. She should therefore be in agreement with my position here, which is simply an application of unconstitutional conditions doctrine to the Religion Clauses. But her substantive commitment to ensuring a "secular public moral order," Sullivan, in this volume, 198 (cited in note 5), overcomes her commitment to a consistent theory of constitutional rights. She argues that the exercise of religion may be subjected to financial "disincentives," id at 213, even though it may not be directly coerced. It is ironic that Sullivan criticizes both the Supreme Court and me for "head[ing] backward toward an eighteenth-century focus on intentional force and away from a twentieth-century understanding that the state has many subtler but equally effective means for controlling religious incentives." Id at 222. My position is precisely the opposite: I contend that the twentieth-century understanding should be applied in both free exercise and establishment contexts. See notes 193-206 and accompanying text (criticizing the narrow conception of coercion under the Establishment Clause); notes 242-46 and accompanying text (criticizing the narrow conception of

2. Free exercise and the rights of conscience.

On the other hand, some would expand the scope of the Free Exercise Clause by treating the free exercise right as a right of personal autonomy or self-definition. Rather than understanding religion as a matter over which we have no control—the demands of a transcendent authority—it has become common to regard religion as valuable and important only because it is *what we choose*. In the words of Justice Stevens, "religious beliefs worthy of respect are the product of free and voluntary choice by the faithful."[247] This treats religion as an individualistic choice rather than as the irresistible conviction of the authority of God.[248]

The most obvious manifestation of this shift is the move to extend free exercise protections to any and all claims arising from "conscience," understood as the reflective judgment of the individual. David A. J. Richards perhaps best exemplifies this move: he argues that constitutional protections for religious freedom are ultimately based on "respect for the person as an independent source of value."[249] Relying on this premise, Richards argues that it is illegitimate to distinguish between the free exercise of religion and the free exercise of any other personal belief or value. Free exercise becomes an undifferentiated right of personal autonomy.

This symposium is not the occasion for discussing whether some other provision of the Constitution might protect an undifferentiated right of personal autonomy. But if we are to understand the theory and principle of the Religion Clauses, we must know what differentiates "religion" from everything else. The essence of "religion" is that it acknowledges a normative authority independent of the judgment of the individual or of the society as

---

prohibition under the Free Exercise Clause). It is Professor Sullivan who advocates a freedom for "religious subcultures to withdraw from regulation" but *not* to be protected from the discriminatory administration of the welfare state. Sullivan, in this volume, 222 (cited in note 5). She advocates a twentieth-century constitutionalism for most rights but an eighteenth-century constitutionalism for religion.

[247] *Jaffree*, 472 US at 53 (footnote omitted).

[248] For a thorough discussion of the Supreme Court's tendency to view religion in terms of choice, see Williams and Williams, 76 Cornell L Rev 769 (cited in note 168). For purposes of the ensuing discussion, I will use the term "God" to denominate the ultimate object of religious devotion, since this is a familiar term. I do not mean to exclude nontheistic religions from the definition of "religion" for purposes of the First Amendment. See Stanley Ingber, *Religion or Ideology: A Needed Clarification of the Religion Clauses*, 41 Stan L Rev 233 (1989).

[249] David A.J. Richards, *Toleration and the Constitution* 142 (Oxford, 1986).

a whole.[250] Thus, the Virginia Declaration of Rights defined religion as the "duty which we owe to our Creator, and the manner of discharging it."[251] Madison said that the law protects religious freedom because the duties arising from spiritual authority are "precedent both in order of time and degree of obligation, to the claims of Civil Society."[252] The Free Exercise Clause does not protect autonomy; it protects obligation.[253]

Of course, the Free Exercise Clause protects religious "choice" in the sense that it recognizes the individual believer as the only legitimate judge of the dictates of conscience; authentic religion may not be coerced by human authority. But the theological concept of "soul liberty," from which this principle derives, is not predicated on any belief in the intrinsic worthiness of individual judgment (which, after the fall and before the acceptance of God's grace, is unregenerate). The concept is based on the view that the relations between God and Man are outside the authority of the state.

Thus, in early challenges to Sunday closing laws under state free exercise clauses, courts consistently rejected claims that it violated the right of conscience for the state to designate Sunday as the day of rest, even though plaintiffs persuasively argued that determining which day is the sabbath is a matter of religious convic-

---

[250] See *United States v Macintosh*, 283 US 605, 633-34 (1931) (Chief Justice Hughes, joined by Justices Holmes, Brandeis, and Stone, dissenting) ("The essence of religion is belief in a relation to God involving duties superior to those arising from any human relation.").

There is an interesting and important parallel to the analysis of homosexual rights, reflected in the general shift from the term "sexual preference" to the term "sexual orientation." It used to be thought that sexuality was entitled to constitutional protection because each person should be free to choose the objects of his or her affection. Now it is more often argued that sexuality is entitled to constitutional protection because it is *not* a choice, but something inherent in the person's nature, which cannot be changed.

[251] Virginia Declaration of Rights of 1776, § 16, reprinted in Poore, ed, 2 *Federal and State Constitutions*, 1909 (cited in note 192).

[252] James Madison, *Memorial and Remonstrance Against Religious Assessments*, reprinted in *Everson*, 330 US at 64.

[253] The Establishment Clause is more a protection for personal autonomy, since it forbids the government to coerce or induce religious observance whether or not the complainant has religious belief to the contrary. It thus protects the right to choose, without regard to any spiritual obligation. But there is no sentiment among liberal commentators to broaden the definition of "religion" under the Establishment Clause, because this broader definition would disable the government from promoting desirable secular values. See Tribe, *American Constitutional Law* § 14-6 at 1185 (cited in note 8). Liberals thus typically treat secular humanism as a "religion" for purposes of free exercise claims (draft exemption, for example) but not for purposes of establishment claims. See id at 1187-88.

tion and conscience.[254] But the same courts distinguished cases in which the plaintiff's own religious doctrine *required* him to work on Sunday.[255] The distinction is subtle but important: free exercise does not give believers the right to choose for themselves to override the socially-prescribed decision; it allows them to obey spiritual rather than temporal authority.

A modern version of this debate is taking place over the claim of a free exercise right to obtain an abortion.[256] In the Utah case now underway,[257] plaintiffs claim that the decision whether to have an abortion is an issue of religiously-informed conscience, and that the state's prohibition of abortions is therefore a violation of free exercise. But plaintiffs do not allege that the law prevents them from complying with the dictates of their own religious persuasion, since their religions do not purport to lay down any such dictates. The plaintiffs assert the right to choose for themselves as autonomous individuals, not the right to conform their conduct to religious law.

This claim must be distinguished from a claim that, under some circumstances, the pregnant woman's religion *requires* her to get an abortion. (Orthodox Jews, for example, believe that an abortion is mandatory if necessary to save the mother's life.[258]) The latter claim, if sincere, is a legitimate free exercise claim, which the government must accommodate unless it has a sufficiently compelling interest in preventing abortion.[259] The Free Exercise Clause does *not* protect the freedom of self-determination (with respect to abortion, working on Sunday, or anything else); it does protect the

---

[254] See *Commonwealth v Wolf*, 3 Serg & Rawle 47 (Pa 1817); *Specht v Commonwealth*, 8 Pa 312 (1848).

[255] *Wolf*, 3 Serg & Rawle at 50; *Specht*, 8 Pa at 326. Similarly, the claim in *Braunfeld* did not rest on the proposition that each individual is entitled to choose whether to work on Sunday, but on the fact that enforced closure on Sunday made it economically infeasible for Saturday sabbatarians to close on Saturday as well, as their religion dictates. *Braunfeld*, 366 US at 602.

[256] See, for example, Ronald Dworkin, *Unenumerated Rights: Whether and How Row Should Be Overruled*, in this volume, 381, 419 (arguing that the Free Exercise Clause protects the right to choose an abortion).

[257] *Jane L. v Bangerter*, 91-C-345 G (D Utah).

[258] David M. Feldman, *Marital Relations, Birth Control, and Abortion in Jewish Law* 275 (Schocken, 1968).

[259] Whether the state's interest in protecting fetal life in cases in which the life of another human being would thereby be threatened is "compelling" is beyond the scope of this Article. On abortion and free exercise more generally, see W. Cole Durham, Jr., Edward McGlynn Gaffney, Douglas Laycock, and Michael W. McConnell. *For the Religious Freedom Restoration Act*, First Things 42, 43 (Mar 1992).

freedom to act in accordance with the dictates of religion, as the
believer understands them.

B. A Pluralist Approach to the Establishment Clause

A pluralist approach to the Establishment Clause requires
more explication, since the Supreme Court has never had a satisfactory Establishment Clause doctrine. The Court's first Establishment Clause case in this century was in 1947,[260] and thereafter the
Court fell quickly into the secularist interpretations that I have
already criticized, most notably the three-pronged *Lemon* test.[261]
Unlike the *Lemon* test, a pluralistic approach would not ask
whether the purpose or effect of the challenged action is to "advance religion," but whether it is to foster religious uniformity or
otherwise distort the process of reaching and practicing religious
convictions. A governmental policy that gives free rein to individual decisions (secular *and* religious) does not offend the Establishment Clause, even if the effect is to increase the number of religious choices. The concern of the Establishment Clause is with
governmental actions that constrain individual decisionmaking
with respect to religion, by favoring one religion over others, or by
favoring religion over nonreligion.

The modern welfare-regulatory state wields three forms of
power that potentially threaten religious pluralism: the power to
regulate religious institutions and conduct, the power to discriminate in distributing state resources, and control over institutions of
culture and education. Each of these powers can, and frequently
does, promote homogeneity of all kinds, and especially with regard
to religion. Too often, however, the Court has interpreted the Establishment Clause to oppose pluralism rather than to foster it by
treating as unconstitutional (1) efforts by the political branches to
reduce the degree to which the regulatory power of the state interferes with the practice of religion, (2) decisions to include religious
individuals and institutions within public programs on an equal
and nondiscriminatory basis, and (3) manifestations of religion
within the publicly-controlled cultural and educational sector, even
in contexts where competitive secular ideologies are given an equal
place. Thus, instead of protecting religious freedom from the incursions of the welfare-regulatory state, the Establishment Clause all
too often was interpreted to exacerbate the problem.

---

[260] *Everson*, 330 US 1.
[261] See Section I.

In these areas, the Supreme Court is moving in a generally positive direction, and it may not be long before the Establishment Clause is no longer a serious obstacle to either accommodation of religious exercise or the equal treatment of religious institutions. The precedential roots of this pluralistic approach, however, go back to the later years of the Burger Court, and especially to opinions by Justices Brennan and Powell in three important cases: *McDaniel v Paty*,[262] *Widmar v Vincent*,[263] and *Witters v Department of Services*.[264] In this section, I will discuss those decision and their importance to the development of the pluralist approach. I will then address the ways in which the Establishment Clause impeded solutions to the modern problems of control over religion through regulation, spending, and cultural influence, and describe the prospects for improvement in recent cases.

1. The roots of the pluralist approach: *McDaniel*, *Widmar*, and *Witters*.

   a) McDaniel v Paty. In *McDaniel*, the Court struck down a provision of the Tennessee Constitution that disqualified clergymen from legislative office.[265] The court below had upheld the provision because it would "prevent those most intensely involved in religion from injecting sectarian goals and policies into the lawmaking process, and thus [would] avoid fomenting religious strife or the fusing of church with state affairs."[266] The plurality of the Supreme Court had no difficulty rejecting this theory on the ground that it lacked any "persuasive support."[267]

Justice Brennan, however, voted to invalidate the exclusion on more interesting and wide-ranging grounds. First, as a doctrinal matter, Justice Brennan maintained that "government may not use religion as a basis of classification for the imposition of duties, penalties, privileges or benefits" *except* when it does so "for pur-

---

[262] 435 US 618 (1978).

[263] 454 US 263 (1981).

[264] 474 US 481 (1985). While these opinions provide a firm and consistent basis for a revised jurisprudence for the Religion Clauses, they failed to gain widespread recognition, in part because Justices Brennan and Powell conspicuously failed to apply the approach in other cases. This gave the impression of confusion and inconsistency rather than of doctrinal advance.

[265] *McDaniel*, 435 US at 627-29.

[266] Id at 636 (Brennan concurring).

[267] *McDaniel*, 435 US at 629.

poses of accommodating our traditions of religious liberty."[268] He further explained his idea of "accommodation":

> [G]overnment may take religion into account . . . to exempt, when possible, from generally applicable governmental regulation individuals whose religious beliefs and practices would otherwise thereby be infringed, or to create without state involvement an atmosphere in which voluntary religious exercise may flourish.[269]

Under this conception, the government must be "religion-blind" *except* when it accommodates religion—i.e., removes burdens on independently adopted religious practice. Brennan's was the first clear statement of the accommodation principle in any Supreme Court opinion.[270]

Second, the Brennan opinion was noteworthy for its treatment of the role of religion in public life. The Tennessee provision was based on the proposition that religion is an inherently sectarian and divisive influence, which must be radically privatized in order to protect the democratic process. This can be seen as a reflection of the Deweyite philosophy, discussed above,[271] which molded Supreme Court thinking during the Warren and Burger periods and underlay the movement to secularize the public sphere. Its principal doctrinal incarnation was the "political divisiveness" element of the entanglement test. The Court explained in *Lemon*:

> Ordinarily political debate and division, however vigorous or even partisan, are normal and healthy manifestations of our democratic system of government, but political division along religious lines was one of the principal evils against which the First Amendment was intended to protect. The potential divisiveness of such conflict is a threat to the normal political process. . . . The history of many countries attests to the hazards of religion's intruding into the political arena.[272]

Without noting its roots in *Lemon*, Justice Brennan took sharp issue with this reasoning in *McDaniel*, stating that it "manifest[ed]

---

[268] Id at 639 (Brennan concurring) (footnote omitted).

[269] Id (footnote omitted).

[270] In *Zorach v Clausen*, the Court upheld an accommodation of religion in the form of a "released time" program in the public schools. 343 US 306, 311-13 (1952). (A released time program permits public schools to release students during the school day so that they may leave the school grounds and go to religious centers for religious instruction or devotional exercises.) But the opinion did not outline a comprehensive accommodation doctrine.

[271] See notes 45-51 and accompanying text.

[272] *Lemon*, 403 US at 622-23 (citations omitted).

patent hostility toward, not neutrality respecting, religion."[273] He denied that the divisiveness of religious entry into political debate is a "threat" to the democratic process. Rather, he said that "religious ideas, no less than any other, may be the subject of debate which is 'uninhibited, robust, and wide-open,' " reminding his readers that "church and religious groups in the United States have long exerted powerful political pressures on state and national legislatures, on subjects as diverse as slavery, war, gambling, drinking, prostitution, marriage, and education."[274] Brennan took the view that religions are among the many points of view held by people of the United States, and that all such points of view are entitled to equal respect and an equal place in the public councils. "Religionists no less than members of any other group enjoy the full measure of protection afforded speech, association, and political activity generally."[275] He warned against using the Establishment Clause "as a sword to justify repression of religion or its adherents from any aspect of public life."[276] Brennan thus saw religion not as a threat to pluralism, but as an essential and legitimate part of it.

b) Widmar v Vincent. In *Widmar*, a public university banned religious student groups from meeting on campus—a privilege extended to all other student groups—on the theory that allowing them to meet would "advance religion" in violation of the Establishment Clause. The university also cited the state constitution's policy of enforcing an even stricter separation of church and state than is required by the federal Constitution.[277] In a sense, the university's policy had some validity: it *does* advance religion to give religious groups free and convenient meeting space; presumably, universities provide facilities for student groups because this will advance the interchange of ideas at their meetings. But Justice Powell's opinion for the majority of the Court recognized that this understanding of "advancement" would commit the government to a policy of discriminating against religion. Since the "forum is available to a broad class of nonreligious as well as religious speakers," Powell noted, any benefit to religion is purely "incidental."[278] Like Brennan's concurrence in *McDaniel*, the decision treated reli-

---

[273] *McDaniel*, 435 US at 636 (Brennan concurring).
[274] Id at 640, 641 n 25.
[275] Id at 641.
[276] Id (footnote omitted).
[277] *Widmar*, 454 US at 270-72, 275.
[278] Id at 274.

gion as an appropriate and legitimate element in the mix of ideas in American life.

    c) Witters v Department of Services. In *Witters*, a blind man challenged the refusal of the Washington Department of Services for the Blind to pay for his program of vocational education, to which he was otherwise statutorily entitled. The State contended that to pay for his religious education would violate the Establishment Clause, because his chosen profession was the ministry and his course of study consisted of a degree program at a Bible college.[279] But the Supreme Court unanimously rejected the state's argument. Although the Bible college at which Witters matriculated was a pervasively sectarian institution and many of the courses for which he was registered contained specifically religious content, the Court held that it would not violate the Establishment Clause for the state to pay the bill.[280] Employing reasoning similar to that in *Widmar*, the opinion for the Court stressed that "[a]ny aid provided under Washington's program that ultimately flows to religious institutions does so only as a result of the genuinely independent and private choices of aid recipients" and "is in no way skewed towards religion."[281] Moreover, the Court noted that the program "creates no financial incentive for students to undertake sectarian education," since the benefits are the same no matter which educational path the student chooses.[282] In short, "the decision to support religious education is made by the individual, not by the State."[283] On the other hand, the opinion for the Court implied that if "any significant portion of the aid expended under the Washington program as a whole [were to] end up flowing to religious education," the program might well be unconstitutional.[284]

    Justice Powell, however—in an opinion apparently supported by four other Justices and hence commanding majority support[285]—argued that the decision should not turn on how many

---

[279] *Witters*, 474 US at 483.

[280] Id at 489.

[281] Id at 487-88 (footnote omitted).

[282] Id at 488.

[283] Id.

[284] Id.

[285] Chief Justice Burger and Justice Rehnquist joined Powell's concurring opinion. Id at 490. Justice O'Connor quoted and endorsed the key passage in Powell's opinion. Id at 493 (O'Connor concurring). Justice White stated that he "agree[s] with most of Justice Powell's concurring opinion with respect to the relevance of *Mueller v Allen*, to this case," while hinting that he adheres to a still more expansive view of the right of the government to aid private schools. Id at 490 (White concurring) (citation omitted).

students choose religious or secular education. According to Powell, "state programs that are wholly neutral in offering educational assistance to a class defined without reference to religion do not violate" the effects prong of the *Lemon* test.[286] The difference between the two opinions is narrow but important. The opinion for the Court in *Witters* was willing to accept religion as one element in the public culture, on nondiscriminatory terms, but *only* when religion was an insignificant minority. Justice Powell, by contrast, was concerned only that the *terms* of the program be "wholly neutral";[287] it did not matter what choices the recipients made.

This line of cases escapes the mistakes of both the emerging Rehnquist Court jurisprudence and that of the Warren and Burger Courts. The decisions did not defer to majoritarian decisionmaking. Indeed, in each of the three cases, the government lost. Justice White's plea in *Widmar* that the States should "be a good deal freer to formulate policies that affect religion in divergent ways"[288] did not attract a single additional vote. Instead, the decisions uphold the principle—to use Madison's language—that religious citizens have "full and equal rights."[289] The opinions also abjure the secularist orientation so common in the other opinions of the Warren and Burger Courts. Whether in the political sphere (Brennan in *McDaniel*), in the interchange of ideas exemplified by the university (*Widmar*), or in the area of government financial assistance (*Witters*), these opinions treat religious perspectives as welcome and legitimate parts of our pluralistic public culture. Although the opinion for the Court in *Witters* hinted that the government-supported sector must remain *predominantly* secular, the opinions were unanimous in rejecting the idea that it must be *entirely* secular. In these opinions, the Justices seem to be moving toward the salutary position that the degree of secularism and of religiosity must be left to the people, not dictated by the Constitution, and not subject to the influence or control of the legislature.

---

[286] Id at 490-91 (Powell concurring).

[287] Neutrality is a subtle and contested idea. For elaborations of this concept of neutrality, see Michael W. McConnell, *Neutrality Under The Religion Clauses*, 81 Nw U L Rev 146 (1986); Laycock, 39 DePaul L Rev 993 (cited in note 162).

[288] *Widmar*, 454 US at 282 (White dissenting).

[289] James Madison (speech of Jun 8, 1789), in Gales, ed, 1 *Annals of Congress* 451 (cited in note 6).

2. Coping with the regulatory state.

As Justice Brennan recognized in *McDaniel*, it is sometimes
necessary for the government to "take religion into account" in order to ensure that government regulation does not infringe religious freedom.[290] While always true to some extent, this has become far more important as government regulation has penetrated
so much more deeply into both private life and the operations of
the non-profit sector. As discussed above, the Rehnquist Court's
adoption of a formal neutrality approach to the Free Exercise
Clause has eliminated constitutional protection for religious individuals and institutions whose practices run contrary to the secular
rules of the modern state. But the Court's more deferential approach to the Establishment Clause has the opposite effect: it permits the political branches wide latitude to soften the effect of regulation on religious practice through appropriate accommodations.
Fortunately, the value of religious liberty is well recognized in the
political sphere, and accommodations are not uncommon, even for
the benefit of relatively small religious groups.

Under the Burger Court, legislative accommodations of religion were treated with suspicion, and not infrequently invalidated
on flimsy pretexts. The Court never held that accommodation is
unconstitutional in principle, but the *Lemon* test made accommodations difficult to defend. Accommodations of religion have no
"secular purpose," if "secular purpose" means a purpose solely relating to nonreligious concerns. The effect of accommodations is to
make the practice of religion easier, and therefore, in all
probability, more widespread. And some accommodations require
the government to make judgments regarding religious beliefs and
needs. This is easily characterized as "entanglement."

Thus, in *Thornton v Caldor, Inc.*,[291] the Court overturned a
Connecticut law accommodating the needs of sabbath-observing
employees on the ground that the supposedly "absolute" language
of the statute could lead to extreme and unconstitutional burdens
on others. This deviated from the usual principles of constitutional
adjudication, since on an "as applied" basis the burden was not
unreasonable and on a "facial" basis the statute was plainly susceptible to constitutional applications. And in *Wallace v Jaffree*,[292]
the Court overturned an Alabama statute accommodating the

---

[290] *McDaniel*, 435 US at 639 (Brennan concurring).
[291] 472 US 703 (1985).
[292] 472 US 38 (1985).

needs of those public school students who wished to begin the
school day with prayer by instituting a moment of silence. Although agreeing that a moment of silence is not generally unconstitutional, the Court overturned this particular statute on the basis
of an out-of-context quotation from a single legislator, uttered after the statute had passed, that the statute was intended to restore
"voluntary prayer" to the Alabama schools. Since the full context
of the legislators' remarks indicated a legitimate purpose[293] (and
since there was no reason to impugn the intentions of the rest of
the legislature), striking down the law was at best an overreaction.
The message conveyed by these decisions was that accommodations would be evaluted with a critical eye.

More recent cases suggest a different posture. I have already
discussed *Corporation of Presiding Bishop v Amos*, in which the
Court unanimously upheld a statute exempting religious organizations from the religious nondiscrimination regulations of Title VII,
which had been struck down by a lower court under *Lemon*. And
in *Smith*, the Court stated in dictum that an exemption for the
sacramental use of peyote would be permissible under the Establishment Clause. *Texas Monthly, Inc. v Bullock* presents a more
ambiguous picture. A divided Court, issuing four inconsistent opinions, struck down a Texas law exempting religious publications
from a sales tax. As Justice Scalia's dissenting opinion demonstrated, a court sympathetic to accommodations could have upheld
the statute on the ground that it resembled what the Court had
held to be constitutionally required in two cases in the 1930s. As
even Justice Blackmun commented, the Court's approach appeared to elevate establishment concerns to the subordination of
free exercise.[294] But the opinion for the plurality—unlike the opinions in *Jaffree* and *Caldor*—took pains to emphasize that properly
drafted accommodations are constitutionally permissible, even
when they go beyond the dictates of the Free Exercise Clause.[295]
Thus, the combined effect of *Amos*, *Smith*, and *Texas Monthly* is
to affirm the legitimacy of exemptions and accommodations
designed to protect religious individuals or organizations from the
infringements of the regulatory state.[296]

---

[293] See id at 86-87 (Burger dissenting).

[294] *Texas Monthly*, 109 S Ct 890, 906 (1989) (Blackmun concurring).

[295] Id at 899-900.

[296] For a more comprehensive analysis of the recent accommodation decisions and justification for the doctrine, see McConnell, (Geo Wash L Rev, forthcoming 1992) (cited in note
233).

3. Equal access to public resources.

One of the most important eighteenth-century abuses against which the no-establishment principle was directed was mandatory support for churches and ministers. This system was support for religion *qua* religion; it singled out religion as such for financial benefit. Secular institutions, activities, and ideologies received no comparable form of assistance. Religious assessments were eliminated in Virginia, Maryland, and most of the southern states by 1789, and in New England by 1834.[297] As the Supreme Court has noted, the struggle against religious assessments was a central event in the development of the philosophy of the Religion Clauses of the First Amendment.[298]

In the ensuing 150 years, the government began to assist in a wide range of charitable and educational activities, formerly left to private (frequently religious) endeavor. Frequently, the government chose to enter these fields not by setting up its own agencies, but by making financial contributions to private institutions that supplied services to the public. Common examples included higher education, hospitals, and orphanages. An advantage of private administration over public was that it preserved diversity, since different institutions would bring a different perspective and approach to the activity. The ultimate beneficiaries thus had a degree of choice. A student interested in a Catholic education could go to a Catholic college; a patient needing to keep to a kosher diet could go to a Jewish hospital; a dying mother wanting her child to be raised as a Protestant could designate a Protestant orphanage. A citizen need not forfeit public benefits as a condition to exercising the religious option. In its only case involving government aid to a religious institution prior to 1947, *Bradfield v Roberts*, the Court held that the religious affiliation of a Catholic hospital was "wholly immaterial" to its right to receive government funds.[299]

When government funding of religiously-affiliated social and educational services became a constitutional issue in the late 1940s, the Court properly looked back at the religious assessment controversy. But it missed the point. The Court did not notice that the assessments against which the advocates of disestablishment inveighed were discriminatory in favor of religion. Instead, the Court concluded that taxpayers have a constitutionally protected

---

[297] See McConnell, 103 Harv L Rev at 1436-37 (cited in note 100).
[298] *Everson*, 330 US at 13.
[299] 175 US 291, 298 (1899).

immunity against the use of their tax dollars for religious purposes.[300] This immunity necessitated discrimination against religion, thus turning the neutrality principle of the assessment controversy on its head.

The Court's analysis failed to recognize the effect of the change in governmental roles. When the government provides no financial support to the nonprofit sector *except for churches*, it aids religion. But when the government provides financial support to the entire nonprofit sector, religious and nonreligious institutions alike, on the basis of objective criteria, it does *not* aid religion. It aids higher education, health care, or child care; it is neutral to religion. Indeed, to deny equal support to a college, hospital, or orphanage on the ground that it conveys religious ideas is to penalize it for being religious. It is a penalty whether the government excludes the religious institution from the program altogether, as in *Lemon*,[301] *Nyquist*,[302] and *Grand Rapids*,[303] or requires the institution to secularize a portion of its program, as in *Tilton v Richardson*,[304] *Roemer*,[305] or *Hunt v McNair*.[306]

The underlying issue is precisely the same as that in *Sherbert v Verner*. The question in *Sherbert* was whether the state could deny benefits to an individual otherwise eligible for unemployment compensation on the ground that she refused to make herself available for work on her sabbath day.[307] The Court recognized that the denial of a benefit, under such circumstances, is equivalent to a "fine" for adhering to her religious convictions.[308] Justice Douglas, a ferocious opponent of nondiscriminatory "aid" to religious institutions, well understood the point in *Sherbert*:

> The fact that government cannot exact from me a surrender of one iota of my religious scruples does not, of course, mean that I can demand of government a sum of money, the better to exercise them. For the Free Exercise Clause is written in

---

[300] See *Everson*, 330 US at 16 ("No tax in any amount, large or small, can be levied to support any religious activities or institutions, whatever they may be called, or whatever form they may adopt to teach or practice religion."). See also *Flast v Cohen*, 392 US 83, 103-04 (1968).

[301] 403 US at 606-07.

[302] 413 US at 761-69.

[303] 473 US at 375-81.

[304] 403 US 672, 676-84 (1971).

[305] 426 US at 755-67.

[306] 413 US 734, 736-49 (1973).

[307] 374 US at 403.

[308] Id at 404.

terms of what the government cannot do to the individual, not in terms of what the individual can exact from the government.

These considerations, however, are not relevant here. If appellant is otherwise qualified for unemployment benefits, payments will be made to her not as a Seventh-day Adventist, but as an unemployed worker. . . . Thus, this case does not involve the problems of direct or indirect state assistance to a religious organization—matters relevant to the Establishment Clause, not in issue here.[309]

The same point applies to nondiscriminatory support for hospitals, colleges, orphanages, and schools. The government supports them not as religious institutions but as colleges, hospitals, orphanages, and schools. To deny benefits to an otherwise eligible institution "forces [it] to choose between following the precepts of [its] religion and forfeiting benefits, on the one hand, and abandoning one of the precepts of [its] religion in order [to obtain support], on the other hand."[310] If the Court was correct to abandon the right-privilege distinction under the Free Exercise Clause, and I believe it was, the Court was illogical and inconsistent to hold to the right-privilege distinction under the Establishment Clause. Equal access to public resources is not a "privilege," and it does not violate the Establishment Clause.

This inconsistent application of the right-privilege distinction is the most fundamental cause of the contradiction between the *Lemon* test and the Free Exercise Clause. *Lemon* assumes an outmoded conception of government aid, which treats equal access as "aid." The Free Exercise Clause, at a minimum (that is, after *Smith*), prohibits discrimination against an institution solely on the ground that it is religious.[311] The *Lemon* test outlaws nondiscriminatory treatment and the Free Exercise Clause requires it.

We must therefore reject the central animating idea of modern Establishment Clause analysis: that taxpayers have a constitutional right to insist that none of their taxes be used for religious purposes. Properly conceived, the taxpayer has a right to insist that the government not give tax dollars to religion *qua* religion, or in a way that favors religion over nonreligion, or one religion over another. But the taxpayer has no right to insist that the govern-

---

[309] Id at 412-13 (Douglas concurring).

[310] *Sherbert*, 374 US at 404.

[311] *Smith*, 110 S Ct at 1599.

ment discriminate against religion in the distribution of public funds. In this pluralistic country, taxpayers come in all varieties of belief and unbelief. To tax everyone, but to dispense money only to secular organizations, is to use government's coercive power to disadvantage religion.[312]

Moreover, it follows that if religious organizations have a constitutional right to equal access to public programs, the government may not condition their access on rules which burden their practice of religion, unless the rules are closely related to the purposes of the program. For example, if the government made grants to organizations providing vocational training, the government could not, in effect, exclude Jewish organizations by requiring all recipients to remain open on Saturday, unless Saturday operations could be persuasively shown to be necessary to the successful conduct of the program. Similarly, if the government provided vouchers for education, the government could not exclude Catholic schools by requiring that recipient schools distribute birth control devices to the students, unless birth control distribution is necessary to education. The test is the same as in any other free exercise case. The threat of loss of funding is an "indirect" burden on the exercise of religion, and cannot be allowed unless there is an overriding governmental purpose. Conditions on spending are indistinguishable in principle from direct regulation.

This does not mean that all participants in government programs have an unlimited constitutional right to engage in religious speech in the context of the program. The test is whether participants have the right to engage in political or other controversial secular speech.[313] Religious speech rights are not superior; nor are they inferior. Thus, in government programs in which grantees are paid to convey a particular message to the public (and no other),

---

[312] See Michael McConnell, *Unconstitutional Conditions: Unrecognized Implications for the Establishment Clause*, 26 San Diego L Rev 255 (1989). Professor Sullivan agrees that there "can be little doubt" that religious speech restrictions on recipients of public funds "would be a disincentive to the exercise of unfettered choice," Sullivan, in this volume, 213 (cited in note 5), and thus would constitute an unconstitutional condition under free speech precedents. Id. She rescues the conditions from this conclusion on the ground that they are "necessitated by the Establishment Clause," which she reads as a "constitutional requirement not to support religious teaching with public funds." Id at 212. But she never explains why she adopts a reading of the Establishment Clause that appears to violate fundamental principles of freedom of speech (let alone free exercise of religion), when it is possible to avoid this conflict by simply interpreting the Establishment Clause as forbidding government preference for religion over nonreligion (or one religion over another), as was done in *Everson*.

[313] In the context of public forum analysis, Justice Stevens advocates a similar position. See *Mergens*, 110 S Ct at 2384 (Stevens dissenting).

religious speech restrictions are permissible and may even be required. In *Bowen v Kendrick*,[314] for example, the federal government made grants to various public and private organizations, including some affiliated with religion, for the purpose of conducting programs to promote responsible attitudes toward sex among adolescents. The government forbade grantees to "teach or promote religion" in the course of the funded programs, and the Supreme Court held that this restriction is mandated by the Establishment Clause. Since this was not a program that permitted free speech about controversial topics of the grantees' choice, but instead one based on structured curricula approved in advance by the federal agency, any claim of free speech rights was properly rejected.[315]

By contrast, it would not be permissible to restrict the rights of artists receiving grants under the National Endowment for the Arts to produce art on religious themes. If artists can convey controversial messages about politics and culture without censorship, it would be unconstitutional to deny them a similar right when they convey messages about religion. Nor was it permissible for the Virginia Supreme Court to deny eligibility for tax-exempt bonds to Liberty Baptist College on the basis of its religious teaching.[316] If secular institutions enjoy the academic freedom to determine the content of their teaching, so should Liberty Baptist. Nor should a college professor be forbidden to discuss his religious beliefs in class or in after-class meetings, when other members of the faculty are free to discuss their personal and professional opinions.[317] Nor should a high school valedictorian's speech be censored on account of its religious content when speakers in other years are permitted to address controversial issues of their choice.[318] That each of these examples has been resolved the other way by lower courts or administrators demonstrates how far we have to go before achieving genuine religious pluralism.

---

[314] 487 US 589 (1988).

[315] The case is similar to *Rust v Sullivan*, 111 S Ct 1759 (1991), in which the government provides grants to groups for the encouragement of pre-conception family planning, and bars speech encouraging abortion.

[316] *Phan v Commonwealth of Virginia*, 806 F2d 516 (4th Cir 1986).

[317] This is the issue in *Bishop v Aronov*, 926 F2d 1066 (11th Cir 1991), petition for cert pending, No 91-286. I am counsel for the petitioner.

[318] *Guidry v Calcasieu Parish School Bd*, 9 Religious Freedom Rptr 118 (E D La 1989), affirmed, 897 F2d 181 (5th Cir 1990).

4.   Government influence over education and culture.

A final threat to religious autonomy arises from governmental control over many of the institutions of education and culture. In an earlier era, when these were under private control, the government's voice was far less prominent in the marketplace of ideas. The influence of government is likely to foster homogeneity with respect to religion, since it is likely to reflect a broadly acceptable, majoritarian view of religion—in short, to support a civil religion.

If it were possible to insist that government be "neutral" in its speech about religion, this would be highly desirable. Unfortunately, in the context of government speech—unlike regulation and spending—"neutrality" is an unattainable ideal.[319] Whenever the government communicates to the people, it will favor some ideas and oppose others. The only truly effective way to reduce government influence on our religious lives through its speech would be to reduce the governmental presence in our cultural and educational institutions. Requirements of accommodation and equal treatment can solve (or at least greatly mitigate) the problems created by the regulatory and spending powers, but there are no real solutions to the problems created by the government's vastly increased role in the culture.

There are three baselines from which the neutrality of government speech might theoretically be evaluated. The first is complete secularization of the public sphere. If the "neutral" position were one in which religion is completely relegated to the private sphere of family and the institutions of private choice, any reference to religion in the public sphere would be a departure from neutrality. This is the position advocated by Professor Sullivan, who says that the solution to the government speech problem is "simple" if we would only "[b]anish public sponsorship of religious symbols from the public square."[320]

Serious enforcement of this position would bring about a radical change in the cultural fabric of the nation. Initial litigation has focused on what have been called "distinctively religious elements,"[321] such as creches, crosses, and menorahs. But multitudes of other symbols, deeply engrained in our public culture, are no less distinctively religious. Christmas trees are symbols of Christmas, too, and many non-Christians (not to mention some Chris-

---

[319] This is my principal area of disagreement with Professor Laycock. See Laycock, 39 DePaul L Rev 893 (cited in note 162).

[320] Sullivan, in this volume, 207 (cited in note 5).

[321] *Lynch*, 465 US at 711 (Brennan dissenting).

Religious Freedom   189

tians) consider them inappropriate for secular institutions.[322] Certainly the star on top of the tree is a religious symbol. And if the star is a religious symbol, so are the pretty lights along the sidewalks of Michigan Avenue in downtown Chicago. Although most of us do not recognize the symbolism, these lights signify the advent of what the gospel of John calls the "true light that enlightens every man."[323] Thanksgiving conveys a religious message, as do the speeches of Abraham Lincoln and the Reverend Martin Luther King, Jr.—which would have to be censored before they could be made a part of public celebrations. Many of our cities have religious names; many of our historic sites reflect religious aspects of the culture. To strip public property of all religious elements (when public property is used to convey secular messages of every kind and description) would have a profoundly secularizing effect on the culture.

The problem with the secularization baseline is that it is not neutral in any realistic sense. A small government could be entirely secular, and would have little impact on culture. But when the government owns the street and parks, which are the principal sites for public communication and community celebrations, the schools, which are a principal means for transmitting ideas and values to future generations, and many of the principal institutions of culture, exclusion of religious ideas, symbols, and voices marginalizes religion in much the same way that the neglect of the contributions of African American and other minority citizens, or of the viewpoints and contributions of women, once marginalized those segments of the society. Silence about a subject can convey a powerful message. When the public sphere is open to ideas and symbols representing nonreligious viewpoints, cultures, and ideological commitments, to exclude all those whose basis is "religious" would profoundly distort public culture.

A useful thought experiment is to imagine what a "neutral" policy toward religion would look like in a socialist state, where the government owned *all* the land and *all* the means of mass communication. In such a world, the government would be constitutionally *required* to erect and maintain churches, synagogues, temples, mosques; to hire priests, ministers, imans, and rabbis; to dissemi-

---

[322] Oddly, the Court has treated Christmas trees as such a "preeminently secular symbol" that they actually *drain* nearby religious symbols of their religious content. *Allegheny*, 492 US at 617, 634. Yet every year the Justices' own law clerks raise an internal fuss over the Christmas tree in the Great Hall of the Supreme Court building

[323] John 1:9 (Revised Standard Version).

nate religious tracts and transmit religious programming; and to display religious symbols on public land at appropriate occasions. If it did not, there would be no opportunity for the practice of religion as traditionally understood. Indeed, a "neutral" state would attempt to replicate the mix of religious elements that one would expect to find if the institutions of culture were decentralized and private—much as the government must do today in the prisons and the military.[324] No one would contend, in a socialist context, that a policy of total secularization would be neutral.

To be sure, we do not live in a socialist state. But we have socialized many of the important avenues for public interchange and the transmission of culture. Within that sphere, total secularization is not a "neutral" answer, either. Even Justice Brennan has warned that too zealous an elimination of religious symbols might appear as "a stilted indifference to the religious life of our people."[325] Thus, there is a growing consensus that the public schools have erred in eliminating from the curriculum virtually all discussion of how religion has influenced history, culture, philosophy, and ordinary life.[326] For the most part, this decision by the schools has reflected a cowardly tendency to avoid anything controversial, but the effect is to create a distorted impression about the place of religion in public and private life. As psychologist Paul Vitz has explained, excluding religious references biases the curriculum "because it makes only the liberal, secular positions familiar and plausible. [Other] positions are made to appear irrelevant, strange, on the fringe, old-fashioned, reactionary."[327]

Some argue for a totally secular public sphere not on the spurious ground that this would be "neutral," but on the ground that the First Amendment committed the United States to a certain public philosophy: a liberal, democratic, secular "civil religion," which is entitled to a preferred status—even a monopoly status—in our public culture.[328] As an historical assertion about

---

[324] Of course, any such attempt would surely fall short of a genuinely decentralized, private pluralism. That is one reason (of many) why liberty is best protected under a regime of limited government.

[325] *Lynch*, 465 US at 714 (Brennan dissenting).

[326] For a summary of research showing that public school curriculum systematically neglects the subject of religion, see McConnell, 1991 U Chi Legal F 123 (cited in note 33).

[327] Paul C. Vitz, *Censorship: Evidence of Bias in Our Children's Textbooks* 77-78 (Servant Books, 1986).

[328] This is the crux of my disagreement with Professor Kathleen Sullivan in this debate. See Sullivan, in this volume, 198-201 (cited in note 5). See also John Mansfield, *The Religion Clauses of the First Amendment and the Philosophy of the Constitution*, 72 Cal L Rev 847 (1984), and Dworkin, in this volume, 381 (cited in note 256).

the meaning of the First Amendment, however, this position is plainly false. Virtually the entire spectrum of opinion at the time of the adoption of the First Amendment expected the citizens to draw upon religion as a principal source of moral guidance for both their private and their public lives.[329] The Establishment Clause prevented the federal government from interfering with the process of opinion formation by privileging a particular institution or set of religious opinions,[330] but it left the citizens free to seek guidance about contentious questions from whatever sources they might find persuasive, religious as well as secular.[331] As a normative proposition, the secularization position must depend on an argument that secular ideologies are superior to religious. But some secular ideologies are divisive, exclusionary, and evil; just as some religious ideologies are tolerant, open-minded, and beneficent (and vice-versa). The republican solution is to leave the choice of public philosophy to the people. There is a great irony in the claim that liberal, democratic, nonsectarian positions have a superior constitutional status to religious positions. Such a position is illiberal (since it denies the people's right to determine what will bring about the good life), undemocratic (since it conflicts with the dem-

---

[329] A few statements from leading figures of the day will give a sense of their attitude. Madison thought that "belief in a God All Powerful wise & good, is so essential to the moral order of the World & to the happiness of man, that arguments which enforce it cannot be drawn from too many sources." Letter from James Madison to Frederick Beasley (Nov 20, 1825), in Gaillard Hunt, ed, 9 *The Writings of James Madison* 229, 230 (G. P. Putnam's Sons, 1910). Washington warned: "Of all the dispositions and habits which lead to political prosperity, religion and morality are indispensable supports. . . . And let us with caution indulge the supposition that morality can be maintained without religion." George Washington, Farewell Address (Sep 17, 1796), reprinted in Henry Commager, ed, *Documents of American History* 169, 173 (Prentice-Hall, 9th ed 1973). Adams maintained that "[o]ur Constitution was made only for a moral and religious people. It is wholly inadequate to the government of any other." Letter from John Adams to the officers of the First Brigade of the Third Division of the militia of Massachusetts (Oct 11, 1798), in Charles Francis Adams, ed, 9 *The Works of John Adams* 228, 229 (Little Brown, 1854).

[330] Thus, Jefferson said that the national government is "interdicted by the Constitution from intermeddling with religious institutions, their doctrines, discipline, or exercises." Letter from Thomas Jefferson to the Reverend Mr. Millar (Jan 23, 1808), in H.A. Washington, ed, 5 *The Writings of Thomas Jefferson* 236, 236-37 (H.W. Derby, 1861). Said Madison: "Religion flourishes in greater purity, without than with the aid of Gov[ernmen]t." Letter from James Madison to Edward Livingston (Jul 10, 1822), in Hunt, ed, 9 *The Writings of James Madison* 98, 103 (cited in note 329). Oliver Ellsworth posited that "[c]ivil government has no business to meddle with the private opinions of the people." Oliver Ellsworth, *Landholder, No. 7* (Dec 17, 1787), reprinted in Kurland and Lerner, eds, 4 *The Founders' Constitution* 639, 640 (cited in note 181).

[331] The prohibition on religious tests for office, US Const, Art VI, ensured that the public councils would be open to persons of all faiths. The government may no more extract a promise that officeholders will decide questions according to secular philosophies than it could extract a promise of adherence to a religious philosophy.

ocratic choices of the people), and sectarian (since it is based on a narrow point of view on religious issues).

A second possible baseline is the degree of religious expression that an "objective observer" would deem appropriate in the public sphere—Justice O'Connor's endorsement test. But this actually states no baseline at all; it is merely a restatement of the question. These issues are passionately contested within our culture. For example, to some (heavily represented in legal academia), inclusion of a nativity scene in a Christmas display on government property is an act of blatant intolerance. With equal sincerity, others (less well represented in legal academia), maintain that deliberate exclusion of a nativity scene from a Christmas display places the prestige and influence of the government in favor of materialism and against religion.[332] The "endorsement test" is justified on the ground that it will ensure that no class of citizens defined by religious perspective is made to feel like an "outsider" to the political community.[333] If so, it is necessary to pay serious attention to both points of view. Both sides are sincere, and both consider themselves in danger of being marginalized. Unfortunately, it is not possible for both to prevail, and there is no objective standpoint for choosing one over the other (that is, no standpoint that both could, in principle, accept). The "objective observer" does not, therefore, offer even a theoretically possible baseline for the evaluation of neutrality.

The indeterminacy of this approach might not, in itself, be a sufficient basis for rejecting it. Other constitutional doctrines are almost equally indeterminate. The special problem of this approach is that it exacerbates religious division and discord by heightening the sense of grievance over symbolic injuries. When religious symbols are upheld, the judicial imprimatur adds to the injury (especially when the standard applied is that of the putative "objective observer"—implying that the losers are not "objective"). When religious symbols are driven from the public square, this alienates a different but equally sincere segment of the population.

---

[332] The record in *Lynch* shows that the mayor and many of the residents of Pawtucket felt this way. The mayor stated at the trial that "for him, as well as others in the city, the effort to eliminate the nativity scene from Pawtucket's Christmas celebration 'is a step towards establishing another religion, non-religion that it may be.'" 465 US at 700 (Brennan dissenting). The district court found that residents viewed the lawsuit against the creche as "'an attack on the presence of religion as part of the community's life.'" Id at 700 n 6 (quoting 525 F Supp 1150, 1162 (D RI 1981)).

[333] This is the justification offered by Justice O'Connor. *Lynch*, 465 US at 688 (O'Connor concurring).

Does anyone believe that the annual outbreak of lawsuits over the symbols of the December holidays advances the cause of religious harmony or civic understanding? When a constitutional doctrine aggravates the very problem it is supposed to solve, without offering hope for resolution, it should be replaced.[334]

The third possible baseline is the state of public culture in the non-government-controlled sector. If the aspects of culture controlled by the government (public spaces, public institutions) exactly mirrored the culture as a whole, then the influence and effect of government involvement would be nil: the religious life of the people would be precisely the way it would be if the government were absent from the cultural sphere. In a pluralistic culture, this is the best of the possible understandings of "neutrality," since it will lead to a broadly inclusive public sphere, in which the public is presented a wide variety of perspectives, religious ones included. If a city displays many different cultural symbols during the course of the year, a nativity scene at Christmas or a menorah at Hannukah is likely to be perceived as an expression of pluralism rather than as an exercise in Christian or Jewish triumphalism. If the curriculum is genuinely diverse, exposing children to religious ideas will not have the effect of indoctrination. Individuals should be permitted to opt out of participating in those religious (or anti-religious) aspects of the program that are objectionable to them on grounds of conscience, but there is no reason to extirpate all religious elements from the entire curriculum. The same is true of the public culture: opt-out rights should be freely accorded, but the general norm should be one of openness, diversity, and pluralism.

If members of minority religions (or other cultural groups) feel excluded by government symbols or speech, the best solution is to request fair treatment of alternative traditions, rather than censorship of more mainstream symbols. If a government refuses to cooperate with minority religious (and other cultural) groups within the community, there may be a basis for inferring that the choice of symbols was a deliberate attempt to use government influence to promote a particular religious position.

Courts should not encourage the proliferation of litigation by offering the false hope that perfect neutrality can be achieved through judicial fine-tuning. Judicial scrutiny should be reserved for cases in which a particular religious position is given such public prominence that the overall message becomes one of conformity

---

[334] Thus, the best resolution of cases in which the plaintiff's claim of injury is weak is not to uphold religious symbols on the merits, but to deny standing to sue.

rather than pluralism. Certainly they should not allow official acts that declare one religion, or group of religions, superior to the rest, or give official sponsorship to symbols or ceremonies that are inherently exclusionary.[335] Particular care should be taken where impressionable children are involved. But courts should be cautious about responding to particular contestable issues in isolation. It is impossible to tell whether a particular event, symbol, statement, or item is an indication of diversity or of favoritism if it is viewed without regard to wider context.[336]

CONCLUSION

The religious freedom cases under the First Amendment have been distorted by the false choice between secularism and majoritarianism, neither of which faithfully reflects the pluralistic philosophy of the Religion Clauses. Instead, the Free Exercise and Establishment Clauses should protect against government-induced uniformity in matters of religion. In the modern welfare-regulatory state, this means that the state must not favor religion over nonreligion, nonreligion over religion, or one religion over another in distributing financial resources; that the state must create exceptions to laws of general applicability when these laws threaten the religious convictions or practices of religious institutions or individuals; and that the state should eschew both religious favoritism and secular bias in its own participation in the formation of public culture. This interpretation will tolerate a more prominent place for religion in the public sphere, but will simultaneously guarantee religious freedom for faiths both large and small.

---

[335] Thus, I agree with the Seventh Circuit's holding that a city may not sponsor a Roman Catholic mass as part of an Italian festival. See *Doe v Village of Crestwood*, 917 F2d 1476 (7th Cir 1990), petition for cert pending, no 1573. The same would not be true of the re-creation of an historic sermon in colonial Williamsburg.

[336] For example, the depiction of a church among the aspects of community life in the city seal of Rolling Meadows, Illinois should not have been held unconstitutional. See *Harris v City of Zion*, 927 F2d 1401 (7th Cir 1991).

Religion and Liberal Democracy

Kathleen M. Sullivan†

It has been a while since Catholics were tarred and feathered or Mormons dispatched by militias and mobs on forced marches to Utah. True, hostility to minority religions has not disappeared entirely: Reverend Sun Myung Moon did time in federal prison for tax crimes, Shree Bhagwan Rashneesh left the country one step ahead of the law, and the International Society for Krishna Consciousness lies largely bankrupt, to name a few examples. But contemporary claims of religious oppression are typically subtler than claims of outright persecution.

For example, Professor Michael McConnell, my opponent in this debate, laments what he depicts as a relentless pattern of "secularization" in which "serious religion—religion understood as more than ceremony, as the guiding principle of life"—has been "shoved to the margins of public life."[1] This secularization, he suggests, is a result of the increasing displacement of religious functions by an expanding welfare state, coupled with two kinds of error by the Supreme Court: (1) it has granted too few religious exemptions from public laws under the Free Exercise Clause; and (2) it has too often excluded religion from public programs in the name of preventing establishment. Professor McConnell would read both Religion Clauses as requiring government to respect a single "baseline": "the hypothetical world in which individuals make decisions about religion on the basis of their own religious conscience, without the influence of government."[2] On this view, the Court should mandate more exemptions and find fewer establishments in order to maintain religious pluralism.

I disagree with both the diagnosis and the cure. To begin, I find any picture of rampant secularization difficult to square with numerous indicators of religion's lively role in contemporary Amer-

---

† Professor of Law, Harvard Law School; Visiting Professor of Law, Stanford Law School. This Article was prepared for *The Bill of Rights in the Welfare State: A Bicentennial Symposium*, held at The University of Chicago Law School on October 25-26, 1991.

[1] Michael W. McConnell, *Religious Freedom at a Crossroads*, in this volume, 115, 126, 127.

[2] Id at 169.

ican social and political life. To name but a few examples, powerful Roman Catholic Archbishops such as John Cardinal O'Connor in New York and Bernard Cardinal Law in Boston exercise substantial political power from the pulpit—they control large constituencies and influence government policies on abortion, AIDS education and prevention, charitable services, and gay rights. Evangelical Protestant ministers such as the Reverend Jerry Falwell and the Reverend Donald Wildmon likewise play an active role in politics, having abandoned earlier fundamentalist approaches favoring retreat from the fallen world rather than engagement with it. Masters of direct mail campaigns experienced at monitoring and boycotting commercial media for "anti-Christian" or "anti-family" themes, Falwell and Wildmon recently mobilized a series of highly effective campaigns against publicly subsidized art they deemed blasphemy or filth. Roman Catholic clerical opposition to a public television documentary about gay protestors at St. Patrick's Cathedral led the Public Broadcasting System to pressure its member stations to take it off the air.[3] And religious convictions and institutions have played a pivotal role in nationwide political activism against abortion.

All of this is fine; such activity is fully protected by the right of free speech,[4] as well as by the right of free exercise.[5] True, the prominence of a few celebrated clergymen does not prove that religious freedom is alive and well, any more than the election of a few black mayors and the judicial interment of Jim Crow signalled an end to race discrimination. The fact of religious resilience does show, however, that if the Court was in the business of wholesale secularization, it has not succeeded. Indeed, religious organizations have thrived in part in opposition to the forces McConnell describes, converting charges of rising secularism into a rallying cry for yet more religious fervor. As McConnell himself concedes, "the resurgence of conservative religious movements among both Protestants and Catholics—and to a lesser extent among Jews—has made religion a more salient force in the political culture."[6]

More fundamental than our disagreement about the facts, however, is our disagreement about the proper reading of the Reli-

---

[3] See Eleanor Blau, *PBS Cancels Act-Up Film*, NY Times C16 (Aug 13, 1991). See also Sharon Bernstein, *KCET Pays Price In Flap With Church*, LA Times F1 (Oct 1, 1991) (San Francisco PBS station ran documentary anyway and lost $55,000 in contributions due to boycott).

[4] See *Widmar v Vincent*, 454 US 263 (1981).

[5] Ministers can even hold political office. See *McDaniel v Paty*, 435 US 618 (1978).

[6] McConnell, in this volume, 134-35 (cited in note 1).

gion Clauses. In Section I, I will outline a reading of the Religion Clauses quite different from McConnell's. In Section II, I will discuss the implications of that interpretation for the Establishment Clause; in Section III, for the Free Exercise Clause.

I. RELIGIOUS BASELINES

The Free Exercise Clause and the Establishment Clause each harbor an unstated corollary. The right to free exercise of religion implies the right to free exercise of non-religion. Just as Caesar may not command one to transgress God's will, he may not command one to obey it. To do either is to run afoul of free exercise. As the Court put it in *Wallace v Jaffree*, "the Court has unambiguously concluded that the individual freedom of conscience protected by the First Amendment embraces the right to select any religious faith or none at all."[7] The "conscience of the infidel [or] the atheist" is as protected as any Christian's.[8]

Just as the affirmative right to practice a specific religion implies the negative right to practice none, so the negative bar against establishment of religion implies the affirmative "establishment" of a civil order for the resolution of public moral disputes. Agreement on such a secular mechanism was the price of ending the war of all sects against all. Establishment of a civil public order was the social contract produced by religious truce. Religious teachings as expressed in public debate may influence the civil public order but public moral disputes may be resolved only on grounds articulable in secular terms.[9] Religious grounds for resolv-

---

[7] 472 US 38, 52-53 (1985) (footnote omitted).

[8] Id at 52. See also John Paul Stevens, *The Bill of Rights: A Century of Progress*, in this volume, 13, 29-30.

[9] See *Harris v McRae*, 448 US 297, 319-20 (1980) (rejecting establishment claim against ban on abortion funding). Specifically, the Court in *Harris* held that a law may be based upon community values that have a religious foundation, but the law must still have a valid secular justification. Id.

It remains debatable whether laws must be secularly motivated in order to satisfy the Establishment Clause, or rather merely susceptible to a post hoc secular rationale. Compare Robert Audi, *The Separation of Church and State and the Obligations of Citizenship*, 18 Phil & Pub Affairs 259, 277-90 (1989) (favoring requirement of secular motivation), with Paul J. Weithman, *The Separation of Church and State: Some Questions for Professor Audi*, 20 Phil & Pub Affairs 52 (1991) (opposing principle of secular motivation as too stringent and favoring requirement of secular rationale). This debate resembles the debate over intent versus meaning or purpose in statutory and constitutional construction. My own view is that an articulable secular rationale is all that is required; a requirement of secular motivation trenches too far on the freedoms of conscience and expression of citizens and legislators.

ing public moral disputes would rekindle inter-denominational strife that the Establishment Clause extinguished.[10]

This reading of the Religion Clauses entails a baseline very different from McConnell's. To McConnell, the proper baseline from which to measure free exercise or establishment violations is undistorted prepolitical religious choice.[11] Government preserves religious liberty best, in his view, if it leaves intact the religious choices that would have been made in the absence of government: "The great evil against which the Religion Clauses are directed is government-induced homogeneity"[12] in matters of religion, and their great virtue, the preservation of the religious diversity or pluralism that emerges from unfettered private choice.[13] In other words, the war of all sects against all is to continue by other means after the truce.

McConnell's view wrongly ignores the affirmative implications of the Establishment Clause. The bar against an establishment of religion entails the establishment of a civil order—the culture of liberal democracy—for resolving public moral disputes. The baseline for measuring Religion Clause violations thus is not "undistorted" prepolitical religious choice. The social contract to end the war of all sects against all necessarily, by its very existence, "distorts" the outcomes that would have obtained had that war continued. Public affairs may no longer be conducted as the strongest faith would dictate. Minority religions gain from the truce not in the sense that their faiths now may be translated into public policy, but in the sense that no faith may be. Neither Bible nor Talmud may directly settle, for example, public controversy over whether abortion preserves liberty or ends life.

The correct baseline, then, is not unfettered religious liberty, but rather religious liberty insofar as it is consistent with the establishment of the secular public moral order. On this view, the exclusion of religion from public programs is not, as McConnell would have it, an invidious "preference for the secular in public

---

[10] It might be objected that separation of church and state is not necessary to extinguish wars of religion; all that is needed is a state monopoly of force. But such a view would ignore the historical correlation between government partiality toward faith and the existence of religious strife. See John Rawls, *The Idea of an Overlapping Consensus*, 7 Oxford J Legal Stud 1, 4 (1987) ("The social and historical conditions of modern democratic regimes have their origins in the Wars of Religion following the Reformation and the subsequent development of the principle of toleration . . . ."). In other words, the end of religious strife requires not just any Leviathan, but a fully agnostic one.

[11] McConnell, in this volume, 169 (cited in note 1).

[12] Id at 168.

[13] Id at 168-69.

affairs."[14] Secular governance of public affairs is simply an entailment of the settlement by the Establishment Clause of the war of
all sects against all. From the perspective of the prepolitical war of
all sects against all, the exclusion of any religion from public affairs
looks like "discrimination." But from the perspective of the settlement worked by the Establishment Clause, it looks like proper
treatment.

What is this civil moral order that the religious truce established? Is it itself a countervailing faith or civil religion? Professor
McConnell at times seems to treat it this way. For example, he
criticizes contemporary Establishment Clause doctrine for favoring
the teaching of "secular humanism" over creationism in public
schools.[15] As he notes, the strategy of "portray[ing] secular ideology as the religion of 'secular humanism' . . . has been a failure."[16]
While the Court readily strikes down as establishment much government approval of religion (too readily in his view), it never
strikes down government "disapproval" of religion, even if that
disapproval amounts to a kind of countervailing faith. McConnell
would correct this asymmetry by reducing secular ideology to the
status of just another competing faith among many in the war of
all sects against all.[17] The perfect mechanism for his vision in the
context of publicly financed education would be a voucher system
in which families could pick and choose among parochial and public schools as a matter of undistorted private religious choice.
"Public" schools presumably would serve as a default option for
atheists.

The culture of liberal democracy may well function as a belief
system with substantive content, rather than a neutral and transcendent arbiter among other belief systems. Various versions of
this argument have been expressed not only by liberalism's critics,

---

[14] McConnell, in this volume, 169 (cited in note 1).

[15] Id at 152. See *Epperson v Arkansas*, 393 US 97 (1968) (invalidating as establishment
a state law forbidding public schools to teach evolution); *Edwards v Aguillard*, 482 US 578
(1987) (invalidating as establishment a state law requiring public schools to teach "creation
science" if they also taught evolution). Compare *Mozert v Hawkins County Board of Education*, 827 F2d 1058 (6th Cir 1987) (rejecting free exercise claim by fundamentalist Christians seeking to prevent their children from being exposed to "secular humanist" values in
public school reading class); *Smith v Bd. of School Commissioners of Mobile County*, 827 F2d
684 (11th Cir 1987) (rejecting establishment challenge to public school curriculum infused
with "secular humanist" tenets). For a discussion of the complexity of this issue, see Nomi
Maya Stolzenberg, *"He Drew A Circle that Shut Me Out": Assimilation, Indoctrination, and
the Paradox of a Liberal Education*, 106 Harv L Rev (forthcoming 1992).

[16] McConnell, in this volume, 152 (cited in note 1).

[17] Id at 190-91.

but by contemporary liberal theorists themselves. On one such view, liberalism's purported procedural neutrality conceals implicit but unstated substantive ends that ought to be flushed out so that people can accept or criticize them.[18] For example, toleration of competing visions of the good is itself a vision of the good; and the idea of equal dignity and respect is itself a substantive rejection of social hierarchy. Another view, developed in the recent work of Professor John Rawls, sees the culture of liberal democracy less as an imperial third force overriding the embedded norms of social subcommunities than as a historically emergent statement of the "overlapping consensus" among them.[19] This view sees the commitment to religious tolerance that ends the war of all sects against all not as a neutral *modus vivendi*, but rather as a substantive recognition that there is more than one path to heaven and not so many as once thought to hell.

Under either of these views, the culture of liberal democracy might well look like a faith to those who disagree with it. For example, suppose a required public school reading text depicts Jane as a wage-earning construction worker and Dick as an unremunerated child-tending househusband. And suppose that a religious community views this a perversion of the sexual division of labor set forth in the book of Genesis. To the religionist, the text undoubtedly looks like an expression of a countervailing faith at odds with her own.[20]

But epistemology does not entail polity. McConnell errs in leaping from one to the other. Even if the culture of liberal democracy is a belief system comparable to a religious faith in the way it structures knowledge, it simply does not follow that it is the equivalent of a religion for political and constitutional purposes. Neither the Bill of Rights, the Republican Party platform, nor the American Civil Liberties Union Policy Guide is the constitutional equivalent of the Ten Commandments, whatever devotion they enjoy from their adherents. The Supreme Court has long drawn a

---

[18] See, for example, Michael Sandel, *Liberalism and the Limits of Justice* (Cambridge, 1982).

[19] Rawls, 7 Oxford J Legal Stud 1 (cited in note 10).

[20] Non-traditional depiction of gender roles was one of the features of the public school reading texts to which fundamentalist parents objected in *Mozert*, 827 F2d at 1061-62. See also Stephen L. Carter, *Evolutionism, Creationism, and Treating Religion as a Hobby*, 1987 Duke L J 977 (interpreting the clash over the teaching of creationism and evolution in the public schools as a clash between faith in God and faith in reason); Stanley Fish, *Liberalism Doesn't Exist*, 1987 Duke L J 997 (reply to Carter) (treating liberalism as an embedded interpretive norm fundamentally at odds with unquestioning religious faith).

distinction between religion and philosophy for purposes of limiting free exercise exemptions: secular pacifists do not get the same breaks from the military draft as pacifist Quakers,[21] and high school dropouts who march to the beat of Henry David Thoreau do not get the same breaks as those who follow the path of their Amish elders.[22] Similarly, a reading text depicting counter-traditional gender roles, while it does inculcate values, does not amount to the establishment of a "religion" of feminism. For constitutional purposes, feminism may be a "faith," but it is not a religion.

The culture of liberal democracy is the overarching belief system for politics, if not for knowledge. Numerous self-limiting features ought to keep at bay any concern that liberal democracy could be a totalistic orthodoxy as threatening as any papal edict. First, the content of the culture of liberal democracy is subject to continual revision in the crucible of pluralistic politics. Liberal democracy may have traditions, but it has no fixed canon or creed. Consider, for example, the vigorous debate now being waged over whether history textbooks in the public schools should shift from a "eurocentric" to a "multicultural" account in light of the rapidly changing demographics of the nation's major cities. Second, the guarantee of free speech ensures that no one may be forced to swear adherence to the culture of liberal democracy any more than to swear oaths of fealty to the Pope.[23] Third, the guarantee of free speech also ensures that religious points of view can participate in the public debate; it is not clear that the public culture of liberal democracy can ever deviate too far from the "overlapping consensus" among social subcultures, including religious subcultures.[24]

If the baseline from which to measure establishment or free exercise violations is the exercise of religious liberty insofar as compatible with the establishment of the secular public order, the secularization of the public order is not "discrimination" against religion. The Court therefore should take a broader view of establishment. But the Court should also take a broader view of free exercise so long as religion does not genuinely threaten to undermine the secular welfare state.

---

[21] See *Gillette v United States*, 401 US 437 (1971).

[22] *Wisconsin v Yoder*, 406 US 205, 215-16 (1972).

[23] *West Virginia State Board of Education v Barnette*, 319 US 624 (1943) (holding that required pledge of allegiance in public schools violated Free Speech Clause).

[24] See Rawls, 7 Oxford J Legal Stud at 2 (cited in note 10).

II. The Establishment Clause

The Establishment Clause clearly forbids a government church, and with it oaths or tithes—that is, enshrinement of official religious belief or exaction of financial support for religion. Contemporary debates over the scope of the Establishment Clause center on just what degree of government action constitutes enshrining official belief or exacting financial support. The trend in both areas has been to permit greater inclusion of religion in public programs.

A. Enshrining Official Belief

In the area of belief, the Court has distinguished three degrees of government favoritism toward religion: "coercion," "endorsement," and "acknowledgement." Religious oaths enforced on pain of criminal penalty would presumably be the paradigm case of impermissible coercion.[25] The Court has considered recitation of prayer or biblical verses in the public school classroom a near equivalent.[26] The Court has treated the public school classroom as a setting particularly rife with coercive potential, given that school attendance is compulsory and that children presumably have not fully developed their faculties of resistance and consent. For similar reasons, the Court has considered the teaching of religious or religiously motivated tenets in the public curriculum the equivalent of forced adherence to a creed,[27] and has been strict in its interpretation of what constitutes such teaching.[28]

Outside of this narrow line of public school cases, however, the Court has been more tolerant of official sponsorship of religious speech and symbols. One key example is its decision permitting clergymen to recite denominational prayers at the opening of state legislative sessions.[29] Other examples are its decisions permitting government to display religious symbols during holiday seasons—first, the nativity scene that is the centerpiece of Christian

---

[25] See *Torcaso v Watkins*, 367 US 488, 495-96 (1961) (holding that oath of belief in God as condition of being notary public was unconstitutional).

[26] *Engel v Vitale*, 370 US 421 (1962); *Abington School District v Schempp*, 374 US 203 (1963); *Wallace v Jaffree*, 472 US 38 (1985).

[27] *Epperson v Arkansas*, 393 US 97 (1968); *Edwards v Aguillard*, 482 US 578 (1987).

[28] *Stone v Graham*, 449 US 39 (1980) (holding that posting Ten Commandments in school was establishment).

[29] *Marsh v Chambers*, 463 US 783 (1983) (rejecting establishment challenge both to prayers and to entire state-sponsored chaplaincy system).

liturgy[30]; later, the menorah that is associated with the Jewish holiday of Chanukah[31]—so long as they are sanitized by surrounding secular symbols.[32] Significantly, in each of these decisions, the Court found that the official recognition of religion in question was a mere "acknowledgement" of the background religious practices of the community, not rising to an "endorsement" of belief, much less to the "coercion" of non-believers.[33]

Even this much accommodation of religion in public life is not enough, however, for some members of the Court. At one time, five Justices supported Justice O'Connor's position that the establishment line should be drawn between impermissible "endorsement" and permissible "acknowledgement,"[34] with "endorsement" defined, at least by Justice O'Connor, as government's transmission of religious messages having exclusionary impact on religious or irreligious minorities.[35] This may be a fine line—for Justice O'Connor it meant that creches alongside reindeer and talking wishing wells in shopping districts were acceptable, while freestanding creches on courthouse steps were not.[36]

At least four Justices on the current Court, led by Justice Kennedy, would go even further and permit government "endorsement" of religion; for them, mere "acknowledgement" is not even a serious case.[37] In a pending case concerning a challenge to the recitation of a prayer at an eighth-grade graduation, the Solicitor General has expressed support for this limitation of Establishment Clause claims to cases of "coercion."[38]

---

[30] *Lynch v Donnelly*, 465 US 668 (1984) (rejecting establishment challenge to government-sponsored display of creche).

[31] *County of Allegheny v ACLU*, 492 US 573 (1989) (rejecting establishment challenge to government-sponsored display of menorah).

[32] See *Lynch*, 465 US at 691-92 (O'Connor concurring), in which Justice O'Connor reasoned that the creche was not an establishment because the surrounding display included secular holiday symbols, such as a Santa Claus house, reindeer pulling Santa's sleigh, candy-striped poles, a Christmas tree, carolers, a clown, an elephant, a sign that said "Season's Greetings," and a "talking" wishing well. The Court explicitly adopted Justice O'Connor's reasoning in *Allegheny*, 492 US at 594-97. There it permitted the menorah because it was surrounded by such secular symbols as a Christmas tree and a sign saluting liberty, id at 614, but forbade a nativity scene because it was not so surrounded. Id at 601-02.

[33] See *Marsh*, 463 US at 792; *Lynch*, 465 US at 692-93 (O'Connor concurring).

[34] See *Allegheny*, 492 US at 595-97 (Blackmun plurality).

[35] See, for example, *Lynch*, 465 US at 688 (O'Connor concurring).

[36] Id at 694 (O'Connor concurring); *Allegheny*, 492 US at 637 (O'Connor concurring).

[37] *Allegheny*, 492 US at 668-74 (Kennedy, joined by Rehnquist, White, and Scalia, dissenting as to invalidation of freestanding creche).

[38] See *Weisman v Lee*, 908 F2d 1090 (2d Cir 1990), cert granted, *Lee v Weisman*, 111 S Ct 1305 (1991).

Professor McConnell likewise favors a narrow test for defining establishment. He rejects Justice O'Connor's "endorsement" test, finds more promise in Justice Kennedy's "coercion" test, but ultimately discards even the "coercion" test for a different "pluralist approach."[39] He does note that "[t]he generation that adopted the First Amendment viewed some form of governmental compulsion as the essence of an establishment of religion."[40] He also cites Locke's distinction that " 'it is one thing to persuade, another to command.' "[41] But he tempers this strict originalist understanding of coercion as force with other historical evidence,[42] allowing him to agree with Justice Kennedy that government speech sometimes may be "coercive": "government does not have free rein to proselytize."[43] Finally, however, he rejects the coercion test in favor of his own proposed "pluralism" test for the Religion Clauses: He defines establishment as government action whose "purpose or probable effect is to increase religious uniformity . . . by forcing or inducing a contrary religious practice."[44] This test clearly goes beyond any force-based definition of coercion.

What government action is sufficient to "induce" religious practice? The answer is not clear. McConnell's theory of religious pluralism fails to resolve the question. It surely would "increase religious uniformity" for government to require a citizen to swear an oath of loyalty to the Pope. But the establishment problem would not disappear if the government offered the oath-taker multiple choices instead—swear an oath to be a Catholic *or* a Baptist, or a member of any sect listed as the genuine article down at the Internal Revenue Service. Defining an establishment requires distinguishing among a range of government means as well as government ends.

What McConnell would *not* regard as establishment is clearer. It seems he would allow significant religious speech and symbolic expression by government short of "proselytization." Absent captive audience problems such as those that exist in public school classroom or graduation settings, he would dismiss claims of dissenters whose only complaint is that they are "irritated," "of-

---

[39] McConnell, in this volume, 175 (cited in note 1).

[40] Id at 154-56.

[41] Id at 159 (quoting from John Locke, *A Letter Concerning Toleration*).

[42] Id at 159 n 201.

[43] Id at 162. Indeed, Professor McConnell suggests that in the pending case of *Lee v Weisman*, the Court should find an establishment in a rabbi's delivery of a graduation invocation at a public school, because the graduation ceremony is inherently coercive. Id at 158.

[44] Id at 169.

fended," or stigmatized by such messages.[45] Indeed he would not have the courts trifle with "perceived messages" of endorsement much at all.[46] Apparently he would allow public-sponsored creches, proximate reindeers or not. Apparently he would also reverse *Edwards v Aguillard* and permit the government to enforce in the public classroom a kind of fairness doctrine for the expression of "a wide variety of perspectives, religious ones included"[47]—even through the mouthpiece of a public teacher.

The trend McConnell backs—of narrowing the test for establishment in the context of government speech and symbols—is exactly the wrong way to go. The establishment of the secular public order forbids government to put its imprimatur of approval on religion through any official action—period. Approving religious "acknowledgement," as both *Marsh v Chambers* and *Lynch v Donnelly* did, is like saying, "a little establishment is okay, but not too much." Both those cases were wrong. Approving religious "endorsement" would be even worse. Neither "acknowledgement" nor "endorsement" can be squared with the Religion Clauses when read in light of their unstated corollaries.

The explanation begins with the Free Exercise Clause. As argued above, the right to free exercise of religion implies the right to free exercise of non-religion. No one may be coerced into worship, any more than out of it. Freedom from coercion *not to* worship may be read to imply freedom from coercion *to* worship—just as current constitutional interpretation finds the right not to speak implied by the right of free speech,[48] and the right to divorce implied by a right to marry.[49] Thus the Free Exercise Clause would forbid the state to coerce minority sects or atheists into contrary beliefs, even without the Establishment Clause.

But the Establishment Clause cannot be mere surplusage. If the Free Exercise Clause standing alone guarantees free exercise of non-religion, the Establishment Clause must do more than bar coercion of non-believers. Thus a "coercion" test for establishment would reduce the Establishment Clause to a redundancy. If the Establishment Clause is to have independent meaning, it must bar something other than coercion of private citizens into confessions of official faith.

---

[45] McConnell, in this volume, 164 (cited in note 1).
[46] Id at 155.
[47] Id at 193.
[48] *Wooley v Maynard*, 430 US 705, 714-15 (1977); *Barnette*, 319 US 624.
[49] *Zablocki v Redhail*, 434 US 374 (1978); *Boddie v Connecticut*, 401 US 371 (1971).

In the context of government speech and symbols, that "something else" is government stamps of approval upon religion. The official agnosticism mandated by the Establishment Clause requires not only even-handed government treatment of private religious groups, but also a standing gag order on government's own speech and symbolism; it prohibits official partiality toward religion. On this reading, the Establishment Clause does more than bar "coercion"; it bars "endorsement" and "acknowledgement" of religion as well.

This disability is unique to the Religion Clauses. No other topic beside religion is off limits to government in the course of its own activities, as opposed to its regulation or imposition of conditions on private activities. There is no political establishment clause.[50] To be sure, the Court's interpretation of the Free Speech Clause to bar government from compelling speech is a partial analogue: Justice Jackson's famous statement in *West Virginia State Board of Education v Barnette* was that government officials may not "force citizens to confess by word or act their faith" in political or religious orthodoxy.[51] But protecting private citizens from forced confessions nearly exhausts this concept in the context of political speech.[52]

In the context of political speech, there is virtually no First Amendment limit on what government may say.[53] The Court has never taken literally the rest of Jackson's "fixed star in our constitutional constellation,"[54] and could not do so. "[O]fficial[s] high or petty" do "prescribe what shall be orthodox in politics, nationalism, religion, or other matters of opinion" all the time in the sense

---

[50] For the reasons that follow, see notes 53-58 and accompanying text, I believe that Professor McConnell's intriguing comparison of the two in *Political and Religious Disestablishment*, 1986 BYU L Rev 405, overstates the similarities.

[51] *Barnette*, 319 US at 642.

[52] I say "nearly" because I believe some constitutional liberties may entail that government may not speak so as to discourage them. Can government teach public schoolchildren the message, "confessions are good for the soul; if you commit a crime, tell all to the police"? This appears at least inconsistent with the Fifth Amendment, if not a violation of it. On the other hand, police officers deliver the same message to criminal suspects all the time, with impunity, so long as they give the *Miranda* warnings. But the point here is that the Establishment Clause *explicitly* prohibits the government from adopting religious positions. Government may or may not adopt a position against the exercise of other rights, but as to religion, it emphatically must not.

[53] While some have criticized this leeway to government, see Mark Yudof, *When Government Speaks: Politics, Law and Government Expression in America* (California, 1983), current interpretation of the First Amendment does not confer anti-propaganda rights on citizens. See *Meese v Keene*, 481 US 465 (1987).

[54] *Barnette*, 319 US at 642.

that they endorse ideas ("prescription" in its weak sense).[55] It is hard to know what government would do if it did not so "speak." "Just say no to drugs," "End racism," and "Have babies, not abortions" are all messages government is free to endorse under current law;[56] it simply may not force private citizens to agree.

The same is not so for religion. The difference between government political speech and government religious speech is illuminated by cases in which individuals invoke the implied First Amendment right "not to speak." In these cases, the inquiry has been, for example, whether forcing citizens to bear such statements as "Live Free or Die" on state-issued automobile license plates is the equivalent of a flag salute or other "forced confession of faith by word or act"—in other words, whether turning a citizen into a billboard for the state's ideology is like using him as a mouthpiece.[57] There has never been serious question, however, that the state could emblazon "Live Free or Die" across the entrance to the state capitol. In contrast, even Justice Kennedy would find "the permanent erection of a large Latin cross on the roof of city hall" an impermissible attempt at government "proselytiz[ation]."[58]

If protection from forced confessions cannot exhaust the meaning of establishment, except by making the Establishment Clause redundant of the Free Exercise Clause, then Justice O'Connor's "endorsement" test comes closer to the mark than Justice Kennedy's "coercion" test. It is true that the application of the "endorsement" test has been unsatisfying. Not to see the creche as sending a message of exclusion to Jews, Muslims or atheists is to see the world through Christian-tinted glasses. Majority practices are myopically seen by their own practitioners as uncontroversial; asking predominantly Christian courts to judge the exclusionary message of creches may be a little like asking an all-male jury to judge a woman's reasonable resistance in a rape case. But the solution is simple: Banish public sponsorship of religious symbols from the public square.[59] That the endorsement test has been needlessly

---

[55] Id.

[56] For the reasons I gave in note 9, I see the third as much more dubious than the first two. *Harris v McRae*, 448 US 297, was mistaken to hold that government may implement a moral preference for childbirth over abortion through a funding program. Because the right of reproductive choice is, at least for now, "fundamental," it is not clear that the lesser disincentive conveyed by mere official exhortation is permissible.

[57] See *Wooley*, 430 US 705.

[58] *Allegheny*, 492 US at 661 (Kennedy dissenting in part).

[59] Thus *Lynch* and *Allegheny* were wrong to uphold the menorah, and *Marsh* was wrong to uphold the practice of opening legislative sessions with a prayer. But we need not melt down the national currency to get rid of "In God We Trust." Rote recitation of God's

complicated and unpersuasively applied does not mean that it asked the wrong question to begin with. The Supreme Court should not eliminate such a test from its Establishment Clause doctrine, but rather should more rigorously enforce it, and indeed extend it to what the Court now calls mere "acknowledgement."

In sum, government-sponsored religious symbols violate the Establishment Clause even if those who object to the symbols are not "coerced" into conversion or false swearing. True, this reading of the Establishment Clause singles out religion from other subject matter—or to the extent religion is a viewpoint, from other viewpoints—for unique exclusion from government speech and symbolism. But that is not invidious "discrimination"; it is simply an entailment of the establishment of the secular public order.

B.   Exacting Financial Support

It is a commonplace that the government plays roles beyond that of policeman in the modern welfare state: Government acts now not only as a regulator but also in significant ways as proprietor, educator, employer, and patron. This expansion of government roles multiplies the opportunities for Establishment Clause conflict over whether government has lent religion impermissible financial support.

The Court's trend in this area—like the trend with religious symbols—has been to move away from the "no aid" position toward greater blessing on religious participation in public programs. The Court's recent decisions have suggested two main approaches government may take to sanitize financial aid to religious beneficiaries of Establishment Clause concerns: first, including religious beneficiaries in a scheme that also extends benefits to other comparable but non-religious beneficiaries[60]; second, allowing private individuals to choose how to use indirect tax benefits instead of centrally directing how cash grants will be used.[61] True, even while allowing fiscal integration of religion into public programs, the

---

name is easily distinguished as a *de minimis* endorsement in comparison with prayer or the seasonal invocation of sacred symbols. The pledge of allegiance is a closer question.

[60] See *Walz v Tax Commission*, 397 US 664 (1970) (upholding property tax exemption to churches as part of broad array of charitable and educational beneficiaries); *Bowen v Kendrick*, 487 US 589 (1988) (upholding grant of federal funds for adolescent sex education to religious organizations as part of broad array of family planning entities).

[61] Compare *Mueller v Allen*, 463 US 388, 399-400 (1983) (permitting parents to deduct parochial school tuition, textbook, and transportation expenses from their taxes), with *Lemon v Kurtzman*, 403 US 602 (1971) (forbidding state to reimburse parochial school teacher salaries and textbooks).

Court has still drawn the line at some forms of physical integration.[62] But several Justices key to thin majorities in such cases are no longer sitting on the Court.

Still, some see the trend in the aid cases as not accommodating enough, and Professor McConnell would appear to be one of them. He would find no establishment when religious organizations participate extensively in public facilities, public grant programs, and public education, so long as the religious organizations participate on an equal basis with secular organizations.[63] As to conditions on benefits, he divides the universe in two: He would forbid conditions if other participants in the program "have the right to engage in political or other controversial secular speech," but not if participants are being recruited to serve as the government's own message-specific mouthpieces.[64] He thus approves of both *Widmar v Vincent*, which requires—on free speech grounds—public schools to grant religious groups equal access to public school classrooms on extracurricular time[65]; and *Bowen v Kendrick*, which allows religious organizations to participate in a federal program to promote sexual abstinence among teenagers.[66] However, he attacks decisions such as *Board of Education v Allen*,[67] which allows government to provide textbooks on secular subjects to parochial schools only if they are the same textbooks used by public schools.[68] In his view, that condition on aid to parochial schools is an unacceptable "seculariz[ation of] their curriculum."[69]

My reading of the Religion Clauses leads me to a different view. I have argued above that one way the Establishment Clause avoids redundancy with the Free Exercise Clause is by barring symbolic government imprimaturs on religion, even in instances short of coercion. A second way in which establishment is more than a doctrine against coerced confession is that it protects individuals from compulsory financial support of other people's reli-

---

[62] See *Grand Rapids School Dist. v Ball*, 473 US 373 (1985) (forbidding state to pay part-time teachers in parochial schools); *Aguilar v Felton*, 473 US 402 (1985) (same). Compare *McCollum v Board of Education*, 333 US 203 (1948) (invalidating voluntary religious instruction for children during school hours on public school grounds), with *Zorach v Clauson*, 343 US 306 (1952) (upholding voluntary religious instruction for children during school hours but *off* public school grounds).

[63] McConnell, in this volume, 185 (cited in note 1).

[64] Id at 186.

[65] 454 US 263.

[66] 487 US 589.

[67] 392 US 236 (1968).

[68] Id at 244-45.

[69] McConnell, in this volume, 133 (cited in note 1).

gion through the tax system—not because such support will coerce conversion, but because it will cause profound divisiveness and offense.[70]

Again, there is an asymmetry between politics and religion. On the political side, the Court has found an implied right to be free of some kinds of financial exactions to support political or ideological speech that is anathema to the payor. The key case is *Abood v Detroit Board of Education*, which held that public employees may be compelled to pay fees for public union representation in collective bargaining but not for the union's political or ideological speech.[71] The Court has extended the principle to compulsory bar associations and certain other entities enjoying some kind of publicly conferred monopoly.[72] But crucially, the Court has never applied or even seriously entertained applying the principle to the tax system.[73] Perhaps payment into a general revenue fund so diffuses any one person's contribution to any government cause that it attenuates any attribution of the government's actions to an individual taxpayer. Or perhaps compulsory taxation does infringe the right against compelled speech, but is overwhelmingly justified by the crippling administrative and revenue burdens of requiring pro rata tax refunds to conscientious objectors to government policy. Whatever the reason, it is clear that the tax system has a bye in *Abood*-type controversies.

Not so for religion. In religion, the Establishment Clause confers a kind of non-disclaimable *Abood* right upon every taxpayer against government expenditures in support of religion—whether through promotion, endorsement, or, in my view, "acknowledgement." Hence the Court concluded in *Flast v Cohen* that the Establishment Clause creates an exception to the usual rule against taxpayer standing.[74] And the remedy in the religion context is injunction, rather than, as in *Abood*, pro rata refund.

Professor McConnell would minimize these distinctions. For example, he analogizes taxpayer objections to government expenditure of public funds to advocate religion to objections by religious opponents of abortion to government subsidization of advocacy of

---

[70] Professor McConnell, in contrast, would forbid only measures that increase religious homogeneity (i.e., foster conversion or lapses), and not measures that offend. Id at 164, 168-69.

[71] 431 US 209, 232, 237 (1977).

[72] *Keller v California*, 496 US 1 (1990).

[73] See Norman L. Cantor, *Forced Payments to Service Institutions and Constitutional Interests in Ideological Non-Association*, 36 Rutgers L Rev 3, 16, 26 (1984).

[74] 392 US 83, 103-06 (1968).

abortion.[75] But government has quite different obligations toward these two sorts of objections. The Constitution mandates that government yield to the first; yielding to the second is a matter of political grace. No taxpayer has a right not to subsidize abortion; all taxpayers have a right not to subsidize religion. True, abortion, like religion, is divisive and controversial, but not all divisive and controversial questions have been privatized by the Constitution; only religious questions have. Abortion may not be turned into a religious question by analogy.[76]

Here lies the crux of my disagreement with Professor McConnell. In my view, the Establishment Clause uniquely privileges the right of conscientious objection to religious activity, speech, or expenditures by government. The key legal consequence is that I view asymmetries that McConnell would describe as discrimination against religion as mandated by the Establishment Clause. In particular, the Establishment Clause will often require excluding religious organizations from public programs, or will necessitate religion-restrictive conditions on their participation.

For example, the Court recently held that, if the government funds a public broadcaster, the Free Speech Clause forbids the government from making "non-editorializing" a condition of public funding.[77] The Court assumed that the broadcaster could not easily segregate its editorializing activity from its other activity—for the sake of the religious parallel, the broadcaster was "pervasively editorializing." This non-segregability made the no-editorials condition an impermissible "penalty" on the other activities supported by private funds.[78] The Court implied that requiring the broadcaster to segregate federally funded non-editorializing activity

---

[75] See Michael W. McConnell, *The Selective Funding Problem: Abortions and Religious Schools*, 104 Harv L Rev 989 (1991). There Professor McConnell, in the third *Harris/ Lemon* permutation (*Harris* was right; *Lemon* was right), suggests that preventing public funding for religious education and for abortions may both be justified as protecting conscientious objectors. Id at 1006-14.

[76] In *Harris v McRae*, 448 US at 319-20, the Court held that denying public medical insurance for abortion while providing it for childbirth does not establish religion, despite the religious motivation of much political opposition to abortion. But neither should free exercise grant religious opponents of abortion the rights of conscientious objectors. The program at issue in *Harris* was an act of political discretion, permissible only under a relaxed standard of review.

[77] *FCC v League of Women Voters*, 468 US 364 (1984) ("*LWV*"). See also McConnell, 104 Harv L Rev at 1016-17 (cited in note 75) (fourth *Harris/Lemon* permutation—*Harris* was right; *Lemon* was wrong).

[78] *LWV*, 468 US at 400.

physically from privately funded editorializing activity would likewise be an impermissible "penalty."[79]

But non-segregability in the religious context rightly cuts the other way. In a "pervasively sectarian" parochial school that cannot segregate religious from secular teaching, there is no way to prevent public tax dollars that go to that school from subsidizing religion, without some condition imposed. Either the state can require that the school stop teaching religious subjects altogether, which will obviously be untenable to the school, or the state can require that the school physically segregate religious from secular teaching.[80]

True, the "no religious teaching" condition is structurally similar to the "no editorializing" condition, and the physical segregation requirements in either case are likely to be prohibitively expensive. But this structural similarity does not decide the case. The "penalty" that is impermissible under the Free Speech Clause in the first case is necessitated by the Establishment Clause in the second. Only thus can government fulfill the constitutional requirement not to support religious teaching with public funds.[81]

---

[79] Id. This implication arose from the way the Court distinguished *Regan v Taxation With Representation*, 461 US 540 (1983) ("*TWR*"). In *TWR*, the Court upheld a "no lobbying" condition on non-profit organizations that received tax-deductible contributions. Id at 545-46. In *LWV*, the Court reasoned that the no-lobbying condition was not a penalty because tax-deductible dollars could still be used by non-lobbying, financially segregated affiliates. *LWV*, 468 US at 399-401.

The Court's view of segregation requirements remains confused. For private funding, the Court has treated even slight financial segregation requirements as a free speech burden requiring strong justification. See *FEC v Massachusetts Citizens for Life, Inc.*, 479 US 238 (1986) (invalidating statute that required organization to keep separate contributions fund for political activities). But for public funding, the Court has permitted financial and even physical segregation requirements as conditions upon the relevant benefit. *TWR*, 461 US at 544 & n 6 (TWR could obtain tax-deductible contributions only for its non-lobbying activity); *Rust v Sullivan*, 111 S Ct 1759, 1774-75 (1991) (upholding a requirement, under Title X of the Public Health Service Act, that a grantee's abortion-related activity be separate from family planning activity receiving federal funds).

[80] The Court required this physical segregation for the parochial schools in *Grand Rapids*, 473 US 303.

[81] A similar argument supports the conclusion that *Harris* was wrong but that *Lemon* was right. Professor McConnell argues that both of the following propositions *cannot* simultaneously be true: that forbidding the government to fund abortions in *Harris* in a public medical insurance program that funds childbirth is an impermissible "penalty" on abortion rights; but that forbidding the government to fund parochial schools in *Lemon* is merely a permissible "nonsubsidy" of parochial schools. Professor McConnell reasons that the two programs were structurally alike: each funded a mutually exclusive substitute for the activity denied funding—the program in *Harris* funded childbirth, while the program in *Lemon* funded public schools. McConnell, 104 Harv L Rev at 1006-14 (cited in note 75). But, while both *Harris* and *Lemon* imposed penalties in the sense that he argues, Professor McConnell

The asymmetrical treatment is an unavoidable feature of the unique demands of the Establishment Clause.

To consider an even more similar parallel, suppose that the government funded general health clinics for pregnant women, provided that the clinics speak favorably of childbirth and do not "encourage, promote, or advocate" abortion, for example by counseling or referring women to have abortions.[82] Compare this program to one in which the government funds religious schools, provided that the school does not "encourage, promote, or advocate" religion, for example by praying on school premises or by referring students to church services. In addition, the school must advise all students of their right to convert to another religion or to no religion. There can be little doubt that in each case, the government's condition would be a disincentive to the exercise of unfettered choice. And it is quite likely that Planned Parenthood in the first case and the Roman Catholic Church in the second would each rather forego the funds than accept the condition. But despite the structural similarity, the two conditions are constitutionally distinct. Whereas the Free Speech Clause should forbid the first, the Establishment Clause should require the second.[83]

Does this asymmetry give secular liberalism the upper hand, or in other words, "discriminate" against religion? It does so no more than the baseline set by the Religion Clauses requires. The Religion Clauses enable government to pursue and endorse a culture of liberal democracy that will predictably clash over many is-

---

curiously overlooks that the penalty in *Lemon* is compellingly justified by the conscientious objection concerns of the Establishment Clause.

[82] This condition differs from the anti-abortion counseling condition on public family planning funds upheld in *Rust*, 111 S Ct 1759. The hypothesized program is one of *general* health care for pregnant women, a universe logically including abortion counseling. In contrast, the Court managed to find the program at issue in *Rust* to be a program limited to "pre-conceptual" counseling about birth control, a universe logically excluding advice about abortion, a "post-conceptual" event. Id at 1772-73. Within the universe of general health care for pregnant women, a condition requiring pro-childbirth advice but forbidding pro-abortion advice would be just the sort of viewpoint discrimination that the Court in *Rust* said was still barred by the First Amendment. Id.

[83] It is not clear that McConnell would disagree with this conclusion. He advocates free speech for religious grantees only where the government has provided a forum for free speech by all grantees (as in *Widmar*, 454 US 263). McConnell, in this volume, 186-87 (cited in note 1). He does not advocate free speech for religious grantees where the government has enlisted private grantees as mouthpieces for a specific government-backed viewpoint (as in *Kendrick*, 487 US 589, where McConnell agrees with the Court's suggestion that religious grantees may preach abstinence but not religion while participating in Adolescent Family Life Act programs). Id. If public education falls on the government speech side of this public forum/government speech dichotomy, then McConnell should permit, if not require, anti-proselytizing conditions.

sues with religious subcultures. The public classroom, for example, may inculcate commitments to gender equality that are incompatible with notions of the natural subordination of women to men drawn by some from the Bible. Protection for religious subcultures lies in exit rights, vigorously protected under the Free Exercise Clause: the solution for those whose religion clashes with a Dick and Jane who appear nothing like Adam and Eve is to leave the public school.[84] The privatization of religion reconciles the two Religion Clauses.

III. FREE EXERCISE

Contemporary legislation rarely evinces outright hostility to religion. Like overt racism, explicit bigotry is hard to find on the face of contemporary laws. When religion is singled out, it is often out of express concern to avoid establishing religion rather than out of hostility.[85] Yet the Supreme Court increasingly has viewed such religious exclusions as overstating the establishment problem and thus as unjustified.[86]

The far more important free exercise problem today comes not from facially discriminatory laws, but rather from facially neutral laws that have a disparate impact on religion by making demands or causing consequences incompatible with religious practice. Most free exercise claims to reach the Supreme Court have been requests for exemption, not invalidation. The analogy in the speech context is challenges to content-neutral laws with an ancillary impact on speech, such as the (unsuccessful) claim in *United States v O'Brien* that a law against draft card mutilation could not constitutionally apply to burning a draft card as a means of political dissent.[87]

---

[84] See *Pierce v Society of Sisters*, 268 US 510 (1925) (upholding right of parents to withdraw children from public schools and educate them privately). Such exit rights are essential not only to the individual liberty of religious parents but also to the flourishing of their communities.

[85] To be sure, the government sometimes does discriminate against minority religions, especially unpopular ones such as Reverend Moon's Unification Church. See, for example, *Larson v Valente*, 456 US 228 (1982) (state's charitable solicitation act was an unconstitutional denominational preference because it exempted from registration and reporting requirements only those religions that receive more than half their total contributions from members).

[86] See *McDaniel*, 435 US 618 (permitting ministers to hold public office); *Widmar*, 454 US 263 (permitting religious organizations to gather on state-owned property); and *Witters v Department of Services*, 474 US 481 (1986) (permitting blind man to receive aid for education at religious college).

[87] 391 US 367 (1968).

The Supreme Court has overwhelmingly rejected free exercise exemption claims. None has succeeded, except in *Wisconsin v Yoder*, which held that Old Order Amish had a free exercise right to withdraw their children from the public schools, compulsory public school attendance notwithstanding;[88] and in the *Sherbert v Verner* line of cases, which held that people unemployed because their religious practices clash with the terms of available employment have a free exercise right to receive unemployment benefits.[89] The Court has used two techniques to reject other claims for exemption from facially neutral laws: First, it has sometimes applied a form of heightened scrutiny, but has found a government interest in the uniform application of the law that outweighs the burden on the religious practice of the claimant.[90] Second, and more typically in recent cases, it has found some reason to forego any searching judicial scrutiny at all.

There have been two variations on the latter approach. In one, the Court has found that a law burdens religion, but has also found that the "restricted environment" to which the law applies, such as the military or prisons, justifies greater deference to government and thus only rationality review.[91] In the other, the Court has found no burden on free exercise of religion in the first place, so as to obviate heightened justification at the threshold. For example, the Court has granted government nearly absolute discretion to conduct its own "internal affairs,"[92] even where the consequences for a religion are devastating. More sweepingly, the Court recently held in *Employment Division v Smith* that free exercise exemption claims from a "neutral law of general applicability" trigger no heightened scrutiny—no matter what the "incidental" impact on

---

[88] 406 US 205 (1972).

[89] *Sherbert v Verner*, 374 US 398 (1963). See also *Thomas v Review Bd. of Indiana Employment Security Division*, 450 US 707 (1981); *Hobbie v Unemployment Appeals Commission of Florida*, 480 US 136 (1987); *Frazee v Illinois Department of Employment Security*, 489 US 829 (1989).

[90] See, for example, *Braunfeld v Brown*, 366 US 599 (1961) (uniform day of rest); *United States v Lee*, 455 US 252 (1982) (uniform contribution to social security system).

[91] See, for example, *Goldman v Weinberger*, 475 US 503 (1986) (rejecting free exercise claim of Jewish officer who sought exemption from military headgear regulations forbidding yarmulke); *O'Lone v Estate of Shabazz*, 482 US 342 (1987) (rejecting free exercise claim of Muslim prisoner who sought exemption from prison security regulations forbidding him to attend Jumu'ah services).

[92] See, for example, *Bowen v Roy*, 476 US 693, 699 (1986) (rejecting free exercise claim by Native American seeking government benefits without assignment of a social security number to his daughter, which he believed would rob her of her soul); *Lyng v Northwest Indian Cemetery Protective Ass'n*, 485 US 439, 448-49 (1988) (rejecting free exercise claim by Native Americans seeking to prevent government foresters from destroying a sacred site).

religious exercise may be.[93] Deliberate targeting of religion will be strictly scrutinized, but government indifference to religious impact—even if negligent—will trigger only rationality review.[94] *Smith* thus amounts not to the *O'Brien*[95] of free exercise law, but rather to its *Washington v Davis*.[96]

Professor McConnell and I fully agree upon the big flaw in *Smith*: it entrenches patterns of de facto discrimination against minority religions. Note that not a single religious exemption claim has ever reached the Supreme Court from a mainstream Christian religious practitioner. Mainstream Christianity does not need judicial help; the legislature is likely already to be obliging. It did not take a lawsuit but only a statute to free sacramental wine from the strictures of Prohibition.[97] Claims for judicial exemption under the Free Exercise Clause, like claims for exemption under the Free Speech Clause, emanate almost invariably from members of relatively politically powerless groups, toward whom the majority is likely to be selectively indifferent or worse. Minority religionists, like political dissenters, rarely have the political muscle to secure exemptions for themselves on the legislative floor.[98] *Smith* wipes out their alternative recourse. The majoritarianism reflected in *Smith* complements the majoritarianism implicit in the permissive establishment cases: It is as if the Court wears blinders, so that it cannot see an establishment of mainstream Christianity and cannot see free exercise violations of anything else.

The Court's retreat on free exercise is related to its retreat on establishment in another respect as well: Both exhibit a retrogressive view of "coercion." A fundamental feature of the modern welfare state is that government can more easily burden rights with-

---

[93] 110 S Ct 1595, 1600 (1990).

[94] Specifically, *Smith* rejected a claim by Native Americans to exempt religiously mandated peyote ingestion from criminal prohibitions on drug use, holding that no heightened scrutiny attaches to claims for exemption from a "generally applicable law that requires (or forbids) the performance of an act that his religious belief forbids (or requires)." Id at 1599. For a strong critique, see Michael W. McConnell, *Free Exercise Revisionism and the* Smith *Decision*, 57 U Chi L Rev 1109 (1990).

[95] See note 87 and accompanying text.

[96] 426 US 229 (1976).

[97] Volstead Act of Oct 28, 1919, 41 Stat 305, codified at 27 USC § 16 (1918), repealed, Act of Aug 27, 1935, 49 Stat 872.

[98] But sometimes they do have the muscle. As *Smith* noted, a number of states voluntarily exempt sacramental peyote use, and Oregon recently joined their number. *Smith*, 110 S Ct at 1606; Or Rev Stat § 475.992(5) (1991). Conversely, it is at least ironic to note that "mainstream Christianity" is today a political alliance, when it was intra-Christian conflict that motivated the Religion Clauses.

out the direct use of force.[99] By heading toward a "coercion" test in establishment while narrowing the definition of "coercion" in free exercise law, however, the Court is returning to a force-based definition of religious injury more appropriate to pre-New Deal government. This reverses the trend which Justice Brennan began in *Sherbert v Verner*, which established a capacious view of "coercion." Recall that in *Sherbert*, the Court held that a denial of unemployment benefits to a Saturday Sabbatarian who lost her job for refusing to work on her sabbath must be strictly scrutinized as the equivalent of a criminal fine on Saturday worship.[100] The key departure in *Sherbert* was to treat the indirect incentives created by a government benefit program as the constitutional equivalent of the use of force.[101] The theory is that one afraid of being denied unemployment benefits will be more likely to work on her Saturday sabbath—it matters little just how much more.

The Court's more recent free exercise cases, however, have shifted the focus back from effects to mechanism, and have resurrected force as the paradigm. In *Bowen v Roy*, the Court rejected a Native American's effort to prevent the government from assigning a social security number to his daughter, despite his belief that it would rob her of her soul. The Court reasoned that religious adherents have no "right to dictate the conduct of the Government's internal procedures."[102] The Court split on a second issue: whether the government could require Mr. Roy to use the soul-robbing social security number as a condition of obtaining Aid to Families with Dependent Children—an issue one might have thought was

---

[99] See Kathleen M. Sullivan, *Unconstitutional Conditions*, 102 Harv L Rev 1413 (1989).

[100] 374 US at 404.

[101] It is a closer question whether establishment concerns justified denying unemployment compensation to Mrs. Sherbert. Writing for the Court, Justice Brennan rejected the dissenters' objection that granting the benefit would amount to a subsidy or windfall to Mrs. Sherbert's religion in violation of the Establishment Clause. Id at 409-10. As I have argued elsewhere, I believe that Brennan's reasoning effectively concedes the sovereignty of Mrs. Sherbert's religion. See Sullivan, 102 Harv L Rev at 1436 & n 84, 1440 (cited in note 99). The baseline for claims of unemployment compensation is involuntary unemployment. If Mrs. Sherbert is deemed voluntarily unemployed because she is choosing religion over work, then giving her (but not other Saturday shirkers) unemployment compensation looks like a subsidy. The denial of unemployment looks like a penalty, however, if Mrs. Sherbert is deemed involuntarily unemployed. Justice Brennan's implicit assumption must have been that the commands of God were no more within Mrs. Sherbert's conscious control than the local unemployment rate, and hence that her unemployment was involuntary. See McConnell, in this volume, 184-85 (cited in note 1), for a full defense of this assumption. There is force, however, to the argument that this assumption gives preferential treatment to religion.

[102] *Bowen*, 476 US at 700.

controlled by *Sherbert*. While Chief Justice Burger's opinion was joined only by Justices Rehnquist and Powell, it reached the merits and found this condition constitutional on grounds that undercut *Sherbert*'s core premise:

> [W]hile we do not believe that no government compulsion is involved, we cannot ignore the reality that denial of such benefits by a uniformly applicable statute neutral on its face is of a wholly different, less intrusive nature than affirmative compulsion or prohibition, by threat of penal sanctions, for conduct that has religious implications.[103]

In *Lyng v Northwest Indian Protective Ass'n*,[104] such reasoning came home to roost. There the Court upheld the government's decision to develop public wilderness in a way that would destroy irretrievably Native American use of the land as a worship site.[105] Writing for the Court, Justice O'Connor (despite her dissent from the Burger opinion in *Roy*) read "prohibition" of free exercise to mean "coercion," and found no coercion.[106] *Lyng* ignored the government's monopoly of a unique worship site, which gave it decisive leverage over the minimal preconditions for the religion's exercise. In such a setting, government indifference becomes the equivalent of prohibitive regulation.[107]

The Court's increasing inattention to effects culminated in *Smith*, which applied deferential review even to a criminal law that literally "prohibited" a religious practice, but not intentionally. In *Smith*, even a coercive mechanism plus a prohibitive effect were not enough so long as the law was facially neutral with respect to religion.

By rejecting disparate impact as a trigger, and by so rarely finding "coercion" or its equivalent in the proprietary actions of the welfare state, the Court has narrowed free exercise too far. The common thread in these cases is an overstated fear of religious anarchy. The most extreme statement is Justice Scalia's in *Smith*: to permit frequent religious exemptions "would be courting anar-

---

[103] Id at 704.

[104] 485 US 439 (1988).

[105] *Lyng*, 485 US at 453.

[106] Id at 450-51.

[107] Compare *Webster v Reproductive Health Services*, 492 US 490, 510 n 8 (1989) (although prohibiting abortions in public hospitals is constitutional in a world with private hospitals, it might be unconstitutional in a world of universal public health care, where denying access to public hospitals for abortions would be the equivalent of a regulatory ban).

chy"—"a system in which each conscience is a law unto itself."[108]
And Scalia found this danger especially potent in a society of many
diverse religious beliefs.[109]

Such reasoning overestimates the practical dangers religious
deviance from conventional practice currently poses to the rule of
law.[110] The error began with *Reynolds v United States*, which disallowed a free exercise claim by Mormons for exemption from a
territorial criminal ban on the practice of polygamy, which was key
to spiritual elevation within their church at the time.[111] The
Court's argument that polygamy was linked to despotic political
regimes, and would have negative external effects on the state-
sanctioned institution of monogamous marriage, seems no more
persuasive than similar domino theories sometimes advanced today
in defense of sodomy laws. Likewise, the conclusion that ceremonial peyote ingestion threatens to undermine the war on drugs
seems widely off the mark, given the small market for the drug and
the self-limiting requirement of religious ceremonial use.

Of course, it is a harder case if the religious practice causes
direct physical harm. For example, should the homicide laws apply
to a cult that reenacts Christ's crucifixion with a real crucifixion of
its own? Assuming a willing adult flagellant—permitting religiously
motivated infliction of harm on children would raise different concerns—it is difficult to make a powerful case that such a cult will
have a major negative effect on others' views of the sanctity of
life.[112] Perhaps even this practice should have free exercise
exemption.

Linking each of these examples is a certain degree of physical
insularity—sects living apart in enclaves demarcated from the civil
order.[113] The Court showed a soft spot for the communal values of

---

[108] *Smith*, 110 S Ct at 1605-06.

[109] Id. To Justice Scalia, the cure of judicial balancing would be as bad as or even worse
than the disease. Id.

[110] Under different social conditions—for example, a society whose religious population
was bipolar rather than pluralistic—I might be less optimistic. In any event, Justice
O'Connor's concurring opinion in *Smith* has the better of the argument: She suggests that if
anarchy really threatens, judicial balancing in favor of the threatened government interest is
capable to stave it off. *Smith*, 110 S Ct at 1611 (O'Connor concurring.)

[111] 98 US 145, 166-67 (1878).

[112] Willing self-sacrifice in the form of unpaid labor, in contrast, may have external
effects on competition and so may justify imposing the minimum wage laws on religious
businesses. See *Tony and Susan Alamo Foundation v Secretary of Labor*, 471 US 290
(1985); William P. Marshall, *In Defense of* Smith *and Free Exercise Revisionism*, 58 U Chi
L Rev 308, 314-15 (1991).

[113] See Robert M. Cover, *Foreword:* Nomos *and* Narrative, 97 Harv L Rev 4 (1983).

such an insular sect in *Yoder*.[114] Religious competition with the values of the secular civil order grows fiercer the more pervasive and integrated the religious practice. For example, when the Roman Catholic and some Protestant churches exclude women from the priesthood, they powerfully and visibly reinforce a social hierarchy rejected in the civil order. But such organizational autonomy is a price of free exercise, so long as it does not impede the functioning of the civil public order. Efforts to inject religious views of gender roles into the public school curriculum, for example, should be rejected.[115]

I thus substantially agree with Professor McConnell on the issue of religious opt-out from regulatory regimes. We both would tolerate more religious "anarchy" than would the Court.[116] We both would generally decline to protect adult "members of the religious community from the consequences of their religious choices."[117]

Where we disagree is on the question of religious opt-out from the redistributive programs of the welfare state. McConnell would grant to religious practitioners extensive withdrawal rights from such programs. For example, he would reverse the Court's unanimous ruling in *United States v Lee* denying the Amish the right to opt out of paying social security taxes,[118] and would likewise reverse the Court's unanimous ruling in *Tony and Susan Alamo Foundation v Secretary of Labor* denying an evangelical religious organization the right to pay workers in its businesses less than the minimum wage.[119] If the Amish believe in caring for their own elderly, he suggests, then they ought not have to pay into the system from which they draw nothing out.[120] The same goes for those "inspired to work for the glory of God for long hours at no pay."[121]

---

[114] 406 US 205. See note 22 and accompanying text.

[115] Thus *Mozert*, 827 F2d 1058, in which the Court rejected the free exercise claim of fundamentalist Christian parents against the exposure of their children to "secular humanism" in a public school, was correct. And *Edwards*, 482 US 578, in which the Court held that creationism may not be given equal time with other accounts of human origins in public schools, was also correct. The "establishment" of the public school curriculum requires that religious tenets be taught elsewhere.

[116] See McConnell, 57 U Chi L Rev at 1145-46 (cited in note 94) (arguing that the government has no power to intervene where the putative injury is internal to the religious community).

[117] See id at 1145.

[118] *Lee*, 455 US 252. McConnell, 57 U Chi L Rev at 1446 (cited in note 94).

[119] *Alamo Foundation*, 471 US 290. See McConnell, 57 U Chi L Rev at 1145-46 (cited in note 94), for his criticism of this decision.

[120] McConnell, 57 U Chi L Rev at 1445 (cited in note 94).

[121] Id at 1145.

Finally, he hints that legislative exemption of religious organizations from the religious antidiscrimination provisions of Title VII are not only permissible under the Establishment Clause, as the Court held in *Corporation of Presiding Bishop v Amos*,[122] but may be mandatory under the Free Exercise Clause.[123] Lurking one step beyond these conclusions is perhaps the view, never quite stated in his articles, that, as a matter of free exercise, those who prefer religious education for their children should not have to pay (through the property tax) for the public schools they do not use. On this view, vouchers permitting private direction of tax funds toward religious education would not only be permissible under the Establishment Clause, but would be mandatory under the Free Exercise Clause.

I do not favor such religious opt-out from the obligations of the welfare state. The reason stems again from my reading of the Religion Clauses outlined above. The affirmative implication of the Establishment Clause is the establishment of the civil public order. That order may appear to religionists to usurp some religious functions: The civil murder laws, not the tenets of Christianity or Islam, settle whether Salman Rushdie may legally be put to death for heresy. As the civil public order expands into greater welfare capacities, it may again appear to religionists to usurp some religious functions: public schools and unemployment benefits displace church classrooms and soup kitchens, all at common expense.

But it is a mistake to see these developments as a penalty on religionists who would rather handle education and charity their own way. All religions gain from the settlement of the war of all sects against all reflected in the establishment of the civil order. Religionists gain from the provision of universal public education even if they withdraw their children to private schools—just as the elderly or childless gain from the education of their fellow citizenry even in the absence of personal family gain. And religionists benefit indirectly from the establishment of universal social insurance programs. Just as religionists must pay for the secular army that engineers the truce among them, they must pay for the other com-

---

[122] 483 US 327 (1987).

[123] See McConnell, in this volume, 170-71 (cited in note 1). Professor McConnell likewise hints that it violates the Free Exercise Clause to require Catholic institutions such as Georgetown University to comply with the District of Columbia human rights law forbidding discrimination against gay and lesbian people. See id at 138 & n 111 (discussing *Gay Rights Coalition v Georgetown University*, 536 A2d 1 (DC App 1987) (en banc)).

mon goods of the civil public order. Thus *Lee* was rightly decided, and vouchers are not compelled.

CONCLUSION

Professor McConnell and I differ more about establishment than about free exercise. Whereas he criticizes "secularists" such as Justice Stevens "who take a strong position on establishment and a weak position on free exercise,"[124] I believe Professor McConnell makes the opposite error: He takes a strong position on free exercise but too weak a position on establishment. The Court has taken a weak position on both. I favor a strong position on both.

The Court's trends under both clauses reflect too narrow a view of "coercion." To be sure, forced oaths amount to establishment, and tarring and feathering members of a hated sect prohibits free exercise, but in the modern welfare state, so does a great deal more. In interpreting the Religion Clauses, the Court is headed backward toward an eighteenth-century focus on intentional force and away from a twentieth-century understanding that the state has many subtler but equally effective means for controlling religious incentives. McConnell agrees with this point halfway: he criticizes the Court's narrowing definition of "coercion" on the free exercise side, and would count a broad range of actions by the welfare state as "burdens" on or "prohibitions" of religious exercise. But he endorses a narrow definition of "coercion" on the establishment side, downplaying how the expansion of the welfare state poses new threats of establishment by means subtler than coercion as well.

Both McConnell and the Court undervalue the Establishment Clause, and in particular, its affirmative implications. Just as the free exercise of religion implies the free exercise of non-religion, so the ban on establishment of religion establishes a civil public order, which ends the war of all sects against all. The price of this truce is the banishment of religion from the public square, but the reward should be allowing religious subcultures to withdraw from regulation insofar as compatible with peaceful diarchic coexistence. And while financial support is withdrawn from religion, religionists may still be required to give financial support to the state, for all religions gain from the truce and the common goods of the civil public order it established. Will this asymmetry have crippling in-

---

[124] McConnell, 57 U Chi L Rev at 1132 & n 108 (cited in note 94).

centive effects on religious practice? The evidence of religious revival points the other way, and suggests we should have more faith in faith.

SPEECH IN THE WELFARE STATE

The New First Amendment Jurisprudence: A Threat to Liberty

Charles Fried[†]

> The first amendment normally has been the friend of left wing values . . . . We should remember too that during the ACLU's early years the organization represented mainly draft resisters and labor organizers, whom Roger Baldwin saw as, and intended to be, the main beneficiaries of his work. So the historical connections between left politics and free speech in this country are obvious.[1]

INTRODUCTION

One would think there is nothing new to say about the First Amendment. The principal lines of doctrine are clear. Government may not suppress or regulate speech because it does not like its content—unless it is obscene or demonstrably defamatory. If government regulates the time, place or manner of speech, it must regulate in a way that does not take sides between competing ideas. And if a government regulation directed at other ends has the effect of restricting speech, that regulation too must be neutral.

---

† Carter Professor of General Jurisprudence, Harvard Law School. Thanks to Richard Fallon, Thomas Grey, Sanford Levinson, and Martha Minow for commenting on earlier drafts, and to Mark Filip and Courtney Wilson for research assistance. This Article was prepared for *The Bill of Rights in the Welfare State: A Bicentennial Symposium*, held at The University of Chicago Law School on October 25-26, 1991.

[1] J.M. Balkin, *Some Realism About Pluralism: Legal Realist Approaches To The First Amendment* 1990 Duke L J 375, 383 (footnotes omitted).

Wonderful intricacies arise in working out the details and boundary lines of these doctrines, but the main principles are clear.

Last summer I lectured on American civil liberties law to a group of young lawyers from the former communist countries of Eastern Europe. These doctrines were clear enough that these lawyers could grasp them readily. They resonated so strongly with universal, liberal (that is liberty-loving) intuitions, that these young men and women found the doctrines entirely natural. At first they were a bit startled that our Supreme Court had declared that we cannot punish those who burn our flag,[2] but on reflection they found it thrilling.

So it is with no pleasure that I note that in this country, in classrooms and law reviews, the great liberal ideal of free expression is under attack. Tyrants have always derided freedom of expression—inspired either by Hitler or Marx and their academic apologists. But as Professor Balkin points out, it had been scholars and activists on the left who worked for the development of First Amendment law.[3] Yet today the theoretical challenge to free speech principles comes from scholars of the left.[4] Since ideas have consequences, and the ideas expressed today in the classrooms and law reviews may tomorrow find their way into judicial opinions, I sound the alarm: to identify and catalogue, to analyze, explain and I hope exorcise this new intellectual attack on liberty. Here, as in a number of other areas, "civic republicanism" is the banner under which this assault on liberty gathers.

A recent article by Professor Owen Fiss of the Yale Law School illustrates this threatening trend.[5] Professor Fiss takes a seemingly uncontroversial premise as his point of departure: The First Amendment's Free Speech Clause was intended to assure the widest possible debate about matters of concern to the community.[6] It is thus a principal engine of democratic or, if you will, republican participation in government. The error Fiss commits right at the outset is to mistake an effect of the principle for the principle itself. The First Amendment protects a liberty—liberty of expression—and it is an effect of this liberty that there is wide

---

[2] *United States v Eichman*, 110 S Ct 2404, 2410 (1990); *Texas v Johnson*, 491 US 397, 402 (1989).

[3] See Balkin, 1990 Duke L J at 383 (cited in note 1).

[4] The ACLU, however, has remained steadfast in this respect.

[5] Owen M. Fiss, *State Activism and State Censorship*, 100 Yale L J 2087 (1991). This article is related to his earlier *Free Speech and Social Structure*, 71 Iowa L Rev 1405 (1986).

[6] Fiss, 100 Yale L J at 2101 (cited in note 5).

and uninhibited discussion of political matters. Similarly, property rights enable markets and the efficiencies they entail. But property is not respected just because of the effect, economic efficiency; rather the effect follows because property rights are respected in principle.

Because Fiss substitutes the effect of liberty for liberty itself, it seems natural for him to claim that the First Amendment may compel making all important channels of public communication available on the widest possible terms—especially providing them to groups and points of view which are deemed insufficiently audible in the public debate.[7] In a benign application of this substitution of effect for principle, Fiss concludes that it would have been unconstitutional for the National Endowment for the Arts not to fund the famous Mapplethorpe photography exhibit.[8] More startlingly, Fiss argues by analogy to the *Prince Edward County* case[9] that in extremis a court might order continued funding of the NEA, if Congress chose to reduce its budget to prevent the NEA from making the controversial grant.

The real trouble begins when this conception of the First Amendment is pressed further to *deny* free speech protection to speakers who wish *not* to pronounce certain views. The speech-as-silence principle has been part of free speech law at least since the flag salute case, *West Virginia State Board of Education v Barnette*[10]—which held that it is unconstitutional to compel an unwilling speaker to speak. The protection of this principle has already been denied to broadcasters, who may be compelled to carry programs they deplore.[11] Fiss's argument entails a denial of this protection to newspapers as well.[12]

---

[7] Id at 2100-01.

[8] Id at 2103-04.

[9] Id at 2105. See *Griffin v School Board of Prince Edward County*, 377 US 218, 233 (1964) ("[T]he District Court [can] require the Supervisors to exercise the power that is theirs to levy taxes to raise funds adequate to reopen, operate, and maintain without racial discrimination a public school system [like] that operated in other counties in Virginia.").

[10] 319 US 624, 642 (1943).

[11] See *Red Lion Broadcasting Co. v FCC*, 395 US 367, 386 (1969), in which the Court held that it was not unconstitutional for the FCC to impose "fairness doctrine" rules on broadcasters requiring both that stations devote a reasonable amount of broadcast time to the discussion of public issues and that each side of a debate be given "fair coverage."

[12] Compare *Miami Herald Publishing Co. v Tornillo*, 418 US 241, 243 n 1, 258 (1974), in which the Court unanimously struck down a Florida statute which required any newspaper that "assail[ed]" a candidate in a political election to print upon demand any response the candidate might have, free of charge, provided the reply took up no more space than the negative comments.

From this it is but a short step to suppression pure and simple. Civic republicans explain the historic exclusion of obscenity from constitutional protection on the ground that obscenity does not contribute to, but rather degrades, public (republican) discourse.[13] Obscenity law is a puzzle, and scholars may be forgiven for this excursion. But the chickens come home to roost when writers as diverse as Robert Bork[14] and Laurence Tribe[15] would extend this analysis to deny First Amendment protection to flag desecration. And UNESCO's infamous "new information order" is upon us indeed as Catharine MacKinnon,[16] Richard Delgado,[17] Charles Lawrence,[18] and Mari Matsuda[19] extend this argument to speech that is offensive and insulting to vulnerable, disfavored (and politically mobilized) groups. MacKinnon and those who follow her not only would strip some forms of uncivil discourse of constitutional protection, but, characterizing them as affirmative *offenses* to constitutional values, they would make these forms of uncivil discourse themselves actionable as denials of constitutional rights.[20]

Straddling these two lines of argument is, in practical terms, the most important case: campaign finance regulation. This includes regulation of citizens' speech in the name of a "fairer" public debate, government subsidies of "under-financed" views, and compelled speech by broadcasters, all to provide platforms for, or

[13] See, for example, Frank I. Michelman, *Law's Republic*, 97 Yale L J 1493, 1532 n 161 (1988); Frank I. Michelman, *Conceptions of Democracy in American Constitutional Argument: The Case of Pornography Regulation*, 56 Tenn L Rev 291, 294 n 8 (1989).

[14] See the report of Judge Bork's testimony before the House Judiciary Committee in Robin Toner, *Bush Allies Push Flag Amendment Before Panel*, NY Times A14 (Jul 20, 1989).

[15] See Laurence H. Tribe, *Give Old Glory A Break: Protect It—And Ideas*, NY Times 19 (Jul 3, 1989); *Statutory and Constitutional Responses to the Supreme Court Decision in* Texas v. Johnson, Hearings before the Subcommittee on Civil and Constitutional Rights of the House Committee on the Judiciary, 101st Cong, 1st Sess 99, 140 (1989) (statement of Professor Laurence H. Tribe, Harvard Law School) ("*Responses to* Texas v. Johnson").

[16] See Catharine A. MacKinnon, *Frances Biddle's Sister: Pornography, Civil Rights, and Speech*, in MacKinnon, *Feminism Unmodified: Discourses on Life and Law* 163, 175-77 (Harvard, 1987); Catharine A. MacKinnon, *Pornography, Civil Rights, and Speech*, 20 Harv CR-CL L Rev 1, 22-24 (1985).

[17] See Richard Delgado, *Words That Wound: A Tort Action for Racial Insults, Epithets, and Name-Calling*, 17 Harv CR-CL L Rev 133, 172-79 (1982).

[18] See Charles R. Lawrence, *If He Hollers Let Him Go: Regulating Racist Speech on Campus*, 1990 Duke L J 431.

[19] See Mari J. Matsuda, *Public Response to Racist Speech: Considering the Victim's Story*, 87 Mich L Rev 2320, 2331-48, 2356-57 (1989).

[20] See Delgado, 17 Harv CR-CL L Rev at 134 (cited in note 17); MacKinnon, 20 Harv CR-CL L Rev at 38-39 (cited in note 16).

to avoid swamping, viewpoints that the government deems insufficiently audible.[21] The Supreme Court in *Buckley v Valeo* proclaimed: "the concept that government may restrict the speech of some elements of our society in order to enhance the relative voice of others is wholly foreign to the First Amendment . . . ."[22] This concept, however, is precisely what some,[23] including the dissenters in *Buckley* and opinions in subsequent cases,[24] have celebrated. This celebration has overlooked the *Buckley* Court's moderate course in allowing campaign expenditure contribution limitations in exchange for generous federal subsidies.

I. History and the First Amendment

American free speech law is as much a product of our history as it is a true deduction from valid premises. Its contours are the result of particular struggles and compromises, played out against the background of familiar doctrinal structures in adjacent fields of public and private law. It is also distinctively American. No other nation claims as fierce and stringent a system of legal protection for speech. It is the strongest affirmation of our national claim that we put liberty ahead of other values. We are still relatively free economically, though circumstances have made many qualifications seem inevitable. But in freedom of expression we lead the world. It is regrettable, but not surprising, that from time to time emergencies or passing tactical concerns lead to proposals to deform this achievement.[25] Far more serious is the disposition to embrace permanent limitations on liberty in deference to other values. Historically, for example, the claims of religion have led to restraints on

---

[21] See *Austin v Michigan Chamber of Commerce*, 110 S Ct 1391, 1408 (1990) (Scalia dissenting) (deploring this aspect of the Court's decision); *Citizens Against Rent Control v Berkeley*, 454 US 290, 298-99 (1981); *First National Bank of Boston v Bellotti*, 435 US 765, 776 (1978); *Buckley v Valeo*, 424 US 1, 14-59 (1976).

[22] 424 US 1, 48-49 (1976).

[23] Cass R. Sunstein, *Free Speech Now*, in this volume, 255; Fiss, 100 Yale L J at 2101-06 (cited in note 5).

[24] *Buckley*, 474 US at 265-66 (White concurring in part and dissenting in part); *Austin*, 110 S Ct at 1397-98 (Marshall writing for the Court); *Citizens Against Rent Control*, 454 US at 310-11 (White dissenting).

[25] See Flag Protection Act, 18 USC § 700 (1989) (held unconstitutional in *Eichman*, 110 S Ct 2404). This Act was only one of several proposed flag-burning statutes and constitutional amendments designed to restrict the scope of First Amendment protection recognized in *Texas v Johnson*, 491 US 397, 420 (1989). See generally, *Responses to* Texas v. Johnson (cited in note 15). Much that was said in favor of these particular flag protection proposals was probably aimed at heading off still worse incursions on the First Amendment. See, for example, id at 55-64 (statement of Professor Walter Dellinger, Duke University Law School).

liberty, as in laws against blasphemy and heresy. In modern times[26] the most constant and menacing manifestation of this disposition invokes the politics of community and equality: a community that politically mobilized agitators seek to impose, and an equality where all are equally subject to the superior authority of some leading class. We have now, as we have had since the time of the Jacobins, a determined band of intellectuals, politicians, and publicists enraged that human material is recalcitrant to their projects to level the condition of all men in the equal service of their particular visions of community. This project is not the pursuit of equality of opportunity, equality before the law, or even the decent instinct to protect all against misery and need. It is the pursuit of equality of results. The partisans of equal subordination to the claims of politics have always been driven to crush what stood in their way: religion,[27] talent, property, science, and most of all, liberty.

It is against this background that I see the elaborate recent campus speech codes.[28] As I shall show, it is hard to credit the claim that these codes are necessary to promote academic values of free and civil inquiry against the ill effects of ugly actions directed against minorities and women. It is more illuminating to see a desire to punish those who blaspheme against community. As with all blasphemy, some of the speech provoking these codes is vulgar, despicable and barely coherent, but this anti-blasphemy response also sweeps up speech that is merely heterodox or vivid.[29]

The difficult theoretical problems presented by the law's treatment of commercial speech, fraud, deception, assault, solicitation, and conspiracy assist the case for these codes, as does the difficulty of accommodating the right of free expression to other private rights. We know that the argument for free speech includes both

---

[26] This does not include wartime and national security concerns. *Schenck v United States*, 249 US 47, 51-53 (1919); *Dennis v United States*, 341 US 494, 511-17 (plurality) (1951); id at 519-56 (Frankfurter concurring); *Scales v United States*, 367 US 203, 228-30 (1961).

[27] Recall the mass murders committed by the Jacobins in Nantes with a mechanized efficiency not to be encountered again until the time of Hitler. Simon Schama, *Citizens: A Chronicle of the French Revolution* ch 17 (Knopf, 1989).

[28] These campus free speech codes are summarized in Comment, *Campus Anti-Slur Regulations: Speakers, Victims, and the First Amendment*, 79 Cal L Rev 919 (1991), David F. McGowan and Ragesh K. Tangri, *A Libertarian Critique of University Restrictions of Offensive Speech*, 79 Cal L Rev 825 (1991). See also Elaine S. Povich, *ACLU Joins Hyde in Free-Speech Fight*, Chi Trib 6 (Mar 12, 1991).

[29] See Dinesh D'Souza, *Illiberal Education: The Politics of Race and Sex on Campus* 129-56 (Free Press, 1991); Stephan Thernstrom, *McCarthyism Then and Now*, 4 Academic Questions 14 (Winter 1990-91).

speaker and audience. It encompasses a speaker's attempts to gain his audience's attention, and thus extends beyond the right to reach a willing audience.[30] What of the potential listener who in some circumstances does not wish to give her attention, or, having given it, wishes to withdraw it? No theory of free speech allows a speaker to pursue his audience into her home, break down her door and unstop her ears. Time, place, and manner restrictions—content neutral—may allow the proper regime of accommodation. But the harassment debate gives this problem a new twist. Are there not settings—the workplace or its analogues: a cafeteria, a hospital, or the campus where one lives and works at getting an education—where a listener is only willing to lend his attention to speech that observes certain limits of decorum and civility? And, if so, are these limits completely captured by traditional time, place, and manner limits? Do these limits not refer to content as well? Some such limits have been acknowledged *ab omnibus et ubique*. But they depend on legal structures, particularly those relating to property rights that are conventional and therefore manipulable.[31] This is apparent in the ebb and flow of decisions about picketing and leafletting in shopping malls and parking lots.[32]

I despair of providing a theoretical basis for free speech that is at once true and elegant. By true I mean that it covers all, and only, those cases that we conclude the First Amendment should cover. By elegant I mean that the theory is a method of analysis that may be used to generate doctrine, rather than a compendium of ad hoc doctrines. However, this is not to say that philosophy and deep political principles cannot illuminate, judge, justify, and constrain legal doctrine. An examination of philosophical and political principles can improve our general understanding of the law and provide insights into the proper foundation of free speech theories.

---

[30] *Cohen v California*, 403 US 15, 21-22 (1971); *NAACP v Claiborne Hardware Co.*, 458 US 886, 928 (1982); *Erznoznik v Jacksonville*, 422 US 205, 208-12 (1975).

[31] It is just at this point that Professor Sunstein, in this volume, 263 (cited in note 23), inserts his knife into the oyster and endeavors to pry it open. It is the whole point of my Article to argue that his effort does not succeed.

[32] See *Marsh v Alabama*, 326 US 501, 509 (1946) (holding that access to the sidewalks of a company-owned town was protected by the First Amendment); *Amalgamated Food Employees Union v Logan Valley Plaza*, 391 US 308, 325 (1968) (holding that picketers enjoy First Amendment protection to demonstrate in a shopping center complex); *Hudgens v NLRB*, 424 US 507, 518-21 (1976) (overruling *Logan Valley*, holding that picketers do not enjoy a First Amendment right to speak at a privately-owned shopping center).

II. FOUNDATIONAL PRINCIPLES

In an important article, Thomas Scanlon points out that philosophical speculation may establish the foundations of a particular topic; for instance the proper measures and limits of distributive justice, the notion of sexual or personal privacy, the propriety of blaming an actor for certain results he causes, or the nature and status of the claim to freedom of expression.[33] He calls the conclusions we reach at this level foundational.[34] They need not be formulated with a mathematical rigor that permits unequivocal applications to the range of concrete circumstances. When we survey those concrete circumstances, we may get a rough idea of how a particular society would look if it embodied the foundational principles. He calls this realization of foundational principles in concrete circumstances the level of policy.[35] Between the foundational and the policy levels stands the level of rights that we recognize in order to approximate these principles in the real world.[36] I have made a similar argument, that "the artificial reason of the law"[37] is necessary to make concrete the abstract, general reflections of philosophy. Philosophy may determine the general orientation of our judgments, but it cannot supply the machinery by which those judgments are instantiated by the law in actual social systems.[38] Ronald Dworkin marks this distinction as between what he calls background rights and institutional rights. I prefer Dworkin's terminology because it shows that at the "foundational" or philosophical level, just as much as at the level of positive law, our values may include rights—moral claims that may not be balanced away

---

[33] Thomas M. Scanlon, Jr., *Freedom of Expression and Categories of Expression*, 40 U Pitt L Rev 519 (1979).

[34] Id at 535.

[35] Id.

[36] Id.

[37] In using this phrase I borrow from Lord Coke, who first coined the term in his famous reply to King James I's assertion that since law was grounded in reason, he should be able to decide cases as well as judges. Lord Coke stated:

> God had endowed his Majesty with excellent science, and great endowments of nature; but His Majesty was not learned in the laws of his realm of England, and causes . . . [of action] are not to be decided by natural reason but by the artificial reason and judgment of law . . . .

12 E Co Rep 63, 65 (James I 1655), reprinted in 77 Eng Rep 1342, 1343 (William Green & Sons, 1907).

[38] See Charles Fried, *The Artificial Reason of the Law or: What Lawyers Know*, 60 Tex L Rev 35, 56-58 (1981). See also Charles Fried, *Is Liberty Possible?*, in Sterling M. McMurrin, ed, *Liberty, Equality, and Law: Selected Tanner Lectures on Moral Philosophy* 91, 134 (Utah, 1987), reprinted from 3 *The Tanner Lectures in Human Values* 89 (Utah, 1982).

in the way that competing interests are readily balanced against each other.[39]

Freedom of expression is properly based on autonomy: the Kantian right of each individual to be treated as an end in himself, an equal sovereign citizen of the kingdom of ends with a right to the greatest liberty compatible with the like liberties of all others.[40] Autonomy is the foundation of all basic liberties, including liberty of expression. There are famous difficulties in defining these spheres of liberty against encroachment by the actions of others—one man's liberty is another's constraint—and many have despaired of deriving any practical conclusions from this principle as it relates to laws bearing on conduct. But the way is much clearer with respect to thought, expression and persuasion. There the claim to liberty runs directly to the foundational. Our ability to deliberate, to reach conclusions about our good, and to act on those conclusions is the foundation of our status as free and rational persons. No conviction forced upon us can really be ours at all. Limits may be put on my actions insofar as my actions impinge on others, but my status as a rational sovereign requires that I be free to judge for myself what is good and how I shall arrange my life in the sphere of liberty that the similar spheres of others leave me.[41] I cede authority to the state to draw the necessary concrete boundaries between our respective spheres of action. But no such necessity requires, indeed self-respect forbids, that I cede to the state the authority to limit my use of my rational powers. That is why lying, while not the most damaging offense to another's moral right, is one of the clearest.[42] It is also why the state has no claim to dominion over our minds: what we believe, what we are persuaded to believe, and (derivatively) what others may try to persuade us to believe.[43]

---

[39] As Dworkin correctly points out, however, sometimes it is proper to balance competing rights. See Ronald Dworkin, *Taking Rights Seriously* ch 4 and appendix (Harvard, 1978).

[40] See Immanuel Kant, *Foundations of the Metaphysics of Morals* (Bobbs-Merrill, 1959); Immanuel Kant, *The Metaphysical Elements of Justice* (Bobbs-Merrill, 1965).

[41] We should not confuse this Kantian definition of autonomy with a completely different notion: the subjectivity of the good. To claim, as Kantians do, that the moral value of the good depends on its being freely chosen and that therefore the capacity to choose is primary, does not imply at all that there are no objective criteria of the good, or that the good is whatever is chosen, nor yet some thesis about the subjectivity of values.

[42] See Charles Fried, *Right and Wrong* ch 3 (Harvard, 1978).

[43] See David A. Strauss, *Persuasion, Autonomy, and Freedom of Expression*, 91 Colum L Rev 334 (1991).

The realization of these foundational rights in the First Amendment law of free expression illustrates the relation of institutions to foundations. The First Amendment does not protect a person from lies or imposition by private individuals. Rather the First Amendment protects against impositions by government—"Congress shall make no law . . . abridging the freedom of speech,"[44] "nor shall any state deprive any person . . . [of his free speech liberties]."[45] The Constitution is hardly concerned with the government lying, and few have argued that you have a constitutional right to have the government refrain from lying to you.[46] Rather, the pressing problems center around government restrictions on speech by others. Indeed, some of the cases in which government might be seen as acting on the Kantian principle—punishing false or misleading speech, or speech designed to circumvent rational evaluation—are just those in which free speech objections to government interference are typically made, though not always successfully. The paradigmatic free speech case is one in which government prevents a person from speaking or punishes him for having spoken—presumably to deter such speech in the future.

The Constitution is concerned only with limits on government, even though a person's autonomy may be assaulted as much if an employer, a neighbor or a family member silences him or stops his access to speech. Other legal norms take care of non-governmental offenses. The background system of private rights goes a long way toward vindicating free speech rights against private actors. John may not interfere with Jane's decision to publish Bill's letter in her newspaper. But neither may Bill complain if Jane decides she does not want to publish that letter. It is her newspaper. I may say what I want at a gathering in my own home, but I have no right to invade your home in order to give a speech there. Free speech values are preserved in this process because of the neutrality of these or-

---

[44] US Const, Amend I.

[45] US Const, Amend XIV, § 1.

[46] What would such a right look like? How would it be vindicated? In limited circumstances defamations by government officials are actionable. *Paul v Davis*, 424 US 693, 701 (1976); *Barr v Matteo*, 360 US 564, 572-74 (1959). But a generalized cause of action for government deception or concealment would, it is feared, make courts actors in controversies that are primarily political. The role of keeping government honest is left to the enterprise of the press and political opponents. The furthest the law of the Constitution has gone has been in *Richmond Newspapers, Inc. v Virginia*, 448 US 555, 575-77 (1980) (extending First Amendment right to receive information by applying it to the right to public access to criminal trials).

dinary background systems of tort, property and criminal law.[47] Perhaps this is why for a long time no one thought to apply constitutional free speech analysis to the law of defamation—unlike criminal libel, where the First Amendment always was thought to apply—until the misuse of that cause of action by the Alabama state police forced latent problems into the open.[48] This is also why commentators have not drawn into question laws against fraud and assault: they protect private rights, and often at the instance of a private party, not the state.

Is this simply an adventitious division of function between constitutional law and common and statutory law? Or is there something *foundational* (in Scanlon's sense) about protection against the government in the free speech area that makes it the proper and sole focus of constitutional limitations? In Max Weber's formula, government represents the monopoly of organized force of the community, that from which there is no escape, the final authority.[49] (Of course there may be powerful groupings in a territory, and sometimes it is these groupings and not the state that have the last word. But that is a pathological condition—at least in a context where state and law and a constitution count for something.[50] If gangs of thugs or warring sects generally predominate over regular authority, then we do not have the context of law or the state at all. And if we do have a state, then the influence of private powers in principle is not inescapable.) The state has the power, for instance, to tax the powerful and redistribute wealth so that new, competing centers of power might grow up. But this is not just a definitional matter. It is fundamental because, as Kant, Rousseau, Locke, and Hobbes each in his own way saw, the state is the only entity to which we delegate this ultimate coercive authority over ourselves. In contractual agreements with

---

[47] Here is what Sunstein's critique, in this volume, 263 (cited in note 23) misses. These background systems are indifferent—blessedly—to the ideological uses to which their beneficiaries would put them. Sunstein's "New Deal" for free speech would make room for systematic manipulation of these background systems to favor their use for "virtuous," "republican" speech.

[48] *New York Times v Sullivan*, 376 US 254, 268 (1964). There were more modest grounds on which the *Sullivan* case might have been decided. There was the obvious fact, for instance, that no reputational harm could possibly have been done to Bull Connor and his men by the New York Times advertisement—so that the punitive and presumed damages could have been seen as the result of the state rather than the parties acting.

[49] See Max Weber, *The Theory of Social and Economic Organization* (translated by A.M. Henderson and Talcott Parsons) (Oxford, 1947); Max Rheinstein, ed, *Max Weber on Law in Economy and Society* ch 13 (Simon and Schuster, 1954).

[50] See H.L.A. Hart, *The Concept of Law* ch 6 (Oxford, 1961).

fellow citizens we make and dissolve arrangements, but we acknowledge in the state a power over us whose authority we may not ignore—except by revolution.

To see this aspect of inescapability, consider the case of a municipal ordinance limiting speech and compare it to blacklisting by a major national media network. The first seems eminently escapable, the latter is everywhere in the national territory. But even that extreme contrast does not quite work. The government, even a municipal government, can make laws to control the broadcast network, and these laws will be effective within its territory; if it may not, that is only because the municipality is subject to another government. In short, the state is different. The state is the law, and the law is final—even when the law appears in the humble guise of a municipal ordinance. That is why our constitutionalism has built into the law a protection for certain fundamental rights against law (the state).

The Constitution protects primarily against state *silencing* of private speech because silencing is distinctive. Silencing invokes the power of the state against both speaker and audience. It stops both mouth and ears. It prevents a transaction between citizens. Classic free speech law privileges speech transactions between citizens as none of the state's business. We acknowledge the state's authority over us in all sorts of situations, but by silencing, the state is asking us to acquiesce in sovereignty over our minds, our rational capacities. That is a deeper kind of subordination than one which at least leaves us free to judge that what the state has done is wrong.

In the case in which the audience does not care to receive the communication, the offense to autonomy is harder to identify. At its limit, where no injury is done to others by the unwanted speech, silencing offends a pure autonomy interest: a right to act (here, speak) where there is no harm to others. But cannot the frustration of the audience's wish that the speaker be silent constitute a kind of harm to it? Perhaps, but not one that should be cognizable in law. It is central to the idea of a fundamental right to liberty that no one should curtail (or ask the state to curtail) the liberty of another when the only reason is disagreement about another's conception of the good. State regulation of unwelcome expression is the punishment of pure ideas or beliefs—the outlawing of having ideas or beliefs, or of letting people know that you have them.[51] This injustice is related, but not identical, to that done in the communicative case. We derive them both from the notion that in a free, just society (a liberal society) no one may be compelled to adopt or to deny any particular theory of the good (although he may be compelled to act on such a theory when communal action is otherwise warranted). This concept of justice limits what we may do to punish unilateral expression and what we may do to forbid communications that may convince an audience to modify its conception of the good.

Private impositions and limitations differ fundamentally from state impositions. First, they issue from the limiting person's own exercise of liberty: the newspaper does not wish to carry my op-ed piece, the private university does not wish to include my intellectual system in its course of study. Second, these limitations derive from other private rights that the limiter might have: rights to privacy, or more commonly, rights to property. A liberal society acknowledges private domains in part to allow the development of individual conceptions of the good.[52] If another individual can invoke the power of the state to override that dominion it is likely to be an illiberal claim of authority by the state to adjudicate between two persons' conceptions of the good. Even a judgment by the state that it would be good for you to hear a speech you do not agree with while you are in your own private space is an illiberal assertion of authority. By contrast, time, place, and manner regulations, which are content-neutral, are not an illiberal assertion of authority, but rather a good faith attempt by the liberal state to adjust zones of privacy without regard to what will be pursued within those zones.

III. Policing the Truth

The foundational status of the state action doctrine answers other questions about the accepted contours of constitutional free speech doctrine. Expressions of opinion are the paradigms of what

---

[51] Robert Bork argues that there is no difference between the state protecting against a neighbor's smoke pollution and the discomfort that some experience when they believe that their neighbors may be using contraceptives in their marital bedroom. Robert H. Bork, *Neutral Principles and Some First Amendment Problems*, 47 Ind L J 1, 7-11 (1971). Ignoring the differences in the route and the mechanism by which your burning tires in your backyard and your reading dirty books in your den may occasion distress to your neighbor is a mistake Bork shares with the civic republicans I criticize here.

[52] We cannot derive the contours of the private domains from any general moral or political principles. All we can derive is that there be some such domains. See Fried, *Is Liberty Possible?* at 127 (cited in note 38).

we protect. Free speech cases often explain that "[t]here is no such thing as a false idea."[53] But why may the state intervene to prohibit or punish factually false statements?[54] Defamation and deception are actionable wrongs, perhaps on the reasoning I have already offered: they vindicate private rights invoked by, or at least on behalf of, private individuals.[55] But the First Amendment precludes punishment for generalized "public" frauds, deceptions, and defamation.[56] In political campaigns the grossest misstatements, deceptions, and defamations are immune from legal sanction unless they violate private rights—that is, unless individuals are defamed.

We should understand the group libel controversy in this light. At common law a group libel is actionable at the instance of a group member only if the generalized libel is adequately pointed and the group sufficiently small so that each member may treat it as the equivalent of an individual defamation.[57] Other liberal societies take a different tack, but one suspects that they are doing so for one of two illiberal reasons. Perhaps they are punishing the wickedness of the person who entertains such sentiments and does not have the decency to keep them to himself. Or perhaps they fear that the group libel will change the values and sentiments of the public, much as a political campaign for a Marxist, Nazi or other palpably evil political cause could be seen as an attempt to corrupt public opinion. From the outset in this country we have

---

[53] See, *Milkovich v Lorain Journal Co.*, 110 S Ct 2695, 2705 (1990); *Hustler v Falwell*, 485 US 46, 51 (1988); *Gertz v Robert Welch, Inc.*, 418 US 323, 339-40 (1974).

[54] See *Milkovich*, 110 S Ct at 2705; *Gertz*, 418 US at 340.

[55] We will have to consider why even this is sufficient to allow a general invocation of state power. An analogous set of arguments might be developed to explain the tort of invasion of privacy and various proprietary actions such as infringement of copyright, publication of trade secrets, or publication of information that a reporter agreed by contract not to release. See *Ruzicka v Conde Nast Publications, Inc.*, 733 F Supp 1289, 1295-1300 (D Minn 1990). By a still more distant analogy, but one that I am inclined to credit, the government itself may have certain proprietary rights which it may protect even if in doing so it restricts speech. See *Snepp v United States*, 444 US 507, 514-16 (1980).

[56] See James Madison, *Report on the Virginia Resolutions*, in 4 *Madison's Works* 544, cited in *Near v Minnesota*, 283 US 697, 713, 717-18, 722-23 (1931). See also *United States v Hudson & Goodwin*, 11 US (7 Cranch) 32 (1812) (holding that there is no federal criminal common law protecting newspaper editors from prosecution under the common-law crime of seditious libel). In this respect our law is distinct from that of other countries—even quite decent liberal ones—which recognize categories of public defamation such as insulting the nation, or the flag, or the head of state. This is why flag desecration laws were so profoundly contrary to the American free speech tradition.

[57] *Neiman-Marcus Co. v Lait* 107 F Supp 96, 100 (S D NY 1952).

generally set our face against such illiberal laws based on such illiberal reasons.[58]

But why do we, along with all liberal nations, treat public deception in a privileged way? Why is there no legal sanction against false accusations against a political program in newspaper editorials? Why may a television commentator misstate the content of a Supreme Court decision or a pronouncement of the President and thereby misinform with impunity? We are familiar with the usual accounts: public debate must be "uninhibited, robust and wide-open,"[59] and the Meiklejohn thesis that the First Amendment protects all speech which bears on matters on which voters have to make decisions.[60] But these accounts seem to announce the conclusion rather than explain why we allow actions for deception and defamation in the private domain but not the public.

The answer must be that in the public domain the state is enforcing a view of the truth about itself. Because it is interested, it cannot be trusted. The public must be left to sort out the truth for itself. Does this mean that the Kantian principle allows a distinction between fact and opinion, at least in principle justifying the imposition of authority in the realm of truth?

We would be willing to delegate to others the task of ferreting out and stopping some forms of deception. However, for other types of potential deception the risk seems too great to allow this delegation. We would be glad to allow an expert to assure the correctness of food labels, claims for medicines and the accuracy of commercial advertising. Compare this to a scenario where the government prevents or punishes the publication of a scientific paper based on false, unreliable, or fabricated data. (Recall the cold fusion episode.) Our reluctance is much greater. We do not allow the suppression of articles about ill-founded diets, exercise programs, or even schemes for making huge fortunes or never having to pay taxes. Books and magazines of this sort may be sold with impunity; yet our intuitions change drastically if the speaker proposes a commercial transaction in which he sells something other than speech.[61]

---

[58] The major departures have been the Alien and Sedition Laws and the prosecution of Eugene Debs, a candidate for President who had received almost a million votes. See *Debs v United States*, 249 US 211 (1919).

[59] *New York Times*, 376 US at 270.

[60] See Alexander Meiklejohn, *Political Freedom: The Constitutional Powers of the People* 26-27 (Harper, 1960).

[61] Note the way we can distinguish the two: the legal sanction must attach to the sale of something other than the speech. If a health food store prominently displays crank articles

At one end of the spectrum are technical questions on which all reasonable, informed persons would agree. The autonomy principle is only implicated when the government seeks to control speech directed to more general or more abstract issues. With these matters, autonomy prohibits irrevocable delegation of the authority to control access to our minds. The issue of commercial fraud illustrates this spectrum. Most would accept the risk of erroneous fact-finding by properly designated government agencies (courts, juries) as a cost of being able to seek redress against others who have cheated us, even though we know that the government agencies might sometimes punish honest and even accurate speech in the process. Where government's own interests are at stake (as in political discussions and the promotion of candidates), however, we withdraw this delegation because of the inherent conflict of interest. This touches on the autonomy principle's objection to allowing the delegee to control the avenues that might lead to the modification or withdrawal of the delegation.

This brings us to the interesting recent development of constitutional protection for commercial speech, itself a victory for the autonomy principle. The initial extension of free speech rights to commercial speech in *Virginia Board of Pharmacy v Virginia Citizens Consumer Council*[62] was bold and correct. It was not, however, radical. The protection from the outset covered only opinion and true speech.[63] In *Linmark Associates, Inc. v Willingboro*, Justice Marshall, for a unanimous Court, explained the issue precisely:

> The [town, in forbidding the posting of "For Sale" and "Sold" signs] acted to prevent its residents from obtaining certain information. . . . The [town] has sought to restrict the free flow of this data because it fears that otherwise homeowners will make decisions inimical to what the [town] views as the homeowners' self-interest and the corporate interest of the township . . . . If dissemination of this information can be restricted, then every locality in the country can suppress any facts that reflect poorly on the locality, so long as a plausible claim can be made that disclosure would cause the recipients of the information to act "irrationally."[64]

---

about the healing powers of lecithin next to the lecithin rack, it is the sale of the lecithin that can be regulated, not the sale of the magazine.

[62] 425 US 748, 770-73 (1976) (statute prohibiting publication of pharmaceutical prices violates the First Amendment).

[63] Id at 771.

[64] 431 US 85, 96 (1977).

The commercial speech cases recognize the autonomy right to make up one's own mind about a proposal that includes no lies. The justifications offered for restricting truthful commercial speech boil down either to a paternalistic claim to control the judgments of even undeceived citizens or, more accurately, to the capture of governmental power by a self-serving faction of commercial actors seeking to entrench its own economic interests. In brushing past these justifications, the Court was not reinstating *Lochner*-era control over economic regulation. Instead, the Court recognized free speech values in an area where they had been overlooked, while using *Lochner*-era arguments to conclude that the state had not met its burden of proof in justifying restrictions on free speech. In pure cases of economic due process like *Lochner*[65] there would be only the Court's economic judgment.

IV. ASSAULT AND WORKPLACE HARASSMENT

The analysis that illuminated the issues of defamation also illuminates the constitutional status of a class of speech that comes closer to the campus speech codes: assaults, threats, and workplace harassment.[66] As we have seen, what made the law of defamation tolerable was the limitation to false speech and the government's limited role as arbiter between conflicting invocations of private rights. But now consider cases in which a person threatens another with physical harm.

The law of assault is grounded not in the communication of information (a threat, after all, is not just a statement of fact), but in the physical imposition for which the assault is a preparatory step.[67] An assault is more like the signal that triggers a criminal act and therefore is punishable as a part of that criminal design.[68] It is

---

[65] *Lochner v New York*, 198 US 45 (1905).

[66] See generally, Kingsley R. Browne, *Title VII as Censorship: Hostile-Environment Harassment and the First Amendment*, 52 Ohio St L J 481 (1991).

[67] See generally, *Claiborne Hardware*, 458 US at 909-11 (so long as means are peaceful, "coercive" and "offensive" speech is protected); *Pipefitters Local Union v United States*, 407 US 385, 421-22 (1972) (discussing election campaign law that prohibited unions from using threats to elicit contributions from members); *Watts v United States*, 394 US 705, 712 (1969) (Fortas dissenting) (hearing should have been held on question of whether threat by inductee to shoot President Johnson was a knowing and willful threat).

[68] Another intellectual puzzle, which the law has dealt with by taking it for granted, is the use of speech to further criminal agreements and enterprises, as when words are used to join a conspiracy, to give orders, or to supply instructions in furtherance of some criminal scheme. In all these cases the law has understood that the words are not being used to express an idea or an attitude so much as they serve as signals and actions. I can help you to build a bomb by supplying parts and helping you assemble them or by giving you the in-

similar to a blackmail letter, for example, which is not primarily a communication of information or a report of an attitude but more a proposal or consummation of a transaction—like the offer or acceptance of a contract. Sexual harassment of the quid pro quo variety (as opposed to the hostile environment type) has some of this quality: it is not the expression of opinion or statement of fact that is objectionable, but rather the offer to exchange workplace advantages for sexual favors.[69]

So it is inapposite to draw analogies between assault and cases of hostile environment harassment or of grave insult—such as in campus hate speech or public flag desecration. The latter are not preparatory to some physical imposition; or if they are, then it is the imposition that makes them wrongful. Instead, what is at work in such cases is the use of speech to cause emotional distress.

Remember that conveying information is not all there is to the free expression principle. Insults may contain a point of view that the speaker is entitled to express and his audience to hear. "Strong and effective extemporaneous rhetoric cannot be nicely channeled in purely dulcet phrases. An advocate must be free to stimulate his audience with spontaneous and emotional appeals . . . ."[70] And if the audience is the object of the insult, the speaker's interest in expression still supplies half of the privilege, which is enough to prevail. Certainly the privilege can't be overcome by the victim's interest in remaining unaware of the speaker's low opinion of him. Hence the difference between receiving harassing phone calls or being bombarded by invective on the street or at work, and the scenario in which one receives a single letter containing the substance of these views. We are not inclined to protect a person against the knowledge of another's bad opinion. Instead, it is the intrusion that is the basis for sanction.

Intrusion embodies the notion of countervailing right. You may not give a political speech in my living room against my will,

---

structions to make the bomb. All this falls outside the bounds of First Amendment protection, but the boundaries may be fuzzy and a sophisticated manipulator of ideas may make something that is squarely in one category look like it is also in the other. But we need not be fooled. For a discussion of the appropriateness of a prior restraint preventing publication of the technical information necessary to build a bomb, see Note, *United States v. Progressive, Inc.: The Faustian Bargain and the First Amendment*, 75 Nw U L Rev 538 (1980). For a thorough and illuminating general exploration of this question see Kent Greenawalt, *Speech, Crime, and the Uses of Language* 81-89, 281-82 (Oxford, 1989).

[69] See *Ellison v Brady*, 924 F2d 872, 879 (9th Cir 1991); *Hirschfeld v New Mexico Corrections Dep't*, 916 F2d 572, 575 (10th Cir 1990); *Dockter v Rudolf Wolff Futures, Inc.*, 913 F2d 456, 461 (7th Cir 1990).

[70] *Claiborne Hardware*, 458 US at 928.

because for quite neutral reasons I have a property/privacy interest in my home. It might also be argued that I have a right to pass along the street without being pursued by unwanted invective. The harasser in this setting is as much an intruder on my privacy as the beggar who corners me on a lonely subway platform.[71] A rule against this sort of harassment is a time, place, and manner restriction, a content-neutral notion that protects against non-consensual intrusions upon one's right to be in a public or other place in relative tranquility. This is much easier to see with respect to workplace harassment: the workplace is not quite your home, but neither is it speakers' corner in Hyde Park. For reasons that are quite content-neutral the law might assign me a right to limit the intrusions I must endure at work to those that relate to my work. The same is true of a college dormitory and some parts of a campus. People should no more be free to pursue me into my dormitory than into my apartment house lobby.[72] This analysis also explains the doctrines about public fora and limited public fora,[73] doctrines that may be seen as attempts to adjust conflicting rights of speakers and the private rights of property owners, audiences, and bystanders.

This institutional adjustment implicates a further institutional principle: restrictions on freedom of expression, if they are to be justified by invocation of some proper governmental purpose (such as protecting countervailing private rights), must be content- and viewpoint-neutral. It is not obvious that this crucial institutional device is a direct manifestation of foundational values. After all, if the government forbids cross burning[74] but not flag burning, the silencing would seem to be as good or as bad, regardless of whether someone else is also silenced. But in fact content-neutrality is the First Amendment's version of a crucial device deployed throughout law to enforce adherence to principle where good purposes are invoked to justify actions that have bad effects. To look only at constitutional law, we require that where legislation makes racial dis-

---

[71] See *Young v New York City Transit Authority*, 903 F2d 146, 152-54 (2d Cir 1990), cert denied, 111 S Ct 516 (1990) (upholding against First Amendment challenge NYCTA prohibitions against all begging and panhandling in certain public transit facilities).

[72] See *Kovacs v Cooper*, 336 US 77, 86 (1949); *Martin v Struthers*, 319 US 141, 143, 148 (1943).

[73] See, for example, *United States v Kokinda*, 110 S Ct 3115, 3118-20 (1990); *Frisby v Schultz*, 487 US 474, 479-81, 484 (1988); *Cornelius v NAACP*, 473 US 788, 799-800 (1985); *Perry Education Ass'n v Perry Local Educators' Ass'n*, 460 US 37, 44-46 (1983).

[74] Compare *In the Matter of the Welfare of R.A.V.*, 464 NW2d 507, 509-11 (Minn 1991), cert granted, *R.A.V. v St. Paul*, 111 S Ct 2795 (1991), with *Eichman*, 110 S Ct at 2410.

tinctions, it be narrowly tailored to a permissible and weighty government purpose;[75] where Congress conditions a federal grant to a state on the state's acceptance of the federal "request" that it adopt a federal policy in an area traditionally reserved to the state (such as the regulation of alcohol), the grant may not be conditioned in a way that is under- or over-inclusive relative to its proper purpose;[76] and uncompensated exactions of property rights from private owners in return for regulatory permissions are valid only if the condition bears a sufficiently close relation to the regulatory purpose.[77] In all of these cases the law assures that important values are not transgressed under the pretext of serving other ends, or even that they not be lightly (though honestly) sacrificed to those other ends.[78] Where the values trenched upon are less weighty, all the law requires is a rational relation to a permissible governmental goal. But no one suggests that the government can so easily justify infringements on free expression.

In some contexts this mix of foundational commitments and their somewhat untidy expression at the institutional level of doctrine would be acceptable and reasonable, and no great commotion would ensue. But the controversy over campus hate speech and the (over)reaction of some institutions has put such common sense accommodations under great pressure. Away from such pressures one would recognize the contingent and even arbitrary nature of some of the lines we must draw to adjust these conflicting rights. That is the nature of legal (institutional) protection for abstract (background) rights and values.

V. CAMPUS SPEECH CODES

If only minor intrusions were at stake it would not have been difficult or controversial to work out a set of rules that marked a person's private (or semi-private) space and condemn incursions

---

[75] *City of Richmond v J.A. Croson Co.*, 488 US 469, 505-08 (1989); *Palmore v Sidoti*, 466 US 429, 432-33 (1984).

[76] *South Dakota v Dole*, 483 US 203, 214-15 (1987) (O'Connor dissenting). O'Connor argues that attaching a condition to highway fund grants such that a portion of a grant to a particular state will be withheld if that state allows alcohol to be sold to minors is under-inclusive because it does not address the lion's share of the problem (adults between twenty-one and thirty), and over-inclusive because it stops teenagers from drinking even when they would not be driving.

[77] *Nollan v California Coastal Commission*, 483 US 825, 834-35 (1987).

[78] This is the law's version of the moral principle of the law of double effect, which suggests that it is more than an institutional device, albeit an important and pervasive one. See generally, Charles Fried, *Right and Wrong—Preliminary Considerations*, 5 J Legal Stud 165,.174-85 (1976); Fried, *Right and Wrong* at 201-05 (cited in note 42).

upon it. But a look at some of the campus speech codes that universities developed in the wake of a widespread campaign for them suggests that the regulators have bigger game in their sights.

Regulations at Michigan, Stanford, Wisconsin[79] and other schools[80] go beyond protecting the privacy of those who work and live in their midst. The University of Michigan regulations, for instance, condemn speech in the classroom, on bulletin boards, in campus fora, in school newspapers and in mailings that

> stigmatizes or victimizes an individual on the basis of race, ethnicity, religion, sex, sexual orientation, creed, national origin, ancestry, age, marital status, handicap or Vietnam-era veteran status, and that . . . [c]reates an intimidating, hostile, or demeaning environment for educational pursuits, employment or participation in University sponsored extra-curricular activities.[81]

What is condemned here is the content of the speech—not the trespass on the space of a reluctant audience which should find some conventional precinct of tranquility.

The ideas the universities condemn are false and offensive, but the universities do not condemn all false and offensive ideas. For example, an invective condemning the United States as an oppressor nation or condemning capitalism as a form of exploitation may be repeated with impunity. The same impunity would extend to invectives directed against students and professors seen as agents, apologists or running dogs of an oppressor nation and of capitalism. Individuals within the community may not espouse some forms of race and gender superiority, but may espouse others. Individuals may advocate Marxism and the most extreme forms of militant feminism. And none of these codes would condemn burning the American flag, even to affront a gathering of veterans or the

---

[79] See *U.W.M. Post, Inc. v Board of Regents of the University of Wisconsin*, 1991 WL 206819 (E D Wis).

[80] See note 28. Of course only public universities are subject to the strictures of the First Amendment, and for the state to restrict the right of private institutions to control discourse in their communities as they saw fit would in itself be a violation of academic freedom (a violation I would expect some of the apologists for this wave of repression to howl most vociferously against). A bill introduced by Congressman Hyde and supported by the ACLU makes this mistake. See L. Gordon Crovitz, *Henry Hyde and the ACLU Propose a Fate Worse than PCness*, Wall St J A15 (May 1, 1991); Povich, Chi Trib at 6 (cited in note 28). It is also true, however, that as members of the academic community we may protest against suppression of speech within it, though not on constitutional grounds.

[81] *The University of Michigan Policy on Discrimination and Discriminatory Harassment by Students in the University Environment* 3 (1988), cited in McGowan and Tangri, 79 Cal L Rev at 920 (cited in note 28).

widows and orphans of soldiers killed in battle. The universities condemn ideas as such: individuals may not express certain views in the way they believe most likely to attract an audience, though precisely the same forms of expression may be used to convey ideas and sentiments less provocative to locally protected sensibilities. This discrimination makes clear that those who promulgate these regulations assign to themselves the authority to determine which ideas are false and which false ideas people may not express as they choose. Breaches of courtesy and good manners may be akin to breaches of content-neutral time, place, and manner regulations, but the benign claim that these regulations simply seek to produce a more courteous community is belied by the fact that not all breaches of courtesy and good manners fall under the ban. Indeed some of the proponents of these codes scorn the idea of content neutrality.[82] The ban is an exercise of power. It shows who is boss. Thus the holders of noxious ideas are suppressed and the rest of the community is impressed and intimidated by this display of political might.

Thomas Grey, one of the drafters of the Stanford code, provides vivid confirmation of my thesis in a short article explaining and justifying that code.[83] He is an evidently decent, reasonable man, quite committed to liberal free speech principles. He begins by acknowledging, as do I, that "civility and courtesy in manner of speech can be required in the classroom from teachers and students alike."[84] I would go further and acknowledge a title to enforce such norms beyond the classroom—in the student unions, dining halls, dormitory meeting rooms and other common places of the university. But Grey is unwilling to enact any such "requirement" in order to deal with the incidents we all deplore. He states without explanation at the outset of his article: "[T]his value is not best pursued by coercive disciplinary regulations of campus-wide application."[85] One is left to wonder why. Toward the end of his

---

[82] See Matsuda, 87 Mich L Rev at 2350-51 (cited in note 19). See also Nat Hentoff, *Stanford and the Speech Police*, Wash Post A19 (Jul 21, 1990).

[83] Thomas C. Grey, *Discriminatory Harassment and Free Speech*, 14 Harv J L & Pub Pol 157 (1991). The Stanford regulation requires three elements to be satisfied to prove an offense: intent to insult or degrade an individual or small group, direct address of the speech to the individual(s), and the use of "insulting or 'fighting words.'" Stanford University, *Fundamental Standard Interpretation: Free Expression and Discriminatory Harassment* 1 (Jun 1990), cited in id at 160-61.

[84] Grey, 14 Harv J L & Pub Pol at 157 (cited in note 83).

[85] Id.

piece, and in another connection, he provides his answer. He concludes that the code he helped draft

> is asymmetrical in the following sense. In those unhappy moments when the contemporary campus becomes a multi-cultural armed camp, the Stanford regulation would prevent me from firing my most powerful verbal assault weapons across racial, sexual, or sexual preference lines. By contrast, people of color, women, and gays and lesbians can use all the words they have at their disposal against me. This result seems an impermissible failure of viewpoint neutrality to some civil libertarians.[86]

This asymmetry would seem to be a defect—an injury not only to traditional free speech principles of content- and viewpoint-neutrality, but also to the value of civility.

That something not quite wholesome is going on here is evident from the labored justification Grey offers for the code's conceded lack of viewpoint and content neutrality. Not only does Grey reject general campus civility codes, he also rejects disciplinary rules based on such "traditionally recognized exceptions to full First Amendment protection like 'defamation,' 'fighting words,' or speech that constitutes 'intentional infliction of emotional distress.' "[87] These latter grounds for regulation might sweep into their net false or unsubstantiated charges of racism or sexism and epithets used against males, whites, or heterosexuals. That is precisely why Grey rejects such grounds of regulation in favor of an analogy to cases brought under Title VII,[88] where the claim is that the employer who allows derogatory epithets creates a work envi-

---

[86] Id at 162.

[87] Id at 158 (footnotes omitted). Grey is actually on somewhat shaky ground. The citation to the fighting words exception is to *Chaplinsky v New Hampshire*, 315 US 568, 573 (1942), but more recent decisions have cast considerable doubt on the vitality of that precedent. See *Brandenburg v Ohio*, 395 US 444, 448 (1969); *Lewis v New Orleans*, 415 US 130, 132 (1974) (distinguishing *Chaplinsky*); *Gooding v Wilson*, 405 US 518, 528 (1972). And for the emotional distress doctrine, Grey's citation asks us to see *Hustler v Falwell*, 485 US 46 (1988). But the *Falwell* decision held that the First and Fourteenth Amendments prohibit public figures from recovering damages for the tort of intentional infliction of emotional distress in the absence of a showing that a publication contained a false statement of fact made with "actual malice"—a standard of proof adopted in "recognition of the fundamental importance of the free flow of ideas and opinions on matters of public interest and concern." Id at 50.

[88] Title VII of the Civil Rights Act of 1964, 42 USC §§ 2000e et seq (1972). Section 2000e-2(d)-(i) prohibits workplace discrimination on the basis of race, color, religion, sex, or national origin.

ronment more hostile to women and minorities and thus discriminates against them in providing employment opportunities.

The analogy is labored, and surprisingly so given the less troublesome and closer analogies that Grey has at hand but rejects. First, the one Supreme Court case cited to support the analogy did not discuss the First Amendment in reviewing a district court's failure to consider a woman's claim that her employer had sexually discriminated by allowing the creation of a workplace environment hostile to female employees.[89] More analytically, the hostile environment cases assume that the employer has both the common law right and the ability to guard against offensive conditions for all of his employees. The employer violates Title VII because of the deficient exercise of his authority (and common law duty) to provide a reasonably dignified work environment for all of his employees. Stanford is not in the position of the Congress of the United States, which passes anti-discrimination laws against the background of state law employment rights and obligations. Its position is rather analogous to the employer who is assumed to be entitled to enforce civility generally—an authority Grey declines to exercise—and who is faulted for failing to enforce it in the one respect which is, by virtue of the Fourteenth Amendment, a subject of federal congressional concern.

Is it unreasonable for me to conclude that one who shrinks from banning from the campus extreme and distressing verbal abuse generally, but will punish insults directed at "blacks, Latinos or gays,"[90] seems more interested in making a political statement and showing political solidarity than in protecting the civility of discourse in the academic community? If you think me churlish in hinting at mauvaise foi where I have demonstrated no more than faulty reasoning, then I ask you to consider what Grey offers in reply: Those, like me, who seek symmetry, content- and viewpoint-neutrality, are guilty of preaching "the *Plessy*[91] doctrine" of separate-but-equal[92] rejected in *Brown v Board of Education*.[93] But here Grey begs the question ferociously. Whether Grey likes it or not (and I suppose he dislikes it very much), there are grounds for saying that modern constitutional doctrine rejects separate-but-

---

[89] *Meritor Savings Bank v Vinson*, 477 US 57, 65-67 (1986). See Grey, 14 Harv J L & Pub Pol at 159 n 10 (cited in note 83).

[90] Grey, 14 Harv J L & Pub Pol at 162 (cited in note 83).

[91] *Plessy v Ferguson*, 163 US 537, 550-51 (1896).

[92] Grey, 14 Harv J L & Pub Pol at 162-63 (cited in note 83).

[93] 347 US 483 (1954).

equal in order to embrace the principle of colorblindness first stated in the *Plessy* dissent,[94] and the grounds are at least as good as those for saying that modern constitutional doctrine endorses the "asymmetry" that moves Grey and his fellow campus Solons.[95]

As you sow, so shall you reap. The result of the kind of asymmetry Grey celebrates is campuses where people falsely deploy raucous charges of racism and sexism not only with impunity but with a fair chance of bringing down censure. Not only does this diminish academic discourse; the reputation of the academy as the haven of free and open discourse also suffers. The sophistries used to defend the various campus speech codes have made intellectuals and academia the deserved butt of public ridicule. The PC jokes may not be very subtle, but they capture something that really is there.

And what are we to make of the argument, first offered by Catharine MacKinnon[96] and since given at least qualified support by Frank Michelman and Cass Sunstein:[97] that some speech must be shut down in the name of free speech because it tends to silence those disparaged by it. MacKinnon does not only make the conventional point that the speech at issue threatens in straightforward ways to drown out or do violence to the victims.[98] If that were the claim, it would come under familiar First Amendment categories—fighting words, incitement to violence, the heckler's

---

[94] This fundamental principle of colorblindness was first presented by Justice John M. Harlan, the lone dissenter in *Plessy*:

[I]n view of the Constitution, in the eye of the law, there is in this country no superior, dominant, ruling class of citizens. There is no caste here. *Our Constitution is colorblind*, and neither knows nor tolerates classes among citizens. In respect of civil rights, all citizens are equal before the law.

163 US at 559 (Harlan dissenting) (emphasis added).

[95] See *J.A. Croson Co.*, 488 US at 493-94 (plurality opinion):

Classifications based on race carry a danger of stigmatic harm. Unless they are strictly reserved for remedial settings they may in fact promote notions of racial inferiority and lead to a politics of racial hostility. . . . [T]he standard of review under the Equal Protection Clause is not dependent on the race of those burdened or benefitted by a particular classification.

"[I agree] in particular with [the plurality's] conclusion that strict scrutiny must be applied to all governmental classification by race, whether or not its asserted purpose is 'remedial' or 'benign.' " Id at 520 (Scalia concurring in the judgment).

[96] MacKinnon, *Feminism Unmodified* at 163-65, 168-71 (cited in note 16).

[97] Michelman, 56 Tenn L Rev at 294-96 (cited in note 13). Cass R. Sunstein, *Pornography and The First Amendment*, 1986 Duke L J 589, 618-24.

[98] MacKinnon also argues that pornography results in violence to the women in the industry because they are often raped, *Feminism Unmodified* at 179-80 (cited in note 16), and to women in general because it traumatizes them, id at 183, and also because it causes some rapes. Id at 184-85.

veto—and could be evaluated in those terms. No, here it is content that is said to silence, and it purportedly does this silencing by causing the audience—both the group disparaged and others in the audience—to entertain certain false opinions: for example, about the capacities, moral situation, and role of women.

Such an argument runs four-square into one of the two convictions at the very heart of free expression: that adult persons should be free to come to whatever opinions of which they may be convinced.[99] The purported silencing of which MacKinnon complains is a silencing that comes about only if women become convinced that they have no right to speak and if others are convinced that women are not worth listening to. This is an odd kind of silencing. Could the Roman Catholic Church complain, then, that Voltaire's diatribes against it deprive it of religious freedom because the faith of believers might be shaken and the willingness of non-believers to entertain its claims lessened? Is Catharine MacKinnon herself silenced by those who deploy good arguments against her? Are her opponents silenced by her good arguments? Of course, MacKinnon thinks her argument applies only when the better established inveigh against the less well-established. But this is irrelevant. If the better off threaten to use force against the less fortunate, that threat, like any threat of illegal or unjust action, is to be condemned. But arguments address the mind and the emotions; they threaten only persuasion. MacKinnon wants a kind of affirmative action in the realm of discourse, and like Robert Bork,[100] ignores the special route by which speech attains its effect. The use of the word silencing here is the kind of when-I-use-words-they-mean-what-I-say gambit that gives academic discourse a bad name.[101]

VI. DEBUNKING THE DROWN-OUT THEORY

It is but a short step from this line of illiberal reasoning to Owen Fiss's thesis that courts may require the state to subsidize access to the public forum by unpopular, unfamiliar, and ill-funded views.[102] Advocates could make the argument in terms of

---

[99] For an excellent critique of MacKinnon's thesis and the sense of those tempted to admire it see Ronald M. Dworkin, *Liberty and Pornography*, NY Rev Books 12, 38 (Aug 15, 1991).

[100] See note 51 and accompanying text.

[101] George Orwell characterized this sort of language use as "consciously dishonest," pointing out that a tyrant might call his regime "democratic" in much the same way. See George Orwell, *Politics and the English Language*, in *A Collection of Essays by George Orwell* 162, 168-69 (Doubleday, 1954).

[102] Fiss, 100 Yale L J at 2087-88 (cited in note 5).

the Meiklejohn thesis of self-government and support for the fullest measure of public controversy,[103] but these are not arguments that we can take seriously. I doubt that Fiss would invoke them to claim support for the very ideas MacKinnon and the University of Michigan authorities would shut down. Rather, the idea is that our society has victimized certain groups—some racial minorities, women, homosexuals—and that justice (if not the Constitution) requires compensation in the public forum as well as everywhere else.

To be sure, if government controlled all the resources, then very little would be left of the value of free speech. There are two responses, however, to this concern. First, as classic liberals have always known but socialists have forgotten, a limited government and a vigorous private sector firmly beyond government's reach are crucial to freedom of the spirit as well as to economic liberty. This is the basis of the old saying that liberty is indivisible. Since community control over resources is the light that beckons on the left, the left—to the extent it cares about freedom of the spirit—must seek out devices that will discipline the government's monopoly in the realm of ideas. But any such device must consist of an official arbiter (that is, a government arbiter) to attempt to distribute access to the public forum. And that device cannot be content-neutral. It must decide which views have been heard too much, which not enough, and which should not be heard at all. The only content-neutral device turns out to be a society in which a significant portion of the resources are in private hands and beyond the reach of government altogether.

Redistributive policies generally are quite compatible with this conception. In fact, as Rawls's theory of justice suggests,[104] this kind of liberty may be one of the best arguments against gross disparities of income, or at least against serious relative deprivation. But let the income distribution be as equal as you please, if a large portion of speech is in private hands, then, on a version of Robert Nozick's Wilt Chamberlain argument,[105] a lot of those resources will end up—as a result of private, individual, and independent

---

[103] Id at 2101.

[104] See John Rawls, *A Theory of Justice* §§ 12, 13, 32 (Harvard, 1971).

[105] In *Anarchy, State, and Utopia*, Robert Nozick demonstrates how liberty justly upsets patterns of equality, arguing that there is nothing unjust about an end-state distribution of resources that may favor one citizen over another (in this case, Wilt Chamberlain, as a result of his athletic prowess), at least where the initial distribution of resources was relatively equal and all income transfers occurred through voluntary transactions. See Robert Nozick, *Anarchy, State and Utopia* 161-64 (Basic, 1974).

choices—supporting the "wrong" speech, and "worthy" speech may be heard hardly at all. Once this occurs, the civic republican arguments we hear today about the corruption of the media and the degraded state of public discourse would be heard again.

Considering the facts of the American world, the whole drown-out thesis is patently absurd. It simply is not the case that no one will publish unpopular views. Information technology is so far advanced that it takes relatively small capital—capital that almost anyone can assemble—to put out one's message in print form. One need only listen to the news and information programming of public broadcasting to hear the broadest array of opinions—with opinions on the left generously represented. If raw, uninterrupted, uninterpreted public affairs reporting is your thing, it is possible in most large cities to overdose on twenty-four hours a day of one or even two C-SPAN channels. Mini-dish satellite broadcasting will reach the humblest home in the most rural setting—as it does already in Europe and parts of the Third World.[106] So what in the world are these people talking about? They cannot literally mean that their messages are drowned out in the sense that those who wish to hear them cannot. It is not as if the networks or The Wall Street Journal were actually jamming the broadcasting of anyone's views. What these people really mean is that not many people are interested; or are not interested for long; or, like myself, if interested are not at all persuaded. In this respect these critics are like annoying children who whine at their parents, "you're not listening to me," when what they mean is, "however much I go on, you don't think I'm right." This whining is dressed up in the self-serving jargon of false consciousness, domination, and cultural hegemonism—a jargon picked up from apologists for Marxism-Leninism—all of which is intended to show how the vulgarity of the competing media is at fault for causing people to ignore the left's more weighty message. What this comes to, of course, is that what some on the left have to say is so boring or so unconvincing that people would rather watch *Wheel of Fortune*. But is that really *Wheel of Fortune*'s fault?

In the end the "drown-out" forced-access thesis is really just a version of fancy arguments that are designed to justify silencing the opposition. What we have is an argument for censorship—this time to avoid the competition, in much the spirit that East European television used to jam Western broadcasts of "Dallas." Or it

---

[106] See generally Ithiel de Sola Pool, *Technologies of Freedom* 44-45, 153, 180 (Harvard, 1983).

is worse: by forcing newspapers to carry articles they do not want and by forcing networks to carry programming that the public will not buy, political entrepreneurs are once more flexing their muscles.

Forced programming is not so much a way of getting a message to the public (the public will probably tune out), as it is a way of showing off power by hoisting flags on other people's flagpoles. The West Virginia Board of Education could not have imagined that by getting Jehovah's Witnesses to salute the flag[107] they were instilling patriotism in them. Instead they were showing off their power by ramming their conception of patriotism down the schoolchildren's throats. This instinct of the civic republican to assert the primacy of community by ramming beliefs and values down people's throats is thus the positive version of the negative instinct to punish those who would speak thoughts the community abhors. Neither compelled professions of faith nor the punishment of blasphemy really seeks to convince; both seek to assert that great communitarian principle: the primacy of politics.

---

[107] See *West Virginia State Board of Education v Barnette*, 319 US 624 (1943).

Free Speech Now

Cass R. Sunstein†

The radio as it now operates among us is not free. Nor is it entitled to the protection of the First Amendment. It is not engaged in the task of enlarging and enriching human communication. It is engaged in making money. And the First Amendment does not intend to guarantee men freedom to say what some private interest pays them to say for its own advantage.

. . .

The radio, as we now have it, is not cultivating those qualities of taste, of reasoned judgment, of integrity, of loyalty, of mutual understanding upon which the enterprise of self-government depends. On the contrary, it is a mighty force for breaking them down. It corrupts both our morals and our intelligence. And that catastrophe is significant for our inquiry, because it reveals how hollow may be the victories of the freedom of speech when our acceptance of the principle is merely formalistic. Misguided by that formalism we Americans have given to the doctrine merely its negative meaning. We have used it for the protection of private, possessive interests with which it has no concern. It is misinterpretations such as this which, in our use of the radio, the moving picture, the newspaper and other forms of publication, are giving the name 'freedoms' to the most flagrant enslavements of our minds and wills.[1]

Alexander Meiklejohn

---

† Karl N. Llewellyn Professor of Jurisprudence, The University of Chicago, Law School and Department of Political Science. This Article was prepared for *The Bill of Rights in the Welfare State: A Bicentennial Symposium*, held at The University of Chicago Law School on October 25-26, 1991. I am grateful to Nancy Eisenhauer for valuable research assistance and to Bruce Ackerman, Akhil Amar, Mary Becker, Lee Bollinger, Elena Kagan, Larry Lessig, Richard Posner, Nancy Rosenbloom, Geoffrey Stone, and David Strauss for helpful comments on a previous draft. Participants in a workshop at Brown University also provided valuable help. A revised version of this essay will appear as chapters 7 and 8 of Cass Sunstein, *The Partial Constitution* (forthcoming 1993).

[1] Alexander Meiklejohn, *Free Speech and Its Relation to Self-Government* 104-05 (Harper & Brothers, 1948).

Even when the words remain the same, they mean something very different when they are uttered by a minority struggling against repressive measures, and when expressed by a group that has attained power and then uses ideas that were once weapons of emancipation as instruments for keeping the power and wealth they have obtained. Ideas that at one time are means of producing social change have not the same meaning when they are used as means of preventing social change.[2]

John Dewey

For those who believe either that the judiciary should play a limited role in American government or that the Constitution's meaning is fixed by the original understanding of its ratifiers, the First Amendment is a particular embarrassment. The current state of free speech in America owes a great deal to extremely aggressive interpretations by the Supreme Court, which has invalidated legislative outcomes on numerous occasions. These decisions cannot be justified by reference to the original understanding of the First Amendment.[3] Such decisions also involve a highly intrusive judicial role in majoritarian politics.

There is some continuity, however, between current practice and the original understanding, and between current practice and principles of democratic government. The continuity lies in the distinctive American contribution to the theory of sovereignty. In England, sovereignty lay with the King. "In the United States," as James Madison explained, "the case is altogether different. The People, not the Government, possess the absolute sovereignty."[4]

---

[2] John Dewey, *The Future of Liberalism*, in John Dewey, 11 *Later Works* 291 (Southern Illinois, 1987).

[3] Indeed, the protection of free speech originally may have been thought to confer primarily a ban against "prior restraints"—licensing systems and other means of requiring prepublication permission from government. See Leonard W. Levy, *Emergence of A Free Press* 272-74 (Oxford, 1985). Under this limited conception of the First Amendment, subsequent punishment for speech usually raises no constitutional problem at all. Id.

Even if this extreme view is incorrect, it seems clear that during the founding period, much of what we now consider "speech" was thought to be unprotected, and speech could be regulated if it could be shown to cause injury or offense. Joseph Story, *A Familiar Exposition of the Constitution of the United States* §§ 445-47 at 316-18 (Regnery Gateway, 1986). In any case it is revealing that during the founding period many people thought that the infamous Sedition Act—making it a crime to libel "the government" and thus criminalizing a wide range of criticism of government—was constitutional. See Philip Kurland and Ralph Lerner, eds, 5 *The Founder's Constitution* (Chicago, 1987).

[4] James Madison, *Report on the Virginia Resolution* (Jan 1800), in Gaillard Hunt, ed, 6 *The Writings of James Madison* 386 (Putnam, 1906).

The placement of sovereignty in the people rather than in the government has important implications for freedom of speech. As Madison understood it, the new conception of sovereignty entailed a judgment that any "Sedition Act" would be unconstitutional.[5] The power represented by such an Act ought, "more than any other, to produce universal alarm; because it is levelled against that right of freely examining public characters and measures, and of free communication among the people thereon, which has ever been justly deemed the only effectual guardian of every other right."[6]

With Madison's pronouncements in mind, we might think of the American tradition of free expression as a series of struggles to understand the relationship between this conception of sovereignty and a system of free speech. The extraordinary protection now accorded to political speech can well be understood as an elaboration of the distinctive American understanding of sovereignty.

My goal in this Article is to defend this basic proposition and to evaluate the current system of free expression in light of it. As we will see, an effort to root freedom of speech in a conception of popular sovereignty shows that our current understandings are off the mark. Those understandings misdirect the basic inquiry, protect speech that should not be protected, and worst of all, invalidate democratic efforts to promote the principle of popular sovereignty under current conditions.

I. THE NEW FIRST AMENDMENT

American children watch a good deal of television—about twenty-seven hours per week[7]—and American television contains a good deal of advertising. For adults, every hour of television contains nearly eight minutes of commercials.[8] For most of its history, the Federal Communications Commission (FCC) imposed limits on the amount of advertising that broadcasters could air on shows aimed at children. In 1984, the FCC eliminated the limits.[9]

In the wake of deregulation, some stations air between eleven and twelve minutes per hour of commercials during children's pro-

---

[5] Id at 386, 406.

[6] Id at 393.

[7] Geoffrey Tooth, *Why Children's TV Turns Off So Many Parents*, US News and World Rep 65 (Feb 18, 1985).

[8] Barbara Gamarekian, *Ads Aimed at Children Restricted*, NY Times D1 (Oct 18, 1990).

[9] Tom Engelhardt, *The Shortcake Strategy*, in Todd Gitlin, ed, *Watching Television* 68, 76 (Pantheon, 1986).

gramming on weekends, and up to fourteen minutes on weekdays.[10] Some shows are actually full-length commercials, because the lead characters are products.[11]

In 1990 Congress imposed, for children's programming, a limit of ten and one half minutes of television commercials per hour on weekends, and twelve minutes on weekdays. President Bush withheld his approval, invoking the First Amendment. According to the President, the First Amendment "does not contemplate that government will dictate the quality or quantity of what Americans should hear—rather, it leaves this to be decided by free media responding to the free choices of individual consumers."[12] The President did "not believe that quantitative restrictions on advertising should be considered permissible . . . ."[13]

Nonetheless, the Children's Television Act of 1990 has become law.[14] It is possible that networks will challenge it on constitutional grounds. Perhaps the constitutional attack will be successful. The plausibility of the argument has affected the debate over controls on children's advertising, and may well have deterred stronger efforts to encourage high-quality broadcasting for children.

This episode reveals that something important and strange has happened to the First Amendment. Whereas the principal First Amendment suits were brought, in the 1940s, 1950s, and 1960s, by political protestors and dissidents, many of the current debates involve complaints by commercial advertisers, companies objecting to the securities laws, pornographers, businesses selling prerecorded statements of celebrities via "900" numbers, people seeking to spend large amounts of money on elections, industries attempting to export technology to unfriendly nations, newspapers disclosing names of rape victims, and large broadcasters resisting government efforts to promote diversity in the media. How has this happened?

To attempt an answer, we must step back a bit. From about 1940 to 1970, American constitutional debate over freedom of expression was divided along clear lines. On one side were those ac-

---

[10] Gamarekian, NY Times § D at 1 (cited in note 8).

[11] On the development of this practice, see Engelhardt, *The Shortcake Strategy* at 70-81 (cited in note 9).

[12] *Statement on the Children's Television Act of 1990*, 26 Weekly Compilation of Presidential Documents 42, 1611-12 (Oct 17, 1990).

[13] Id at 1612.

[14] The President did not veto the bill but allowed it to become law without his signature. He did not explain why he did not veto it. Id at 1611-12.

cepting what came to be the dominant position, a form of First Amendment "absolutism." On the other side were the advocates of "reasonable regulation." One could identify the two sides by their commitment to, or rejection of, four central ideas.

The first idea is that the government is the enemy of freedom of speech. Any effort to regulate speech, by the nation or the states, is threatening to the principle of free expression. More subtly, an effort to regulate speech is defined as a governmental attempt to interfere with communicative processes, taking the existing distribution of entitlements—property rights, wealth, and so on—as a given. I will discuss this point in more detail below.[15]

The second idea is that we should understand the First Amendment as embodying a commitment to a certain form of neutrality. Government may not draw lines between speech it likes and speech it hates. All speech stands on the same footing. Thus the protection accorded to speech extends equally to Communists and Nazis, the Ku Klux Klan and the Black Panthers, Martin Luther King, Jr. and George Wallace. Government should ensure that broadcasters, newspapers, and others can say what they wish, constrained only by the impersonal pressures of the marketplace. This conception of neutrality among different points of view is the government's first commitment.

The third idea is that we should not limit the principle of free expression to political speech, or to expression with a self-conscious political component. It is extremely difficult to distinguish between political and nonpolitical speech. Any such distinction is likely to reflect illegitimate partisan politics.[16] Thus the free speech principle extends to more than self-conscious efforts to contribute to democratic deliberation. It extends equally to sexually explicit speech, music, art, and commercial speech. Under this view, the First Amendment sets out a principle not limited to its particular historical wellsprings. "Speech," in the First Amendment, means all speech.

The final idea is that any restrictions on speech, once permitted, have a sinister and inevitable tendency to expand. Principled limits on government are hard to articulate; to allow one kind of restriction is in practice to allow many other kinds as well. "Slippery slope" arguments therefore deserve a prominent place in the theory of free expression. As far as possible, "balancing" ought to

---

[15] See Section II.

[16] See Steven H. Shiffrin, *The First Amendment, Democracy, and Romance* 48-53 (Harvard, 1990).

play no role in free speech law. Judges should not uphold restrictions on speech simply because the government seems to have good reasons for the restriction in the particular case. They must protect against the likely effect of the decision on future government action.

In the past quarter-century these four principles have commanded enormous respect. The press insisted on them with special enthusiasm. It was joined by many teachers in law schools and political science departments, and by numerous litigators, most notably the American Civil Liberties Union.

One can easily identify the components of the opposing position.[17] On this view, balancing is an inevitable part of a sensible system of free expression, and "reasonable regulation" should be upheld. The meaning of the First Amendment should be determined by reference to its history, in particular by reference to the relatively limited aims of the Framers and the complexities of the Supreme Court's own precedents. Certain categories of speech—advocacy of crime, especially dangerous speech, commercial speech, hate speech, sexually explicit speech, and libel—fall outside the First Amendment altogether. The government, according to this view, plays a role in maintaining a civilized society. This means that it may guard, for example, against the degradation produced by obscenity or the risks posed by speech advocating overthrow of the government. Large-scale neutrality makes no sense.

From the perspective of the 1990s, it may be hard to remember the vigor and tenacity with which the opposing camps struggled over their respective positions. The basic commitments of the absolutist view are now clichés, even dogma. Despite that view's novelty and the lack of direct historical support on its behalf, it has won a dramatic number of victories in the Supreme Court. This is so especially with restrictions of speech on the basis of its content, where special scrutiny is now routine, except in quite narrow categories of excluded speech.[18] Thus constitutional protection has been accorded to most commercial speech; to most sexually explicit speech; to many kinds of libel; to publication of the names of rape victims; to the advocacy of crime, even of violent overthrow of the government; to large expenditures on electoral campaigns; to

---

[17] Much of this is stated in Robert H. Bork, *Neutral Principles and Some First Amendment Problems*, 47 Ind L J 1, 21-22 (1971).

[18] Content-neutral restrictions are of course subject to a form of balancing. See generally Geoffrey R. Stone, *Content-Neutral Restrictions*, 54 U Chi L Rev 46, 48-50 (1987).

corporate speech; in all likelihood to hate speech; and of course to flag burning.[19]

It is not an overstatement to say that, taken all together, these developments have revolutionized the law of free expression. For many, the new law is an occasion for a sense of triumph and, perhaps, a belief that the principal difficulties with First Amendment law have been solved. The remaining problems are thought to be ones of applying hard-won doctrinal wisdom to ever-present threats of censorship.

In the last decade, however, the commitments that emerged from the last generation of free speech law have come under extremely severe strain. Emerging controversies have appeared over such issues as campaign finance regulation, hate speech, "dial-a-porn," the securities laws, scientific speech, nude dancing, commercial advertising, selective funding of expression, pornography, and regulation designed to produce quality and diversity in broadcasting. With these developments, previous alliances have come apart. Sometimes the new disputes seem to resurrect the belief in "reasonable regulation." Often they draw one or more of the four basic commitments of the absolutists into sharp question.

The ironies in all this are abundant. The new coalitions have spurred plausible arguments of hypocrisy, with free speech advocates claiming that the new challengers abandoned the liberal commitment to free speech as soon as the commitment became inconvenient, or required protection for unpopular causes. Indeed, it has been charged that, for many, the commitment to free speech stands revealed as contingent and convenient, and not principled at all.

On the other hand, the enthusiasm for broad application of free speech principles to the new settings is ironic as well. The constitutional protection accorded to commercial speech, for example, is relatively new. Justices Douglas and Black,[20] probably the most vigorous advocates of free expression in the history of the Court, rejected protection for commercial speech, as did many others. The notion that the First Amendment protects libel of ethnic groups, or

---

[19] *Virginia Board of Pharmacy v Virginia Citizens Consumer Council*, 425 US 748, 770 (1976) (commercial speech); *New York Times Co. v Sullivan*, 376 US 254, 265-66 (1964) (libel); *Florida Star v BJF*, 491 US 524, 533-34 (1989) (names of rape victims); *Brandenburg v Ohio*, 395 US 444, 447-48 (1969) (advocacy of illegality); *Buckley v Valeo*, 424 US 1, 22-23 (1976) (campaign expenditures); *First National Bank of Boston v Bellotti*, 435 US 765, 776 (1978) (corporate speech); *Miller v California*, 413 US 15 (1973) (obscenity); *Texas v Johnson*, 491 US 397 (1989) (flag-burning).

[20] See *Valentine v Chrestensen*, 316 US 52, 54-55 (1942).

hate speech, is a quite modern development, if it is a development at all. Until recently, no one thought that the First Amendment cast any doubt on the securities laws. Until the last few decades, the states had very broad authority to regulate sexually explicit material. And the interaction of the free speech principle with campaign spending and broadcasting surely raises complex and novel issues.

Under these circumstances, it seems peculiar to insist that any regulatory efforts in these areas will endanger "the First Amendment" or inevitably pave the way toward more general incursions on speech. Insistence on the protection of all words seems especially odd when it is urged by those who otherwise proclaim the need for judicial restraint, for the freeing up of democratic processes from constitutional compulsion, and for close attention to history. These ideas would seem to argue most powerfully against reflexive invocation of the First Amendment.

Current law, then, faces a new set of constitutional problems, raising issues that have shattered old alliances and that promise to generate new understandings of the problem of freedom of expression. In this Article, I propose and evaluate two responses to the current state of affairs. The two responses have the same source. That source is the distinctive American contribution to the theory of sovereignty.

The first proposal calls for a New Deal with respect to speech. It applies much of the reasoning of the New Deal attack on the common law to current questions of First Amendment law. Such an approach would produce significant changes in existing understandings of the nature of the free speech guarantee. It would call for a large-scale revision in our view of when a law "abridges" the freedom of speech. At a minimum, it would insist that many imaginable democratic interferences with the autonomy of broadcasters or newspapers are not "abridgements" at all. The New Deal for speech would also argue that such autonomy, because it is guaranteed by law, is itself sometimes an abridgement. I believe that there is much to be said in favor of this approach, and in certain, well-defined settings, it should be accepted.

The second proposal is less dramatic. It proclaims that the First Amendment is best understood by reference to the democratic process. The overriding goal of the amendment, rightly perceived, is to protect politics from government. This view would clarify a number of current controversies without fundamentally changing existing law. I conclude that this approach should also be adopted, notwithstanding the likely apprehension from those accustomed to "slippery slope" arguments in the First Amendment context.

Ultimately, I argue that an insistence that the First Amendment is fundamentally aimed at protecting democratic self-government, combined with modest steps in favor of a New Deal for speech, would resolve most of the current problems in free speech law without seriously compromising the First Amendment or any other important social values. But in order to reach this conclusion, it will be necessary to abandon, or at least qualify, the basic principles that have dominated judicial and academic thinking about speech in the last generation.

II. A New Deal for Speech?

A. Background

Perhaps we need a New Deal for speech, one that would parallel what the New Deal provided to property rights during the 1930s, and that would be rooted in substantially similar concerns.[21] A brief review follows.

---

[21] Something of this general sort is suggested in Onora O'Neill, *Practices of Toleration*, in Judith Lichtenberg, ed, *Democracy and the Mass Media* 155 (Cambridge, 1990); Thomas M. Scanlon, Jr., *Content Regulation Reconsidered*, in id at 331; Owen M. Fiss, *Free Speech and Social Structure*, 71 Iowa L Rev 1405 (1986); Owen M. Fiss, *Why the State?*, 100 Harv L Rev 781 (1987); J.M. Balkin, *Some Realism About Pluralism: Legal Realist Approaches to the First Amendment*, 1990 Duke L J 375. For reasons suggested below, I do not go so far as Fiss in this direction; my treatment overlaps with the approach outlined in O'Neill, Scanlon, and Balkin.

Many of the concerns expressed here were set out long ago in The Commission on Freedom of the Press, *A Free and Responsible Press* (Chicago, 1947). That Commission, headed by Robert Hutchins and Zechariah Chafee, Jr., included among its members John Dickinson, Harold Lasswell, Archibald MacLeish, Charles Merriam, Reinhold Niebuhr, and Arthur Schlesinger. It did not recommend legal remedies for the current situation, but it suggested the need for private measures to control novel problems.

> The press has been transformed into an enormous and complicated piece of machinery. As a necessary accompaniment, it has become big business. . . . The right of free public expression has therefore lost its earlier reality. Protection against government is now not enough to guarantee that a man who has something to say shall have a chance to say it. The owners and managers of the press determine which persons, which facts, which versions of the facts, and which ideas shall reach the public.

Id at 15-16. For a recent statement to similar effect, see James S. Fishkin, *Democracy and Deliberation: New Directions for Democratic Reform* 33 (Yale, 1991):

> [T]he system of free expression cannot be evaluated merely in terms of whether some positions are forcibly suppressed. Crucial voices may fail to achieve an effective hearing without the need to silence any of them. In a modern, technologically complex society, access to the mass media is a necessary condition for a voice to contribute to the national political debate. Unless the media permit the full range of views that have a significant following in the society to get access to the media on issues of intense inter-

Before the New Deal, the Constitution was often understood as a constraint on government "regulation." In practice, this meant that the Constitution was often invoked to prohibit governmental interference with existing distributions of rights and entitlements.[22] Hence minimum wage and maximum hour laws were seen as unjustifiable exactions—takings—from employers for the benefit of employees and the public at large.[23] The Due Process Clause insulated private arrangements from public control, especially if the government's goals were paternalistic or redistributive. In operating under the police power, government must be neutral in general, and between employers and employees in particular. A violation of the neutrality requirement, thus understood, would count as a violation of the Constitution.

On the pre-New Deal view, existing distributions marked the boundary not only between neutrality and partisanship, but between inaction and action as well. Government inaction consisted of respect for existing distributions. Government action was understood as interference with them. The rallying cry "laissez-faire" embodied such ideas. The fear of, and more important, the very conception of "government intervention" captured this basic approach.

The New Deal reformers argued that this entire framework was built on fictions. Their response is captured in President Roosevelt's references to "this man-made world of ours"[24] and his insistence that "we must lay hold of the fact that economic laws are not made by nature. They are made by human beings."[25] The pre-New Deal framework treated the existing distribution of resources and opportunities as prepolitical, when in fact it was not. It saw minimum wage and maximum hour laws as introducing government into a private or voluntary sphere. But the New Dealers

---

est to proponents of those views, then the full realization of political equality has fallen short.

[22] Two qualifications are necessary. First, redistribution through taxation—most notably by way of the poor laws and other welfare measures—was permissible. Second, some forms of regulation were permissible even if they had redistributive features. The "police power," for example, extended to protection of workers' health, although the Court was sometimes skeptical that a health justification was plausible. See, for example, *Lochner v New York*, 198 US 45, 57-58 (1905).

[23] See *Adkins v Children's Hospital*, 261 US 525, 558 (1923); *Lochner*, 198 US at 57-58. Of course minimum wage and maximum hour legislation has complex redistributive consequences; it does not simply transfer resources from employers to employees.

[24] Franklin D. Roosevelt, Message to Congress, June 8, 1934, reprinted in Robert B. Stevens, ed, *Statutory History of the United States: Income Security* 61 (Chelsea House, 1970).

[25] 1 *The Public Papers of Franklin D. Roosevelt* 657 (Russell & Russell, 1938).

pointed out that this sphere was actually a creation of law. Rules of property, contract, and tort produced the set of entitlements that ultimately yielded market hours and wages.[26]

To New Deal reformers, the very categories of "regulation" and "government intervention" seemed misleading. The government did not "act" only when it disturbed existing distributions. It was responsible for those distributions in the first instance. What people owned in markets was a function of the entitlements that the law conferred on them. The notion of "laissez-faire" thus stood revealed as a conspicuous fiction.

To the extent that property rights played a role in market arrangements—as they inevitably did—those arrangements were a creature of positive law, including, most notably, property law, which gave some people a right to exclude others from "their" land and resources.[27] On this view, market wages were a result of legal rules conferring rights of ownership on certain groups. Rather than superimposing regulation on a realm of purely voluntary interactions, minimum wage laws substituted one form of regulation for another.

The fact that an existing distribution is not natural or prepolitical provides no argument against it.[28] When one regulatory system is superimposed on another, it is not true that all bets are off, or that we cannot evaluate them in constitutional terms, or for their ability to diminish or to increase human liberty, or other things we value. Here the New Deal reformers were often too cava-

---

[26] Nothing said here denies that people often work for what they have. They acquire property independently of legal rules, in the sense that their own effort contributes to getting them whatever they have. While legal rules create preconditions for acquiring property and may help along the way, they do not operate in a vacuum from individual initiative. In this sense, the existing distribution of resources and opportunities is emphatically not simply the creation of law; it is instead a result of a complex interaction between law and many other things, including individual effort. The New Dealers did not deny these propositions.

[27] Dewey, 11 *Later Works* at 291 (cited in note 2). Amartya Sen, *Poverty and Famines, An Essay on Entitlement and Deprivation* (Oxford, 1981), is a striking contemporary illustration of similar ideas. Sen demonstrates that famines are not only or always a result of a decrease in the supply of food. Instead, they are a result of social choices, prominent among them legal ones, deciding who is entitled to what. Sen notes:

> Finally, the focus on entitlement has the effect of emphasizing legal rights. Other relevant factors, for example market forces, can be seen as operating *through* a system of legal relations (ownership rights, contractual obligations, legal exchanges, etc.). The law stands between food availability and food entitlement. Starvation deaths can reflect legality with a vengeance.

Id at 165-66. This claim can be understood as a special case of the New Deal understanding of "laissez-faire."

[28] See John Stuart Mill, *On Liberty and Other Essays* 182 (MacMillan, 1926) ("conformity to nature, has no connection whatever with right and wrong").

lier.[29] A system of private property is a construct of the state, but it is also an important individual and collective good. In general, a market system—for property or for speech—promotes both liberty and prosperity, and its inevitable origins in law do not undermine that fact.

To their basic point, then, the New Dealers added a claim that existing distributions were sometimes inefficient or unjust.[30] Different forms of governmental ordering had to be evaluated pragmatically and in terms of their consequences for social efficiency and social justice. The fact that markets are a creature of law meant not that they were impermissible, but that they would be assessed in terms of what they did on behalf of the human beings subject to them. Markets would not be identified with liberty in an a priori way; they would have to be evaluated through an examination of whether they served liberty or not.

The New Dealers were not socialists; they generally appreciated the contributions of markets to prosperity and freedom.[31] At the very least, however, a democratic judgment that markets constrained liberty—embodied in a law calling for maximum hours or minimum wages—was plausible and entitled to judicial respect.

B. Theory

These ideas have played little role in the law of free speech. For purposes of speech, contemporary understandings of neutrality

---

[29] There are many contemporary analogues. See, for example, Allan C. Hutchinson, *The Three "R's": Reading/Rorty/Radically*, 103 Harv L Rev 555, 558-63 (1989) (apparently arguing that contingency is a reason for change); Anthony E. Cook, *Beyond Critical Legal Studies: The Reconstructive Theology of Dr. Martin Luther King, Jr.*, 103 Harv L Rev 985, 990-91 (1990) (same).

Compare the following statement, very much in the spirit of the New Deal, in Morris R. Cohen, *Property and Sovereignty*, 13 Cornell L Q 8, 14 (1927):

> [T]he recognition of private property as a form of sovereignty is not itself an argument against it. Some form of government we must always have. . . . At any rate it is necessary to apply to the law of property all those considerations of social ethics and enlightened public policy which ought to be brought to the discussion of any just form of government.

[30] Compare Robert L. Hale, *Coercion and Distribution in a Supposedly Noncoercive State*, 38 Pol Sci Q 470, 471-74 (1923), who rightly draws attention to coercive characteristics in the law of property, but assumes that this insight establishes more than it does. Regulatory interference with market arrangements does not disturb an otherwise prepolitical status quo, but it may produce inefficiency and unfairness. A good deal of theoretical and empirical work is necessary to assess any particular interference. Of course many of the New Deal reforms produced unanticipated adverse consequences.

[31] Not always, though, and not enough. See especially the enthusiasm for cartels in the "first" New Deal, discussed in Ellis W. Hawley, *The New Deal and the Problem of Monopoly* 270-80 (Princeton, 1966).

and partisanship, or government action and inaction, are identical to those that predate the New Deal.[32]

One response to the recent First Amendment controversies would be to suggest that they confirm the wisdom of the New Deal reformation on this score. On this view, American constitutionalism, with respect to freedom of expression, has failed precisely to the extent that it has not taken that reformation seriously enough. I do not mean to suggest that speech rights should be freely subject to political determination, as are current issues of occupational safety and health, for example. I do not mean to suggest that markets in speech are generally abridgements of speech, or that they usually disserve the First Amendment. I do mean to say that in some circumstances, what seems to be government regulation of speech actually might promote free speech, and should not be treated as an abridgement at all. I mean also to argue, though more hesitantly, that what seems to be free speech in markets might, in some selected circumstances, amount to an abridgement of free speech.

A general clarification is necessary at the outset. It will be tempting to think that the argument to follow amounts to a broad and puzzling plea for "more regulation" of speech. Many of the practices and conditions I will challenge are commonly taken to involve private action, and not to implicate the Constitution at all. We generally treat the practices of broadcasters and managers of newspapers as raising no constitutional question; it is "regulation" of "the market" that is problematic. In fact there should be enthusiastic agreement—for reasons of both text and principle[33]—that the First Amendment is aimed only at governmental action, and that private conduct raises no constitutional question. The behavior of private broadcasters by itself poses no legal problem. It seems clear too that to find a constitutional violation, one needs to show that governmental action has "abridged the freedom of speech." That action must take the form of a law, a regulation, or behavior by a government official.

---

[32] The major qualification is the remarkable decision in *Red Lion Broadcasting Co. v FCC*, 395 US 367, 390, 393-94 (1969), in which the Court upheld the fairness doctrine against First Amendment attack. See text accompanying notes 49-53.

[33] The text of course says that "Congress" shall make no law abridging the freedom of speech, and the Fourteenth Amendment, taken to incorporate the First, applies its proscriptions to "states." In principle, the limitation of the Constitution to state action has the salutary consequence of helping to constitute and free up a private sphere from legal disabilities. See text accompanying notes 33-34 (discussing what counts as the private sphere).

But if the lesson of the New Deal is taken seriously, it follows, not that the requirement of state action is unintelligible or incoherent, but that governmental rules lie behind the exercise of rights of property, contract, and tort, especially insofar as common law rules grant people rights of exclusive ownership and use of property. From this it does not follow that private acts are subject to constitutional constraint, or even that legally-conferred rights of exclusive ownership violate any constitutional provision. To repeat: The acts of private broadcasters raise no First Amendment issue. Private acts exist; they are not subject to the First Amendment.

To find a constitutional violation, it is necessary to identify some exercise of public power, and to show that it has compromised some constitutional principle. But property law always lies behind markets. Displacement of property law may be constitutional. New efforts to promote greater quality and diversity in broadcasting, for example, are claims for a new regulatory regime, not for "government intervention" where none existed before. And property law might itself violate the First Amendment.

Another clarification is in order. I have suggested that legal rules lie behind private behavior, and it will be tempting to think that this suggestion dissolves the state action limitation. If private exclusion of speech is made possible by law, does it not turn out that the First Amendment invalidates private behavior after all? Is not all private action therefore state action? The answer is that it is not. A private university, expelling students for (say) racist speech, is not a state actor. The trespass law, which helps the expulsion to be effective, is indeed state action. The distinction matters a great deal. The trespass law, invoked in this context, is a content-neutral regulation of speech in a place that is not plausibly a public forum. This regulation does not violate the First Amendment. By contrast, the behavior of the university is content-based, and if engaged in by a public official, would indeed violate the First Amendment. We always need to identify the exercise of public power. Without it, there is no free speech issue, even on the New Deal view. And such power, when identified, often raises no serious constitutional issue when it takes the content-neutral form of protecting ownership rights.

What I want to suggest here is, first and foremost, that legal rules that are designed to promote freedom of speech and that interfere with other legal rules—those of the common law—should not be invalidated if their purposes and effects are constitutionally valid. It may also follow that common law rules are themselves subject to constitutional objection if and when such rules "abridge the freedom of speech" by preventing people from speaking at certain times and in certain places.

For the moment, these general proposals must remain abstract; I will particularize them below. And while the proposals might seem unconventional, they have a clear foundation in no lesser place than *New York Times Co. v Sullivan*,[34] one of the defining cases of modern free speech law. There the Court held that a public official could not bring an action for libel unless he could show "actual malice," defined as knowledge of or reckless indifference to the falsity of the statements at issue.[35] The *Sullivan* case is usually taken as the symbol of broad press immunity with respect to criticism of public officials. More importantly, observers often understand *Sullivan* to reflect Alexander Meiklejohn's conception of freedom of expression[36]—a conception of self-government connected to the American conception of sovereignty and built on the need to ensure that the government does not inhibit political expression.

It is striking that in *Sullivan*, the lower court held that the common law of tort, and more particularly libel, was not state action at all, and was therefore entirely immune from constitutional constraint.[37] A civil action, on this view, involves a purely private dispute. The Supreme Court quickly disposed of this objection. The use of public tribunals to punish speech is conspicuously state action.[38] What is interesting is not the Supreme Court's rejection of the argument, but the fact that the argument could even be made by a state supreme court as late as the 1960s. How could reasonable judges perceive the rules of tort law as purely private?

The answer lies in the persistence of the pre-New Deal understanding that the common law simply implements existing rights or private desires, and does not amount to "intervention" or "action" at all. The view that the common law of property should be taken as prepolitical and just, and as a refusal to use government power—the view that the New Deal repudiated—was the same as

---

[34] 376 US 254 (1964).

[35] Id at 280, 283.

[36] See Meiklejohn, *Free Speech and its Relation to Self-Government* at 14-19, 22-27 (cited in note 1). The link is made explicitly in William J. Brennan, Jr., *The Supreme Court and the Meiklejohn Interpretation of the First Amendment*, 79 Harv L Rev 1, 12-14, 19 (1965).

[37] *New York Times Co. v Sullivan*, 144 S2d 25, 40 (Ala 1962). It is notable that in *Sullivan*, the government was not a party—something that distinguishes the case from most others in which First Amendment objections have been raised. But to see this as meaning that there is no state action is simply another version of the problem discussed in the text.

[38] *Sullivan*, 376 US at 265.

the view of the state supreme court in *Sullivan*. Reputation, after all, is a property interest. Just as in the pre-New Deal era, the state supreme court did not see the protection of that interest as involving government action at all.

The Supreme Court's rejection of that claim seemed inevitable in *Sullivan*, and this aspect of the case is largely forgotten. But courts base much of current law on precisely the forgotten view of that obscure state court. We might even generalize from *Sullivan* the broad idea that courts must always assess the protection of property rights through the common law pragmatically, in terms of its effects on speech.[39]

Consider, for example, the issues raised by a claimed right of access to the media. Suppose that most broadcasters deal little or not at all with issues of public importance, restricting themselves to stories about movie stars or sex scandals. Suppose too that there is no real diversity of view on the airwaves, but instead a bland, watered-down version of conventional morality. If so, a severe problem for the system of free expression is the governmental grant of legal protection—rights of exclusive use—to enormous institutions compromising Madisonian values. Courts usually do not see that grant of power—sometimes made through the common law, sometimes through statute—as a grant of power at all, but instead treat it as purely "private." Thus the exclusion of people and views from the airwaves is immunized from constitutional constraint, on the theory that the act of exclusion is purely private. By

---

[39] See O'Neill, *Practices of Toleration* at 177-78 (cited in note 21).

[N]o society can institutionalize zero-regulation of public discourse. The choice can only be between differing patterns of regulation. . . . No society can guarantee that all communicators will be able to express every possible content in every possible context. Supposed attempts to do this by laissez-faire communications policies merely assign the regulation of communication to nonstate powers. They secure a particular configuration of freedom of expression, which may leave some unable to find their voices and does not guarantee the expression of diverse views. A better and less abstract aim for a democratic society is a set of practices that enables a wide range of communication, especially of public communication, for all.

There is a difference between *Sullivan* and the cases that follow. In *Sullivan*, the property right was not asserted by someone who was simultaneously speaker and owner. In cases that involve a claimed right of access to the media, the ownership right that prevents others from speaking is held by someone who is himself expressing something. But it is unclear why this difference should be decisive. The question is whether the legal vindication of the property right is constitutionally acceptable.

Note also that the shopping center cases, see notes 117-19, really are close to *Sullivan*, for they too involve the use of a property interest protected at common law to stop speech. The only differences are that (a) libel law is content-based, as property law is not, and (b) libel law is aimed particularly at speech whereas property law allows the exclusion of everyone, whether a speaker or not.

contrast, rights of access to the media are thought to involve governmental intervention into the private sphere.[40]

In *Sullivan*, the Supreme Court said, as against a similar claim, that courts should inspect common law rules for their conformity with the principle that government may not restrict freedoms of speech and press. "The test is not the form in which state power has been applied but, whatever the form, whether such power has in fact been exercised."[41]

We can apply this understanding to current problems. If we regard the First Amendment as an effort to ensure that people are not prevented from speaking, especially on issues of public importance, then current free speech law seems ill-adapted to current conditions. Above all, the conception of government "regulation" misstates certain issues and sometimes disserves the goal of free expression itself. Some regulatory efforts, superimposed on the established regulation through common law rules, may promote free speech. Less frequently, the use of statutory or common law rules to foreclose efforts to speak might themselves represent impermissible content-neutral restrictions on speech. We must judge both reform efforts and the status quo by their consequences, not by question-begging characterizations of "threats from government."

It is tempting to understand this argument as a suggestion that the New Dealers were concerned about private power over working conditions, and that modern courts should take more interest in the existence of private power over expression or over democratic processes.[42] But this formulation misses the real point, and does so in a way that suggests its own dependence on pre-New Deal understandings. The problem is not that private power is an obstacle to speech; even if it is, private power is not a subject of the First Amendment. Nor would it be accurate to say that employer power was the true concern for the New Dealers. The real problem is that public authority creates legal structures that restrict speech, that new exercises of public authority can counter the existing restrictions, and that any restrictions, even those of the common law, must be assessed under constitutional principles precisely because they are restrictions.

Consider, for example, a case in which the owners of a large shopping center exclude from their property war protestors who

---

[40] See text accompanying notes 56-57.

[41] *Sullivan*, 376 US at 265.

[42] It is sometimes so argued. See David Strauss, *Persuasion, Autonomy, and Freedom of Expression*, 91 Colum L Rev 334, 361-68 (1991).

believe that the center is the best place to draw attention to their
cause. The Supreme Court has said that the situation does not implicate the First Amendment, since it does not involve government
regulation of speech. Private property owners have simply barred
people from their land.[43]

In fact, this is a poor way to understand the situation; it was
the state court's view in *Sullivan*. The owners of the shopping
center may exclude the protestors only because government has
conferred on them a legal right to do so. The conferral of that right
is an exercise of state power. It is *this* action that restricts the
speech of the protestors. Surely it is a real question whether the
grant of exclusionary power violates the First Amendment, at least
in circumstances in which it eliminates the only feasible way of
making a protest visible to members of a community.

Or consider a case in which a network decides not to sell advertising time to a group that wants to discuss some public issue or
to express some dissident view. Under current law, the refusal
raises no First Amendment question, in part because a number of
the justices—perhaps now a majority—believe that there is no
"state action."[44] But government gives broadcasters property
rights in their licenses, and their exercise of those rights is a function of law in no subtle sense. It is generally salutary to have a
system in which government creates ownership rights or markets
in speech, just as in property. The point is not that markets are
bad, but that a right of exclusive ownership in a television network
is governmentally conferred. The exclusion of the would-be speakers is made possible by the law of civil and criminal trespass,
among other things. It is thus a product of a governmental
decision.

A market system in which only certain speakers express only
certain views is a creation of law. The questions are (1) whether
reform efforts eliminating adverse effects of exclusive ownership
rights by conditioning the original grant are consistent with the
First Amendment, or (2) whether the government grant of exclusive ownership rights itself violates the First Amendment. We cannot answer such questions by saying that ownership rights are governmental; we need to know the purposes and effects of the grant.

---

[43] *Lloyd Corp. v Tanner*, 407 US 551, 570 (1972); *Hudgens v NLRB*, 424 US 507, 519-
21 (1976).

[44] *CBS, Inc. v Democratic National Committee*, 412 US 94 (1973). There only three
Justices said that there was no state action. Id at 114-210. But those three justices may now
represent the majority view. See *Flagg Bros., Inc. v Brooks*, 436 US 149, 163 (1978).

And we cannot answer that question a priori or in the abstract; we need to know a lot of details.

One might respond that the Constitution creates "negative" rights rather than "positive" ones, or at least that the First Amendment is "negative" in character, granting a right to protection against the government, not to subsidies from the government. The claim certainly captures the conventional wisdom, and an argument for a New Deal for speech must come to terms with it.

There are two responses. First, and most fundamentally, no one is asserting a positive right in these cases. Instead, the claim is that government sometimes cannot adopt a content-neutral rule that imposes a (negative) constraint on who can speak and where they can do so. When someone with view X cannot speak on the networks, it is because the civil and criminal law prohibits him from doing so. This is the same problem that underlies a wide range of familiar claims in content-neutral cases. Consider a ban on door-to-door soliciting. An attack on content-neutral restrictions is not an argument for "positive" government protection. It is merely a claim that courts must review legal rules stopping certain people from speaking in certain places under First Amendment principles. In fact the response that a New Deal for speech would create a "positive right" trades on untenable, *Lochner* era distinctions between positive and negative rights.[45]

The second response is that the distinction between negative and positive rights fails to explain even current First Amendment law.[46] There are two obvious counterexamples. The Supreme Court has come very close to saying that when an audience becomes hostile and threatening, the government is obligated to protect the speaker. Under current law, reasonable crowd control measures are probably constitutionally compelled, even if the result is to require

---

[45] To say this is not to say that the distinction itself is untenable. We can understand a positive right as one that requires for its existence some act by government and a negative right as one that amounts merely to an objection to some such act. There is nothing incoherent about this distinction. I argue here against the view that an objection to rights of exclusive ownership is a call for a positive right. In fact that objection is mounted against something that government is actually doing, and is therefore about a negative right. See generally, Jeremy Waldron, *Homelessness and the Issue of Freedom*, 39 UCLA L Rev 295, 304-15 (1991) (arguing that property law invades negative rights of the homeless).

[46] It also fails to explain constitutional law in general. The Eminent Domain Clause creates a positive right to governmental protection of property. The Contracts Clause creates a right to governmental protection of contractual agreements. In both cases, the Constitution is violated by a governmental withdrawal from the scene.

a number of police officers to come to the scene.[47] The right to speak may well include a positive right to governmental protection against a hostile private audience.

The area of libel provides a second example. By imposing constitutional constraints on the common law of libel, the Court in effect has held that those who are defamed must subsidize speakers, by allowing their reputations to be compromised to the end of broad diversity of speech. Even more, the Court has held that government is under what might be seen as an affirmative duty to "take" the reputation of people whom the press defames in order to promote the interest in free speech. The First Amendment requires a compulsory, governmentally produced subsidy of personal reputation (a property interest) for the benefit of speech.[48]

These cases reveal that the First Amendment, even as currently conceived, is no mere negative right. It has positive dimensions. These dimensions consist of a command to government to take steps to ensure that legal rules according exclusive authority to private persons do not violate the system of free expression. In a hostile audience case, the government is obliged to protect the speaker against private silencing. In the libel cases, the government is obliged to do the same thing—to provide extra breathing space for speech even though a consequence is an infringement on the common law interest in reputation. It is incorrect to say that the First Amendment creates merely a right to fend off government censorship as conventionally understood.

In any case, a broadcasting system in which government confers on networks the right to exclude certain points of view might well raise a constitutional question. The creation of that right is parallel to the grant of a right to a hostile audience to silence controversial speakers, subject only to the speakers' power of self-help through the marketplace (including the hiring of private police

---

[47] See, for example, *Kunz v New York*, 340 US 290, 294-95 (1951); *Edwards v South Carolina*, 372 US 229, 231-33 (1963); *Cox v Louisiana*, 379 US 536, 550 (1965); *Gregory v Chicago*, 394 US 111, 111-12 (1969). See also Scanlon, *Content Regulation Revisited* at 337-39 (cited in note 21); and Fiss, 100 Harv L Rev at 786 (cited in note 21), discussing this point.

[48] See Richard Epstein, *Was* New York Times v. Sullivan *Wrong?*, 53 U Chi L Rev 782 (1986) (discussing libel as a form of "taking"). A qualification is necessary here. To decide whether there is a subsidy one needs a baseline. To see reputation as part of the initial set of endowments is to proceed in good common law fashion; and any social contract version of this idea (the state must protect certain rights in return for the decision of citizens to leave the state of nature) supports the same view. But it would be possible to say that on the correct theory, people do not have such an antecedent right to reputation, and therefore no subsidy is involved in the libel cases.

forces). In the hostile audience setting, it is insufficient to say that any intrusion on the speaker is private rather than governmental. It is necessary instead to evaluate the consequences of the system by reference to the purposes of the First Amendment—just as it is necessary to evaluate the consequences of any system in which property rights operate to hurt some and benefit others.

None of this demonstrates that the creation of property rights in broadcasting fails to produce broad diversity of views and an opportunity for opposing sides to speak. If property rights do produce these effects, a market system created by law is constitutionally unobjectionable on the merits. This is a question of fact, on which courts should give considerable deference to other branches. But it is imaginable that a market system will have less fortunate consequences—an issue to which I return below. At least a legislative judgment opposed to free markets might, on the appropriate factual record, warrant judicial respect.

Consider the Court's remarkable opinion in the *Red Lion* case.[49] There the Court upheld the fairness doctrine, which required[50] broadcasters to give attention to public issues and provide a chance for those with opposing views to speak. In *Red Lion*, the Court actually seemed to suggest that the doctrine was constitutionally compelled. According to the Court, the fairness doctrine would "enhance rather than abridge the freedoms of speech and press," for free expression would be disserved by "unlimited private censorship operating in a medium not open to all."[51] The Court suggested that:

> [A]s far as the First Amendment is concerned those who are licensed stand no better than those to whom licenses are refused. A license permits broadcasting, but the licensee has no constitutional right to be the one who holds the license or to monopolize a radio frequency to the exclusion of his fellow citizens. There is nothing in the First Amendment which prevents the Government from requiring a licensee to share his frequency with others and to conduct himself as a proxy or fiduciary with obligations to present those views and voices which are representative of his community and which would otherwise, by necessity, be barred from the airwaves.

---

[49] *Red Lion Broadcasting Co. v FCC*, 395 US 367 (1969).

[50] For the most part, the requirement was theoretical only. In practice the doctrine was rarely enforced. See Robert M. Entman, *Democracy Without Citizens* 104-06 (Oxford, 1989).

[51] *Red Lion*, 395 US at 375, 392.

. . .

> [T]he people as a whole retain their interest in free speech by
> radio and their collective right to have the medium function
> consistently with the ends and purposes of the First Amend-
> ment. It is the right of the viewers and listeners, not the right
> of the broadcasters, which is paramount. It is the purpose of
> the First Amendment to preserve an uninhibited marketplace
> of ideas in which truth will ultimately prevail, rather than to
> countenance monopolization of that market, whether it be by
> the Government itself or a private licensee. It is the right of
> the public to receive suitable access to social, political, es-
> thetic, moral, and other ideas and experiences which is crucial
> here. That right may not constitutionally be abridged either
> by Congress or by the FCC.[52]

This vision of the First Amendment does not stress the autonomy of broadcasters with current ownership rights. Instead it emphasizes the need to promote democratic self-government by ensuring that people are presented with a broad diversity of views
about public issues. A market system may compromise this goal. It
is hardly clear that "the freedom of speech" is promoted by a regime in which people may speak if and only if other people are
willing to pay enough to hear them.

This argument applies most conspicuously to broadcasters,
since the role of the government in allocating licenses is obvious.
But it has force with respect to newspapers as well: Their property
rights also amount to a legally-conferred power to exclude others.
Simply as a matter of fact,[53] that power is a creature of the state.
In general, this is hardly bad; but we must assess the resulting system in terms of its consequences for speech.

If all this is correct, the first two commitments of current First
Amendment law come under severe strain. The idea that threats to

---

[52] Id at 389-90 (citations omitted). Compare this suggestion:

> It was time to move away from thinking about broadcasters as trustees. It was time to
> treat them the way almost everyone else in society does—that is, as businesses. . . .
> [T]elevision is just another appliance. It's a toaster with pictures.

Bernard D. Nossiter, *The FCC's Big Giveaway Show*, The Nation 402 (Oct 26, 1985) (statement of Mark Fowler, former Chairman of the Federal Communications Commission).

[53] This point is not a criticism of a system of private property. To say that a system is
state-created is not to disparage it. See text accompanying notes 28-31. A system of private
property is an individual and collective good—in large part because it immunizes citizens
from dependence on the state and in that way creates the preconditions for prosperity, democracy, and citizenship. This point is not in any way inconsistent with those suggested in
the text.

speech come from government is correct, but as conventionally understood, it is far too simple. Sometimes threats come from what seems to be the private sphere, but those threats are fundamentally a product of legal entitlements that enable some private actors but not others to speak and to be heard. When this is so, these legal entitlements pose a large risk to a system of free expression, one not readily visible to current law.

Second, the idea that government should be neutral among all forms of speech seems correct in the abstract. But as frequently applied it is as implausible as the idea that government should be neutral between the associational interests of blacks and those of whites under conditions of segregation,[54] or between the freedom of employers and workers under conditions in which market pressures drive hours dramatically up and wages dramatically down.[55] The difficulty with this conception of neutrality is that it takes existing distributions of resources and opportunities as the baseline for decision.

The most important problem here is that neutrality between different points of view is frequently thought to be exemplified in the use of economic markets to determine access to the media and thus an opportunity to be heard. This form of neutrality actually embodies a collective choice. The choice is captured in the use of the market and the creation of particular legal standards for its operation that ensure that some will be unable to speak or to be heard, and at the same time that others will be permitted to dominate expressive outlets. Markets are generally good things, both for ordinary products and for speech. But when the legal creation of a market has harmful consequences for free expression—and it sometimes does—then we must reevaluate it in light of free speech principles.

C. Practice

A core insight of the *Red Lion* case is that the interest in legally protected private autonomy from government is not always connected with the interest in democratic self-governance. To immunize broadcasters from government control may not be consistent with quality and diversity in broadcasting. If so, it is not consistent with the First Amendment's own commitments.

---

[54] See Herbert Wechsler, *Toward Neutral Principles of Constitutional Law*, 73 Harv L Rev 1, 13-14, 33-34 (1959).

[55] *Lochner*, 198 US at 52-53, 64; *Adkins*, 261 US at 558, 560-61.

We could generate, from the suggested First Amendment "New Deal," a large set of proposals for constitutional reform. I describe those proposals in summary fashion here. A more detailed discussion would be necessary in order fully to come to terms with any one of them.

1. Regulation of broadcasting.

For much of its history, the Federal Communications Commission ("FCC") has imposed on broadcast licensees the "fairness doctrine." As noted, the fairness doctrine requires licensees to devote time to issues of public importance, and it creates an obligation to broadcast speech by people of diverse views.

The last decade has witnessed a mounting constitutional assault on the fairness doctrine. One reason for the doctrine was the scarcity of licenses, but licenses are no longer scarce; indeed, there are far more radio and television stations than major newspapers. The FCC recently concluded that the fairness doctrine violates the First Amendment because it is a government effort to tell broadcasters what they may say. On this view, the fairness doctrine represents impermissible government intervention into voluntary market interactions.[56] It violates the government's obligation of "neutrality," defined as respect for market outcomes. Influential judges and scholars have reached the same conclusion.[57] The mode of analysis, in particular the notions of neutrality and inaction, is the same as that of the pre-New Deal Court.

The Constitution forbids any "law abridging the freedom of speech."[58] But is the fairness doctrine such a law? Certainly we cannot establish the proposition merely by a reference to the constitutional text. To its defenders, the fairness doctrine promotes "the freedom of speech" by ensuring more access to the airwaves and more diversity of views than the market provides. The fact that the market responds to consumption choices does not solve the problem.[59] The FCC's attack on the fairness doctrine closely parallels pre-New Deal understandings. It asserts, without a full look at the real-world consequences of different regulatory strate-

---

[56] See *In re Complaint of Syracuse Peace Council*, FCC 88-131, FCC Rcd 2035, 64 Rad Reg (P&F) 1073 (Apr 7, 1988); Entman, *Democracy Without Citizens* at 102-03 (cited in note 50) (statement of Chairman Dennis Patrick).

[57] See Lucas A. Powe, Jr., *American Broadcasting and the First Amendment* 214-15 (California, 1987).

[58] US Const, Amend I.

[59] See text accompanying notes 106-07.

gies, that the doctrine involves governmental interference with an otherwise purely law-free and voluntary private sphere.

Those entrusted with interpreting the Constitution should instead deal with the fairness doctrine by exploring the relationships among a market in broadcasting, alternative systems, and the goals, properly characterized, of a system of free expression.[60] On the one hand, a market will provide a fair degree of diversity in available offerings, especially in a time of numerous outlets. So long as the particular view is supported by market demand, it should find a supplier. The broadcasting status quo is far preferable to a system of centralized command-and-control regulation, at least if such a system sharply constrains choice. Markets do offer a range of opinions and options. A command-and-control system, if it restricted diversity of view and attention to public affairs, would indeed abridge the freedom of speech. Nothing I have said argues in favor of governmental foreclosure of political speech.

We might therefore distinguish among three scenarios. First, the market might itself be unconstitutional if it could be shown that existing property rights produce little political discussion or exclude certain views.[61] For reasons suggested below, courts should be cautious here, in part because the issue turns on complex factual issues not easily within judicial competence. Second, regulation of the market might well be upheld, as against a First Amendment challenge, if the legislature has made a considered judgment, based on a record, that the particular regulation will promote First Amendment goals.[62] Third, regulation of the market might be invalidated if it discriminates on the basis of viewpoint, or if it can be shown that the regulation actually diminishes attention to public affairs or diminishes diversity of view. On this latter, highly factual question, the legislature is entitled to a presumption of constitutionality.[63]

---

[60] See Scanlon, *Content Regulation Reconsidered* at 350 (cited in note 21):

The case for or against such powers must be made out on the basis of their consequences. Statutes requiring that opponents of newspaper or television editorials be given the opportunity to reply are not, on the face of it, inconsistent with the right of freedom of expression. Everything depends on what the consequences of such statutes would be as compared with the likely alternatives.

See also Commission on Freedom of the Press, *A Free and Responsible Press* at 23-24 (cited in note 21) ("the great agencies of mass communication should regard themselves as common carriers of public discussion. . . . all the important viewpoints and interests in the society should be represented in its agencies of mass communication").

[61] See text accompanying notes 111-13.

[62] See text accompanying notes 66-109.

[63] See *Red Lion*, 395 US 367.

Importantly, a market will make it unnecessary for government officials to oversee the content of material in order to assess its value. The fact that a market removes official oversight counts strongly in its favor. The restrictions of the market are content-neutral. The restrictions of the fairness doctrine, or any similar alternative, are content-based.

On the other hand, a market in communications generates a range of problems. Imagine, for example, that we allocated the right to speak to those people whose speech other people are willing to pay to hear—in other words, through a pricing system, like that used to allocate soap, or cereal, or cars. This system would prevent people from speaking if other people were not willing to pay enough for them to do so. Surely this would seem a strange parody of democratic aspirations—the stuff of science fiction, rather than self-government. It would be especially perverse insofar as it would foreclose dissident speech—expression for which people are often unwilling to pay. But in many respects, this is precisely the system we have. The FCC allocates broadcasting licenses very much on the basis of private willingness to pay.[64]

In one respect our system is even worse, for programming content is affected not merely by consumer demand, but also by the desires of advertisers. Viewers are thus the product as well as the users of broadcasting, and this introduces some additional distortions.[65] In any case, the First Amendment issues must depend in large part on the details.

a) The facts. Much information has been compiled on the content of local television news, which began, incidentally, as a direct response to the requirements of the FCC's fairness doctrine.[66] Local news programming devotes very little time to genuine news. Instead, it covers stories about movies and television programs and sensationalized disasters of little general interest.[67] "The search for emotion-packed reports with mass appeal has led local television news to give extensive coverage to tragedies like murders, deaths in

---

[64] To be sure, there are many ways to present speech regardless of willingness to pay; for example, one can distribute leaflets. If those ways were sufficient to serve Madisonian ideals, there would be no reason to worry about the broadcast media. But in practice, it seems unlikely that there is sufficient attention to public affairs, and diversity of view, in other media to pick up the slack.

[65] See Section II.C.1.b.

[66] See Phyllis Kaniss, *Making Local News* 102 (Chicago, 1991).

[67] See Entman, *Democracy Without Citizens* at 110-15 (cited in note 50).

fires, or plane crashes, in which they often interview survivors of victims about 'how they feel.' "[68]

During a half-hour of news programming, no more than eight to twelve minutes involves news. Each story that does involve news typically ranges from twenty to thirty seconds.[69] Even the news stories tend to focus on fires, accidents, and crimes instead of issues of government and policy.[70] Discussions of governmental policy are further de-emphasized during the more popular evening show.[71] Coverage of government does not tend to describe the content of relevant policies, but instead focuses on sensational and often misleading "human impact" anecdotes.[72] In addition, there has been great emphasis on "features"—dealing with popular actors, or entertainment shows, or even stories focusing on the movie immediately preceding the news.[73] Economic pressures seem to be pushing local news in this direction even if reporters might prefer to deal with public issues more seriously.

With respect to network news, the pattern is similar. In 1988, almost sixty percent of the national campaign coverage involved "horse race" issues—who was winning, who had momentum—while about thirty percent involved issues and qualifications. In the crucial period from January to June, 1980, one network offered about 450 minutes of campaign coverage, of which no less than 308 minutes dealt with the "horse race" issues.[74]

It is notable in this regard that for presidential candidates, the average block of uninterrupted speech fell from 42.3 seconds in 1968 to only 9.8 seconds in 1988.[75] There is little sustained coverage of the substance of candidate speeches; instead attention is placed on how various candidates are doing. Citizenship is exceedingly unlikely to flourish in this environment.

There has been an increase in stories about television and movies and a decrease in attention to questions involving government and its obligations. In 1988, there was an average of thirty-eight minutes per month of coverage of arts and entertainment

---

[68] Kaniss, *Making Local News* at 110 (cited in note 66).

[69] Id at 111. If a reporter is giving the story, the range is one to three minutes. Id.

[70] Id at 114.

[71] Id at 118.

[72] Id at 120-21.

[73] Id at 129-30.

[74] Fishkin, *Democracy and Deliberation* at 63 (cited in note 21).

[75] Kiku Adatto, *Sound Bite Democracy: Network Evening News Presidential Campaign Coverage, 1968 and 1988* 4 (Research Paper R-2) (Harvard, John F. Kennedy School of Government, 1990) (on file with U Chi L Rev).

news; in the first half of 1990, the average was sixty-eight minutes per month.[76] According to one person involved in the industry, "by the necessity of shrinking ratings, the network news departments have had to, if not formally then informally, redefine what is news."[77] According to the Executive Producer of NBC's Nightly News, "A lot of what we used to do is report on the back and forth of how we stood against the Russians. But there is no back and forth anymore. I mean nobody is talking about the bomb, so you have to fill the time with the things people *are* talking about."[78]

There is evidence as well of advertiser influence over programming content, though at the moment the evidence is largely anecdotal.[79] No conspiracy theory appears plausible; but some recent events are quite disturbing. There are reports that advertisers have a large impact on local news programs, especially consumer reports. In Minneapolis, a local car dealer responded to a story about consumer problems with his company by pulling almost one million in advertisements. He said: "We vote with our dollars. If I'm out trying to tell a good story about what I'm doing and paying $3000 for 30 seconds, and someone's calling me names, I'm not going to be happy."[80] Consumer reporters have increasingly pointed to a need for self-censorship. According to one, "we don't even bother with most auto-related stories anymore"; according to another, "I won't do the car-repair story, or the lemon story . . . . It's not worth the hassle."[81]

A revealing recent episode involved the effort by Turner Broadcasting Systems (TBS) and the Audubon Society to produce a program dealing with the "spotted owl" controversy between loggers and environmentalists in the Pacific Northwest. Believing that the program was biased, a group representing the logging community did not want TBS to air it. As a result, all of the eight advertisers (including Ford, Citicorp, Exxon, and Sears) pulled their sponsorship of the program. TBS aired the program, but lost the $100,000 spent on production.[82] And NBC had severe difficulties

[76] J. Max Robins, *Nets' Newscasts Increase Coverage of Entertainment*, Variety 3, 63 (Jul 18, 1990).

[77] Id at 3.

[78] Id at 63.

[79] See the discussion of a forthcoming report from the Center for the Study of Commercialism in G. Pascal Zachary, *All the News? Many Journalists See A Growing Reluctance to Criticize Advertisers*, Wall St J A1 (Feb 6, 1992). The report describes growing newspaper attentiveness to advertiser views on stories.

[80] Steven Waldman, *Consumer News Blues*, Newsweek 48 (May 20, 1991).

[81] Id.

[82] *Advertisers Drop Program About the Timber Industry*, NY Times 32 (Sep 23, 1989).

finding sponsors for its television movie, "Roe v. Wade." Fearful of boycotts by religious groups, hundreds of sponsors solicited by NBC refused to participate.[83] It seems highly unlikely that advertisers could be found for any program adopting a "pro-life" or "pro-choice" perspective, or even for a program attempting a balanced discussion of the issues.[84]

Consider children's television. Educational programming for children simply cannot acquire sponsors; such programming can be found mostly on PBS.[85] In the 1960s, the FCC issued recommendations and policy statements calling for "programming in the interest of the public" rather than "programming in the interest of salability."[86] In 1974, it concluded that "broadcasters have a special obligation to serve children," and thus pressured the industry to adopt codes calling for educational and informational programs.[87] In 1981, the new FCC Chair, Mark Fowler, rejected this approach. For Fowler, "television is just another appliance. It's a toaster with pictures."[88]

Shortly thereafter, network programming for children dramatically decreased,[89] and programs based on products increased. According to one critic, by 1986 children's television had become "a listless by-product of an extraordinary explosion of entrepreneurial life forces taking place elsewhere—in the business of creating and marketing toys."[90] In 1983, cartoons based on licensed characters accounted for fourteen programs; by 1985, the number rose to over forty.[91] It continued to increase. Most of the resulting shows for children are quite violent, and the violence has increased since deregulation. Statistical measures will of course be inadequate, but it is at least revealing that before 1980, there were 18.6 violent acts per hour in children's programs, whereas after 1980, the number

---

[83] Verne Gay, *NBC v Sponsors v Wildmon Re: Telepic "Roe v Wade"*, Variety 71 (May 10, 1989).

[84] Id at 82.

[85] Children and Television, Hearing before the Subcommittee on Telecommunications, Consumer Protection, and Finance, House of Representatives, 98th Cong, 1st Sess 36-37 (Mar 16, 1983) (statements of Bruce Christensen, President of the National Association of Public Television Stations).

[86] Englehardt, *The Shortcake Strategy* at 75 (cited in note 9).

[87] Id.

[88] Nossiter, The Nation at 402 (cited in note 52).

[89] From 11.3 to 4.4 hours per week; there was no regularly scheduled children's series during the usual after-school time slot. Englehardt, *The Shortcake Strategy* at 76 (cited in note 9).

[90] Id at 70.

[91] Id.

increased to 26.4 acts per hour.[92] Children's daytime weekend programs have consistently been more violent than prime-time shows.[93] Few of these shows have educational content. They are often full-length advertisements for products.

More generally, there is a high level of violence on all television programming.[94] Seven of ten prime time programs depict violence. During prime time in 1980, there was an average of between five and six violent acts per hour. By 1989, the number increased to 9.5 acts per hour. In 1980, ten shows depicted an average of more than ten acts of violence per hour; by 1989, the number was sixteen; the high mark was in 1985, with twenty-nine such shows. Violence on children's television has been found to increase children's fear and also to contribute to their own aggression.[95]

Empirical studies show that news and entertainment programming sometimes discriminates on the basis of sex. A 1986 study of network news stories found that when women appear as "private individuals," they are most frequently depicted as falling in the category "family members; that is, they were the mothers or other relatives of hostages, gunmen, spies, afflicted children, and the like."[96] Next most frequent was the appearance of women as victims, including battered women, stabbing victims, and residents of areas affected by earthquakes and toxic waste sites.[97] When women are used as speaking subjects on a public issue, it is often to speak against a position traditionally associated with women. Thus Christie Hefner was used as a prominent critic of an anti-pornography report, and a woman doctor was used to defend a company policy of transferring women out of jobs dealing with hazardous chemicals.[98] One study of situation comedies and crime drama programs in 1975 found that women were often portrayed in subordinate roles.[99]

---

[92] Sources for this discussion are George Gernber and Nancy Signorielli, *Violence Profile 1967 through 1988-89: Enduring Patterns* 9 (Pennsylvania, 1990).

[93] Id.

[94] Id at 9-10.

[95] See Jerome L. Singer, and Dorothy G. Singer, and Wanda S. Rapaczynski, *Family Patterns and Television Viewing as Predictors of Children's Beliefs and Aggression*, 34 J Commun 73, 87-88 (1984).

[96] Lana F. Rakow and Kimberlie Kranich, *Woman As Sign in Television News*, 41 J Commun 8, 14 (1991).

[97] Id.

[98] Id at 17.

[99] Judith Lemon, *Women and Blacks on Prime-Time Television*, 27 J Commun 70, 73 (1977).

Children's programming frequently consists exclusively of male characters, and when a female character is added "a group of male buddies will be accented by a lone female, stereotypically defined."[100] On this pattern, "the female is usually a little-sister type," or "functions as a girl Friday to . . . male superheroes."[101] Thus "[g]irls exist only in relation to boys."[102] Of major dramatic characters in one survey, women made up only sixteen percent, and "females were portrayed as younger than males, more likely to be married, less active and with lower self-esteem."[103]

b) Correctives and the First Amendment. Regulatory strategies cannot solve all of these problems, but they could help. At least some regulatory strategies should not be treated as abridgements of the freedom of speech.

It might be suggested that in an era of cable television, the relevant problems disappear. People can always change the channel. Some stations even provide public affairs broadcasting around the clock. In this light, a concern about the market status quo might seem to amount to a puzzling rejection of freedom of choice. Both quality and diversity can be found in light of the dazzling array of options made available by modern technology. Why should we not view a foreclosure of expressive options as infringing freedom of speech?

There are several answers. First, information about public affairs has many of the characteristics of a public good, like national defense or clean air.[104] It is well-known that if we rely entirely on markets, we will have insufficient national defense and excessively dirty air. The reason is that both defense and clean air cannot be feasibly provided to one person without simultaneously being provided to many or all. In these circumstances, each person has inadequate incentives to seek, or to pay for, the right level of national defense or clean air. Acting individually, each person will "free ride" on the efforts of others. No producer will have the appropri-

---

[100] Katha Pollitt, *The Smurfette Principle*, NY Times 6-22 (Apr 7, 1991).

[101] Id.

[102] Id.

[103] John Corry, *Briefs on the Arts: Children's TV Found Dominated by White Men*, NY Times C14 (Jul 15, 1982).

[104] See Daniel A. Farber, *Free Speech Without Romance: Public Choice and the First Amendment*, 105 Harv L Rev 554, 558-62 (1991). Information is not a pure public good, for it is often feasible to provide it to those who pay for it, and copyright and patent laws can guarantee appropriate incentives for its production. But it does have much in common with pure public goods.

ate incentive for production. The result will be unacceptably low levels of the relevant goods.

Much the same is true of information, especially with respect to public affairs. The benefits of a broad public debate, yielding large quantities of information—through coverage of public issues, disclosure of new facts and perspectives, and diversity of view—accrue simultaneously to many or all people. Once information is provided to one person, or to some of them, it is also provided to many others too, or it can be so provided at minimal cost. The production of information for any person thus yields large external benefits for other people as well. But—and this is the key point—the market provides no mechanism to ensure that these benefits will be adequately taken into account by those who produce the information, in this case the newspaper and broadcasting industries.

At the same time, the benefits of informing one person—making him an effective citizen—are likely to accrue to many other people as well, through that person's contribution to multiple practices and conversations, and to political processes in general. But the external benefits, for each person, will not be taken into account in individual consumption choices.

Because of the "public good" features of information, no single person has sufficient incentive to "pay" for the benefits that he receives. The result will be that the market will produce too little information. Reliance on media markets will therefore have some of the same difficulties as reliance on markets for national defense or environmental protection. For this reason, a regulatory change, solving the collective action problem, is justified, at least in principle.

It might be thought that the distinctive characteristics of the broadcasting market provide at least a partial solution. Because advertisers attempt to ensure large audiences, viewers are commodities as well as or instead of consumers. In these circumstances, it is not as if individual people are purchasing individual pieces of information. Instead, advertisers are aggregating individual preferences in seeking popular programming and, in that sense, helping to overcome the collective action problem. Under this view, any kind of regulatory change is therefore unnecessary.

The problem with this response is that the advertisers' desire to attract large audiences does not adequately serve the goal of overcoming the public good problem with respect to information about public affairs. A program with a large audience may not be providing information at all; consider most of network television.

As we have seen, advertisers may even be hostile to the provision of the relevant information. Their economic interests often argue against sponsorship of public service or controversial programming, especially if the audience is relatively small, but sometimes even if it is large. The external benefits of widely-diffused information about politics are thus not captured in a broadcasting market. The peculiarities of the broadcasting market do overcome a kind of collective action problem, by providing a system for aggregating preferences. But they do not respond to the crucial difficulty. Thus far, then, it seems plain that the broadcasting market will produce insufficient information about public issues.

So much for the public good issue. The second problem with reliance on the large number of outlets is that sheer numbers do not explain why there is a constitutional objection to democratic efforts to increase quality and diversity by ensuring better programming on individual stations. Even with a large number of stations, there is far less quality and diversity than there might be. Perhaps people can generate at least a partial solution by changing the channel. But why should the Constitution be thought to foreclose a collective decision to experiment with new methods for achieving their Madisonian goals?

The third problem with relying on decreasing scarcity is that it is important to be extremely cautious about the use, for constitutional and political purposes, of the notion of "consumer sovereignty." Consumer sovereignty is the conventional economic term for the virtues of a free market, in which commodities are allocated through consumer choices, as measured through the criterion of private willingness to pay. Those who invoke free choice in markets are really insisting on consumer sovereignty. But Madison's conception of "sovereignty" is the relevant one for First Amendment purposes, and that conception has an altogether different character.

On the Madisonian view, sovereignty entails respect not for private consumption choices, but for the considered judgments of the citizens. In a well-functioning polity, laws frequently reflect those judgments—what might be described as the aspirations of the public as a whole.[105] Those aspirations can and often do call for markets themselves. But they might also diverge from consumption choices—a familiar phenomenon in such areas as environmen-

---

[105] See Howard Margolis, *Selfishness, Altruism, and Rationality, A Theory of Social Choice* 17-25 (Cambridge, 1982); Jon Elster, *Ulysses and the Sirens* 141-46 (Cambridge, 1979).

tal law, protection of endangered species, social security, and antidiscrimination law. Democratic aspirations should not be disparaged. Democratic liberty should not be identified with "consumer sovereignty." And in the context at hand, the people, acting through their elected representatives, might well decide that democratic liberty, calling for quality and diversity of view in the mass media, is more valuable than consumer sovereignty.

Finally, private broadcasting selections are a product of preferences that are themselves a result of the broadcasting status quo, and not independent of it. In a world that provides the existing fare, it would be unsurprising if people generally preferred to see what they are accustomed to seeing. They have not been provided with the opportunities of a better system. When this is so, the broadcasting status quo cannot, without circularity, be justified by reference to the preferences.[106] Preferences that have adapted to an objectionable system cannot justify that system. If better options are put more regularly in view, we might well expect that at least some people would be educated as a result, and be more favorably disposed toward programming dealing with public issues in a serious way.

It is tempting but inadequate to object that this is a form of "paternalism" unjustifiably overriding private choice. If private choice is a product of existing options, and in that sense of law, the inclusion of better options, through new law, does not displace a freely produced desire. At least this is so if the new law has a democratic pedigree. In such a case, the people, in their capacity as citizens, are attempting to implement aspirations that diverge from their consumption choices.

For those skeptical about such arguments, it may be useful to note that many familiar democratic initiatives—including, for example, term limitations for elected offices—are justified on precisely these grounds. The fact that voters can reject a two-term president is hardly a decisive argument against the two-term rule. The whole point of the rule is to reflect a precommitment strategy. To those who continue to be skeptical, it is worthwhile to emphasize that the Constitution is itself a precommitment strategy, and that this Constitution includes the First Amendment.

What strategies might emerge from considerations of this sort? There is a strong case for public provision of high quality programming for children, or for obligations, imposed by govern-

---

[106] See Jon Elster, *Sour Grapes* 109-40 (Cambridge, 1983).

ment on broadcasters, to provide such programming.[107] The provision of free media time to candidates would be especially helpful, simultaneously providing attention to public affairs and diversity of view, while overcoming the distorting effects of "soundbites" and financial pressures. More generally, government might award "points" to license applicants who promise to deal with serious questions or provide public affairs broadcasting even if unsupported by market demand. Government might require purely commercial stations to provide financial subsidies to public television or to commercial stations that agree to provide less profitable high quality programming.

It is worthwhile to consider more dramatic approaches as well. These might include a compulsory hour of public affairs programming per evening, rights of reply, reductions in advertising on children's television, content review of children's television by nonpartisan experts, or guidelines to encourage attention to public issues and diversity of view.

Of course there will be room for discretion, and abuse, in making decisions about quality and public affairs. There is thus a legitimate concern that any governmental supervision of the sort I have outlined would pose risks more severe than those of the status quo. The market, surrounded by existing property rights, may restrict speech; but at least it does not entail the sort of substantive approval or disapproval, or overview of speech content, that would be involved in the suggested "New Deal." Surely it is plausible to respond that the relative neutrality of the market minimizes the role of public officials, in a way that makes it the best of the various alternatives.

There are three responses. The first is that the current system itself creates extremely serious obstacles to a well-functioning system of free expression. The absence of continuous government supervision should not obscure the point. With respect to attention to public issues, and diversity of view, the status quo disserves Madisonian goals.

The second point is that it does indeed seem plausible to think that such decisions can be made in a nonpartisan way, as is currently the case for public television. Regulatory policies have helped greatly in the past. They are responsible for the very creation of local news in the first instance. They have helped increase the quality of children's television. Public television, which offers a

---

[107] See Amy Gutmann, *Democratic Education* 238-55 (Princeton, 1987).

wide range of high quality fare, owes its existence to governmental involvement. We have no basis for doubting that much larger improvements could be brought about in the future. Nor is there any reason grounded in evidence—as opposed to market theology—to think that a regulatory solution of this sort would inevitably be inferior to the current system.

The third point is that any regulations would be subject to First Amendment scrutiny. Viewpoint discrimination would be invalid under normal standards. Any content regulation must have a high degree of generality and neutrality. These requirements would be satisfied by a broad requirement that public affairs programming, or free time for candidates, be provided; they would be violated by a requirement that (for example) feminists, pro-lifers, or the Democrats in particular must be heard. And the legislature must generate a factual record to support any regulatory alternative to the existing regime.

How might these points bear on the constitutional question? A law that contained suitable regulatory remedies might promote rather than undermine "the freedom of speech," at least if we understand that phrase in light of the distinctive American theory of sovereignty. The current system does not promote that understanding. Instead, it disserves and even stifles citizenship.

I have not argued that government should be free to regulate broadcasting however it chooses. As noted, regulation designed to excise a particular viewpoint of course would be out of bounds. More draconian controls than those I have described—for example, a requirement of public affairs broadcasting around the clock—would raise more serious questions. But at the very least, legislative "fairness doctrines" would not raise serious doubts.[108] Legislative efforts to restructure the marketplace might even be seen as the discharge of the legislature's constitutional duty, a duty

---

[108] Consider Meiklejohn, *Free Speech and Its Relation to Self-Government* at 16-17 (cited in note 1):

> [C]ongress is not debarred from all action upon freedom of speech. Legislation which abridges that freedom is forbidden, but not legislation to enlarge and enrich it. The freedom of mind which befits the members of a self-governing society is not a given and fixed part of human nature. It can be increased and established by learning, by teaching, by the unhindered flow of accurate information, by giving men health and vigor and security, by bringing them together in activities of communication and mutual understanding. And the federal legislature is not forbidden to engage in that positive enterprise of cultivating the general intelligence upon which the success of self-government so obviously depends. On the contrary, in that positive field the Congress of the United States has a heavy and basic responsibility to promote the freedom of speech.

that courts are reluctant, for good institutional reasons, fully to enforce.[109] We might understand the courts' unwillingness to require something like a fairness doctrine to be a result of the judiciary's lack of a democratic pedigree and limited remedial power. A legislature faces no such institutional limits. Its actions might therefore be seen as a response to genuine, though underenforced, constitutional obligations.

2. Campaign finance.

Many people have justified restrictions on campaign expenditures as an effort to promote political deliberation and political equality by reducing the distorting effects of disparities in wealth. On this view, such laws promote the system of free expression by ensuring that less wealthy speakers do not have much weaker voices than wealthy ones. But some have forcefully challenged campaign finance laws as inconsistent with "the marketplace of ideas." Indeed, some say these laws effect a kind of First Amendment taking from rich speakers for the benefit of poor ones. On this rationale, the Supreme Court invalidated certain forms of campaign finance regulation in *Buckley v Valeo*.[110] In the crucial passage, the Court said that "the concept that government may restrict the speech of some elements of our society in order to enhance the relative voice of others is wholly foreign to the First Amendment . . . ."[111]

Buckley reflects pre-New Deal understandings. We should view it as the modern-day analogue of *Lochner v New York*:[112] a decision to take the market status quo as just and prepolitical, and to use that decision to invalidate democratic efforts at reform. Reliance on markets is governmental neutrality. Use of existing distributions for political expenditures marks out government inaction.

From what I have said thus far, it should be clear that elections based on those distributions are actually subject to a regulatory system, made possible and constituted through law. That law consists, first, in legal rules protecting the present distribution of wealth, and more fundamentally, in legal rules allowing candidates to buy speech rights through markets.

---

[109] See Lawrence Gene Sager, *Fair Measure: The Legal Status of Underenforced Constitutional Norms*, 91 Harv L Rev 1212, 1239-42 (1978).

[110] 424 US 1, 58-59 (1976).

[111] Id at 48-49.

[112] 198 US 45, 53 (1905).

Because it involves speech, *Buckley* is even more striking than *Lochner*. Efforts to redress economic inequalities, or to ensure that they do not translate into political inequalities, should not be seen as impermissible redistribution, or as the introduction of government regulation where it did not exist before. Instead we should evaluate campaign finance laws pragmatically in terms of their consequences for the system of free expression. There are some hard questions here. The case for controls on campaign expenditures is plausible but hardly clearcut.[113] An inquiry into these considerations would raise issues quite different from those invoked by the *Buckley* Court.

3.   Private right of access.

If it were necessary to bring about diversity and attention to public matters, a private right of access to the media might even be constitutionally compelled. The notion that access will be a product of the marketplace might be constitutionally troublesome.[114] I have suggested that a democratic polity allowing people to speak in accordance with the amount of resources that other people are willing to pay in order to hear them makes a mockery of democratic ideals. With respect to much important and influential speech, our current system of free expression has just that feature in practice.

Suppose, for example, that a group objecting to a war, or to the practice of abortion, seeks to purchase advertising time to set out its view. Suppose too that the purchase is refused because the networks object to the message. It is plausible that the law that makes the refusal possible violates the First Amendment, at least

---

[113] Consider John Rawls, *The Basic Liberties and Their Priority*, in Sterling M. McMurrin, ed, *Liberty, Equality and Law, Selected Tanner Lectures on Moral Philosophy* 76 (Utah, 1987):

> The Court fails to recognize the essential point that the fair-value of the political liberties is required for a just political procedure, and that to insure their fair-value it is necessary to prevent those with greater property and wealth, and the greater skills of organization which accompany them, from controlling the electoral process to their advantage. . . . On this view, democracy is a kind of regulated rivalry between economic classes and interest groups in which the outcome should properly depend on the ability and willingness of each to use its financial resources and skills, admittedly very unequal, to make its desires felt.

But such regulation might be objectionable on other grounds, for example, that it operates in purpose or effect as a kind of incumbent protection measure. This is of course a quite different point from that in *Buckley*.

[114] See the discussion in Meiklejohn, *Free Speech and its Relation to Self-Government* at 104-05 (cited in note 1), of the failure "of the commercial radio."

if other outlets are unavailable or are far less effective. Effectiveness is important because if speech involving public affairs or diverse views is not widely heard, the Madisonian system will be severely undermined.

If the courts ought to deny a right of access, it is largely for institutional reasons. Such a right would strain judicial competence in light of the courts' limited factfinding and policymaking capacities. But it is not clear that these considerations should be decisive.

4. Conventional constitutional claims.

What I have said so far suggests that we need to reassess the constitutional claims of television and radio broadcasters quite generally.[115] In general, the production of most television shows is not a contribution to democratic deliberation, or even a means of self-expression, but instead a fairly ordinary business decision. The broadcast of such shows bears faint resemblance to the production of works for which the First Amendment was designed to provide protection. From the standpoint of liberty, regulatory intrusions on these business decisions do not always abridge the freedom of speech. Indeed, the broadcast media in many respects set out a new orthodoxy on social and political questions—making serious criticisms, from the left and the right, invisible or seem too silly or invidious to deserve consideration.[116]

I do not mean to suggest that broadcasters should be regulable under the same standards applied to, say, employers. Broadcasters are engaged in speech, and this fundamentally alters the inquiry. But we should not disable a constitutional democracy from responding to the current situation. A constitutional amendment en-

---

[115] Compare John Dewey, *The Public and its Problems* 184 (Gateway, 1946):
We have but touched lightly and in passing upon the conditions which must be fulfilled if the Great Society is to become a Great Community; a society in which the ever-expanding and intricately ramifying consequences of associated activities shall be known in the full sense of that word, so that an organized, articulate Public comes into being. The highest and most difficult kind of inquiry and a subtle, delicate, vivid and responsive art of communication must take possession of the physical machinery of transmission and circulation and breathe life into it. When the machine age has thus perfected its machinery it will be a means of life and not its despotic master. Democracy will come into its own, for democracy is a name for a life of free and enriching communion. . . . It will have its consummation when free social inquiry is indissolubly wedded to the art of full and moving communication.

[116] It is interesting to compare this phenomenon with the recent attention given to the phenomenon of "political correctness." In any culture there are ideas about what is politically correct, and in our culture these ideas reflect the conventional political morality of television and radio. Serious criticism of that political morality, from any point of view, sometimes counts as beyond the pale.

acted in order to ensure democratic self-determination need not bar a democratic corrective.

5.   Exclusive property rights.

The creation of rights of exclusive use of property raises constitutional problems when people are thereby deprived of a chance to present their views to significant parts of the public. Courts should review the creation of such rights under the standards applied to content-neutral classifications. That is, courts should apply some form of balancing to the use of property law to exclude people from places plausibly indispensable for free and open discussion. Government should have to show that the adverse consequences on the exercise of rights of free speech were justified by important governmental interests.

This would entail a new look at the "shopping center" cases.[117] In these cases, people sought to use the shopping center to engage in political protest. They claimed that access to those grounds was necessary if the public was to hear a certain point of view. Their claim is the same as that which underlies the notion, accepted by the Court, that the state may not ban leafletting or door-to-door solicitation.[118] In view of the role of the shopping center in many areas of the country, a right of access seems fully justified.

It follows that insofar as newspapers invoke the civil and criminal law to prevent people from reaching the public, we might be able to regulate them, in a viewpoint-neutral way, without abridging the freedom of speech.[119] If the government seeks to promote quality and diversity in the newspapers, courts should uphold mild regulatory efforts, especially in view of the fact that many newspapers operate as de facto monopolies.

6.   The public forum doctrine.

We would also have to rethink the public forum doctrine.[120] Current law appears to take roughly the following form. The state may not close off streets, parks, and other areas held open to the

---

[117] *Amalgamated Food Employees Union v Logan Valley Plaza*, 391 US 308, 324-25 (1968); *Lloyd Corp. v Tanner*, 407 US 551, 567-70 (1972); *Hudgens v NLRB*, 424 US 507, 521-23 (1976).

[118] See, for example, *Schneider v State*, 308 US 147, 165 (1939) (leafletting); *Martin v Struthers*, 319 US 141, 145-49 (1943) (door-to-door solicitation).

[119] This claim casts doubt on the outcome, or at least the rationale, in *Miami Herald Publishing Co. v Tornillo*, 418 US 241, 254-58 (1974).

[120] See *Hague v CIO*, 307 US 496, 514-18 (1939) (Roberts writing for a plurality); *Clark v Community for Creative Non-Violence*, 468 US 288, 293-99 (1984).

public "from time immemorial"; here the public has earned a kind of First Amendment easement. Courts will uphold reasonable regulations, but government cannot eliminate the basic right of access. The same rules apply to other areas if they have been "dedicated" to the public, that is, if the state has generally opened them for expressive activities. But still other areas—and this is a very large category—need not be open at all. Courts will uphold any restrictions so long as they are minimally rational.

This system turns on common law rules. It gives access if the area has been "dedicated," by tradition or practice, for public access, and this determination is based on whether, at common law, the area in question was held open.[121] In a period in which streets and parks were principal places for communicative activity, this historical test was sensible functionally. It well served the goal of the public forum doctrine, which was the creation of access rights to places where such rights were most effective and crucial.

The streets and parks no longer carry out their common law roles. Other areas—mailboxes, airports, train stations, broadcasting stations—are the modern equivalents of streets and parks. It is here that current doctrine is ill-suited to current needs. To keep the streets and parks open is surely important, but it is not enough to allow broadly diverse views to reach the public. For this reason the Court should abandon the common law test and look instead to whether the government has sufficiently strong and neutral reasons for foreclosing access to the property.[122] Certainly airports and train stations should be open to communicative efforts.

7. Content-based versus content-neutral restrictions.

We would also need to reassess the distinction between content-based and content-neutral restrictions on speech—the most central distinction in contemporary free speech law.

Under current law, the Court views with considerable skepticism any law that makes the content of speech relevant to restriction. If, for example, Congress tries to prevent speech dealing with a war from appearing on billboards, it is probably acting unconstitutionally. By contrast, if Congress bars all speech on billboards, courts will subject the measure to a balancing test, because this type of restriction on speech is content-neutral. It does not skew

---

[121] See *Davis v Massachusetts*, 167 US 43, 47-48 (1897), where this idea is explicit.
[122] *Grayned v Rockford*, 408 US 104, 115-18 (1972).

the thinking process of the community, and it is unlikely to reflect an impermissible governmental motivation.[123]

There is a great deal to be said in favor of this conception of neutrality.[124] In certain respects, however, it reproduces the framework of the *Lochner* era. It takes the market status quo as natural and just insofar as it bears on speech. It sees partisanship in government decisions to alter that status quo, and neutrality in decisions that basically respect it. But there may be no neutrality in use of the market status quo when the available opportunities are heavily dependent on wealth, on the common law framework of entitlements, and on the sorts of outlets for speech that are made available, and to whom. In other words, the very notions "content-neutral" and "content-based" seem to depend on taking the status quo as if it were preregulatory and unobjectionable.

At least two things follow. The first is that many content-neutral laws have content-differential effects.[125] They do so because they operate against a backdrop that is not prepolitical or just. In light of an unjust status quo, rules that are content-neutral can have severe adverse effects on some forms of speech. Greater scrutiny of content-neutral restrictions is therefore appropriate.[126] Above all, courts should attend to the possibility that seemingly neutral restrictions will have content-based effects. The government's refusal to allow Lafayette Park (across the street from the White House) to be used as a place for dramatizing the plight of the homeless[127] is a prominent example.

Second, we should draw into question a familiar justification for skepticism about content-based regulation of speech. That justification is that such regulation "skews" the marketplace of ideas.[128] This idea has two infirmities. First, we do not know what a well-functioning marketplace of ideas would look like. The preconditions of an economic marketplace can be specified by neoclassical economics; the same is not true for the preconditions of a system of free expression.[129] Second, the idea depends on taking the "marketplace" as unobjectionable in its current form. If it is already skewed, content-based regulation may be a corrective. It

---

[123] Geoffrey R. Stone, *Content Regulation and the First Amendment*, 25 Wm & Mary L Rev 189, 202, 208-09, 217-18, 227-28 (1983).

[124] Id.

[125] Id at 217-27.

[126] See Stone, 54 U Chi L Rev at 82 (cited in note 18).

[127] *Clark*, 468 US at 289, 295-99.

[128] See Stone, 54 U Chi L Rev at 55 (cited in note 18).

[129] See Strauss, 91 Colum L Rev at 349 (cited in note 42).

would be exceptionally surprising if there were no such skewing. The point bears especially on the debate over pornography, where critics often say that the "preregulatory" status quo is in fact a regulatory system—one that is skewed in favor of sexual inequality.[130]

In general, the existence of an unjust status quo is not a good reason to allow content regulation. For one thing, any inquiry into the speech status quo is probably beyond governmental capacity. There is a serious risk that judicial or legislative decisions about the relative power of various groups, and about to whom redistribution is owed, will be biased or unreliable. Judgments about who is powerful and who is not must refer to some highly controversial baseline. The resulting judgments are not easily subject to governmental administration. Indeed, government will inevitably be operating with its own biases, and those biases will affect any regulatory strategy. This risk seems unacceptable when speech is at stake.

What is distinctive about regulation of speech is that such regulation forecloses the channels of change; it prevents other views from being presented at all. Instead of allowing restrictions, we should encourage efforts to promote a better status quo.[131] I have discussed some of these in connection with the broadcasting market.

8. "Unconstitutional conditions"?

Finally, it would be necessary to reemphasize that there are limits on government's power to affect deliberative processes through the use of government funds. On this point, it is exceptionally hard to unpack the Court's cases. Some of these decisions suggest that when allocating funds, government cannot discriminate on the basis of point of view. It would follow that government could not allocate funds only to people who will speak in favor of a certain cause. Other cases draw a distinction between a "subsidy" and a "penalty," permitting government to refuse to subsidize speech, but prohibiting government from penalizing it.

The Court's most recent decision suggests that so long as the government is using its own money and is not affecting "private"

---

[130] See Catharine A. MacKinnon, *Francis Biddle's Sister: Pornography, Civil Rights and Speech*, in MacKinnon, *Feminism Unmodified: Discourses on Life and Law* 163-97 (Harvard, 1987).

[131] Of course it is necessary to defend the characterization of any change as a "restriction." See Section II.B.

expression, it can channel its funds however it wishes. The problem in *Rust v Sullivan*[132] arose when the Department of Health and Human Services issued regulations banning federally funded family planning services from engaging in (a) counseling concerning, (b) referrals for, and (c) activities advocating abortion as a method of family planning. The plaintiffs claimed that these regulations violated the First Amendment, arguing that the regulations discriminated on the basis of point of view.

The Court disagreed. In the key passage, it said,

> The Government can, without violating the Constitution, selectively fund a program to encourage certain activities it believes to be in the public interest, without at the same time funding an alternate program which seeks to deal with the problem in another way. In so doing, the Government has not discriminated on the basis of viewpoint; it has merely chosen to fund one activity to the exclusion of the other.[133]

In response to the claim that the regulations conditioned the receipt of a benefit on the relinquishment of a right, the Court said that "here the government is not denying a benefit to anyone, but is instead simply insisting that public funds be spent for the purposes for which they were authorized."[134]

Rust seems to establish the important principle that government can allocate funds to private people to establish "a program" that accords with the government's preferred point of view. In fact the Court seems to make a sharp distinction between government coercion—entry into the private realm of markets and private interactions—and funding decisions. So made, this distinction replicates pre-New Deal understandings. But there is no fundamental distinction among the law that underlies markets, the law that represents disruption of markets, and the law that calls for funding

---

[132] 111 S Ct 1759 (1991).

[133] Id at 1772. The Court added:

To hold that the Government unconstitutionally discriminates on the basis of viewpoint when it chooses to fund a program dedicated to advancing certain permissible goals, because the program in advancing those goals necessarily discourages alternate goals, would render numerous government programs constitutionally suspect. When Congress established a National Endowment for Democracy to encourage other countries to adopt democratic principles . . . it was not constitutionally required to fund a program to encourage competing lines of political philosophy such as Communism and Fascism.

Id at 1773.

[134] Id at 1774.

decisions. Courts must assess all of them in terms of their purposes and effects for free speech.[135]

Notwithstanding the apparent implications of *Rust*, it would be intolerable to say that government can target funds, or jobs, or licenses, or anything else that it owns only for speech with which it agrees. Suppose, for example, that the government decides to fund only those projects that speak favorably of Democrats. However government is acting, the First Amendment constrains the purposes for which government may act, and the effects of its actions. The notion that the First Amendment is directed only at criminal punishment or civil fines depends on an outmoded notion of what government does, and on a pre-New Deal understanding of "interference" with constitutional rights. A government decision to sponsor speech favorable to one or another party platform would run afoul of a central commitment of the First Amendment.

For this reason funding decisions that discriminate on the basis of viewpoint are at least ordinarily impermissible.[136] The proposition that government may allocate funds however it chooses is rooted in anachronistic ideas about the relationship between the citizen and the state. It poses a genuine threat to free speech under modern conditions.

D. Conclusion: A New Deal For Speech

A reformulation of First Amendment doctrine of this general sort has much to be said in its favor. Above all, such a reformulation would reinvigorate processes of democratic deliberation, by

---

[135] This is not to say that we should treat funding decisions the same as other decisions. From first principles, the development of constitutional limits on funding that affects speech raises exceedingly complex issues, and I restrict myself to a few observations here. A key feature of funding is that government must be selective in dispensing money, and the inevitability of selection means that certain judgments will be acceptable here that would not be acceptable elsewhere. With respect to the arts, for example, judgments involving esthetics and subject matter seem unavoidable. A more detailed discussion of government funding of speech and the arts can be found in Cass R. Sunstein, *Why the Unconstitutional Conditions Doctrine is An Anachronism*, 70 B U L Rev 593, 610-15 (1990).

[136] *Rust v Sullivan* is an unusual case, on its facts. (1) It plausibly involves "private speech"—counseling—rather than public or political speech. Private speech is subject to more deferential scrutiny. See *Connick v Myers*, 461 US 138 (1983). (2) It involves the abortion context, where the government has a legitimate interest in protecting fetal life. See *Maher v Roe*, 432 US 464 (1977). (3) The speech restriction in *Rust* might be seen as ancillary to the prohibition on government funding of abortion. For these reasons we may doubt whether *Rust* will extend to viewpoint discrimination with respect to public, political speech; instead, it involved a limitation on a governmentally funded private counseling program.

ensuring greater attention to public issues and greater diversity of treatment of those issues.

Some qualifications are necessary here. A system of markets in speech—surrounded by the law of property, contract, and tort—has major advantages over other forms of regulation. Such systems are content-neutral, at least on their face. This is an important point, above all because in markets, no government official is authorized to decide, in particular cases, who will be allowed to speak. There is no need to emphasize the risk of bias when government decides that issue.

In addition, markets are highly decentralized. With respect to both the print and electronic media, there are numerous outlets. Someone unable to find space in the New York Times or on CBS may well be able to find space elsewhere. A great advantage of a market system is that other outlets generally remain available. At least some other forms of regulation do not have this salutary characteristic. In any case it is important to ensure that any regulation does not foreclose certain points of view.

But our current system of free expression does not serve the Madisonian ideal. Free markets in expression are sometimes ill-adapted to the American revision of the principle of sovereignty. If we are to realize that principle, a New Deal for speech, of the sort outlined above, would be highly desirable.[137]

---

[137] There is no argument here that government may silence "the powerful" to protect "the powerless." Such a position would create a legitimate risk that judicial or legislative decisions about the relative power of various groups, and about who should receive redistribution, will be biased or unreliable. Judgments about who is powerful and who is not must refer to some baseline. That baseline will of course be politically contested. When the powerful are free to redistribute speech, it is likely they will distribute it in ways that advantage them. The resulting judgments are not easily subject to governmental administration. This risk seems unacceptable.

Moreover, we should regard a decision to silence the views of the powerful as an objectionable interference with freedom, even if it might promote the goal of equality. Well-off people might not have any strong claim of right to distributions of wealth and property that the common law grants them; but surely they have a right to complain if they are silenced. It is obvious that what they have to say may turn out to be correct, may spur better approaches to current problems, or may add a great deal to the debate simply by virtue of the reasons offered by those who respond.

These are the most conventional Millian arguments for the distinctiveness of speech. See Mill, *On Liberty* at 20-21 (cited in note 28). They do not apply to the recommendations set out here. These recommendations turn not on "power" or on "silencing the powerful," but on the application of First Amendment scrutiny to all legal rules.

III. An Alternative Proposal: The Primacy of Politics

Instead of or in addition to renovating the free speech tradition in this way, we might offer a more cautious proposal. The most fundamental step would involve an insistence on the original idea that the First Amendment is principally about political deliberation.[138] The fact that words or pictures are involved is not, standing by itself, a sufficient reason for full constitutional protection. Bribery, criminal solicitation, threats, conspiracies, perjury—all these are words, but they are not by virtue of that fact entitled to the highest level of constitutional protection. They may be regulated on the basis of a lesser showing of harm than is required for political speech.[139] They are not entirely without constitutional protection—they count as "speech"—but they do not lie within the core of the free speech guarantee.[140]

A. Theory

1. The two-tier First Amendment; and a note on autonomy.

In order to defend this proposal, we must explore whether there should be a two-tier First Amendment. The view that some forms of speech are less protected than others is frequently met with alarm. Notwithstanding its controversial character, this view derives strong support from existing law. Indeed every Justice has expressed some such view within the last generation.

---

[138] See Meiklejohn, *Free Speech and Its Relation to Self-Government* at 94 (cited in note 1):

> The guarantee given by the First Amendment is not . . . assured to all speaking. It is assured only to speech which bears, directly or indirectly, upon issues with which voters have to deal—only, therefore, to the considerations of matters of public interest. Private speech, or private interest in speech, on the other hand, has no claim whatever to the protection of the First Amendment.

[139] Alexander Meiklejohn, the greatest philosopher of the First Amendment, was emphatic on the point, distinguishing between "a private right of speech which may on occasion be denied or limited, though such limitations may not be imposed unnecessarily or unequally" and "the unlimited guarantee of the freedom of public discussion." Id at 39. "There are, then, in the theory of the Constitution, two radically different kinds of utterances. The constitutional status of a merchant advertising his wares, of a paid lobbyist fighting for the advantage of his client, is utterly different from that of a citizen who is planning for the general welfare." Id.

[140] Here I depart from Meiklejohn, who believed that nonpolitical speech was not covered by the First Amendment at all. Much of the analysis in this section is devoted to an exploration of how to protect nonpolitical speech in a two-tier First Amendment.

For example, the Supreme Court accords less than complete protection to commercial speech.[141] It excludes obscenity from First Amendment protection altogether.[142] It treats libel of private persons quite differently from libel of people who are public figures.[143] The fact that the First Amendment does not protect conspiracies, purely verbal workplace harassment of individuals on the basis of race and sex, bribery, and threats appears to owe something to a distinction between political and nonpolitical speech.

The Court has yet to offer a clear principle to unify the categories of speech that it treats as "low value." Indeed the apparent absence of a unifying principle is a source of continuing frustration to scholars of free speech law. But at least it seems clear that all the categories of low-value speech are nonpolitical.[144]

Thus far, then, we see that the Supreme Court understands the First Amendment to have two tiers. But is a two-tier First Amendment inevitable, or desirable? It does indeed seem that any well-functioning system of free expression must ultimately distinguish between different kinds of speech by reference to their centrality to the First Amendment guarantee.[145]

For example, courts should not test regulation of campaign speeches under the same standards applied to misleading commercial speech, child pornography, conspiracies, libel of private persons, and threats.[146] If the same standards were applied, one of two results would follow, and both are unacceptable.[147]

The first possible result would be to lower the burden of justification for governmental regulation as a whole, so as to allow for restrictions on misleading commercial speech, private libel, and so forth. If this were the consequence, there would be an unaccept-

---

[141] *Central Hudson Gas v Public Service Commission of New York*, 447 US 557, 562-63 (1980); *Posadas de Puerto Rico Associates v Tourism Co.*, 478 US 328, 340 (1986).

[142] *Miller v California*, 413 US 15, 23 (1973) ("categorically settled").

[143] *Gertz v Robert Welch, Inc.*, 418 US 323, 342-48 (1974); see also *Milkovich v Lorain Journal Co.*, 110 S Ct 2695, 2703-04 (1990).

[144] This is so at least in the sense that I understand the term "political" here.

[145] See Thomas M. Scanlon, Jr., *Freedom of Expression and Categories of Expression*, 40 U Pitt L Rev 519 (1979).

[146] Id at 537-39.

[147] It is tempting, and possible, to classify some speech as unprotected because it is "really" action. But this is unhelpful. Conspiracies and bribes are speech, not action. If they are to be treated as action—that is, if they are not to be protected—it is because of their distinctive features. This is what must be discussed. The word "action" is simply a placeholder for that unprovided discussion.

ably high threat to political expression. A generally lowered burden of justification would therefore be intolerable.

The second possible result is that courts would apply the properly stringent standards for regulation of political speech to commercial speech, private libel, and child pornography. The central problem with this approach is that it would mean that government could not control speech that should be regulated. A system in which the most stringent standards were applied across the board would mean that government could not regulate criminal solicitation, child pornography, private libel, and false or misleading commercial speech, among others. The harms that justify such regulation are real, but they are insufficient to permit government controls under the extremely high standards applied to regulation of political speech. If courts are to be honest about the matter, an insistence that "all speech is speech" would mean that they must eliminate many currently unobjectionable and even necessary controls—or more likely that judgments about value, because unavoidable, would continue to be made, but covertly.

If courts must draw a distinction between low- and high-value expression, the many efforts to understand the First Amendment as a protection of "autonomy" may be doomed to failure.[148] Some have suggested, for example, that the free speech principle guards the autonomy of speakers or of listeners.[149] I must be tentative here, but it seems likely that any autonomy-based approach would make it difficult or impossible to distinguish between different categories of speech.[150] Autonomy, taken in the abstract, seems to argue in favor of similar protection of all, or most, forms of speech.[151]

---

[148] See Thomas Scanlon, *A Theory of Freedom of Expression*, 1 Phil & Pub Aff 204, 214-15 (1972); Strauss, 91 Colum L Rev at 353-60 (cited in note 42); Martin H. Redish, *The Value of Free Speech*, 130 U Pa L Rev 591, 625 (1982). Especially notable, it is for this reason that Scanlon revised his own earlier position, see Scanlon, 40 U Pitt L Rev at 533-34 (cited in note 145); See also Charles Fried, *The New First Amendment Jurisprudence: A Threat to Liberty*, in this volume, 225, 233.

[149] Strauss, 91 Colum L Rev at 335-36 (cited in note 42).

[150] It might be tempting to ask whether the speech in question is cognitive or affective, and to accord protection only to the former. Some of the Court's opinions can be so read. See, for example, *Chaplinsky v New Hampshire*, 315 US 568, 573-74 (1942). But such an approach would be unacceptable. It would disregard the fragility of the distinction between the affective and the cognitive; see Martha C. Nussbaum, *Love's Knowledge, Essays on Philosophy and Literature* 291-97 (Oxford, 1990). There are important affective components of much political speech, or speech that is high-value by any measure; and many forms of speech accorded a lower-level of protection—like commercial speech and private libel—are surely cognitive.

[151] But see note 153.

Moreover, an approach rooted in a norm of autonomy makes it difficult to understand what is special about speech.[152] Many acts, like most speech, serve the goal of autonomy as it is usually understood by advocates of an autonomy-based conception of the First Amendment.[153] If autonomy in the abstract is the principle, there appears to be nothing distinctive about speech to explain why it has been singled out for constitutional protection. An approach to the First Amendment that does not account for the distinctiveness of speech would be untrue to constitutional text and structure.

2. The case for the primacy of politics.

We must still decide by what standard courts might accomplish the task of distinguishing between low-value and high-value speech. To support an emphasis on politics, we need to define the category of political speech. For present purposes I will treat speech as political *when it is both intended and received as a contribution to public deliberation about some issue.* It seems implausible to think that words warrant the highest form of protection if the speaker does not even intend to communicate a message; the First Amendment does not put gibberish at the core even if it is taken, by some in the audience, to mean something.[154] By requiring intent, I do not mean to require a trial on the question of subjective motivation. Generally this issue can be resolved simply on the basis of the nature of the speech at issue. By requiring that the speech be received as a contribution to public deliberation, I do not mean that all listeners or readers must see the substantive content. It is sufficient if some do. Many people miss the political message in some forms of political speech, especially art or literature. But if no one sees the political content, it is hard to understand why the speech should so qualify.

Finally, the requirements are in the conjunctive, though in almost all cases speech that is intended as a contribution to public deliberation will be seen by some as such. The fact that speech is

---

[152] Bork, 47 Ind L J at 25 (cited in note 17).

[153] It would be possible, however, to have a more refined conception of autonomy. Under such a conception, autonomy is not a right to say and do what you "want," but instead, to have the social preconditions for autonomy, understood as a form of self-mastery. This notion may well allow distinctions among different forms of speech. See C. Edwin Baker, *Human Liberty and Freedom of Speech* 37-46 (Oxford, 1989); Cass R. Sunstein, *Preferences and Politics*, 20 Phil & Pub Aff 3, 11-14 (1991). But it will be very hard to make this a principle for speech.

[154] See R. George Wright, *A Rationale from J.S. Mill for the Free Speech Clause*, 1985 S Ct Rev 149.

so seen by some is insufficient if it is not so intended; consider, for example, commercial speech, obscenity, or private libel. If some people understand the speech in question to be a contribution to public deliberation, it cannot follow that the speech qualifies as such for constitutional purposes, without treating almost all speech as political and therefore destroying the whole point of the two-tier model. Of course the definition I have offered leaves many questions unanswered, and there will be hard intermediate cases. I offer it simply as a starting point for analysis.

An approach that affords special protection to political speech, thus defined, is justified on numerous grounds. Such an approach receives firm support from history—not only from the Framers' theory of free expression, but also from the development of that principle through the history of American law. There can be little doubt that suppression by the government of political ideas that it disapproved, or found threatening, was the central motivation for the clause. The worst examples of unacceptable censorship involve efforts by government to insulate itself from criticism. Judicial interpretations over the course of time also support a political conception of the First Amendment.[155]

This approach seems likely as well to accord with our initial or considered judgments about particular free speech problems. Any approach to the First Amendment will have to take substantial account of those judgments, and adjust itself accordingly.[156] It seems clear that such forms of speech as perjury, bribery, threats, misleading or false commercial advertising, criminal solicitation, and libel of private persons—or at least most of these—are not entitled to the highest degree of constitutional protection. No other approach unifies initial or preliminary judgments about these matters as well as a political conception of the First Amendment.

In addition, an insistence that government's burden is greatest when political speech is at issue responds well to the fact that here government is most likely to be biased. The presumption of dis-

---

[155] See Levy, *Emergence of a Free Press* at 266-70 (cited in note 3). Original understanding and the tradition of legal interpretation, however, are not decisive. The same support could be found for an unacceptably narrow view of the Equal Protection Clause, the history of which suggests validation of much discrimination on the basis of sex and even race. But a position is surely strengthened if it can draw on a good historical pedigree.

[156] Thus it is not unprincipled or merely convenient to adjust a theory when it proves to deal inadequately with particular cases. Sometimes the adequacy of the theory is itself tested by how well it conforms to initial or considered judgments about particular outcomes. See John Rawls, *A Theory of Justice* 48-51 (Harvard, 1971) (discussing reflective equilibrium).

trust of government is strongest when politics are at issue.[157] It is far weaker when government is regulating (say) commercial speech, bribery, private libel, or obscenity. In such cases there is less reason to suppose that it is insulating itself from criticism.[158]

Finally, this approach protects speech when regulation is most likely to be harmful. Restrictions on political speech have the distinctive feature of impairing the ordinary channels for political change; such restrictions are especially dangerous.[159] If there are controls on commercial advertising, it always remains possible to argue that such controls should be lifted. If the government bans violent pornography, citizens can continue to argue against the ban. But if the government forecloses political argument, the democratic corrective is unavailable. Controls on nonpolitical speech do not have this uniquely damaging feature.

Taken in concert, these considerations suggest that government should be under a special burden of justification when it seeks to control speech intended and received as a contribution to public deliberation. To be sure, there are some powerful alternative approaches. Perhaps we should conclude that speech is entitled to protection if it involves rational thought. This would extend beyond the political to include not merely literary and artistic work, but commercial and scientific expression as well. But there would be serious problems with any such approach. For example, we should probably not give technological data with potential military applications the same degree of protection as political speech; nor should we give misleading commercial speech the same protection as misleading political speech.

Alternatively, one might think that the free speech principle includes any representation that reflects deliberation or imagination in a way that is relevant to the development of individual capacities.[160] No one has fully elaborated an approach of this sort. It

---

[157] See Frederick Schauer, *Free Speech: a Philosophical Enquiry* 35, 39, 45 (Cambridge, 1982).

[158] As work in public choice theory has shown, there are possible bad incentives elsewhere too. For example, restrictions on commercial advertising might be an effort by a well-organized group to eliminate competition. But this does not distinguish regulation of speech from regulation of anything else, and so it provides no special reason to be suspicious of government regulation of speech. Regulation of political speech, by contrast, raises the specter of governmental efforts to suppress criticism of its own conduct and is therefore more likely to be biased.

[159] See John Hart Ely, *Democracy and Distrust: A Theory of Judicial Review* 75-77 (Harvard, 1980).

[160] This idea could reflect Aristotelian ideas involving the development of individual capacities. See Amartya Sen, *Commodities and Capabilities* (Elsevier Science, 1985);

would carry considerable promise. But such an approach would make it hard to distinguish between scientific and political speech. It also might protect such things as child pornography.

Much work must be done to elaborate and evaluate alternatives of this sort. But a conception of free speech that centers on democratic governance appears to be the best way to organize our considered judgments about cases likely to raise hard First Amendment questions.

If the First Amendment offers special protection to political speech, we must of course reject the proposition that all forms of speech stand on the same ground. It would be necessary to draw distinctions between obscenity and political protest, or misleading commercial speech and misleading campaign statements, or proxy statements and party platforms. We must resort far less readily to the view that a restriction on one form of speech necessarily will lead to restriction on another.

3. Counterarguments.

The difficulties with a political conception of the First Amendment are not unfamiliar; they raise all of the questions that produced the current First Amendment preoccupation with line-drawing. How, for example, are we to treat the work of Robert Mapplethorpe, the music of a rock group, or nude dancing? Both commercial speech and pornography are political in the crucial sense that they reflect and promote a point of view, broadly speaking ideological in character, about how to structure important things in the world. The recent attack on pornography has drawn close attention to its political character, and thus ironically might be thought to invalidate efforts to regulate it.[161]

Is it so clear that speech that has nothing to do with politics is not entitled to First Amendment protection? Must we exclude music or art or science?[162] Surely it is philistine[163] or worse to say that

---

Martha Nussbaum, *Aristotelian Social Democracy*, in R. Bruce Douglass, Gerald M. Mara, and Henry S. Richardson, eds, *Liberalism and the Good* 203 (Routledge, 1990). The idea has no clear defenders in current legal writing.

[161] See *American Booksellers Association, Inc. v Hudnut*, 771 F2d 323, 325 (7th Cir 1985).

[162] See Meiklejohn, *Free Speech and Its Relation to Self-Government* at 99-100 (cited in note 1):

We have assumed that the studies of the "scholar" must have, in all respects, the absolute protection of the First Amendment. But with the devising of "atomic" and "bacteriological" knowledge for the use of, and under the direction of, military forces, we can now see how loose and inaccurate, at this point, our thinking has been. . . . It may be,

the First Amendment protects only political platforms. Often the deepest political challenges to the existing order can be found in art, literature, music, or sexual expression.[164] Sometimes government attempts to regulate these things for precisely this reason.

These are hard questions without simple solutions. I will venture only some brief remarks in response. The first is that we should not take the existence of hard line-drawing problems to foreclose an attempt to distinguish between political and nonpolitical speech. If the distinction is otherwise plausible, and if systems that fail to make it have severe problems, the difficulty of drawing lines is acceptable.

Even more fundamental, there is no way to operate a system of free expression without drawing lines. Not everything that counts as words or pictures is entitled to full constitutional protection. The question is not whether to draw lines, but how to draw the right ones.

Second, we should understand broadly the category of the political. The definition I have offered would encompass not simply political tracts, but all art and literature that has the characteristics of social commentary—which is to say, much art and literature.[165] Much speech is a contribution to public deliberation despite initial appearances. In addition, it is important to create a large breathing space for political speech by protecting expression even if it does not fall unambiguously within that category. Both *Ulysses* and *Bleak House* are unquestionably political for First Amendment purposes. The same is true of Robert Mapplethorpe's work, which attempts to draw into question current sexual norms and practices, and which bears on such issues as the right of privacy and the antidiscrimination principle.

To say this is emphatically not to say that speech that has political consequences is by virtue of that fact "political" in the constitutional sense. Obscenity is political in that it has political well-springs and effects; the same is true of commercial speech and

---

therefore, that the time has come when the guarding of human welfare requires that we shall abridge the private desire of the scholar—or of those who subsidize him—to study whatever he may please. . . . As I write these words, I am not taking a final stand on the issue which is here suggested. But I am sure that the issue is coming upon us and cannot be evaded. In a rapidly changing world, another of our ancient sanctities—the holiness of research—has been brought under question.

[163] See Richard A. Posner, *Sex and Reason* (Harvard, 1992).

[164] Sex is familiarly a metaphor for social rebellion. See, for example, George Orwell, *Nineteen Eighty-Four* 126-27 (Harcourt, 1949).

[165] See generally Nussbaum, *Love's Knowledge* (cited in note 150).

even bribery—certainly bribery of public officials. An employer's purely verbal sexual or racial harassment of an employee surely has political consequences, including the creation of a disincentive for women and blacks to go to that workplace at all. But these forms of speech are not by virtue of their effects entitled to the highest form of constitutional protection. To say that speech is political for First Amendment purposes because it has political causes and effects is to say that nearly all words or pictures are immunized from legal regulation without the gravest showing of clear and immediate harm. For reasons suggested above, that cannot be right.

For purposes of the Constitution, the question is whether the speech is a contribution to social deliberation, not whether it has political effects or sources. Thus, for example, there is a distinction between a misogynist tract, which is entitled to full protection, and pornographic movies, some of which are in essence masturbatory aids and not entitled to such protection. Personal, face-to-face racial harassment by an employer of an employee is not entitled to full protection,[166] while a racist speech to a crowd is. There is a distinction between a racial epithet and a tract in favor of white supremacy. An essay about the value of unregulated markets in oil production should be treated quite differently from an advertisement for Texaco—even if an oil company writes and publishes both.

The definition I have offered would exclude a wide variety of speech from the category of high-value expression, and for this reason might be thought to pose an unacceptable danger of censorship. A more general response to the suggestion that the core of the First Amendment involves politics and democracy is that this theory would provide fragile safeguards for art, music, literature, and perhaps much of commercial entertainment. A First Amendment that offers so little protection to so much might be embarrassingly weak and thin. If the exclusion of such materials results ' from a theory of free speech that the Constitution's text does not compel, perhaps the Court should repudiate that theory.

In fact, however, there would remain room for powerful First Amendment challenges to most regulatory efforts. No speech can be regulated on the basis of whim or whimsy. Something stronger than rationality review, though weaker than "strict scrutiny," is

---

[166] This is a harder question if it is not personal. It could, however, still count as harassment under current law. See Balkin, 1990 Duke L J at 414-28 (cited in note 21), on "captive audience" ideas in this setting.

and should be applied to low-value expression. Thus, for example, commercial speech occupies an intermediate category, regulable when government can show a good reason and a solid connection between the means of regulation and the reason in question. The same should be true for scientific speech and private libel.

In addition, the government may not regulate speech—or anything else—on the basis of constitutionally disfavored justifications. Frequently, the reason for regulating speech will be disfavored even if the speech is low-value. Courts could not permit the regulation of pornography if the purpose of the regulation is to repress a message rather than to redress genuine harms.[167] The First Amendment makes certain reasons for regulation illegitimate, and this is so even if those reasons are invoked against low-value speech.

Government may not regulate speech of any kind if the reason is that it disapproves of the message or disagrees with the idea that the speech expresses. Regulation can be justified only by reference to genuine harms. An effort to regulate music because it is "offensive," or because it stirs up passionate feeling, would run afoul of the Free Speech Clause. Of course there will be hard cases in which courts have to decide whether a legitimate justification is at work. The resolution of these cases cannot be purely mechanical. But even if we understand the First Amendment as centrally concerned with political speech, there is little reason to fear that this understanding would permit a large increase in official censorship.

B. Practice

This approach would not entail substantial change in existing law. It would help us deal with the new controversies, but generally would not unsettle resolution of the old ones. The Court has already created categories of speech that are less protected or unprotected. But the Court has not given a sense of the unifying factors that justify the creation of these categories. It is highly revealing that political speech never falls within them, and that all speech that does so is usually not political in the sense that I understand the term. The principal difference between the approach I suggest

---

[167] It is sometimes said that the goal of anti-pornography laws is to suppress pornography's message about women. If this were the reason for such laws, they would indeed be unconstitutional. I do not enter that debate here. See Cass Sunstein, *Neutrality in Constitutional Law (With Special Reference to Pornography, Abortion, and Surrogacy)*, 92 Colum L Rev 1, 18-29 (1992) (discussing harm-based arguments for pornography regulations).

and current law is the explicit statement that nonpolitical speech occupies a lower tier—a statement that the Court has yet to make. For reasons suggested below, it is unclear that even this would make much of a difference.

There are several areas of controversy, however, where this approach would likely lead to different results than those reached under current law. The suggested approach would mean that libel of public figures not involved in governmental affairs—famous actors, for example—would not be subject to special constitutional disabilities. Current law sharply constrains celebrities from bringing libel actions.[168] But there is no special interest in protecting the "breathing space" of the press in discussing athletes or movie stars. On what principle must a legal system provide special "breathing space" to untruths about famous people?[169] The test for special protection should be whether the matter bears on democratic governance, not whether the plaintiff is famous.

Treatment of sexually explicit speech also would diverge from current doctrine. Under current law, such speech usually receives protection[170] if it has significant social value, even if scientific or literary rather than political. An emphasis on the political foundations of the First Amendment appears to threaten this basic protection. But under the approach I suggest, courts should invalidate regulation of sexually explicit speech in most cases. As discussed in more detail below, such regulation usually would be unsupportable by reference to a legitimate justification.[171]

The securities laws would raise no serious question. Indeed, many of the controversies with which I began would be resolved fairly automatically. The only real exception is hate speech, which plausibly has political content in that it is a self-conscious statement about how to resolve current political controversies. The analysis would depend on the extent to which something labelled as "hate speech" is actually intended or received as a contribution

---

[168] *Gertz v Robert Welch, Inc.*, 418 US 323, 342 (1974).

[169] A possible response would be that many famous people have governmental associations of some sort, and the notion of "public figures" is designed to overcome the difficulties of case-by-case inquiries. Also, many people not involved in government are involved in activities in which the public is legitimately concerned on democratic grounds. Consider attempted bribery of public officials by corporate executives. Probably the best approach, suggested by Justice Marshall, would involve an inquiry into whether the issue is one of legitimate public interest or concern. See *Rosenbloom v Metromedia, Inc.*, 403 US 29, 43-44 (1971) (Marshall concurring).

[170] *Miller v California*, 413 US 15, 26 (1973).

[171] Literature is generally protected, see text accompanying note 165. With the regulation of sexually explicit speech, illegitimate motives are likely to be at work.

to thought about a public matter. This approach might deprive speech of protection if it amounts to simple epithets, showing visceral contempt. On an analogy to the obscene telephone call, a public university can prevent students and teachers from using words in a way that is not plausibly part of social deliberation about an issue. But racist, homophobic, or sexist speech, even if offensive and harmful, would not be regulable so long as it is plausibly part of the exchange of ideas. It follows that the speech codes of public universities are generally unconstitutional, except insofar as they apply to the narrow category of epithets.[172]

This approach would also suggest that government may regulate some forms of scientific speech. For example, the government could regulate the export of technology with military applications. This is so even though the showing of harm is in such cases insufficient under the standards properly applied to political speech.[173]

What of art and literature? The fact that they are frequently political—combined with the severe difficulty of evaluating their political quality on an ad hoc basis—argues powerfully in favor of the view that generally art and literature should be taken as "core" speech. When government seeks to censor art or literature, it is almost always because of the political content, making the censorship impermissible. Even when art or literature stands outside the core, government cannot attempt to regulate speech because it disagrees with the message. The First Amendment requires a legitimate justification. A legitimate justification is almost always lacking.

This approach would solve most of the current First Amendment problems without making it necessary to enter into complex debates about power and powerlessness, or about neutrality in constitutional law. It would also draw on history, on the best theories about the function of the free speech guarantee, and on a sensible understanding about when government is least likely to be trustworthy.

IV. NOTES ON FOUNDATIONS: DELIBERATIVE DEMOCRACY

Thus far I have not said anything general about the functions of the free speech guarantee or about the conception of democracy

---

[172] See Cass R. Sunstein, *Ideas, Yes; Assaults, No*, The American Prospect 35, 37-38 (Summer 1991).

[173] See Cass R. Sunstein, *Government Control of Information*, 74 Cal L Rev 889, 905-12 (1986).

that we should take it to embody. A few remarks are therefore in order.

We might understand the American constitutional system to create a deliberative democracy.[174] This is a system that combines a degree of popular accountability with a belief in deliberation among representatives and the citizenry at large. The system is not designed solely to allow the protection of private interests and private rights. Even more emphatically, its purpose is not to furnish the basis for struggle among self-interested private groups. That notion is anathema to American constitutionalism.

Instead, the system is intended to ensure discussion and debate among people who are differently situated, in a process through which reflection will encourage the emergence of general truths.[175] A distinctive feature of American republicanism is hospitality toward heterogeneity, rather than fear of it. Indeed, it was along this axis that the antifederalists and federalists most sharply divided. Thus the antifederalist Brutus insisted: "In a republic, the manners, sentiments, and interests of the people should be similar. If this be not the case, there will be a constant clashing of opinions; and the representatives of one part will be continually striving against those of the other."[176] Alexander Hamilton responded that in a heterogeneous republic, discussion will be improved; "the jarring of parties" will "often promote deliberation."[177] The Federalists did not believe that heterogeneity would be an obstacle to political discussion and debate. On the contrary, they thought that it was indispensable to it.

In the American tradition, politics is not a process in which desires and interests remain frozen, before or during politics. Indeed, some suggested early on that national representatives should take instructions from their constituents and vote accordingly. The First Congress rejected the proposal on the ground that it would destroy the purpose of the meeting.[178] That purpose was to ensure an exchange of views, one that would actually change opinions. We should understand the protection accorded to free speech in this

---

[174] Joseph M. Bessette, *Deliberative Democracy: The Majority Principle in Republican Government*, in Robert A. Goldwin and William A. Schambra, eds, *How Democratic is the Constitution?* 102, 112-16 (American Enterprise Institute, 1980); Cass R. Sunstein, *Interest Groups in American Public Law*, 38 Stan L Rev 29, 45-48 (1985).

[175] This is a pragmatic conception of truth. See, for example, William James, *Pragmatism and the Meaning of Truth* 78-79 (Harvard, 1935).

[176] Brutus in Herbert J. Storing, ed, *The Complete Antifederalist* 369 (Chicago, 1980).

[177] Federalist 70 (Hamilton) in *The Federalist Papers* 471, 475 (Wesleyan, 1961).

[178] Joseph Gales, ed, 1 *Annals of Congress* 733-45 (Gales and Seaton, 1834).

view. Its overriding goal is to allow judgments to emerge through general discussion and debate.

This view does not depend on a sharp distinction between public interest and private interest, or on an insistence that private interest should not be a motivation for political action. We need only to claim that the provision of new information, or alternative perspectives, can lead to new understandings of what interests are and where they lie.

In this sense, conceptions of politics as an aggregation of interests, or as a kind of "marketplace," inadequately capture the American system of free expression. Aggregative or marketplace notions disregard the extent to which political outcomes are supposed to depend on discussion and debate, and on the reasons offered for or against the various alternatives. The First Amendment is the central constitutional reflection of the commitment to these ideas. It is part and parcel of the constitutional commitment to citizenship. This commitment must be understood in light of the American conception of sovereignty, placing governing authority in the people themselves.

The proposals set out above flow directly from this conception of the First Amendment. The belief that politics lies at the core of the amendment is an outgrowth of the more general structural commitment to deliberative democracy. The concern for ensuring the preconditions for deliberation among the citizenry is closely associated with this commitment. The proposals suggested here thus fit with the highest aspirations of the constitutional commitments of which the First Amendment is the most tangible expression.

Through this route, we have come far from the basic ideas that characterize current thinking about free speech. The aversion to line-drawing with respect to speech seems to lead to insoluble conundrums. It is better to be candid about the matter and to insist that as far as the First Amendment is concerned, all speech is not the same. Threats to free speech do come from government, but the general understanding of what this means is far off the mark. Such threats do take the form of conventional, highly visible censorship. But they also take the form of what is in some respects the same thing—the allocation by government of rights of property, ownership, and exclusion that determine who can speak and who cannot, and that involve the use of civil and criminal law to protect the rights of exclusion. Government neutrality is the right aspiration, but properly understood, neutrality does not mean respect for rights of speech as these can be vindicated in light of the existing distribution of rights and entitlements. It is thus necessary to reform all of the commitments that, with respect to speech, have come to represent the conventional wisdom in many circles.

CONCLUSION

Over the last forty years, the American law of freedom of speech has experienced a revolution. The revolution has accomplished enormous good. A return to the pre-1950 law of free speech certainly would not provide a better understanding of the free speech principle, or sufficiently serve other valuable social goals to justify abandonment of the current approach. In the bicentennial year of the Bill of Rights—a period in which appreciation for freedom of speech is exploding throughout the world—it is more than appropriate to celebrate our tradition of liberty, and to recognize the extent to which it is an extraordinary and precious achievement.

At the same time, a crucial part of that achievement involves the dynamic and self-revising character of the free speech tradition. Our existing liberty of expression owes much of its content to the capacity of each generation to rethink and to revise the understandings that were left to it. To the economists' plea that "the perfect is the enemy of the good," we might oppose Dewey's suggestion that "the better is too often the enemy of the still better."[179] The conception of free speech in any decade of American history is often quite different from the conception twenty years before or after.

An adherence to current understandings is inadequate to resolve current controversies, and it threatens to protect both more and less free speech than it should. It is inadequate for current controversies, because it is poorly adapted to the problems raised by campaign finance regulation, scientific speech, regulation of broadcasting, government funding, content-neutral restrictions on speech, hate speech, commercial advertising, and pornography. It protects more than it should, because it includes, within the category of protected expression, speech that serves few or none of the goals for which speech is protected, and that causes serious social harms. It protects less than it should, because current doctrine does not sufficiently serve the central goal of producing a deliberative democracy among political equals. Ironically, the existing system owes many of its failures to the supposed mandates of contemporary conceptions of the First Amendment.

---

[179] See John J. McDermott, ed, *The Philosophy of John Dewey* 652 (Chicago, 1973).

In this Article I have suggested two changes in existing understandings; both of them derive from the American contribution to the theory of sovereignty. First, some forms of apparent government intervention into free speech processes can actually improve those processes. We should not understand these as an objectionable intrusion into an otherwise law-free social sphere. In these ways, such intervention should not always be taken as an impermissible "abridgement" of the free speech right. Efforts of this sort do not represent "positive" government action intruding on constitutionally protected "negative" liberty.[180]

Instead these proposals entail a democratic recognition of the dangers to free speech posed by content-neutral restrictions that limit access to arenas in which expression should occur. Current doctrine generally recognizes the risks posed by content-neutral restrictions. The gap lies in the unwillingness to see that the speech "market" is a product of law subject to legislative improvements and to First Amendment constraints. A salutary recognition that decentralized markets generally are indispensable to promote liberty—for products and for speech—is not inconsistent with the basic claim. Nor is that recognition inconsistent with the view that the creation of markets might, on some occasions and in some settings, itself be an abridgement of free speech.

Second, we should understand the free speech principle to be centered above all on political thought. In this way the free speech principle should always be seen through the lens of democracy. Government may regulate other forms of speech not on a whim, and not for illegitimate reasons, but on the basis of a lesser showing of harm.

Taken together, these principles would bring about significant changes in the legal treatment currently accorded to electoral campaigns, electronic broadcasting, and the assertion of ownership rights in order to exclude political speech. In their most modest form, the principles would provide a major step toward resolving current free speech controversies without requiring serious revisions in existing law. Rightly understood, these principles might counteract the novel, sometimes invisible, and often serious obstacles that now lie in the path of free speech in America, and that promise to do so in an increasingly threatening way in the twenty-first century.

---

[180] Here the analysis in Fiss, 71 Iowa L Rev at 1423-24 (cited in note 21), seems to be off the mark.

LEVELS OF GENERALITY IN CONSTITUTIONAL INTERPRETATION

Liberating Abstraction

Bruce Ackerman†

This is a great moment in world history. From Berlin to Moscow, the news is full of the restless striving of a renascent liberalism. For the first time in a long time, all of Europe resonates with the great liberal themes of freedom and equality under law. Great movements bring great dangers: a mobilized liberalism must compete with resurgent nationalisms, obscurantisms, theocracies. But the new demagogues seem less formidable than Hitler or Lenin or even Mussolini. Though we are in for lots of disappointments, I open my New York Times with something that feels like genuine hope. Will Johannesburg or Havana or Peking successfully manage the formidable challenges of liberal transformation? Maybe the answer will be "no," but this is the first time since 1848[1] when liberals could seriously ask the question.

Against this background, there is something puzzling about the path of American constitutional law. As in so many other places, American politics in the 1980s witnessed a resurgence of individualistic rhetoric. Reaganism was the most serious expression of this impulse in the half-century since the New Deal. And yet, when we look at the way the new Republicanism is translating itself into constitutional law, we find only paradox: the Supreme Court is not busily at work renewing and reviving constitutional

---

† Sterling Professor of Law and Political Science, Yale University. This Article was prepared for *The Bill of Rights in the Welfare State: A Bicentennial Symposium*, held at The University of Chicago Law School on October 25-26, 1991.

[1] I say 1848, rather than 1918, since even the most passionate Wilsonian recognized that Lenin's vision would be a very formidable competitor during the decades ahead.

317

commitments to individual freedom. It seems bent on glorifying the powers of the state and diminishing the constitutional protection of individual rights. Except to those fully socialized into the law-business, it must seem odd to find one of the leading legal intellectuals of the Reagan Revolution, Judge Frank Easterbrook, arguing in favor of liberating big government from an expansive interpretation of the Bill of Rights; while I come from the liberal legal academy to argue that judges like Easterbrook should be defending individual freedom. Why this odd relationship between Reaganite politics and Republican law? Why is the new Republican court leaving it to defenders of big government, like myself, to emphasize the fundamental importance of fundamental rights?

I haven't gotten to the bottom of this one. Since the question threatens to become one of the leading constitutional paradoxes of the 1990s, it will serve as my entry into the present subject. Specifically, I will argue that the statism of the new Republican court expresses itself in a fundamental asymmetry in its attitude toward legal abstraction. In interpreting the power-granting side of the Constitution, today's Court exhibits no hesitation about the liberating power of abstraction. It shows no serious inclination to question the New Deal transformation of a *federal* government with limited powers into a *national* government with plenary powers at home and abroad. Instead, the Court saves all its doubts about abstract thought for the rights-granting side of the Constitution. This asymmetry—abstract powers, but particular rights—shows the authoritarian bias in the emerging pattern of Supreme Court decisions. Time and again, the Court authorizes the activist state to assault fundamental constitutional rights in ways that evade the narrowing judicial focus.[2]

This asymmetry would be troubling enough if it were "only" a matter of legal method. It is a single Constitution we are interpreting—both when it speaks about powers and when it speaks about rights. Nobody who takes interpretation seriously should feel free to split the text in two, and approach the fragments in radically different ways—unless he is prepared to tell us why.

Take Justice Scalia for example. For all his disdain for abstraction when the subject is fundamental rights, the Justice plays a very different tune when he talks about the separation of powers.[3] He does not let the absence of a "Separation of Powers

---

² See Charles A. Reich, *The Individual Sector*, 100 Yale L J 1409 (1991).

³ See *Mistretta v United States*, 488 US 361, 416-27 (1989) (Scalia dissenting).

Clause" block his interpretive path.[4] Like any other good reader of a text, he reads clauses and paragraphs together as he tries to convince us that Articles One, Two and Three express a fundamental commitment to separation—and proceeds to think about the meaning of this commitment in a highly abstract way. Like many others, I am unpersuaded by the particular abstractions Justice Scalia deploys in his interpretation of "checks and balances." My asymmetry point, however, is analytically distinct from this disagreement. I simply ask him to explain why he scoffs at Justice Douglas's celebrated search amongst the "penumbras" of the Bill of Rights in *Griswold*,[5] but invites us to conduct an analogous search amongst the penumbras of Articles One, Two, and Three in *Morrison*.[6]

Since I am not debating Justice Scalia in these pages, I will defer a serious assessment of his particular form of selective abstraction for another time.[7] It will be enough to engage Frank Easterbrook in a serious dialogue in the hope that he might reassess his very selective aversion to abstraction and generalization in constitutional law. This endeavor requires, at the outset, a search for common ground—which, happily, has not proved very difficult. When I considered Easterbrook's efforts as a judge, I found that I agreed with his most important decision touching the Bill of Rights: *American Booksellers Association, Inc. v Hudnut*.[8]

The case assessed an Indianapolis ordinance that expressed a strong feminist line on the suppression of pornography. Rather than focusing on "obscene" materials without redeeming social

---

[4] The absence of such a provision was by no means unintentional. Madison had originally proposed that the First Congress codify its commitment to the separation of powers in the following constitutional amendment:

> The powers delegated by this constitution are appropriated to the departments to which they are respectively distributed: so that the legislative department shall never exercise the powers vested in the executive or judicial nor the executive exercise the power vested in the legislative or judicial, nor the judicial exercise the powers vested in the legislative or executive departments.

See Bernard Schwartz, 2 *The Bill of Rights: A Documentary History* 1028 (Chelsea House, 1971). While Madison's proposal passed the House as part of the original Bill of Rights, it failed in the Senate. Id at 1146. Since the Senate did not publish its proceedings, we do not know the reason why it failed. We do know that, in the House, opposition came from two directions: Mr. Sherman opposed the amendment as "altogether unnecessary" while Mr. Livermore thought the "clause subversive of the constitution." Id at 1117.

[5] *Griswold v Connecticut*, 381 US 479, 484 (1965).

[6] *Morrison v Olson*, 487 US 654, 697-734 (1988) (Scalia dissenting).

[7] See the useful critique of Justice Scalia's views in Laurence H. Tribe and Michael C. Dorf, *On Reading the Constitution* 97-106 (Harvard, 1991).

[8] 771 F2d 323 (7th Cir 1985), aff'd without opinion, 475 US 1001 (1985).

value, the ordinance conceived the "pornography" problem in self-consciously political terms. It sought to suppress sexually explicit messages that "discriminated" against women by portraying them in subordinate positions.[9] So long as subordination was the theme, the work's other values would not save it from Indianapolis's ban.[10] Sexual explicitness was not "pornographic" so long as it expressed egalitarian attitudes on the gender question.[11]

This was, transparently, the kind of case that led Easterbrook to desert the academy for the bench. *American Booksellers* provided a chance to rise above statutory detail on the appellate dockets and consider a fundamental challenge fundamentally; a chance to show how a thoughtful representative of the Republican judiciary should respond to a legislative success of the academic left.[12] How to begin to write the opinion?

I join Easterbrook at this moment of judicial self-definition, and applaud his choice of a starting point. After stating the facts of the case, Easterbrook begins neither with the latest decisions of the Supreme Court, nor with the wisdom of the Founding Fathers. He begins in the middle: with Robert Jackson's great opinion in the second Flag Salute Case, *West Virginia State Board of Education v Barnette*.[13] This strikes me as an inspired choice, and one that other recent judicial appointees support as they investigate the legacy of the past half-century.[14] The debate between Jackson and Frankfurter in the Flag Salute Cases implicates far more than the meaning of the flag or even of the First Amendment. It marks a crucial turning point in the theory and practice of judicial review—one that deserves a more central role than *Carolene Product*'s famous footnote of 1938,[15] or *Palko*'s talk of "ordered liberty" in 1937.[16] The famous slogans we owe to *Carolene* and *Palko* were merely trial balloons—dicta suggesting that the New Deal Court might one day come up with a general approach to limiting the awesome powers of the modern state. *Barnette*, however, takes these promises seriously. Not only does the Court actually protect

---

[9] 771 F2d at 324.

[10] Id at 325.

[11] Id.

[12] A principal drafter of the Indianapolis ordinance was Catharine MacKinnon, presently a Professor of Law at the University of Michigan.

[13] 319 US 624 (1943).

[14] See, for example, *Texas v Johnson*, 491 US 397, 420-21 (1989) (Kennedy concurring).

[15] *United States v Carolene Products Co.*, 304 US 144, 152-53 n 4 (1938) (suggesting different levels of judicial scrutiny of the constitutionality of legislation depend on its subject matter).

[16] *Palko v Connecticut*, 302 US 319, 324-25 (1937).

individual rights, but it does so only after Felix Frankfurter forces the Justices to struggle self-consciously with the asymmetry problem with which I began: how abstractly should judges read the Bill of Rights, given that they accept the New Deal decision to read the Constitution's "Bill of Powers" at the highest levels of abstraction?

Within the context of the New Deal in general, and Frankfurter's opinions in particular, Jackson's decision in *Barnette* marks a very fundamental turn indeed—toward a powerful statement of a distinctive problem confronting the modern judiciary. I call this the problem of intergenerational synthesis and explore why it led Jackson to reaffirm the power of abstraction in interpreting the Bill of Rights. I conclude by asking why Easterbrook, though he turns to Jackson at his moment of professional self-definition in *American Booksellers*, seems to be a very selective abstractionist.

My test case will be *Bowers v Hardwick*.[17] I suggest that a consistent embrace of the Jacksonian position should lead Easterbrook to the dissenters' position in *Bowers*. I do not hope to convince him to sign any of the dissents written in the case. As before, my aim is to talk to him in a language that he understands, the language of property and contract, and to convince him that he should be urging his colleagues to overrule *Bowers*. This effort to engage Easterbrook in serious dialogue will, I hope, illustrate the paradox with which I began: Why is the Republican Court so intent upon aggrandizing the authority of activist government against the claims of individual freedom?

I. THE BILL OF POWERS

Nowadays, even Robert Bork and Richard Epstein accept—after appropriate grumbling[18]—the New Deal reading of the Bill of Powers contained in Article One, Section Eight of the Constitution. For Robert Jackson, things stood differently. In 1942, the proper interpretation of the Bill of Powers was very much a live issue. During the same Term he wrote *Barnette*, he also handed down *Wickard v Filburn*[19] for a unanimous court.

---

[17] 478 US 186 (1986) (holding state anti-sodomy law constitutional).

[18] See Robert H. Bork, *The Tempting of America: The Political Seduction of the Law* 158 (Free Press, 1990); Richard A. Epstein, *The Proper Scope of the Commerce Power*, 73 Va L Rev 1387, 1454-55 (1987).

[19] 317 US 111 (1942).

322   *Bruce Ackerman*

A.   Jackson, Abstraction, and the Commerce Power

Wickard examined the effort of the national government to regulate a farmer who was growing a trivial quantity of wheat for on-farm use.[20] Even though the crop would never leave the farm, Justice Jackson empowered national bureaucratic regulation by reading the Commerce Clause at a breathtaking level of abstraction: "[i]f we assume that [the wheat] is never marketed, it supplies a need of the man who grew it which would otherwise be reflected by purchases in the open market. Home-grown wheat in this sense competes with wheat in commerce."[21] This highly abstract equation of opportunity cost with commerce allowed the national government to place all significant human activity within its constitutional grasp.[22] By unanimously embracing this abstractionist reading, the New Deal Court rang the death-knell for traditional notions of limited national government expressed in leading cases of the Republican era like *Hammer v Dagenhart*.[23]

When the New Deal Court unanimously overruled the case-law of the Republican era, it repudiated the old idea of limited government with all of the decisiveness of a formal constitutional amendment.[24] Lawyers would quickly treat cases like *Hammer* with the kind of disdain they reserve for decisions, like *Dred Scott*,[25] that have been reversed through mobilized constitutional politics. How, they would soon ask themselves, could the Old Court of the 1930s have ever thought it worthwhile to fight desperate battles in defense of "mechanical" distinctions between "direct" and "indirect" effects on interstate commerce?

---

[20] Id at 114.

[21] Id at 128.

[22] This implication became even more emphatic when the Warren Court relied on the New Deal's expansion of the Commerce Clause to legitimate the Civil Rights Act of 1964 in *Heart of Atlanta Motel v United States*, 379 US 241, 253-62 (1964). The abstract reading of the Commerce Clause thus served to codify the two great successes of constitutional politics in the modern era: the New Deal and the Civil Rights Movement.

[23] 247 US 251 (1918), overruled by *United States v Darby*, 312 US 100, 116 (1941).

[24] Unanimity in *Wickard* was important. If a single Republican justice remained on the bench to contest the New Deal vision, he would keep the old "direct-indirect" distinctions alive on the pages of the United States Reports. Savvy lawyers would be obliged to keep abreast of these dissents, since they could never know when the new judicial majority would split, leaving the Republican vote to play a decisive role. See Bruce Ackerman, *We The People: Transformations* ch 9 (forthcoming).

[25] *Scott v Sandford*, 60 US (19 Howard) 393 (1856).

B. Founding Father?

As we approach the flag salute cases, however, it is important to recall the remarkable way that Jackson's abstractionist reading uprooted the modern Constitution from one of its deepest historical roots. To reawaken this sense of rupture and discontinuity, allow me to tell a story from the life of our greatest constitutionalist, James Madison.

The date is March 3, 1817, the day before President Madison leaves the White House. As his last official service to the nation, he leaves a revealing state paper. It is his final veto—the sixth of his presidency and the eighth in the history of the Republic (Washington contributed the other two).[26] As these numbers suggest, vetoes were taken seriously in those days. They were not normal instruments of presidential government. They were reserved for especially weighty anxieties.[27]

In the President's case, these were occasioned by the passage of a bill to establish a fund "for constructing roads and canals."[28] Madison had no problem with the intrinsic merits of the proposal. He placed his veto entirely on high constitutional ground: " 'The power to regulate commerce among the several States' cannot include a power to construct roads and canals," the veto advises, "without a latitude of construction departing from the ordinary import of the terms . . . ."[29] The entire veto is well worth reading,[30]

---

[26] See Benjamin Perley Poore, ed, *Veto Messages of the Presidents of the United States, With the Action of Congress Thereon* 16-18 (GPO 1886), published as Senate Mis Doc No 53, 49th Cong, 2d Sess (1887).

[27] See Bruce Ackerman, *We the People: Foundations* 68-69 (Belknap, 1991). This view of the veto power arose from a very different understanding of the presidential office, usefully explicated by James W. Ceaser, *Presidential Selection: Theory and Development* ch 1 (Princeton, 1979), and Ralph Ketcham, *Presidents Above Party: The First American Presidency, 1789-1829* chs 5-7 (North Carolina, 1984).

[28] Poore, *Veto Messages* at 16 (cited in note 26).

[29] Id at 17. The text of this veto is perhaps most easily found in Jefferson Powell, *Languages of Power: A Source Book of Early American Constitutional History* 313-14 (Carolina Academics, 1991). We owe a debt of gratitude to Professor Powell, who has recently made materials readily available to modern readers interested in the controversy that provoked Madison's veto. See id at 311-25.

[30] Especially its remarkable explanation of why the road-building program is not authorized by the grant of power to Congress to "provide for the common defense":

> To refer the power in question to the clause "to provide for the common defense and general welfare," would be contrary to the established and consistent rules of interpretation, as rendering the special and careful enumeration of powers, which follow the clause, nugatory and improper. Such a view of the Constitution would have the effect of giving to Congress a general power of legislation, instead of the defined and limited one hitherto understood to belong to them, the terms "common defense and general welfare" embracing every object and act within the purview of a legislative trust.

but this punchline is mind-boggling enough. Here is *the* Founding Father reserving his last official words to warn us against the dangerous abstraction needed to suppose that federal support for roads and canals was a necessary and proper way "to regulate Commerce . . . among the several States." And yet the New Deal Court simply erased these Madisonian anxieties from legal consciousness—to the point where "conservatives" like Frank Easterbrook deny the very existence of the problem.[31]

I do not wish to urge reconsideration of Robert Jackson's wrenching break with the constitutional past. We should see the truth for what it is: the New Deal Democrats gained the mobilized consent of a majority of the American people to a fundamental constitutional transformation—a reorganization no less profound than the one successfully achieved by the Reconstruction Republicans. If the Court had stood by its Madisonian views of the national government, Congress was prepared to amend the Constitution formally.[32] By making its "switch in time," the New Deal Court made this drastic action seem unnecessary.[33] With Jackson's abstractifying opinion in *Wickard*, the new judicial majority ful-

---

Poore, *Veto Messages* at 17 (cited in note 26).

I have placed a copy of this passage in the glove compartment of my car. It serves as marvelous therapy whenever I am threatened by drowsiness while driving on the interstate. I simply stop at the next roadside rest, retrieve this bit of Madisonian wisdom from the glove compartment, and am jolted into another hour of reasonably alert confrontion with the perplexities of life on the National System of Interstate Defense Highways.

[31] See Frank H. Easterbrook, *Abstraction and Authority*, in this volume, 349, 369: "[I] do not locate the advance of federal power in the New Deal. It occurred in *McCulloch v Maryland*. . . . Everything after that was a matter of details." In fact, Marshall's opinion in *McCulloch* is far more cautious than Easterbrook supposes in its affirmation of national powers. Note, for example, Marshall's warning that the Court would intervene if Congress, "under the pretext of executing its power, pass[ed] laws for the accomplishment of objects not entrusted to the government." *McCulloch v Maryland*, 17 US (4 Wheat) 316, 423 (1819). For a critique of the present mythification of Marshall's nationalism, see Ackerman, *We the People: Foundations* chs 2-3 (cited in note 27).

[32] I shall discuss the congressional debate over the need for constitutional amendment and its relationship to Roosevelt's Court-packing plan, in the next volume of Ackerman, *We the People: Transformations* (cited in note 24).

[33] In Jackson's words:

What we demanded for our generation was the right consciously to influence the evolutionary process of constitutional law, as other generations had done. And my generation has won its fight to make its own impression on the Court's constitutional doctrine. It has done it by marshalling the force of public opinion against the old Court through the court fight, by trying to influence the choice of forward-looking personnel, and most of all, by persuasion of the Court itself.

Robert H. Jackson, *The Struggle for Judicial Supremacy: A Study of a Crisis in American Power Politics* xiv (Knopf, 1941).

filled a term of the constitutional bargain that permitted the Court to survive the 1937 crisis with its powers untouched.[34]

Rather than questioning *Wickard*, I want simply to emphasize how it sets the stage for Jackson's confrontation with the modern asymmetry problem in *Barnette*: *given* the historical victory of an abstract understanding of constitutional powers, how should modern lawyers read the Constitution's rights-granting provisions? Should we approach the Constitution asymmetrically, reading the Bill of Rights (and other fundamental texts) in the same particularistic way in which Madison had read the original Bill of Powers?[35]

II. The Bill of Rights: The Flag Salute Cases

Even if Jackson had not authored *Wickard*, he could hardly avoid these questions in deciding *Barnette*. Felix Frankfurter had placed them at the very center of the Court's first response to the flag salute problem.[36] Frankfurter's opinion for the Court in *Gobitis* is well known and widely excoriated amongst civil libertarians. How, they ask, could this New Dealer turn his back so quickly on

---

[34] See Ackerman, *We the People: Foundations* chs 2, 4, 5 (cited in note 27).

[35] A cautionary note: Since *Barnette* involved a suit against West Virginia, not the United States, it raises additional fundamental questions. Even if it is assumed that Jackson was right to read the Bill of Rights at a very high level of abstraction, we must also ask ourselves about his approach to the "incorporation" problem. Was he right to impose his abstract interpretation of the Bill of Rights on the states as well as the federal government, or should he have watered down the guarantees of the Bill when applying it to the exercise of state power?

Unfortunately, Judge Easterbrook confuses these two questions when he objects to my argument on the ground that "[m]ost contemporary debates about abstraction do not concern federal power. They have to do with state power." Easterbrook, in this volume, 369 (cited in note 31). Insofar as this is true, Easterbrook is making a serious mistake in suggesting that federalist concerns are relevant to the abstraction problem. If federalist values trouble Easterbrook, he should reserve them for a critique of Jackson's decision, followed by a host of more recent judges, to incorporate most of the Bill of Rights through the Fourteenth Amendment. As the second Justice Harlan famously emphasized, it would be a fatal error to allow federalist concerns to water down the guarantees of the Bill of Rights since this would liberate the federal government, as well as the states, from these constitutional limitations. See *Duncan v Louisiana*, 391 US 145, 183 n 21 (1968) (Harlan dissenting); *Ker v California*, 374 US 23, 45-46 (1963) (Harlan concurring in the result). Better by far to rethink incorporation than to dilute the Bill of Rights.

This is not the place to do justice to the problems raised by the incorporation debate. See Ackerman, *We the People: Foundations* 86-99 (cited in note 27). My point is simply that if Judge Easterbrook wants to enter this debate in defense of Harlanesque views on incorporation, he should try to do so in a way that avoids the mistakes that Harlan condemns.

[36] *Minersville School District v Gobitis*, 310 US 586 (1940), overruled by *Barnette*, 319 US at 642.

his liberal past and uphold compulsory flag-saluting in his first major opinion?

A.   Frankfurter's Asymmetry

This question is best treated as a rhetorical one because it proceeds on a false premise. Frankfurter is not going against the grain of the New Deal in deciding the case against the Jehovah's Witnesses. Instead, *Gobitis* should be read as an especially pure example of the New Deal approach to the Bill of Rights, which builds upon the New Deal revolution in the theory of government power.[37]

Frankfurter's opinion organizes post-*Lochner*ian rights-talk around two New Deal ideas. The first is democracy:

> Except where the transgression of constitutional liberty is too plain for argument, personal freedom is best maintained—so long as the remedial channels of the democratic process remain open and unobstructed—when it is ingrained in a people's habits and not enforced against popular policy by the coercion of adjudicated law.[38]

The second is expertise:

> The influences which help toward a common feeling for the common country are manifold. Some may seem harsh and others no doubt are foolish. Surely, however, the end is legiti-

---

[37] This explanation is more plausible than one that views Frankfurter as acting out of some deep psychological deficiency. See Richard Danzig, *Justice Frankfurter's Opinions in the Flag Salute Cases: Blending Logic and Psychologic in Constitutional Decisionmaking*, 36 Stan L Rev 675 (1984). See also Robert A. Burt, *Two Jewish Justices: Outcasts in the Promised Land* 42-43 (California, 1988). Though Danzig recognizes that "Justice Frankfurter was strongly influenced by the ideas inherent in the opinions . . . that rejected the notion of close judicial oversight of New Deal legislation," Danzig, 36 Stan L Rev at 720 n 132, he does not criticize these ideas: "I [do not] detect any decisive error of logic in Felix Frankfurter's flag salute opinions." Id at 722. Instead, he "explains" Frankfurter's opinion by rooting it in a remarkably unsympathetic psychological portrait of the Justice as a rootless cosmopolitan. Id at 690-718.

My emphasis is different. Frankfurter and Jackson do differ on a crucial issue of legal "logic": should we draw our powerful legal abstractions only from the New Deal or from the Founding and Reconstruction as well? Cosmopolitan Jews are not fated to answer this question in Frankfurter's manner, nor are small-town Protestants predisposed toward Jackson's answer. As lawyers and judges, we owe our fellow citizens more than the reflex reenactment of our particular ethnic and religious heritages. We can and should use constitutional law to carve out a common public space in which we may affirm our identity as American citizens, fated by a common past to determine a common future—and to recognize that, for all their transparent differences, both Frankfurter and Jackson still have something to say to us as we continue their conversation about our public identity.

[38] *Gobitis*, 310 US at 599.

mate. And the effective means for its attainment are still so uncertain and so unauthenticated by science as to preclude us from putting the widely prevalent belief in flag-saluting beyond the legislative power.[39]

Frankfurter is using the very same abstractions—democracy and expertise—that Robert Jackson employed one year later to liberate New Deal Democracy from a limiting construction of the enumerated powers. Just as Jackson in *Wickard* allowed an "expert" Agricultural Adjustment Act administrator to restrict a farmer's consumption of homegrown wheat in order to implement a democratic judgment about the interstate economy, Frankfurter in *Gobitis* allowed an "expert" board of education to implement a democratic judgment about national solidarity. One may question the expert judgment of either agency. In both cases, though, the New Deal answer should be the same: in the absence of a "clear mistake" in means-end rationality, fight it out in democratic politics, not in the courts.

Since Jackson had not yet come to the Court when the first Flag Salute Case was decided, we don't know whether he would have been persuaded by Frankfurter's arguments for minimizing the scope of the Bill of Rights. We do know that every New Dealer then on the bench—Black, Reed, Douglas, and Murphy—did go along, as did every non-Roosevelt appointee except Stone. Moreover, when Frankfurter's colleagues deserted him in *Barnette* in 1943, his New Deal elegance consoled him in his famous dissent.[40] After opening with a passionate peroration, the dissent begins its technical-legal analysis by quoting a New Deal dissent in *United States v Butler*, one of the Old Court's last desperate struggles on behalf of a Madisonian understanding of limited national powers.[41] Frankfurter then denies that there is any fundamental difference between the New Court's defense of liberty in the public school

---

[39] Id at 598. Frankfurter's opinion contributes another characteristic New Deal invocation of legislative expertise:

> To stigmatize legislative judgment in providing for this universal gesture of respect for the symbol of our national life in the setting of the common school as a lawless inroad on that freedom of conscience which the Constitution protects, would amount to no less than the pronouncement of pedagogical and psychological dogma in a field where courts possess no marked and certainly no controlling competence.

Id at 597-98.

[40] *Barnette*, 319 US at 646-71 (Frankfurter dissenting).

[41] Id at 647-48 (quoting *United States v Butler*, 297 US 1, 79 (1936) (Stone dissenting)).

and the Old Court's defense of property.[42] He urges his colleagues
to remember 1937,[43] and to keep faith with the bargain that left
them their powers of judicial review.

This New Deal mix of democracy and expertise—call it the
ideal of "democratic managerialism"—retains a strong hold on the
modern legal mind.[44] It remains an important source of the modern propensity toward an asymmetric reading of the Constitution,
in which the Bill of Rights is constrained by an understanding of
the democratic managerial imperatives underlying the Bill of Powers. It is all the more important, then, to see how Jackson responds
to the challenge.

B.   Jackson's Reply: Intergenerational Synthesis

A key Jacksonian text is worth reciting:

True, the task of translating the majestic generalities of the
Bill of Rights, conceived as part of the pattern of liberal government in the eighteenth century, into concrete restraints on
officials dealing with the problems of the twentieth century, is
one to disturb self-confidence. These principles grew in soil
which also produced a philosophy that the individual was the
center of society, that his liberty was attainable through mere
absence of governmental restraints, and that government
should be entrusted with few controls and only the mildest
supervision over men's affairs. We must transplant these
rights to a soil in which the *laissez-faire* concept or principle
of non-interference has withered at least as to economic affairs, and social advancements are increasingly sought through
closer integration of society and through expanded and
strengthened government controls. These changed conditions
often deprive precedents of reliability and cast us more than
we would choose upon our judgment. But we act in these matters not by authority of our competence but by force of our
commissions.[45]

---

[42] Id at 648.

[43] Id at 652.

[44] The most important statement of this ideal is found in John Hart Ely, *Democracy
and Distrust: A Theory of Judicial Review* (Harvard, 1980). Other scholars' works are also
profoundly marked by democratic managerialism. Robert Bork's well-known book, *The
Tempting of America*, for example, is more heavily influenced by this New Deal ideal than
by any constitutional principle articulated by the Founding Federalists during the 1780s.
See Bork, *Tempting* (cited in note 18).

[45] *Barnette*, 319 US at 639-40.

Begin by considering how much common ground this text reveals. Jackson, no less than Frankfurter, bears witness to the great constitutional revolution in which they both had been eager participants: "the *laissez-faire* concept or principle of non-interference has withered at least as to economic affairs." Hence he is happy to memorialize the transformation in opinions like *Wickard* that empower the activist regulatory state to pursue the general welfare.[46]

But he is not willing to go further—from powers to rights. While the New Deal shattered the old foundations, Jackson denies that his generation intended to completely remove the old constitutional philosophy from the modern constitutional understanding. Instead, he calls on the Court to make sense of the Constitution as the work of different generations, each contributing different ideas and ideals into an evolving whole. In a phrase, the task is one of "intergenerational synthesis." The aim is to "translat[e]" the "majestic generalities" of "the eighteenth century" into "concrete restraints on officials dealing with the problems of the twentieth century." The challenge is to "transplant" the "principle of non-interference" into a constitutional order in which "social advancements are increasingly sought through closer integration of society and through expanded and strengthened government controls."

Frankfurter, in contrast, treats the constitutional transformation of the 1930s as if it had worked a total revolution in our constitutional law. He insists that the New Deal model of democratic managerialism should be the measure of all things, and that judges should rewrite previous constitutional history so as to emphasize only those features that are consistent with the reigning ideas of the Roosevelt Revolution.[47] Frankfurter's approach allows for clarity in doctrinal derivation because all legal ideas can be related to a single generation's cluster of organizing concepts. The trouble is that his approach distorts the character of the modern Constitution, which is the cumulative product of the constitutional politics of many generations, not the exclusive handiwork of any one of them.

Or so Jackson persuaded himself—and, more importantly, the other triumphant New Dealers who sat with him on the bench in 1943. From where these men sat, Frankfurter seemed the model

---

[46] See text accompanying notes 19-25.

[47] His treatment of the Founding in *Barnette*, id at 652-54, provides an instructive example of this Whiggish technique, which I elsewhere analyze as a "myth of rediscovery." See Ackerman, *We the People: Foundations* chs 2-3 (cited in note 27); and Ackerman, *We the People: Transformations*, chs 8-11 (cited in note 24).

legal ideologue who insists upon totalizing the transforming character of the particular intellectual movement to which he has committed his life. After thinking over Frankfurter's proposal, however, most New Dealers in 1943 were content to read their
generation as supporting only a revolutionary reform, not a total
revolution. For them, the questions were how to identify the shattered fragments of the constitutional order that had survived the
New Deal transformation, and how to integrate these fragments
into the brave new world of "closer integration of society . . . and
strengthened government controls" that Americans had built for
themselves in the 1930s.

C.   Earlier Challenges in Intergenerational Synthesis

This was not the first time the Supreme Court had faced such
a problem. The Civil War, no less than the Great Depression, had
led Americans to give their sustained support to a constitutional
politics of revolutionary reform—reform which was expressed in
the three Reconstruction Amendments. As the movement in support of Reconstruction crested, a newly reconstituted Republican
Court confronted the same questions as the New Deal Court: How
comprehensive was the revolutionary reform after all? How much
of the old order had been repudiated? How much old law could or
should be integrated into the new regime? The Reconstruction
Court's response was similar to that of the New Deal Court.

In its first encounter with the challenge of synthesis, the Republican Court expressed the very same sense of anxiety and responsibility later voiced by Jackson for the newly reconstituted
Democratic Court. Justice Miller set up the problem of intergenerational synthesis he confronted in the *Slaughter-House Cases* of
1873:

> We do not conceal from ourselves the great responsibility
> which this duty devolves upon us. No questions so far-reach-
> ing and pervading in their consequences . . . have been before
> this court during the official life of any of its present
> members.
> . . . Twelve articles of amendment were added to the Federal
> Constitution soon after the original organization of the gov-
> ernment under it in 1789. Of these all but the last were
> adopted so soon afterwards as to justify the statement that
> they were practically contemporaneous with the adoption of
> the original; and the twelfth, adopted in eighteen hundred
> and three, was so nearly so as to have become, like all the

others, historical and of another age. But within the last eight years three other articles of amendment of vast importance have been added by the voice of the people to that now venerable instrument.[48]

Miller, like Jackson, finds himself on the other side of a yawning break in constitutional time. He must somehow synthesize a recent constitutional transformation of "vast importance" into a very different constitutional order built in "another age." Of course, the ideals that inspired nineteenth-century Americans in the aftermath of the Civil War were very different from those that gained decisive popular support in response to the Great Depression. The Reconstruction Republicans had won a decisive victory for previously controversial ideas of nationhood, liberty, and equality. The New Deal Democrats gained much larger popular majorities for their vision of activist regulation by expert bureaucracies, superintended by democratic politicians responsive to an "open and unobstructed" electoral process.

Despite crucial substantive differences, the two Courts both emphasized the distinctive interpretive problem facing them: how to do justice to the most recent transformation in constitutional principles, while integrating the achievements of earlier generations of Americans into a meaningful whole.

D. A Closer Look at Intergenerational Synthesis

Jackson's answer: We should refuse to look upon New Deal ideals of democratic managerialism as if they were the only powerful abstractions guiding modern constitutional law. Instead, we should view them as part of a larger whole, in which the contributions of earlier generations justify robust abstractions that should constrain the operation of these New Deal ideals.

Since I will offer Jackson's performance in *Barnette* as a model for constitutional adjudication[49] in general, it is best to begin by sketching the broad outlines of this project in intergenerational synthesis. After all, neither the First Amendment nor the entire Bill of Rights is the only fragment from the Founding and Reconstruction that has survived the constitutional politics of the twentieth century. Before exploring *Barnette* more closely, it would be wise to view the entire range of problems to which Jackson's methods might serve as a guide.

---

[48] *Slaughter-House Cases*, 83 US 36, 67 (1873).
[49] See Section II.E.

For this purpose, think of the modern Constitution as a series
of ideals constructed through the successful constitutional politics
of different generations. From the Founding, at least four ideals
have survived the transformations of two centuries: first, *higher
lawmaking*—the people can give new marching orders to the normal politicians who govern in their name; second, *separation of
powers*—no elected politician may normally monopolize authority,
but must convince many other representatives of the people to go
along before a new law can be validated; third, *federalism*—states,
no less than the federal government, exercise power delegated by
the people; and fourth, *fundamental rights*, including those expressly reserved by the people in the original Constitution and the
Bill of Rights.

Following in the footsteps of Miller and Jackson, however,
modern judges interpret the meaning of these constitutional
themes in the light of other ideals validated during the great mobi-
lizations of the nineteenth and twentieth centuries. Since Reconstruction, for example, judges have sought to reconcile the Founding federalism with the new sense of nationhood affirmed in the
aftermath of the Civil War, and the new affirmations of universal
liberty and equality that became the birthright of all Americans.
Since the New Deal, judges have tried to preserve these Reconstruction ideals within the framework of a powerful activist state
authorized to intervene in many areas of social life whenever
elected politicians find that bureaucratic management will serve
the general welfare.[50]

Nobody really expects the Justices to integrate all of the constitutional ideals of the Founding, Reconstruction, and New Deal
in a single Moment of Grand Synthesis. Such a Herculean effort
would outstrip the limits of the human mind. Such an expectation
would also be hubristic in its implication that a single judge, or
even an entire interpretive community, could wholly escape the
limits of its own time and place. Despite our best efforts at synthe-

---

[50] In singling out the great transformations achieved during Reconstruction and the
New Deal, I do not deny the contributions of other generations in the construction of the
modern constitutional order. From the triumphs of Jeffersonian and Jacksonian Democracy
before the Civil War, through the victories of the Progressives and the Women's Movement
during the middle republic, through the Civil Rights Revolution of the modern era, each
generation has made its mark. My simplified triangular schema is complicated enough to
make my point that the synthetic mission marked out in *Barnette* is a formidable one,
requiring judges to reflect deeply upon the complex web of affirmations made at different
times and places by the American people. See Ackerman, *We the People: Foundations* chs
3-6 (cited in note 27).

sis, future generations of judges will, by virtue of their different historical perspectives on our nation's formative events, win insights that elude us today.

Modern judges have sought synthetic insight in a more realistic way: by using the case method as the engine for an ongoing process of collective deliberation. Each judicial effort at intergenerational synthesis is partial in at least two senses. First, even the greatest cases undertake a fundamental re-examination of only a few of the constitutive themes of constitutional law. *Barnette*, for example, focuses on the relationship between the New Deal ideal of democratic managerialism and the Founders' Bill of Rights, leaving other synthetic issues to other cases.

This first kind of incompleteness leads to another. Over time, as the Court explores different lines of partial synthesis, it will gain a new perspective on the synthetic exercises of the past, which will allow it to revisit older syntheses with new insights. No partial synthesis is good for all time. Each opinion, no matter how important, is but a sentence in an ongoing legal conversation. Judges, driven by the pragmatic imperative to decide a never-ending stream of cases, are required by individual litigants to revisit the tensions generated by the different ideals affirmed by different generations of the American people as they confronted different challenges to their constitutional identities. Because different sides will win if they can convince the Court to extend the leading ideals of different periods of constitutional politics to the case at hand, opposing lawyers regularly pit Founding federalism against Reconstruction equality, New Deal managerialism against the ideals of liberty expressed at the Founding and Reconstruction, and so forth.

The result is an ongoing contest between advocates of the Founding, Reconstruction, and New Deal for primacy in the field of legal contestation. No advocate ousts the others from the conversation, but each seeks to persuade the Justices (and the rest of us) to give greater weight to the themes and concerns most vividly expressed during one or another of these great jurisgenerative periods. This agon, I should emphasize, is motivated by each party's self-interest. The reason that one side emphasizes the Founding, and the other emphasizes the New Deal, has everything to do with their efforts to win the case. The larger test of success is whether, over many cases, lawyers and judges can elaborate convincing lines

of synthesis which integrate intergenerational tensions into meaningful doctrinal wholes.[51]

The process of legal abstraction plays a crucial role within the
ongoing effort at synthesis. It provides a vital medium through
which the continuous struggle among the partisans of the Founding, Reconstruction, and the New Deal is conducted. In the courtroom, each lawyer tries to win her case by abstracting those aspects of these crucial jurisgenerative eras which suggest that the
emerging lines of synthesis should be drawn in her favor. The judicial patterns of response to particular abstractions provide an index of the power of each past generation to make its constitutional
ideals an enduring part of modern law.

E. Jackson's Contribution

Within this framework I return to the Flag Salute Cases. As
we have seen, Justice Frankfurter's opinions represent a remarkably pure case of New Deal hegemony.[52] He seeks to express his own
generation's contribution by elaborating the powers of the democratic managerial state at a high level of abstraction, while trivial-
izing all previous contributions that cannot be understood within
New Deal terms. Thus, he is entirely willing to recognize the meaning of the Bill of Rights insofar as it might be instrumental in
keeping "the remedial channels of the democratic process . . . open
and unobstructed."[53] Similarly, he is willing to tolerate intervention when democratic managers make "clear mistakes" in means-
end rationality. But Frankfurter is unwilling to accept the thought
that New Deal themes should be constrained by abstractions
drawn from the constitutional politics of *previous* genera-

---

[51] Of course, this dynamic effort at ongoing synthesis is but an interpretive possibility.
Time may lead instead to judicial arbitrariness and interpretive confusion: in one case, New
Deal ideas of democratic managerialism may triumph over Founding ideals of the Bill of
Rights; and in the next, apparently similar, case, the reverse is true. Rather than trying to
reconcile conflicting "lines of cases," the Court acts in the way legal realists say is both
inevitable and desirable—rejecting the synthetic imperative and glorying in the judicial
freedom wrought by doctrinal indeterminacy.

It is important to determine whether American judges have, by and large, followed the
path of the law described in the text or in this footnote. Moreover, there is only one way to
find out: we should take the interpretive hypothesis seriously and read the Justices' work
with charity. Can one see them elaborating large synthetic patterns over time? If not, then
the realist/crit hypothesis wins. If so, the argument proceeds to a second stage more
favorable to the interpretivist: why does the realist/crit insist on ignoring the patterns of
juridical meaning that intelligent reading reveal?

[52] See Section II.A.

[53] *Gobitis*, 310 US at 599.

tions—generations whose enthusiasm for the activist welfare state was modest, to say the least.[54]

This is the premise that Jackson is at pains to deny:

> The very purpose of a Bill of Rights was to withdraw certain subjects from the vicissitudes of political controversy, to place them beyond the reach of majorities and officials and to establish them as legal principles to be applied by the courts. One's right to life, liberty, and property, to free speech, a free press, freedom of worship and assembly, and other fundamental rights may not be submitted to vote; they depend on the outcome of no elections.[55]

Note the exercise in holistic reading that has, since the time of Marshall, signalled the introduction of powerful constitutional abstractions. Jackson refuses to cut up the Bill of Rights into little bits and pieces. He urges us to study the Bill, taken as a whole, and use it to re-present the Founding contribution to the new world of constitutional meaning inaugurated by the New Deal. As he approaches his particular problem, his claims for the Bill's enduring relevance are no less emphatic. For him, the First Amendment is to be understood as a norm of compelling generality and abstraction.

As always, Frankfurter provides a useful foil in considering generality. His dissent in *Barnette* points out that parents who deeply object to flag-saluting have the option of sending their children to private schools that dispense with this requirement.[56] For him, this private-sector option helps make it constitutionally permissible for the state to require ritual professions of loyalty.[57]

---

[54] A fuller treatment of Frankfurter's particular effort at synthesis would move far beyond his Flag Salute opinions. On the one hand, his treatment of reapportionment as a "political question," see *Colegrove v Green*, 328 US 549, 552-56 (1946), sits awkwardly with his recognition in *Gobitis* of the importance of keeping the "channels of the democratic process . . . open and unobstructed." 310 US at 599. On the other hand, his willingness to use the Due Process Clause as a source of substantive norms, see *Rochin v California*, 342 US 165, 169-74 (1952), is in tension with the hard line he took in *Barnette* a decade earlier. Since my focus here is on Jackson, not Frankfurter, I will have to save a fuller treatment of these Frankfurterian themes for another time. See Bruce Ackerman, *The Common Law Constitution of John Marshall Harlan*, 36 NY L Sch L Rev (forthcoming 1992).

[55] *Barnette*, 319 US at 638. Jackson's final line is, I think, an exaggeration. Since the Bill of Rights can be amended, its continuing vitality could well "be submitted to vote"—as, for example, President Bush's effort to repeal the First Amendment with regard to flagburning suggests. I elaborate on this theme in *We the People: Foundations* chs 1, 11 (cited in note 27).

[56] *Barnette*, 319 US at 656-57.

[57] Id at 657-58.

Jackson rejects this gambit. He thinks that the Bill of Rights should not be treated as a weighty constraint only when the activist state intervenes in the private sector; its powerful abstractions should also constrain state action within the expanding *public* sector.[58] As in other great synthetic cases of the early modern period—most notably *Brown v Board of Education*[59]—the constitutional limits on the public sector are developed in a case involving the schools. But the theme invites yet further generalization: democratic management of public institutions, no less than intervention in the private sector, must contend with competing principles drawn from the Founding and Reconstruction.

Within this framework, Jackson defines the mission of the First Amendment:

> If there is any fixed star in our constitutional constellation, it is that no official, high or petty, can prescribe what shall be orthodox in politics, nationalism, religion, or other matters of opinion or force citizens to confess by word or act their faith therein.[60]

Notice the "if." As the New Deal transformation has swept away so much of the old order, it is not at all clear whether any fixed stars remain in our constitutional constellation. *If*, however, it remains plausible to use the Founding as a check on the New Deal, Jackson's celestial imagery suggests that we must appreciate the great distance separating us from the eighteenth century. His gesture toward a distant but "fixed" star recalls Justice Miller's recognition that the Founders' Constitution is "of another age."[61] Neither Miller nor Jackson imagines that Madison, or anybody from the eighteenth century, could help him out on his particular problem. Madison lived in a world where states still established religions, where public schooling was hardly known, where we had not fought the Civil War and had not won the Reconstruction Amendments. The only way *credibly* to re-present the Founding contribution in the twentieth century is through "majestic general-

---

[58] See his opinion in *Barnette*, 319 US at 635-36 (answering in the negative the question whether "a ceremony [flag saluting] so touching matters of public opinion and political attitude may be imposed upon the individual by official authority under powers committed to any political organization under our Constitution.").

[59] 347 US 483 (1954). For a discussion, see Ackerman, *We the People: Foundations* ch 6 (cited in note 27). See also *Everson v Board of Education*, 330 US 1 (1947) (relationship of Establishment Clause to state funding for parochial education).

[60] *Barnette*, 319 US at 642.

[61] *Slaughter-House Cases*, 83 US at 67.

ities," which challenge us to make them meaningful premises in our effort to do justice to the concrete problems of activist government.

Jackson's opinion cautions us against any mechanical understanding of this process. He refuses to categorize *Barnette* as a "free exercise" case and thus protect the Witnesses' rights on the basis of a formulaic reading of a single clause. While this much is evident from the text,[62] Jackson's next step requires more careful attention. For it is equally mistaken to understand him as "applying" a mechanistic understanding of the clause protecting "free speech." There is not a single day in the life of school children when they are not forced to speak and write in ways that meet with their teachers' approval. And if they don't say and do the "right things" in oral drill and written examination, school authorities can punish them very severely without violating their constitutional rights. Indeed, if any compendious label will serve to mark Jackson's fixed star, I think "privacy" serves at least as well as "free speech." While the activist state may coercively shape the behavioral and intellectual repertoire of each young American through long years of "public education,"[63] each child has the fundamental right to turn his back on the symbols of national identity so eagerly impressed upon him by his teachers. He has the right to tell his classmates, and his fellow citizens more generally, that he insists upon standing apart from the common rituals of citizenship they find so deeply meaningful—that the Constitution protects his right "to be let alone," and to search for fundamental meaning in fora far removed from the common civic culture.

It is better yet to beware all labels, and focus instead on Jackson's fundamental interpretive proposal. We must continue to read the Bill of Rights, and other great texts of the eighteenth and nineteenth centuries, as a source of liberating abstractions that might serve as a counterweight to the claims of democratic managerialism. "We must transplant these rights to a soil in which the *laissez-faire* concept or principle of non-interference has withered at least as to economic affairs, and social advancements are increas-

---

[62] *Barnette*, 319 US at 635-36.

[63] Moreover, even if parents choose to withdraw their children from the public schools they can hardly insulate "private" education from pervasive state control. While a certain degree of curricular freedom is constitutionally required, see, for example, *Meyer v Nebraska*, 262 US 390, 402-03 (1923), the extent to which "private" schools may exempt themselves from onerous state minima remains an open question.

ingly sought through closer integration of society and through expanded and strengthened government controls."[64]

III. EASTERBROOK'S CONTRIBUTION?

A. The Paradox Revisited

This is, at least, Frank Easterbrook's view of the matter as he confronts his moment of judicial truth in *American Booksellers*.[65] In seeking to explain why Indianapolis's sweeping prohibition of pornography was unconstitutional, Easterbrook can find no better place to start than a word-for-word recitation of Jackson's gesture toward a "fixed star."[66] What follows is a compelling effort to follow in Jackson's footsteps by insisting on the right of all Americans to pursue a private life of the spirit even though a majority may find that life degrading.[67]

I am puzzled, then, that Judge Easterbrook returns to academia in these pages to profess anxiety about the role of abstraction in constitutional law. He is much too wise to spend his time challenging the decisive New Deal victory for an abstract reading of the Bill of Powers. Surely he is not willing to stumble where even Robert Bork and Richard Epstein fear to tread.[68] Does he propose, then, to renounce his opinion in *American Booksellers* and embrace the ideal of managerial democracy with the New Deal fervor of a Felix Frankfurter? Equally unlikely. Easterbrook's reliance on Jackson was no makeweight. It reflects an interpretive imperative that both of us share. We both aim to put the New Deal Revolution in its place—neither making too much of it nor too little. Thus, we both accept Jackson's opinion in *Wickard* as putting the quietus on sharp Madisonian limits on the powers of the ac-

---

[64] *Barnette*, 319 US at 640.

[65] *American Booksellers Ass'n, Inc. v Hudnut,* 771 F2d 323 (7th Cir 1985). See text accompanying notes 8-16.

[66] 771 F2d at 327.

[67] While I find much to praise in Easterbrook's opinion, I do have a serious problem with it. It lies in his monocular concentration on a single one of the "fixed stars" that seems relevant to his problem. An even better opinion would have thoughtfully confronted—as Easterbrook did not—Catharine MacKinnon's effort to guide doctrinal development in this area by reference to a very different "fixed star": the principle of equality affirmed two generations after the Founding at Reconstruction.

MacKinnon, however, suffers from an equal and opposite deficiency in her exercises in constitutional navigation: she peripheralizes the libertarian aspect of the Founding with the same spectacular intensity that Easterbrook uses to blot out the potential significance of Reconstruction. I am still searching for a deeper sense of synthetic understanding than either Easterbrook or MacKinnon attempts or provides.

[68] See note 18 and accompanying text.

tivist welfare state. At the same time, we follow Jackson in seeking to place the revolutionary reforms codified by *Wickard* into a larger constitutional context within which the enduring principles of Reconstruction and the Founding play a fundamental role. Only if judges continue to thematize these earlier affirmations with the vigor that Easterbrook displays in *American Booksellers* will the ideals of the Bill of Rights continue to compete on relatively equal terms with New Deal ideals of democratic managerialism.

I now return to the paradox with which I began. If Easterbrook and I basically don't disagree about the role of abstraction in constitutional law, surely we *do* disagree about something. What might that something be? My bewildered reply: at least so far as constitutional law is concerned, Frank Easterbrook is a bigger New Dealer than I am, and so is more reluctant to use the Bill of Rights as a source of powerful abstractions constraining the claims of democratic managerialism. This may seem paradoxical because I would also be prepared to use the (more limited) powers of activist government more aggressively on a whole range of legislative matters than Easterbrook would tolerate.

B. The *Lochner* Myth

Right now I am more interested in elaborating the paradox than in resolving it. A systematic approach would invite Judge Easterbrook to read the entire Bill of Rights in the same spirit of robust abstractionism with which he reads the First Amendment. It will be enough here to concentrate on one obvious place where Easterbrook lets his anxieties about abstraction get the better of him—in his acceptance of the familiar New Deal myth about *Lochner v New York*.[69] On this view, the *Lochner* Court was simply imposing its own hard-nosed capitalist values upon a populace who, even in 1905, was already yearning for New Deal leadership. Justice Peckham and company were not engaged in the business of constitutional interpretation; they were pulling decisions out of thin air. In the words of Justice Black, they were engaged in some obscurantist project in "natural law."[70] To borrow from Justice White, perhaps the most emphatic New Dealer now on the bench:[71]

---

[69] 198 US 45 (1905).
[70] *Griswold*, 381 US at 514-15 (Black dissenting).
[71] See *INS v Chadha*, 462 US 919, 967-1003 (1983) (White dissenting).

340	*Bruce Ackerman*

The Court is most vulnerable and comes nearest to illegitimacy when it deals with judge-made constitutional law having little or no cognizable roots in the language or design of the Constitution. That this is so was painfully demonstrated by the face-off between the Executive and the Court in the 1930's, which resulted in the repudiation of much of the substantive gloss that the Court had placed on the Due Process Clauses . . . .[72]

Substantive due process: the oxymoron itself suggests the phantasmic quality of the *Lochner* era on the New Deal rendering. If Easterbrook holds this view of *Lochner*, I'm not surprised that he worries about the "right" level of abstraction appropriate in constitutional cases. If the judicial protection of "liberty" involves "constitutional law having little or no cognizable roots in the language or design of the Constitution," perhaps the "right" level of abstraction in *these* cases should be "zero." If anything, Justice White is fainthearted in describing the lessons of the New Deal-Old Court struggle: why should the Courts safeguard *any* rights unrooted in the larger "text or design"?[73]

But this familiar line of reasoning is based on a false historical premise. The *Lochner* Court was not making it up: the Contract and Property Clauses are no more, but no less, a part of the Constitution than are the Free Speech and Establishment Clauses. Peckham's decision in *Lochner*, no less than Jackson's decision in *Barnette*, has deep intellectual roots in our most successful movements of constitutional politics. Freedom of contract is deeply entrenched in the Free Labor and Abolitionist sources of the Reconstruction Amendments, with roots that run as deep as the Enlightenment and Commonwealth ideas that provide the interpretive context for the Founding Bill of Rights.[74] When *Lochner*

---

[72] *Bowers v Hardwick*, 478 US 186, 194-95 (1986).

[73] See Frank H. Easterbrook, *Substance and Due Process*, 1982 S Ct Rev 85, 125.

[74] A fuller treatment would consider the Founders' understanding of the Property and Contract Clauses before the constitutional politics of the nineteenth century transformed the original Constitution. See Ackerman, *We the People: Foundations* at 63-67, 101-04 (cited in note 27). *Lochner* was unthinkable as a constitutional interpretation until Reconstruction made it seem a plausible synthetic response to the task of reconciling the Founding concerns with federalism and Republican commitments to Free Labor and Abolitionist principles. See id at 86-103. The most sensitive recent discussion of these matters is William E. Forbath, *The Ambiguities of Free Labor: Labor and the Law in the Gilded Age*, 1985 Wis L Rev 767, 772-800. As Forbath emphasizes, *Lochner*ism was by no means the only plausible interpretation of the historical experience culminating in the Reconstruction Amendments. For example, if the Populists had won the crucial Presidential election of 1896, their judicial appointees would have interpreted the tradition in ways far more conge-

was decided in 1905, moreover, Americans had decisively repudiated the Populist effort to transform the emerging laissez-faire economy.[75] Indeed, Teddy Roosevelt had a very hard time gaining support for very modest efforts to control big time capitalism.[76] It is simply anachronistic to suppose that the courts of the *Lochner* era were engaging in an utterly undemocratic and noninterpretive form of value imposition.[77]

Rather than spending more time criticizing the New Deal myth about *Lochner*, I want to invite Easterbrook to join me in taking a more sympathetic view of the interpretive enterprise that the justices of the middle republic attempted during their long march from Reconstruction to the New Deal. After all, if liberal Democrats like myself can face up to the anachronistic character of this New Deal myth, why should conservative Republicans resist intellectual rapprochement with the *Lochner* Court?

C. Easterbrook's Options

The task for a judge like Easterbrook, of course, is to define the implications for practical decisionmaking were he to undertake this interpretive turn. So far as I can see, Judge Easterbrook has two basic choices: he can follow Richard Epstein or he can follow me.[78]

---

nial to the rights of organized labor. See id at 800-17. But this point only establishes that *Lochner* wasn't inevitable, not that it was radically noninterpretive.

Just as modern constitutionalists minimize the nineteenth-century foundations of a property-contract understanding of constitutional liberty, so too we tend to exaggerate the continuity between the modern understanding of free speech and its eighteenth-century roots. See Leonard W. Levy, *Emergence of a Free Press* (Oxford, 2d rev ed 1985). To forestall predictable misunderstanding, I hardly wish to suggest that there is *no* continuity between the eighteenth and twentieth centuries. To the contrary, it is precisely Jackson's aim to convince us that, by approaching the Bill of Rights at an appropriately abstract level, we may grasp the sense in which twentieth-century case law carries on, under vastly different circumstances, the motivating concerns of the eighteenth-century Framers. My point is simply to suggest that my proposed application/of the Contract and Property Clauses in *Bowers v Hardwick*, see Section II.D., is no more, but no less, grounded in the constitutional affirmation of the past as Easterbrook's application of the First Amendment in *American Booksellers*.

[75] See James L. Sundquist, *Dynamics of the Party System: Alignment and Realignment of Political Parties in the United States* 134-69 (Brookings, rev ed 1983).

[76] See John Morton Blum, *The Republican Roosevelt* 73-87 (Atheneum, 3d ed 1974).

[77] Or so I have argued, at tedious length, elsewhere. Ackerman, *We the People: Foundations* ch 4 (cited in note 27). For an analysis of *Lochner* that goes quite far in questioning the New Deal myth, see Laurence H. Tribe, *American Constitutional Law* 584-86, 769-72 (Foundation, 2d ed 1988); Tribe and Dorf, *On Reading the Constitution* at 65-66 (cited in note 7).

[78] When faced with such grim alternatives, perhaps he will find his own "third way"?

First, for Richard Epstein: If *Lochner* was good law when it was decided, it remains good law today. So let's get on with the great task of our generation—the destruction of the constitutional legacy of the New Deal. Forward to yesterday.[79]

Second, for me: The reason you are a judge, and other Reagan nominees aren't, is that you recognize that Epstein is calling for a constitutional revolution that has not gained the mobilized support of the American people.[80] Whatever the Reagan Revolution accomplished, it failed to win a popular mandate that would justify an effort by its judicial appointees to repudiate the Roosevelt Revolution. Robert Jackson should remain Easterbrook's "fixed star"—both the Jackson of *Wickard* and the Jackson of *Barnette*.

Nonetheless, this is the 1990s, not the 1940s. Perhaps Judge Easterbrook can take advantage of his historical perspective to recognize some things that enthusiastic New Dealers like Jackson did not emphasize in the heat of their constitutional struggle. In particular, the Old Court's emphasis on private property and freedom of contract was not nearly so aberrant as the New Deal Court proclaimed. Granted, New Deal Democracy suceeded in repudiating property and contract talk as a way of constraining governmental regulation of the marketplace. Nonetheless, the ideas of property and contract have a far broader range of application than merely to the marketplace. Perhaps, following Jackson in *Barnette*, Easterbrook should be able to "transplant these rights [of property and contract] to a soil in which the *laissez-faire* concept or principle of non-interference has [not] withered"?[81]

D.   The Test Case: *Bowers v Hardwick*

Consider *Bowers v Hardwick*.[82] Two adults want to arrange their affairs to their mutual advantage. They seek to exclude others who wish to invade their private spaces for the purpose of disrupting their consensual arrangements—to make the couple worse off, not better off, as they themselves understand "better" and "worse." This is stuff the Old Court described in the language of property and contract, only they talked this way mostly in cases

---

[79] See Richard A. Epstein, *Takings: Private Property and the Power of Eminent Domain* 281-82 (Harvard, 1985).

[80] Bernard Siegan, for example, owes the failure of his nomination to the Court of Appeals to his Epsteinian views on the Takings Clause. See, for example, Editorial, *An Injudicious Choice for Judge*, NY Times 26 (Mar 5, 1988) ("[t]he courts are the wrong place for such extreme views").

[81] 319 US at 640.

[82] 478 US 186 (1986).

involving the marketplace.[83] *Lochner* protected the right of workers, not lovers, to move their bodies around ovens, not bedrooms,
for as many hours a week as they and their employers believed
mutually advantageous.

But any reasonably competent lawyer can see that the same
basic legal ideas are at play in *Lochner* and *Bowers*: property, conceived as the right to exclude others, and contract, conceived as
the right to arrange mutually advantageous terms for association.
The parallel should be especially obvious to a lawyer-economist
like Frank Easterbrook, whose entire academic career has been devoted to the property-contract paradigm. Easterbrook's particular
specialty has been corporation law, where he has been quite creative in analyzing the modern firm as if it were little more than an
especially dense "nexus of contracts."[84] If Easterbrook has the imagination to view "General Motors" as just another name for a
"nexus of contract," it should be child's play for him to see how a
homosexual couple can use the language of property and contract
to express their legal interests.[85] Quite true, most lawyers call *Bowers* a case involving "privacy" and "freedom of intimate association," not "property" and "contract." But these conventional labels shouldn't stop Easterbrook from applying the property-
contract paradigm to *Bowers* any more than it stopped him in the
case of "corporations" like General Motors.

Indeed, it doesn't require fancy law and economics to grasp
the point. In their great essay of 1890 introducing "privacy" into
the legal lexicon, Warren and Brandeis were perfectly aware that

---

[83] However, the Court did not reserve this language *exclusively* for cases involving the
marketplace. See, for example, *Meyer v Nebraska*, 262 US 390, 400 (1923) (invalidating
statute forbidding teaching of foreign languages and placing an instructor's and parents'
rights to contract for instruction "within the liberty of the [Fourteenth] Amendment");
Pierce v Society of Sisters, 268 US 510, 535 (1925) (invalidating statute mandating public
school attendance and recognizing private schools' property rights in maintaining the patronage of students).

[84] See Frank H. Easterbrook and Daniel Fischel, *The Economic Structure of Corporate
Law* 12 (Harvard, 1991).

[85] The standard framework for defining property relationships within the field of law
and economics does not discriminate between traditional economic relationships and those
typically described by the language of "privacy." So far as lawyer-economists are concerned,
a rights-holder has a *property* interest if the law requires others to gain his consent before
invading the right in question. See Guido Calabresi and A. Douglas Melamed, *Property
Rules, Liability Rules, and Inalienability: One View of the Cathedral*, 85 Harv L Rev 1089,
1092 (1972). Plainly, the petitioners in *Bowers* were claiming a property right in this sense.
Moreover, other members of the Chicago School of Law and Economics have spent a great
deal of time analyzing family relationships in contractualist terms. See Gary S. Becker, *A
Treatise on the Family* ch 2 (Harvard, 1991).

they could have achieved their objectives by dispensing with their neologism.[86] They explicitly note that their point would prevail if the profession would begin to speak not of privacy, but of "[t]he right of property in its widest sense, including all possession, including all rights and privileges, and hence embracing the right to an inviolable personality."[87] Rather than taking this conceptual route, however, Warren and Brandeis chose to split "the right of property in its widest sense" into two components: they kept the name of "property" to mark the market-based conception that nineteenth-century lawyers used at common law and equity, and they applied the new label "privacy" to mark the legitimate exclusion of outsiders in non-market contexts.

Warren's and Brandeis's proposal to split "property in its widest sense" into two legalistic boxes—"market property" and "privacy"—has had many fateful consequences in twentieth-century law. Most importantly, the two-box approach made it easier for the legal mind to accommodate itself to increasing regulation of market property. However intensive public regulation in this area might be, lawyers could explain to themselves that they might continue to protect more intimate relationships through the new doctrine of "privacy." Similarly, lawyers could endorse the intensive regulation of "contracts" in the marketplace, while protecting more intimate contractual relationships under the heading "freedom of intimate association."[88] Perhaps the pragmatic advantages engendered by this systematic doubling of doctrinal categories have proven substantial; perhaps not. But surely, there is no gain in forgetting the more abstract ideas—"property and contract in their

---

[86] Samuel D. Warren and Louis Brandeis, *The Right to Privacy*, 4 Harv L Rev 193 (1890).

[87] Id at 211. See also: "We must therefore conclude that . . . the principle which has been applied to protect these rights [of privacy] is in reality not the principle of private property, *unless that word be used in an extended and unusual sense.*" Id at 213 (emphasis supplied). Of course, if the authors had convinced their audience to expand property-talk, rather than speak in terms of "privacy," the "extended" conception of property would have long since lost its "unusual" character.

[88] Kenneth Karst recognizes that "[w]e pay a price" for refusing to recognize the relationship between the modern language of "intimate association" and *Lochner*ian talk of "freedom of contract." See his characteristically sensitive essay, Kenneth L. Karst, *The Freedom of Intimate Association*, 89 Yale L J 624, 664-65 (1980). Nonetheless, even he does not explore this relationship with the energy he displays in other parts of his important essay.

widest sense"—when we go about construing the meaning of the Constitution.[89]

New Dealers like Justices Black and White are wrong, then, to treat "privacy" and "intimate association" as concepts that have "little or no cognizable roots in the language . . . of the Constitution."[90] And essays, like Richard Posner's in this issue, continue this error by treating *Bowers* as if it involved the question of "unenumerated rights."[91] To the contrary, the special place of contract and property is *explicitly* enumerated in our Constitution. The challenge is simply to grasp the way in which "privacy" and "freedom of intimate association" express these constitutional commitments to "property" and "contract" after the New Deal transformation has stripped *market*-property and *market*-contract of their constitutionally privileged position. While I am an admirer of Justice Douglas's opinion in *Griswold v Connecticut*,[92] he unnecessarily weakens his argument by treating "privacy" as if it were only a "penumbra" of other explicit guarantees of the Bill of Rights.[93] Though a holistic reading of the Bill of Rights does indeed support Douglas's claim, it should serve as a preliminary for the main point: "privacy" is simply a word that modern lawyers have used to describe a vital aspect of "property in its widest sense"—and hence is appropriately at the *center* of the modern Takings Clause.[94] Similarly, Justice Brennan missed an opportunity to use the Contract Clause in *Eisenstadt v Baird*, when he led the Court to protect the fundamental right of each American to arrange the terms of his sexual engagements to mutual advantage.[95] No less than Douglas, Brennan was too traumatized by the

---

[89] A powerful essay by Margaret Jane Radin, *Property and Personhood*, 34 Stan L Rev 957 (1982), serves as the best modern introduction to this use of the Takings Clause. See also Bruce Ackerman, *Private Property and the Constitution* chs 2, 4 (Yale, 1977).

[90] *Bowers*, 478 US at 194.

[91] Richard A. Posner, *Reasoning From the Top Down and From the Bottom Up: The Question of Unenumerated Constitutional Rights,* in this volume, 433.

[92] 381 US 479 (1965). See Ackerman, *We the People: Foundations* at ch 6 (cited in note 27).

[93] 381 US at 484.

[94] See Radin, 34 Stan L Rev 957 (cited in note 89), and Ackerman, *Private Property* at chs 2, 4 (cited in note 89).

[95] 405 US 438 (1972). On the surface at least, Brennan relied on a construction of the Equal Protection Clause, holding that there were insufficient grounds for a statute denying unmarried individuals access to contraceptives which married couples could claim by right under *Griswold*. To make this argument credible, however, he found himself speaking in a language with contractualist overtones.

It is true that in *Griswold* the right of privacy in question inhered in the marital relationship. Yet the marital couple is not an independent entity with a mind and heart of

Court Crisis of the 1930s to allow himself to admit the extent to
which he was engaged in the Jacksonian project of "transplant[ing]
. . . rights"—rights of property and contract—"to a soil in which
the *laissez-faire* concept or principle of non-interference has
withered at least as to economic affairs."[96]

But, as Easterbrook's presence on the bench attests, a new judicial generation is rising to prominence. In contrast to Black or
Douglas, White or Brennan, the New Deal Revolution is not a central part of this generation's lived experience. It is simply an important, but not all-important, historical reality. While perfectly
prepared to live with the activist regulatory state, the Easterbrooks
of the world are not prepared to love it. They are, moreover,
equipped with intellectual tools that allow them to understand
non-market institutions in terms of property and contract. Their
challenge is synthesis: to use their conceptual tools to express a
renewed appreciation of the fundamental place of liberty in the
American constitutional tradition without destroying the constitutional foundations of the modern state.

E.   Final Thoughts: Pollution/Commerce, Privacy/Property

Perhaps a final analogy will help smooth the way. This one
returns to my first point—the need for symmetry in the treatment
of rights and powers. From this vantage, my proposal for *Bowers*
invites courts to use the very same level of abstraction in dealing
with "privacy" that they already use in legitimating novel uses of
federal power. Consider, for example, the untroubled way in which
courts have authorized the national government to embark on a
multifaceted assault on the pollution problem. In dealing with the
Clean Air Act,[97] nobody worries about the lack of an explicit grant
of power to "regulate pollution" in the Constitution. In the post-
New Deal era, it is enough to point to the power to regulate "commerce," and pass on to more interesting constitutional questions.

But more thoughtful consideration suggests that the relationship of "pollution" to "commerce" is, as a matter of legal method,

---

its own, but an association of two individuals each with a separate intellectual and
emotional makeup. If the right of privacy means anything, it is the right of the *individual*, married or single, to be free from unwarranted governmental intrusion into matters so fundamentally affecting a person as the decision whether to bear or beget a
child.

Eisenstadt, 405 US at 453. Because Brennan understood the case in equal protection, rather
than contractualist, terms, he did not expand on this line of thought.

[96] *Barnette*, 319 US at 640.

[97] Clean Air Act, 42 USC §§ 7401 et seq (1989).

remarkably analogous to the relationship of "privacy" to "property." First, treating "pollution" as if it involves "commerce" requires a more abstract understanding of the term than even *Wickard* involved. It was at least *possible* for the farmer in *Wickard* to sell his home-grown wheat in the marketplace, and thus participate in interstate commerce. The only problem was that the farmer didn't want to enter the marketplace. In contrast, there is no marketplace for pollution at all. If "commerce" covers this exercise of power, the idea must be stripped of all its usual connotations of "buying" and "selling." The only sense in which "pollution" involves "commerce" is that it is often, but not always, the outcome of market production, and its federal regulation will alter competitive relationships that would otherwise exist. Yet this very extended sense of "opportunity cost" suffices to place "pollution" comfortably within the category of "commerce" as the modern legal mind understands the term. If this is so, why does it seem so hard to define "property" at a sufficient level of abstraction so as to embrace Hardwick's "privacy" right? If anything, the relationship between these two ideas is closer than anything that binds "commerce" and "pollution." The core of both "privacy" and "property" involves the same abstract right: the right to exclude unwanted interference by third parties. The only real difference between the two concepts is the kind of relationship that is protected from interference—"property" principally protects market relationships while "privacy" protects more spiritual ones. Yet surely this fact should not prevent recognition of "privacy" as a dimension of constitutional "property in its widest sense."

We can push the analogy further. In both the case of "commerce" and the case of "property," the explicit text, if particularistically interpreted, only covers cases involving relatively straightforward market relationships. In treating these two concepts abstractly so as to include "pollution" and "privacy," modern constitutional law has permitted modern government to reinterpret its fundamental purposes in ways that undoubtedly would have surprised the Founding generation. Though founded in the Commerce Clause, the federal concern with "pollution" is by no means exhausted by economic concerns, however abstractly understood. There is a different concern at work—a concern for ecological integrity which is quite alien to any of the central aims of the Founders. Whatever was motivating the generations who fought the Revolution and the Civil War, it definitely wasn't the protection of the wilderness.

Once again, the relationship between "property" and "privacy" is less strained. While "privacy," like "pollution," directs our attention to non-market values, at least the particular value it protects—individual freedom—isn't absent from the writings of the Federalist Founders and Reconstruction Republicans. If lawyers find it so easy to read "commerce" to embrace ecology, it seems very odd that they should suddenly have "originalist" worries when reading "property" to embrace privacy. The question remains: *Why* this asymmetry between powers and rights?

Conclusion

At the end of his great dissent in *Bowers v Hardwick*, Justice Blackmun searches the past for signs of a better future. Remarkably enough, he repairs to the same fixed star that inspires Judge Easterbrook:

> It took but three years for the Court to see the error in its analysis in [*Gobitis*]. . . . I can only hope that here, too, the Court soon will reconsider its analysis and conclude that depriving individuals of the right to choose for themselves how to conduct their intimate relationships poses a far greater threat to the values most deeply rooted in our Nation's history than tolerance of nonconformity could ever do.[98]

It is not too late for Judge Easterbrook to hear this warning. The tides of political fortune, and his own intellectual gifts have granted him a position of judicial leadership. Will he lend his formidable talents to a deeper accommodation of the Bill of Rights to New Deal claims of managerial democracy? Or will his gesture toward Jackson's "fixed star" seem increasingly empty with the passage of time—as he leads the rising generation of judges to embrace a statist reading of the Bill of Rights that Jackson thought he had buried at the moment of the welfare state's greatest promise?

---

[98] 478 US at 213-14 (Blackmun dissenting).

Abstraction and Authority

Frank H. Easterbrook†

Our Constitution creates a government of laws and not of men. The distinction is more than slogan. It is embedded in structure. Congress must proceed by law, using intelligible standards and principles with sufficient breadth to be more than bills of attainder. Rules are proposed, debated, voted on, and published. Process matters: failure at any step means no law. There are no common law crimes. Sudden changes in norms may transgress the Ex Post Facto Clause, the Due Process Clause, or both. Executive officials must act under standards they can defend in public (and before courts); judges too must support their decisions by reasons of general application.

Yet the law teems with devices that defeat uniformity and predictability. Laws may create plastic standards. They may, for example, charge an agency to act in the "public interest, convenience, and necessity." Judges attempt to define "unreasonable" restraints of trade. Balancing tests blossom in constitutional law—although lists of factors do not create "tests," for a combination of a lack of weights for the factors and the tension in a 200-year stock of precedent enables judges to go any which way. As society becomes more complex and public actors—Presidents, administrators, legislators, judges—have less time to spend on each subject, it becomes both tempting and essential (if business is to be finished at all) to muddle through with standards rather than rules. Even in theory it is difficult to know when a rule is preferable to a standard;[1] in practice neither information nor time permits a confident choice.[2] Language itself is too crude for full specifica-

† Judge, United States Court of Appeals for the Seventh Circuit; Senior Lecturer, The Law School, The University of Chicago. This Article was prepared for *The Bill of Rights in the Welfare State: A Bicentennial Symposium*, held at The University of Chicago Law School on October 25-26, 1991. © 1991 by Frank H. Easterbrook. I thank Thomas Collier, G. Michael Halfenger, Alan J. Meese and Richard A. Posner for helpful comments on an earlier draft.

[1] Isaac Ehrlich and Richard A. Posner, *An Economic Analysis of Legal Rulemaking*, 3 J Legal Stud 257 (1974). See also Donald Wittman, *Prior Regulation versus Post Liability: The Choice Between Input and Output Monitoring*, 6 J Legal Stud 193 (1977).

[2] See Frank H. Easterbrook, *What's So Special About Judges?*, 61 U Colo L Rev 773, 778-82 (1990).

tion even if there were time and data. So the objective of announcing rules in advance, and applying them mechanically to fact, cannot be achieved.

That decision by rule is an objective of law—even a supposition of our constitutional system—cannot be denied. That decision by rule is a benefit cannot be doubted.[3] How far short will we fall? That depends in part on how general are our norms. Sometimes it is said that the more abstract the statement, the more discretion in each case; the more discretion, the less "law" remains in the system. Abstraction (the "reasonable person" approach of tort law) may liberate courts from rules, license ex post appreciations and "fair" divisions of the stakes; concrete rules establish incentives ex ante and restrain discretion later on. Sometimes, however, the more general norm is the more constraining—and the persons who seek to boost the level of generality at one time trumpet the virtues of the concrete at others.

How should we choose? Unless there is an answer, we should abandon hope of government by law. Anyone casting a glance over the constitutional landscape would encounter many different levels of abstraction. Judges (not to mention legislatures) read most of the power-granting provisions, such as the Commerce Clause, quite broadly. It is difficult to name anything that falls outside legislative power—neither a loaf of bread nor an x-ray.[4] Judges read many of the power-limiting provisions at a lower level of generality. The Contracts Clause, for example, applies not to the institution of contracts but to agreements signed before a law setting up a new rule.[5] A legislature thus may regulate contracts as it pleases, provided it is prepared to wait for those in existence to expire. And despite the functional equivalence between laws adjusting "rights" and those altering "remedies," a legislature may suspend or even extinguish remedies for unkept promises.[6] Treating the grants as broad and the limits as pinpricks has enlarged the power of the government dramatically; reading the limitations broadly and the grants narrowly is lexically possible and would have the opposite

---

[3] See Antonin Scalia, *The Rule of Law as a Law of Rules*, 56 U Chi L Rev 1175, 1179-80 (1989) (emphasizing not only certainty for those affected by law and reduction in the role of the politics of the judge but also the value of rules in helping judges stand against majoritarian pressure in difficult times).

[4] *Wickard v Filburn*, 317 US 111 (1942); *Summit Health, Ltd. v Pinhas*, 111 S Ct 1842 (1991).

[5] *Ogden v Saunders*, 25 US (12 Wheat) 213, 265-68 (1827).

[6] *Home Building & Loan Ass'n v Blaisdell*, 290 US 398, 429-30, 440-42 (1934).

effect.[7] You need a justification for doing one or the other. This is a conference about the Bill of Rights, so I pay disproportionate attention to the amendments to the Constitution but shall not neglect Bruce Ackerman's challenge[8] to produce a theory of abstraction adequate to both the power-granting and the power-limiting clauses.

I.

Consider some examples from recent decisions under the Bill of Rights.

Michael H. v Gerald D. required the Court to decide whether the Due Process Clause entitles a father to visit his child over the protest of the mother and her husband.[9] The Justices debated whether a biological father has a "fundamental right" to visitation, a question all believed depended in substantial measure on "tradition." Traditions are constructs and may be described in many ways. *Michael H.* precipitated one of the few explicit discussions of the abstraction question. Justice Scalia, for himself and Chief Justice Rehnquist, contended that the Court should select "the most specific level at which a relevant tradition protecting, or denying protection to, the asserted right can be identified."[10] Finding this level might be hard, Justice Scalia conceded, but anything else would be arbitrary. Justice Scalia inquired whether there is a tradition of allowing adulterous fathers to interfere with families and found none. Justice Brennan, writing for Justices Marshall and Blackmun as well, rejoined that generality is no more arbitrary than specificity and proceeded to define the tradition as the right of biological parents to raise their children, coupled with "freedom not to conform"[11]—presumably a fundamental right to commit adultery. With "freedom not to conform" as a "fundamental right," the Court holds the whip hand, for *all* law abridges this

---

[7] See *United States v E.C. Knight Co.*, 156 US 1, 12 (1895) (reading the commerce power specifically, to mean transportation but not manufacturing); *Lochner v New York*, 198 US 45 (1905) (treating broadly implicit limits on state power over commerce, so that a general "liberty of contract" forbids what the Contract Clause itself allows under *Ogden*). Richard Epstein is the leading contemporary exponent of the view that the power-granting clauses *should* be read narrowly and the power-restraining ones broadly. Richard A. Epstein, *The Proper Scope of the Commerce Power*, 73 Va L Rev 1387 (1987).

[8] Bruce Ackerman, *Liberating Abstraction*, in this volume, 317.

[9] 491 US 110 (1989).

[10] Id at 127-28 n 6.

[11] Id at 141 (Brennan dissenting).

freedom, and a judge may deem insufficient the justification asserted by the state for any rule at all.[12]

Cases such as *Michael H.* show the importance of picking a level of generality. By choosing narrowly the Court may find no problem in the law. By choosing broadly the Court may find a problem with any law it pleases—invoking "tradition" to demonstrate that adultery and other things that society has long deprecated are actually *protected* by some traditional freedom, that practices traditionally scorned and punished are no different from practices traditionally praised, such as providing a home for one's grandchild.[13] By reserving the right to choose a level of generality to fit the circumstances, as Justices O'Connor and Kennedy did,[14] the Court makes a virtue of "the understandable temptation to vary the relevant tradition's level of abstraction to make it come out right."[15] Justices O'Connor and Kennedy worried that a rule for selecting a level of generality would change the outcome of some cases. Exactly so, but it is less than clear why that should be troubling.

Although *Michael H.* vividly demonstrates the importance of the level of abstraction, the Justices' dispute was driven by the need to identify a "tradition," which would be used to define a fundamental right. If you assume that the purpose of that enterprise is to increase the number of protected interests, then "it is crucial to define the liberty at a high enough level to permit unconventional variants to claim protection."[16] If you believe that tradition serves to restrict the powers of judges to pursue their vision of a good society, then you will choose a lower level of generality. In either case the selection depends on conclusions about the role of "tradition" in due process analysis rather than about the function of abstraction in understanding the Constitution itself.

---

[12] Justice Blackmun took a similar tack dissenting in *Bowers v Hardwick*, 478 US 186, 199 (1986), in asserting that the sodomy statute interfered with the "right to be let alone." As all law interferes with a "right" stated at this level of abstraction, if the "right to be let alone" is deemed "fundamental" then all law is unconstitutional (at least there is a strong presumption of unconstitutionality, and only an interest deemed weighty by judges would suffice to justify the law). Even Professor Tribe finds this unacceptably general. Laurence H. Tribe and Michael C. Dorf, *Levels of Generality in the Definition of Rights*, 57 U Chi L Rev 1057, 1065-67 (1990).

[13] *Moore v City of East Cleveland*, 431 US 494 (1977).

[14] *Michael H.*, 491 US at 132 (O'Connor concurring).

[15] John Hart Ely, *Democracy and Distrust: A Theory of Judicial Review* 61 (Harvard, 1980). See also John Hart Ely, *Another Such Victory: Constitutional Theory and Practice in a World Where Courts are no Different From Legislatures*, 77 Va L Rev 833 (1991).

[16] Laurence H. Tribe, *American Constitutional Law* 1428 (Harvard, 2d ed 1988).

Let us pause for clarification. Words such as "general" and "abstract" are—general. Professor Ackerman and I use them in different ways. He treats a statement of a right as "more general" when the upshot is greater protection of the claim of liberty. (Put to one side that claims of entitlement often conflict, so that it is not possible to tell which outcome protects rights more fully.) Justice Brennan's view in *Michael H.* is more general than Justice Scalia's in this sense. It is more general in a second sense as well: its statement abstracts away from facts and consequences, not only applying to more cases (all familial relations) but also depending less on the specifics of the underlying dispute. I use "abstract" or "general" in this second sense. The rule "motorists must use reasonable care when driving" is highly general—much more so than the rule "motorists must obey the speed limit and must drive more slowly during rain." The more abstract rule may call for detailed inquiries later (what, after all, is "reasonable care" in the circumstances?) or may not (the rule "do not discriminate on account of a speaker's viewpoint" eliminates the sort of balancing after the fact that is common in tort law). Justice Brennan's abstract statement of familial rights did not eliminate the need to inquire into the nature and justification of the state's regulation. Sometimes the point of a highly abstract statement is to set up the occasion for weighing interests and justifications, sometimes high abstraction eliminates that possibility. This is a rich source of confusion, but one I try to minimize.

Harmelin v Michigan[17] presents a generality question without the complication of fundamental rights. The Eighth Amendment forbids the imposition of cruel and unusual punishments. Michigan prescribes life in prison without possibility of parole for anyone caught possessing more than 650 grams of cocaine. Do the two conflict? The most specific reading of "cruel and unusual punishments" is that the Eighth Amendment, like similar language in the Declaration of Rights of 1689 after the Glorious Revolution in England, forbids *judges* to impose punishments that are not authorized by law.[18] We could read the language more generally to prevent the legislature from devising cruel or freakish *modes* of punishment, such as drawing and quartering or burning at the stake, neither of which ever got a foothold in the United States. Still more generally we could understand this language to address

---

[17] 111 S Ct 2680 (1991).

[18] See Anthony F. Granucci, *"Nor Cruel and Unusual Punishments Inflicted": The Original Meaning*, 57 Cal L Rev 839 (1969).

modes of punishment that, although once common, have become
less so and are also widely viewed as cruel. Then the clause polices
outliers among states, a function it now serves in capital cases. At a
more general level still, the clause is unrelated to either history or
contemporary practice and forbids kinds of punishment (say, fifty
years in prison for a no-funds check) that modern penological theory does not support, even if many states prescribe it. Yet another
boost would forbid any punishment "cruel" by *any* measure—case-
by-case review of proportionality between offense and punishment.
This last approach requires judges to devise and apply their own
theory of criminal sanctions, which may or may not be accepted by
legislatures, the populace, or the academy.

Justice Scalia, writing once again for himself and Chief Justice
Rehnquist, discarded the British practice on the ground that the
lack of common law offenses in the United States meant that the
cruel and unusual punishments clause had to apply to legislatures.[19] He settled on the next-more-general approach, a ban on
cruel modes of punishment unknown in the United States. Justices
O'Connor, Kennedy, and Souter were uncomfortable with this approach and came to Justice Scalia's result without endorsing his
method.[20] Justice White, carrying with him Justices Blackmun and
Stevens, looked through the other end of the telescope and found a
principle of case-by-case proportionality. To the modern ear "cruel
and unusual" sounds case-specific. Although some historical evidence supports Justice Scalia, Justice White thought that it
"would hardly be strong enough to come close to proving an affirmative decision against the proportionality component."[21] Justice
Scalia rejoined:

> Surely this is an extraordinary method for determining what
> restrictions upon democratic self-government the Constitution
> contains. It seems to us that our task is not merely to identify
> various meanings that the text "could reasonably" bear, and
> then impose the one that from a policy standpoint pleases us
> best. Rather, we are to strive as best we can to select from
> among the various "reasonable" possibilities *the most plausi-
> ble* meaning. We do not bear the burden of "proving an af-

---

[19] *Harmelin*, 111 S Ct at 2691. He did not consider the possibility that the Bill of
Rights, including the Eighth Amendment, is the reason why there are no common law
crimes. Accomplishing its task without a struggle does not liberate an amendment for some
other battle. (Justice Scalia also overlooked our one common law crime: contempt of court.)

[20] Id at 2702-09 (Kennedy concurring).

[21] Id at 2710 (White dissenting).

firmative decision against the proportionality component,"
ibid.; rather, Justice White bears the burden of proving an affirmative decision in its favor. For if the Constitution does not
affirmatively contain such a restriction, the matter of proportionality is left to state constitutions or to the democratic
process.[22]

This passage makes an important point: you can't have a theory of
constitutional interpretation divorced from a theory of judicial review. Section III returns to this subject.

If you conclude from *Harmelin* that boosting the level of generality is a way to increase the protection of liberties, you are
wrong. Maryland allows children to testify in criminal trials by
closed circuit television. That way the child doesn't need to look
her accused abuser in the eye. Five Justices concluded in *Maryland v Craig*[23] that this satisfied the Confrontation Clause of the
Sixth Amendment. They asked: "Why do we have confrontation?",
to which they answered, roughly, "so that defendants may receive
fair trials." Having boosted the level of abstraction well beyond
confrontation, the majority asked: "Did this defendant get a fair
trial?", to which it answered "yes." That was that.

Confrontation vanished in the shuffle. Justice Scalia made this
point in dissent, pursuing his regular program of keeping abstraction under control but now with strange bedfellows: Justices Brennan, Marshall, and Stevens.[24] The real Constitution does not say
"All trials must be fair." It contains a series of rules, which the
drafters anticipated would produce fair trials. Justice Scalia emphasized the rule (confrontation) while the majority emphasized
the hoped-for effects.

Boosting the level of generality—in *Craig* by emphasizing the
purposes and effects of a rule—can be a method of liberating
judges *from* rules. Sometimes the practitioners of the method use
it to find "traditions" that would startle students of American society; sometimes they use it to keep the Constitution in tune with
modern tastes. Views can be liberal (as the high-generality approach was in *Harmelin*) or conservative (as it was in *Craig*).
Nothing in the method of abstraction prefers one over the other.

To see this consider three cases in which the Court's champion
of specificity showed up on the side of generality. In the first, *Em-*

---

[22] Id at 2692 n 6 (emphasis in original). *Another* footnote 6 (see *Michael H.* above).
Why do the most important ideas in today's opinions appear in footnotes?

[23] 110 S Ct 3157 (1990).

[24] Id at 3172-73 (Scalia dissenting).

ployment Division v Smith, Justice Scalia wrote for the Court, adopting the principle that any rule neutral with respect to religion satisfies the Free Exercise Clause of the First Amendment.[25] Here is a highly abstract approach: a simple rule covers the whole field. *Smith* held that a state may ban the use of peyote, even as a sacrament—the equivalent of holding that a state may forbid the use of wine in a Catholic mass.[26] Chief Justice Rehnquist and Justices White, Stevens, and Kennedy joined Justice Scalia; Justices Brennan, Marshall, Blackmun, and O'Connor all promoted a more particularistic reading of the text.[27] In the second case, *City of Richmond v J.A. Croson Co.*,[28] Justice Scalia concluded that all racial classifications are forbidden by the Fourteenth Amendment. He treated the Equal Protection Clause as the source of a simple but exceedingly general rule—government may not use race as a ground of decision except to undo the effects of an earlier adverse decision based on the same criterion—although Justice Scalia's colleagues shied away from or rejected that level of abstraction. In the third, Justice Scalia joined Justice Brennan in *Texas v Johnson*, which held unconstitutional a prohibition on flag desecration.[29] Justice Brennan stated the scope of the Free Speech Clause at a high level of generality—the government may not take adverse action because of the viewpoint of a communication—and thereaf-

---

[25] 110 S Ct 1595, 1600-02 (1990).

[26] *Smith* contains a footnote (footnote 5) at least as provocative as the footnotes 6 in *Michael H.* and *Harmelin*. See notes 10 and 22 and accompanying text. The majority trotted out a parade of horribles in which judicial line-drawing concerning accommodation would displace legitimate democratic choices. When responding to Justice O'Connor's contention, id at 1612-13 (O'Connor concurring), that reasonable judges could avoid these horribles, while a neutrality rule would enforce obnoxious laws, the majority remarked:

> [T]he cases we cite have struck "sensible balances" only because they have all applied the general laws, despite the claims for religious exemption. In any event, Justice O'Connor mistakes the purpose of our parade: it is not to suggest that courts would necessarily permit harmful exemptions from these laws (though they might), but to suggest that courts would constantly be in the business of determining whether the "severe impact" of various laws on religious practice (to use Justice Blackmun's terminology) or the "constitutiona[l] significan[ce]" of the "burden on the particular plaintiffs" (to use Justice O'Connor's terminology) suffices to permit us to confer an exemption. It is a parade of horribles because it is horrible to contemplate that federal judges will regularly balance against the importance of general laws the significance of legal practice.

Id at 1606 n 5. This sounds the theme of note 6 in *Harmelin*: that there is a link between generality and the institution of judicial review.

[27] Id at 1606-15 (O'Connor concurring in the judgment), 1615-23 (Blackmun dissenting).

[28] 488 US 469, 520-25 (1989) (Scalia concurring in the judgment).

[29] 491 US 397 (1989).

ter had little trouble. Justices Marshall, Blackmun, Scalia, and Kennedy joined his opinion.[30]

In these three cases the high level of abstraction twice leads to condemnation (*Croson* and *Johnson*), and once shelters the state law (*Smith*). If we ask instead whether boosting the level of generality protects the champions of civil liberties, the answer is unambiguously "yes" in *Johnson*, unambiguously "no" in *Smith*, and debatable in *Croson*—for there are civil liberties claims on both sides of such cases. I have nothing to say about the merits of these cases (or any others); in each there were respectable arguments for divergent positions,[31] and in each it was possible to choose a level of abstraction to achieve almost any desired outcome. Nothing in the text of the Equal Protection Clause answers the critical question: "Equal with respect to *what*?"[32] One reading of the clause is that it deals only with the use of law to protect citizens, so that if the state penalizes the murder of white citizens it must penalize the murder of black citizens and so protect their lives by deterring crime. Under this reading, it has *nothing* to say about racial preferences in doling out public contracts.[33] (Substantive entitlements, on this view, are the province of the Privileges and Immunities Clause.) Increasing levels of abstraction apply the Equal Protection Clause to any use of race that hurts black persons (the "separate but equal" approach) through any use of a poorly justified classification of any kind, with many stops in between. You can't get the right level of abstraction from the words, and the justices have been selective in their use of history.

---

[30] Id at 398. The same majority in *United States v Eichman*, 110 S Ct 2404 (1990), rebuffed a renewed legislative effort to prohibit flag-burning.

[31] The neutrality position in *Smith*, for example, derives from the work of Philip B. Kurland, *Religion and the Law* (Chicago, 1962), and has at least one adherent on the far left of the intellectual spectrum. Mark Tushnet, *"Of Church and State and the Supreme Court": Kurland Revisited*, 1989 S Ct Rev 373. Other careful students of the First Amendment believe that the Free Exercise Clause requires accommodation of some religious practices and on that ground have been critical of *Smith*. See, for example, Douglas Laycock, *The Remnants of Free Exercise*, 1990 S Ct Rev 1; Michael W. McConnell, *Free Exercise Revisionism and the* Smith *Decision*, 57 U Chi L Rev 1109 (1990). See also Michael W. McConnell, *The Origins and Historical Understanding of Free Exercise of Religion*, 103 Harv L Rev 1410, 1420 (1990). But see William P. Marshall, *In Defense of* Smith *and Free Exercise Revisionism*, 58 U Chi L Rev 308 (1991), to which Professor McConnell has replied in Michael W. McConnell, *A Response to Professor Marshall*, 58 U Chi L Rev 329 (1991).

[32] See Peter Westen, *The Empty Idea of Equality*, 95 Harv L Rev 537 (1982).

[33] Although it would have something to say about unequal application of the death penalty, making *McCleskey v Kemp*, 481 US 279 (1987), one of the few equal protection cases in the original sense to reach the Court.

Justice Scalia, who discoursed on history at length in *Harmelin*, said nothing about constitutional history in *Smith* and little in *Croson*. Perhaps no history beyond the Civil War was necessary in *Croson*, for the Fourteenth Amendment was designed to get states out of the business of awarding or withholding benefits on the basis of race. Yet four Justices carried a similar principle over to the federal government in *Metro Broadcasting, Inc. v FCC*,[34] although after the Civil War the federal government made extensive use of race as a basis of benefits (the Freedmen's Bureau was a race-conscious enterprise!), and no Equal Protection Clause applies to the federal government. For textualists finding *any* warrant for applying equal protection principles to the national government is a high, perhaps insuperable, hurdle.[35] To apply such principles at their highest level of generality without a textual hook is quite a feat—one unremarked in *Metro Broadcasting*.

We have seen all four squares of the matrix: general and specific, rights-protecting and rights-denying. Cases fill each, and all of the Justices can be found at one time or another in each square. None chooses consistently. Levels of generality are high sometimes, low at other times; history that may constrain (or boost) abstraction is sometimes used, sometimes bypassed. I suggest in Section III that the appearance of inconsistency is misleading; at all events I do not disparage opening efforts to address a complex subject that has been overlooked for the bulk of the Court's history. Better an incomplete discussion than the pretense that there is no problem.

Movements in the level of constitutional generality may be used to justify almost any outcome. It is correspondingly important that we have a consistent theory of choice. Perhaps there is one—one that explains (at least illuminates) the different Justices' varying approaches, or one that would justify a different line altogether. Section II examines several proposals;[36] Section III offers my own perspective.

---

[34] 110 S Ct 2997 (1990). Chief Justice Rehnquist and Justices O'Connor, Scalia, and Kennedy would have applied a highly abstract version of the Equal Protection Clause to a federal program awarding a preference to minority applicants for broadcast licenses. Id at 3028-47.

[35] See Robert H. Bork, *The Tempting of America: The Political Seduction of the Law* 83-84 (Free Press, 1990).

[36] Careful readers will notice that I say nothing about the developing school of legal pragmatism. See, for example, Richard A. Posner, *The Problems of Jurisprudence* 71-123, 454-69 (Harvard, 1990); Daniel A. Farber, *Legal Pragmatism and the Constitution*, 72 Minn L Rev 1331 (1988). My excuse is that with the exception of Frederick Schauer, *Playing by the Rules* (Oxford, 1991), the pragmatists do not tackle the abstraction question. Although

II.

Traditional. Most judges and justices, most of the time, act as if every text contains its own rule for the level of abstraction. All you have to do is read. Justice Black was a loud exponent of this view, but you did not have to be an absolute textualist to find the approach congenial. Seeing that there is even a *question* is the novelty.

Robert Bork has offered one of the best contemporary defenses of the traditional way of solving the generality problem. He treats the level of generality as part of the meaning of the text. For most constitutional provisions "the level of generality which is part of their meaning is readily apparent."[37] When it is not—when the rule is stated broadly (for example, "equal protection of the laws")—"a judge should state the principle at the level of generality that the text and historical evidence warrant."[38] Bork does not recommend peering inside the minds of the drafters. Their thoughts are unknowable. Anyway, they left us their *words*, their rule of decision, and not their *thoughts*; only the words passed through the process of ratification. Thus the question becomes the level of generality the ratifiers and other sophisticated political actors at the time would have imputed to the text.[39] We inquire not what the drafters thought their rule would accomplish (a dead end version of private meaning we could call "expectationism"), but what their rule is. Rules may have surprising implications when applied to novel facts; often the implications of a rule elude its drafters. Thus Bork is consistent in concluding that the Fourteenth Amendment forbids segregation even though its authors might have accepted separate-but-equal, and that the First Amendment curtails libel actions even though defamation actions were common in 1791.[40] Because the meaning of a text lies in its

---

pragmatists believe that there are "rules" and that decision by rule sometimes is best, they deny both that rules are essential to the judicial office and that it is possible to locate the proper level of abstraction. (Schauer, who is more attracted to rules and believes the subject may be tractable, calls himself a formalist rather than a pragmatist.)

[37] Bork, *Tempting* at 149 (cited in note 35).

[38] Id.

[39] Michael J. Perry spells out the argument more fully than I can do here, giving Bork the credit that many other liberal scholars deny him by discussing only a caricature of his argument. See Michael J. Perry, *The Legitimacy of Particular Conceptions of Constitutional Interpretation*, 77 Va L Rev 669, 675-84 (1991).

[40] See Bork, *Tempting* at 74-84 (cited in note 35); *Ollman v Evans*, 750 F2d 970, 996 (DC Cir 1984) (en banc) (Bork concurring).

interpretation by an interpretive community, an objective reader-centered approach produces an objective level of generality.[41]

You can go a long way with this approach. Many provisions of the Bill of Rights proclaim their level of generality. The Seventh Amendment cries out for narrow, historical reading; the Fourth (with its mention of reasonableness) for more abstraction. But other amendments resist this approach—and they resist it even if we look to the meaning the words would have had for the legal community at the time of drafting.

Take the Eighth Amendment and the problem of *Harmelin*. All would be simple if "cruel and unusual punishment" in the Eighth Amendment means exactly what it means in the Declaration of Rights of 1689. The American interpretive community of 1791 did not hear the words so, however. Members of Congress talked as if the restriction would apply to legislatures and would prevent beastly punishments (in one example, the cropping of ears).[42] What makes a punishment beastly? That it is a barbaric *type* of punishment, no matter the provocation? That a penalty that sometimes is all right is wicked as applied to this crime (twenty lashes for walking your dog without a leash)? Is the benchmark the sensibilities of 1791 or 1971? If these questions had been put to the interpretive community of 1791, they might have been answered. But they were not put to it; perhaps they did not occur to it. So different levels of abstraction may be fully consistent with the discourse of the drafters; nothing enables us to distinguish. Bork takes exactly this view of the Equal Protection Clause when concluding that the Fourteenth Amendment forbids racial segregation of schools: the rule has meanings that may differ from the expectations of its authors.

This recognition, too, is a centerpiece of modern philosophy of language. Even the *speaker* does not exhaust the meaning of the expression until possible applications have been exhausted. Someone using the expression "plus" to refer to an operation on numbers may mean addition but could refer instead to the rule: "If both numbers are less than 10,000, add them; otherwise give up."[43]

---

[41] In this Bork shares much with twentieth-century philosophers of language. See, for example, Ludwig Wittgenstein, *Philosophical Investigations* §§ 201-65 (Basil Blackwell, 1953), although for reasons I take up below, see text accompanying notes 48-54, the identification of the interpretive community is a stumbling block.

[42] I bypass references to the history, which may be found in Granucci, 57 Cal L Rev 839 (cited in note 18), and the opinions in *Harmelin*, 111 S Ct 2680.

[43] See Saul A. Kripke, *Wittgenstein on Rules and Private Language: An Elementary Exposition* 8-18 (Harvard, 1982).

An external interpretive community could discover whether the speaker embraced a rule carrying addition past 10,000 by asking questions and evaluating the answers. Old texts foil that process. Because official action by states *favoring* racial minorities was unheard of in 1871, we do not know (and cannot reconstruct) how the interpretive community of that era would have understood the Fourteenth Amendment. Therefore we cannot tell for a case such as *Croson* whether the right level of generality is "no official use of race" or "no use of race to harm minorities," or some additional possibility.[44] A problem neither appreciated nor discussed is not resolved; texts do not settle disputes their authors and their contemporary readers could not imagine.

Worse: the founding generation itself understood that their texts left many matters open and preferred practice over textual interpretation as a way of settling them.[45] James Madison, for example, believed that even in conjunction the Commerce Clause and the Necessary and Proper Clause did not authorize Congress to create a national bank. Yet he signed the legislation creating the second Bank of the United States, remarking that the accommodations of the political branches in the exercise of their powers pointed more surely to meaning than did his personal view.[46] In the 46th Federalist Madison defends the allocation of powers as malleable:

> If . . . the people should in future become more partial to the federal than to the State governments, the change can only result from such manifest and irresistible proofs of a better administration, as will overcome all their antecedent propensities. And in that case, the people ought not surely to be precluded from giving most of their confidence where they may discover it to be most due . . . .[47]

---

[44] Perry, 77 Va L Rev at 677-79 (cited in note 39), makes this point so well that repetition would be otiose.

[45] See H. Jefferson Powell, *The Original Understanding of Original Intent*, 98 Harv L Rev 885 (1985). Although Powell's assessment is not free from controversy, see Charles A. Lofgren, *The Original Understanding of Original Intent?*, 5 Const Comm 77 (1988), no one doubts that constitutional debate and practice in the first fifty years gave substantial weight to the working structure of government and did not rely exclusively on texts or their interpretation.

[46] Contrast his speech on the floor of the House on February 2, 1791 opposing the first proposal with his decision in 1816 to sign the legislation. See Jefferson Powell, *Languages of Power: A Source Book of Early American Constitutional History* 37-40, 293-95 (Carolina Academic, 1991).

[47] Federalist 46 (Madison) in Benjamin Fletcher Wright, ed, *The Federalist* 329, 331 (Belknap, 1961).

Designed for an unknown future, the Constitution accommodates change. The power to accommodate implies grave difficulty in using the community of ratifiers to fix a single level of generality.

Modified Traditional. If we cannot consult the interpretive communities of bygone years, perhaps we can turn to the one with us today. Ronald Dworkin, Owen Fiss, and Harry Wellington, among others, propose putting the abstraction question to the contemporary legal community.[48] Although the answer may depart from the one the original community may have given, it has the virtue of objectivity—of being a consensus answer rather than one personal to the interpreter, and therefore of conforming to the ideal of law. The method tracks the recommendations of scholars such as Hans-Georg Gadamer, whose hermeneutics stress the ability (indeed, necessity) of texts to adapt as their readership changes.[49]

Applying methods of literary interpretation to legal texts is, however, no cure. Styles of literary interpretation exalt creativity, indeterminacy, novelty.[50] Readers use texts to enlarge their horizons. Judges, by contrast, use texts to impose obligations—to order persons to do things, pay money, go to jail. An approach that helps people broaden their minds does not justify sending them to jail; *that* depends on the idea that there are rules. "Let a thousand flowers bloom" is the right cast of mind for literary interpretation; attractive ideas will take root and others wither; it would be silly to have only one "approved" understanding of a poem or novel. Certainty and uniformity are important in law; our theory of legal obligation does not admit the possibility that one text has many meanings. I have elsewhere thrown cold water on the proposition

---

[48] Ronald Dworkin, *Law's Empire* 87-90 (Belknap, 1986); Owen M. Fiss, *Objectivity and Interpretation*, 34 Stan L Rev 739 (1982); Harry H. Wellington, *Interpreting the Constitution: The Supreme Court and the Process of Adjudication* ch 8 (Yale, 1990). Compare Anthony T. Kronman, *Living in the Law*, 54 U Chi L Rev 835 (1987).

[49] Hans-Georg Gadamer, *Truth and Method* xxiv (Crossroad, 2d rev ed 1989). See also William N. Eskridge, Jr., *Gadamer/Statutory Interpretation*, 90 Colum L Rev 609 (1990) (recommending a similar approach for statutes), and T. Alexander Aleinikoff, *Updating Statutory Interpretation*, 87 Mich L Rev 20 (1988) (suggesting a "nautical model" of statutory interpretation in which the enacting body charts a course and the current crew changes that course as necessary).

[50] Anyone who doubts this should consult the work of Stanley Fish, whose presence on the law faculty at Duke has played an important role in introducing lawyers to the hermeneutical methods of the other parts of today's universities. See, for example, Stanley Fish, *Is There a Text in this Class? The Authority of Interpretive Communities* (Harvard, 1980); Stanley Fish, *Doing What Comes Naturally: Change, Rhetoric, and the Practice of Theory in Literary and Legal Studies* (Duke, 1989).

that legal and literary interpretation should use the same methods, and in this belief have good company.[51]

Let us assume that a legal community is more apt than a literary one to produce answers to hard questions. Why are judges the proper persons to interrogate the legal community and pronounce its answers? Judges have tenure in large measure to insulate them from swings of contemporary opinion, the better to make them faithful to decisions taken in the past. If these decisions are to be updated, better to have the revision performed by those who are sensitive to the contemporary will—administrative officials, Congress, the President. Although judges are more apt to be dispassionate than are political officials, their dispassion need not lead them to be more faithful to the median view of the contemporary legal culture; it may lead them to be more faithful to their *own* views. This is the dark side of tenure.[52] To the extent it influences judges, achieving objectivity is impossible.

If the living legal community is indeed the right benchmark, it is tempting to ask: why a *constitution*? A written constitution—the instrument that separates us from the United Kingdom, where living majorities mold traditions and thus governmental institutions to suit tastes—is designed to be an anchor in the past. It creates rules that bind until a supermajority of the living changes them. You can imagine change by the living in ways other than those described; after all, our Constitution was ratified without the unanimity required by the Articles of Confederation.[53] That constitutional change requires a supermajority sustained over an extended period cannot be doubted, however—for to doubt it is to doubt the ability of the past *ever* to constrain the present, and thereby to destroy the source of the judges' claim to countermand the will of contemporary majorities. Yet putting questions about the level of abstraction to today's legal community dispenses with both the supermajority requirement and the need for some stability in that opinion (which must endure long enough to obtain a

---

[51] Frank H. Easterbrook, *Approaches to Judicial Review*, in Jack David and Robert McKay, eds, *The Blessings of Liberty: An Enduring Constitution for a Changing World* 147, 148-50 (Random House, 1989). See also Richard A. Posner, *Law and Literature: A Misunderstood Relation* ch 5 (Harvard, 1988); Paul Brest, *Interpretation and Interest*, 34 Stan L Rev 765, 769-73 (1982); Thomas C. Grey, *The Constitution as Scripture*, 37 Stan L Rev 1, 2-3 (1984); Richard S. Kay, *Adherence to the Original Intentions in Constitutional Adjudication: Three Objections and Responses*, 82 Nw U L Rev 226, 238-40 (1988).

[52] See generally Easterbrook, 61 U Colo L Rev 773 (cited in note 2).

[53] See Akhil Reed Amar, *Philadelphia Revisited: Amending the Constitution Outside Article V*, 55 U Chi L Rev 1043, 1047 (1988).

two-thirds vote in both chambers of Congress and a majority in three-fourths of the states' legislatures, a process that takes considerable time).

At all events, if we are to query the living legal community, *which* one? You get very different answers to the cases presented in Section I from scholars, practitioners, and judges. In the United States judges are selected from such divergent parts of the profession that it is a mistake to speak even of a judicial interpretive community. A judge devoted to selecting a modern interpretive community external to his own preferences may play the field. Who receives the (hypothetical) question about the right level of generality in *Harmelin*, *Croson*, or *Johnson*? Choosing a hypothetical interlocutor determines the answer.[54] Add to this the fact that the judge not only chooses the recipient of the question but also supplies the answer (it is a hypothetical community and hypothetical question, after all!) and you have no useful guidance.

I do not mean by this that you *never* get useful answers; many questions in law have determinate answers (or a substantial range of determinacy). Rather, the point is that we deem a constitutional question interesting and difficult when our hypothetical community gives different answers. The process therefore does not usefully constrain interpretation and cannot repair the difficulties with the traditional view, which looks to the interpretive community at the time of enactment.

Consistency. One variant of modified traditionalism deserves special attention. Laurence Tribe and Michael Dorf, in the most ambitious analysis of the abstraction problem to appear in the legal literature, contend that the court should treat the Bill of Rights as a coherent whole and generalize to examples that were not contemplated at the time.[55] A statement fails when the Court must ignore the rationales of other amendments or cases describing particular instances. Thus a "right to be let alone" is too general, because it makes earlier cases sustaining particular laws inexplicable. But a "tradition of protecting the marital unit against claims of adulterous natural fathers" is too specific, because it cannot rationalize earlier cases acknowledging, say, a right to contraception by unmarried couples.

---

[54] A point I make with respect to statutes in Frank H. Easterbrook, *The Role of Original Intent in Statutory Interpretation*, 11 Harv J L & Pub Pol 59, 62-65 (1988).

[55] Tribe and Dorf, 57 U Chi L Rev at 1059-64 (cited in note 12). See also Laurence H. Tribe and Michael C. Dorf, *On Reading the Constitution* 73-80 (Harvard, 1991).

This is a variant rather than an independent proposal because it expressly depends on the propriety of using methods of literary interpretation[56] and attempts to construct a contemporary interpretive community—the one reflected in recent decisions of the Supreme Court. I find much to admire in this attempt to make the point of reference more specific (and more accessible), thereby cutting down on judges' ability to influence outcomes by going community-shopping. Any step in the direction of objectivity is welcome.

As a variant, however, the Tribe-Dorf proposal suffers from most of the difficulties of its lineage. Their efforts to repair the defects of this category of methods creates new problems. The authors patch over some difficulties by assuming that "the issues of interpretation that arise in construing the words of the Bill of Rights are *identical* to those that arise in the fundamental rights context,"[57] although most members of today's interpretive community (including those who sit on the Court) believe that there is a substantial difference between legal claims based on constitutional text and those that are not. Tribe and Dorf patch over other difficulties by assuming consistency and calling for a combination of interpolation and extrapolation. Yet you can demand consistency in the treatment of new cases only if the existing stock of rules (and precedents) is consistent. You cannot take out more consistency than you put in. Given two inconsistent propositions (in the text or the cases), you can show or refute any proposition at all.

Tribe and Dorf assume but do not demonstrate that the stock of reference points is consistent. Why should we expect it to be consistent? The Third, Fourth, and Seventh Amendments operate on dramatically different planes of generality. Interpolating to the Due Process Clause of the Fifth does not yield one of these rather than another. If Justice Scalia prefers the historical approach of the Seventh Amendment, while Justice Brennan uses the reasonableness standard of the Fourth for a benchmark, is either one "wrong?" Maybe so, if precedent marks a clear choice and speaks as our interpretive community. Yet where is the choice? You cannot get five pages into the Tribe-Dorf article without encountering a glaring inconsistency: the difference between constitutional protection of abortion in *Roe v Wade*[58] and the failure in *Bowers v*

---

[56] Id at 1072-77.
[57] Id at 1061 (emphasis added).
[58] 410 US 113 (1973).

Hardwick[59] to include sodomy within the same class. These are irreconcilable decisions—Tribe and Dorf think so, I think so,[60] the Justices themselves think so. At least seven of the Justices who voted in *Bowers* would have treated the abortion and sodomy questions identically: Justices Brennan, Marshall, Blackmun, and Stevens, by protecting both; Justices Burger, White, and Rehnquist (perhaps Justice O'Connor too), by protecting neither. Only Justice Powell saw a difference—adhering to *Roe* while joining the majority in *Bowers*—and he is reputed to have changed his mind about *Bowers* after he left the Court.

The contrast between abortion and sodomy illustrates a problem in making decisions by majority vote, as the Court does (and as the Constitutional Convention, Congress, and the ratifying state bodies do). Even if every member of a body behaves consistently, the collectivity will generate inconsistent results.[61] How pervasive the inconsistency may be is a subject of legitimate debate;[62] that we are doomed to have *some* is beyond all debate. Inconsistency embedded in the stock of precedents—one that now fills more than 500 volumes—disables proposals to extrapolate consistently from these opinions. The Constitution is a series of compromises, starting with the Great Compromise between the large and small states (equal suffrage in the Senate) that made political union possible, and the three-fifths compromise over questions of representation. Prudence rather than unifying principle shaped the initial document and all of its amendments.

Moreover, it is difficult to believe that Tribe and Dorf embrace one of the principal implications of their view: strict path dependence, in which the meaning of the Constitution varies with the order in which cases reach the Court. Suppose *Bowers* had been decided in 1973 and the abortion question had come up for its initial decision in 1986.[63] Then consistent application of the prece-

---

[59] 478 US 186 (1986).

[60] See Frank H. Easterbrook, *Implicit and Explicit Rights of Association*, 10 Harv J L & Pub Pol 91, 92-93 (1987).

[61] Kenneth J. Arrow, *Social Choice and Individual Values* 59-60 (John Wiley, 1951). For applications to courts see Frank H. Easterbrook, *Ways of Criticizing the Court*, 95 Harv L Rev 802, 813-32 (1982); Lewis A. Kornhauser and Laurence G. Sager, *Unpacking the Court*, 96 Yale L J 82, 109-10 n 37 (1986); Herbert Hovenkamp, *Arrow's Theorem: Ordinalism and Republican Government*, 75 Iowa L Rev 949 (1990).

[62] Daniel A. Farber and Philip P. Frickey, *Law and Public Choice: A Critical Introduction* ch 2 (Chicago, 1991), provides a careful assessment of the state of the literature.

[63] An unlikely supposition, as only the outcome of *Roe* made *Bowers* a case worth litigating. Still, it is a thought experiment worth pursuing, as no one wants a form of constitutional adjudication in which judges always must *increase* their degree of "creativity" and

dents implies the absence of any fundamental right of intimate association. The abortion case would be simple after the sodomy case: if the Constitution does not protect sexual activities that have few effects on unconsenting parties, it does not protect decisions that affect the welfare of other family members and the potential child. Would Tribe and Dorf conclude that their method compelled the Court to decide against abortion in 1986 if it had decided against sodomy in 1973? Not at all; they would not (and need not) because there are contrary strands in the contraception cases. Neither result of the abortion case could be reached by simple extrapolation.

And so it is with the other subjects. You cannot get to *Harmelin* (or its opposite), to *Croson*, or to most of the other cases discussed in Section I by assuming that the interpretive community is the body of recent precedents. *Texas v Johnson* comes closest to being a "determined" outcome, although four justices did not agree and managed to cite a goodly number of recent cases that make the abstract principle "there shall be no viewpoint discrimination" (the one to which the majority adhered in *Johnson*) look like an overstatement of the body of precedent. "No viewpoint discrimination" is a *good* principle on many grounds and one I find congenial,[64] but it cannot be produced by simple interpolation of precedent.

Adding a dollop of the Ninth Amendment to the stew of precedent, as Tribe and Dorf propose, does no better at producing consistency. The Ninth Amendment reads: "The enumeration in the Constitution, of certain rights, shall not be construed to deny or disparage others retained by the people." This tells us that there *are* rights not spelled out; John Hart Ely is right to say that an originalist must take this text seriously even if it is uncomfortably vague.[65] Still, rights "retained" implies an historical inquiry, just as the Seventh Amendment (the "right of trial by jury shall be

---

depart still farther from the text—an approach that would be compelled if every case built on the last one and urged "a little more" departure, followed by extrapolation. We must therefore imagine a sequence in which the first case simply asks the Court to confirm the conventional wisdom (in 1973 and before, that sodomy is not a fundamental right) and the second case seeks a departure (in this example, the arrival of the abortion question for the first time in 1986).

[64] See *American Booksellers Ass'n v Hudnut*, 771 F2d 323, 327-28 (7th Cir 1985), aff'd without opinion, 475 US 1001 (1986).

[65] Ely, *Democracy and Distrust* at 34-41 (cited in note 15). See also Randy E. Barnett, ed, *The Rights Retained by the People: The History and Meaning of the Ninth Amendment* (George Mason, 1989).

preserved") has precipitated historical inquiry.[66] There is no right level of generality at which to read history—we are back to *Harmelin*—and no reason to suppose that historical investigation would produce clues that could promote consistent adjudication.

Countervailing Rights. Bruce Ackerman asks us to abandon this pursuit and take up a different subject. He seeks consistent treatment of the level of generality of the power-granting clauses and the power-denying clauses. The New Deal settled the question for the power-granting clauses. Once the Commerce Clause is taken to authorize Congress to control whatever has an indirect effect on commerce, the national government may do almost anything a majority in Congress thinks proper. Unless the power-constraining clauses (except the Contracts and Takings Clauses!) also expand, the original balance is undone, and perhaps the people will be undone. How ironic if the judges who, like me, are most skeptical of governmental power should accept the power-expanding half of this equation, reject the power-limiting half, and end up as statists.

The force driving this argument is the belief that Something Big happened in 1933-53: an unwritten amendment to the Constitution incorporating the New Deal and authorizing a great enlargement of federal power.[67] I confess to doubting the equivalence of written and unwritten amendments to the Constitution. Perhaps this marks me as a throwback. So be it. Shouldn't good interpreters of this document strive to exemplify the eighteenth-century mind? (Well, maybe the nineteenth-century mind; let us not forget 1871.) Too, I wonder why the discarding of the written provisions of the Constitution in favor of unwritten amendments implies anything about *judicial power*. If the document no longer binds us in some respects, why does it govern in others? Political systems can survive without textual anchors in centuries past—most of the liberal democracies do so quite nicely. If we have cast aside the limited power-granting clauses and the explicit limits in the Contracts and Takings Clauses, it does not follow that judges should make extravagant claims in the name of still other clauses.

---

[66] See *Richmond Newspapers, Inc. v Virginia*, 448 US 555, 579-80 n 15 (1980) (Burger) (invoking the Ninth Amendment as collateral support for the proposition that the press's traditional access to criminal trials is constitutionally protected even though the right to a "speedy and public trial" identified in the Sixth Amendment belongs exclusively to the accused).

[67] See Bruce A. Ackerman, *We the People: Foundations* (Belknap, 1991).

Ackerman seeks to attract me to his enterprise by placing one of my judicial heroes in the vault of his pantheon. He treats the second Justice Jackson as the model interpreter of the New Deal Constitution.[68] But which Robert Jackson should we emulate: the generalizer of the flag salute cases and the Japanese removal cases,[69] or the anti-generalizer of *Terminiello* and the steel seizure cases?[70] I think Jackson one of the nation's greatest Justices, not only because of his eloquence and his support for the liberties established in the text of the Bill of Rights, but also because he doubted the omniscience of judges and the warrant for expansive claims of judicial power. Jackson was an enforcer, not a creator, of rights, and Ackerman would cast him in a different role.

Even Ackerman's strong appeal to our common denominator does not lead me to embrace his approach to abstraction. For I do not locate the advance of federal power in the New Deal. It occurred in *McCulloch v Maryland*,[71] more than a century earlier, when the Court invoked the Necessary and Proper Clause to hold that Congress could establish a national bank. Everything after that was a matter of details. Important details to be sure, as majorities occasionally could loose a bolt of lightning at a law or three.[72] But these were temporary setbacks, notches in an upward-sloping graph.[73] Dramatic boosts to national power came from the railroads, telegraphs, and other instruments that knitted the nation together (the optimal size of government grows as transportation and communication become cheaper) and two *real* constitutional amendments that made the federal government the locus of control: the Sixteenth, creating the personal income tax, and the Seventeenth, ending state legislatures' selection of senators. It is not proper for courts to rein in the effects of changing economic conditions or express amendments augmenting national power.

Most contemporary debates about abstraction do not concern federal power. They have to do with state power. And the states

---

[68] Ackerman, in this volume, 334-38 (cited in note 8).

[69] *West Virginia State Board of Education v Barnette*, 319 US 624 (1943); *Korematsu v United States*, 323 US 214, 242-48 (1944) (Jackson dissenting).

[70] *Terminiello v Chicago*, 337 US 1, 13-37 (1949) (Jackson dissenting); *Youngstown Sheet & Tube Co. v Sawyer*, 343 US 579, 634-55 (1952) (Jackson concurring).

[71] 17 US (4 Wheat) 316 (1819).

[72] Even in the heyday of *Lochner*ian substantive due process and the nadir of the commerce power, most laws by state and federal governments were favorably received in the Supreme Court. See David P. Currie, *The Constitution in the Supreme Court: The Second Century, 1888-1986* 47-50 (Chicago, 1990).

[73] *E.C. Knight*, 156 US 1, for example, was effectively undone by *Swift & Co. v United States*, 196 US 375 (1905), before a decade was out.

did not receive their powers from the Constitution. They owe their powers to the consent and acquiescence of their own people. State power *decreased* during the New Deal—not only because of the augmentation of national power, but also because the steady decline in the costs of transportation and communication made states less important. Two hundred years ago states could impose taxes or regulate commerce with few obstacles. Now the people and firms will respond to state and local regulation by taking their business (or themselves) elsewhere.

As insularity fell, so did inroads on civil liberties. In 1787 seven states had established churches; all were dis-established long before the Supreme Court applied the First Amendment to the states in 1940.[74] The Court's role in civil liberties (with the exception of its holdings about race relations) has been that of a follower, not a leader. It extirpates in the name of the Constitution practices that have already disappeared or dwindled among the states. It obliterates outliers.[75]

The slow but steady erosion in the powers of the states should lead Ackerman to recommend that the Court decrease the level of generality and do less to interfere with state actions. Federalism was an important part of the original design, which would suffer at Ackerman's hands. He proposes to use the decrease in state power attributable to a changing economy as the fulcrum of a still further decrease at the hands of the judiciary. Yet it should be significant for him that most of the ways in which states affect personal liberties (for example, impose life sentences for crime, punish flag-burning, limit fathers' access to their biological children, use race as a ground of decision, regulate sexual activity) are unrelated to the issues of the New Deal. States did not acquire their power to put people in jail from the Franklin Roosevelt Administration. These are old issues, prudential and moral disputes present at the foundation. Ackerman does not persuade me that the level of abstraction appropriate to the problems in *Harmelin, Michael H., Croson, Johnson,* and *Craig* should be different in 1891 and 1991. *Smith* is a better case for Ackerman; Oregon denied Smith unemployment compensation after his discharge for smoking peyote.

---

[74] *Cantwell v Connecticut,* 310 US 296, 303 (1940) (applies the Free Exercise Clause to the states); *Everson v Board of Education,* 330 US 1, 15 (1947) (applies the Establishment Clause to the states).

[75] See generally Gerald N. Rosenberg, *The Hollow Hope: Can Courts Bring About Social Change?* (Chicago, 1991); Cass R. Sunstein, *Three Civil Rights Fallacies,* 79 Cal L Rev 751, 765-69 (1991); Frank H. Easterbrook, *Bills of Rights and Regression to the Mean* (forthcoming 1992).

Unemployment compensation *is* an invention of the welfare state, and local programs are so underwritten by the Treasury that they are effectively federal. Yet in *Smith* the Court took Ackerman's advice and used a high level of abstraction—much to his dismay, I should think.

Is It All Incoherent? My survey of the terrain of approaches did not produce a reliable way to select a plane of generality on which to locate a constitutional rule. Perhaps there is no way at all to do this. Dean Brest, for example, believes that the abstraction problem defeats all efforts to construct a system of adjudication by neutral principles.[76] As Brest put it, the quest for "objectivity in legal interpretation [is] on a par with the fantasy of a single, objective reading of *Hamlet* or of Balinese culture."[77] Many other thoughtful persons have come to the same conclusion.

Brest's claim is overstated if he means that it is impossible to select the level of generality for *any* rule on a principled basis. *Hamlet* and Balinese culture are substantially more complex than most legal rules, and simplicity promotes understanding—even if imperfect.[78] If we really can't settle on the right level of generality, we will have a difficult time explaining why people must pay the piper for failing to anticipate the judges' disposition. Brest's claim is unanswerable, however, if limited to the category of cases the legal culture deems "hard" at a particular time. They are hard precisely *because* the kit of legal tools cannot produce agreement among those competent in their use. There is no way out of this conclusion. The question is: what do we make of it?

III.

Multiple legitimate levels of abstraction imply multiple legitimate meanings of the text. The problems that concern us today were not settled in the past and encoded in authoritative rules; they must be settled by the living.

Who among the living? Anyone reading a law review "knows" that this means judges. The author starts with the assumption that

---

[76] Paul Brest, *The Fundamental Rights Controversy: The Essential Contradictions of Normative Constitutional Scholarship*, 90 Yale L J 1063, 1084-85, 1091-92 (1981).

[77] Brest, 34 Stan L Rev at 771 (cited in note 51).

[78] See Kent Greenawalt, *How Law Can Be Determinate*, 38 UCLA L Rev 1 (1990); Kay, 82 Nw U L Rev at 248-50, 273-84 (cited in note 51). See also Margaret Jane Radin and Frank Michelman, *Pragmatist and Poststructuralist Critical Legal Practice*, 139 U Pa L Rev 1019, 1046-54 (1991) (defending, albeit tepidly, the proposition that there can be understandable rules).

the judge will decide—*that* was settled by *Marbury v Madison*[79] in 1803—and then displays a range of meanings that could be imputed to the text, imploring judges to select the best one. Judicial opinions often have the same flavor. Judges' right to the final say having been established long ago, the plasticity of old texts becomes a platform for an enlargement of discretion.

When interpreting the Constitution it is tempting to see how far old texts can be pressed—for any limitations, any at all, create at least some possibility of horrible deeds slipping into the cracks. A sophisticated lawyer worried about abuses starts with the text and identifies its purposes and consequences. Next comes a move to a level of abstraction selected so that the rule governs whatever may threaten these interests to any degree. That move eliminates loopholes, but at the expense of making the rule so universal that it occupies the field of governmental action. Then the judge announces that "reasonable" limitations on the interests so identified will be respected, and no others. What is "reasonable," except what is wise? Interests conflict and overlap, so that to choose generality in a way that focuses attention on interests is to give judges an essentially political role.[80]

If indeed the Constitution deputizes judges to settle all hard legal issues, then inability to settle on a level of abstraction greatly but properly enlarges the judicial role in governance. If it does not, then the sequence should be reversed. Instead of assuming power and then searching for a level of abstraction, the court should search for that degree of generality capable of justifying a *judicial* role. Unless it is possible to find an answer that adequately differentiates judicial from political action, the judge should allow political and private actors to proceed on their way—that is, the judge should honor the structural features of the Constitution allocating powers to states and to political actors who have followed the approved forms such as bicameral approval.

Judges, more than other political actors, must answer the question why anyone should obey. The President has the Army, Congress the purse. Judges have reason. They could assemble political coalitions for protection; the Supreme Court has a formida-

---

[79] 5 US (1 Cranch) 137 (1803).

[80] See T. Alexander Aleinikoff, *Constitutional Law in the Age of Balancing*, 96 Yale L J 943, 984-95 (1987); *Miller v Civil City of South Bend*, 904 F2d 1081, 1129-30 (7th Cir 1990) (en banc) (Easterbrook dissenting), rev'd as *Barnes v Glen Theatre, Inc.*, 111 S Ct 2456 (1991); *American Jewish Congress v City of Chicago*, 827 F2d 120, 137-40 (7th Cir 1987) (Easterbrook dissenting).

ble constituency (including the press, which relies on the Court to protect speech and repays the debt by rallying to the Court's defense). But other political actors can appeal to the same constituencies, which will not lift a finger to defend judges who march to their own drummer. Judges must persuade other political actors, and the public at large, that courts produce net benefits; only that demonstration makes it sensible for others to obey judicial decisions as a rule, enforcing even edicts that a political majority believes unsound. The rule of law attracts formidable support only so long as people believe that there is a rule *of law* and not a rule *by judges*. The need to persuade society to obey sets bounds on judicial creativity; it is most unlikely that obedience will long be forthcoming to an institution that appears to be subcommittee chairmen wearing robes.

Whether or not obedience endures, there remains the question of justification. Public power in the United States depends on law. Everyone exercising the power of the state needs a legal justification, not just a moral or prudential one—the cop making an arrest, the bureaucrat denying an application for welfare benefits or collecting a tax, the commissioner dissolving a merger, the cabinet secretary reducing the number of landing slots at an airport, everyone. When rules cannot limit the exercise of authority, we define justification as process (for example, approval by both houses of Congress and the signature of the President). You can describe a society where public acceptance of official demands is a complete justification for those demands. In nations without constitutions (the United Kingdom, for example), tradition and authority merge. Our republic was founded on contractarian premises, however, and no one holding power here asserts that public acquiescence is sufficient.

Everyone needs a justification. "Everyone" includes judges. *Especially* judges, who insist that other public officials scrupulously observe the limits on their own power even when prudence might justify additional powers.[81] *Especially* judges, who alone have tenure of office, something justified if at all by the tendency of tenure to make them more faithful to decisions taken in the past at the expense of convenience today. *Especially* judges, whose charge is the maintenance of the rules of the game and the faithful implementation of decisions taken under its rules. As judges (and scholars) demand that political officials justify their acts with more

---

[81] See, for example, *INS v Chadha*, 462 US 919 (1983); *Youngstown*, 343 US 579.

than a claim of prudence, so judges must supply no lesser justification for their own acts.

How did it come to be that judges have any role in reviewing decisions taken by other branches? That power is not conferred expressly in the Constitution. It was inferred from the constitutional structure. And the way in which it was inferred informs our understanding of the abstraction problem.[82]

The major premise of *Marbury v Madison* is that the Constitution is law—the supreme law, binding on all organs of government, and sufficiently clear to be enforceable as law. Chief Justice Marshall gives the ex post facto clause as an example and asks rhetorically whether in case of clear conflict one applies the retrospective criminal law. Another premise is that the Constitution includes a hierarchy—that it is supreme over statutes and treaties. Finally, Marshall argues that every public official owes a duty, by virtue of his oath if not the written nature of the document, to follow the supreme law in the event of conflict. Written instruments are meant to have bite; and our Constitution not only is written but also establishes a system of limited government. If there are limits then there are boundaries to be patrolled.[83] Otherwise our government is not limited after all.

Problems lurk in this explanation. It begs the critical question: why must political actors pay more attention to the judges' views than the judges pay to the legislature's? Chief Justice Marshall's implicit answer is that the constitutional hierarchy binds all branches, that to demonstrate the argument for the meaning of the Constitution is to produce acquiescence. Congress and the President must follow the Court because the same syllogism that drives the Court's action drives everyone else's. That is, there are understandable rules. They were laid down in the past and govern us still. To have identified the rule is to have identified the reason why all must obey. The Supreme Court's decision about the content of the rules prevails because of the definition of a *rule*, given to all alike.

Judicial review under *Marbury* is a search for rules.[84] If the age or generality of the text frustrates the statement of a rule, then

---

[82] See Easterbrook, *Approaches to Judicial Review* (cited in note 51).

[83] Id at 178-80. See Sylvia Snowiss, *Judicial Review and the Law of the Constitution* ch 4 (Yale, 1990), explaining the difference between this justification of judicial review and the more limited approach some state courts had taken.

[84] See Stephen L. Carter, *Constitutional Adjudication and the Indeterminate Text: A Preliminary Defense of an Imperfect Muddle*, 94 Yale L J 821 (1985); Stephen L. Carter, *Constitutional Improprieties: Reflections on* Mistretta, Morrison, *and Administrative Gov-*

it also defeats the claim of judicial power. If the living must indeed chart their own course, then the question is political, outside the domain of judicial review. You cannot have a view that denies the power of the past to rule today's affairs yet asserts that Article III still binds. Judicial review depends on the belief that decisions taken long ago are authoritative. The judges' duty is "to declare all acts contrary to the manifest tenor of the Constitution void."[85] This assumes that the document *has* a "manifest tenor." The writers and ratifiers thought it did. We broke from England by having rules—and therefore enforcement—instead of having only practices and consensus that are always in political evolution, and therefore not enforceable by judges.

Marbury teases judicial review from structure rather than language. It therefore necessarily admits the possibility of other inferential, structural claims—a possibility that quickly developed in the intergovernmental tax immunity doctrine of *McCulloch*. Structural arguments can enlarge review further. Perhaps judicial review flows from the terror of the alternative: chaos. So it seemed to Holmes, who opined that the Republic would dissolve if the federal courts did not have the power to declare state laws unconstitutional.[86] So it seemed to Learned Hand, whose argument goes:

> [I]t was probable, if indeed it was not certain, that without some arbiter whose decision was final the whole system would have collapsed . . . . The courts were undoubtedly the best 'Department' in which to vest such a power, since by the independence of their tenure they were least likely to be influenced by diverting pressure. It was not a lawless act to import into the Constitution such a grant of power.[87]

Such a line of argument has a corollary, which Hand acknowledged:

> [I]t was absolutely essential to confine the power to the need that evoked it: that is, it was and always has been necessary to distinguish between the frontiers of another 'Department's' authority and the propriety of its choices within those fron-

---

ernment, 57 U Chi L Rev 357, 364-76 (1990); Antonin Scalia, *Originalism: The Lesser Evil*, 57 U Cin L Rev 849 (1989).

[85] Federalist 78 (Hamilton) in Wright, ed, *The Federalist* 489, 491 (cited in note 47).

[86] Oliver Wendell Holmes, *Collected Legal Papers* 295-96 (Peter Smith, 1952).

[87] Learned Hand, *The Bill of Rights: The Oliver Wendell Holmes Lectures, 1958* 29 (Harvard, 1962).

tiers. The doctrine *presupposed that it was possible to make such a distinction*, though at times it is difficult to do so.[88]

One thing this version of the claim for judicial power cannot do is justify novelties. Will the Republic fall apart if some states use capital punishment and others do not? If some states permit sodomy and others prohibit the practice? The argument from chaos cannot establish that diversity of practice about debatable moral questions is baleful. Quite the contrary. Many visions of utopia entail great diversity of moral views and the power of people to choose their polity. Our particular governmental structure recognizes the value of different solutions (in different cities and states) to debatable questions. This is not so that states may "experiment," which implies that we will converge on a single answer to every problem. It is, rather, because people differ in tastes and moral views, both of which evolve. Divergent practices and the power to choose (or move) are important elements of liberty.

The need to produce a theory of meaning that is also adequate to justify the judicial role constrains the level of abstraction. It implies a search for a common denominator, in which judges enforce, against the contrary views of other governmental actors, only the portion of the text or rule sufficiently complete and general to count as law.[89] Several of the cases in Section I yield quickly to this approach. *Michael H.* involved an extra-textual claim, and it was correspondingly hard to locate any legal principle requiring every state and local government to adopt the same rule. This implies a low level of abstraction, for a highly general approach along Justice Brennan's lines dispenses altogether with the need to justify judicial power and dispense by assumption with the possibility of different legitimate answers. *Johnson* and *Craig* are the flip side: here there are strong textual claims to be honored. Justice Brennan's majority opinion in *Johnson* invoked a legal norm; the dissenters sought to particularize the subject in order to evade it. Just the opposite happened in *Craig*, where the majority increased the level of abstraction in order to evade a strictly legal claim: that whatever could be said about the accuracy of the verdict, it had been reached without *confrontation*. The majority in *Craig*, as it seems to me, sought to improve on rather than enforce the Sixth Amendment. *Harmelin* also is straightforward. To observe, as the

---

[88] Id at 29-30 (emphasis added). See also id at 66-77.

[89] See Bork, *Tempting* at 166-67 (cited in note 35); Easterbrook, *Approaches to Judicial Review* at 161 (cited in note 51); Kay, 82 Nw U L Rev at 248-50 (cited in note 51).

dissenters did in support of a general proportionality rule, that neither text nor history proves an argument *against* such a rule is to invert the theory of review, doing nothing at all to support a judicial role. It may be that a rule limited to barbaric modes of punishment will have limited contemporary effect, but it is not possible to make greater demands in the name of *law*.

Cases such as *Smith* are tougher. Neutrality between religion and secular affairs is at once a highly general rule and one that minimizes the judicial role. It is easy to see why a majority found it attractive. Yet free "exercise" implies more than free "belief": Michael McConnell makes a strong case that the drafters and ratifiers used this word to signify accommodation of religious practice.[90] Boosting the level of abstraction to achieve a neutrality rule produces the most modest claims of judicial power—maybe too modest, just as *Craig* denied judicial authority through this device. In *Croson* and *Metro Broadcasting*, greater abstraction (e.g., "make no use of race") reduces judicial *discretion* but increases judicial *power* relative to the other branches. It is the claim of judicial power that must be justified; although a reduction in judicial discretion is desirable, we do not get there unless the scope of authority has first been established. Again the level of generality may be excessive in relation to either textual or historical support.[91]

You will notice that I have omitted two lines of argument that appear over and over. One is that to settle on *any* approach to selecting the level of abstraction is to allow some hideous outcomes—capital punishment for the common cold and like abominations. Rules have borders; if there are borders people may take advantage; thus there should be no bright lines. The other sally is that settling on any one approach makes a fossil of the Constitution. As the world is changing, it would be regrettable to have governmental institutions strangled by a skeletal hand from the past.

Arguments of both flavors are common. Both are inconsistent with the premise of *Marbury*. They assert that the Constitution is not law—indeed, shouldn't be law. Maybe so, but what then is the justification of judicial power? Why is updating to be done by persons who cannot be removed from office and have been insulated from contemporary society? Having knocked out our legal system's premier justification, the proponents of these arguments need to

---

[90] McConnell, 103 Harv L Rev at 1488-90 (cited in note 31).

[91] I repeat the caveat from Section I. Determining the *right* answer in hard cases such as *Smith* and *Metro Broadcasting* would require a substantive investigation—one of the kind Professor McConnell has conducted and I have not.

provide a substitute and typically do not. It is hard to find judges willing to say in public that *Marbury* is wrong and that they have a different justification of the judicial role.

As soon as you distinguish judicial from political power, you have a short and satisfactory answer to the problem of the dead hand. As the drafting of the Constitution becomes remote judicial power is harder to justify (because it is harder to point to rules of law), but the ability of the political branches of the government to keep in touch with the times *increases*. All judges can do is intervene to *negate* a political choice. When they decline to do this, the ability of political society to keep up with the times is unimpeded. Congress gained plenary legislative powers not only from popular will (recall Madison's argument in Federalist No. 46) but also from judicial inability to identify a rule of law defining the limits of "commerce."

The terror of the slippery slope looms larger. Horsewhipping for double parking; zoning laws eliminating churches; freedom to use your business rival's trademark (if Johnson can burn the flag, why can't Wendy's erect golden arches?). Surely judges *must* be able to prevent such abuses; the need to do this counsels against any rule of adjudication. Even Justice Scalia, our leading textualist, does not resist this siren's song.[92] He should; the parade of horribles is nothing but an argument against rules and serves (if indulged) to undermine rather than strengthen the claim for judicial review.

Horribles have lurked in the background for a long time. Here is one from Madison's Federalist 10, perhaps the greatest document of political theory penned on this side of the Atlantic.

> The influence of factious leaders may kindle a flame within their particular States, but will be unable to spread a general conflagration through the other States. A religious sect may degenerate into a political faction in a part of the Confederacy; but the variety of sects dispersed over the entire face of it must secure the national councils against any danger from that source. A rage for paper money, for an abolition of debts, for an equal division of property, or for any other improper or wicked project, will be less apt to pervade the whole body of the Union than a particular member of it . . . .[93]

---

[92] Antonin Scalia, *Assorted Canards of Contemporary Legal Analysis*, 40 Case W Res L Rev 581, 590-93 (1989-90); *Harmelin*, 111 S Ct at 2697 n 11.

[93] Federalist 10 (Madison) in Wright, ed, *The Federalist* at 129, 136 (cited in note 47).

Madison tells us that paper money is wicked—but not to worry, the national government will be immune to its lure. It didn't work out that way, although the transition was not exactly smooth.[94]

Marbury does not contain an assertion along the lines of: "Why, if there were no judicial review we might end up with paper money; and as that is too horrible to contemplate . . . ." It is missing because it is no argument. At any instant some laws will be unthinkable. The jurisprudence of horribles is based on that fact. Yet the political climate changes; what is too horrible to contemplate in 1787 comes to pass during the Civil War. By the time the bottom of the slippery slope is reached, society no longer views the result as horrible. The exercise—whether it involves pointing a finger at paper money, or at the regulation of a farmer's baking wheat into bread, or at some rule that outrages contemporary thought—is no more than a truism. It gets its entire emotional punch by ignoring the possibility of cultural change.[95]

Hypothetical horribles start from the belief that a legislature has done what *no* reasonable person could want. Such a supposition is possible only if the political process has collapsed. If indeed the process has collapsed, only judicial review can prevent disaster. Once you introduce the possibility that the laws look horrible only because the writer has assumed away the possibility of cultural change, it is harder to justify the assumption that the law is a product of political collapse and correspondingly hard to justify tinkering with the level of abstraction *now*, for a *real* law, in order to maintain discretion to deal with a horror that may never come to pass (and, if it does, won't be viewed as horrible). It was the fear of horribles, coupled with Chief Justice Marshall's slogan that "the power to tax involves the power to destroy"[96] that led to an unjustifiably sweeping rule of tax immunities from which the Court is beating a retreat.[97] We should be able to learn from experience.

Arguments of this genus may have greater utility when the Court is addressing the anachronistic law—one that could never be passed today but that is kept in place by a dedicated interest

---

[94] Compare *Hepburn v Griswold*, 75 US (8 Wall) 603 (1870), with *The Legal Tender Cases*, 79 US (12 Wall) 457 (1871) (overruling *Hepburn*), and *Norman v Baltimore & Ohio RR*, 294 US 240 (1935) (the Gold Clause cases). See also David P. Currie, *The Constitution in the Supreme Court: The First Hundred Years, 1789-1888* 320-29 (Chicago, 1985).

[95] See Paul Gewirtz, *The Jurisprudence of Hypotheticals*, 32 J Legal Educ 120 (1982).

[96] *McCulloch*, 17 US at 431.

[97] See *Washington v United States*, 460 US 536 (1983), among many similar recent cases. *Garcia v San Antonio Metropolitan Transit Authority*, 469 US 528, 540-43 (1985), implies that the entire body of cases from *McCulloch* forward was misbegotten.

group despite the injuries it inflicts on a larger (but more diffuse) populace. I do not deny a modest role for what Henry Monaghan has called constitutional common law:[98] the "remand" of obsolete laws to the legislature, with the understanding that a contemporary legislative view prevails over the judges' assessment of the demands of modern society. The Court achieved something of the sort when *Furman v Georgia* effectively required states to start from scratch with capital punishment laws.[99] This echo of Justice Holmes's rejoinder to Chief Justice Marshall ("Not while this Court sits.")[100] is a far cry from a general power of superintendence lest laws that seem outrageous to judges commend themselves to the population.

IV.

My point in the end is simple. Meaning depends on the purpose to which we put it. The Constitution can mean one thing in a classroom and another in a courtroom. Constitutional principles may serve as moral or prudential arguments about how a community should conduct itself. Judges seek not enlightenment but right answers, the core meaning within which further debate is ruled out. That core will be smaller than the scope of all constitutional interests and proprieties. In the end, the power to countermand the decisions of other governmental actors and punish those who disagree depends on a theory of meaning that supposes the possibility of right answers.

So you can't view abstraction in the abstract. You must search for a level of generality simultaneously suited to the Constitution and to the judicial role. One that will be neither broad nor narrow all of the time, neither pro- nor con- state power. We must demand not that it conform to the reader's political theory, but that it be law.

---

[98] Henry P. Monaghan, *The Supreme Court, 1974 Term—Foreword: Constitutional Common Law*, 89 Harv L Rev 1 (1975).

[99] 408 US 238 (1972).

[100] *Panhandle Oil Co. v Mississippi*, 277 US 218, 223 (1928) (Holmes dissenting) ("The power to tax is not the power to destroy while this Court sits.").

THE CONCEPT OF UNENUMERATED RIGHTS

Unenumerated Rights: Whether and How
Roe Should be Overruled

Ronald Dworkin†

Judge Posner and I have been asked to debate the subject of unenumerated rights. I am at a disadvantage, because I think that the distinction between enumerated and unenumerated constitutional rights, a distinction presupposed by our assignment, is bogus. I shall explain why, but it would be unfair to end my contribution to the expected debate with that explanation. The topic "unenumerated rights" on a conference menu leads the audience to expect some discussion of abortion, the most violently debated constitutional issue of our era. So I shall try to explain how that constitutional issue should be resolved once the distinction between enumerated and unenumerated rights is safely shut up with other legal concepts dishonorably discharged for bad philosophy.

I. The Real Bill of Rights

We are celebrating the Bill of Rights, which we take to include the Civil War Amendments. I begin by asking you, in your imagination, to *read* that part of the Constitution. Some parts of the

---

† Professor of Law, New York University, and Professor of Jurisprudence and Fellow of University College, Oxford University. ©1992 by Ronald Dworkin. This Article is based on a much expanded version of remarks at *The Bill of Rights in the Welfare State: A Bicentennial Symposium*, held at The University of Chicago Law School on October 25-26, 1991. I would like to thank Arnand Agneshwar, Alice Hofheimer, Sharon Perley, and Richard Posner for very helpful information, comments and advice, and also to thank the Filomen D'Agostino and Max E. Greenberg Research Fund of New York University Law School.

Bill of Rights are very concrete, like the Third Amendment's prohibition against quartering troops in peacetime. Others are of medium abstraction, like the First Amendment's guarantees of freedom of speech, press, and religion. But key clauses are drafted in the most abstract possible terms of political morality. The Fourteenth Amendment, for example, commands "equal" protection of the laws, and also commands that neither life nor liberty nor property be taken without "due" process of law. That language might, in some contexts, seem wholly concerned with procedure—in no way restricting the laws government might enact and enforce, but only stipulating how it must enact and enforce whatever laws it does adopt. Legal history has rejected that narrow interpretation, however, and once we understand the constitutional provisions to be substantive as well as procedural, their scope is breathtaking. For then the Bill of Rights orders nothing less than that government treat everyone subject to its dominion with equal concern and respect, and that it not infringe their most basic freedoms, those liberties essential, as one prominent jurist put it, to the very idea of "ordered liberty."[1]

II. THE NATURAL READING OF THE BILL OF RIGHTS

On its most natural reading, then, the Bill of Rights sets out a network of principles, some extremely concrete, others more abstract, and some of near limitless abstraction. Taken together, these principles define a political ideal: they construct the constitutional skeleton of a society of citizens both equal and free. Notice three features of that striking architecture. First, this system of principle is comprehensive, because it commands both equal concern and basic liberty. In our political culture these are the two major sources of claims of individual right. It therefore seems unlikely that anyone who believes that free and equal citizens would be guaranteed a particular individual right will not also think that our Constitution already contains that right, unless constitutional history has decisively rejected it. That is an important fact about constitutional adjudication and argument, to which I shall return.

Second, since liberty and equality overlap in large part, each of the two major abstract articles of the Bill of Rights is *itself* comprehensive in that same way. Particular constitutional rights that follow from the best interpretation of the Equal Protection Clause, for example, will very likely also follow from the best interpreta-

---

[1] Justice Cardozo in *Palko v Connecticut*, 302 US 319, 325 (1937).

tion of the Due Process Clause. So (as Justice Stevens reminded us in the address which opened this conference)[2] the Supreme Court had no difficulty in finding that, although the Equal Protection Clause does not apply to the District of Columbia, racial school segregation in the District was nevertheless unconstitutional under the Due Process Clause of the Fifth Amendment, which does apply to it. Indeed, it is very likely that, even if there had been no First Amendment, American courts would long ago have found the freedoms of speech, press, and religion in the Fifth and Fourteenth Amendments' guarantees of basic liberty.

Third, the Bill of Rights therefore seems to give judges almost incredible power. Our legal culture insists that judges—and finally the justices of the Supreme Court—have the last word about the proper interpretation of the Constitution. Since the great clauses command simply that government show equal concern and respect for the basic liberties—without specifying in further detail what that means and requires—it falls to judges to declare what equal concern really does require and what the basic liberties really are. But that means that judges must answer intractable, controversial, and profound questions of political morality that philosophers, statesmen, and citizens have debated for many centuries, with no prospect of agreement. It means that the rest of us must accept the deliverances of a majority of the justices, whose insight into these great issues is not spectacularly special. That seems unfair, even frightening. Many people think that judges with that kind of power will impose liberal convictions on less-liberal majorities. But they are equally likely to impose conservative convictions on less-conservative majorities, as the Supreme Court did in *Lochner*, and is now doing again in, for example, its affirmative action decisions. The resentment most people feel about unelected judges having that kind of power is bipartisan.

III. Constitutional Revisionism

In any case, many academic constitutional theorists have for a long time thought that their main job is to demonstrate to themselves, the legal profession, and the public at large that the Constitution does not mean what it says—that it does not, properly understood, actually assign that extraordinary and apparently unfair power to judges. The revisionist strategy is a simple one. It denies

---

[2] Justice John Paul Stevens, *The Bill of Rights: A Century of Progress*, in this volume, 13, 20.

that the Bill of Rights has the structure I said was its natural interpretation. It aims to picture it differently, not as defining the skeleton of an overall conception of justice, but as only an antique list of the particular demands that a relatively few people long ago happened to think important. It hopes to turn the Bill of Rights from a constitutional charter into a document with the texture and tone of an insurance policy or a standard form commercial lease.

In one way this collective revisionist effort has been remarkably successful. It has achieved the Orwellian triumph, the political huckster's dream, of painting its opponents with its own shames and vices. It has persuaded almost everyone that turning the Constitution into an out-of-date list is really *protecting* that document, and that those who stubbornly read the Constitution to mean what it says are the actual inventors and usurpers. Even judges who accept the broad responsibility the Constitution imposes on them still adopt the misleading names their revisionist opponents assign them. They call themselves "activists," or "noninterpretivists," or champions of "unenumerated rights," who wish to go "outside" the "four corners" of the Constitution to decide cases on a "natural law" basis.

In that important political way, the massive effort to revise and narrow the Bill of Rights has been successful. But in every substantive way, it has failed—not because it has constructed coherent alternative interpretations with unattractive consequences, but because it has failed to construct any coherent alternative interpretations at all.

Part of the revisionist effort has not even attempted an alternative *interpretation*. I refer to what I call the "external" revisionist strategy, which does not propose an account of what the Constitution itself actually means, but rewrites it to make it more congenial to what the revisionists consider the best theory of democracy. In its rewritten version, the Constitution leaves as much power to government as is possible, consistent with genuine majority rule and with what the text of the Constitution uncontroversially forbids. Learned Hand held a version of this theory,[3] and John Hart Ely has provided its most elaborate form.[4] The external revisionist strategy plainly begs the question. "Democracy" is itself the name of an abstraction: there are many different conceptions of democracy, and political philosophers debate which is the most

---

[3] See, for example, Learned Hand, *The Bill of Rights* (Harvard, 1958).

[4] See John Hart Ely, *Democracy and Distrust: A Theory of Judicial Review* (Harvard, 1980).

attractive. The American conception of democracy is whatever form of government the Constitution, according to the best interpretation of that document, establishes. So it begs the question to hold that the Constitution should be amended to bring it closer to some supposedly purer form of democracy.[5]

For the most part, however, the revisionists have indeed tried to disguise their revisionism as only "better" interpretations of the actual Constitution. They argue that the natural interpretation I described—that the Constitution guarantees the rights required by the best conceptions of the political ideals of equal concern and basic liberty—is not in fact the most accurate interpretation. They say that that natural interpretation neglects some crucial *semantic* fact, some property of language or communication or linguistic interpretation which, once we grasp it, shows us that the abstract language of the great clauses does not mean what it seems to mean. Constitutional scholars have ransacked the cupboard of linguistic philosophy to find semantic constraints of that character and power. They found in that cupboard, for example, the important idea that what philosophers call the "speaker's meaning" of an utterance may differ from the meaning an audience would likely assign the utterance if it were ignorant of any special information about the speaker.

Some constitutional lawyers try to transform that point into a so-called "framers' intention" theory of constitutional interpretation. They argue that the great constitutional clauses should be understood, not to declare abstract moral requirements, as they do if read acontextually, but in the supposedly different and much less expansive sense which some presumed set of "framers" supposedly "intended."

That suggestion is self-destructive, however, as Robert Bork's unsuccessful attempt to defend it (largely by abandoning it) in his recent book shows.[6] We must take care to make a distinction on which the philosophical idea of speaker's meaning crucially depends: the distinction between what someone means to say and what he hopes or expects or believes will be the consequence for the law of his saying it. Many of the framers undoubtedly had dif-

---

[5] See Ronald Dworkin, *A Matter of Principle* ch 2 (Harvard, 1985); Ronald Dworkin, *Law's Empire* ch 10 (Harvard, 1986); and Ronald Dworkin, *Equality, Democracy and the Constitution: We the People in Court*, 28 Alberta L Rev 324 (1990).

[6] See Robert H. Bork, *The Tempting of America: The Political Seduction of the Law* (Free Press, 1990) (especially chapters 7, 8, and 13). See also Ronald Dworkin, *Bork's Jurisprudence*, 57 U Chi L Rev 657, 663-74 (1990), for my review of Bork's book.

ferent beliefs from mine about what equality or due process requires, just as my beliefs about that differ from yours. They
thought that their abstract commands about equality and due process had different legal implications for concrete cases from the
implications you or I think those abstract commands have. But it
does not follow that they meant to *say* anything different from
what you or I would mean to say if we used the same words they
did. We would normally use those words to say, not that government is forbidden to act contrary to the speakers' own conceptions
of equality and justice, but that it is forbidden to act contrary to
the soundest conception of those virtues. All the evidence (and
common sense) suggests that that is what they meant to say as
well: they meant to use abstract words in their normal abstract
sense. If so, then strict attention to speakers' meaning only reinforces the broad judicial responsibility that the revisionists hope to
curtail.

IV. ENUMERATED AND UNENUMERATED RIGHTS

The distinction I am supposed to be discussing, between enumerated and unenumerated rights, is only another misunderstood
semantic device. Constitutional lawyers use "unenumerated rights"
as a collective name for a particular set of recognized or controversial constitutional rights, including the right of travel; the right of
association; and the right to privacy from which the right to an
abortion, if there is such a right, derives. They regard this classification as marking an important structural distinction, as the terms
"enumerated" and "unenumerated" obviously suggest. If the Bill
of Rights only enumerates *some* of the rights necessary to a society
of equal concern and basic liberty, and leaves other such rights unmentioned, then judges arguably have only the power to enforce
the rights actually enumerated.

Some lawyers accept the distinction, but deny the inference
about judicial power. They say that judges *do* have the power to
enforce unenumerated rights, and claim that the Court has often
done so in the past. But lawyers who argue in this way have conceded a very great deal to their opponents who deny that judges
should have this kind of power. Their opponents are then able to
say that judges have no *authority* to add to the enumerated. If we
allow judges to roam at will beyond the "four corners" of the Constitution, they add, we abandon all hope of limiting judicial power.
That is the argument made by Justice White in *Bowers v Hardwick*, for example, to explain why the Court should not recognize a

right of homosexual sodomy.[7] He said that judge-made constitutional law was particularly suspect when it had "little or no cognizable roots in the language or design of the Constitution";[8] and he
presumably had in mind the putative right of abortion, as well as
that of homosexual sodomy.

So the distinction between enumerated and unenumerated
rights is widely understood to pose an important constitutional issue: the question whether and when courts have authority to enforce rights not actually enumerated in the Constitution as genuine
constitutional rights. I find the question unintelligible, however, as
I said at the outset, because the presumed distinction makes no
sense. The distinction between what is on some list and what is not
is of course genuine and often very important. An ordinance might
declare, for example, that it is forbidden to take guns, knives, or
explosives in hand luggage on an airplane. Suppose airport officials
interpreted that ordinance to exclude canisters of tear gas as well,
on the ground that the general structure of the ordinance, and the
obvious intention behind it, prohibits all weapons that might be
taken aboard and used in hijacks or terrorism. We would be right
to say that gas was not on the list of what was banned, and that it
is a legitimate question whether officials are entitled to add
"unenumerated" weapons to the list. But the distinction between
officials excluding pistols, switch-blades and hand-grenades on the
one hand, and tear gas on the other, depends upon a semantic assumption: that tear gas falls within what philosophers call the *reference* of neither "guns" nor "knives" nor "explosives."

No comparable assumption can explain the supposed distinction between enumerated and unenumerated constitutional rights.
The Bill of Rights, as I said, consists of broad and abstract principles of political morality, which together encompass, in exceptionally abstract form, all the dimensions of political morality that in
our political culture can ground an individual constitutional right.
The key issue in applying these abstract principles to particular
political controversies is not one of reference but of *interpretation*,
which is very different.

Consider the following three constitutional arguments, each of
which is very controversial. The first argues that the Equal Protection Clause creates a right of equal concern and respect, from
which it follows that women have a right against gender-based discriminations unless such discriminations are required by important

---

[7] 478 US 186 (1986).
[8] Id at 193-94.

state interests. The second argues that the First Amendment grants a right of symbolic protest, from which it follows that individuals have a right to burn the American flag. The third argues that the Due Process Clause protects the basic freedoms central to the very concept of "ordered liberty," including the right of privacy, from which it follows that women have a constitutional right to abortion. By convention, the first two are arguments (good or bad) for enumerated rights: each claims that some right—the right against gender discrimination or the right to burn the flag—is an instance of some more general right set out, in suitably abstract form, in the text of the Constitution. The third argument, on the other hand, is thought to be different and more suspect, because it is thought to be an argument for an unenumerated right. The right it claims—the right to an abortion—is thought to bear a more tenuous or distant relationship to the language of the Constitution. It is said to be at best implied by, rather than stated in, that language.

But the distinction cannot be sustained. Each of the three arguments is interpretive in a way that excludes the kind of semantic constraints the distinction assumes. No one thinks that it follows just from the meaning of the words "freedom of speech" either that people are free to burn flags, or that they are not. No one thinks it follows just from the meaning of the words "equal protection" that laws excluding women from certain jobs are unconstitutional, or that they are not. In neither case does the result follow from the meanings of words in the way it follows from the meaning of "gun" that it refers to pistols but not to canisters of gas. Nor are the three arguments different in how they are interpretive. Each conclusion (if sound) follows, not from some historical hope or belief or intention of a "framer," but because the political principle that supports that conclusion best accounts for the general structure and history of constitutional law. Someone who thinks that this manner of constitutional argument is inappropriate—who thinks, for example, that framers' expectations should play a more decisive role than this view of constitutional argument allows—will have that reservation about all three arguments, not distinctly about the third. If he thinks that the third argument is wrong, because he abhors, for example, the idea of substantive due process, then he will reject it, but because it is wrong, not because the right it claims would be an unenumerated one.

In his reply to my remarks, Judge Posner constructs a Socratic dialogue in which the straight man is brought to see that "speech" in the First Amendment includes flag burning, though Posner concedes that the argument might have gone the other way.[9] He does not construct a parallel dialogue in which another dupe is made to agree that gender is a suspect category under the Equal Protection Clause, though it is easy to see how that second dialogue might go. And it would be equally easy to construct a third dialogue ending with a straight man's startled recognition that abortion is, after all, a basic liberty protected by the Due Process Clause. Posner does suggest that this argument might take us "further" from the text. But the metaphor of distance is wholly opaque in this context: it means or suggests nothing. Posner cannot mean, for example, that a right to abortion is further away from the Constitution's language than a right against gender-discrimination is, in the sense that "tear gas" is further from the meaning of "gun" than "pistol" is. "Pistol" is closer because "gun" refers to a pistol and does not refer to tear gas. But since neither a right to abortion nor a right against gender-discrimination follow from the meanings of textual words, neither can be closer to or further from the text than the other in that sense.

It is sometimes said that the Constitution does not "mention" a right of travel, or of association, or of privacy, as if that fact explained why these rights are usefully classified as unenumerated. But the Constitution does not "mention" flag burning or gender discrimination either. The right to burn a flag and the right against gender-discrimination are supported by the best interpretation of a more general or abstract right that is "mentioned." It is true that the phrase "right to privacy" is itself more abstract than the phrase "right to burn a flag as protest," and that the former phrase therefore figures more in the conversation and writing of constitutional scholars than the latter. But these facts reflect accidents (or highly contingent features) of usage. Scholars have found it useful to develop a name of middling abstraction—the right of privacy—to describe a stage in the derivation of particular concrete rights from the even more abstract rights named in the constitutional text. But it hardly follows that those concrete rights—including the right to abortion—are more remote from their textual beginnings than are concrete rights—such as the right to burn a flag—that are derived by arguments that do not employ names for rights of middling abstraction. Constitutional lawyers might well have adopted the middling terms "right of symbolic protest" or "right of gender equality" in the way they have

---

[9] Richard A. Posner, *Legal Reasoning From the Top Down and From the Bottom Up: The Question of Unenumerated Constitutional Rights*, in this volume, 433, 437-38.

adopted "right of privacy." It is hardly a deep fact of constitutional structure that they have not.

I must be clear. I am not arguing that the Supreme Court
should enforce unenumerated as well as enumerated constitutional
rights, any more than I meant to argue, in my remarks about
speaker's meaning, that the Court is right to ignore or modify what
the framers said. I mean that the distinction between enumerated
and unenumerated rights, as it is commonly used in constitutional
theory, makes no sense, because it confuses reference with
interpretation.

I should say—to complete this exercise in provocation—that I
take much the same view of a variety of other distinctions popular
among constitutional lawyers, including those Posner discusses in
his reply. He distinguishes between what he calls a "top-down"
and a "bottom-up" method of legal reasoning, and also between a
"clause-by-clause" and a "holistic" approach. He apparently regards the second of these distinctions as more important than the
first. Though he says he agrees with me that "there isn't much to
bottom-up reasoning,"[10] he thinks that I am wrong to criticize
Bork's "clause-by-clause" approach,[11] and also that I would do better to make my own arguments about abortion more explicitly
"holistic."[12]

Neither of the two distinctions makes any sense, however. We
cannot understand a particular precedent, for example, except by
construing that decision as part of a more general enterprise, and
any such constructive interpretation must, as I argued at length in
Law's Empire, engage the kind of theoretical hypothesis characteristic of what Posner calls top-down reasoning.[13] So bottom-up reasoning is automatically top-down reasoning as well. The same
point also erodes the distinction between clause-by-clause and holistic constitutional interpretation. Legal interpretation is *inherently* holistic, even when the apparent target of interpretation is a

---

[10] Id at 435.

[11] Id at 439-40. Posner objects to my claim that Bork has no coherent constitutional
philosophy, that Bork has theories of particular clauses, but not of the Constitution as a
whole. But Bork does not, as Posner says he does, distrust general theory. On the contrary,
Bork claims a perfectly general, comprehensive, constitutional theory. He claims that all of
the Constitution, not just particular clauses, are exhausted by the intentions of the Framers,
and he argues for that global theory by appealing to a single, global theory of democracy
and a single, global account of what law, by its very nature, is like. Bork does not have a
coherent constitutional philosophy, as I argued in *Bork's Jurisprudence*, 57 U Chi L Rev
657 (cited in note 6). But that is not because he does not claim one.

[12] Posner, in this volume, 444-45 (cited in note 9).

[13] Dworkin, *Law's Empire* (cited in note 5). See particularly id at 65-68.

single sentence or even a single clause rather than a document. Any interpreter must accept interpretive constraints—assumptions about what makes one interpretation better than another—and any plausible set of constraints includes a requirement of coherence. An interpretation of the Bill of Rights which claims that a moral principle embedded in one clause is actually rejected by another is an example not of pragmatist flexibility, but of hypocrisy.

V. Law's Integrity

Where do we stand? The most natural interpretation of the Bill of Rights seems, as I said, to give judges great and frightening power. It is understandable that constitutional lawyers and teachers should strive to tame the Bill of Rights, to read it in a less frightening way, to change it from a systematic abstract conception of justice to a list of discrete clauses related to one another through pedigree rather than principle. These efforts fail, however, and are bound to fail, because the text and history of the Bill of Rights will not accept that transformation. They are bound to fail, moreover, in a paradoxical and disastrous way. Because the semantic distinctions on which the efforts are based have no sense as they are used, they are powerless themselves to define any particular set of constitutional rights. As the recent history of the Court amply demonstrates, a judge who claims to rely on speaker's meaning, "enumeration," or a preference for clause-by-clause interpretation must actually choose which constitutional rights to enforce on grounds that have nothing to do with these semantic devices, but which are hidden from view by his appeal to them. The search for limits on judicial power ends by allowing judges the undisciplined power of the arbitrary.

Posner's reply acknowledges that fact, with typical candor. He says that the semantic devices beloved of conservative lawyers "could end up with a document that gave answers only to questions that no one was asking any longer,"[14] and that judges who say they are constrained by those useless devices will necessarily decide according to their own "personal values,"[15]—according, he says, to what makes them "puke."[16] His own personal values en-

---

[14] Posner, in this volume, 446 (cited in note 9).

[15] Id at 449.

[16] Id at 447. Posner takes this phrase—which gives new meaning to the old realist thesis that the law is only what the judge had for breakfast—from Holmes. I should say that though I understand Posner's hagiographic admiration for that jurist, I do not share it. Holmes wrote like a dream. His personal conversion from the view that the First Amend-

dorse "stretching" the Due Process Clause to yield *Griswold*, and, if I read correctly between the lines, *Roe v Wade* as well. But he knows that other judges have stronger stomachs about society dictating sexual morality: their puke tests will flunk affirmative action programs instead.[17] The idea that the Constitution cannot mean what it says ends in the unwelcome conclusion that it means nothing at all.

What is to be done? We can finally, after the 200 years we celebrate in this symposium, grow up and begin to take our actual Constitution seriously, as those many nations now hoping to imitate us have already done. We can accept that our Constitution commands, as a matter of fundamental law, that our judges do their best collectively to construct, re-inspect and revise, generation by generation, the skeleton of liberal equal concern that the great clauses, in their majestic abstraction, demand. We will then abandon the pointless search for mechanical or semantic constraints, and seek genuine constraints in the only place where they can actually be found: in good argument. We will accept that honest lawyers and judges and scholars will inevitably disagree, sometimes profoundly, about what equal concern requires, and about which rights are central and which only peripheral to liberty.

We will then acknowledge, in the political process of nomination and confirmation of federal judges, what is already evident to anyone who looks: that constitutional adjudicators cannot be neutral about these great questions, and that the Senate must decline to confirm nominees whose convictions are too idiosyncratic, or who refuse honestly to disclose what their convictions are. The second stage of the Thomas confirmation hearings was, as most people now agree, physically revolting. But the first stage was intellectually revolting, because candidate and senators conspired to pretend that philosophy had nothing to do with judging, that a nominee who said he had abandoned convictions the way a runner sheds clothing was fit for the office he sought.[18]

---

ment must be limited to a Blackstonian condemnation of prior restraint to the radically different view that it must be understood as a much more abstract and general principle, was an epochal event in American constitutional history. But most of his gorgeous epigrams were the vivid skins of only very lazy thoughts, and his philosophical pretensions, almost entirely in service of an unsophisticated, deeply cynical form of skepticism, were embarrassing—as I believe the metaphysical observations Posner includes in his own new collection of Holmes's writings demonstrate. See Richard A. Posner, *Introduction,* in Richard A. Posner, ed. *The Essential Holmes* xvii-xx (Chicago, 1992).

[17] I discuss Posner's own recommendations in note 22.

[18] Ronald Dworkin, *Justice for Clarence Thomas,* NY Rev Books 41 (Nov 7, 1991).

The constitutional process of nomination and confirmation is an important part of the system of checks through which the actual Constitution disciplines the striking judicial power it declares. The main engines of discipline are intellectual rather than political, however, and the academic branch of the profession has a responsibility to protect that intellectual discipline, which is now threatened from several directions. Of course, we cannot find a formula which will guarantee that judges will all reach the same answer in complex or novel or crucial constitutional cases. No formula can protect us from a *Lochner*, which Posner tells us stinks, or from a *Bowers*. The stench of those cases does not lie in any jurisdictional vice or judicial overreaching. After a near century of treating *Lochner* as a whipping-boy, no one has produced a sound mechanical test that it fails. The vice of bad decisions is bad argument and bad conviction; all we can do about those bad decisions is to point out how and where the arguments are bad. Nor should we waste any more time on the silly indulgence of American legal academic life: the philosophically juvenile claim that, since no such formula exists, no one conception of constitutional equality and liberty is any better than another, and adjudication is only power or visceral response.[19] We must insist, instead, on a principle of genuine power: the idea, instinct in the concept of law itself, that whatever their views of justice and fairness, judges must also accept an independent and superior constraint of *integrity*.[20]

Integrity in law has several dimensions. First, it insists that judicial decision be a matter of principle, not compromise or strategy or political accommodation. That apparent banality is often ignored: The Supreme Court's present position on the politically sensitive issue of affirmative action, for example, cannot be justified on any coherent set of principles, however conservative or unappealing.[21] Second, integrity holds vertically: a judge who claims a particular right of liberty as fundamental must show that his claim is consistent with the bulk of precedent, and with the

---

[19] See Ronald Dworkin, *Pragmatism, Right Answers and True Banality*, in Michael Brint, ed, *Pragmatism and Law* (forthcoming 1992). See Posner, in this volume, 447 (cited in note 9).

[20] I discuss integrity at considerable length in *Law's Empire* at ch 7 (cited in note 5).

[21] I believe that Professor Fried unwittingly demonstrated this incoherence in defending the position in his recent book. See Charles Fried, *Order and Law: Arguing the Reagan Revolution—A Firsthand Account* (Simon & Schuster, 1991), and my review of this book in Ronald Dworkin, *The Reagan Revolution and the Supreme Court*, NY Rev Books 23 (Jul 18, 1991). See also Fried's letter to the editor and my letter in reply, in NY Rev Books 65 (Aug 15, 1991).

main structures of our constitutional arrangement. Third, integrity holds horizontally: a judge who adopts a principle must give full weight to that principle in other cases he decides or endorses.

Of course, not even the most scrupulous attention to integrity, by all our judges in all our courts, will produce uniform judicial decisions, or guarantee decisions you approve of, or protect you from those you hate. Nothing can do that. The point of integrity is principle, not uniformity: We are governed not by a list but by an ideal, and controversy is therefore at the heart of our story. We are envied for our constitutional adventure, and increasingly imitated, throughout the democratic world: in Delhi and Strasbourg and Ottawa, even, perhaps, in the Palace of Westminster, and perhaps tomorrow or the day after, in Moscow and Johannesburg. In all those places people seem ready to accept the risk and high promise of government by ideal, a form of government we created in the document we celebrate. We have never fully trusted that form of government. But unless we abandon it altogether, which we will not do, we should stop pretending that it is not the form of government we have. The energy of our best academic lawyers would be better spent in making, testing, and evaluating different conceptions of liberal equality, to see which conception best fits our own history and practice. They should try to guide and constrain our judges by criticism, argument, and example. That is the only way to honor our great constitutional creation, to help it prosper.[22]

---

[22] Posner describes my account of integrity-based constitutional reasoning as "holistic" and "top-down." He says it is "too ambitious, too risky, too contentious." Posner, in this volume, 446 (cited in note 9). He says that when judges are called upon to interpret the great abstract moral clauses of the Constitution they should react as their "conscience" demands: they should cite the abstract moral language of these clauses to strike down only what they instinctively find "terribly unjust." Id at 447. He would not require a judge to provide much, if anything, by way of a principled explanation of how or why he believes a law unjust, or to aim at consistency of principle even himself, from one day to the next, let alone with decisions other judges have made on other days. His views, as always, are striking and powerful. But how can he think that advice less "risky," or less likely to produce "contentious" decisions, than the more familiar advice that judges should at least do their best, as their time and talent allows, to discipline their initial reactions by accepting those responsibilities?

Is Posner right, at least, that his proposals are less "ambitious" because less "holistic?" He says judges should declare statutes unconstitutional, on moral grounds, only when there is a "compelling practical case" for doing so. Id at 447. The word "practical" is a familiar obscuring device in pragmatist philosophy: it is meant somehow to suggest, with no further argument, that moral decisions can be based not on "reason" but on more hard-headed sounding "experience" in the shape of obvious social needs. But Posner's extended discussion of *Griswold* shows that Connecticut's ban on contraceptives was not impractical but unjust. That will be true in almost every case in which a Posnerian judge's "can't helps" are in play: his decision will engage his moral convictions, not his practical good sense. Posner

VI.   Abortion: What is the Argument About?

In the discussion of abortion that I promised, I shall try to illustrate the role that integrity should play in legal argument. I begin by briefly summarizing claims about the constitutional status of that issue that I have argued elsewhere,[23] and will argue in much more detail in a book about abortion and euthanasia now in manuscript.[24] A woman, I assume, has a constitutionally protected right to control the use of her own body. (I shall later consider the constitutional source of that right.) Therefore a pregnant woman has a right to an abortion unless her state's government has some legitimate and important reason for prohibiting it. Many people think governments do have such a reason, and would have no difficulty in saying what it is.

A state must make abortion a crime, they say, in order to protect human life. That is indeed what many state officials have said, in preambles to regulatory statutes, in legal briefs and in political rhetoric. That is, moreover, what the Supreme Court justices who dissented in *Roe v Wade*, or who later announced their view that it is wrong, say a state's reason for forbidding abortion is. And even justices and lawyers who support that decision say something similar. In his opinion for the Court in *Roe v Wade*, Blackmun recognized that a state had an interest in protecting what he called "fetal life."[25] He said that a state's interest in protecting life did not

---

insists, however, that his moral convictions are discrete "instincts," not the product of some comprehensive theory of the entire Constitution. But the distinction is mysterious in this context, because any judge's opinions about whether a ban on contraception is profoundly unjust, or maximum-hours legislation deeply unfair, or affirmative action an insult to the very idea of equal citizenship, will reflect and be drawn from much more general opinions and attitudes that will also fix his reactions to other legislation he tests "viscerally" against other clauses, at least if he is acting in moral good faith on any of these occasions. If any judge's immediate reaction really was one off—if it really was just a response to one set of facts with no implications for others—it would not be a response of *conscience* at all, but only a whim or a tic.

So Posner's contrast between clause-by-clause and holistic adjudication seems wildly overdrawn. He uses the reason-passion vocabulary of eighteenth-century philosophical psychology. But he has in mind, not an epistemological distinction between different mental faculties judges might use, but a contrast between two views of judicial responsibility. He rejects integrity, which insists that judges do the best they can to exhibit a principled basis for their decisions, in favor of a different standard that encourages them to keep that basis dark. I do not claim, in the discussion of abortion that follows, that integrity produces only one plausible view, or that it can end controversy. But I shall claim, at several points, that integrity rules out some accommodations that politics or weariness or even laziness might recommend, accommodations I fear Posner's unbuttoned license would guarantee.

[23] See Ronald Dworkin, *The Great Abortion Case*, NY Rev Books 49 (Jun 29, 1989).
[24] This book, to be published by Alfred Knopf in 1993, is not yet titled.
[25] 410 US 113, 163 (1973).

give it a compelling reason for prohibiting abortion until the third
trimester, but he conceded that it did have that interest throughout pregnancy.[26] The premise on which so many people rely is,
however, dangerously ambiguous, because there are two very different aims or purposes a state might have, each of which might be
described as protecting human life. A good part of the confusion
that surrounds both the legal and the moral argument about abortion is the result of ignoring that ambiguity. Consider the difference between two kinds of reasons a government might have for
prohibiting murder within its territory. First, government has a responsibility to protect the rights and interests of its citizens, and
chief among these, for most people, is an interest in staying alive
and a right not to be killed. I shall call this a derivative reason for
prohibiting murder, because it presupposes and derives from individual rights and interests. Government sometimes claims, second,
a very different kind of reason for prohibiting murder. It sometimes claims a responsibility not just to protect the interests and
rights of its citizens, but to protect human life as an objective or
intrinsic good, a value in itself, quite apart from its value to the
person whose life it is or to anyone else. I shall call this responsibility a detached one, because it is independent of, rather than a
derivative of, particular people's rights and interests.

If government does have a detached responsibility to protect
the objective, intrinsic value of life, then its laws against murder
serve both its derivative and detached responsibility at once. They
protect the rights and interests of particular victims, and they also
recognize and respect the intrinsic value of human life. In some
cases, however, the two supposed responsibilities might conflict:
when someone wishes to kill himself because he is in terrible pain
that doctors cannot relieve, for example, or when relatives wish to
terminate the mechanical life support of someone who is perma-
nently unconscious. In such cases, suicide or terminating life support might be in the best interests of the person whose life ends, as
he or his relatives think it is. These acts nevertheless seem wrong
to many people, because they think that any deliberate killing, or
ever allowing someone to die who might be kept alive longer, is an
insult to the intrinsic value of human life. It makes a great difference, in such cases, whether a government's legitimate reasons for
protecting human life are limited to its derivative concern, or
whether they include a detached concern as well. If the latter, then

---

[26] Id at 162-64.

government is entitled to forbid people from ending their lives, even when they rightly think they would be better off dead.

We have identified two different claims a state that proposes to forbid abortion in order to protect human life might be making: a derivative claim and a detached claim. The derivative claim presupposes that a fetus already has rights and interests. The detached claim does not, though it does presuppose that the intrinsic value of human life is already at stake in a fetus's life. You will notice that I did not describe either of these claims as claims about when human life begins, or about whether a fetus is a "person," because those runic phrases perpetuate rather than dissolve the ambiguity I described.

Though scientists disagree about exactly when the life of any animal begins, it seems undeniable that in the ordinary case a fetus is a single living creature by the time it has become implanted in a womb, and that it is human in the sense that it is a member of the animal species *Homo sapiens*. It is, in that sense, a human organism whose life has begun. It does not follow that it also has rights and interests of the kind that government might have a derivative responsibility to protect. Nor that it already embodies the intrinsic value of a human life that a government might claim a detached responsibility to guard. But when people say that a fetus is already a living human being, they often mean to make either or both of these further claims.

"Person" is an even more ambiguous term. We sometimes use it just as a description (in which use it is more or less synonymous with human being) and sometimes as a term of moral classification, to suggest that the creatures so described have a special moral standing or importance that marks them out from other species. So someone who said that a just-conceived fetus is already a person might simply mean that it is a member of the human—rather than some other animal—species. Or he might mean, not just that a fetus is alive and human, but that it already has that special kind of moral importance. But even the latter claim is ambiguous in the way I described. It might mean that a fetus is already a creature with the interests and moral rights we take persons, as distinct from other creatures, to have. Or it might mean that a fetus is already a creature whose life has the intrinsic moral significance the life of any person has. So the clarity of the public debate is not improved by the prominence of the questions "Is a fetus a person?" or "When does human life begin?" We do better to avoid that language so far as we can. I suggest that we consider, instead, whether states can justify anti-abortion legislation on one of the two grounds—derivative or detached—that I described.

Most people think that the great constitutional debate about abortion in America is obviously and entirely about a state's derivative grounds. They think the argument is about whether a fetus is a person in the sense in which that means having a right to life. That is why one side claims, and the other denies, that abortion is murder. (Some might add that the detached ground I described is too mysterious or metaphysical even to make sense, let alone to provide a plausible ground for anti-abortion legislation.) Not just the political argument, but the legal and academic discussion as well, seems to assume that view of the controversy. Lawyers and philosophers discuss whether a fetus is a person with rights. They speculate about whether abortion is morally permissible even if a fetus does have a right to life. But they almost all assume that if it does not, then there is no moral objection even to consider.

In the following two sections I shall assess the constitutional argument understood in that familiar and popular way. I shall interpret the claim that states have a responsibility to protect life to mean that they have a derivative responsibility to protect the right to life of a fetus. I shall argue, however, that if we do understand the dispute that way, then the constitutional argument is a relatively simple one. On that basis, *Roe* was not only correct but obviously correct, and its many critics are obviously wrong. I conclude that the constitutional debate about abortion is actually *not* about whether a fetus has rights and interests. It must be understood, if at all, as about the different claim I just conceded some people may find mysterious: that a state can legitimately claim a detached responsibility to protect the intrinsic value of human life.

VII. Is a Fetus a Constitutional Person?

The national Constitution defines what we might call the constitutional population. It stipulates who has constitutional rights that government must respect and enforce, and therefore whose rights government must take into account in curtailing or limiting the scope of other people's constitutional rights in cases of conflict. States would of course have a derivative reason for forbidding abortion if the Constitution designated a fetus as a constitutional person, that is, as a creature with constitutional rights competitive with those of a pregnant woman. Our analysis must therefore begin with a crucial threshold question. Is a fetus a constitutional person? In *Roe v Wade*, the Supreme Court answered that question in the only way it could: in the negative. If a fetus is a constitutional person, then states not only *may* forbid abortion but, at least in some circumstances, *must* do so. No justice or prominent politician has even advanced that claim.

It is true, as a number of legal scholars have pointed out, that the law does not generally require people to make any sacrifice at all to save the life of another person who needs their aid. A person ordinarily has no legal duty to save a stranger from drowning even if he can do so at no risk to himself and with minimal effort.[27] But abortion normally requires a physical attack on a fetus, not just a failure to come to its aid. And in any case parents are invariably made an exception to the general doctrine. Parents have a legal duty to care for their children; if a fetus is a person from conception, a state would discriminate between infants and fetuses without any justification if it allowed abortion but did not permit killing infants or abandoning them in circumstances when they would inevitably die.[28] The physical and emotional and economic burdens of pregnancy are intense, but so are the parallel burdens of parenthood.

We may safely assume, then, that the national Constitution does not declare a fetus to be a constitutional person whose rights may be competitive with the constitutional rights of a pregnant woman. Does this leave a state free to decide that a fetus shall have that status within its borders? If so, then *Roe v Wade* could safely be reversed without the politically impossible implication that states were required to prohibit abortion. The Supreme Court could then say that while some states have chosen to declare fe-

---

[27] These scholars argue that for that reason anti-abortion laws are unconstitutional even if a fetus is considered a person, and they would certainly reject my much stronger claim that in that event many laws permitting abortion would be unconstitutional. The legal arguments rely on a famous and influential article about the morality of abortion by Judith Jarvis Thompson: *A Defense of Abortion*, 1 Phil & Pub Aff 47 (1971). The legal arguments applying Thompson's views to constitutional law are best and most persuasively presented in Donald H. Regan, *Rewriting* Roe v. Wade, 77 Mich L Rev 1569 (1979). Thompson does not argue that every pregnant woman has a right to an abortion, even if a fetus is a person, but only that some do, and she recognizes that a woman who voluntarily risks pregnancy may not have such a right. In any case, her arguments assume that a pregnant woman has no more moral obligations to a fetus she is carrying, even if that fetus is a person with rights and therefore her son or daughter, than anyone has to a stranger—to a famous violinist a woman might find herself connected to for nine months because he needs the use of her kidneys for that period in order to live, for example.

[28] In the article cited in the preceding note, Regan questions the analogy between abortion and infanticide on the ground that parents have the option of arranging an adoption for their child. Regan, 77 Mich L Rev at 1597 (cited in note 27). But that is not inevitably true: minority infants, in particular, may not be able to find adoptive homes, and their parents are not permitted to kill them, or abandon them in circumstances that will inevitably lead to their death, whenever they can in fact make no alternative arrangement.

tuses persons within their jurisdiction, other states need not make the same decision.

There is no doubt that a state can protect the life of a fetus in a variety of ways. A state can make it murder for a third-party intentionally to kill a fetus, as Illinois has done, for example, or "feticide" for anyone willfully to kill a quickened fetus by an injury that would be murder if it resulted in the death of the mother, as Georgia has. These laws violate no constitutional rights, because no one has a constitutional right to injure with impunity.[29] Laws designed to protect fetuses may be drafted in language declaring or suggesting that a fetus is a person, or that human life begins at conception. The Illinois abortion statute begins, for example, by declaring that a fetus is a person from the moment of conception.[30] There can be no constitutional objection to such language, so long as the law does not purport to curtail constitutional rights. The Illinois statute makes plain, for example, that it does not intend to challenge or modify *Roe v Wade* so long as that decision remains in force.[31]

So qualified, a declaration that a fetus is a person raises no more constitutional difficulties than states raise when they declare, as every state has, that corporations are legal persons and enjoy many of the rights real people do, including the right to own property and the right to sue. States declare that corporations are persons as a shorthand way of describing a complex network of rights and duties that it would be impossible to describe in any other way, not as a means of curtailing or diminishing constitutional rights that real people would otherwise have.

The suggestion that states are free to declare a fetus a person, and thereby justify outlawing abortion, is a very different matter, however. That suggestion assumes that a state can curtail some persons' constitutional rights by adding new persons to the constitutional population. The constitutional rights of one citizen are of course very much affected by who or what else also has constitutional rights, because the rights of others may compete or conflict with his. So any power to increase the constitutional population by

---

[29] It is a separate question whether a state would violate the Eighth Amendment if it punished feticide with the death penalty. Though Illinois does use the death penalty, the statute making the killing of a fetus murder rules out that penalty for that crime. Homicide of an Unborn Child, Ill Rev Stat ch 38, ¶ 9-1.2(d) (1989).

[30] Abortion Law of 1975, id at ch 38, ¶ 81-21(1).

[31] Id.

unilateral decision would be, in effect, a power to decrease rights the national Constitution grants to others.

If a state could not only create corporations as legal persons, but endow each of those corporations with a vote, it could impair the constitutional right of ordinary people to vote, because the corporations' votes would dilute theirs. If a state could declare trees to be persons with a constitutional right to life, it could prohibit publishing newspapers or books in spite of the First Amendment's guarantee of free speech, which could not be understood as a license to kill. If a state could declare the higher apes to be persons whose rights were competitive with the constitutional rights of others, it could prohibit its citizens from taking life-saving medicines first tested on those animals. Once we understand that the suggestion we are considering has that implication, we must reject it. If a fetus is not part of the constitutional population, under the national constitutional arrangement, then states have no power to overrule that national arrangement by themselves declaring that fetuses have rights competitive with the constitutional rights of pregnant women.

I am uncertain how far Posner disagrees with that conclusion. He says that states can indeed create new persons. But he adds that it remains an open question how far they can treat these new persons' interests as if they were the interests of real people. This leaves mysterious what he thinks creating a new person amounts to. Perhaps he means only to agree with me that though a state can create persons for a variety of purposes, it cannot thereby acquire a power to abridge constitutional rights that it would not otherwise have had.

That position would be consistent with the examples he offers. He says, for example, that states can create property and liberty in ways that affect people's procedural rights under the Due Process Clause.[32] These are not, however, powers to decrease constitutional rights by adding competing rights-holders to the constitutional scheme. They are powers to create new rights under state law that, once created, satisfy standing conditions for constitutional protection without decreasing the constitutional rights of others. He also says that states can decide whether "death means brain death" or "a stopped heart"[33] and that it follows that they can "decide when life begins."[34] A state can certainly decide when life begins and

---

[32] Posner, in this volume, 444 (cited in note 9).
[33] Id.
[34] Id.

ends for any number of reasons, as I said a moment ago. It can fix the moment of death for purposes of the law of inheritance, for example, just as it can declare that life begins before birth in order to allow people to inherit through a fetus. But it cannot change constitutional rights by its decisions about when life begins or death happens. It cannot escape its constitutional responsibilities to death-row prisoners by declaring them already dead, or improve its congressional representation by declaring deceased citizens still alive for that purpose. I cannot think of any significant constitutional rights that would be curtailed by treating someone as dead when his brain was dead, however. So none of Posner's examples suggest that he really accepts the position I reject.

Nor, I dare say, do many of even the strongest opponents of *Roe v Wade* really accept it, because it is inconsistent with other views they hold. Chief Justice Rehnquist, who dissented in that case, had "little doubt" that a state could not constitutionally forbid an abortion that was necessary to save a pregnant woman's life.[35] Of course, if a state could declare a fetus a constitutional person, it could prohibit abortion even when the pregnancy threatens the mother's life, just as it normally forbids killing one innocent person to save the life of another.

VIII. Do Fetuses Have Interests?

Consider this argument, however. "Even if a fetus is not a constitutional person, and states have no power to make it one, a state can nevertheless legislate to protect a fetus's interests, just as it can legislate to protect the interests of dogs, who are not constitutional persons either." States can protect the interests of non-persons. But it is extremely doubtful whether a state can appeal to such interests to justify a significant abridgement of an important constitutional right, such as a pregnant woman's right to control her own body. It can do that only in deference to the rights of other constitutional persons, or for some other "compelling" reason.

But it is important to see that this argument fails for another reason as well: a fetus has no interests before the third trimester. Not everything that can be destroyed has an interest in not being destroyed. Smashing a beautiful sculpture would be a terrible insult to the intrinsic value that great works of art embody, and also very much against the interests of people who take pleasure in see-

---

[35] 410 US at 173 (Rehnquist dissenting).

ing or studying it. But a sculpture has no interests of its own; a savage act of vandalism is not unfair to *it*. Nor is it enough, for something to have interests, that it be alive and in the process of developing into something more mature. It is not against the interests of a baby carrot that it be picked early and brought to table as a delicacy. Nor even that it is something that will naturally develop into something different or more marvelous. A butterfly is much more beautiful than a caterpillar; but it is not better for the caterpillar to become one. Nor is it enough, for something to have interests, even that it is something *en route* to becoming a human being. Imagine that, just as Dr. Frankenstein reached for the lever that would bring life to the assemblage of body parts on the table before him, someone appalled at the experiment smashed the apparatus. That act, whatever we think of it, would not have been harmful to the assemblage, or against its interests, or unfair to it.

These examples suggest that nothing has interests unless it has or has had some form of consciousness—some mental as well as physical life.[36] Creatures that can feel pain of course have an interest in avoiding it. It is very much against the interests of animals to subject them to pain, in trapping them or experimenting on them, for example. Causing a fetus pain would be against its interests too. But a fetus cannot feel pain until late in pregnancy, because its brain is not sufficiently developed before then. Even conservative scientists deny that a fetal brain is sufficiently developed to feel pain until approximately the twenty-sixth week.[37]

---

[36] Catholic doctrine, it is true, now holds that a fetus is endowed with an eternal soul at conception, and has interests for that reason. (Earlier in its history the Church held that God ensouled a fetus at some point after conception: at forty days for a male and eighty for a female, and that abortion before that point, though wrong because it violated the intrinsic value of God's creation, was not murder. Laurence H. Tribe, *Abortion: The Clash of Absolutes* 31 (Norton, 1990).) That argument offers a counter-example to my claim that nothing can have interests without a brain, though not to my more general claim that nothing can have interests without some form of consciousness, because I assume that a soul, which can suffer, is itself a special form of consciousness. If someone accepts this argument, then he does have a reason for insisting that a fetus (or more accurately the soul it contains) has an interest in continuing to live. But states are not entitled to act on reasons of theological dogma.

[37] See Clifford Grobstein, *Science and the Unborn: Choosing Human Futures* 130 (Basic, 1988):

> To provide a safe margin against intrusion into possible primitive sentience, the cortical maturation beginning at about thirty weeks is a reasonable landmark until more precise information becomes available.
>
> Therefore, since we should use extreme caution in respecting and protecting possible sentience, a provisional boundary at about twenty-six weeks should provide safety against reasonable concerns. This time is coincident with the present definition of viability . . . .

Of course many things that are against people's interests cause them no physical pain. Someone acts against my interests when he chooses someone else for a job I want, or sues me, or smashes into my car, or writes a bad review of my work, or brings out a better mousetrap and prices it lower than mine, even when these things cause me no physical pain, and, indeed, even when I am unaware that they have happened. In these cases my interests are in play not because of my capacity to feel pain but because of a different and more complex set of capacities: to enjoy or fail to enjoy, to form affections and emotions, to hope and expect, to suffer disappointment and frustration. I do not know when these capacities begin to develop, in primitive or trace or shadowy form, in animals including humans. Infants may have them in at least primitive form, and therefore so may late-stage fetuses, whose brains have been fully formed. But of course such capacities are not possible before sentience, and therefore, on conservative estimates, not before the twenty-sixth week.

We must beware the familiar but fallacious argument that abortion must be against the interests of a fetus, because it would have been against the interests of almost anyone now alive to have been aborted. Once a creature develops interests, then it becomes true, in retrospect, that certain events would have been against those interests if they had happened in the past. It obviously does not follow that these events were therefore against interests someone had *when* they happened. Suppose we assume that it was good for me that my father was not sent on a long business trip the night before my parents conceived me, rather than, as in fact happened, two days later. It does not follow that it would have been bad for anyone, in the same way, had he left on the earlier date. There never would have been anyone for whom it could have been bad.

Of course, when a fetus is aborted, there is something for whom someone might think this bad, a candidate, as it were. But the fetus's existence makes no difference to the logical point. If the fact that I would not now exist had my father left early does not entail that there was some creature for whom it would have been bad if he had, as it plainly does not, then the fact that I would not exist if I had been aborted doesn't entail that either. Whether abortion is against the interests of a fetus must depend on whether the fetus itself has interests, not on whether interests will develop if no abortion takes place.

This distinction may help explain what some observers have found puzzling. Many people who believe that abortion is morally permissible nevertheless think it wrong for pregnant women to smoke or drink or otherwise to behave in ways injurious to a child they intend to bear. Critics say that this combination of views is contradictory: since killing something is worse than injuring it, it cannot be wrong to smoke and yet not wrong to abort. But if a woman smokes during pregnancy, someone will later exist whose interests will have been seriously damaged by her behavior. If she aborts, no one will exist against whose interests that will ever have been.

IX. The Real Issue in *Roe v Wade*

An important conclusion follows from my argument so far: If the only issue at stake in the constitutional debate was whether states could treat a fetus as a person whose rights are competitive with those of a pregnant woman, then *Roe v Wade* would plainly be right. But that is not the only issue at stake, and (though this is widely misunderstood) that is not even the central issue in the underlying national debate about the *morality* of abortion. Most people, it is true, say that both the moral and the legal debate turns on some question about the moral personality, or rights, or interests of a fetus. They say that it turns, for example, on whether a fetus is a metaphysical or moral person, or whether a fetus has interests of its own, or how its interests should rank in importance with those of a pregnant woman, or some other question of that sort. In fact, however, most people's actual views about the morality of abortion in different circumstances make no sense if we try to understand these views as flowing from a set of consistent answers they give to questions about fetal personhood or rights or interests.

Most people think, for example, that abortion is always morally problematic, and must never be undertaken except for very good reason, but that it is nevertheless sometimes justified. Some think it justified only to save the life of the mother. Other overlapping but non-identical groups think it justified in other circumstances as well: to protect the mother from non-life threatening physical impairment, for example, or in cases of rape and incest, or in cases of serious fetal deformity. Some people who think abortion always morally problematic also think it justified when childbirth would severely cripple a mother's chances for a successful life herself. Many people also think that a pregnant woman should be free to decide about abortion for herself, even when she chooses abortion in circumstances in which they believe it morally impermissible. None of these complex positions flows from a consistent an-

swer to the question whether a fetus is a moral person, or how its
interests compare in importance to other people's interests.

Most people's views about abortion can only be understood as
responses to a very different set of issues. They assume that
human life is *intrinsically* valuable, and worthy of a kind of awe,
just because it is human life. They think that once a human life
begins, it is a very bad thing—a kind of sacrilege—that it end pre-
maturely, particularly through someone's deliberate act. That assumption does not presuppose that the creature whose life is in
question is a person with rights or interests, because it does not
suppose that death is bad *for* the creature whose life ends. On the
contrary, the assumption explains why some people think suicide
morally wrong even in circumstances in which they believe suicide
would be best for the person who dies. Most people take a parallel
view about the destruction of other things they treat as sacrosanct,
which plainly involve no moral personhood: works of art, for example, and particular animal species. Our attitude toward the destruction of human life has the same structure, though it is, understandably, much more intense.

Though most people accept that human life is sacrosanct, and
must be respected as such, the American community is divided
about what that respect actually requires in the kinds of circumstances I just described: rape, incest, fetal deformity, and cases in
which motherhood would have a serious and detrimental impact on
the potential mother's own life. Some Americans think that respect
for life forbids abortion in some or all of these circumstances;
others think that respect for life recommends and even requires
abortion in some or all of them.[38] As I argue in the forthcoming
book I mentioned, these differences reflect profound differences in
people's views about the relative importance of divine, natural and
human contributions to the overall intrinsic value of a human life.
They also reflect, as Kristin Luker has argued, different convictions about the appropriate lives for women to lead in our society.[39] The public is deeply divided about these matters. It is divided, however, not into two bitterly opposed groups—one of
which affirms and the other of which denies that a fetus is a person—but in a much more complex way, because judgments about
whether abortion dishonors or respects the intrinsic value of life in
different circumstances involve a large variety of separate issues.

---

[38] *McRae v Califano*, 491 F Supp 630, 727-28 (E D NY), rev'd as *Harris v McRae*, 448
US 297 (1980).
[39] Kristin Luker, *Abortion and the Politics of Motherhood* ch 8 (California, 1984).

So what I take to be the uncontroversial propositions that a fetus is not a constitutional person, and that a state may not enlarge the category of constitutional persons, do not, after all, entail that *Roe v Wade* was right. Neither paintings nor animal species nor future human beings are constitutional persons. But no one doubts that government can treat art and culture as having intrinsic value, or that government can and should act to protect the environment, endangered animal species, and the quality of life of future generations of people. The majority in a community can levy taxes that will be used to support museums. It can forbid people to destroy their own buildings if it deems these to be of historical or architectural value. It can prohibit building or manufacturing that threatens endangered species or that will injure future generations. Why should a majority not have the power to enforce a much more passionate conviction—that abortion is a desecration of the inherent value that attaches to every human life?

So the most difficult constitutional issue in the abortion controversy is whether states can legitimately claim a detached interest in protecting the intrinsic value, or sanctity, of human life. Does our Constitution allow states to decide not only what rights and interests people have and how these should be enforced and protected, but also whether human life is inherently valuable, why it is so, and how that inherent value should be respected? We cannot dispose of that question in the quick way some liberals might prefer: we cannot say that an individual woman's decision whether or not to have an abortion affects only herself (or only herself and the fetus's father) and that it is therefore none of the community's business which decision she makes. Individual decisions inevitably affect shared collective values. Part of the sense of the sacred is a sense of taboo, a shared sense of horror at desecration, and it is surely harder to maintain a sense of taboo about abortion in a community in which others not only reject the taboo but violate it openly, especially if they receive official financial or moral support. It is plainly more difficult for a parent to raise his or her children to share the conviction that abortion is always a desecration in such a community than in one in which abortion is branded a crime.

The constitutional question I describe therefore lies at the intersection of two sometimes competing traditions, both of which are part of America's political heritage. The first is the tradition of religious and personal freedom. The second is a tradition that assigns government responsibility for guarding the public moral space in which all must live. A good part of constitutional law consists in reconciling these two ideas. What is the appropriate balance in the case of abortion?

X. Government's Legitimate Concerns

One idea deployed in both the majority and dissenting opinions in *Roe* might have seemed mysterious: that a state has an interest in "protecting human life." I have now assigned a particular sense to that idea. A community has an interest in protecting the sanctity of life—in protecting the community's sense that human life in any form has enormous intrinsic value—by requiring its members to acknowledge that intrinsic value in their individual decisions. But that statement is ambiguous. It might describe either of two goals, and the distinction between them is extremely important. The first is the goal of responsibility. A state might aim that its citizens treat decisions about abortion as matters of moral importance, that they recognize that fundamental intrinsic values are at stake in their decision, and that they decide reflectively, not out of immediate convenience but out of examined conviction. The second is the goal of conformity. A state might aim that all its citizens obey rules and practices that the majority believes best capture and respect the sanctity of life, that they abort only in circumstances, if any, in which the majority thinks abortion is appropriate or at least permissible.

These goals of responsibility and conformity are not only different; they are antagonistic. If we aim at responsibility, we must leave citizens free, in the end, to decide as they think right, because that is what moral responsibility entails. If, on the other hand, we aim at conformity, we deny citizens that decision. We demand that they act in a way that might be contrary to their own moral convictions, and we discourage rather than encourage them to develop their own sense of when and why life is sacred.

The traditional assumption that states have a derivative interest in preventing abortion, which I have rejected, submerges the distinction between the two goals. If a fetus is a person, then of course the state's dominant goal must be to protect that person, just as it protects all other people. The state must therefore subordinate any interest it has in developing its citizens' sense of moral responsibility to its interest that they reach, or at least act on, a particular moral conclusion: that killing people is wrong.

But when we shift the state's interest, as we have, to its interest in protecting a particular intrinsic value, then the contrast and opposition between the two goals moves into the foreground. The sanctity of life is, as I said, a highly contestable value. What it requires in particular cases is controversial: when a fetus is deformed, for example, or when having a child would seriously depress a woman's chance to make something valuable of her own life. Does a state protect a contestable value best by encouraging people to accept the value *as* contestable, with the understanding that they are responsible for deciding for themselves what it means? Or does the state protect that value best by itself deciding, through the political process, which interpretation is the right one, and then forcing everyone to conform? The goal of responsibility justifies the first choice; the goal of conformity the second. A state cannot pursue both goals at the same time.

I can think of no reason, grounded in a plausible conception of either equal concern or basic liberty, why government should not aim that its citizens treat decisions about human life and death as matters of serious moral importance. The benefits of such a policy are evident and pervasive. So in my view the Constitution allows states to pursue the goal of responsibility; but only in ways that respect the distinction between that goal and the antagonistic goal of wholly or partly coercing a final decision. May a state require a woman contemplating abortion to wait twenty-four hours before the operation? May it require that she receive information explaining the gravity of a decision to abort? May it require a pregnant teen-age woman to consult with her parents, or with some other adult? Or a married woman to inform her husband if she can locate him? Must the government provide funds for abortion if, and on the same terms as, it provides funds for the costs of childbirth for those too poor to bear those costs themselves? Constitutional lawyers have tended to discuss these issues as if they were all governed by *Roe*, as they would be if the only pertinent issue were whether a fetus is a person. If that were the only issue, and if *Roe* is right that a fetus is not a constitutional person, then on what ground could a state require women contemplating abortion to wait, or to discuss the question with an adult? On what ground could Congress aid women who wanted to bear their fetuses but not those who wanted to abort?

Much of the media discussion about how far the Supreme Court has amended *Roe* in its recent decisions presupposes that questions about responsibility and questions about conformity are tied together in that way. That explains why the Court's decision

in *Webster*[40] was widely viewed as in itself altering *Roe*,[41] why the
New York Times said that the Third Circuit's recent *Casey* decision upholding a comprehensive Pennsylvania regulatory statute
assumed that *Roe* would soon be overturned,[42] and why so many
commentators expect the Supreme Court, which has agreed to review the Third Circuit decision, to use that opportunity further to
narrow *Roe* or perhaps to overrule it altogether, even though the
Court requested parties only to brief issues the Third Circuit had
actually addressed.[43]

Many of these commentators say that *Roe* gave women a fundamental right to abortion, which states need a compelling reason
to curtail, and that *Webster* undermined *Roe*, and *Casey* will undermine it further, by allowing states to curtail the right without
such a reason. But when we understand *Roe* as I suggest, this analysis becomes too crude. The fundamental right *Roe* upheld is a
right against conformity. It is a right that states not prohibit abortion before the third trimester, either directly or through undue
burdens on a woman's choice to abort. *Roe* itself did not grant a
right, fundamental or otherwise, that states not encourage responsibility in the decision a woman makes or that states not display a
collective view of which decision is most appropriate.

It is a further question, certainly, whether a particular regulation—say, a mandatory waiting period or mandatory notification
or consultation—makes abortion much more expensive or dangerous or difficult to secure, and so does unduly burden the right
against conformity.[44] And of course I agree that it would be naive
to read the Court's recent decisions as carrying no threat to *Roe* at
all. The past statements of at least four justices, and the likely
views of the two newest appointees, are threatening indeed. But we
do no favor to the crucial right *Roe* recognized by insisting that

[40] *Webster v Reproductive Health Services*, 492 US 490 (1989).

[41] Professor Tribe, for example, says that "[i]f constitutional law is as constitutional
law does, then after *Webster*, *Roe* is not what it once was." Tribe, *Abortion* at 24 (cited in
note 36).

[42] See Michael de Courcy Hinds, *Appeals Court Upholds Limits For Abortions*, NY
Times A1 (Oct 22, 1991), discussing *Planned Parenthood v Casey*, 947 F2d 682 (3d Cir
1991), cert granted in part by 60 USLW 3388 (1992), and in part by 60 USLW 3446 (1992).
In fact the majority opinion in *Casey* assumed the distinction between responsibility and
conformity I defend in the text, and interpreted Justice O'Connor's "undue burden" test in
Webster, 492 US at 529-31 (O'Connor concurring), to presuppose that distinction as well.

[43] See, for example, Sheryl McCarthy, *Climactic Battle Is at Hand*, Newsday 5 (Jan 22,
1992); *Washington Brief*, Natl L J 5 (Feb 3, 1992).

[44] In *Casey*, the Third Circuit, claiming to follow Justice O'Connor, proposed that the
pertinent test should be whether the regulation imposed an "undue burden" on a woman's
right to have an abortion if after reflection she wished one. 947 F2d at 695-97, 706-07.

every decision pro-life groups applaud is automatically another nail in *Roe*'s coffin.

The real question decided in *Roe*, and the heart of the national debate, is the question of conformity. I said that government sometimes acts properly when it coerces people in order to protect values the majority endorses: when it collects taxes to support art, or when it requires businessmen to spend money to avoid endangering a species, for example. Why (I asked) can the state not forbid abortion on the same ground: that the majority of its citizens thinks that aborting a fetus, except when the mother's own life is at stake, is an intolerable insult to the inherent value of human life?

XI. CONFORMITY AND COERCION

I begin my reply to that question by noticing three central and connected reasons why prohibiting abortion is a very different matter from conservation or aesthetic zoning or protecting endangered species. First, the impact on particular people—pregnant women—is far greater. A woman who is forced by her community to bear a child she does not want is no longer in charge of her own body. It has been taken over for purposes she does not share. That is a partial enslavement, a deprivation of liberty vastly more serious than any disadvantage citizens must bear to protect cultural treasures or to save troubled species. The partial enslavement of a forced pregnancy is, moreover, only the beginning of the price a woman denied an abortion pays. Bearing a child destroys many women's lives, because they will no longer be able to work or study or live as they believe they should, or because they will be unable to support that child. Adoption, even when available, may not reduce the injury. Many women would find it nearly intolerable to turn their child over to others to raise and love. Of course, these different kinds of injury are intensified if the pregnancy began in rape or incest, or if a child is born with grave physical or mental handicaps. Many women regard these as not simply undesirable but terrible consequences, and would do almost anything to avoid them. We must never forget that a great many abortions took place, before *Roe v Wade*, in states that prohibited abortion. These were illegal abortions, and many of them were very dangerous. If a woman desperate for an abortion defies the criminal law, she may risk her life. If she bows to it, her life might be destroyed, and her self-respect compromised.

Second, it is a matter of deep disagreement within our culture, as I said, what someone who is anxious to respect the intrinsic value of human life should therefore do about abortion. There is no parallel disagreement in the case of the other values I mentioned. No one could plausibly claim that respect for future generations sometimes means leaving the planet uninhabitable for them or that respect for animal species sometimes means allowing their extinction. When the law requires people to make sacrifices for those values, it requires them, at most, to sacrifice for something that they do not believe to be important, but that the rest of the community does. They are not forced to act in ways that they think are not only disadvantageous to them but ethically wrong.[45] A woman who must bear a child whose life will be stunted by deformity, or a child who is doomed to an impoverished childhood and an inadequate education, or a child whose existence will cripple the woman's own life, is not merely forced to make sacrifices for values she does not share. She is forced to act not just in the absence of, but in defiance of, her own beliefs about what respect for human life means and requires.

Third, our convictions about how and why human life has intrinsic importance, from which we draw our views about abortion, are much more fundamental to our overall moral personality than the other convictions about inherent value I mentioned. They are decisive in forming our opinions about all life-and-death matters, including not only abortion but also suicide, euthanasia, the death penalty and conscientious objection to war. Their power is even greater than this suggests, moreover, because our opinions about how and why our *own* lives have intrinsic value crucially influence every major choice we make about how we should live.[46] Very few people's opinions about architectural conservation or endangered species are even nearly so foundational to the rest of their moral personality, even nearly so interwoven with the other major structural convictions of their lives.

These interconnections are most evident in the lives of people who are religious in a traditional way. The connection between their faith and their opinions about abortion is not contingent but constitutive: their convictions about abortion are shadows of more general foundational convictions about why human life itself is im-

---

[45] Of course, government sometimes forces people to do what they think wrong—to pay taxes that will be used to fight a war they think immoral, for example. But in such cases government justifies coercion by appealing to the rights and interests of other people, not to an intrinsic value those who are coerced believe requires the opposite decision.

[46] See Ronald Dworkin, *Foundations of a Liberal Equality*, in 11 *The Tanner Lectures on Human Values* 1 (Utah, 1990).

portant, convictions at work in all aspects of their lives. A particular religion, like Catholicism, could not comprehensively change its views about abortion without becoming a significantly different faith, organized around a significantly different sense of the ground and consequences of the sacrosanct character of human life. People who are not religious in the conventional way also have general, instinctive convictions about whether, why and how any human life—their own, for example—has intrinsic value. No one can lead even a mildly reflective life without expressing such convictions. These convictions surface, for almost everyone, at exactly the same critical moments in life—in decisions about reproduction and death and war. Someone who is an atheist, because he does not believe in a personal god, nevertheless has convictions or at least instincts about the value of human life in an infinite and cold universe, and these convictions are just as pervasive, just as foundational to moral personality, as the convictions of a Catholic or a Moslem. They are convictions that have, in the words of a famous Supreme Court opinion, "a place in the life of its possessor parallel to that filled by the orthodox belief in God . . . ."[47]

For that reason we may describe people's beliefs about the inherent value of human life, beliefs deployed in their opinions about abortion, as *essentially* religious beliefs. I shall later try to defend that claim as a matter of constitutional interpretation: I shall argue that such beliefs should be deemed religious within the meaning of the First Amendment. My present point is not legal but philosophical, however. Many people, it is true, think that no belief is religious in character unless it presupposes a personal god. But many established religions—some forms of Buddhism and Hinduism, for example—include no commitment to such a supreme being. Once we set aside the idea that every religious belief presupposes a god, it is doubtful that we can discover any defining feature that all but only religious beliefs have. We must decide whether to classify a belief as religious in a less rigid way: by asking whether it is similar in content to plainly religious beliefs.[48] On that test, the belief that the value of human life transcends its value for the creature whose life it is—that human life is objectively valuable from the point of view, as it were, of the universe—is plainly a religious belief, even when it is held by people

---

[47] *United States v Seeger*, 380 US 163, 166 (1965).

[48] Kent Greenawalt, *Religion as a Concept in Constitutional Law*, 72 Cal L Rev 753 (1984); George Freeman III, *The Misguided Search for the Constitutional Definition of "Religion"*, 71 Georgetown L J 1519 (1983).

who do not believe in a personal deity. It is, in fact, the most fundamental purpose of traditional religions to make exactly that claim to its faithful, and to embody it in some vision or narrative that makes the belief seem intelligible and persuasive.

Religion in that way responds to the most terrifying feature of human life: that we have lives to lead, and death to face, with no evident reason to think that our living, still less how we live, makes any genuine difference at all. The existential question whether human life has any intrinsic or objective importance has been raised in many ways. People ask about the "meaning" or "point" of life, for example. However it is put, the question is foundational. It cannot be answered by pointing out that if people live in a particular recommended way—observing a particular moral code, for example, or following a particular theory of justice—this will make them, individually or collectively, safer or more prosperous, or that it will help them fulfill or realize their human nature, as understood in some particular way. The existential question is deeper, because it asks why any of that matters.

In that way beliefs about the intrinsic importance of human life are distinguished from more secular convictions about morality, fairness and justice. The latter declare how competing interests of particular people should be served or adjusted or compromised. They rarely reflect any distinctive view about why human interests have objective intrinsic importance, or even whether they do.[49] That explains why people with very different views about the meaning or point of human life can agree about justice, and why people with much the same views about that religious issue can disagree about justice dramatically. Of course many people believe that fairness and justice are important only because they think that it is objectively important how a human life goes.[50] But their particular views about what justice requires are not, for that reason, themselves views about why or in what way that is true.

Religions attempt to answer the deeper existential question by connecting individual human lives to a transcendent objective value. They declare that all human lives (or, for more parochial

---

[49] John Rawls, for example, distinguishes his own and other theories of justice from what he calls comprehensive religious or ethical schemes; political theories of justice, he says, presuppose no opinion about what is objectively important. In particular, they presuppose no opinion about if or why or in what way it is intrinsically important that human life continue or prosper, though of course political theories of justice are compatible with a great variety of such opinions. See John Rawls, *Justice as Fairness, Political not Metaphysical*, 14 Phil & Pub Aff 223 (1985).

[50] See Dworkin, *Foundations of a Liberal Equality* (cited in note 46).

religions, the lives of believers) have objective importance through some source of value outside human subjective experience: the love of a creator or a redeemer, for example, or nature believed to give objective normative importance to what it creates, or a natural order understood in some other but equally transcendental way. People who think that abortion is morally problematic, even though a fetus has no interests of its own, all accept that human life is intrinsically, objectively valuable. Some think that human life is intrinsically important because it is created by a god, others because human life is the triumph of nature's genius, and others because human life's complexity and promise is in itself awe-inspiring. Some people in each of these groups believe that because human life has intrinsic importance abortion is always, or almost always, wrong. Others in each group have reached a contrary conclusion: that abortion is sometimes necessary in order truly to respect life's inherent value.[51] In each case the belief affirms the essentially religious idea that the importance of human life transcends subjective experience.

XII. The Right of Procreative Autonomy

These three ways in which abortion is special, even among issues that involve claims about inherent value, suggest an interpretation of the much-discussed constitutional right of privacy. That constitutional right limits a state's power to invade personal liberty when the state acts, not to protect rights or interests of other people, but to safeguard an intrinsic value. A state may not curtail liberty, in order to protect an intrinsic value, (1) when the decisions it forbids are matters of personal commitment on essentially religious issues, (2) when the community is divided about what the best understanding of the value in question requires, and (3) when the decision has very great and disparate impact on the person whose decision is displaced.[52]

I should say again (though by now you will be tired of the point) that the principle of privacy I just defined would not guarantee a right to abortion if a fetus were a constitutional person

---

[51] *McRae*, 491 F Supp at 690-702. I develop this point at length in the forthcoming book I mentioned earlier.

[52] I do not mean that no stronger constitutional right of personal autonomy can be defended as flowing from the best interpretation of the Constitution as a whole. Indeed I think a significantly stronger right can be. But I shall not defend any principle broader than the more limited one just described, because that principle is strong enough to ground a right of privacy understood to include a right to procreative autonomy.

from the moment of conception. The principle is limited to circumstances in which the state claims authority to protect some inherent value, not the rights and interests of another person. But once we accept that a fetus is not a constitutional person, and shift the ground of constitutional inquiry to the different question of whether a state may forbid abortion in order to respect the inherent value of human life, then the principle of privacy plainly does apply.

It applies because ethical decisions about procreation meet the tests the principle provides. That is why procreative decisions have been collected, through the common law method of adjudication, into a distinct principle we might call the principle of procreative autonomy. That principle, understood as an application of the more general principle of privacy, provides the best available justification for the Court's decisions about contraception, for example. In the first of these cases—*Griswold v Connecticut*[53]—the Justices who made up the majority provided a variety of justifications for their decision. Justice Harlan said that laws forbidding married couples to use contraceptives violated the Constitution because they could only be enforced by police searching marital bedrooms, a practice that struck him as repulsive to the concept of ordered liberty.[54]

This justification was inadequate even for the decision in *Griswold*—a prohibition on the purchase or sale of contraceptives could be enforced without searching marital bedrooms, just as a prohibition on the sale of drugs to or the use of drugs by married couples can be enforced without such a search. And it was plainly inadequate for the later decisions in the series. In one of these, Justice Brennan, speaking for the Court, offered a different and more general explanation. "If the right of privacy means anything," he said, "it is the right of the *individual*, married or not, to be free from government intrusion into matters so fundamentally affecting a person as the decision whether to bear or beget a child."[55]

I take the principle of procreative autonomy to be an elaboration of Brennan's suggestion. It explains the sense in which individual procreative decisions are, as he said, fundamental. Many decisions, including economic decisions, for example, have serious

---

[53] 381 US 479 (1965).

[54] Id at 500 (Harlan concurring) (referring to his dissent in *Poe v Ullman*, 367 US 497, 539-45 (1961)).

[55] *Eisenstadt v Baird*, 405 US 438, 453 (1972) (emphasis in original).

and disparate impact. Procreative decisions are fundamental in a different way, because the moral issues on which a procreative decision hinges are religious in the broad sense I defined. They are issues touching the ultimate point and value of human life itself. The state's power to prohibit contraception could plausibly be defended only by assuming a general power to dictate to all citizens what respect for the inherent value of human life requires: that it requires, for example, that people not make love except with the intention to procreate.

The Supreme Court, in denying the specific power to make contraception criminal, presupposed the more general principle of procreative autonomy I am defending. That is important, because almost no one believes that the contraception decisions should now be overruled. It is true that Bork had challenged *Griswold* and the later decisions in speeches and articles before his nomination.[56] But during his hearings, he hinted that *Griswold* might be defended on other grounds.[57]

The law's integrity demands, as I said, that principles necessary to support an authoritative set of decisions must be accepted in other contexts as well. It might seem an appealing political compromise to apply the principle of procreative autonomy to contraception, which almost no one now thinks the states can forbid, but not to apply it to abortion, which powerful conservative constituencies violently oppose. But the point of integrity—the point of law itself—is exactly to rule out political compromises of that kind. We must be one nation of principle: our Constitution must represent conviction, not the tactical strategies of justices anxious to satisfy as many political constituencies as possible.

Integrity does not, of course, require that justices respect principles embedded in past decisions that they and others regard as *mistakes*. It permits the Court to declare, as it has several times in the past, that a particular decision or string of decisions was in error, because the principles underlying those decisions are inconsistent with more fundamental principles embedded in the Constitution's structure and history. The Court cannot declare everything in the past a mistake: that would destroy integrity under the pretext of serving it. It must exercise its power to disregard past

---

[56] See, for example, Robert H. Bork, *Neutral Principles and Some First Amendment Problems*, 47 Ind L J 1, 7-10 (1971).

[57] Nomination of Robert H. Bork to be Associate Justice of the Supreme Court of the United States, Hearings Before the Senate Committee on the Judiciary, 100th Cong, 1st Sess 250 (Sep 16, 1987). See Ethan Bonner, *Battle for Justice* 221-22, 260 (Norton, 1989).

decisions modestly. But it must also exercise that power in good faith. It cannot ignore principles underlying past decisions it purports to approve, decisions it would ratify if asked to do so, decisions almost no one, not even rabid critics of the Court's past performance, now disapproves or regards as mistakes. The contraception cases fall into that category, and it would be both dangerous and offensive for the Court cynically to ignore the principles presupposed in those cases in any decision it now reaches about abortion.

So integrity demands general recognition of the principle of procreative autonomy, and therefore of the right of women to decide for themselves not only whether to conceive but whether to bear a child. If you remain in doubt, then consider the possibility that in some state a majority of voters will come to think that it shows *disrespect* for the sanctity of life to continue a pregnancy in some circumstances—in cases of fetal deformity, for example. If a majority has the power to impose its own views about the sanctity of life on everyone, then the state could *require* someone to abort, even if that were against her own religious or ethical convictions, at least if abortion had become physically as convenient and safe as, for example, the vaccinations and inoculations states are now recognized as having the power to require.

Of course, if a fetus were a person with a right to live, it would not follow from the fact that one state had the right to forbid abortion that another would have the right to require it. But that does follow once we recognize that the constitutional question at stake in the abortion controversy is whether a state can impose a canonical interpretation of the inherent value of life on everyone. Of course it would be intolerable for a state to require an abortion to prevent the birth of a deformed child. No one doubts, I think, that that requirement would be unconstitutional. But the reason why—because it denies a pregnant woman's right to decide for herself what the sanctity of life requires her to do about her own pregnancy—applies with exactly equal force in the other direction. A state just as seriously insults the dignity of a pregnant woman when it forces her to the opposite choice, and the fact that the choice is approved by a majority is no better justification in the one case than in the other.

XIII. Textual Homes

My argument so far has not appealed to any particular constitutional provision. But, as I said, the general structure of the Bill of Rights is such that any moral right as fundamental as the right of procreative autonomy is very likely to have a safe home in the Constitution's text. Indeed, we should expect to see a principle of that foundational character protected not just by one but by several constitutional provisions, because these must necessarily overlap in the way I also described.

The right of procreative autonomy follows from any competent interpretation of the Due Process Clause and of the Supreme Court's past decisions applying that clause. I have already indicated, in my discussion of the contraception cases, my grounds for that claim. I shall now argue, however, for a different and further textual basis for that right. The First Amendment prohibits government from establishing any religion, and it guarantees all citizens the free exercise of their own religion. The Fourteenth Amendment, which incorporates the First Amendment, imposes the same prohibition and the same responsibility on the states. These provisions guarantee the right of procreative autonomy. I do not mean that the First Amendment defense of that right is stronger than the Due Process Clause defense. On the contrary, the First Amendment defense is more complex and less demonstrable as a matter of precedent. I take it up because it is, as I shall try to show, a natural defense, because it illuminates an important dimension of the national debate about abortion, and because the argument for it illustrates both the power and the constraining force of the ideal of legal integrity.

Locating the abortion controversy in the First Amendment would seem natural to most people, who instinctively perceive that the abortion controversy is at bottom essentially a religious one. Some of you may fear, however, that I am trying to revive an old argument now rejected even by some of those who once subscribed to it. This argument holds that since the morality of abortion is a matter of controversy among religious groups, since it is declared immoral and sinful by some orthodox religions—conspicuously the Catholic Church—but permissible by others, the old idea of separation of church and state means that government must leave the subject of abortion alone. That would indeed be a very bad argument if states were permitted to treat a fetus as a person with rights and interests competitive with the rights of a pregnant woman. For the most important responsibility of government is to identify the differing and sometimes competing rights and interests of the people for whom it is responsible, and to decide how these rights may best be accommodated and these interests best served. Government has no reason to abdicate that responsibility just because (or when) organized religion also takes an interest in those matters. Religious bodies and groups were among the strongest campaigners against slavery, and they have for centuries sought social justice, the eradication of suffering and disease, and a vast variety of other humanitarian goals. If the distinction between church and state barred government from also taking up those goals, the doctrine would paralyze government altogether.

But we are now assuming that the issue whether a fetus is a person with rights and interests of its own has already been decided, by secular government, in the only way that issue can be decided under our constitutional system. Now we are considering a different constitutional issue: whether states may nevertheless prohibit abortion in order to endorse a controversial view about what respect for the intrinsic value of human life requires. That is not an issue about who has rights, or how people's competing interests should be balanced and protected. If states are forbidden to prohibit conduct on the ground that it insults the intrinsic value of human life, they are not therefore disabled from pursuing their normal responsibilities. On the contrary, it is one of government's most fundamental duties, recognized throughout Western democracies since the eighteenth century, to insure that people have a right to live their lives in accordance with their own convictions about essentially religious issues. So the reasons for rejecting the bad argument I described are not arguments against my suggestion that the First Amendment forbids states to force people to conform to an official view about what the sanctity of human life requires.

We must now consider arguments for that suggestion. It is controversial how the Establishment and Free Exercise Clauses should be interpreted, and the Supreme Court's rulings on these clauses are somewhat unclear.[58] I cannot offer an extended consideration of those rulings here, and my immediate purpose is not to compose a full and detailed legal argument for the First Amendment defense, but rather to indicate the main structural lines of that defense. Any satisfactory interpretation of the Religion Clauses of the amendment must cover two issues. First, it must fill out the phrase "free exercise of religion" by explaining which features make a particular belief a religious conviction rather than a non-religious moral principle or a personal preference. Second, it must interpret "establishment" by explaining the difference between secular and religious aims of government.

---

[58] See Greenawalt, 72 Cal L Rev 753 (cited in note 48); Freeman, 71 Georgetown L J 1519 (cited in note 48).

Difficult cases arise when government restricts or penalizes conduct required by genuinely religious convictions, but for the secular purpose of serving and protecting other people's interests.[59] Such cases require courts to decide how far the right of free exercise prevents government from adopting policies it believes would increase the general secular welfare of the community. It is a very different matter, however, when government's only purpose is to support one side of an argument about an essentially religious issue. Legislation for that purpose which substantially impaired anyone's religious freedom would violate both of the First Amendment's Religion Clauses at once.

Of course, if a fetus were a constitutional person, with interests government is obliged and entitled to protect, then legislation outlawing abortion would fall into the first of these categories even if convictions permitting or requiring abortion are genuinely religious in character. Such legislation would plainly be constitutional: rights of free exercise would not extend to the killing of a fetus any more than they extend to human sacrifice in religious ritual. But a fetus is not a constitutional person. If people's convictions about what the inherent value of human life requires are religious convictions, therefore, any government demand for conformity would be an attempt to impose a collective religion, and the case would fall into the second category.

What makes a belief a religious one for purposes of the First Amendment? The great majority of eighteenth-century statesmen who wrote and ratified the Constitution may have assumed that every religious conviction presupposes a personal god. But, as the Supreme Court apparently decided in *United States v Seeger*, that restriction is not now acceptable as part of a constitutional definition of religion, in part because not all the major religions represented in this country presuppose such a being.[60] Once the idea of

---

[59] We can regard the Supreme Court's decision in *Smith v Employment Division*, 494 US 872 (1990), as an example of that kind of case, whether or not we agree with the decision.

[60] 380 US 163. The Court in that case construed a statute rather then the Constitution. But since the Court's decision contradicted the evident statutory purpose, commentators have assumed that the Court meant to imply that the statute was constitutional only if so construed.

In a recent book, which I received while this Article was in galleys, Professor Peter Wenz argues for a ground of distinction between religious and secular opinions that is different from the two possible distinctions I mention here (which he calls "epistemological"). He accepts the traditional view, that the argument over abortion is about whether a fetus is a person, but insists that the question whether an early fetus is a person is a religious one because it cannot be decided "entirely" on the basis of "methods of argumentation that are

religion is divorced from that requirement, however, courts face a difficulty in distinguishing between religious and other kinds of conviction. There are two possibilities: a conviction can be deemed religious because of its content—because it speaks to concerns identified as distinctly religious—or because it has very great subjective importance to the person who holds it, as orthodox religious convictions do for devout believers. In *Seeger*, the Court suggested that a scruple is religious if it has "a place in the life of its possessor parallel to that filled by the orthodox belief in God of one who clearly qualifies for the exemption."[61] That statement, taken by itself, is ambiguous. It might mean that a conviction is religious if it answers the same questions that orthodox religion answers for a believer, which is a test of content, or that it is religious if it is embraced as fervently as orthodox religion is embraced by a devout believer, which is a test of subjective importance.

The opinion as a whole is indecisive about which of these two meanings, or which combination of them, the Court intended, and the ambiguity has damaged the development of constitutional law in this area. In any case, however, a subjective importance test is plainly inadequate, by itself, to distinguish religious from other forms of conviction, or indeed from intensely felt preferences. Even people who are religious in the orthodox way often count plainly non-religious affiliations, like patriotism, as equally or even more important. Some test of content is at least necessary, and may be sufficient.

I argued, earlier, that a belief in the objective and intrinsic importance of human life has a distinctly religious content. Convictions that endorse that objective importance play the same role, in providing an objective underpinning for concerns about human rights and interests, as orthodox religious beliefs provide for those who accept them. Several of the theologians the Court cited in *Seeger* made the same claim. The Court called the following statement from the Schema of a recent Ecumenical Council, for example, "a most significant declaration on religion": "Men expect from the various religions answers to the riddles of the human condi-

---

integral to our way of life." Peter Wenz, *Abortion Rights as Religious Freedom* 131 (Temple, 1992). I agree with the conclusion he reaches: that the abortion debate is primarily a religious one governed by the First Amendment. But his test is not acceptable, because government must make and impose decisions on a wide variety or moral issues about which people disagree profoundly, and which cannot be decided on empirical grounds or by appeal to any convictions shared by everyone or by methods that are in any other way "integral" to any collective way of life.

[61] Id at 165-66.

tion: What is man? What is the meaning and purpose of our lives?"[62]

I can think of no plausible account of the content a belief must have, in order to be religious in character, that would rule out convictions about why and how human life has intrinsic objective importance, except the abandoned test that requires a religious belief to presuppose a god. It is, of course, essential that any test of religious content allow a distinction between religious beliefs, on the one hand, and non-religious political or moral convictions, on the other. I have already suggested, however, how the belief that human life has intrinsic objective importance, and other beliefs that interpret and follow directly from that belief, differ from most people's opinions about political fairness or the just distribution of economic or other resources.[63]

We can see the distinction at work in the Supreme Court's disposition of the conscientious objector cases. In *Seeger*, the Court presumed that the Constitution would not allow exempting men whose opposition to all war was based on theistic religion but not men whose similar opposition was grounded in a non-theistic belief. In *Gillette*, on the other hand, the Court upheld Congress's refusal to grant exemption to men whose opposition to war was selective, even to those whose convictions condemning a particular war were supported by their religion.[64] Though the Court offered various practical grounds for the distinction, these were unpersuasive. The distinction can in fact be justified—if it can be justified at all—only by supposing that though a flat opposition to all war is based on a conviction that human life as such is sacred—which is a distinctly religious conviction—selective opposition is at least normally based on considerations of justice or policy, which justify killing in some cases but not others, and which are not themselves religious in content even when they are endorsed by a religious group. As the Court said,

> A virtually limitless variety of beliefs are subsumable under the rubric, "objection to a particular war." All the factors that might go into nonconscientious dissent from policy, also might appear as the concrete basis of an objection that has roots in conscience and religion as well. Indeed, over the realm of pos-

---

[62] See *Draft Declaration on the Church's Relations with Non-Christians*, in Council Daybook 282 (Vatican II, 3d Sess, 1965), quoted and cited in *Seeger*, 380 US at 181-82 & n 4.

[63] See text accompanying notes 49-51.

[64] *Gillette v United States*, 401 US 437.

sible situations, opposition to a particular war may more likely be political and nonconscientious, than otherwise.[65]

So the popular sense that the abortion issue is fundamentally a religious one, and some lawyers' sense that it therefore lies outside the proper limits of state action, is at bottom sound, though for reasons somewhat more complex than is often supposed. It rests on a natural—indeed irresistible—understanding of the First Amendment: that a state has no business prescribing what people should think about the ultimate point and value of human life, about why life has intrinsic importance, and about how that value is respected or dishonored in different circumstances. In his reply, Posner objects that if my view of the scope of the Free Exercise Clause were correct, government could not forbid "an aesthete to alter the exterior of his landmark house."[66] But he has misunderstood my view: he apparently thinks that I use a test of subjective importance to identify religious convictions. He points out, as a *reductio ad absurdum* of my argument, that "economic freedom *is* a religion" to a variety of libertarians,[67] suggesting that taxation, which libertarians find particularly offensive, would on my argument violate their religious freedom.

I argued, however, that convictions about the intrinsic value of human life are religious on a test of content, not subjective importance. A law forbidding people to tear down Georgian houses does not raise essentially religious issues, no matter how much some people would prefer to build post-modern pastiches instead, because that law does not presuppose any particular conception of why and how human life is sacred, or take a position on any other matter historically religious in character.[68] It is even plainer that my argument would not justify exempting Milton Friedman from tax on grounds of his free-market faith. Government collects taxes in order to serve a variety of secular interests of its citizens, not to declare or support a particular view about any essentially religious

---

[65] Id at 455 (footnotes omitted). The Court also endorsed, as on a careful view supporting the distinction between universal and selective opposition, the government's claim that opposition to a particular war necessarily involves judgment that is "political and particular" and "based on the same political, sociological, and economic factors that the government necessarily considered" in deciding whether to wage war. Id at 458 (citing government's brief).

[66] Posner, in this volume, 444 (cited in note 9).

[67] Id at 443.

[68] Such laws do raise other issues about intrinsic value, and in some extremely unusual circumstances might violate a more powerful form of the principle of privacy than the weak form I described and defended.

matter. It is, of course, true that some people resist paying taxes for reasons that do implicate their convictions about the intrinsic value of human life. Some people refuse to pay taxes to finance war on that basis, for example. In such cases compulsory taxation does plausibly impair the free exercise of religion. But the problem falls into the first of the two categories I distinguished, and the appropriate balancing sustains the tax, given the limited character of the infringement of free exercise and the importance of uniform taxation.

I conclude that the right to procreative autonomy, from which a right of choice about abortion flows, is well grounded in the First Amendment.[69] But it would be remarkable, as I said, if so basic a right did not figure in the best interpretation of constitutional liberty and equality as well. It would be remarkable, that is, if lawyers who accepted the right did not think it fundamental to the concept of ordered liberty, and so protected by the Due Process Clause, or part of what government's equal concern for all citizens requires, and so protected by the Equal Protection Clause. Posner is amused that different scholars who endorse a right of procreative autonomy have offered a variety of textual homes for it: he says that in my account, *Roe v Wade* "is the Wandering Jew of constitutional law."[70] But of course, as he would agree, it is hardly an embarrassment for that right that lawyers have disagreed about which clause to emphasize in their arguments for it. Some constitutional lawyers have an odd taste for constitutional neatness: they want rights mapped uniquely onto clauses with no overlap, as if redundancy were a constitutional vice. Once we understand, however, that the Bill of Rights is not a list of discrete remedies drawn up by a parsimonious draftsman, but a commitment to an ideal of just government, that taste makes no more sense than the claim that freedom of religion is not also liberty, or that the protection of freedom for everyone has nothing to do with equality.

---

[69] I should mention a complexity. I have been arguing that many women's decisions about abortion reflect convictions, which may well be inarticulate, about whether abortion or childbirth would best respect what they believe intrinsically valuable about human life. That is not necessarily true of all women who want abortions, however, and the free exercise claim might therefore not be available, as a matter of principle, for everyone. But states could not devise appropriate and practicable tests for discriminating among women in that way, and in any case prohibition would be the establishment of an essentially religious position, even in cases when it worked to outlaw abortion for someone whose grounds were not religious in any sense.

[70] Posner, in this volume, 441 (cited in note 9).

XIV. Dignity and Concern

I pause for a brief summary. We must abandon the traditional way of understanding the constitutional argument about abortion. It is not an argument about whether a fetus is a person. It is rather a dispute about whether and how far government may enforce an official view about the right understanding of the sanctity of human life. I described a constitutional right—the right of procreational autonomy—which denies government that power. I suggested that this right is firmly embedded in our constitutional history. It is the best available justification of the "privacy" cases, including the contraception cases. Those cases are conventionally understood as residing, by way of textual home, in the Due Process Clause of the Fourteenth Amendment. I argued that they might also rest on the Religion Clauses of the First Amendment.

Posner suggests that my argument is more powerful construed holistically, that is, as an argument about what the Constitution as a whole requires. I do not, as I said, see a difference between clause-by-clause and holistic interpretations of the Bill of Rights. But I nevertheless accept the spirit of his suggestion—that it is important to notice the place the right I have been describing holds not only in the structure of the Constitution, but in our political culture more generally. Cardinal in that culture is a belief in individual human dignity: that people have the moral right—and the moral responsibility—to confront for themselves, answering to their own conscience and conviction, the most fundamental questions touching the meaning and value of their own lives. That assumption was the engine of emancipation and of racial equality, for example. The most powerful arguments against slavery before the Civil War, and for equal protection after it, were framed in the language of dignity: the cruelest aspect of slavery, for the abolitionists, both religious and secular, was its failure to recognize a slave's right to decide issues of value for himself or herself. Indeed the most basic premise of our entire constitutional system—that our government shall be republican rather than despotic—embodies a commitment to that conception of dignity.

So the principle of procreative autonomy, in the broad sense, is a principle that any remotely plausible explanation of our entire political culture would have to recognize. It is also a principle we would want our Constitution to contain even if we were starting on a clean slate, free to make any constitution we wanted. I want to guard against an interpretation of my argument that I would disown, however. It does not suppose that people either are or should be indifferent, either as individuals or as members of a political community, to the decisions their friends or neighbors or fellow citizens or fellow human beings make about abortion. On the contrary it recognizes several reasons why they should not be indifferent. As I have already noticed, individual choices together create a moral environment that inevitably influences what others can do. So a person's concern for his own life, and for that of his children and friends, gives him a reason for worrying about how even strangers treat the inherent value of human life. Our concern that people lead good lives is not naturally limited, moreover, nor should it be, to concern for our own lives and those of our family. We want others, even strangers, not to lead what we regard as a blighted life, ruined by a terrible act of desecration.

But the most powerful reason we have for wanting others to respect the intrinsic value of human life, in the way we think that value demands, is not our concern for our own or other people's interests at all, but just our concern for the value itself. If people did *not* think it transcendently important that human lives not be wasted by abortion, then they would not have the kind of commitment my argument assumes people do have. So of course Americans who think that almost all abortion is immoral must take a passionate interest in the issue: liberals who count such people as deranged busybodies are insensitive as well as wrong. Nevertheless, we must insist on religious tolerance in this area, as in other issues about which people once cared just as passionately and in the same way, and once thought sufficiently important to wage not just sit-ins but wars. Tolerance is a cost we must pay for our adventure in liberty. We are committed, by our Constitution, to live in a community in which no group is deemed clever or spiritual or numerous enough to decide essentially religious matters for everyone else. If we have genuine concern for the lives others lead, moreover, we will also accept that no life is a good one lived against the grain of conviction, that it does not aid someone else's life but spoils it to force values upon him he cannot accept but can only bow before out of fear or prudence.

XV. *Roe* Reconsidered

We must now take a fresh look at *Roe v Wade*. *Roe* did three things. First, it re-affirmed a pregnant woman's constitutional right of procreative autonomy, and declared that states do not have the power simply to forbid abortion on any terms they wish. Second, it recognized that states nevertheless do have a legitimate interest in regulating abortion. Third, it constructed a detailed regime for balancing that right and that interest: it declared, roughly, that states could not forbid abortion for any reason in the first trimester of pregnancy, that they could regulate abortion in the second trimester only out of concern for the health of the mother, and, finally, that they could outlaw abortion altogether after fetal viability, that is, after approximately the beginning of the third trimester. We must inspect those three decisions against the background of our argument so far.

Our argument confirms the first decision. The crucial issue in the constitutional abortion controversy is not whether a fetus is a person—*Roe* was plainly right in holding that a fetus is not a person within the meaning of the Constitution—but whether states have a legitimate power to dictate how their members must respect the inherent value of life. Since any competent interpretation of the Constitution must recognize a principle of procreative autonomy, states do not have the power simply to forbid abortion altogether.

Roe was also right on the second score. States do have a legitimate interest in regulating the abortion decision. It was mysterious, in *Roe* and other decisions, what that interest was. Our account identifies it as a legitimate interest in maintaining a moral environment in which decisions about life and death, including the abortion decision, are taken seriously, treated as matters of moral gravity.

It remains to consider whether *Roe* was right on the third score. Does the trimester scheme it announced allow states to pursue their legitimate interests while adequately protecting a pregnant woman's right of autonomy? That trimester scheme has been criticized as arbitrary and overly rigid, even by some lawyers who are sympathetic to the narrowest decision in *Roe*: that the Texas statute was unconstitutional. Why is the point of viability the crucial point? We might put that question in two ways. We might ask why viability should mark the earliest time at which a state is entitled to prohibit abortion. If it can prohibit abortion then, why not earlier, as a majority of citizens in some states apparently wish? Or we might ask why viability should mark the end of a woman's right to protection. If a state cannot prohibit abortion before viability, then why may it prohibit it after that point? Both questions challenge the point of viability as arbitrary though from different directions. I shall first pursue the second form of the question. What happens at viability to make the right I have been describing—the right of procreative autonomy—less powerful or effective?

Two answers to that question might figure in any defense of the *Roe v Wade* scheme. First, at about the point of viability, but not much before, fetal brain development may be sufficient to allow pain.[71] So at the point of viability, but not much before, a fetus can sensibly be said to have interests of its own. That does not mean, I must emphasize, that a state is permitted to declare a fetus a person at that point. The question who is a constitutional person, with independent constitutional rights in competition with the rights of others, must be decided nationally, as I argued. But a state may nevertheless act to protect the interests even of creatures—animals, for example—who are not constitutional persons, so long as it respects constitutional rights in doing so. So at the point of viability, the state may claim a legitimate derivative interest that is independent of its detached interest in enforcing its collective conception of the sanctity of life.

Second, choosing the point of viability gives a pregnant woman, in most cases, ample opportunity to reflect upon and decide whether she believes it best and right to continue her pregnancy or to terminate it. Very few abortions are performed during the third trimester—only about .01 percent[72]—and even fewer if we exclude emergency abortions necessary to save a mother's life, which almost no one wants to prohibit even near the end of pregnancy. It is true that a very few women—most of whom are very young women—are unaware of their pregnancy until it is nearly complete. But in almost all cases, a woman knows she is pregnant in good time to make a reflective decision before viability. That suggests that a state does not violate most women's right to choose by insisting on a decision before that point, and it also suggests an important reason why a state might properly so insist.

It is an almost universal conviction that abortion becomes progressively morally more problematic as a fetus develops towards the shape of infanthood, as the difference between pregnancy and infancy becomes more a matter of location than development. That widespread conviction seems odd so long as we suppose that whether abortion is wrong depends only on whether a fetus is a person from the moment of conception. But the belief is compelling once we realize that abortion is wrong, when it is, because it

---

[71] See Grobstein, *Science and the Unborn* at 54-55 (cited in note 37).

[72] *Facts in Brief: Abortion in the United States* (Alan Guttmacher Institute, 1991). See also Stanley K. Henshaw, *Characteristics of U.S. Women Having Abortions, 1982-83*, in Stanley K. Henshaw and Jennifer Van Vort, eds, *Abortion Services in the United States: Each State and Metropolitan Area, 1984-85* 23 (Alan Guttmacher Institute, 1988).

insults the sanctity of human life. The insult to that value is greater when the life destroyed is further advanced, when, as it were, the creative investment in that life is greater. Women who have a genuine opportunity to decide on abortion early in pregnancy, when the impact is much less, but who actually decide only near the end, may well be indifferent to the moral and social meaning of their act. Society has a right, if its members so decide, to protect its culture from that kind of indifference, so long as the means it chooses do not infringe the right of pregnant women to a reflective choice.

Taken together, these two answers provide, I believe, a persuasive explanation of why government is entitled to prohibit abortion, subject to certain exceptions, after the sixth month of pregnancy. But do they provide an answer to the question asked from the other direction? Why may government not prohibit abortion earlier? The first answer would not justify any much earlier date, because, as I said, the central nervous system is not sufficiently developed much before the end of twenty-six weeks of pregnancy to admit of pain.[73] But must that be decisive? The second answer does not depend on attributing interests to a fetus, and, by itself, seems an adequate justification of state power to prohibit abortion after a sufficiently long period. Would women not have a sufficient opportunity to exercise their right of autonomy if they were forbidden abortion after just five months? Four? Three?

Blackmun chose a point in pregnancy that he thought plainly late enough to give women a fair chance to exercise their right, in normal circumstances, and that was salient for two other reasons, each captured in the overall explanation I gave. As I said, viability seems, on the best developmental evidence, the earliest point at which a fetus might be thought to have interests of its own, and the point at which the natural development of a fetus is so far continued that deliberately waiting until after that point seems contemptuous of the inherent value of life. These three factors together indicate viability as the most appropriate point after which a state could properly assert its interests in protecting a fetus's interests, and in responsibility. Blackmun's decision should not be overruled. So important a decision should not be overruled, after nearly twenty years, unless it is clearly wrong, and his was not clearly wrong. On the contrary, the arguments for choosing viability as the key date remain impressive.

---

[73] See note 37.

But it is important to acknowledge that a different test, bringing the cut-off date forward by some period, would have been acceptable if it had afforded women enough time to exercise their right to terminate an unwanted pregnancy. Of course, the earlier the cut-off time, the more important it would be to provide realistic exceptions for reasons the mother could not reasonably have discovered earlier. Suppose that the Court had substituted for the fixed scheme of *Roe*, not another fixed scheme, but rather a constitutional standard drafted in terms of overall reasonableness, which the federal courts would enforce case-by-case. Such a standard might have provided, in effect, that any prohibition would be unconstitutional if it did not provide women a reasonable time to decide upon an abortion after discovering that they were pregnant, or after discovering medical information indicating defects in the fetus or an increased risk to the mother of pregnancy, or other facts pertinent to the impact of childbirth on their lives.

In the end, as Blackmun no doubt anticipated, the Court would have had to adopt more rigid standards that selected at least a *prima facie* point in pregnancy before which prohibition would be presumptively unconstitutional. But the Court might have developed those standards gradually, perhaps deciding, in the first instance, that any statute that forbade second-term abortions would be subject to strict scrutiny to see whether it contained the exceptions necessary to protect a woman's right to a reflective choice. That approach still would have struck down the Texas law in *Roe*. It would also strike down the equally strict laws that some states and Guam have recently adopted, each hoping to provide the lawsuit that will end *Roe*.

Would it make much practical difference if the Supreme Court now substituted such a case-by-case test for *Roe*'s rigid structure? A case-by-case test might not, in fact, much reduce legal abortion. In 1987, only ten percent of abortions took place in the second trimester,[74] and many of these were on medical or other grounds that would still be permitted in any legislation acceptable under the more flexible test I have described. If a more flexible test were adopted, publicity might bring home to more women the impor-

---

[74] The U.S. Bureau of the Census reports that ten percent of the 1,559,100 abortions performed in 1987 occurred at thirteen or more weeks gestational age. U.S. Department of Commerce, Economics and Statistics Administration, Bureau of the Census, *The Statistical Abstract of the United States* 71 (111th ed 1991). Since about .01% of all abortions are performed after twenty-four weeks, see note 72 and accompanying text, it can be inferred that about 9.99% of the abortions performed in 1987 occurred in the second trimester.

tance of deciding and acting early. Medical developments in the technology of abortion might soon increase the percentage of very early abortions anyway. For instance, the abortion pill being developed in France, RU 486, which permits a safe abortion at home early in pregnancy, will allow pregnant women a more private method of abortion, if they decide and act in a timely way.[75] Of course, no statute that banned that pill would be constitutional, even under the more flexible standard.

I believe, as I said, that *Roe v Wade* should not be substantially changed. The line it draws is salient and effectively serves the legitimate state purpose of promoting a responsible attitude toward the intrinsic value of human life. But the most important line, as I said, is the line between that legitimate goal and the illegitimate goal of coercion. It will be disappointing, but not intolerable, if *Roe* is amended in some such way as I have been discussing. But it would be intolerable if *Roe* is wholly reversed, if the constitutional right of procreative autonomy is denied altogether. Some of you already think that recent appointments to the Court, and recent decisions by it, signal a dark age for the American constitutional adventure, that this symposium should have been convened as a wake, not as a celebration. I hope that your bleak judgment is premature. But it will be confirmed, spectacularly, if the Supreme Court declares that American citizens have no right to follow their own reflective convictions in the most personal, conscience-driven and religious decisions many of them will ever make.

---

[75] The RU 486 pill may in any case defuse the public controversy by reducing the need for abortion clinics that act as magnets for protesters, as in Wichita.

Legal Reasoning From the Top Down and From the Bottom Up: The Question of Unenumerated Constitutional Rights

Richard A. Posner†

I. TOP-DOWN AND BOTTOM-UP REASONING

I want to approach the subject of my debate with Professor Dworkin—unenumerated constitutional rights—by distinguishing two types of legal reasoning: what I shall call reasoning from the top down and reasoning from the bottom up. In top-down reasoning, the judge or other legal analyst invents or adopts a theory about an area of law—perhaps about all law—and uses it to organize, criticize, accept or reject, explain or explain away, distinguish or amplify the existing decisions to make them conform to the theory and generate an outcome in each new case as it arises that will be consistent with the theory and with the canonical cases, that is, the cases accepted as authoritative within the theory. The theory need not be, perhaps never can be, drawn "from" law; it surely need not be articulated in lawyers' jargon. In bottom-up reasoning, which encompasses such familiar lawyers' techniques as "plain meaning" and "reasoning by analogy," one starts with the words of a statute or other enactment, or with a case or a mass of cases, and moves from there—but doesn't move far, as we shall see. The top-downer and the bottom-upper do not meet.

I am associated with several top-down theories. One, which is primarily positive (descriptive), is that the common law is best understood on the "as if" assumption that judges try to maximize the wealth of society. Another, primarily normative, is that judges should interpret the antitrust statutes to make them conform to the dictates of wealth maximization. In the development of the lat-

---

† Judge, United States Court of Appeals for the Seventh Circuit; Senior Lecturer, The University of Chicago Law School. This is a slightly expanded text of my talk at *The Bill of Rights in the Welfare State: A Bicentennial Symposium,* held at The University of Chicago Law School on October 25-26, 1991. The reader should bear in mind that it was prepared for oral delivery. I thank Ronald Dworkin, Frank Easterbrook, Lawrence Lessig, Andrew Schapiro, and Cass Sunstein for many helpful comments.

ter theory, Robert Bork—Dworkin's *bête noire*[1]—was a pioneer.
Bork called his theory "consumer welfare maximization,"[2] but that
is just a reassuring term for wealth maximization. He divided the
Supreme Court's antitrust cases into a main tradition informed by
the principles of wealth maximization and a deviant branch of that
tradition, and he argued for lopping off the branch.[3]

Dworkin himself is prominently associated with a theory of
constitutional law that makes such law the expression of liberalism, weighted with egalitarianism.[4] Richard Epstein has a
broadly similar view of constitutional law but he weights his liberalism not with egalitarianism but with economic freedom.[5] John
Hart Ely has a different but equally ambitious theory of constitutional law, one that yokes the various clauses together to draw the
plow called promoting the values of a representative democracy.[6]
Bruce Ackerman has still another.[7] A famous common-law top-
downer from an earlier generation was Christopher Columbus
Langdell.[8] And before him Hobbes.

Yet legal reasoning from the bottom up is the more familiar,
even the more hallowed, type.[9] The endlessly repeated refrain of
modern judicial opinions that in interpreting a statute the judge
must start with its words is in this tradition. And we all remember
our first day in law school, when we were asked to read for each
course not an overview or theoretical treatment of the field but a
case—a case, moreover, lying in the middle rather than at the historical or logical beginning of the field. Those of us who are judges
also remember our first day in that job, when we were handed a

[1] See the following works by Ronald Dworkin: *Reagan's Justice*, NY Rev Books 27
(Nov 8, 1984); *The Bork Nomination*, NY Rev Books 3 (Aug 13, 1987); *From Bork to Kennedy*, NY Rev Books 36 (Dec 17, 1987); and *Bork's Jurisprudence*, 57 U Chi L Rev 657
(1990).

[2] Robert H. Bork, *The Antitrust Paradox: A Policy at War With Itself* 7 (Basic, 1978)
("the only legitimate goal of antitrust is the maximization of consumer welfare").

[3] See Robert H. Bork, *The Rule of Reason and the Per Se Concept: Price Fixing and
Market Division (Part I)*, 74 Yale L J 775 (1965); Robert H. Bork, *The Rule of Reason and
the Per Se Concept: Price Fixing and Market Division (Part II)*, 75 Yale L J 375 (1966).

[4] See, for example, Ronald Dworkin, *Taking Rights Seriously* (Harvard, 1977).

[5] See, for example, Richard A. Epstein, *Property, Speech and the Politics of Distrust*, in
this volume, 41.

[6] See John Hart Ely, *Democracy and Distrust: A Theory of Judicial Review* (Harvard,
1980).

[7] See, for example, Bruce Ackerman, *We the People: Foundations* (Belknap, 1991).

[8] See, for example, Christopher Columbus Langdell, *A Selection of Cases on the Law of
Contracts* (Little Brown, 1871) (preface).

[9] For a classic statement, see Edward H. Levi, *An Introduction to Legal Reasoning*
(Chicago, 1949).

sheaf of briefs in cases from fields we may have known nothing about and told that in a few days we would be hearing oral argument and would then take our tentative vote.

There is a question whether legal reasoning from the bottom up amounts to much. Dworkin thinks not. His extensive writings evince little interest in the words of the Constitution, or in its structure (that is, in how its various parts—the articles, sections, clauses, and amendments—work together), in the texture and details of the complex statutes that his works discuss, such as Title VII of the Civil Rights Act of 1964,[10] or in any extended body of case law, let alone in the details of particular cases. His implicit legal universe consists of a handful of general principles embodied in a handful of exemplary, often rather bodiless, cases.

I do not myself see the law in quite that way but I agree there isn't much to bottom-up reasoning.[11] We don't ever really "start" from a mass of cases or from a statute or from a clause of the Constitution. To read a case, to read a statute, a rule, or a constitutional clause presupposes a vast linguistic, cultural, and conceptual apparatus. And more: You don't see judicial opinions that say, for example, "On page 532 of Title 29 of the U.S. Code appears the following sentence . . . ." The opinion invariably gives you the name of the statute ("The Sherman Act provides . . ." or "ERISA provides . . .") and immediately you are primed to react to the words in a particular way. And if, as is so common, the case or statute or other enactment is unclear, and maybe even when it seems quite clear, the reader, to extract or more precisely to impute its meaning, must *interpret* it; and interpretation, we now know, is as much creation as discovery.

Nor is it clear what it means to reason "from" one case to another, the heart of bottom-up reasoning in law. It sounds like induction, which from Hume to Popper has taken hard knocks from philosophers. Actually, most reasoning by analogy in law is an oblique form of logical reasoning. Cases are used as sources of interesting facts and ideas, and hence as materials for the creation of a theory that can be applied deductively to a new case. But not as the *exclusive* materials for the creation of the theory; that would unjustifiably exclude whole worlds of other learning and insight.

Reasoning by analogy also has an empirical function. If case A is canonical within your theory, and along comes case B, and the theory implies that the outcome of B should be different from A,

---

[10] Ronald Dworkin, *A Matter of Principle* 316-31 (Harvard, 1985).
[11] See Richard A. Posner, *The Problems of Jurisprudence* ch 2 (Harvard, 1990).

you had better be sure that the two outcomes are logically consistent; otherwise you have a problem with the theory. So cases accepted within a theory provide testing instances for its further application. But there must be a theory. You can't just go from case to case, not responsibly anyway. You can't say: I have no theory of privacy or due process or anything else, but, given *Griswold*,[12] *Roe*[13] follows. You have to be able to say what in *Griswold* dictates *Roe*. *Griswold* doesn't tell you how broadly or narrowly to read *Griswold*.

II. UNENUMERATED RIGHTS AND THE TWO METHODS OF REASONING

All this may be too compressed to carry conviction. But I'm not centrally interested here in showing the limitations of bottom-up reasoning. I am more interested in reminding you of its established place in our legal tradition and in relating it to the issue of unenumerated rights. The relation is this. The issue of unenumerated rights looks quite different when you approach it bottom up than when you approach it from the top down.

Start with top-down. If we wanted to take a top-down approach to the Constitution we might proceed as have Dworkin, and Epstein, and Ely, and many others, each in his own way, by creating from a variety of sources—the text, history, and background of the Constitution (with the text given no particular primacy, because people who are sophisticated about interpretation know that text doesn't come first in any illuminating sense), the decisions interpreting the Constitution, and sundry political, moral, and institutional values and insights—a comprehensive theory of the rights that the Constitution should be deemed to recognize. Armed with such a theory one can select a main tradition of cases and discard or downplay the outliers and thus decide new cases in a way that will be consistent both with the theory and with the (duly pruned) precedents.

If I were to attempt such a project I might come out a good deal closer to Professor Dworkin than many in this audience would think possible. I consider myself a liberal, albeit in the classical tradition, the tradition of John Stuart Mill, Herbert Spencer, and Milton Friedman, rather than in the newer, welfarist or redistributive sense pioneered by John Rawls; and if I weight economic free-

---

[12] *Griswold v Connecticut*, 381 US 479 (1965).

[13] *Roe v Wade*, 410 US 113 (1973).

dom more and equality less than Dworkin, and perhaps, owing to a different temperament, to different experiences in the law, or whatever, would be more timid than he about assertions of judicial power and more inclined than he to give the states room for experimentation, the practical differences might be small, especially in the areas of personal rights such as freedom of speech, religious freedom, and sexual and reproductive liberty. And then indeed, as Dworkin says in the very interesting article that he has prepared for this debate, the right to use contraceptives and the right to burn the American flag (provided you own the flag you burn) would be seen to stand on the same plane as far as the distinction between enumerated and unenumerated rights is concerned.[14]

The distinction has no significance to a comprehensive constitutional theory. The theory may use the text as one of its jumping-off points (*one of*, not *the*), but it goes beyond and eventually submerges textual distinctions, because, on the approach I am describing, specific constitutional rights such as the right to burn flags or to use contraceptives come out of the theory rather than (directly) out of the text.

The situation is different if you follow a bottom-up approach. For then you start by paging through the Constitution and you will find nothing that seems related to contraception, sex, reproduction, or the family. You will find no mention of the flag either but you will find a reference to freedom of speech, and it is easy to move analogically from literal speech to flag burning, as in the following interior Socratic dialogue:

"I see nothing here about flags or about the use of fire. Speech is verbal. Flag-burning is not a verbal act."

"Well, to begin, must speech be oral? Is sign language speech? If so, doesn't this show that speech goes beyond words, to include gestures? And what about communicating with semaphores? Semaphores *are* flags, as a matter of fact."

"I fully agree that sign language and semaphores are speech, but they are merely different methods from spoken language of encoding words—as is Morse code, or writing itself."

"Since we're talking about the flag-*burning* issue, what about the chain of fires that in Aeschylus's great play *Aga-*

---

[14] Ronald Dworkin, *Unenumerated Rights: How and Whether* Roe *Should be Overruled*, in this volume, 381, 388-89.

memnon are used to signal the fall of Troy to Clytemnestra hundreds of miles away?"

"Well, that's not quite speech because the fires don't encode a particular form of words, but they do communicate a simple message."

"Is the essence of constitutionally protected speech, then, the communication of a message?"

"Yes."

"So the signal fires would be protected (provided there were no safety concerns, etc.)?"

"Surely."

"But doesn't flag-burning, when employed as an element of a protest or a demonstration rather than as a method of discarding a piece of worn-out cloth or starting a (literal) conflagration, communicate a message?"

"Well, I suppose so, but it involves the destruction of property and that's different."

"People are allowed to destroy their own property, aren't they? And this isn't wanton destruction; it's consumption; it's just like the destruction of a forest to produce the Sunday *New York Times*. Isn't it?"

"I guess you're right."

This method of "proof" may well be spurious. It shows that there is a sense of "speech" that embraces flag burning—just as there is a sense of the word that embraces a right of association and a right not to be forced to express support for a cause one disfavors.[15] But it doesn't furnish a reason for adopting that sense rather than a narrower one. For that, one must range wider and consider the differences, not just the similarities, between burning a flag and engaging in the other forms of communication that the courts have held to be constitutionally protected. One must, in fact, develop or adopt a theory of free speech and then apply it to the case at hand. The development of such a theory was Bork's project in his famous 1971 *Indiana Law Journal* piece,[16] which he later retracted in part.[17]

---

[15] See *NAACP v Alabama*, 357 US 449, 460 (1958); *West Virginia State Board of Education v Barnette*, 319 US 624, 633 (1943).

[16] Robert H. Bork, *Neutral Principles and Some First Amendment Problems*, 47 Ind L J 1 (1971).

[17] Nomination of Robert H. Bork to be Associate Justice of the Supreme Court of the United States, Hearings Before the Senate Committee on the Judiciary, 100th Cong, 1st Sess 269-71 (Sep 16, 1987).

III. The Scope of the Theory: Holistic or Clause-by-Clause?

But even after we acknowledge that bottom-up reasoning is not reasoning but is at best preparatory to reasoning and that legal reasoning worthy of the name inescapably involves the creation of theories to guide decision, we are left with the question of the appropriate scope of such theories. Must they embrace entire fields of law, such as federal constitutional law or the common law? Must they, perhaps, embrace all of law? Or can they be limited to narrower slices of legal experience, such as particular clauses of the Constitution, or particular statutes, or clusters of related statutes? Can they be so limited even if this results in theories that are not consistent with one another, so that you have clauses sometimes pulling in different directions?

Professor Dworkin answers the last two questions "no." An interpretation of individual clauses that fails to achieve consistency of principle across clauses is illegitimate. A theory of constitutional law must take in the whole Constitution, or at least the whole of the Bill of Rights plus the Fourteenth Amendment—must to that extent be coherent, holistic.[18] For his basic criticism of Bork is that Bork has no constitutional philosophy.[19] But as Dworkin well knows, Bork is famous for his theory of free speech, and for his theory of antitrust as well.[20] And these are very much top-down theories. Bork doesn't go case to case. He derives an overarching principle which he then applies to the cases, discarding many. But his theories are tied to specific provisions; they lack the political and moral generality and ambition that Dworkin prizes. Bork's

---

[18] [T]he Supreme Court has a duty to find some conception of protected liberties, some statement defining which freedoms must be preserved, that is defensible both as a political principle and as consistent with the general form of government established by the Constitution.

Dworkin, *Reagan's Justice*, NY Rev Books at 30 (cited in note 1). Or, as he has put it elsewhere, "[t]he system of [constitutional] rights must be interpreted, so far as possible, as expressing a coherent vision of justice." Ronald Dworkin, *Law's Empire* 368 (Belknap, 1986). The qualification "so far as possible" enables Dworkin to make room for some pragmatic compromises. See, for example, id at 380-81.

[19] "[I] am interested . . . in a different issue: not whether Bork has a persuasive or plausible constitutional philosophy, but whether he has any constitutional philosophy at all." Dworkin, *The Bork Nomination*, NY Rev Books at 3 (cited in note 1). Bork's "constitutional philosophy is empty: not just impoverished and unattractive but no philosophy at all." Id at 10. "[H]e believes he has no responsibility to treat the Constitution as an integrated structure of moral and political principles . . . ." Id. "[H]e has no theory at all, no conservative jurisprudence, but only right-wing dogma to guide his decisions." Id.

[20] The first sentence of Bork's 1971 *Indiana Law Journal* article begins: "A persistently disturbing aspect of constitutional law is its lack of theory . . . ." Bork, 47 Ind L J at 1 (cited in note 16).

only *general* theory of constitutional law is—*distrust* of general theory.

The question of the proper scope of a constitutional theory connects with a topic discussed in the preceding debate, about what level of generality of the Framers' intentions should guide judges in interpreting the Constitution.[21] If you ask what is the intention behind the Equal Protection Clause, you find that it was both to benefit blacks in some ways but not others and to promote an ideal of equality that may be inconsistent with aspects of the more specific intention (for example, that the blacks were entitled only to political, and not to social, equality with whites). The choice of which intention to honor determines for example whether the Supreme Court was correct to outlaw racial segregation in public schools. But it is a question about the level of generality of intention behind a single clause. To pass beyond that to intentions concerning the Constitution as a whole, a sheaf of documents written at different times and covering a variety of discrete topics, is to enter cloudcuckooland. This is not to disparage the holistic approach but to distinguish it from an approach that depends on the Framers' intentions, whether broadly or narrowly construed. Yet it will be a demerit of the holistic approach, in the eyes of many legal professionals, that it cuts free from the Framers' intentions.

IV. IMPLICATIONS FOR *ROE V WADE*

The issue of holistic versus clause-by-clause is not merely aesthetic or methodological. Despite the efforts that Dworkin makes to ground *Roe v Wade* in a particular clause of the Constitution, he cannot have great confidence that the rights he especially cherishes can be generated by theories limited to individual clauses, such as the Due Process Clause, *Roe*'s original home. The substantive construal of that clause stinks in the nostrils of modern liberals and modern conservatives alike, because of its association with Dred Scott's case[22] (though in fact it played only a small role in that decision) and with *Lochner*[23] and the other freedom of contract cases, because of its formlessness, because of its being rather buried in the Fifth Amendment (making one wonder whether it can be all that important—though, granted, it is featured more

---

[21] A topic to which Dworkin has made important contributions. See, for example, Dworkin, *Taking Rights Seriously* at 134-37 (cited in note 4); Dworkin, *A Matter of Principle* at 48-50 (cited in note 10); Dworkin, 57 U Chi L Rev at 663-74 (cited in note 1).

[22] *Scott v Sandford*, 60 US (19 How) 393 (1857).

[23] *Lochner v New York*, 198 US 45 (1905).

prominently in the Fourteenth Amendment), and because it makes a poor match with the right to notice and hearing that is the procedural content of the clause. If we must go clause by clause in constructing our constitutional theory (actually theor*ies*, on this approach), we are conceding, Dworkin must believe, too much rhetorical ammunition to the enemies of the sexual liberty cases.

Could the Ninth Amendment dissolve the tension between the clause-by-clause and holistic approaches? It is a chunk of the text, after all. It says, "The enumeration in the Constitution, of certain rights, shall not be construed to deny or disparage others retained by the people." Could this be a warrant for judges to recognize new rights, both against the federal government and against the states? There is an extensive literature on this question,[24] but it has had little impact because, with rare exceptions, neither the clause-by-clausers nor the holists are happy with basing decisions on the Ninth Amendment. The reason is that the amendment does not identify any of the retained rights, or specify a methodology for identifying them. If it gives the courts anything, it gives them a blank check. Neither the judges nor their academic critics and defenders want judicial review to operate *avowedly* free of any external criteria. Even "due process" and "equal protection" seem directive compared to the Ninth Amendment—or to "privileges and immunities," another constitutional orphan. So, not only is there not enough textual support for unenumerated constitutional rights, there is too much textual support for them.

The tension between the clause-by-clause approach and the holistic approach is stark in Dworkin's discussion of *Roe v Wade*. Despite the many insightful and even moving observations that he offers about the abortion problem,[25] he is not able to find a clause in which the right to an abortion can be made to fit comfortably, though he tries very hard to find one. In his account, as in that of his predecessors in the effort to rationalize the decision, *Roe v Wade* is the Wandering Jew of constitutional law. It started life in

---

[24] See, for example, Randy E. Barnett, ed, *The Rights Retained by the People: The History and Meaning of the Ninth Amendment* (George Mason, 1989).

[25] Not all of which I agree with, however. (For the reasons, see my book *Sex and Reason* ch 10 (Harvard, 1992).) For example, that "a great many abortions took place, before *Roe v Wade*, in states that prohibited abortion." Dworkin, in this volume, 411 (cited in note 14); that Catholicism "could not comprehensively change its views about abortion without becoming a significantly different faith," id at 413; or that illegal abortions are "dangerous," id at 411. And I don't understand why the Constitution must be interpreted to give *conclusive* weight to a woman's desire that her fetus die rather than that it be carried to term and turned over "to others to raise and love." Id at 411.

the Due Process Clause, but that made it a substantive due process case and invited a rain of arrows. Laurence Tribe first moved it to the Establishment Clause of the First Amendment, then re-canted.[26] Dworkin now picks up the torch but moves the case into the Free Exercise Clause, where he finds a right of autonomy over essentially religious decisions.[27] Feminists have tried to squeeze *Roe v Wade* into the Equal Protection Clause.[28] Others have tried to move it inside the Ninth Amendment (of course—but if I am right it has no "inside"); still others (including Tribe) inside the Thirteenth Amendment.[29] I await the day when someone shovels it into the Takings Clause, or the Republican Form of Government Clause (out of which an adventurous judge could excogitate the en-tire Bill of Rights and the Fourteenth Amendment), or the Privi-leges and Immunities Clause. It is not, as Dworkin suggests, a mat-ter of the more the merrier; it is a desperate search for an adequate textual home, and it has failed. I cannot adequately explain the reasons for this conclusion here,[30] but I will give the flavor of them by glancing briefly at the equal protection argument, which Catha-rine MacKinnon,[31] Sylvia Law,[32] Cass Sunstein,[33] and others have pressed.

The argument begins by noting that a law forbidding abor-tions weighs more heavily on women than on men. Granted. But a difference in treatment does not violate the Equal Protection Clause if it is justifiable, and this particular difference in treatment seems, at first glance anyway, justified by the fact that men and women are, by virtue of their biology, differently situated in rela-tion to fetal life. To show that the difference is not substantially related to an important governmental interest, and is therefore un-constitutional under the prevailing standard for reviewing sex dis-

---

[26] See Laurence H. Tribe, *American Constitutional Law* 1349-50 & nn 87-88 (Founda-tion, 2d ed 1988) (acknowledging "shift in the author's thinking" between 1973 and 1978).

[27] Dworkin, in this volume, 419 (cited in note 14).

[28] See notes 31-33 and accompanying text.

[29] Laurence H. Tribe, *The Abortion Funding Conundrum: Inalienable Rights, Affirma-tive Duties, and the Dilemma of Dependence*, 99 Harv L Rev 330, 337 (1985); Andrew Kop-pelman, *Forced Labor: A Thirteenth Amendment Defense of Abortion*, 84 Nw U L Rev 480 (1990).

[30] For a fuller discussion, see chapter 12 of my book, *Sex and Reason* (cited in note 25).

[31] See Catharine MacKinnon, *Toward a Feminist Theory of the State* 184-94 (Harvard, 1989); Catharine A. MacKinnon, *Feminism Unmodified: Discourses on Life and Law* 93-102 (Harvard, 1987); Catharine MacKinnon, *Reflections on Sex Equality Under Law*, 100 Yale L J 1281, 1309-28 (1991).

[32] Sylvia A. Law, *Rethinking Sex and the Constitution*, 132 U Pa L Rev 955 (1984).

[33] Cass R. Sunstein, *Neutrality in Constitutional Law (With Special Reference to Por-nography, Abortion, and Surrogacy)*, 92 Colum L Rev 1 (1992).

crimination challenged under the Fourteenth Amendment, requires consideration of the benefits to the fetus and the costs to
others, an intractable inquiry or at least one that the proponents of
Roe v Wade do not wish to undertake.

The door to that inquiry cannot be slammed shut by arguing
that, whatever justifications *might* be offered for laws forbidding
abortion, the support for those laws *in fact* comes from people who
want to keep women down; and an invidious purpose can condemn
a law. Realistically, an invidious purpose can condemn only a trivial law, such as a law imposing a poll tax or requiring a literacy test
for prospective voters; courts are not going to deprive the people of
essential legal protection just because some of the supporters of
such laws (laws criminalizing rape, for example) had bad motives.
The principal support for anti-abortion laws, moreover, comes not
from misogynists or from "macho" men (Don Juan would favor
abortion on demand because it would reduce the cost of sex), but
from men and women who, whether or not Roman Catholic (many
of them of course are Roman Catholic), believe on religious
grounds in the sanctity of fetal life. That is not a sexist or otherwise discriminatory or invidious belief, even though it is positively
correlated with a belief in the traditional role of women, a role that
feminists, with much support in history, consider subordinate. No
doubt for many opponents of abortion, opposition to abortion is
commingled with opposition to a broader set of practices and values—call it feminism. But for many supporters, abortion on demand is the very symbol of feminism. Should the courts take sides
in this clash of symbols?

Behind symbols, ideology, even religious belief may lie concrete interests. The debate over abortion, and over the sexual and
reproductive freedom of women more broadly, is in part a debate
between women who lose and women who gain from that freedom.
The sexually freer that women are, the less interest men have in
marriage, and women specialized in household rather than market
production are therefore harmed. This is a clash of interests, and
in a democratic system legislatures rather than courts are generally
considered the proper arenas for resolving such clashes.

Dworkin takes a different tack. He considers a person's view of
the sanctity of life a religious view even if the person is an atheist;
and he says that the government cannot, without violating the
Free Exercise Clause, make a person act on one religious view
rather than another. Well, fine, but if "religion" is to be understood so broadly, then we must allow for a religion of free markets
(economic freedom *is* a religion to Murray Rothbard, Milton and

David Friedman, Friedrich Hayek, Ayn Rand, Richard Epstein, and perhaps even Robert Nozick, whom, by the way, Dworkin has acknowledged as a fellow liberal[34]), a religion of animal rights, of environmentalism, of art, and so on. An ordinance that forbade an aesthete to alter the exterior of his landmark house would thus be an infringement of religious freedom. Dworkin's expansive notion of religion actually dissolves the distinction he wants to draw between restrictions on abortion and other restrictions on personal freedom.

Dworkin is able to make abortion a matter of the varying opinions that Americans hold about the sanctity of life, rather than an issue of life or death, only because he will not allow states to define the fetus as a person and therefore abortion as murder. (If he did allow this, he would not be able to distinguish abortion from infanticide.) Yet the states are allowed to decide what is property and (in the case of prisoners for example) what is liberty, for purposes of the Due Process Clause; why not what is a person? Can't a state decide that death means brain death rather than a stopped heart? And if it can decide when life ends why can't it decide when life begins? Here by the way is an illustration of one of the modest functions I assigned earlier to bottom-up reasoning, that of testing the consistency of our thought.

An Illinois statute makes abortion murder,[35] and on the civil side wrongful death.[36] The Supremacy Clause prevents its application to abortions privileged by *Roe v Wade*, but with that qualification the constitutionality of the statute cannot be doubted. It shows that the states are already in the business of defining human life. They can, thus, classify a fetus as a human being, and the question is then—because I do not think the state's declaration of personhood should be conclusive (what if it declared a meat loaf a person?)—the strength of the state's interest in protecting that newly recognized human being against various menaces to it.

Quite apart from the specific objections that can be made to Dworkin's attempt to ground a right of abortion in the Free Exercise Clause, it blurs his holistic approach. There is no actual inconsistency, because his interpretation of the Free Exercise Clause draws on values derived from his reflections on other provisions in the Constitution, consistent with his insistence on the integrity of

---

[34] See Bryan Magee, *Three Concepts of Liberalism: A Conversation with Ronald Dworkin*, New Republic 41, 47 (Apr 14, 1979).

[35] Homicide of an Unborn Child, Ill Rev Stat ch 38, ¶ 9-1.2 (1989).

[36] Wrongful Death Act, id at ch 70, ¶ 2.2.

the document as a whole. But his position would be clearer, and I think more persuasive, if he were content to derive a right of abortion from his general theory of constitutional law, in which the clauses merge and lose their distinctness and the issue of the right of abortion becomes the place of such a right in the liberal theory of the state—and I agree that it has the place in that theory that Dworkin assigns to it. *Griswold*, the first of the sexual liberty cases, actually started down this road. For we recall how Justice Douglas, albeit in his usual slipshod way, tried to extract a general (or at least generalizable) principle of sexual liberty from a collection of seemingly unrelated constitutional clauses.[37] But no judge has picked up this particular spear and tried to throw it farther.

V. A Role For Conscience; A Basis in Fact

The arguments against the holistic approach are familiar. The basic one is that it gives judges in a democracy (perhaps in any polity) too much discretion. When you think of all those constitutional theories jostling one another—Epstein's that would repeal the New Deal, Ackerman's and Sunstein's that would constitutionalize it, Michelman's that would constitutionalize the platform of the Democratic Party, Tushnet's that would make the Constitution a charter of socialism, Ely's that would resurrect Earl Warren, and some that would mold constitutional law to the Thomists' version of natural law—you see the range of choice that the approach legitimizes and, as a result, the instability of constitutional doctrine that it portends. It is no good saying that Epstein is wrong, or Michelman is wrong, or St. Thomas is wrong; the intellectual tools do not exist for administering a death blow to these theories (to *all* of them, at any rate). Logic, science, statistical inquiry, the lessons of history, shared intuitions—none of these techniques of either exact or practical reasoning can slay them, or even wound them seriously in the eyes of those drawn to them for reasons of temperament or personal experience. If the only constraints on constitutional decisionmaking are good arguments, the embarrassment is the number and strength of good arguments on both sides—on many sides—of the hot issues.

Heat is important here. If you're indifferent to the outcome of a dispute, you'll weigh up the arguments on both sides and give the nod to the side that has the stronger arguments, even if the weaker side has good arguments too. But if you have a strong emotional

---

[37] *Griswold*, 381 US at 484-86.

commitment to one side or another, it would be not only unnatural, but imprudent, to abandon your commitment on the basis of a slight, or even a not so slight, preponderance of arguments against your side. Our deepest commitments are not so weakly held. Hence there can be practical indeterminacy about an issue even if a disinterested observer would not think the competing arguments evenly balanced.[38]

A comprehensive theory of constitutional law is apt to step on the toes of many deeply held commitments without being supportable by decisive arguments. That is why the situation with respect to constitutional theory is one of practical indeterminacy, driving the cautious jurist back into the clause-by-clause approach. It is much easier to impute a purpose to a particular clause and then use that purpose both to generate and circumscribe the meaning of the clause—which is all I meant in speaking of Bork's "theories" of free speech and of antitrust—than to impute a purpose to the Constitution as a whole. The problem with the modest approach is that it opens up large gaps in constitutional protection. As the eighteenth century recedes, and the original text becomes a palimpsest overlaid with the amendments of two centuries, not only the vision but the very identity of the Founders blurs and by going clause by clause one could end up with a document that gave answers only to questions that no one was asking any longer. Americans like to think that the Constitution protects them even against political enormities that don't fit comfortably into one clause or another. This is the practical appeal of an approach that makes of the Constitution a tire that seals up automatically when it is punctured or gashed. In 1791 such an approach might well have been otiose; the modest top-down, the ambitious top-down, the bottom-up approaches might all have coincided. No more. They diverge further with every passing year, and the ambitious top-down approach becomes more attractive with every passing year. It is not just academic fashion that has made constitutional theorizing a bigger activity today than a century ago.

I would abandon, however, as too ambitious, too risky, too contentious, the task of fashioning a comprehensive theory of constitutional law, an "immodest" top-down theory intended to guide judges.[39] At the same time I would allow judges to stretch clauses—even such questionable candidates as the Due Process

---

[38] See Posner, *The Problems of Jurisprudence* at 124-25 (cited in note 11).

[39] The qualification "theory intended to guide judges" is vital. Academic theories have academic value, and can moreover point to or highlight facts that can alter judges' thinking,

Clause—when there is a compelling practical case for intervention. This was Holmes's approach, and later that of Cardozo, Frank-furter, and the second Harlan. Holmes said (privately, to be sure) that a law was constitutional unless it made him want to "puke."[40] If we follow this approach we must be careful not to appoint judges whose stomachs are too weak. Of course he was not speaking literally; nor am I. The point is only that our deepest values (Holmes's "can't helps"[41]) live below thought and provide warrants for action even when we cannot give those values a compelling or perhaps any rational justification. This point holds even for judicial action—although I may think this only because it makes a judge happier in his job. He knows that he won't have to ratify a law or other official act or practice that he deeply feels to be terribly unjust, even if the conventional legal materials seem not quite up to the job of constitutional condemnation. He preserves a role for conscience.

It is easy for legal professionals and intellectuals of every stripe to ridicule this approach—which, by the way, transcends both top-down and bottom-up reasoning by locating a ground for judicial action in instinct rather than in analysis. They can ridicule it for its shapelessness (shades of substantive due process!), its subjectivity, its noncognitivism, its relativism, its foundationlessness, its undemocratic character unredeemed by pedigree or principle. But the alternatives are unpalatable (to continue the digestive metaphor); and maybe what was good enough for Holmes should be good enough for us. And it need not, perhaps—this alternative approach that I am discussing—be quite as shapeless, as subjective, as visceral as I have implied. Certainly it need not be inarticulate (in this respect the digestive metaphor is inapt); Holmes was the most eloquent judge in the history of this country, perhaps of any country. And it can be—it should be—informed through empirical inquiry more searching than is normal in judicial opinions. Simple prudence dictates that before you react strongly to some-

---

just as economic theory can help us interpret the recent events in eastern Europe and the Soviet Union as a refutation of socialism.

[40] See Philippa Strum, *Louis D. Brandeis: Justice for the People* 361 (Harvard, 1984) ("[Justice Brandeis] told [his law clerks] that Justice Holmes employed a simple rule of thumb for judging the constitutionality of statutes, summed up in Holmes's question, 'Does it make you puke?' ").

[41] See Letter of Oliver Wendell Holmes, Jr., to Harold J. Laski (Jan 11, 1929), in Mark DeWolfe Howe, ed, 2 *Holmes-Laski Letters* 1124 (Harvard, 1953) ("when I say that a thing is true I only mean that I can't help believing it—but I have no grounds for assuming that my can't helps are cosmic can't helps").

thing you try to obtain as clear an idea as possible of what that something is.

The *Griswold* case, for example, in part because of the excellent brief of the lawyers for the birth control clinic (one of whom was Thomas Emerson of the Yale Law School faculty), provided an opportunity—which the Court didn't take—to deploy pertinent data in support of a professionally more respectable precedent than what emerged from Douglas's majority opinion and the concurrences. The brief highlights some striking facts which subsequent research[42] has confirmed. One is that statutes forbidding contraceptives had been passed in a wave in the late nineteenth century but had been repealed in all but two states, Connecticut and Massachusetts, in both of which repeal, though repeatedly attempted, had been blocked by the vigorous lobbying of the Catholic Church working on the large Catholic population in both states. But while the statute had remained on the books, the only efforts to enforce it—and they were entirely successful—were directed against birth control clinics, whose clientele was dominated by the poor and the uneducated; middle-class women preferred to go to their private gynecologist for contraceptive advice and devices. So the clinics were closed down and of course abortion was illegal at the time, making the sexual and reproductive dilemmas of poor women acute, while middle-class women had unrestricted access to contraceptives, and probably to safe illegal abortions as well if contraception failed, but it was less likely to fail for them.

And remember that the law made no distinction between married and unmarried persons; it could be thought therefore to burden marriage—specifically marriage by the poor and the working class—and to do so arbitrarily. The law had been founded on Protestant (indeed, such are the ironies of history, on anti-Catholic) concern with fornication, adultery, and prostitution, and with the immorality of immigrants and of the lower class generally, though it may actually have discouraged marriage—and fostered immorality—among the poor; and its survival owed everything to a belief, by 1965 limited essentially to Catholics and by no means shared by all of them, that it is sinful to impede the procreative outcome of an act of sexual intercourse.

The law, in sum, was sectarian in motive and rationale, capriciously enforced, out of step with dominant public opinion in the country, genuinely oppressive, and, I think it fair to say, a national

---

[42] See my discussion in chapters 7 and 12 of *Sex and Reason* (cited in note 25).

embarrassment—as would be a law forbidding remarriage, or limiting the number of children a married couple may have, or requiring the sterilization of persons having genetic defects, or denying the mothers of illegitimate children parental rights, or forbidding homosexuals to practice medicine, or forbidding abortion even when necessary to spare a woman from a crippling or debilitating illness, or requiring the tattooing of people who carry the AIDS virus, or—coming closest to *Griswold* itself—requiring married couples to have a minimum number of children unless they prove they're infertile. It is not the worst thing in the world to have judges who are willing to strike down such laws in the name of the Constitution. The sequelae to *Griswold* show that the risks in this approach are enormous too, but smaller I think than the risks that would be entailed by the totalizing approach that Professor Dworkin defends with such elegant tenacity.

Dworkin believes that only his approach can prevent constitutional doctrine from changing with every change in the composition of the Court. This exaggerates both the possibility of cogent theorizing at the high level of abstraction implied by the holistic approach and the fidelity of judges, especially Supreme Court Justices, whose decisions are unreviewable, to the doctrines (as distinct from narrow holdings) of their predecessors. Nothing but *force majeure* can prevent judges from giving vent to their political and personal values, if that is what they want to do.

I remind you, in support of my suggested approach, that judicial decision precedes articulate theory—because the duty to resolve the dispute at hand is primary—that few judges (few anybody) are equipped to create or even evaluate comprehensive political theories, that our judges are generally not appointed on the basis of their intellectual merit, and that instinct can be a surer guide to action than half-baked intellectualizing. I know that I seem to be indulging in paradox in proposing an approach that accepts the role of personal values in adjudication and asks only that they be yoked to empirical data. This may seem a strange match indeed. But personal values, while influenced by temperament and upbringing, are not independent of adult personal experience; and research—into facts, not into what judges have said in the past—can be a substitute for experience, can bring home to a judge the realities of a law against contraception or against abortion or against sodomy. That at least has been my own experience. It may not be typical. Yet I think it is apparent that most judges can handle facts better than they can handle theories. Of course that is what bottom-up reasoners say in defense of their approach.

Bottom-up reasoning *pretends*, however, to be—reasoning. I ask you to join with me in abandoning that pretense.

In doing so we will make room for the greatest judge in the history of our law, and probably the greatest scholar. I refer of course to Holmes—who also had the finest *philosophical* mind in the history of judging. His most famous judicial opinion is his dissent in *Lochner*.[43] But, judged by the usual principles of legal reasoning, it is a flop, because it illustrates Holmes's inveterate tendency "to substitute epigrams for analysis: instead of taking *Lochner* as the opportunity to show what the due process clause was all about, Holmes contented himself with the smug assertion that the clause did not 'enact Mr. Herbert Spencer's Social Statics.' "[44] I agree: "It is not, in short, a good judicial opinion. It is merely the greatest judicial opinion of the last hundred years."[45] There is something wrong with the conventional principles of legal reasoning. They miss the vital essence of legal growth and insight.

I remind you finally that I am speaking primarily of areas of constitutional law in which constitutional history and text give out. In an area such as freedom of speech, where we have a text and a history and a long case experience, the materials are at hand for the creation of a theory, albeit clause-bound, that will guide future decisions; and so, perhaps, with such questions as whether and what types of sex discrimination fall under the ban of the Equal Protection Clause.[46] In areas to which the constitutional text and history and a long decisional tradition cannot fairly be made to speak, such as that of sexual rights, we must either renounce a judicial role or suffer the judges to fall back on their personal values enlightened so far as they may be by a careful study of the pertinent social phenomena. Neither top-down nor bottom-up legal reasoning can finesse this painful choice.

---

[43] 198 US at 74.

[44] David P. Currie, *The Constitution in the Supreme Court: The Second Century: 1888-1986* 82 (Chicago, 1990). See also id at 81-82, 130.

[45] Richard A. Posner, *Law and Literature: A Misunderstood Relation* 285 (Harvard, 1988).

[46] There are, of course, many areas outside of constitutional law where field-specific theories are entirely feasible: torts, contracts, and antitrust are examples.

INTERDISCIPLINARY APPROACHES

The Politics of Women's Wrongs and the Bill of "Rights": A Bicentennial Perspective

Mary E. Becker†

The language of the Bill of Rights is almost entirely gender neutral and its provisions have always applied to some women.[1] But free white men of property designed the Bill of Rights in a political process from which they excluded most Americans and all women. Not surprisingly, the Bill of Rights served and serves the interests of such men better than the interests of others.

Legal constitutional literature, whether from the right or the left, tends to be celebratory rather than critical.[2] But in looking back on the Bill of Rights during this bicentennial year, women and many men outside the propertied white male class should be ambivalent. In this Article, I assess the Bill of Rights from the per-

---

† Professor of Law, The University of Chicago Law School. This Article is the written version of the Katz Lecture given at The University of Chicago Law School on October 24, 1991. I thank Pauline Bart, Cynthia Bowman, Jill Fosse, Marcella David, Rochelle Dreyfus, Laurie Feldman, Stephen Gilles, Mary Ann Glendon, Wendy Gordon, Hendrick Hartog, Lynne Henderson, Jennifer Hertz, Linda Hirschman, Elena Kagan, Linda Kerber, Larry Kramer, Norval Morris, Judith Resnik, Carol Rose, Vicki Schultz, Kenneth Simmons, Geoffrey Stone, Cass Sunstein, Nadine Taub, Morrison Torrey, Robin West, John Wiley, and workshop participants at the Chicago Feminist Colloquium, UCLA Law School, Emory Law School, University of Miami Law School, NYU Law School, Northwestern Law School, and the University of Wisconsin Law School for helpful comments on earlier drafts and Paul Bryan, Jennifer Hertz, Elizabeth Rosenblatt, William Schwesig and Charles Ten Brink for research and other assistance. Research support was provided by the Russell Baker Scholars Fund and the Russell J. Parsons Faculty Research Fund of the University of Chicago and by the Morton C. Seely Fund and the Jerome S. Weiss Faculty Research Fund.

[1] The Bill of Rights is almost entirely free of gendered language. It speaks repeatedly of "person" or "people." The Fifth Amendment contains one "himself" and the Sixth Amendment one "him" and two "his's." Thus, one has the right not to be "compelled in any criminal case to be a witness against *himself*," US Const, Amend V (emphasis added); the right of the criminal defendant "to be confronted with the witnesses against *him*; to have compulsory process for obtaining witnesses in *his* favor, and to have the Assistance of Counsel for *his* defense," US Const, Amend VI (emphasis added). But the clauses containing these references were understood as applying to "free" women from the first.

[2] See, for example, John Paul Stevens, *The Bill of Rights: A Century of Progress*, in this volume, 13; Charles Fried, *The New First Amendment Jurisprudence: A Threat to Liberty*, in this volume, 225; Cass R. Sunstein, *Free Speech Now*, in this volume, 255; Michael W. McConnell, *Religious Freedom at a Crossroads*, in this volume, 115; and Kathleen M. Sullivan, *Religion and Liberal Democracy*, in this volume, 195.

spective of women and other outsiders, with special emphasis on its continuing impact on women's political participation. I offer three kinds of criticisms in discussing specific clauses.

First, and most important, I make a point that is not normative or prescriptive but merely critical: the Bill of Rights does less to solve the problems of women and nonpropertied men than to solve the problems of men of property, especially white men of property. Some clauses, such as the Fifth Amendment right to "property," originally did not help most women, or helped only trivially, or had vastly different meanings for women and men. Often this disparity continues. Some provisions overlook much more serious problems for women than the problems they address. Consider, for example, women's Fourth Amendment right "to be secure in their persons, houses, papers, and effects against unreasonable [governmental] searches and seizures."[3] The Fourth Amendment neither gives women security in their homes from husbands nor ensures that government treat marital rape like other rapes and assaults. Indeed, at the time the Fourth Amendment was adopted, and in many jurisdictions today, husbands and lovers could and can rape "their" women without criminal consequences.

Some provisions operate differently for women and men in the sense that they perpetuate women's subordinate status. Although many historical inequities would have persisted without the Bill of Rights, the Bill magnifies these inequities. For example, the Religion Clauses permit substantial subsidies from government to mostly-patriarchal religious organizations—organizations that continue to be important socializing institutions for children.

Second, although the Bill of Rights may not *cause* a given problem, it sometimes impedes legislative reform. We revere the Bill of Rights;[4] its invocation legitimates the status quo. For example, the Second Amendment assists the National Rifle Association in preventing stringent federal gun control legislation. Thus, although gun control might be good for women, and is favored by most women,[5] the Second Amendment impedes its adoption.

My third point concerns politics. Several provisions of the Bill of Rights have continuing political effects, impeding women's effec-

[3] US Const, Amend IV.

[4] See, for example, Hendrik Hartog, *The Constitution of Aspiration and "The Rights That Belong to Us All"*, 74 J Amer Hist 1013 (1987).

[5] Katherine M. Jamieson and Timothy J. Flanagan, eds, *Sourcebook of Criminal Justice Statistics* 110, Table 2.43 (US Dept of Justice, 1987).

tive political participation today. Consider, for example, *Buckley v Valeo*, which held unconstitutional spending limits on individuals directly engaging in political speech, thus constitutionalizing the right of the rich to participate in the political process more effectively than the poor.[6] And women are, of course, disproportionately poor.[7]

More fundamentally, the Bill of Rights is inadequate in guaranteeing women the exercise of governmental power. Given that women were excluded from the process that produced the Bill of Rights and that few women occupy high government positions today, we should question the legitimacy of our purported democracy. Surely we would question whether another government was truly democratic if a majority group, other than women, had never held the top executive position and comprised only six percent of the national legislature.[8] Only six percent of governors are women.[9] Women hold only eighteen percent of state-wide elective offices.[10] Women occupy only 18.1 percent of state legislative seats.[11]

Women are similarly under-represented in judicial positions at the state and federal levels. At the state level, only 2.8 percent of the law-trained trial court judges are women; 5.5 percent of intermediate appellate state judges are women.[12] On state supreme courts, 5.89 percent of justices are women; 0.56 percent are minority women.[13] At the federal level, women comprise only 4.07 percent of administrative law judges; seven percent of district court judges; eight percent of appellate judges; and 11.11 percent of the

---

[6] 424 US 1, 58-59 (1976).

[7] See, for example, 163 *Current Population Reports: Consumer Income: Poverty in the United States: 1987*, 118-19 (US Bureau of the Census, 1989).

[8] See Center for the American Woman and Politics (CAWP), *Fact Sheet: Women in Elective Office 1991*, Table 2 (Eagleton Institute, 1991) (on file with U Chi L Rev).

[9] *The World Almanac and Book of Facts 1992* 596-99 (World Almanac, 1991).

[10] CAWP, *Fact Sheet: Statewide Elective Executive Women 1991* 1 (Eagleton Institute, 1991) (on file with U Chi L Rev).

[11] Id.

[12] Telephone conversation with Dixie Noble, National Association of Women Judges, Williamsburg, Virginia (Oct 3, 1991) (notes on file with U Chi L Rev). This data was current as of the date of the call for the intermediate and appellate state courts. The data on trial court judges is from 1985. I have not been able to find data on minority judges in other categories.

[13] Id.

Supreme Court. No women serve as senior appellate judges and less than two percent of the senior trial judges are women.[14]

Two points recur in my criticisms of various clauses. The Bill of Rights incorporates a private-public split[15] with only negative rights under a limited government. As a result, women's activities and concerns—from economic rights to religion—seem beyond the proper scope of government. That women are poorer than, and subordinate to, men appears "natural" and pre-political. Because of the private-public split, the Bill of Rights protects a number of institutions that are not entirely good for women from governmental interference and effective reform, such as the media. Because the Bill of Rights incorporates only "negative" rights, it includes no provision guaranteeing, or even defining as an important concern of national government, the economic and educational rights so important to women as caretakers. Indeed, women in the United States have fewer economic and educational supports than in any other North Atlantic nation.

To a large extent, my criticisms could apply to any written set of cryptic, abstract, and negative rights enforced by judges. Any such scheme will better protect the powerful against government action harmful to their interests than the less powerful, who need protection against the powerful as well as against the government. In part, this is because abstract rights enforced by judges, regardless of their wording, are unlikely to make radical changes in the distribution of power and resources.[16] The less powerful need many concrete, positive rights. These rights require detailed implementation schemes and the expenditure of funds. Judges are not likely to order either when enforcing abstract clauses. For example, no matter how a constitution states its equality provision, it is unlikely that the provision would lead judges to restructure the social security system so as to provide equivalent old-age security to breadwinners and homemakers.[17]

---

[14] Id. For discussions of this problem, see Carl Tobias, *The Federal Judiciary Engendered*, 5 Wis Women's L J 123 (1990); Judith Resnik, *"Naturally" Without Gender: Women, Jurisdiction and the Federal Courts*, 66 NYU L Rev (forthcoming 1992).

[15] For a discussion of the inconsistencies in the way we look at the public-private split, see Frances E. Olsen, *The Family and the Market: A Study of Ideology and Legal Reform*, 96 Harv L Rev 1497 (1983).

[16] See, for example, Gerald N. Rosenberg, *The Hollow Hope: Can Courts Bring About Social Change?* (Chicago, 1991); Mary E. Becker, *Prince Charming: Abstract Equality*, 1987 S Ct Rev 201.

[17] See Mary E. Becker, *Obscuring the Struggle: Sex Discrimination, Social Security, and Stone, Seidman, Sunstein & Tushnet's* Constitutional Law, 89 Colum L Rev 264, 271-85 (1989).

We cannot, therefore, expect a piece of paper to produce justice for women or other disadvantaged groups.[18] I nevertheless suggest a number of ways in which the Bill of Rights could be improved through interpretation or amendment. For example, courts could redefine, or legislatures amend, the Religion Clauses of the First Amendment to prohibit government subsidies to religions that close the ministry to women. Courts could read the Free Speech Clause of the First Amendment to allow content-based governmental regulation of some sexist and racist speech, or subsidies for nonsexist speech.

Some of my points focus on the underclass, rather than women as such. It is impossible to separate the interests of women from those of their class and race. When, for example, justice is denied the urban underclass in the criminal "justice" system, women inevitably suffer even though most of those caught directly in the system are men. Women suffer the destruction of their communities as well as the destruction of the men and boys who are, or might have been, in their lives.

In the Conclusion, I make several general points not directed at specific provisions of the Bill of Rights. An ideal Constitution or Bill of Rights would contain a substantive sex equality provision. At a minimum, such a provision could require judges to take into account detrimental impact on women when approaching other constitutional provisions as well as legislation and other governmental action.[19]

In the Conclusion, I address more basic structural problems with the Constitution and the Bill of Rights. First, I note that our constitutional structure, with its emphasis on individual rights conceived in absolutist and negative terms, particularly property rights, contributes to a culture in which the kinds of economic rights women need are difficult to achieve. Mary Ann Glendon makes this point in her most recent book.[20] Absolutist individual rights are almost inevitably negative limits on government. Giving constitutional sanctity to negative rights only, with a central role for property rights, reinforces American faith in rugged individualism which is so incompatible with the needs of children and their caretakers.

---

[18] See, for example, Rosenberg, *The Hollow Hope* at 10-13 (cited in note 16): Becker, 1987 S Ct Rev 201 (cited in note 16).

[19] See note 301 and accompanying text.

[20] Mary Ann Glendon, *Rights Talk: The Impoverishment of Political Discourse* 14, 24-25 (Free Press, 1991).

I also discuss some of the ways in which our constitutional structure is countermajoritarian. The Framers deliberately devised a government that would protect the propertied minority from oppression by the propertyless majority.[21] We should see it as a problem of democracy that, to date, women have not exercised their share of governmental power. I suggest that other governmental structures and electoral systems might be more democratic.[22]

In as many sections, I discuss seven clauses or sets of clauses in the Bill of Rights: the Religion Clauses[23] and Free Speech Clause[24] of the First Amendment; the right to bear arms of the Second Amendment;[25] protections against misuse of the criminal justice system in the Fourth, Fifth, and Sixth Amendments;[26] the right to be secure in one's home under the Fourth Amendment;[27] the property right of the Fifth Amendment;[28] and the Due Process right of the Fifth Amendment, together with the jury provisions of the Sixth and Seventh Amendments.[29] I begin with the first two clauses of the First Amendment, which "guarantee" freedom of religion. I discuss the religion clauses in greater depth than the others because there have been so few explorations in the legal literature of the problems religion poses for women.[30]

I. RELIGIOUS FREEDOM

The Bill of Rights begins with the First Amendment's Religion Clauses: "Congress shall make no law respecting an establishment of religion, or prohibiting the free exercise thereof."[31] All of my criticisms apply to both of these provisions. Religious freedom has meant, and means, vastly different things to women and men. In a number of ways this freedom secures to men rights superior to

---

[21] Jennifer Nedelsky, *Private Property and the Limits of American Constitutionalism: The Madisonian Framework and Its Legacy* 220-22 (Chicago, 1990).

[22] See notes 293-300 and accompanying text.

[23] See Section I.

[24] See Section II.

[25] See Section III.

[26] See Section IV.

[27] See Section V.

[28] See Section VI.

[29] See Section VII.

[30] For examples of articles that do discuss the patriarchal nature of religion, see Judith C. Miles, *Beyond* Bob Jones: *Toward the Elimination of Governmental Subsidy of Discrimination by Religious Institutions*, 8 Harv Women's L J 31 (1985); Kathleen A. McDonald, *Battered Wives, Religion, and Law: An Interdisciplinary Approach*, 2 Yale J L and Feminism 251 (1990); Judith Resnik, *On the Bias, Feminist Reconsiderations of the Aspirations of Our Judges*, 61 S Cal L Rev 1877, 1918-21 (1988).

[31] US Const, Amend I.

those secured to women. As I discuss below, religion perpetuates and reinforces women's subordination, and religious freedom impedes reform. The Religion Clauses allow substantial government subsidies of religion, such as exemptions from income and property taxes and awards of government contracts, thus assisting religion in perpetuating the subordination of women. Religious freedom also impedes women's effective political participation.

I divide the discussion of religion into four parts. I begin with a discussion of the ways in which religious practices and doctrine contribute to traditional attitudes towards women and their appropriate roles. Next, I discuss positive aspects of the relationship between religion and women: religion has often empowered women and has responded to and reflected the beliefs and values of women, who are, in general, more religious than men. Third, I consider empirical evidence on the relationship between religion and women's subordinate status. This evidence indicates that, despite the positive potential of religion and the ways in which women shape religion, mainstream Christian religions in the United States tend to contribute to women's subordinate status and to retard women's ability to participate fully and effectively in political life. I discuss several examples of current governmental subsidies of mostly-patriarchal religion. I conclude the Section by suggesting that the Religion Clauses be interpreted or amended to minimize their countermajoritarian effect while still preserving the positive potential of religion.

A. Religion and Patriarchy

The religious freedom clauses do not have the same meaning for women and men. For the Framers, the social reality of religious freedom meant their own freedom and the freedom of other men of their race and class to develop, govern, and control religion free of state interference. Even men of other races and classes could be religious leaders. For example, prior, even, to emancipation separate black churches developed led by black preachers.[32] These separate churches laid the foundation for an autonomous African-American Christianity.[33]

Religious freedom has not had this meaning for women. Religious leaders have been overwhelmingly male from the time the

---

[32] See, for example, Eugene D. Genovese, *Roll, Jordan, Roll: The World the Slaves Made* 255-79 (Pantheon, 1974).

[33] Id at 280.

Bill of Rights was passed until the present day. Many religious groups, including Mormons, Roman Catholics, and Orthodox Jews, still close the ministry to women. Other groups allow female ministers, but women still lead those groups in relatively low numbers, especially in the organizational hierarchy or at the head of large and important congregations.[34]

Male control of religious leadership has a number of negative effects. Only men are able to use positions as religious leaders to rise in the social hierarchy and to become leaders in their communities. The absence of women in leadership positions suggests to younger women and girls that women are not capable of leadership. Most important, because mainstream religious leadership has been and remains so dominated by men, mainstream religion inevitably incorporates male perspectives and bias against women. As one (male) student of comparative religion put it, "regardless of what a religion teaches about the status of women, or what its attitudes toward sex might be, if women are excluded from the institutions and positions that influence society, a general misogynism seems to result."[35] Religions thus contribute to women's subordinate status, not only within religious communities' hierarchies, but also in the broader culture.

At the time the Bill of Rights was passed, mainstream American religions taught the subordination of women openly and without embarrassment. For example, the Reverend Amos Chase described women's divinely ordained position of inferiority in a funeral sermon in Litchfield, Connecticut in 1791:

> A woman of fine feelings cannot be insensible that *her constitutional condition is secondary and dependant [sic] among men.* Nor can she long want conviction that the sure way to avoid any evil (to the thus dependant) [sic] is *to yield the front of battle to a hardier sex.*[36]

Religion was often used to legitimate the use of the state's power to enforce women's inferior social position. For example, in

---

[34] See, for example, Keith A. Roberts, *Religion in Sociological Perspective* 291-94 (Wadsworth, 2d ed 1990).

[35] Vern L. Bullough, *The Subordinate Sex: A History of Attitudes Toward Women* 134 (Illinois, 1973).

[36] Amos Chase, *On Female Excellence, or a Discourse in which Good Character in Women is Described, Occasioned by the Death of his Wife* 12 (delivered at Litchfield, March 6, 1791), as quoted in Nancy Falik Cott, *In the Bonds of Womanhood: Perspectives on Female Experience and Consciousness in New England 1780-1830* 99 (1974) (unpublished Ph.D. dissertation, Brandeis University (Waltham)) (on file with U Chi L Rev).

Bradwell v Illinois, the Supreme Court upheld a statute barring women from the practice of law, with three concurring justices using divine law to justify a man-made law by which men gave themselves a monopoly in the practice of law.[37]

Today, mainstream religions in the United States remain patriarchal in many ways. I begin with a discussion of substantive problems with religious doctrines and practices from the perspective of women.[38] The Religion Clauses have given men a comparatively greater ability to develop meaning, values, and morality based on an authority independent of government and made in their image. Although religion means much to women, it has not meant this.

1. Creation, male gods, and Eve.

All mainstream religious traditions in the United States replace the wonder of women's reproductive power with stories of creation by a male god.[39] In one of the two creation myths in Genesis, God created Eve out of Adam's rib to be his partner (rather than a being with her own purposes).[40] Eve tempts Adam and her reproductive power becomes a punishment for sin in the story of the fall.[41] Because of her sin, God declares Adam her master.[42] Christianity adds, as a prerequisite to true life, rebirth through redemption by a male god.[43]

Although there is an occasional use of female imagery in the Judeo-Christian tradition—in the Wisdom literature, for example[44]—the gods of that tradition are overwhelmingly male. The Christian "God the Father" is the ultimate male warrior: utterly

---

[37] 83 US (16 Wallace) 130, 132, 139 (1872).

[38] I have organized the discussion in the subsection in seven points, some of which apply to Jews and Christians, others of which apply only to Christians. Because most religious Americans are Jews or Christians, and because my space is limited, I examine only these traditions.

[39] Beverly Wildung Harrison, *Our Right to Choose: Toward a New Ethic of Abortion* 60-61 (Beacon, 1983); Mary Daly, *Gyn/Ecology: The Metaethics of Radical Feminism* 73-89 (Beacon, 1990).

[40] Genesis 2:18-23 (New English Bible). A less sexist version of creation is presented in the first story of creation. See Genesis 1:26-28.

[41] Genesis 3:16-19 (New English Bible):
   To the Woman he said: "I will increase your labor and your groaning, and in labour you shall bear children. You shall be eager for your husband, and he shall be your master."

[42] See id.

[43] Harrison, *Our Right to Choose* 59-61 (cited in note 39); Daly, *Gyn/Ecology* at 83-89 (cited in note 39).

[44] See, for example, The Wisdom of Solomon 10: 1-19 (New English Bible).

alone and without need for others or the ability to empathize with them, the unmoved mover.[45] More than the language ascribes maleness; the Old Testament God typifies the masculine warrior hero in western culture, violent and overpowering, striking down his enemies.[46] Jesus is, by contrast, often very feminine,[47] but his gender is clearly male. Although Mary sometimes has near-divinity status, she is a singularly passive and subservient god.

It is easy to dismiss this complaint as silly or unimportant. The effect of male gods goes unnoticed because it is so ubiquitous, and is effective because so consistent with male domination in our culture. If you look around, you will see widespread and severe under-representation of women in positions of power, as gods, in the ministry, as heroes, and as authorities, whether in religion or sports or the military or the evening news. Some of these problems are discussed elsewhere in this article.[48] The cumulative effect is a double message to girls. On one level, they hear, "you're equal, you're equal, you're equal." But when they observe the world around them, on television, in their history books, in their story books, in literature or religion, girls receive a different message: "you're not, you're not, you're not." Almost exclusively, they see males as active heroes and in positions of power and honor. Not surprisingly, girls and young women have less self-esteem and confidence than boys and men.[49]

Men in our culture fail to appreciate the advantages of having gods in their image. But women who can imagine a female god, despite indoctrination in religions with male gods, can sense the power of such images. Someone raised in the white Judeo-Christian tradition has extreme difficulty imagining a female god. But

---

[45] For feminist insight on the vision of "God the Father" as a male figure, see Catherine Keller, *From a Broken Web: Separation, Sexism and Self* 38-40, 86-87 (Beacon, 1986); Carol P. Christ, *Laughter of Aphrodite: Reflections on a Journey to the Goddess* 93-101 (Harper & Row, 1987); Susan Brooks Thistlethwaite, *Sex, Race, and God: Christian Feminism in Black and White* 109-25 (Crossroad, 1989).

[46] See, for example, Psalm 7:12-13 (New English Bible): "He sharpens his sword,/ strings his bow and makes it ready./He has prepared his deadly shafts and tipped his arrows with fire."

[47] For a discussion of the more feminine Jesus, central to the devotional life of many Christian women, white and black, see text accompanying notes 87-88.

[48] See text accompanying notes 152-59, 200, for example.

[49] American Association of University Women, *Shortchanging Girls, Shortchanging America: A nationwide poll to assess self esteem, educational experiences, interest in math and science, and career aspirations of girls and boys ages 9-15* graph B (following p 5) (Greenberg-Lake Analysis Group, 1991) (in elementary school, girls' self-esteem is 79% of boys'; in middle school and high school, 60% (calculation from figures in graph B)).

just a glimpse of the Goddess can be startling and empowering.[50] Mainstream American religions have not offered women what they offer men: the ability as leaders to develop powerful images of gods like themselves.

2. Emphasis on family stability.

In addition, all mainstream religious traditions emphasize family stability. Inequities exist in most families today, however, where women generally work more hours a week than their husbands because of the husbands' failure to share the second shift—housework. Emphasis on family stability, at least without an equal emphasis on the need for change within families, reinforces current advantages of both power and leisure that men enjoy within families. Religion encourages women to live with the status quo rather than destabilizing it by insisting on equality. For battered women, this emphasis reinforces their tendency to think only of the needs of others[51] and to try to keep the "family together at all costs—even the woman's life."[52] Again, religion does not do the same thing for women and men.

3. Fundamentalism, orthodoxy, and women's subordinate status.

Today, fundamentalist and orthodox religious groups, such as fundamentalist Christians, continue to teach, explicitly or implicitly, that women should be subordinate to men. For example, fundamentalist Christians still often state overtly that wives should submit to husbands. In *The Total Woman*, Marabel Morgan describes the "biblical remedy for marital conflict": " 'wives must submit to [their] husbands' leadership in the same way [they] submit to the Lord,' " citing Paul's letter to the Ephesians.[53] Orthodox Jews state less explicitly that wives should submit to husbands, but orthodox belief and practice implies women's inferiority in at least four different ways. First, Judaism is phallocentric:

---

[50] Catherine Keller discusses parallels between the opening of Genesis and earlier Babylonian creation myths and concludes that the earlier Goddess is reflected in certain words in Genesis. I was thrilled (and amazed at how thrilling it was) to find such a revelation in the words I had been taught to revere as a child. See Keller, *From a Broken Web* at 80-88 (cited in note 45).

[51] Robin West, *The Difference in Women's Hedonic Lives: A Phenomenological Critique of Feminist Legal Theory*, 3 Wis Women's L J 81, 98 (1987).

[52] Lenore E. Walker, *The Battered Woman* 164 (Harper & Row, 1979).

[53] Marabel Morgan, *The Total Woman* 69 (Revell, 1973) (quoting *The Living Bible* Ephesians 5:22 (Tyndale House, 1971)).

a mark on the penises of baby boys symbolizes "Abraham's everlasting covenant with his god." The phallus is thus sanctified.[54]

Second, Jewish marriage and divorce law do not treat women and men as equals.[55] In both, women are passive, men are active. In an Orthodox wedding, the bride says nothing. A divorce is something a man effects and gives to a woman; she cannot remarry unless he agrees to divorce her. Although she can demand a divorce, and he *should* then give it to her, among the strictly Orthodox she often has little recourse if he refuses.

Third, the obligation to worship and to study Torah, central to the lives of Orthodox men, is less important for women, though women should know enough Torah to be able to educate their children. Implicit is the message that she counts less. Indeed, for purposes of the minyan (the quorum needed for certain prayers), she does not count at all. Her husband begins the day by thanking God that he was not born a woman. (Thereby, according to the least objectionable meaning, expressing gratitude that he is called to worship God and study Torah).[56]

Fourth, the Jewish faith relegates women to serving others, rather than recognizing them as creatures with important spiritual lives.[57] Orthodox men serve God through prayer and study. Orthodox women serve God through serving others. For very Orthodox women, much of this service consists of cooking and cleaning under circumstances made onerous by dietary laws.[58]

Fundamentalist religious groups encourage or require women to fulfill traditional roles, including economic dependence on husbands and serving others in the home. Yet economic dependence on individual men weakens women's position within marriage. The combination of traditional roles and fundamentalists' unusually strong emphasis (relative even to other mainstream religious groups) on family stability lessens fundamentalist women's ability to object to traditional relationships between the sexes. Again, the

---

[54] Batya Bauman, *Women-identified Women in Male-identified Judaism*, in Susannah Heschel, ed, *On Being a Jewish Feminist: A Reader* 88, 91 (Schocken, 1983).

[55] Saul Berman, *The Status of Women in Halakhic Judaism*, in Elizabeth Koltun, ed, *The Jewish Woman: New Perspectives* 114, 115 (Schocken, 1976).

[56] Thena Kendall, *Memories of an Orthodox Youth* in Heschel, ed, *On Being a Jewish Feminist: A Reader* 96, 97-98 (cited in note 54).

[57] Berman, *The Status of Women in Halakhic Judaism* at 116 (cited in note 55).

[58] Kendall, *Memories of an Orthodox Youth* (cited in note 56). At the same time giving spiritual significance to women's work and the way it is done is in some ways positive, according importance and value to women.

main point is that religion does not offer women what it offers
men.

4.   The core of Christianity: forgiving and suffering.

All strands of Christianity urge forgiving. Christianity teaches
that the virtuous person forgives even the unpardonable. Quoting
Matthew 18:22, Marabel Morgan advises wives to forgive "seventy
times seven."[59] Christianity also places a high value on suffering,
the archetype being Jesus's suffering during the crucifixion.

Forgiving and valuing suffering are not effective strategies for
an oppressed group to force social change. These activities reinforce existing power disparities and encourage the disempowered
to accept their real-world disadvantages as spiritual advantages.

Forgiving and valuing suffering are particularly dangerous
strategies for battered women.[60] Such teachings encourage battered
women (who are all too likely to believe their batterers who ask
forgiveness and swear they will never do it again) to stay in extremely destructive relationships. Religious counselors often advise
battered women to "pray for guidance, become better women, and
go home and help their husbands 'become more spiritual and find
the Lord.' "[61]

Even more perversely, the Christian valuation of suffering encourages women to accept abuse. Christian theology glorifies vic-
timization, posing special hazards to women because society, as
well as Christianity, assigns them the "suffering-servant role."[62]
Joanne Carlson Brown and Rebecca Parker make this point
powerfully:

> Christianity has been a primary—in many women's lives *the*
> primary—force in shaping our acceptance of abuse. The cen-
> tral image of Christ on the cross as the savior of the world
> communicates the message that suffering is redemptive. If the
> best person who ever lived gave his life for others, then, to be
> of value we should likewise sacrifice ourselves. Any sense that
> we have a right to care for our own needs is in conflict with

---

[59] Morgan, *The Total Woman* at 144 (cited in note 53) (citing King James Version of
the Bible).

[60] See McDonald, 2 Yale J L and Feminism 251 (cited in note 30).

[61] Walker, *The Battered Woman* at 23 (cited in note 52).

[62] Joanne Carlson Brown and Rebecca Parker, *For God So Loved the World?*, in Joanne
Carlson Brown and Carole R. Bohm, eds, *Christianity, Patriarchy, and Abuse: A Feminist
Critique* 1, 3 (Pilgrim, 1989).

being a faithful follower of Jesus. Our suffering for others will save the world.[63]

Thus, the values at the core of the Christian tradition reinforce and contribute to women's suffering and subordination.

5. Female sexuality and mothering.

Traditionally, Judaism has linked women's bodies with uncleanliness, regarding menstrual blood and childbirth as polluting. Prior to menopause, the Jewish faith deems a woman unclean for two weeks of every month: while she is menstruating and for seven days thereafter until she has "undergone ritual purification in a mikveh" (ritual bath).[64] After childbirth, purification of the woman's body is also necessary.[65] Instead of celebrating women's reproductive power, Judaism perceives women's bodies (and women themselves) as unclean and polluted.

Judaism nevertheless sees marriage (and sexuality) as a positive experience, a necessary part of life for an observant member of the community. The blessing given the newborn child is to grow up to Torah, marriage, and good deeds. Orthodox congregations do not hire unmarried rabbis nor do they usually hire unmarried cantors.

Christianity more consistently approaches women's bodies and sexuality negatively, linking women with sexuality and sexuality with imperfection and sin.[66] For example, Clement of Alexandria wrote that for women, "the very consciousness of their own nature must evoke feelings of shame."[67] The equation of women with sex may seem odd, since men seem more interested in genital sex than women do. But, from the perspective of heterosexual men who feel sexual desire but regard sexual intercourse as "filthiness" and "disgustingness" (the terms belong to St. Thomas Aquinas[68]), there is a certain logic in regarding women as the source of the evil. Were there no women, these men would not be tempted to engage in such repulsive activities.[69]

---

[63] Id at 2.

[64] Paula Hyman, *The Other Half: Women in the Jewish Tradition*, in Koltun, ed, *The Jewish Woman* 105, 110-11 (cited in note 55).

[65] Heschel, ed, *On Being a Jewish Feminist: A Reader* 286 (cited in note 54) (glossary entry for *mikvah* at back of book).

[66] Bullough, *The Subordinate Sex* at 97-101 (cited in note 35).

[67] Uta Ranke-Heinemann, *Eunuchs for the Kingdom of Heaven: Women, Sexuality, and the Catholic Church* 127 (Doubleday, 1990) (quoting *Paedagogus* II, 33, 2.).

[68] Id at 194.

[69] Bullough, *The Subordinate Sex* at 84 (cited in note 35).

During much of Christian history, all sexual intercourse, even within marriage, was tainted. Augustine and Thomas Aquinas regarded original sin as transmitted via sexual intercourse (even when unaccompanied by pleasure).[70] For centuries, active sexuality ranked inferior to celibacy, and often was regarded as sinful even within marriage.[71] For example, Augustine regarded any married person who requested sex for pleasure, rather than procreation, as committing a venial sin.[72]

The equation of women with sexuality and sexuality with impurity and sin remains strong in Roman Catholicism, with its all-male celibate clergy and its rejection of contraception (which permits sex for pleasure). Most other Christian denominations permit clergy to marry, regard the married life as consistent with holiness, and permit contraception. But traces of the equation of women with sex and sex with sin persist. For example, most Christian denominations still insist on a belief in the Virgin Birth. The Virgin Birth distances ordinary women from the Christian ideal: ordinary reproduction and mothering are tainted. If Mary is "pure" because she never had sex, all other mothers are impure because they did. Again, religious doctrine offers different things to women and men. In the areas of sexuality and reproduction, religion stresses female impurity and male creative power.

6.   Christian sin and virtue.

Christianity defines as sin what is most likely to be the sin of men: putting one's own development and needs ahead of others. It defines as virtue self-sacrificing love.[73] But self-sacrifice is often women's sin. Christianity thus encourages women to do what society encourages them to do as caretakers and nurturers: hide their own talents and find fulfillment vicariously through service to the talents of others. This very sacrifice tends to be the sin of women, who are too likely to dissipate themselves "in activities which are merely trivial" in the service of others.[74] A woman's greatest temp-

---

[70] Ranke-Heinemann, *Eunuchs for the Kingdom of Heaven* at 192-93 (cited in note 67).

[71] Id at 27-28.

[72] Id at 95.

[73] There is only one gospel parable about failing to develop one's talents. See Matthew 25:14-30 (New English Bible). In contrast, the gospels are full of verses on the need for humility. Christian churches continue to define sin primarily as pride rather than hiding.

[74] Valerie Saiving, *The Human Situation: A Feminine View*, in Carol P. Christ and Judith Plaskow, eds, *Womanspirit Rising: A Feminist Reader in Religion* 25, 38 (Harper & Row, 1979). Keller carries this insight further, noting that "God the Father" is the embodiment of Christian (male) sin. See Keller, *From a Broken Web* at 38-40 (cited in note 45).

tation is to hide her talents rather than develop them, sacrificing her development as an autonomous self in order to serve others. A woman who does this is:

> guilty of the sin of hiding; inasmuch as she has poured herself into vicarious living, inasmuch as she has denied her sense of self in total submission to husband/father/boss or in total self-giving to children, job, or family, she has been guilty of the sin of hiding. As she has been afraid to dream a dream for herself as well as for others, and as she has trained herself to live a submerged existence, she has hidden from her full humanity.[75]

Thus, the dominant conceptions of both Christian virtue and sin discourage women from developing as autonomous beings. Focusing on men's sin as *the* sin and extolling women's sin as virtue is a likely result of male domination of a religious tradition. Theology, like theory, is in large part autobiography. For most men, Christianity has correctly identified sin and virtue. Following Christian teaching helps men to become better people. But men have neither the insight nor any incentive to define women's sin in a way that will encourage women to become more self-interested. Instead, men define sin in a way that encourages women to sin rather than to work against their real temptations. It is possible to have it both ways; Christianity could give equal emphasis to both women's sin (hiding) and men's sin (pride), stressing the need to avoid *both*. Had women participated equally as leaders in Christianity, it is likely that Christianity would do so rather than perpetuate "woman's bondage to her hiddenness."[76] To reiterate my major point, religion does not mean for women what it means for men.

7. Christianity and traditional roles for women: Mary the mother.

Mainstream Christian religions present, as ideal, traditional images of women as caretakers, nurturers, servants of others.[77] Mary, the most prominent woman, is the most traditional and submissive of women: "I am the Lord's servant; as you have spoken, so

---

See also Susan Nelson Dunfee, *The Sin of Hiding: A Feminist Critique of Reinhold Niehbuhr's Account of the Sin of Pride*, 65 Soundings 316 (1982).

[75] Dunfee, 65 Soundings at 321-22 (cited in note 74).

[76] Id at 322.

[77] See, for example, Jerome L. Himmelstein, *The Social Basis of Antifeminism: Religious Networks and Culture*, 25 J Scientific Study Religion 1, 8 (1986).

be it.''[78] In contrast to the portrayal of women in a singular traditional role, men are seen in many roles: God, savior, prophet, religious leader, father, etc. Again religion offers different things to
men and women. It offers men a greater range of more powerful
roles.

These problems in mainstream religions, particularly Christian
religions, are deeply embedded in religious belief and practice.
These religions cannot eliminate the sexism easily; the use of gen-
der-neutral language will not eradicate deeper problems. A number
of commentators consider America's religious traditions "to be our
most deep-seated cause of patriarchy."[79] Nevertheless, religion has
been and is a positive influence in many women's lives. It is a
source of meaning for women more than for men, despite its patriarchal nature. I next consider the positive aspects of the complex
relationship between women and religion. This exploration balances my critical discussion of religion. It does not, however, de-
tract from my main point. Religious freedom has not given women
and men the same ability to develop an extra-governmental authority for meaning, values, and morality.

B. Religion as a Positive Force in Women's Lives

In this Section, I discuss two positive aspects of religion for
women. First, I explore ways in which religion has empowered
women. Second, I explore ways in which religion has been affected
by and reflects women's beliefs and values.

1. Religion often empowers women.

Throughout history, religion has been a source of power for
individual women. Like men, many women, from Joan of Arc to
African American women preachers in the nineteenth century,[80]
have found an authority in religion to support unconventional
choices. Religious activities and organizations offered women

---

[78] Luke 1:38 (New English Bible) (Mary's reply to the angel Gabriel when informed
that she will have a son, though she is a virgin).

[79] Anne Barstow Driver, *Religion*, 2 Signs 434, 434 (1976) (review essay). See also, for
example, John Wilson, *Religion in American Society: The Effective Presence* 264 (Prentice
Hall, 1978) ("Religion is probably the single most important shaper of sex roles."); Himmelstein, 25 J Scientific Study Religion at 7-12 (cited in note 77).

[80] For the stories of some of the latter, see, for example, Bert James Loewenberg and
Ruth Bogin, eds, *Black Women in Nineteenth-Century American Life* (Penn State, 1976);
William L. Andrews, ed, *Sisters of the Spirit: Three Black Women's Autobiographies of the
Nineteenth Century* (Indiana, 1986); Jean McMahon Humez, ed, *Gifts of Power: The Writ-
ings of Rebecca Jackson, Black Visionary, Shaker Eldress* (Massachusetts, 1981).

meaningful and respectable work in public life when many women were otherwise relegated to their homes. Women in religious orders received educations and achieved independence denied to most women. Activists in the suffrage and abolition movements first organized and pushed for change through their churches.[81] Some religious groups, particularly Quakers, produced exceptionally high numbers of women leaders.[82] During the nineteenth century, women used movements with religious overtones and membership, such as the temperance, voluntary motherhood, and social purity movements, to try to better the condition of women in a variety of ways.[83] Although many of these women used religious networks and ideals in their organizing, they were rarely religious leaders as such. Their ability to restructure religious belief and practice was therefore limited.

Religion continues to play a positive role in the lives of many women today. Most religious Christian women today, and more women than men, regard their religious commitment as a positive experience.[84] In the next Section, I explore some of the reasons why Christianity, despite and even because of its sexism, appeals disproportionately to women.[85]

2. Religion reflects women's traditional roles and values.

Religious values are, in many ways, more consistent with women's roles than men's. A man's duty to support his family by succeeding in the competitive world of a market economy conflicts

---

[81] See, for example, Eleanor Flexner, *Century of Struggle: The Woman's Rights Movement in the United States* (Harvard, rev ed 1975); Marjorie Wall Bingham, *Women and the Constitution: Student Textbook* 23-24 (Communicorp, 1990); Nancy A. Hewitt, *Women's Activism and Social Change: Rochester, New York, 1822-1872* 43-44 (Cornell, 1984).

[82] Bingham, *Women and the Constitution* at 22-24 (cited in note 81).

[83] See, for example, Linda Gordon, *Woman's Body, Woman's Right: A Social History of Birth Control in America* 116-20, 131-32 (Penguin, 1977); Elizabeth B. Clark, *Religion and Rights Consciousness in the Antebellum Woman's Rights Movement*, in Martha Albertson Fineman and Nancy Sweet Thomadsen, eds, *At the Boundaries of Law: Feminism and Legal Theory* 188 (Routledge, 1991); Carolyn De Swarte Gifford, *Women in Social Reform Movements*, in Rosemary Radford Ruether and Rosemary Skinner Keller, eds, 1 *Women and Religion in America: The Nineteenth Century* 294 (Harper & Row, 1981); Nancy F. Cott, *The Bonds of Womanhood: "Woman's Sphere" in New England, 1780-1835* 149-54 (Yale, 1977).

[84] Robert Wuthnow and William Lehrman, *Religion: Inhibitor or Facilitator of Political Involvement Among Women?*, in Louise A. Tilly and Patricia Gurin, eds, *Women, Politics, and Change* 300, 302 (Russell Sage Foundation, 1990). Indeed, "[w]omen are 18 points more likely than men to say that their religious commitment has been a positive experience." Id.

[85] Jews are as likely to be men as women. See George Gallup, Jr., *Religion in America 50 Years: 1935-1985*, in The Gallup Report No 236 at 34 (1985).

somewhat with the virtues of mainstream Christianity. Christianity calls for humility, service to others, obedience to the laws of God (rather than the market), generosity to the poor and unfortunate, and forgiving and forgetting. These virtues better match women's traditional roles as mothers, nurturers, and enablers responsible for making home a "haven" from the heartless world of the market.

I noted earlier that Christian sin is sin for men: pride and putting oneself first. For women, real sin tends to be forgetting one's own needs and living through others, the sin of "hiding," of failing to use one's talents. Ironically, Christianity extols women's sin—self-sacrifice and vicarious fulfillment—as the primary virtue. But precisely because self-sacrifice is women's real sin, the Christian notions of sin and virtue resonate with women. Christianity gives positive meaning to women's behavior as subordinates and victims.

Women's culture and rules of conduct also identify and proscribe the sin of pride. In her recent book, *You Just Don't Understand*,[86] Deborah Tannen studied the ways groups of girls and groups of boys interact. For girls, interaction is about sharing feelings and experiences, about empathy. Girls tend to consider it socially inappropriate to put oneself forward as superior, to out-distance one's friends in any way. Unusual success is something one apologizes for or explains away. Boys tend to see interaction as essentially about establishing hierarchy, out-distancing one's friends both in games and in other activities, using words to demonstrate that because of one's success, one out-ranks another. Given these differences, Christian sin will seem odd to boys, and out of touch with reality. For girls, Christian sin resonates with their social norms, which proscribe precisely the same thing as Christian sin. In other words, Christian virtues of service and self-sacrifice resonate deeply with girls' culture and with what girls are told they should do in order to be good wives and mothers. They make less sense for boys because they are inconsistent with boys' culture and with the traditional breadwinner role in a rough-and-tumble market economy. Thus, the appeal of Christianity is precisely its danger for women. Had more Christian theologians and preachers been women, Christianity might give equal emphasis to women's sin, and resonate with women's culture no more than with men's.

---

[86] Deborah Tannen, *You Just Don't Understand: Women and Men in Conversation* (William Morrow, 1990).

In Christianity, the evangelical emphasis on inner feelings and the emotional cult of Jesus also appeals greatly to women. Evangelical movements dominated Protestantism in America in the nineteenth century and profoundly changed the content of all mainstream Christian denominations,[87] shifting the devotional focus of many from a macho "God the Father" incapable of empathy to a very feminine and empathetic Jesus. For many women, religion fills an important emotional void. Educated in heterosexual romance,[88] but unable to find a satisfactory male lover, women find in religion the romantic emotional union they long for and cannot find in a relationship with a man.

The Christian emphasis on suffering, as exemplified by the crucifixion, valorizes traditionally feminine masochism of the sort Freud would recognize. In part, the appeal of Christianity to women arises from its ability to give meaning to the suffering and pain of their own lives; to give meaning to all suffering and subordination.

Jewish traditions are feminine in another sense, one not shared by most Christian sects: religious rituals in the home are of great importance. Women are ultimately responsible for such rituals. This emphasis sanctifies the space traditionally reserved for women and gives significance to women's caretaking activities, especially as cooks and organizers of family holidays and rituals.

In addition, both Judaism and Christianity protect and support women in important ways. Both legitimate and value women's traditional roles. Both developed economic protections for wives and mothers. For example, canon law developed the obligations of a husband, separated from wife and children, to pay alimony and child support. These obligations became the basis of secular family law's economic supports for divorced women.[89] Orthodox Judaism provides a number of property protections for a divorced wife.[90] In addition, the secular idea of equality—which has been important

---

[87] See Claude Welch, 1 *Protestant Thought in the Nineteenth Century: 1799-1870* 22-30 (Yale, 1972); Cott, *The Bonds of Womanhood* at 128-37 (cited in note 83). For another view of Jesus as feminine, see Roberts, *Religion in Sociological Perspective* at 284 (cited in note 34).

[88] On the importance of romance to women, see, for example, Dorothy C. Holland and Margaret A. Eisenhart, *Educated in Romance: Women, Achievement and College Culture* (Chicago, 1990); Keller, *From a Broken Web* at 15-16 (cited in note 45).

[89] See Mary Ann Glendon, *State, Law and Family: Family Law in Transition in the United States and Western Europe* 312-13 (North-Holland, 1977).

[90] See, for example, Daniel I. Leifer, *On Writing New Ketubot*, in Koltun, ed, *The Jewish Woman* 50 (cited in note 55).

in giving women a basis for arguing for social change—may have its origins in Christian ideas and ideals.

Although many feminists have left patriarchal religions because of the difficulty of reconciling their beliefs about women with traditional religious beliefs and practices,[91] many other women and feminists work from within to make religions less sexist and more responsive to, and reflective of, the human condition. Within Jewish and Christian congregations, feminists are working in many ways and on many levels to make religions more responsive to women's needs. For example, feminists challenge the focus on the male sin of pride in Christianity to include the female sin of "hiding,"[92] which is the "underdevelopment or negation of self."[93] Feminists also bring insights to evangelical Christianity (including fundamentalist evangelical groups),[94] Roman Catholicism,[95] Judaism,[96] and the study of early Christianity.[97] This outpouring of feminist insights and criticisms of mainstream religions indicates the deep attachment many women feel toward religion, even when they see its sexism.

The positive aspects of the relationship between women and religion and women's deep attachment to religion do not negate my central concern: religious freedom has not meant the same thing for women and men. Indeed, this discussion has demonstrated the close link between religion's appeal to women and its danger for women. Religion values women's traditional roles, including subordination and even suffering. Religion also offers emotional fulfillment, rather than requiring women to find fulfillment through the development of their abilities. Thus, religion reinforces women's subordinate status. It does not, of course, have this effect for men, who dominate both religion and society in general. In the next Section, I explore the empirical literature on the effect of religion on

---

[91] Wuthnow and Lehrman, *Religion* (cited in note 84).

[92] See Dunfee, 65 Soundings 316 (cited in note 74). See notes 74-76 and accompanying text.

[93] Saiving, *The Human Situation* at 37 (cited in note 74). See also Keller, *From a Broken Web* at 12, 39-40, 190 (cited in note 45).

[94] See Judith Stacey, *Brave New Families: Stories of Domestic Upheaval in Late Twentieth Century America* 139-46 (Basic, 1990) (reviewing writings of evangelical feminists).

[95] See generally Anne E. Carr, *Transforming Grace: Christian Tradition and Women's Experience* (Harper & Row, 1988); Rosemary Radford Ruether, *Sexism and God-Talk: Toward a Feminist Theology* (Beacon, 1983).

[96] See, for example, Koltun, ed, *The Jewish Woman* (cited in note 55).

[97] See, for example, Elisabeth Schussler Fiorenza, *In Memory of Her: A Feminist Theological Reconstruction of Christian Origins* (Crossroad, 1983).

political issues important to women and on women's political participation.

C. Empirical Evidence: Religion and Women

Religious Christians are more likely than other Americans to take positions inconsistent with women's equality. Those who attend Christian services frequently are more likely to oppose abortion, the Equal Rights Amendment, paternity leave, affirmative action quotas, government support of day care, women keeping their birth name or using the title "Ms.," and allowing girls on boys' sports teams.[98] Indeed, Christian "church attendance is generally more strongly related to [these] antifeminist beliefs than are education, income, occupational status, class, age, residence, and most other social traits."[99] Findings like these have been replicated in study after study.[100]

The evidence on the relationship between Jewish religious commitment and attitudes toward women is ambiguous. Female supporters of feminism are likely to have had parents who were Jewish, atheist, or agnostic and are more likely to be Jewish, athe-

---

[98] Himmelstein, 25 J Scientific Study Religion 1, 9-10 (cited in note 77). In another study, Christian church attendance was found to be correlated with traditional answers to two questions about the desirability of a traditional division of labor and power with women taking the domestic, subordinate role, and with two traditional answers about the consequences for children of maternal employment. Karen Oppenheim Mason and Yu-Hsia Lu, *Attitudes Toward Women's Familial Roles: Changes in the United States, 1977-1985*, 2 Gender & Soc 39, 43, 49-51 (1988).

[99] Himmelstein, 25 J Scientific Study Religion at 13 (cited in note 77).

[100] See id (looking at data amassed in a number of studies, including data from general population surveys, and concluding that antifeminist attitudes are rooted in Christian religious networks); Merlin B. Brinkerhoff and Marlene M. MacKie, *Religious Denominations' Impact Upon Gender Attitudes: Some Methodological Implications*, 25 Rev Religious Research 365, 365 (1984) ("denomination, the typology, and attendance [at Christian religious services] tend to be more strongly correlated to gender attitudes than age or education"); Ross K. Baker, Laurily K. Epstein and Rodney D. Forth, *Matters of Life and Death: Social, Political, and Religious Correlates of Attitudes on Abortion*, 9 Amer Pol Q 89 (1981) (approval of abortion found to be "a function of intensity of religious adherence"); Mary Y. Morgan, *The Impact of Religion on Gender-Role Attitudes*, 11 Psych Women Q 301 (1987) (religious devoutness most important variable for predicting five measured dimensions of gender-role attitudes); Carol Mueller and Thomas Dimieri, *The Structure of Belief Systems Among Contending ERA Activists*, 60 Soc Forces 657, 664-65 (1982) (activist opponents of state ERA in Massachusetts in 1975 were all members of a church or parish; most proponents were not); Kent L. Tedin, *Religious Preference and Pro/Anti Activism on the Equal Rights Amendment Issue*, 21 Pac Sociol Rev 55, 64 (1978) (study of activists involved in state deliberations on national ERA in Texas in spring of 1975; anti-ERA activists tended to belong to conservative denominations).

ist, agnostic, or Unitarian themselves.[101] But these studies confound secular Jewish people who identify with their ethnic heritage and those who are religious. It is not clear whether religious Jews are less sexist than religious Christians.[102] Given the content of Orthodox belief and practice,[103] it is possible that at least some religious Jews possess more sexist views than secular Jews.

To be sure, there is some variation among Christian denominations with respect to issues important for women's equality.[104] For example, researchers using 1980 data found that 85.7 percent of Jews, 64.3 percent of Catholics, 59.8 percent of Fundamentalist Protestants, 59.2 percent of other Protestants, and twenty-five percent of Mormons supported the Equal Rights Amendment.[105] One study of students at Utah State University demonstrated that Mormon students have much less favorable attitudes toward nontraditional roles for women than do other students.[106] Across Christian denominations, however, researchers have "clearly, con-

---

[101] J.A. Dempewolff, *Some Correlates of Feminism*, 34 Psych Rep 671, 671 (1974). I have not found studies examining various strands of Judaism to see if they differ on this point. Even religious Jews may be relatively egalitarian as a result of stress on the Israeli norm of sexual equality (which exists at least on the level of American rhetoric). See Andrea Dworkin, *Israel: Whose Country Is It Anyway?*, Ms. 69, 73 (Sep/Oct 1990).

[102] Of those who identified themselves as Jewish in a 1975 study, only 38% were members of a synagogue and only 32% attended services. Steven M. Cohen, *American Modernity & Jewish Identity* 56 (Tavistock, 1983). In 1989, Christians were 21-26% more likely to attend service than Jews. See Tom W. Smith, *Counting Flocks and Lost Sheep: Trends in Religious Preference Since World War II*, in GSS Social Change Rep No 26, 53, 55 (National Opinion Research Center University of Chicago, 1991).

[103] See notes 58, 64-65 and accompanying text.

[104] See Himmelstein, 25 J Scientific Study Religion at 7 (cited in note 77) ("Jews and the unaffiliated are distinctly more liberal on both ERA and abortion than either Protestants or Catholics. Protestants tend to be slightly more supportive of abortion and less supportive of ERA than Catholics. Fundamentalist and conservative Protestants are more likely to oppose both than are liberal protestants."). Himmelstein reviewed a number of population studies. See also Brinkerhoff and MacKie, 25 Rev Religious Research at 374 (cited in note 100) (some variation in gender attitudes found by Christian denomination: Mormons and Pentecostals most traditional in terms of attitudes though in terms of division of household labor and family power, Mormons among most egalitarian); Val Burris, *Who Opposed the ERA? An Analysis of the Social Bases of Antifeminism*, 64 Soc Sci Q 305, 308-10 (1983); Baker, Epstein, and Forth, 9 Amer Pol Q at 99 (cited in note 100) (denominational variation only modest on approval of abortion; key factor found to be intensity of religious adherence).

[105] Burris, 64 Soc Sci Q at 309 (cited in note 104). See also Glenna Spitze and Joan Huber, *Effects of Anticipated Consequences on ERA Opinion*, 63 Soc Sci Q 323, 326 (1982) (national sample: Catholics, Jews, and those without a religious affiliation more favorable to ERA than Protestants).

[106] Moshe Hartman and Harriet Hartman, *Sex-role Attitudes of Mormons vs. Non-Mormons in Utah*, 45 J Marriage & Family 897, 899 (1983).

sistently"[107] found a strong correlation between church attendance and opposition to the ERA[108] and abortion:[109] "Religious involvement has a conservative effect [on ERA and abortion attitudes] no matter what the denomination or its doctrines (though the magnitude of the effect varies)."[110] Religious devoutness has greater predictive power with respect to five dimensions of gender-role attitudes among women undergraduates than self esteem, assertiveness, mother's education, or mother's employment. The greater the woman's devoutness, the more traditional her notions about sex roles.[111]

---

[107] Himmelstein, 25 J Scientific Study Religion at 7 (cited in note 77).

[108] See, for example, Burris, 64 Soc Sci Q at 309-10 (cited in note 104); Baker, Epstein, and Forth, 9 Amer Pol Q at 99-101 (cited in note 100) (survey of New Jersey voters: opposition to ERA correlates with strength of religious attachment, regardless of whether respondent Catholic or Protestant); Louis Bolce, Gerald De Maio, and Douglas Muzzio, *ERA and the Abortion Controversy: A Case of Dissonance Reduction*, 67 Soc Sci Q 299, 306, 310 (1986) (Center for Political Studies National Election Study Data: traditionalist early supporters of ERA reversed positions as they experienced cognitive dissonance; white religious people especially likely to switch from pro-ERA to anti-ERA); David W. Brady and Kent L. Tedin, *Ladies in Pink: Religion & Political Ideology in the Anti-ERA Movement*, 56 Soc Sci Q 564, 575 (1976) (study of anti-ERA activists in Texas: 98% church members; 66% Fundamentalist Protestant; 25% other Protestant; 92% religion very important).

There are feminist reasons why one might oppose the ERA. See generally Becker, 1987 S Ct Rev at 214-24, 215 n 49 (cited in note 16). The empirical research consistently finds a correlation between religious commitment and, not just opposition to the ERA, but more generally opposition to change in women's roles and status. See notes 98-116 and accompanying text. In fact, the states that refused to ratify the ERA were states in which women were generally worse off than the states in which the ERA was ratified. See David C. Nice, *State Opposition to the Equal Rights Amendment: Protectionism, Subordination, or Privatization*, 67 Soc Sci Q 315, 324-25 (1986) (states supporting ERA had lower divorce rates; better AFDC benefit levels; better control of domestic violence; were less likely to have women on death row; were less likely to have called for banning abortion; were less likely to have required school segregation). This suggests that opposition was not grounded on a commitment to women's welfare, but an opposition to increased status for women. Id at 326-27.

[109] See, for example, Baker, Epstein, and Forth, 9 Amer Pol Q at 99-100 (cited in note 100) (survey of New Jersey voters: opposition to abortion correlates with *strength* of religious attachment, rather than with being a Catholic or Protestant); Sharon Marmon and Howard A. Palley, *The Decade After Roe Versus Wade: Ideology, Political Cleavage, and the Policy Process*, in Gwen Moore and Glenna Spitze, eds, 2 *Research in Politics and Society: Women and Politics: Activism, Attitudes, and Office-Holding* 181, 194 (1986) ("Among Catholics and Protestants who are frequent and regular churchgoers, church attendance strongly correlates with opposition to abortion on demand, a correlation which is considerably stronger with respect to Catholics than to Protestants.").

[110] Himmelstein, 25 J Scientific Study Religion at 8 (cited in note 77). This author notes that "differences are more marked for Catholicism than for Protestants and for the more conservative protestants than the less conservative ones, but they are present across the board." Id at 7.

[111] Morgan, 11 Psych Women Q at 305-06 (cited in note 100). Morgan measured five gender-role attitudes:

Interestingly, the correlation between Christian religious commitment and sexist attitudes contrasts with the relationship between such commitment and racist attitudes. Although moderately active Christians are, on the average, more racist than those who do not attend church, the most committed church members are as tolerant of racial minorities as non-members.[112] By contrast, church members are more sexist than the nonaffiliated, and the most committed churchmembers are the most sexist.[113]

The reader may object that religious activities (or perhaps Christian religious activities) do not "cause" antifeminist or other political attitudes or acceptance of traditional women's roles. Rather, those with traditional attitudes are more likely to be members of religious groups, especially conservative religious groups. Thus, self selection explains the correlation between religious involvement and antifeminist beliefs.

But children are not born with either sex-role attitudes or religious commitments. Rather, they are socialized within religious communities and by parents with certain beliefs. There is a high correlation between one's religious training as a child and one's religious commitment as an adult. For example, ninety-one percent of those "raised as Baptists say they are Baptists today."[114] For Episcopalians, the figure is ninety percent; for Lutherans, eighty-nine percent; for Methodists, seventy-four percent; for Presbyterians, seventy-two percent; for Catholics, eighty-one percent; for Jews, eighty-six percent; for those with no religion, forty-four percent.[115] The fact that parents so successfully socialize their chil-

---

(a) familial roles, i.e., mothers' and fathers' roles pertaining to household division of labor and care of children; (b) extrafamilial roles, i.e., roles of men and women regarding career commitment, decisionmaking, and leadership ability; (c) male/female stereotypes, i.e., beliefs about the innate characteristics of men and women such as male superiority and female dependency; (d) social change as related to sex roles, i.e., changes in social structure necessary for equality in male/female roles such as equal pay and equal job opportunities . . . ; and [(e)] gender-role preferences for role of wife, i.e., the role of a woman in relationship to her husband when she is working outside the home.

Id at 302 (citations omitted).

[112] Richard L. Gorsuch and Daniel Aleshire, *Christian Faith and Ethnic Prejudice: A Review and Interpretation of Research*, 13 J Scientific Study Religion 281, 285 (1974). "The more intrinsically religious, nonfundamentalistic, and theologically discriminating persons were also more tolerant." Id at 281. See also Keith A. Roberts, *Religion in Sociological Perspective* 261-79 (Wadsworth, 2d ed 1990).

[113] Roberts, *Religion in Sociological Perspective* at 280-300 (cited in note 112).

[114] *Public Opinion Report: America: Land of the Faithful* 96, 101 n (American Enterprise, 1990).

[115] Id (again, the figure for Jews would include both religious and secular Jews). I am not asserting that adults *never* choose religion. Fifty-six percent of those raised without

dren into their religion means that we cannot regard correlations between sexist attitudes and religious beliefs as the result of self-selection by autonomous adults. To the extent religious beliefs correlate with antifeminist beliefs, sexual equality for younger generations conflicts with religious freedom for older generations.[116]

Further, to the extent "autonomous" adults do chose religion, the correlation between church devotion and antifeminist political views should be troubling because of the unavailability of any non-sexist religious tradition in the American mainstream. Adults have only a limited set of options—a set that does not include any tradition in which women have been leaders in appropriate levels for any period of time (let alone the millenia over which mainstream religious traditions have developed). If a nonsexist religion *were* part of the American mainstream, we would live in a culture rather different from the present one, and "autonomous" adults in that culture would likely make quite different choices from those made by "autonomous" adults in this culture. That people choose from the options available to them cannot justify the range of options.

The studies already cited suggest that mainstream Christian religions contribute to women's subordinate status in society at large: churchgoers are more likely to take antifeminist positions on political issues important to women.[117] Mainstream Christian religions also impede women's success as politicians. Researchers have found a negative correlation between fundamentalist membership within a state and female representation in the state legislature.[118] A study of female candidates running for state and national office from New York city and two neighboring counties found Catholic women underrepresented and Jewish women overrepresented.[119]

Churches also engage directly in politics. Protestant and Catholic organizations are often used to rally opposition to feminist is-

---

religion nevertheless have a religious affiliation as adults. My point is that particular religious beliefs are passed on from one generation to the next; one cannot, therefore, assert that religious beliefs are the result of choice by "autonomous" adults. If all children were raised without religion, fewer would be associated with religious organizations as adults (and more would be feminists as adults).

[116] *Wisconsin v Yoder*, 406 US 205, 241-46 (1972) (Douglas dissenting in part) (pointing out that religious freedom of high school-age Amish children may conflict with their parents' religious freedom).

[117] See text accompanying notes 98-111.

[118] See, for example, Thomas J. Bolgy, John E. Schwarz, and Hildy Gottlieb, *Female Representation and the Quest for Resources: Feminist Activism and Electoral Success*, 67 Soc Sci Q 156, 161 (1986).

[119] Nikki R. Van Hightower, *The Recruitment of Women for Public Office*, 5 Amer Pol Q 301, 311 (1977).

sues, and thereby have a very direct impact on politics.[120] Catholic prelates have been more willing to criticize female Catholic politicians (as compared to men) for failing to follow official doctrine.[121] Yet many Protestant and Catholic organizations enjoy significant tax and postage advantages over women's political organizations such as NOW PAC.

The empirical work on religion and women examined in this Section shows that religion is a political problem for women. Christian religious values support the sexual status quo. Christians disproportionately favor antifeminist positions. In part, this is because sexism pervades religious doctrines and practices in content and effect. In part it is because religious organizations are political actors and are led by men. In the next subsection, I examine the extent to which government subsidizes religion despite its antidemocratic effects.

D. Government Support for Religion

In the United States, we have neither separation of church and state nor state neutrality toward religion. Rather, the government contributes significantly to religions. I briefly give three examples: 1) *Lynch v Donnelly*[122] ("the creche case"); 2) tax and postage advantages; and 3) income tax-free housing subsidies for "ministers of the gospel." In each of these examples, the governmental subsidy is troubling for two reasons. The first is a general objection: subsidies to mainstream religions contribute to women's subordinate status generally and within the political system. The second is an objection to more specific practices. In the creche case, the government subsidized a sexist image. In the case of tax and postal subsidies, religions, which mobilize opposition to feminist issues, receive benefits denied women's political organizations. And housing subsidies reinforce and magnify discriminatory employment practices within religious organizations.

The reader may object that the Bill of Rights does not *cause* the problems in these three areas: it does not mandate the display of sexist imagery on government property, require tax exemptions from generally applicable taxes, or require housing subsidies. In-

---

[120] See, for example, Kenneth D. Wald, Dennis E. Owen, and Samuel S. Hill, Jr., *Churches as Political Communities*, 82 Amer Pol Sci Rev 531, 533-34 (1988); Himmelstein, 25 J Scientific Study Religion at 8 (cited in note 77).

[121] See, for example, Geraldine A. Ferraro with Linda Bird Francke, *Ferraro: My Story* 222 (Bantam, 1985).

[122] 465 US 668 (1984).

deed, the housing subsidy may be unconstitutional under the Establishment Clause.[123] My point is that, except for the housing subsidy, the Bill of Rights does not *prohibit* these subsidies. When they are held unconstitutional, as in the housing subsidy case, it is not because they discriminate against women. Indeed, the conflict between religious freedom and equality for women is not even visible in the literature or caselaw of the First Amendment.

1. *Lynch v Donnelly.*

In *Lynch v Donnelly* the Supreme Court held that the Establishment Clause does not prohibit a merchants' association in Pawtucket, Rhode Island, from erecting a creche (along with a number of other symbols, including a clown, an elephant, and a teddy bear) in a public park.[124] This governmental subsidy for religion—allowing public property to be used for the display of religious symbols—is not neutral with respect to sex for two reasons. First, most religion is patriarchal and governmental subsidies of religion will, therefore, reinforce patriarchal traditions. Second, an image of the Holy Family displayed on government property raises a more particular set of problems.

The relationship between Mary and Jesus embodies a male fantasy of the ideal mother-son relationship. Jesus is more important; he is the son of God. Mary, as a mere mortal, exists to serve him. Jesus will grow to be a powerful and active male with an important mission. Mary plays only a passive supporting role. The birth of Jesus had nothing to do with his mother's sexual pleasure or even sexuality. The reproductive agency of "God the Father" overshadows the reality of female reproductive power.[125] Admittedly, the virgin Mary is a positive female image—it might be worse to have no women at all. Moreover, both men and women are supposed to emulate the ideal of submission to the will of God. But, as noted earlier, the message of submission to God's will addresses men's sin (pride) more than women's sin (passivity) and Mary's virginity is a denial of female sexuality and reproductive power.[126] This message is a barrier to women's equality and effec-

---

[123] See note 134 and accompanying text.

[124] 465 US at 685. The Court has subsequently held that a creche not surrounded by animals or other secular symbols cannot be constitutionally placed on government property. *County of Allegheny v ACLU*, 492 US 573, 621 (1989).

[125] See, for example, Daly, *Gyn/Ecology* at 83 (cited in note 39).

[126] See text accompanying notes 73-74, especially Saiving, *The Human Situation* (cited in note 74).

tive political participation because it reinforces men's superior status and political dominance.[127]

Of course, the sexism in the imagery of the creche is likely to have only trivial consequences, compared with much more harmful sexist imagery, such as pornography and advertising aimed at selling clothes or beauty products to women by making women feel inadequate. For this reason, I would not recommend excluding such religious symbols from government property because of the harm they cause to women. But the sexism in such symbols should not remain invisible in legal analysis. And perhaps such sexism should justify compensatory "affirmative" action.

2. Tax and postage breaks for religious organizations.

Although religious organizations and feminist political organizations both act politically on issues important to women, such as abortion, they do not receive equal treatment in terms of either taxes or postage rates. The Constitution permits the government to subsidize antifeminist religious organizations yet deny equal treatment to feminist political organizations.

To illustrate this point, I compare the treatment of the Catholic Church, a politically active religious organization, and the treatment of a feminist political action organization, NOW PAC. The government treats these two organizations similarly in terms of income tax on organizational income: both are exempt, since NOW PAC is a nonprofit organization.[128] But all states exempt the Catholic Church from paying property taxes for churches.[129] Many states exempt all church-owned property used exclusively for religious purposes.[130] Most states exempt the Catholic Church from

---

[127] See Section I.B.2.

[128] 26 USC § 527(a).

[129] Richard R. Hammar, *Pastor, Church & Law* 378 (Gospel Publishing, 1983). In order to qualify for federal income tax exemptions, a religious corporation must not intervene or participate directly in political campaigns at all (i.e., it cannot support or oppose specific candidates). Id at 340-41. Nor is the organization allowed to undertake "substantial efforts to influence legislation." Id at 336-40. There is no bright line for determining when such efforts are substantial. Id. The Catholic Church has never lost its tax exempt status despite the fact that it teaches a position on abortion inconsistent with legislation allowing women to choose and despite the use of church networks and events to rally opposition to abortion rights. Nor did the Catholic Church lose its status when prelates attacked Geraldine Ferraro because of her position on abortion. See Ferraro, *My Story* at 211-39 (cited in note 121).

[130] Hammar, *Pastor, Church & Law* at 378 (cited in note 129). Others exempt parsonages in addition to churches. Id.

sales taxes, use taxes, and personal property taxes as well.[131] NOW PAC must pay these taxes. Contributors to the Catholic Church can deduct their contributions from income in calculating income tax.[132] Contributors to NOW PAC cannot. The Catholic Church can take advantage of subsidized mail rates which are unavailable to NOW PAC.[133]

Subsidies to mostly patriarchal religions are not gender neutral in two obvious respects. First, they are equivalent to taxpayer funding of sexist institutions. Second, these subsidies have political effects that are detrimental to women.

3.   Income tax treatment of housing for "ministers of gospel."

The Internal Revenue Code permits a "minister of the gospel" to exclude housing costs or a housing allowance from income for tax purposes.[134] As interpreted by the courts and the IRS, this exemption is available only to ordained ministers and those holding equivalent positions in congregations without ordained clergy.[135]

Like other governmental subsidies of religion, this policy is troubling on two levels. First, it subsidizes only institutions that are mostly patriarchal because it subsidizes only religious workers and not other people. Second, because of the specifics of the provision, it magnifies traditional discrimination by religious groups with respect to leadership positions, giving the benefit only to those religious workers who are likely to be male: people who are either ordained ministers or the functional equivalent.[136] Women's traditional roles in congregations—as teachers, support staff, etc.—do not qualify under this provision, even when the women are full-time employees.[137] Although this provision of the federal

---

[131] See *Texas Monthly, Inc. v Bullock*, 489 US 1, 29, 30 n 2, 32 n 3 (1989) (Scalia dissenting) (lists many state exemptions from sales and use taxes). The majority struck down a Texas exemption from sales and use taxes that applied only to religious periodicals and not to "similar" charitable or educational organizations. Id at 25.

[132] 26 USC § 170(b)(1)(A)(ii).

[133] See 39 USC § 3626 (1991). Second and third class rates are available at a discount to religious, educational, scientific, philanthropic, agricultural, labor, veterans, and fraternal organizations if they are nonprofit and meet other requirements. 39 USC § 3626(a)(1) (1991) (incorporating former code sections 39 USC §§ 4358, 4359, 4421, 4422, 4452, and 4554). Qualified political committees may also mail at the discounted third class rates, but must be part of a political party. See 39 USC §§ 3626(e)(1) and 3626(2)(A). NOW PAC would not qualify, nor would any other women's organization since no women's political party exists.

[134] 26 USC § 107.

[135] See IRS Rev Rule 78-301 (Jewish cantor qualified as "minister of the gospel").

[136] Treas Reg § 1.107-1(a).

[137] IRS Private Letter Ruling 8614010 (unordained teachers did not qualify).

tax code is probably vulnerable to constitutional challenge in light of a 1989 Supreme Court case holding that a tax exemption applicable *only* to religious activities is unconstitutional,[138] it remains in effect. And if the Court does overrule it, I doubt that discrimination against women religious workers will inform the decision.

There are no estimates of the total taxpayer subsidies for religious organizations through postage and tax breaks including the housing exemption, but the amount is quite large. One recent case involved over $100,000 in sales taxes imposed on the Jimmy Swaggart Ministries' sales of religious materials through the mail over a period of about eight years in a single state.[139] In fiscal year 1985, Congress appropriated $723.6 million to subsidize postage for qualifying organizations; about forty-five percent of the qualifying organizations were religious.[140] Total annual government subsidies to religious organizations in the United States as a result of exemptions and direct subsidies must be well in the billions.

I have discussed three ways in which government supports mostly patriarchal religions: through the display of religious symbols on government property; through tax and postage breaks for religious organizations; and through exemptions from income tax for housing allowances for ministers of the gospel. This is not, of course, an exhaustive list. Myriad federal and state laws and policies support religion. I mention two others briefly as illustrations of the breadth of the problem, though many more exist. First, governments routinely hire religious organizations to perform governmental services, such as caring for abused or neglected families and children, sometimes in religious institutions.[141] Second, the Supreme Court has permitted federal funding of religious counseling programs on teenage sexuality,[142] though such programs reflect religious organizations' sexist attitudes toward sexuality, especially those of the Catholic Church.

---

[138] *Texas Monthly*, 489 US at 25.

[139] See Brief for Appellant 8-9, *The Jimmy Swaggart Ministries v Board of Equalization of California* S Ct No 88-1374, 493 US 378 (1990).

[140] See Richard Kielbowicz and Linda Lawson, *Reduced-Rate Postage for Nonprofit Organizations: A Policy History, Critique, and Proposal*, 11 Harv J L & Pub Pol 347, 398-99 (1988).

[141] See, for example, *Catholic Agency to Operate Youth Shelter*, Chi Trib 3 (May 13, 1988) (describing temporary shelter and more permanent institution for abused or delinquent children to be run by Catholic Charities); *State Seeks to Overhaul its Shelters*, Chi Trib 5 (Jul 28, 1989) (describing a child intake center for young neglected or abused children run by Catholic Charities: Columbus-Maryville Reception Center).

[142] *Bowen v Kendrick*, 487 US 589, 621 (1988).

484   Mary E. Becker

True, government receives services in exchange under these kinds of programs, but hiring sexist religious organizations to perform governmental functions is not sex-neutral. Such contracts support religion and increase its power. Indeed, such programs often give governmental power as well as money to religion.

In this Section, I have discussed both the positive and negative aspects of mainstream religion for women and the relevant empirical evidence. As I stressed in the Introduction, my major point is purely critical: the religion clauses of the First Amendment do not have the same meaning for women and men. These clauses have not empowered women as much as men to develop an autonomous source of authority, meaning, value, and morality independent of the state. Instead, these clauses shield from state regulation deeply patriarchal institutions which impede women's political effectiveness in a democracy. Indeed, the Religion Clauses, at least as currently interpreted, allow the government to magnify the subordinating effects of religion by subsidizing it and giving governmental power to religious activities. There has been too little appreciation of this point in the legal literature. I know of no other discussion of this point, though there is some appreciation of the conflict between religious freedom for parents and children's interests in education or health care.[143]

We cannot expect the Bill of Rights to establish all the social rights women need. I do, however, suggest a change that we could implement by interpretation or amendment. In interpreting the First and Fourteenth Amendments, the Court could hold unconstitutional tax subsidies, tax exemptions, or the award of government contracts to religions that discriminate overtly and admittedly on the basis of sex in hiring leaders.

On this view, the Constitution compels a *Bob Jones* approach to religions that discriminate on the basis of sex in leadership positions. In *Bob Jones*, the IRS denied charity status to a religious university that discriminated on the basis of race.[144] The religious university prohibited interracial dating because the religion disapproved of interracial marriage. The Supreme Court held that the denial of charity status to such an institution was statutorily permissible. The case is understood to indicate that the Supreme

---

[143] See, for example, *Wisconsin v Yoder*, 406 US 205, 242-46 (1972) (Douglas dissenting) (pointing out that religious freedom of high school-age children may conflict with their parents' religious freedom); *In re Eric B. v Ted B.*, 189 Cal App 3d 996, 1008-09 (1987) (blood transfusion ordered for child whose parents' religion would not permit it).

[144] *Bob Jones University v United States*, 461 US 574, 604-05 (1983).

Court does not regard the IRS interpretation of the statute as unconstitutional. If the Court had regarded the IRS interpretation as unconstitutional, it would have interpreted the statute to avoid the constitutional problem. Thus, a denial of a benefit to a religious organization that admittedly and overtly discriminates on the basis of race does not violate either of the Religion Clauses.

The Constitution may *compel* this approach in the context of race. The grant of a tax advantage to a racist university is state action. And in both *Shelly v Kraemer*,[145] involving government enforcement of a racially exclusionary covenant, and *Burton v Wilmington Parking Authority*,[146] involving the government's grant of a lease to a racially discriminatory restaurant, the Supreme Court held that similar private racial discrimination was impermissible when accompanied by similar state action.[147]

This approach could and should extend to banning tax exemptions and postal subsidies and the award of government contracts to religious organizations that close leadership positions to women. Like anti-miscegenation policies (*Bob Jones*), and segregation in housing (*Shelley*) and in places of public accomodation such as restaurants (*Burton*), keeping women out of leadership positions denies women the opportunity to participate in society as equals. Keeping women out of religious leadership positions precludes a necessary prerequisite for religious freedom to mean as much to women as to men. For example, the sexist imagery of the creche, whether on government property or elsewhere, is less likely to change if women are not religious leaders. At the same time, denying benefits to religions that overtly close leadership positions to women would not involve greater governmental entanglement with religion than denying benefits to religious universities with anti-miscegenation policies. Under this interpretation, the Constitution would prohibit benefits only to religions or religious institutions which overtly and admittedly deny women religious autonomy and free exercise.

Thus, the Court could regard a *Bob Jones* approach as constitutionally compelled when religions close leadership positions to women. Grants of tax exemptions or subsidies or government contracts to such organizations are state action and the state cannot discriminate on the basis of sex without an exceedingly strong justification. Religious liberty cannot justify the exemption, since

---

[145] 334 US 1 (1948).
[146] 365 US 715 (1961).
[147] *Shelley*, 334 US at 23; *Burton*, 365 US at 726.

these organizations deny women the religious liberty they offer men. To be sure, denial of such subsidies will "hurt" religions that close leadership to women just as the denial of tax exempt status hurt Bob Jones University.[148] Our unwillingness to take action with respect to this blatant sex discrimination reflects our priorities. At present, religious freedom for some men and women justifies affirmative support for institutions subordinating women and denying women full religious freedom. At the very least, we should rethink our decision to *foster* such institutions.

We could modify the Constitution to proscribe religious subsidies altogether, or even to require state regulation of religion to eliminate sexism. I would not, however, favor these approaches. I think that all people need sources of authority outside government. Too much government control would preclude the ability of religion to perform that function. My only suggested change in this area is, therefore, exceedingly moderate.

II. FREE SPEECH AND PRESS

Amendment I to the Constitution guarantees "freedom of speech" and freedom "of the press."[149] In a society with a mass culture, where institutions of the "press" wield immense power, the freedom of the press assumes particular importance. The First Amendment views the "press" (television, movies, videos, books, video games) as largely beyond the reach of government regulation. Yet the "press," particularly its most powerful organ, television, impedes the democratic functioning of our political system. I discuss this problem in terms of both race and sex.[150] In addition, a "free" market in speech means that the market, governed by ability to pay, determines who can speak.

Although white men are a minority in this country, television presents a world in which white men are the majority of the popu-

---

[148] For an argument that distinguishing between religions that overtly discriminate and those that do not is a violation of the Establishment Clause (and *Bob Jones* was therefore wrongly decided), see Miles, 8 Harv Women's L J 31 (cited in note 30) (arguing that all subsidies to religions should therefore end).

[149] US Const, Amend I.

[150] In each case, there can be no absolutely firm evidence of causation. For example, correlations are always ambiguous since television viewing may not cause the observed trait but rather be related to other factors that cause both the observed trait and television viewing. I assume, for this discussion, that television does influence viewers' attitudes, especially the attitudes of young viewers.

lation as well as socially dominant.[151] As one group of researchers expressed it, "[t]he prominent and stable overrepresentation of well-to-do white males in the prime of life dominates prime time."[152] In 1989, only twenty-nine percent of the leads in feature films were for actresses. And a number of those parts were prostitutes, though prostitutes are a very small part of the population of women.[153] Minorities and women rarely appear as authorities on television.[154] When women do appear as authorities, they frequently espouse positions regarded as anti-women.[155] Television and films *about* caretaking portray men more often than women in the lead caretaking roles, contributing to the invisibility and undervalvation of women as caregivers.[156]

Media sports pervade American culture, and almost all sports heroes are male. Women's team sports do not receive national television coverage. When women do appear in popular sports events, such as Olympic gymnastics or ice skating, aesthetics—watching the female body in motion in a revealing costume—dominate. Even women tennis stars (the most visible non-Olympic women athletes in the national media) are held to an aesthetic standard more demanding, especially with respect to weight, than that applied to men.[157]

The visual media (film, television, magazines) inevitably stress appearance. But for women, the standard of beauty is both more demanding and of more singular importance than for men. In part, this is because women are more often defined as sex objects. Even when not presented *solely* as sex objects (for example, when portrayed as a business person with a briefcase in a credit card advertisement), women are almost always young and beautiful. The

---

[151] See, for example, Matilda Butler and William Paisley, *Women and the Mass Media: Sourcebook for Research and Action* 78 (Human Sciences, 1980) (reporting that in the thirteen studies of the relative appearance of women and men over a twenty year period, the appearance of women became less frequent; overall, men were 72% of all characters and women 28%; one study found that 79% of all white characters were men and 90% of all black characters were men).

[152] George Gerbner, et al, *Charting the Mainstream: Television's Contributions to Political Orientations*, 32 J Commun 100, 106 (1982).

[153] Gene Siskel, *It's the Streep Mystique*, Chi Trib Arts 4 (Sep 2, 1990).

[154] For example, most voice overs in commercials are male voices. See Butler and Paisley, *Women and the Mass Media* at 69-70 (cited in note 148).

[155] See Sunstein, in this volume, 284 (cited in note 2).

[156] See Judith Posner, *Where's Mom? With more men in the kitchen, TV mothers fade from the screen*, 49 Media & Values 6 (1989). On the undervaluation of women's caretaking in the context of child custody standards, see Mary E. Becker, *Maternal Feelings: Myth, Taboo, and Child Custody,* 1 S Cal Rev L & Women's Stud (forthcoming 1992).

[157] See John Feinstein, *Hard Courts* 201-02 (Villard, 1991).

ubiquitous message confirms reality: a woman's body determines her value, even as a business professional.[158] Advertising is particularly damaging to women; it sells products to women by making women feel inadequate.[159]

Pornography—sexually explicit material presenting women's subordination as sexy—exemplifies the politics of sexuality in the media. Andrea Dworkin states: "The major theme of pornography as a genre is male power, its nature, its magnitude, its use, its meaning. . . . Male power is the raison d'etre of pornography; the degradation of the female is the means of achieving this power."[160] And pornographic themes—that women are sex objects available for male pleasure at all times—pervade mainstream media such as MTV and visual advertising.[161]

Children's television programs are actually more sexist than programs for adults. A 1982 study found that women and minorities appeared even less in children's television than in prime time. When present, women were "portrayed in a more stereotyped manner in children's programming than in prime-time programming."[162] Children's television has not improved since 1982. As of late April, 1991, no Saturday morning children's show featured a girl heroine.[163] The networks had cancelled the only Saturday morning cartoon show with a female lead because only girls were watching the show.[164] Girls will watch shows with boys in leading roles, but boys will not watch shows with female leads.[165] Many shows, like *Garfield*, are essentially all male; others may have one female, under the "Smurfette principle." The Smurfette principle presents "a group of male buddies . . . accented by a lone female, stereotypically defined."[166] The message: "boys are the norm, girls the variation; boys are central, girls peripheral; boys are individuals, girls types."[167] Children's television also emphasizes the impor-

---

[158] See generally, Naomi Wolf, *The Beauty Myth: How Images of Beauty Are Used Against Women* (Morrow, 1991); Robin Tolmach Lakoff and Raquel L. Scherr, *Face Value: The Politics of Beauty* (Routledge & Kegan Paul, 1984).

[159] Wolf, *The Beauty Myth* at 276-77 (cited in note 158).

[160] Andrea Dworkin, *Pornography: Men Possessing Women* 24-25 (Dutton, 1989).

[161] See, for example, Fred Pelka, *"Dreamworlds": How the Media Abuses Women*, 21 On The Issues 20 (1991).

[162] John Corry, *Children's TV Found Dominated by White Men*, NY Times C14 (Jul 15, 1982).

[163] Lynn Hecht Schafran, *The Smurfette Principle*, NY Times 6-12 (Apr 28, 1991).

[164] Id.

[165] Bill Carter, *Children's TV, Where Boys Are King*, NY Times A1 (May 1, 1991).

[166] Katha Pollitt, *The Smurfette Principle*, NY Times 6-22 (Apr 7, 1991).

[167] Id.

tance of physical appearance for girls.[168] Children's video games are worse: when female humans appear, which is rare, they are in need of rescue by the male hero. Female figures in such games are rarely active.[169]

American media, particularly television, film, and video games, promote violence. Most of the empirical evidence on the effect of television and film violence indicates that it stimulates, rather than purges, aggression.[170] Media violence almost always takes place in the context of stereotypical sex roles. It is rare for a woman to use violence other than as an agent of a man or as a crazy person. Military video games present military activities in an abstract context, without blood or pain or suffering. The military use video "games" as training devices, and civilians use them as recreational activities.[171]

As a result of free speech in the media—as well as sexist speech elsewhere in the culture—women face three problems. First, the media silences women. This is true on the most literal level. For example, whether in news, sports, or other programs, it is overwhelmingly men who speak on television. When women do speak, they usually speak others' words rather than their own. And when women are authorities, they tend to espouse anti-women positions.[172]

The media free market is not a market without censors, though the censors are not governments. Women's speech is censored directly by media executives and by advertisers who control the substantive content of articles and programs in magazines and on television.[173] Women's speech is censored indirectly by media

---

[168] See Butler and Paisley, *Women and the Mass Media* at 150-51 (cited in note 151).

[169] Eugene F. Provenzo, Jr., *Video Kids: Making Sense of Nintendo* 61 (Harvard, 1991):

> In a sample of 100 video arcade games, [Terri] Toles determined that 92 percent of the games did not include any female roles, and that of the remaining 8 percent of the games, 6 percent had females assuming "damsel in distress" roles and 2 percent in active roles. Interestingly, in the case of the two females who do take active roles, neither is human—one being a Mama Kangaroo attempting to retrieve her child and the second a feminized blob, Ms. Pac-Man.

[170] See, for example, L. Rowell Heusmann and Neil M. Malamuth, *Media Violence and Antisocial Behavior: An Overview* 42(3) J Soc Issues 1 (1986).

[171] Provenzo, *Video Kids* at 132-35 (cited in note 169); Terri Toles, *Video Games and American Military Ideology*, in Vincent Mosco and Janet Wasko, 3 *Critical Communications Review: Popular Culture and Media Events* 207, 217-21 (Ablex, 1985).

[172] See text accompanying note 155.

[173] See Sunstein, in this volume, 282 (cited in note 2); Gloria Steinem, *Sex, Lies & Advertising*, Ms. 18 (Jul/Aug 1990).

portrayals of feminists as irrational, unattractive, man-hating lesbians.[174]

Second, market speech harms women more than men by impeding women's ability to develop as autonomous individuals. In a world of inequality, where men control a disproportionate share of resources and women have a disproportionate need for resources because of their responsibility for children, it often pays for women to present themselves as attractive sex objects. But women also internalize the beauty standard and judge themselves inadequate. In a 1984 *Glamour* survey, seventy-five percent of women between the ages of eighteen and thirty-five believed they were fat, though only twenty-five percent were fat by medical standards. More "heartbreaking," and a greater barrier to women's autonomous selfhood, "respondents chose losing ten to fifteen pounds above success in work or in love as their most desired goal."[175] Because of the implicit and explicit messages they receive about their abilities and worth, women have lower self-esteem and confidence than men. Pornography teaches women through concrete physical experience and example that they are worthless and that they exist to service men.

The third problem for women is the media focus on violence and its glorification. This culture of violence is alien to more women than men. Men use violence against women more than women use it against men.[176] The media's glorification of violence, together with the video-game mentality visible during the Gulf War, encourages citizens to view United States military aggression as a spectator sport, one in which men dominate.

These problems exist not only for American women but also for women throughout the world, given the high levels at which we export American media. People in other cultures viewing western media are likely to associate feminism with the pervasive images of women in western media, and hence with the sexualization of women. As a result, women in other cultures encounter more difficulty in objecting to their status; they can easily be tarred as "feminists," decadent as well as disloyal because western. American media thus silences women in other societies, forcing them to betray

---

[174] See Paula Kamen, *Feminist Fatale: Voices from the "Twentysomething" Generation Explore the Future of the "Women's Movement"* 63-74 (Donald I. Fine, 1991).

[175] Wolf, *The Beauty Myth* at 185-86 (cited in note 158).

[176] See text accompanying notes 170-71.

either their sex or their culture.[177] In addition, the allure of western glamor makes it more difficult for many women and girls to become autonomous selves, rather than the playthings western media suggests women are.[178]

These problems impede women's political success in the United States and elsewhere. "Free" speech in a market means that those with the ability to pay are able to speak the most. This is true for political speech. Women are poorer than men and have greater economic responsibility for children. These realities mean men have more disposable income to spend on political speech. Current case law constitutionally protects this differential.[179]

Speech and effective communication are necessary preconditions for having one's needs recognized in the political process. Low self-esteem compounds this differential, since it translates into feelings that one is not entitled to more.[180] Particularly in an individualistic culture such as the United States, low self-esteem and feelings of disentitlement impede solutions which must be both structural and political, such as the support systems women need and enjoy in the rest of the North Atlantic community of nations.[181]

The media's cultivation of violence also has political effects. Women oppose violence more than men do; the glorification of violence impedes action to suppress it, such as passage of gun control legislation or refusal to go to war.

The reader may object that the Free Speech Clause protects feminist speech today just as it protects other speech, and that

---

[177] See, for example, Leila Ahmed, *Feminism and Feminist Movements in the Middle East, A Preliminary Exploration: Turkey, Egypt, Algeria, People's Democratic Republic of Yemen*, in Azizah al-Hibri, ed, *Women and Islam* 153, 162 (Pergamon Press, 1982).

[178] One writer has noted that the combination of Western exports of media violence and weaponry to third world countries "satiate[s] the Third World in patterns of brutality." Sissela Bok, *Alva Myrdal: A Daughter's Memoir* 346 (Addison-Wesley, 1991). In *A Daughter's Memoir*, Bok discusses her mother's acceptance of the Nobel Peace Prize in 1982. The speech discusses these themes generally. See Alva Myrdal, *Disarmament, Technology and the Growth in Violence*, reprinted in *Les Prix Nobel 1982: Nobel Prizes, Presentations, Biographies and Lectures* 222, 228 (Acmquist & Wiksell, 1983).

[179] *Buckley v Valeo*, 424 US 1 (1976) (invalidating campaign expenditure ceilings, ensuring that those with more funding have a larger political voice).

[180] See Linda Gordon, *What Does Welfare Regulate?*, 55 Soc Res 609, 623 (1988):

Women's movements have had a particularly erratic, discontinuous history. This is because women's sense of entitlement is tenuous, easily reinterpreted as selfish, women being raised to define their virtue in terms of selflessness.

[181] See, for example, Sylvia Ann Hewlett, *When the Bough Breaks: The Cost of Neglecting Our Children* 173-82 (Basic, 1991); Sheila B. Kamerman and Alfred J. Kahn, *What Europe Does for Single-Parent Families*, 93 Pub Int 70 (Fall 1988).

without this protection, women pressing for change would be worse off. But a comparison of government censorship of feminist speech in England and the United States suggests that the American Free Speech Clause is not the critical factor when feminist speech is permitted. England has no written constitution and hence no Free Speech Clause. Historically, both England and the United States censored much feminist speech, even simple information about birth control, during the nineteenth and early twentieth centuries.[182] Neither country's government censors private feminist speech. The United States, however, does censor some feminist speech today: doctors receiving certain federal funding cannot mention abortion to a pregnant woman, even when abortion is the safest available treatment.[183] This comparison suggests that the source of government's unwillingness to censor private feminist speech is not the Free Speech Clause.

The Free Speech Clause does not, in and of itself, cause the problems "free" speech creates for women. England, for example, has no Free Speech Clause and yet has sexist speech. My main point is that the Free Speech Clause does more for men than for women, protecting speech that supports patriarchy. In addition, the Free Speech Clause impedes needed reform. It makes many direct forms of regulation of sexist speech unconstitutional. It also gives constitutional legitimacy to opponents' arguments even when the Constitution might not bar such reform.

I suggest a number of ways in which we could interpret or amend the Free Speech Clause to avoid or lessen the problems discussed in this Section. We could redefine or amend the Free Speech Clause to allow more equitable limits on spending for political speech.[184] The Free Speech Clause could be redefined or amended to allow government to regulate speech in ways suggested by Andrea Dworkin, Catharine MacKinnon, Mari Matsuda, and Cass Sunstein. For example, Dworkin and MacKinnon would give those harmed by pornography a right to damages.[185] Matsuda suggests that the United States should limit racist hate speech, as do

---

[182] Elizabeth Barrett Browning was censored in the United States (Boston) and England. Contraceptive information was banned in both countries. Anne Lyon Haight, *Banned Books: Informal Notes on Some Books Banned for Various Reasons at Various Times and in Various Places* 49, 63-64, 74-75, 77 (Bowker, 1970).

[183] See *Rust v Sullivan*, 111 S Ct 1759, 1767 (1991).

[184] This interpretation would necessarily overrule *Buckley*, 424 US 1.

[185] See Andrea Dworkin and Catharine A. MacKinnon, *Pornography and Civil Rights: A New Day for Women's Equality* 139-41 (Dworkin/MacKinnon, 1988) (model anti-pornography ordinance).

other liberal democracies (including England).[186] Sunstein suggests that government intervention should be permissible if it does not abridge speech but rather expands the market in speech by subsidizing or otherwise enabling speech that would not otherwise be heard.[187] Under Sunstein's "New Deal for Speech," for example, it might be permissible for the FCC to take sexism or ownership by women into account in licensing.[188] In addition, Sunstein suggests that the free speech principle should be understood to be centered above all on political deliberation.[189] Under this approach, other forms of speech may be regulated for illegitimate reasons, but on the basis of a lesser showing of harm.[190]

Perhaps we should amend the Bill of Rights to make such reform seem possible. The African National Congress (ANC) draft Bill of Rights, for example, includes both a free speech provision[191] and a provision that "[e]ducational institutions, the media, advertising and other social institutions shall be under a duty to discourage sexual and other types of stereotyping."[192] In addition, the ANC draft Bill of Rights includes an affirmative action provision that would seem to permit government funding of, or preferences for, women's speech or nonsexist speech,[193] and another authorizing restrictions of racist or sexist speech.[194]

In this Section, I have discussed problems that "free" speech in a market economy poses for women. Women are silenced.

---

[186] Mari J. Matsuda, *Public Response to Racist Speech: Considering the Victim's Story*, 87 Mich L Rev 2320, 2346-47, 2380-81 (1989).

[187] Sunstein, in this volume, 267-69 (cited in note 2).

[188] See *Metro Broadcasting, Inc. v FCC*, 110 S Ct 2997 (1990) (upholding constitutionality of requirement that transfers of certain "distress sale" licenses go to minority-controlled firms). The example is mine, rather than Sunstein's, and he might not agree.

[189] Sunstein, in this volume, 301 (cited in note 2).

[190] Id.

[191] African National Congress, *A Bill of Rights for a Democratic South Africa—Working Draft for Consultation*, Art 4, § 1 (on file with U Chi L Rev) ("There shall be freedom of thought, speech, expression and opinion, including a free press which shall respect the right to reply.").

[192] Id at Art 7, § 5.

[193] Id at Art 13, § 1 ("Nothing in the Constitution shall prevent the enactment of legislation, or the adoption by any public or private body of special measures of a positive kind designed to procure the advancement and the opening up of opportunities, including access to education, skills, employment and land, and the general advancement in social, economic and cultural spheres, of men and women who in the past have been disadvantaged by discrimination.").

[194] Id at Art 14, § 4 (". . . the State may enact legislation to prohibit the circulation or possession of materials which incite racial, ethnic, religious, gender or linguistic hatred, which provoke violence, or which insult, degrade, defame or encourage abuse of any racial, ethnic, religious, gender or linguistic group.").

Women have difficulty developing as autonomous selves with as much confidence as men. And women live in a culture permeated by male violence. I have suggested a number of reforms that should be considered. If the First Amendment cannot be interpreted to allow such reforms, we should consider changing it, since the problems impede women's ability to participate effectively in the political system.

III. THE RIGHT TO BEAR ARMS

The drafters of the Constitution saw the ability of armed citizens to oppose national government as an important check on the misuse of federal governmental power, with its "standing army of lackeys and hirelings (mercenaries, vagrants, convicts, aliens, and the like)."[195] The Second Amendment to the Constitution guarantees "the right of the people to keep and bear Arms."[196] This amendment has one of three meanings: either it grants states the right to organize citizens into state militias, or it grants individual citizens the right to bear arms (against the state and one another), or it grants both.[197] Each of these readings is troubling from the perspective of women.

A. State Militias

One reading of the Second Amendment is that it limits the ability of the federal government to limit state militias: citizens have the right to bear arms for the state.[198] But the right of states to organize militias of citizens has meant that only men may bear arms in military organizations, even after women received the vote and became, one might have thought, full citizens.[199] Women are still forbidden to bear arms in combat units, both in state militias and in the national armed services; women may serve in the militia

---

[195] Akhil Reed Amar, *The Bill of Rights as a Constitution*, 100 Yale L J 1131, 1163 (1991).

[196] US Const, Amend II.

[197] Wendy Brown, *Guns, Cowboys, Philadelphia Mayors, and Civic Republicanism: On Sanford Levinson's* The Embarrassing Second Amendment, 99 Yale L J 661, 662 (1989); Sanford Levinson, *The Embarrassing Second Amendment*, 99 Yale L J 637, 644-45, 648-51, 655-56 (1989); John E. Nowak, Ronald D. Rotunda, and J. Nelson Young, *Constitutional Law* § 10.2 n 4 (West, 3d ed 1986). Elaine Scarry has argued that the right of citizens to bear arms is inconsistent with the use of nuclear weapons. Elaine Scarry, *War and the Social Contract: Nuclear Policy, Distribution, and the Right to Bear Arms*, 139 U Pa L Rev 1257 (1991).

[198] Levinson, 99 Yale L J at 644-45 (cited in note 197); Brown, 99 Yale L J at 661-62 (cited in note 197).

[199] See Amar, 100 Yale L J at 1202-03 (cited in note 195).

and federal services only in limited numbers and in limited positions.[200]

Were women fully integrated in combat units in state militia, they would almost certainly serve in combat when state units are called up to fight at the federal level during national emergencies, given the integrated structure of the military. The state militia, together with the national army, navy, marines, and air force, form the United States military. Both the state militia and national armed services are delineated in Article I of the Constitution. It mentions the "organized"[201] state militia (or national guards) and the federal armed services. The state National Guards are under the command of the governors[202] unless called into the service of the United States by the President pursuant to his power under Article II, § 2.[203] The Congress has the power to organize, arm, and discipline the state militia (National Guard) and to govern "such Part of them as may be employed in the Service of the United States."[204] But the states have the reserved power to appoint officers to the militia (National Guard) and to train them "according to the discipline prescribed by Congress." In addition, Congress and the President have the power to raise and deploy federal armies. At the drafting of the Bill of Rights, the militia referred to male citizens drafted at the local or state level (citizen-soldiers) and the federal armies referred to volunteers (mercenaries).[205]

When the United States engages in war, the state National Guards are routinely called and integrated into active forces, both combat and noncombat. National Guard units served in World War I, World War II, the Korean War, Panama,[206] and the Gulf War. National Guard units have often played heroic roles in for-

---

[200] See, for example, *Women in Uniform*, Boston Globe 3 (Jun 19, 1991) ("Women constituted 11 percent of U.S. armed forces as of December 1990"); *Letters to the Editor* USA Today 11A (Jul 2, 1991) (52% of Army jobs open to women; 97% of Air Force jobs; 59% of Navy jobs; 20% of Marine jobs).

[201] There is also the unorganized militia, but it does not seem to be of any practical importance today. The unorganized militia is defined in the United States Code as consisting "of all able-bodied males" 17 to 44 who are, or have declared their intent to be, citizens of the United States unless they are members of the organized militia or of the federal armed forces. 10 USC §§ 311, 312 (1991).

[202] Richard Halloran, *With Roots in State and in Past, Guard Has Many Missions*, NY Times A16 (Aug 23, 1988).

[203] US Const, Art II, § 2. Article I, § 8 provides that Congress cannot appropriate money for the army "for a longer Term than two Years."

[204] US Const, Art I, § 8.

[205] Amar, 100 Yale L J at 1168 (cited in note 195).

[206] Halloran, NY Times at A16 (cited in note 202); Rudy Abramson, *U.S. Again Looks to the Reservists*, LA Times A1 (Aug 23, 1990) (only a few National Guard units served in

eign wars. For example, in World War I, the earliest troops in combat, and those who saw the most combat, were National Guards, including the famous "42d (Rainbow) Division composed of Guard units from many states, including the 69th Infantry Regiment from New York."[207] The government mobilized the National Guards for World War II prior to any draft, and over a year before the country entered the war. Many played important combat roles. For example, the 38th Infantry Division fought in the Philippines.[208] Today, the reserves play a central role in defense strategy. They are an integral part of any fighting force, capable of being quickly deployed and integrated with active troops, as illustrated by past wars.[209] Thus the full integration of women into the National Guard would mean full integration into the federal forces unless the various branches reorganized to limit women's integration into combat. That should be impermissible if women have a right to be treated as full citizen-soldiers.

As Akhil Amar has noted, militia service, along with jury service and voting, are political rights and obligations of citizens in a democracy.[210] Exclusion of women from militia service in combat denies women the obligations of full citizenship. This denial inevitably translates into disadvantaging women as citizens by depriving them of power they would otherwise share more equally with men. I discuss two concrete problems for American women.

First, keeping women out of combat maintains the image of the male warrior, who is superior to physically passive women who need his protection and cannot resist his violence.[211] This is important on many levels: in terms of the effect of these images on the culture in general and in terms of the lives of individual women and men. The military trains men to operate within a macho culture with the belief that they are superior to women. New male recruits are called "girls" and "ladies" until they earn a masculine label.[212] They march to a sexist and racist cadence: "I don't know

---

Vietnam, in part because of a perceived need to keep them available in the event they were needed in Europe).

[207] Halloran, NY Times A16 (cited in note 202).

[208] Id (this is the unit in which Vice President Quayle later served).

[209] Abramson, LA Times 1A (cited in note 206).

[210] See Amar, 100 Yale L J at 1202-03 (cited in note 195); Kenneth L. Karst, *The Pursuit of Manhood and the Desegregation of the Armed Forces*, 38 UCLA L Rev 499, 499-500 (1991).

[211] See generally Karst, 38 UCLA L Rev 499 (cited in note 210).

[212] Christine L. Williams, *Gender Differences at Work: Women and Men in Nontraditional Occupations* 69 (California, 1989).

but I've been told, Eskimo pussy is mighty cold."[213] They learn about venereal diseases from "Suzy Rottoncrotch."[214] Pictures of nude women are common.[215] In the late 1980s, Marine recruits at Parris Island, South Carolina, marched behind a sign with a naked woman on it and another with a skull and crossbones and the words "kill, rape, pillage, burn."[216] The boys and men trained in this system interact with women both within and outside the military. Men who chant these cadences and learn to consume pornography in the military become husbands, fathers, employees, employers, voters and politicians. Their experiences in the military are likely to make them less willing to accept women as leaders or to sympathize with the problems of women constituents.

The other side of this coin is that keeping women out of combat positions in the military supports the taboo against women using force, especially lethal force. The socialization of girls and women encourages them to be less physically aggressive than boys and men, and boys and men are socialized to expect girls and women to be passive in response to their violence.[217] It is revealing that current military rules do not exclude women from combat zones (i.e., do not keep women out of danger), but rather keep women from using lethal force.[218] Maintaining male control of le-

---

[213] Id.

[214] Id.

[215] Id. The author of this study reports that "[i]n the lounge of the student squadron where I interviewed female pilots, pictures of nude women and 'Playboy' insignias were tacked on the walls." In civilian life, such workplaces would constitute sexual harassment. See, for example, *Ellison v Brady*, 924 F2d 872 (9th Cir 1991); *Robinson v Jacksonville Shipyards, Inc.*, 760 F Supp 1486 (M D Fla 1991).

[216] *Marines' 'rape' slogan draws fire*, Wisc State J 7A (Oct 4, 1989).

[217] See Williams, *Gender Differences at Work* at 54 (cited in note 212) (policies that prohibit women from direct combat but expose them to indirect combat constitute a male protection racket); Pauline Burt and Patricia O'Brien, *Stopping Rape: Successful Survival Strategies* (Pergamon, 1985) (study of many connections between passivity and rape). See also Jalna Hanmer and Elizabeth Stanko, *Stripping Away the Rhetoric of Protection: Violence to Women, Law and the State in Britain and the U.S.A.*, 13 Intl J Soc L 357, 370 (1985) ("Essentially women in today's society are caught in a bind; male violence to women forces women to turn to men for protection.").

[218] See Williams, *Gender Differences at Work* at 54 (cited in note 212). During the Panamanian invasion, women drove other soldiers under sniper fire and one woman, Captain Linda Bray, led a military police company in a firefight. *2 Army Women Being Investigated for Disobeying Order in Panama*, NY Times A20 (Jan 21, 1990). An uproar followed over whether in fact Captain Bray had led troops in combat (in violation of military rules) and whether women *should* be allowed in combat positions. There was, however, no discussion of whether women should be kept out of combat zones as long as in noncombat positions, such as driving under sniper fire. See, for example, Tony Kornheiser, *Capt. Bray and a Dogged Assault*, Wash Post D1 (Jan 12, 1990); Judy Mann, *The Battle Has Just Begun*, Wash Post C3 (Jan 5, 1990). Several enlisted women in the military police were also in

thal force clearly preserves male interests both with respect to control of the military itself (a powerful institution in its own right) and with respect to men's power over women through physical intimidation throughout society.

Integrating women into the military would change the way we raise girls and decrease male violence against women. We treat girls and boys differently even as infants and children. As babies, boys are more likely to be tossed about. We expect boys to be tough and not to cry. We treat girls as more physically vulnerable and expect them to be less active physically. Girls' sports programs are different from boys': serious girls' sports are rarely aggressive contact team sports. Were women present in the military and in combat positions in proportion to their presence in the population, we probably would treat girls differently. There probably would be less violence against women, because women would be less passive physically and because military training would be less sexist. There is, for example, evidence that men who are or have been in the military are more likely to batter their wives.[219] Were women and men trained in the same system, they would be more likely to interact as equals elsewhere.

Women's exclusion from combat units in the military also increases the rate at which our soldiers rape women from the "other" side during war.[220] Our soldiers would be less likely to rape if half their comrades were women. Although we do not tend to hear much about this problem, it does happen many times in most wars.[221] We should consider it in assessing the costs and benefits of including women in the military.

The second major problem, and an extremely troubling one in a democracy, is that the exclusion of women from the draft and from combat positions in state militia and federal forces supports many barriers, erected by government itself, to women's participation in government and political life. The exclusion of women from combat means that women have less authority in government than

---

combat attacking Panamanian defense headquarters, thus raising controversy. See Wilson Ring, *Women Led U.S. Troops into Battle; Captain's Platoon Took PDF Target*, Wash Post A1 (Jan 3, 1990); Molly Moore, *Combat Role to be Sought for Women; Panama Experience Prompts Schroeder*, Wash Post A25 (Jan 4, 1990). See also Colman McCarthy, *Women at War, a Foolish First*, Wash Post F2 (Jan 14, 1990) ("What kind of society are we when similar opportunity in killing is the standard for equality.").

[219] See Del Martin, *Battered Wives* 52-53 (Glide, 1976); Walker, *The Battered Woman* at 36-37 (cited in note 52).

[220] Susan Brownmiller, *Against Our Will: Men, Women and Rape* 64-65 (Simon & Schuster, 1975).

[221] Id at 31-32.

men. Because of the exclusion, only men can be military heros. Women political candidates cannot boast of combat service, which voters regard as a credential for public office. Women within legislative bodies are regarded as having less authority on military matters than their male colleagues because they have not "been there;" they are regarded as less qualified to serve on military oversight committees and as having less authority if on such committees.

The military services deny women equal employment opportunities because they both limit the numbers of women in the services, and they deny women the combat experience necessary for promotion to high rank. Because they are so often present in token numbers, women in the services are subject to more sexual harassment than they would be in a more integrated organization.[222] No woman has ever been a member of the Joint Chiefs of Staff. Nor is any woman likely to be as long as women are not present in the military, in all positions, in proportion to their presence in the population.

It may be that women are more pacifist than men. If so, excluding women from combat disarms women's pacifism. Their resistance means less because it has fewer consequences. For example, women protesting the war in Vietnam had less authority because they did not have draft cards to burn and tended therefore (and for a host of other reasons) to be relegated to subservient positions in anti-war organizations.[223] Women in Congress who oppose military action have less authority because they have not been in combat. They, unlike Senator Kerrey, cannot oppose a military action with the authority of a recipient of the Congressional Medal of Honor who has lost a leg in combat.[224]

In addition, both federal and state governments have created a large number of preferences for veterans. Under these preferences, many positions in state and federal government are held mostly by men. For example, proportionately, even fewer federal administra-

---

[222] Karst, 38 UCLA L Rev at 525 (cited in note 210); Susanne Fowler, *Breaking Ranks: Rape, Harassment Claimed by Cadets* Chi Trib Womanews 1 (Oct 20, 1991) (allegations of sexual harassment in military training program at Texas A&M).

[223] Sara Ruddick has examined many of the arguments for including women in the military to serve peace and concludes that this is an inappropriate strategy because such interests can best be "cultivated in pacifist organizations." See Sara Ruddick, *Pacifying the Forces: Drafting Women in the Interests of Peace*, 8 Signs 471, 485-86 (1983). But, as Jennifer Hertz pointed out to me, Ruddick ignores the ways in which women's exemption from combat "disarms" them within pacifist organizations and denies them the same authority as pacifist men who have so much more to lose by resistance to military service.

[224] John Cassidy, *Democrats Run for Cover as Bush Fever Grips US*, Sunday Times 14 (London) (Mar 17, 1991).

tive law judges are women (5.41 percent) than federal Supreme Court (11.11 percent), federal Courts of Appeal (10.11 percent), or federal District Court judges (8.69 percent) because the federal veterans' preference applies to administrative law judges.[225] In many states, there are preferences for veterans in state employment as well.[226] Some state governments are almost entirely male at high levels for the same reason.[227] Thus, as a result of discrimination in military service, women are less likely to wield governmental power in nonelective offices.[228]

The reader may object that paying for military service is a valid governmental purpose, and that veterans' preferences are simply one form of compensation. But veterans' preferences for governmental employment are not the equivalent of compensation schemes. Such preferences give men an edge in running government and exclude women from power on the basis of a factor linked by government itself to sex. In addition, such policies are anti-democratic, creating a government based on a sort of military aristocracy rather than a government open to all.

I have discussed two ways in which the exclusion of women from combat hurts women. The exclusion contributes to cultural images and the social reality of violent male warriors and physically passive women in need of their protection. It also creates numerous barriers to women's participation in government and political life. As the framers of the Second Amendment realized, "ultimate political power" lies "with those who control the means of force."[229]

There are, of course, a number of arguments that can be made against full integration of women into the armed services and National Guard. Most women, even most women in the military today, oppose mandatory combat service. Most career military

---

[225] The data on women judges is based on a phone call to Dixie Noble, National Association of Women Judges, Williamsburg, Virginia (Oct 3, 1991) (notes on file with U Chi L Rev). 5 USC § 3105 (1991) authorizes agencies to appoint administrative law judges; 5 CFR § 930.203(e) (1990) instructs that agencies should accept highest rated applicants for Administrative Law Judge positions "augmented . . . by veteran preference."

[226] Veterans' organizations also receive postal subsidies denied to women's organizations. 39 USC § 3626 (1991).

[227] See, for example, *Personnel Administrator of Massachusetts v Feeney*, 442 US 256, 283 (1979) (Marshall dissenting) (majority upheld veterans' preferences in Massachusetts despite fact that 98% of veterans were male and virtually all desirable state civil service employment positions were consequently held by men).

[228] See id (as a result of Massachusetts's preference for veterans, "desirable state civil service employment [is] an almost exclusively male prerogative").

[229] David C. Williams, *Civic Republicanism and the Citizen Militia: The Terrifying Second Amendment*, 101 Yale L J 551, 553 (1992).

women want to engage in combat service, but ordinary enlisted women do not.[230] The military is perhaps the most masculinist institution in our society; its values and its focus on physical violence are alien to most women. Nevertheless, until women are full citizens—citizen soldiers on the same basis as men—women will have less power in government and outside it. They will lack power in waging peace as well as war, and will face restricted employment opportunities both in the military and in government.

Today's interpretation of the Bill of Rights does not require that women be accorded full citizenship. We should interpret the Second Amendment, especially in light of the Fourteenth and Nineteenth Amendments, as extending the right to bear arms in state militia to women. At a minimum, the Fourteenth Amendment should bar veterans' preferences in state employment as long as women do not receive equal treatment in the military. It is absurd to regard injury as justifying injury as when overt government discrimination against women in one area justifies non-merit based standards that exclude most women from many government jobs.

B.   The Right of Individual Citizens to Bear Arms

The other possible meaning of the Second Amendment, either as an alternative reading or in combination with the reading given above,[231] is that it limits the ability of both the state and federal governments to regulate gun ownership. In other words, it grants individuals a right to bear arms, arms which may be used, perhaps illegally, against other individuals or the state.[232] Although it is extremely difficult to compare rates of violence internationally because of reporting differences, the United States is clearly much

---

[230] Most (about 75% of those interviewed by one reporter in Panama) female officers believed that women should be able to volunteer for combat. But only a quarter of that sample thought "that women should be compelled to enter combat units, just as men are." Charles Moskos, *Army Women* Atlantic Monthly 7, 77 (Aug 1990). In contrast, about 75% of enlisted women thought that women should not be allowed into combat. Only 25% thought that women should be able to volunteer for combat. No enlisted women "favored forcing women into combat assignments." Id.

[231] Amar argues, as noted earlier, that the Second Amendment means both the right of the individual citizen to bear arms and of the states to organize their citizens into militia. See Amar, 100 Yale L J at 1162-73 (cited in note 195).

[232] Although it is not clear whether the Second Amendment would ban legislation banning private ownership of guns (see, for example, Levinson, 99 Yale L J at 640 (cited in note 197)), the Second Amendment does appear to make even regulation more difficult, by giving those who want guns to remain unregulated a *constitutional* argument and rallying cry.

more violent than other countries.[233] Although there is no way to prove this point, it seems likely that the Second Amendment reflects and reinforces the unusual levels of violence in our culture. Moreover, violence harms women and other groups more than it harms men like the founding fathers.

Violence devastates poor inner city communities, which are made more deadly by the availability of guns. Women in the inner cities where crime is highest lead lives circumscribed by violence. Intolerable levels of violence victimize them and those they love. They must worry before going outside at night, or even during the day in some areas.[234] They worry about their children getting safely through the school day and back home. Many see their sons join the violent underworld of drugs and gangs with deadly results: "[T]he number one cause of death for African-American males between the ages of fifteen and twenty-four is murder."[235] Men like the founding fathers—propertied white men—do not live in these neighborhoods and are not as likely to be victims or perpetrators of violence as are poor women and men.

To the extent the Second Amendment protects individuals' rights to own guns, or assists the NRA in resisting effective gun control legislation, the Second Amendment is a countermajoritarian impediment to women's effective use of the political system. Men are not only more likely to own guns than women, they are also more likely to oppose gun control.[236] For example, in 1985, fifty percent of men but only twelve percent of women owned guns.[237] In 1986, fifty-five percent of women, but only thirty-nine percent of men, favored laws banning the sale and possession of handguns in their own community.[238] Women and men have conflicting interests and opinions concerning gun regulation, and the Constitution enshrines, at least on a rhetorical level, a male norm.[239]

---

[233] See, for example, James D. Wright, et al, *Weapons, Crime, and Violence in America: A Literature Review and Research Agenda* 2-4 (US Dept of Justice, 1981).

[234] Margaret T. Gordon and Stephanie Riger, *The Female Fear* 8-22 (Free Press, 1989).

[235] Randolph N. Stone, *Crisis in the Criminal Justice System*, 8 Harv BlackLetter J 33, 39 (1991).

[236] Katherine M. Jamieson and Timothy J. Flanagan, eds, *Sourcebook of Criminal Justice Statistics* 109-11, Tables 2.38-2.43 (US Dept of Justice, 1987).

[237] Id at 109, Table 2.38.

[238] Id at 110, Table 2.43.

[239] See Brown, 99 Yale L Rev at 663-64 (cited in note 197). For evidence that gun control laws can decrease violence, see Elisabeth Scarff, *Evaluation of the Canadian Gun Control Legislation: Final Report* 36, 39, 42, 53, 63, 65, 66, 68 (Ministry of the Solicitor General of Canada, 1983); *Gun Control Laws in Foreign Countries* 88-94, 135-36, 157-60 (Law Li-

Changes to the Second Amendment in light of my criticisms are easy to imagine. An amendment or new interpretation could allow effective national bans on gun ownership by individuals. Alternatively, if the Second Amendment affords citizens the right to bear arms in state militia, that right should be extended to all citizens, regardless of sex.

IV. Criminal Justice System Protections

The Bill of Rights contains a number of provisions designed to guard against governmental misuse of the criminal justice system. The Fourth Amendment proscribes unreasonable searches and seizures.[240] The Fifth Amendment provides for indictment by a grand jury for serious crimes and for due process in criminal trials.[241] The Sixth Amendment guarantees the accused a right to a trial by jury in criminal cases, and the assistance of counsel for his defense.[242] The drafters intended these provisions to guard against misuse of the criminal justice system by government, particularly criminal prosecution of government critics.[243]

Nothing in the Bill of Rights or the Fourteenth Amendment guards against systemic racism in the operation of the criminal justice system, or against its systematic misuse to "solve" problems associated with racism and poverty. In making these points, the emphasis in this section differs somewhat from the emphasis in other sections. Here, I stress that the Bill of Rights does less for poor minorities than it does for propertied white men. In other sections, I stress that the Bill of Rights does less for women than for men. This shift is appropriate even though my major concern is the latter. Although most of those caught in the criminal "justice" system are men, the problems with the way the system operates in poor minority communities pose major problems for women in those communities. One cannot separate the interests of poor minority women and men; their fates are intertwined in ways without precise parallel to white women and men, particularly propertied white women and men. Women who live in communities destroyed by drugs and by the "war" on drugs are devastated by the destruc-

---

brary, Library of Congress, 1981) (evidence from Britain mixed, but both Japan and Sweden, which have strict gun control laws, have low rates of murders involving firearms).

[240] US Const, Amend IV.

[241] US Const, Amend V.

[242] US Const, Amend VI.

[243] Amar, 100 Yale L J at 1175-99 (cited in note 195).

tion around them even though they themselves are less likely to go to prison than are their sons, lovers, and husbands.

At the time the Bill of Rights was enacted, whites were free to enter the home and batter, rape, or kill African Americans with impunity. This was particularly true for African Americans who were slaves, but even free or freed African Americans were often subject to white violence without the criminal law protection afforded white men (and white women in some contexts).[244] At the same time, black people, particularly slaves, were often punished for alleged crimes without any evidence of guilt. For African Americans in 1791, the criminal "justice" system was part of the problem, and the Bill of Rights did nothing to end these systemic abuses.

Racism persists within the criminal justice system.[245] African American women receive less protection from the criminal justice system than white women. When African American women are raped, their rapists are less likely to serve time than the rapists of white women.[246] Defendants in rape prosecutions often succeed by suggesting that the woman was a prostitute, and this may be especially effective when women live, as poor and African American women often must, in neighborhoods where prostitutes are on the streets. African Americans, women as well as men, more often fall into the police net because they fit the drug courier image,[247] are more likely to be treated roughly or beaten severely by the police,[248] and are more likely to be arrested. States are most likely to

---

[244] See, for example, *State v Weaver*, 3 NC 70, 71 (1798) (justifiable homicide for master to kill slave or freed servant who forcefully resists master's use of force to compel obedience).

[245] I only outline problems in the criminal justice system here. I am not an expert in criminal law and cannot provide the in-depth discussion these issues deserve. For a fuller discussion of these problems, I refer the reader to work by others. Stone, 8 Harv Black-Letter L J 33 (cited in note 235); Stephen J. Schulhofer, *Access to Justice for the American Underclass*, The World & I 463, 469-75 (Jun 1991); Sheri Lynn Johnson, *Unconscious Racism and the Criminal Law*, 73 Cornell L Rev 1016 (1988); Randall L. Kennedy, *McCleskey v. Kemp: Race, Capital Punishment, and the Supreme Court*, 101 Harv L Rev 1388 (1988); Samuel R. Gross, *Race and Death: The Judicial Evaluation of Evidence of Discrimination in Capital Sentencing*, 18 UC Davis L Rev 1275 (1985).

[246] Generalized from data that finds that black offenders are sentenced most harshly when their victims are white, Alfred Blumstein, et al, eds, 1 *Research on Sentencing: The Search for Reform* 101 (National Academic Press, 1983). See also Gary D. LaFree, *The Effect of Sexual Stratification by Race on Official Reactions to Rape*, 45 Am Soc Rev 842, 852 (1980).

[247] Editorial, *Bringing Sanity to Seizure Laws*, Chi Trib 2 (Sep 1, 1991).

[248] See, for example, Frank Clifford and John L. Mitchell, *Incident Gives City a National Black Eye; Image: Old Memories of Free-Swinging Cops Are Revived*, LA Times B1 (Mar 7, 1991) (reporting on Rodney Glen King police beating incident in Los Angeles).

impose the death penalty on African American defendants whose victims were white.[249]

Moreover, the criminal justice system is used today to "solve" problems caused by poverty—drugs and drug-related crime. As Randolph Stone has noted, "[t]he war on drugs has devastated the criminal justice system" as well as "some segments of the African-American community."[250] Today, "the judicial system has become an assembly line."[251] Most defendants do not receive trial by jury or the opportunity to confront witnesses against them.[252] Because judges are pressured to treat cases summarily, counsel is more important than ever. But effective assistance of counsel is often denied, particularly to the poor or those accused of drug-related crimes. Public defenders handle unmanageable caseloads.[253] In places without public defenders, poor defendants must rely on court-appointed counsel, who are often required to work pro bono or for token fees.[254]

Once dragged into the criminal "justice" net, the consequences can be devastating, even if police and prosecutors lack sufficient evidence to proceed to trial. Under federal law and many states' laws, if the police suspect that property is related to drugs, they can seize it on grounds as slight as those required for a search warrant:[255] probable cause to believe that the property was involved in illegal activities.[256] Seizure of property makes it more difficult to

---

[249] *McCleskey v Kemp*, 481 US 279, 286-87 (1987).

[250] Stone, 8 Harv BlackLetter L J at 36 (cited in note 235).

[251] Id at 34.

[252] For a description of the problem, see Schulhofer, *The World & I* at 474 (cited in 245) (As a result of our resource decisions, "85-90 percent of criminal convictions are obtained by guilty plea.").

[253] See Stone, 8 Harv BlackLetter L J at 34 (cited in note 235):

Lawyers in our felony trial division [Cook County Public Defender's office] have one hundred pending cases, while those in our Homicide Task Force handle twenty-three pending murder cases each; one-third to one-half of those homicide cases are death penalty cases.

[254] See Schulhofer, The World & I at 469-75 (cited in note 245).

[255] See, for example, Walter J. Van Eck, *The New Oregon Civil Forfeiture Law*, 26 Willamette L Rev 449, 476-78 (1990); Thomas E. Payne, *An Introduction to Civil Forfeiture in Mississippi: An Effective Law Enforcement Tool or Cash Register Justice?*, 59 Miss L J 453, 463 (1989); Steven L. Kessler, *Quo vadis? Assessing New York's Civil Forfeiture Law*, 4 Touro L Rev 253 (1988).

[256] The federal civil forfeiture provision is at 21 USC § 881. For a discussion, see Barry Tarlow, *Forfeiture Trends*, 15 The Champion 42 (Nov 1991); Mark A. Jankowski, *Tempering the Relation-Back Doctrine: A More Reasonable Approach to Civil Forfeiture in Drug Cases*, 76 Va L Rev 165 (1990); G. Richard Strafer, *Civil Forfeitures: Protecting the Innocent Owner*, 37 U Fla L Rev 841 (1985); Gerard E. Lynch, *RICO: The Crime of Being a Criminal (parts III & IV)*, 87 Colum L Rev 920 (1987); Terrance G. Reed, *The Defense Case for RICO Reform*, 43 Vand L Rev 691, 701-11 (1990); Jeffrey M. Evans, *"Civil" For-*

hire counsel either to recover the property or for criminal defense. Given the fiscal crunch facing most law enforcement systems, these statutes create powerful incentives for misuse of seizure without trial.

Using the criminal justice system to battle problems caused by poverty and racism results in a prison population that is half African American men.[257] There are more African American men in prison than in college.[258] The incarceration rate in the United States is now the highest known in the world: 426 prisoners per 100,000 population. South Africa is second with a rate of 333 per 100,000 and the Soviet Union third with a rate of 268 per 100,000. Most of the world has much lower rates. For example, Western European rates are 35-120 per 100,000.[259]

Although poor pregnant addicts cannot find the in-patient medicaid-funded rehabilitation treatment they need, they are increasingly subject to criminal prosecution for delivering drugs to minors.[260]

The misuse of the criminal justice system to address problems of poverty and racism has political effects. People wrongly convicted of many crimes cannot vote in state elections while serving time and in most states even thereafter.[261] More importantly, keeping the poor impoverished—rather than dealing with poverty effectively—means keeping them politically ineffective. The poor, disproportionately, do not vote and do not participate in political life.[262]

The protections in the Bill of Rights against misuse of the criminal justice system do not "cause" these problems. But the Bill of Rights does less to guard against misuse of the criminal justice system to combat problems of poverty and racism than it does to guard against misuse of the criminal justice system to silence political dissidents. Furthermore, the misuse of the Bill of Rights to

---

feitures Under State RICO Laws: A Legislative Attempt to Circumvent the Constitution, 8 Crim Just J 293 (1986).

[257] Stone, 8 Harv BlackLetter L J at 35 (cited in note 235).

[258] Though one year in prison costs as much as an education at a four-year college. Id.

[259] Mark Mauer, *Americans Behind Bars: A Comparison of International Rates of Incarceration* 4-5 (The Sentencing Project, 1991). Incarceration rates have been dropping in the Soviet Union. Ten years ago they were estimated to be about 25% to 100% higher than current estimates. Id at 4, 6.

[260] See Michelle Oberman, *Sex, Drugs, Pregnancy and the Law: Rethinking the Problems of Pregnant Women Who Use Drugs*, Hastings L Rev (forthcoming 1992).

[261] *Shepard's Lawyer's Reference Manual* 575-95 table A-31 (1983) (survey of voter qualifications).

[262] See text accompanying notes 271-73.

facilitate the war on drugs has undermined specific constitutional guarantees as applied to poor minorities, especially those accused of drug involvement, by denying them a fair trial with effective assistance of counsel. Thus the general protections of the Bill of Rights against misuse of the system have been effectively destroyed by the drug war for many poor people, who are subjected to assembly-line justice without effective counsel. Finally, the Bill of Rights does not provide any affirmative economic or educational protections for the poor, protections which might ensure that problems of poverty be effectively addressed.

An interpretation of or amendment to the Bill of Rights might lessen these problems by directly addressing the economic and educational needs of the poor and by providing provisions more effective at ensuring justice for all within the criminal justice system. After discussing the "property" right enshrined in the Fifth Amendment, I suggest a number of positive economic and educational rights that we could incorporate in the Bill of Rights.[263] In addition, the Bill of Rights could include provisions guaranteeing effective assistance of counsel and fair trials. For example, we could interpret effective assistance of counsel as proscribing the seizure of assets used to pay counsel and as requiring reasonable caseloads for public defenders and reasonable fees for court-appointed counsel.[264] At a minimum, government should be prevented from seizing assets without a trial, and money paid to a lawyer prior to execution of a judgment should be no more coverable than money paid to any other creditor. We could obtain this result by reasonable interpretation of the Fifth Amendment's Takings Clause.

V. SECURITY AT HOME

The Fourth Amendment provides that "[t]he right of the people to be secure in their persons, houses, papers, and effects, against unreasonable searches and seizures, shall not be violated." White male heads of family during the revolution and today face threats to physical security at home from two kinds of intruders: government actors and criminals. The criminal law has been used to protect against the latter, if not always effectively; the Fourth Amendment guards against the former.

---

[263] See text accompanying notes 274-80.

[264] For these and additional suggestions, see Schulhofer, The World & I at 475 (cited in note 245).

Women, by contrast, face a third major source of physical insecurity within the home: battery and rape by someone who lives in the home—their sexual partners. Yet we have never accorded protection against domestic violence at the level accorded other crimes of violence. The Fourth Amendment does not address domestic violence. The Fourth Amendment protects women against governmental assault, but leaves governments free to treat "domestic" assaults differently from other crimes. Indeed, the criminal codes of many states still deny equal criminal protection to wives who are raped by their husbands.[265] Although some states have eliminated this distinction, others have extended it to nonmarried cohabitants.[266]

These inequities have political consequences. Women who fear violence redefine themselves as wanting to give what might otherwise be taken away, instead of asserting their own interests,[267] particularly in a politically effective way. Women who are abused within their most intimate relationships are less able to assert their interests within those relationships. Abused women are unlikely to press strongly for change in the political arena, especially when their interests conflict with the interests of the abuser.

In large part, my criticism is simply that the Fourth Amendment does less for women than it has done for white men, who drafted it. Protected by the criminal justice system from attacks by criminals, they added the Fourth Amendment to protect themselves from governmental intrusion. The Fourth Amendment is much less thorough in providing the protections needed by women. It allows government, police, and prosecutors to treat domestic violence differently from other violence. Indeed, the Constitution allows government to treat marital rape as noncriminal. The Fourth Amendment may have affirmatively made women worse off by giving a constitutional foundation to the notion that a "man's home is his castle."

One can easily imagine improvements in the Bill of Rights from the perspective of violence against women. The Bill of Rights could include an equality standard for sex that would require the state to respond to domestic violence in the same way it responds to other crimes, and to proscribe marital rape.[268] Such constitu-

---

[265] See Robin West, *Equality Theory, Marital Rape, and the Promise of the Fourteenth Amendment*, 42 U Fla L Rev 45, 46-48, 46 n 6 (1990).

[266] See id at 48 n 11.

[267] See West, 3 Wis Women's L J at, 93-111 (cited in note 51).

[268] See generally West, 42 U Fla L Rev 45 (cited in note 265).

tional provisions would not by themselves revolutionize how police, prosecutors and jurors treat intersexual domestic violence, but they might contribute to changed attitudes. They would, moreover, ensure some of the prerequisites for effective control of domestic violence.

VI. PROPERTY

The Fifth Amendment provides that "[n]o person shall . . . be deprived of life, liberty, or property, without due process of law; nor shall private property be taken for public use without just compensation."[269] There are a number of problems with this provision from the perspective of minorities and women. First, and most dramatically, at the time the Bill of Rights was adopted in 1789, slaves *were* property. They were protected as property of others; they could have no property themselves. This provision of the Fifth Amendment was an instrument of oppression for African American women and men.

Second, at the time of the passage of the Bill of Rights, married women could not own or control property. Thus, the Fifth Amendment protected only the property of men and single women.

Third, the protection of "property" meant and means the privileging of existing distributions, no matter how dubious. Consider, for example, the property rights of the newly-freed people vis-à-vis the property rights of their former owners. The fields cleared and cultivated by the freed people belonged to the owners. The buildings and plantations built by the freed people belonged to the owners.

Fourth, while "property" has always included realty and the goods produced by the kinds of labor in which most men spend their working lives, we have never recognized women's reproductive and domestic labor as property. Women's caretaking impedes women's ability to accumulate property in three distinct ways: (1) caretaking itself does not tend to produce property; (2) caretaking tends to limit one's ability to earn property; and (3) caretaking tends to require consumption of property. As a result, women have fewer resources than men and are far more likely to be poor.[270]

Lack of property precludes effective political participation. The poor vote less often, are less politically active, and have fewer

---

[269] US Const, Amend V.

[270] See, for example, 163 *Current Population Reports: Consumer Income: Poverty in the United States: 1987* 118-19 (US Bureau of the Census, 1989) (slightly under 11% of all families are poor, though 34% of families headed by women are poor).

resources with which they can influence elections. It is more difficult for the poor to make contributions to candidates likely to represent their interests or to spend money themselves to advance
candidates or political positions. Yet the Constitution protects the
ability of the rich to spend more politically.[271] Although seventy-
six percent of those making over $50,000 a year vote, only thirty-
eight percent of those making less than $5,000 a year vote.[272] Re-
gistration is structured so as to discourage registration by the
poor.[273]

Provisions in a Bill of Rights could lessen these problems. A
Bill of Rights could provide for positive economic rights, ensuring
women economic supports and safety nets as effective as those
available to men. Such a Bill of Rights would be more detailed and
specific, less elegant, brief, and abstract, than the Bill of Rights we
have today. Against this aesthetic loss must be balanced the benefit to women and children, who form the majority of Americans. In
addition, a society in which women have more power would be
more democratic. Its government would have greater legitimacy.[274]

Affirmative economic rights could include a right to health
care under a national and universal health care system (the details
of which would be specified by legislation); a requirement of a family allowance (tied to some independent economic indicator, such
as a fractional percentage of gross national product); caretaking
leave with wage support as part of the unemployment insurance
system (with support required at the level generally provided for
unemployment compensation); government-financed child care; a
requirement that social security benefits be, on average, the same
for women and men (within a limited level of tolerance);[275] a right
to a decent education (with a ban on financing schools through
property taxes and a requirement that per pupil expenditures be
uniform throughout the United States);[276] and a requirement that
breadwinners and homemakers be treated the same with respect to

---

[271] *Buckley v Valeo*, 424 US 1 (1976).

[272] Garry Wills, *'New Votuhs'*, NY Rev Books 3, 3 (Aug 18, 1988).

[273] Id.

[274] See Linda Gordon, *What Does Welfare Regulate?* 55 Soc Res 609, 629 (1988).

[275] For a discussion of the many structural problems in the social security system, see
Mary E. Becker, 89 Colum L Rev 264 (cited in note 17).

[276] In New Jersey, where the state supreme court has interpreted the state Constitution
as banning differential school funding levels based on local property taxes, "per-pupil expenditures are still $2,880 in poor districts and $4,029 in wealthy districts." Hewlett, *When
the Bough Breaks* at 58 (cited in note 181). See generally id at 56-61, 246-49.

all substantive standards for disability.[277] A ban on abortion should be seen as a taking (of women's reproductive labor) for government purposes without compensation.[278] The Bill of Rights should also include a right to abortion, fully paid by the state, in light of (inter alia) the economic consequences of childbearing for women.

Further, the Bill of Rights should make family law a matter within the control of the national government and not the states. Gender relations in the family are of primary importance for a just society.[279] Setting a framework for just relationships should be a priority for national government; living within such a framework should be a prerogative of national citizenship.[280]

Like other provisions of the Bill of Rights, the Takings Clause of the Fifth Amendment does much more for men than for women, favoring men's productive labor over women's reproductive labor. The Due Process Clause of the Fifth Amendment also favors men's experiences, by enshrining as the "rule of law" a legal system developed by and for elite white men. In the next Section, I examine this provision and contrast it with the jury provisions, which now provide for the participation of all in applying the laws developed by the few.

VII. Due Process and the Jury Provisions

The Fifth Amendment provides for "due process" before any person is deprived of "life, liberty, or property."[281] The Sixth and Seventh Amendments provide for a jury trial in criminal and civil cases.[282] The "due process" guaranteed by the Fifth Amendment thus entitled its framers, mostly elite white men, to the procedures

[277] Social Security has different substantive disability standards for homemakers and breadwinners. See Becker, 89 Colum L Rev at 269 (cited in note 17).

[278] In making this point, I do not suggest that women's reproductive ability should be treated in all respects like alienable property rights. Indeed, I think it a mistake to commodify women's bodies by creating a market for their reproductive labor. For a discussion of the problems with a market approach, see Margaret Jane Radin, *Market-Inalienability*, 100 Harv L Rev 1849 (1987); Cass R. Sunstein, *Neutrality in Constitutional Law (with Special Reference to Pornography, Abortion, and Surrogacy)*, 92 Colum L Rev 1 (1992). I am merely stating that government should not be able to take women's reproductive labor without compensation by banning abortion. Women's reproductive labor should, however, be inalienable.

[279] See generally Susan Moller Okin, *Justice, Gender, and the Family* (Basic, 1989).

[280] I am indebted to Hendrik Hartog for this idea.

[281] US Const, Amend V.

[282] US Const, Amends VI and VII. In civil cases, the right applies "where the value in controversy shall exceed twenty dollars." US Const, Amend VII.

and substantive rules of a legal system developed by and for people like themselves. At that time, women and African Americans could not participate as either lawyers or judges.

Today, the legal system remains one developed by and for propertied white men, with strong, built-in, conservative tendencies, in the form of well-developed substantive rules combined with rules favoring precedent.[283] As I have described,[284] the overwhelming majority of legislators and judges continue to be men. "Due process" continues to mean something quite different for propertied white men and other groups.

The Sixth Amendment provides that "[i]n all criminal prosecutions, the accused shall enjoy the right to a speedy and public trial, by an impartial jury. . . ."[285] At the time the Bill of Rights was enacted, neither women nor slaves were allowed on juries. As early as 1880, however, the Supreme Court held that states could not overtly exclude African Americans from juries under the Fourteenth Amendment.[286] But African Americans were effectively excluded throughout the South until relatively recently. Juries were drawn from voter rolls which—until the 1960s—included few African Americans. And in the North as well as the South, African Americans could be excluded on the ground of race from any particular jury prior to the Supreme Court's 1965 Fourteenth Amendment decision in *Swain v Alabama*[287] and its 1986 decision in *Batson v Kentucky*.[288] Since these cases, it has been unconstitutional to exclude African Americans or other racial minorities either from jury lists or from a particular jury because of race.

A more limited set of rules has developed with respect to sex.[289] The Supreme Court found overt limitations on women's presence in jury pools to be unconstitutional under the Fourteenth Amendment in 1975.[290] But several lower courts have refused to

---

[283] See, for example, Lois G. Forer, *Unequal Protection: Women, Children, and the Elderly in Court* (Norton, 1991) (retired judge discussing the many ways in which legal rules developed by white male judges adversely affect women, children, and the elderly).

[284] See text accompanying notes 8-14.

[285] US Const, Amend VI.

[286] *Strauder v West Virginia*, 100 US 303, 310 (1880).

[287] 380 US 202 (1965).

[288] 476 US 79 (1986).

[289] See generally Shirley S. Sagawa, Batson v Kentucky: *Will It Keep Women on the Jury?*, 3 Berkeley Women's L J 14 (1987/1988); Note, *Sex Discrimination in the* Voir Dire *Process: The Rights of Prospective Female Jurors*, 58 S Cal L Rev 1225 (1985).

[290] *Taylor v Louisiana*, 419 US 522 (1975). See also *Duren v Missouri*, 439 US 357 (1979). The Supreme Court has held that jury exclusions violate the Sixth Amendment only when capital sentencing occurs. See *Lockhart v McCree*, 476 US 162 (1986).

hold unconstitutional the exclusion of women from jury panels even if the exclusion is on the basis of sex.[291] Thus, the right to trial by a jury selected without discrimination on the basis of sex remains unavailable to women. Further, minority women remain without effective protection on the basis of race *and* sex.[292]

I suggest three changes to the Bill of Rights in the areas of due process and jury selection. First, in civil cases there should be the same protections against sex discrimination in jury selection as for race.[293] Second, women and minorities should be protected from sex or race discrimination by prosecutors in challenging jurors in criminal cases. Indeed, we might ban all peremptory challenges by prosecutors.[294]

Third, judges and legislators, as well as jurors, should represent the population. We require that juries be representative with respect to race and somewhat representative with respect to sex, but have no constitutional provisions regarding judges or legislators. This is so even though the law developed and applied by judges and legislators is all the process that is "due" in any dispute before a jury or a judge. For any group other than white men, who is on the bench or in the legislature is more important than who is on the jury.

The Bill of Rights could require that judges represent the population with respect to sex and race. The African National Congress (ANC) Draft Bill of Rights includes a provision that "the judiciary shall be transformed in such a way as to consist of men and women drawn from all sectors of . . . society."[295] The Bill of Rights could provide that women's representation in legislatures at appro-

---

[291] See, for example, *United States v Hamilton*, 850 F2d 1038, 1042 (4th Cir 1988); *State v Olivera*, 534 A2d 867, 870 (RI 1987). See also *State v Gilmore*, 511 A2d 1150, 1159 n 3 (NJ 1986). Even when women are on jury panels, they tend to be less influential than the men on the jury. See Nancy S. Marder, *Gender Dynamics and Jury Deliberations*, 96 Yale L J 593, 597-98 (1987).

[292] Minority women should, one would think, be entitled to *more*, not less, protection because of their dual disadvantages. See generally, Judy Scales-Trent, *Black Women and the Constitution: Finding Our Place, Asserting Our Rights*, 24 Harv CR-CL L Rev 9 (1989). See also Kimberle Crenshaw, *Demarginalizing the Intersection of Race and Sex: A Black Feminist Critique of Antidiscrimination Doctrine, Feminist Theory and Antiracist Politics*, 1989 U Chi Legal Forum 139.

[293] See *Edmonson v Leesville Concrete Co., Inc.*, 111 S Ct 2077, 2079 (1991) (race can not be basis for excluding juror in civil case). Structural changes may also be needed to accommodate women's different approaches to dispute resolution. See Laura Gaston Dooley, *Sounds of Silence on the Civil Jury*, 26 Valp U L Rev 405 (1991).

[294] See, for example, Albert W. Alschuler, *The Supreme Court and the Jury: Voir Dire, Peremptory Challenges, and the Review of Jury Verdicts*, 56 U Chi L Rev 153, 232 (1989).

[295] ANC, *A Bill of Rights for a Democratic South Africa* Art 14, § 7 (cited in note 191).

priate levels is of prime importance in a democracy, and authorize
Congress to enact a Voting Rights Act for Women. Such an act
could offset the political problems women face as a result of freedoms we all value, such as freedom of religion and speech. If we
had separate voting districts for women and men, women would be
represented in legislatures in rough proportion to their presence in
the population.[296] Women tend to hold elective office in higher
numbers in multi-member districts,[297] under proportional representation,[298] and with internal party quotas for women candidates.[299] Our parties already have internal sex-based quotas for
their national committees, and the Democrats have experimented
with quotas for convention delegates. Our parties could be en-
couraged to experiment with such quotas by government funding
tied to the number of women running in open elections.[300]

CONCLUSION

The Bill of Rights serves the interests of those most like its
drafters: relatively elite white men who tend to own more than
their share of "property." Other groups—particularly women, the
poor, and people of color—have fewer of their needs addressed by
this revered document. I have shown three kinds of problems with
the provisions of the Bill of Rights.

My major point has been critical: the Bill of Rights does less
for other groups than it does for those in the class of propertied
white men; often it perpetuates or even magnifies social inequities
rather than eliminating them. When this happens, the Bill of
Rights becomes part of the problem, rather than the solution. Second, the Bill of Rights is often an impediment to reform; this is

---

[296] This is more or less the result with respect to racial minorities under the remedial
scheme of the Voting Rights Act. See, for example, Voting Rights Act Extension, S Rep No
97-417, 97th Cong, 2d Sess 1000-10 (1982).

[297] See, for example, Susan Welch and Albert K. Karnig, *Correlates of Female Office
Holding in City Politics*, 41 J Pol 478, 486-87 (1979); Janet Clark, et al, *Women as Legislative Candidates in Six States*, in Janet A. Flammang, ed, *Political Woman* 141, 154 (Sage,
1984).

[298] See Anne Phillips, *Engendering Democracy* 80-83 (Pennsylvania, 1991). There are
disadvantages to proportional representation. Proportional representation, like divided government, tends to mean weak government. See Arend Lijphart, *Democracies: Patterns of
Majoritarian and Consensus Government in Twenty-One Countries* 107-26, 150-68 (Yale,
1984).

[299] Phillips, *Engendering Democracy* at 83-89 (cited in note 298).

[300] For example, the national parties could be given so much in federal funds for each
woman in an open election for the House, double that amount for open Senate races, and
triple that amount for open governor races.

particularly true for the First Amendment's Free Speech Clause and the Second Amendment insofar as it prevents gun control legislation. Third, the problems ignored or even perpetuated by the Bill of Rights have political consequences for women and other outsider groups. More fundamentally, the Bill of Rights has done too little to ensure that women, a majority group, can exert their interests effectively in the political system.

I have suggested a number of changes to the individual provisions of the Bill of Rights, changes that we could implement either as interpretations or as amendments. These changes would make the Bill of Rights more responsive to the needs of women and other outsider groups and should produce a more effective democratic structure.

In this Conclusion, I add three more general criticisms. First, part of the problem is that the Constitution contains no strong provision on sex discrimination. If such a provision were in the Bill of Rights, it might help judges balance other rights, such as free exercise of religion, against the right of women to social equality. Such a provision should be a right to substantive, not formal, equality.[301] In addition, as in the ANC Draft Bill of Rights,[302] the Bill of Rights should ban discrimination on the basis of sexual orientation, both because lesbian and gay people are a vulnerable group needing protection,[303] and because compulsory heterosexuality is a form of discrimination against women.[304]

---

[301] See, generally Catharine A. MacKinnon, *Toward a Feminist Theory of the State* 215-49 (Harvard, 1989); Catharine A. MacKinnon, *Reflections on Sex Equality Under Law*, 100 Yale L J 1281 (1991).

[302] See ANC, *A Bill of Rights for a Democratic South Africa*, Art 7 § 2 (cited in note 191) ("Discrimination on the grounds of gender, single parenthood, legitimacy of birth or sexual orientation shall be unlawful."). The European Human Rights Commission has interpreted the European Human Rights Convention as banning punishment for at least private homosexual acts between consenting adults. See Glendon, *Rights Talk* at 146-58 (cited in note 20).

However, I realize that a judicially enforced abstract right to sex equality would not do much for women. The drive for its adoption would drain scarce resources from more effective strategies for change. See, for example, Rosenberg, *The Hollow Hope* (cited in note 16); Becker, 1987 S Ct Rev 201 (cited in note 16). I do not, therefore, suggest we should seek such a right at the present time. I merely mention that, in a Constitution anywhere near ideal, we would have a substantive sex equality provision.

[303] See Bruce A. Ackerman, *Beyond* Carolene Products, 98 Harv L Rev 713, 730-31 (1985); Janet E. Halley, *The Politics of the Closet: Towards Equal Protection For Gay, Lesbian, and Bisexual Identity*, 36 UCLA L Rev 915, 916 n 5 (1989).

[304] See Sylvia A. Law, *Homosexuality and the Social Meaning of Gender*, 1988 Wis L Rev 187, 187 (1988); John Stoltenberg, *You Can't Fight Homophobia and Protect the Pornographers at the Same Time—An Analysis of What Went Wrong in* Hardwick, in Dorchen Leidholdt and Janice G. Raymond, eds, *The Sexual Liberals and the Attack on*

Second, the Bill of Rights and other provisions of the Constitution have created a structure posing obstacles to the implementation of the sorts of economic support systems and safety nets present in every other North Atlantic nation. Mary Ann Glendon makes this point powerfully and persuasively in her most recent book.[305] Several features of our Constitution have reinforced the individualism so dominant in our culture: the absolutist wording of individual rights in the Bill of Rights; the failure of the Bill of Rights to include any positive economic rights; and the focus of both the Constitution and the Bill of Rights on *limited* government as the guarantor of liberty. Given these elements in our constitutional structure, it is not surprising that initial attempts at social legislation in this country were declared unconstitutional as violations of the Contracts Clause, a variation on the property right protected in the Fifth Amendment.[306] We abandoned this approach during the New Deal,[307] but by then the United States was far behind the Continent in providing economic support systems. The gap persists today.[308] Had we *no* written constitution so that a *Lochner* era never happened we might live today in a more just society.[309]

My third and last general criticism has been made before by Jennifer Nedelsky, among others. Because the Framers focused on protection of private property as the key to liberty, they devised a "democratic" anti-majoritarian governmental structure. They saw the major problem of democracy as the "problem of majority oppression."[310] The solution was to create barriers to ordinary people's participation, including multiple levels of government and

---

Feminism 184 (Pergamon, 1990); MacKinnon, *Toward a Feminist Theory of the State* at 57 (cited in note 301); Adrienne Rich, *Compulsory Heterosexuality and Lesbian Experience*, in Rich, *Blood, Bread, and Poetry* 23 (Norton, 1986).

[305] See Glendon, *Rights Talk* at 106-08 (cited in note 20). For a discussion of the symbolic power of the Constitution, see Hendrik Hartog, *The Condition of Aspiration and "The Rights That Belong to Us All"*, 74 J Amer Hist 1013 (1987).

[306] See, for example, *Lochner v New York*, 198 US 45 (1905).

[307] *West Coast Hotel Co. v Parrish*, 300 US 379 (1937) (overruling *Lochner*).

[308] Glendon, *Rights Talk* at 32-46 (cited in note 20). For a brief discussion of economic supports in Europe, see Sheila B. Kamerman and Alfred J. Kahn, *What Europe does for Single-Parent Families*, 93 Pub Int 70 (Fall 1988).

[309] It is also possible that we would live in a fascist dictatorship. For an argument that a constitution should include provisions "designed to work against precisely those aspects of a country's culture and tradition that are likely to produce harm through that country's ordinary political process," see Cass R. Sunstein, *On Property and Constitutionalism*, 17 U Chi L Econ Working Paper No 3 (2d series 1991).

[310] Jennifer Nedelsky, *Private Property and the Limits of American Constitutionalism: The Madisonian Framework and its Legacy* 220-22 (Chicago, 1990).

rule by a distant elite.[311] In addition, the Constitution limited directly the ability of less-distant state governments to experiment with the basic structure of the economy.[312]

Seeing the problem of democracy as the problem of majority oppression of the propertied minority is particularly inappropriate from the perspective of women. Women are a majority of the population, who have never controlled or even exercised their proportionate share of influence. Surely we should regard men's domination of positions of power within government as at least *a* problem of democracy in light of women's ability to vote during the last seventy-one years.

We should consider whether other governmental structures and electoral systems would be more democratic. Three independent branches of government minimize governmental action, preserving the status quo. A requirement of coordination among three independent branches is countermajoritarian and conservative. Action is easier in parliamentary systems which integrate the legislative and executive power. We also should consider other electoral systems, such as the ones suggested above.[313]

These are not all pragmatic proposals for change. Members of our legislative bodies are not likely to change the way the game is played when they have won under existing rules. My point is that our governmental structure is not ideal from the perspective of women, other outsider groups, or, indeed, democracy. We could imagine better structures, and many are in place in some parts of the world. We should not be exporting ours, as is, to Eastern Europe.

How should we assess a constitutional structure or a Bill of Rights? I suggest that we should consider, along with other factors, how well the system facilitates women's political participation, poverty rates (especially for women and children), physical safety, and incarceration rates. Measured by these standards, our constitutional system must be found wanting.

---

[311] Id.

[312] Id.

[313] See text accompanying notes 295-300.

Rights in Twentieth-Century Constitutions

Mary Ann Glendon†

Although this symposium has treated the subject of the Bill of Rights in the welfare state primarily within the context of American constitutional law, it is instructive and appropriate to compare the American experience with the experiences of other liberal democratic welfare states. Indeed, if a symposium on this subject had been held in 1991 at a university anywhere except in the United States, its approach almost certainly would have been cross-national from beginning to end. Most of the participants, no doubt, would have been invited to explore how some countries—for example, Canada, Denmark, France, Germany, Italy, Japan, Norway, and Sweden—have managed, more or less successfully, to remain simultaneously committed to political and civil rights, a well-developed welfare state, and a system of constitutional control of legislative and executive action. There would probably have been a session or two devoted to the transition of the East European countries from socialism to constitutional social democracy. Another major topic would have been how commitments made in international human rights instruments have affected national legal systems. Finally, in all likelihood, there would have been sessions devoted to two special cases: first, England, a welfare state without a system of judicial review or a bill of rights (in the modern sense); and second, the United States, a country with a venerable rights tradition and a strong system of judicial review, but with a minimalist welfare state.

In this article, I cannot present such an extended comparative survey. My goal is rather to advance the proposition that American thinking about rights and welfare would benefit from examining the experiences of other liberal democracies,[1] and to speculate about the insights that might emerge from such a comparative

† Professor of Law, Harvard University. The University of Chicago, B.A.; J.D.; M.Comp.L. This Article was prepared for *The Bill of Rights in the Welfare State: A Bicentennial Symposium*, held at The University of Chicago Law School on October 25-26, 1991. The helpful comments of Professor Aviam Soifer of Boston University Law School are gratefully acknowledged.

[1] In this Article, I concentrate mainly on nations whose experience is most similar to our own: countries at levels of social and economic development comparable to ours; and

analysis. I do not claim that we will find abroad any answers to the great questions debated by the participants in this symposium. Rather, the benefits I have in mind are more like those to which the great French historian, Fernand Braudel, was referring when he once said:

> Live in London for a year, and you will not get to know much about the English. But through comparison, and in the light of your surprise, you will suddenly come to understand some of the more profound and individual characteristics of France, which you did not previously understand because you knew them too well.[2]

Taking my cue from Braudel, I will reflect, first, on some of the "more profound and individual characteristics" of the United States that we often overlook—because we know them so well. I will then consider some of the special difficulties posed by our distinctive experience with rights and welfare. Finally, I will suggest that heightened awareness of how our country's experience is distinctive can alert us to opportunities for improvement—opportunities that seem, at least theoretically, to be more available to us than to policymakers elsewhere.

I. AMERICAN DISTINCTIVENESS

Many of the issues vigorously debated at this symposium owe their very existence to the simple chronological fact that, when our Constitution and Bill of Rights were adopted, the welfare state as we know it was not even a twinkle in the eyes of the Founding Fathers. Because the overwhelming majority of the world's constitutions have been adopted within the past thirty years,[3] there are few other countries where scholars need to ask questions like the following: How does our eighteenth-century design for government fit with our modern regulatory state? Does it matter which branches of government take the lead in deciding what adaptations are necessary? Is it a problem that our welfare state, such as it is, continues to develop without any specific constitutional impetus?

---

countries where welfare states co-exist with a strong commitment to individual liberty and the rule of law.

[2] Fernand Braudel, *Histoire et Sciences Sociales: La Longue Durée*, Annales: Economies, Sociétés, Civilisations 725, 737 (1958).

[3] Three-quarters of the approximately 160 single-document constitutions in the world today have been adopted since 1965. Lis Wiehl, *Constitution, Anyone? A New Cottage Industry*, NY Times B6 (Feb 2, 1990) (citing Professor Albert P. Blaustein of the Rutgers Law School).

Or, does the deep structure of the Fourteenth Amendment—say, the idea of "protection"—provide a constitutional lodestar for the welfare state after all? The age of our Bill of Rights is thus foremost among the features that distinguish the United States with respect to rights and the welfare state. The first ten amendments to the Constitution, backed up by judicial review, were in place long before our legislatures began to attend systematically to the health, safety, and well-being of citizens. In most other liberal democracies, the sequence has been just the reverse. In Canada, France, and Germany, for example, the foundations of the welfare state were in place well before regimes of constitutional rights appeared.[4]

A second distinguishing feature is that the American Constitution, unlike the constitutions of most other liberal democracies, contains no language establishing affirmative welfare rights or obligations.[5] A third factor is the conspicuous unwillingness of American governments to ratify several important international human rights instruments to which all the other liberal democracies have acceded. And finally there is the unusual structure of our welfare state, which, much more than elsewhere, leaves pensions, health insurance, and other benefits to be organized privately, mainly through the workplace, rather than directly through the public sector. I will elaborate briefly upon the first three of these factors.

A.   Rights Before Welfare

We Americans are justly proud of our long tradition of protecting individual rights, celebrated in this bicentennial year of the Bill of Rights. We also take patriotic satisfaction in that, prior to 1945, we were one of very few countries that protected constitutional rights through judicial review. However, it is worth recalling that American courts seldom exercised the power of judicial review

---

[4] Expanded suffrage in the French Third Republic and fear of militant socialism in Bismarck's Germany in the late nineteenth century led those countries to adopt factory legislation, rudimentary social welfare laws, and statutes regulating commerce and public utilities.

France adopted a limited form of constitutional control only in 1958, and Canada established judicial review only in 1982. In Germany, though some courts in the Weimar Republic had claimed the power to rule on the constitutionality of laws, constitutional review did not become a significant feature of the legal order until 1951, when the Federal Constitutional Court was established in what was then West Germany. Donald P. Kommers, *The Constitutional Jurisprudence of the Federal Republic of Germany* 6-11 (Duke, 1989).

[5] Louis Favoreu, *La Protection des Droits Economiques et Sociaux dans les Constitutions*, in *Conflict and Integration: Comparative Law in the World Today* 691-92 (Chuo, 1989).

claimed in *Marbury v Madison*[6] until the turn of the century, and
then the courts deployed the power in a way that may well have
impeded the development of the welfare state here for decades.[7] In
the *Lochner* era, when the American Supreme Court engaged in its
first sustained adventure with judicial review, legislators in the rest
of the industrialized world were busily constructing their infant
welfare states on the basis of statutes broadly similar in spirit to
those our Court was striking down.[8]

It was not until the active period of constitution-making following World War II that other nations widely adopted bills of
rights and institutional mechanisms to enforce them.[9] At that time,
the majority of liberal democratic countries opted for variants of a
system developed in pre-war Austria that has come to be known as
the "European model" of constitutional control.[10] The principal
feature that distinguishes the "European" from the "American"
model is that, under the former, constitutional questions must be
referred to a special tribunal that deals only or mainly with such
matters. Constitutional adjudication is off-limits for other courts in
such countries. It is only in the United States, and in the relatively
small group of countries that have adopted the "American model,"
that ordinary courts have the power to rule on constitutional questions in ordinary lawsuits. Many nations that have adopted the
European model are still further distanced from our system by the
fact that constitutional questions may be presented to the consti-

---

[6] 5 US (1 Cranch) 137 (1803).

[7] As James Q. Wilson has noted,

In the first seventy-five years of this country's history, only 2 federal laws were held
unconstitutional; in the next seventy-five years, 71 were. Of the roughly 900 state laws
held to be in conflict with the federal Constitution since 1789, about 800 were overturned after 1870. In one decade alone—the 1880s—5 federal and 48 state laws were
declared unconstitutional.

James Q. Wilson, *American Government: Institutions and Policies* 83 (Heath, 3d ed 1986).

[8] See, for France, Leon Duguit, *Law in the Modern State* 32-67 (Allen & Unwin, 1919)
(translated by Frida and Harold Laski); and for England, A.V. Dicey, *Lectures on the Relation Between Law & Public Opinion in England During the Nineteenth Century* 259-302
(Macmillan, 1914). See generally Alexander Alvarez, *Dominant Legal Influences of the Second Half of the Century*, in *The Progress of Continental Law in the Nineteenth Century*,
11 Continental Legal Hist Series 31, 52-56 (Little, Brown, 1918).

[9] For a concise survey of the development of judicial review, see Louis Favoreu, *American and European Models of Constitutional Justice*, in David S. Clark, ed, *Comparative
and Private International Law: Essays in Honor of John Henry Merryman* 105 (Duncker &
Humbolt, 1990).

[10] For a discussion of why the American model was widely regarded as unsuitable for
transplant, see id at 106-11, and Mauro Cappelletti, *Judicial Review in the Contemporary
World* 53-66 (Bobbs-Merrill, 1971).

tutional tribunal only by other courts *sua sponte*, or by political authorities, but not by private litigants.[11]

Even among the handful of countries that have adopted a form of the "American model" of judicial review—such as Canada, Japan, and the Republic of Ireland—the United States remains unique. For in those nations, neither the supreme courts nor the lower courts thus far have exercised their powers of judicial review with such frequency and boldness as their American counterparts have exercised at both the state and federal levels. Indeed, to foreigners, the recent burgeoning of state court constitutionalism and the innovative use of injunctions by federal district courts beginning in the 1960s are two of the most remarkable features of the American legal system. Even if judicial activism in the Supreme Court has subsided somewhat in recent years,[12] the relative readiness of American judges at all levels of jurisdiction to deploy their powers of judicial review in the service of a variety of social aims has made the United States the model of a particularly adventurous form of judicial rights protection.

B.   What Counts as a Right?

A renowned European legal historian recently compiled a list he described as representing the "basic inventory" of rights that have been accepted by "most western countries" at the present time.[13] The list includes, first and foremost; human dignity; then personal freedom; fair procedures to protect against arbitrary governmental action; active political rights (especially the right to vote); equality before the law; and society's responsibility for the social and economic conditions of its members.[14] An American reader of this list is apt to be struck both by the omission of property rights, and by the inclusion of affirmative welfare obligations. Yet the list cannot be faulted as description of the law on the books of "most western countries." Welfare rights (or responsibili-

---

[11] Favoreu, *American and European Models* at 112-13 (cited in note 9). But Germany is an exception. There the bulk of the caseload of the Constitutional Court consists of constitutional complaints by private citizens. Kommers, *Constitutional Jurisprudence* at 32-33 (cited in note 4).

[12] I use the word "somewhat" advisedly. See, for example, *Missouri v Jenkins*, 110 S Ct 1651 (1990), in which the Supreme Court in dicta authorized a lower federal court, as part of a desegregation plan, to direct a local school district to levy taxes for capital improvements to schools, even without the normal requirement that the voters approve.

[13] Franz Wieacker, *Foundations of European Legal Culture*, 37 Am J Comp L 1, 29 (1989).

[14] Id.

ties) have become a staple feature of post-war international declarations[15] and have been accorded a place beside traditional political and civil liberties in the national constitutions of most liberal democracies.[16] It is the eighteenth-century American Constitution that, with the passage of time, has become anomalous in this respect.

As Gerhard Casper has pointed out, these differences regarding the rights that are accorded constitutional status in various countries are not merely a function of the age of the documents establishing those rights. To a great extent, the differences are legal manifestations of divergent, and deeply rooted, cultural attitudes toward the state and its functions.[17] Historically, even eighteenth- and nineteenth-century continental European constitutions and codes acknowledged state obligations to provide food, work, and financial aid to persons in need.[18] And continental Europeans today, whether of the right or the left, are much more

[15] See, for example, the *United Nations Universal Declaration of Human Rights*, adopted by the General Assembly on December 10, 1948:

Article 22

Everyone, as a member of society, has the right to social security and is entitled to realization, through national effort and international cooperation and in accordance with the organization and resources of each State, of the economic, social, and cultural rights indispensable for his dignity and the free development of his personality.

Article 25

Everyone has the right to a standard of living adequate for the health and well-being of himself and his family, including food, clothing, housing and medical care and necessary social services, and the right to security in the event of unemployment, sickness, disability, widowhood, old age or other lack of livelihood in circumstances beyond his control.

The *United Nations Covenant on Economic, Social and Cultural Rights* was opened for signature in December 1966 and came into force a decade later after being ratified by nearly ninety countries, but not, so far, by the United States. The United States did, however, sign the *Universal Declaration* and the *Helsinki Final Act of 1975* (which like the *Universal Declaration* calls for a nonbinding commitment to stated human rights). See generally Richard B. Lillich, *United States Ratification of the United Nations Covenants*, 20 Ga J Intl & Comp L 279 (1990); Louis B. Sohn, *United States Attitudes Toward Ratification of Human Rights Instruments*, 20 Ga J Intl & Comp L 255 (1990).

[16] The formulations vary from the bare recitation in the German Basic Law of 1949 that the Federal Republic of Germany is a "social" state (Article 20), to detailed lists of specific social and economic rights such as those contained in the constitutions of France, Italy, Japan, Spain, and the Nordic countries.

[17] Gerhard Casper, *Changing Concepts of Constitutionalism: 18th to 20th Century*, 1989 S Ct Rev 311, 318-19 (the Continental concept of the "state" is closer to the Anglo-American notion of the "welfare state" or the "administrative state"). See also Leonard Krieger, *The German Idea of Freedom: History of a Political Tradition* (Beacon, 1957).

[18] See Casper, 1989 S Ct Rev at 319-21 (cited in note 17). Early constitutions used the language of obligation rather than of rights: for example, "It is incumbent on the authorities of the State to create conditions which make it possible for every person who is able to work to earn his living by his work." Norwegian Constitution of 1814, § 110, reprinted in Gisbert

likely than Americans to assume that governments have affirmative duties actively to promote the well-being of their citizens.[19] The leading European conservative parties, for example, accept the subsidization of child-raising families, and the funding of health, employment, and old age insurance at levels most Americans find scarcely credible.[20] By contrast, it is almost obligatory for American politicians of both the right and the left to profess mistrust of government.

These divergent attitudes toward the state have found constitutional expression in what are sometimes called "negative" and "positive" rights. The American Bill of Rights is frequently described as a charter of "negative" liberties, protecting certain areas of individual freedom from state interference.[21] Judge Posner has succinctly stated the position: "The men who wrote the Bill of Rights were not concerned that the federal government might do too little for the people, but that it might do too much to them."[22] The Supreme Court, while willing to accord procedural due process protection to statutory welfare entitlements, has consistently declined to recognize constitutional welfare rights.[23] Chief Justice Rehnquist's opinion in *DeShaney v Winnebago County Department of Social Services* reaffirmed that the Due Process Clause of the Fourteenth Amendment was "a limitation on the State's power to act, not . . . a guarantee of certain minimal levels of safety and security."[24]

These statements contrast markedly with the attitudes of the post-World War II European constitution-makers who supple-

---

H. Flanz, *Norway*, in Albert P. Blaustein and Gisbert H. Flanz, eds, 13 *Constitutions of the Countries of the World* 8 (Oceana, 1976).

[19] "[The state achieves legitimacy] not so much through its constitution as through the active, welfare-providing administration." Casper, 1989 S Ct Rev at 325 & n 69 (cited in note 17) (quoting a treatise by a former constitutional law professor now serving on the German Constitutional Court).

[20] See William Pfaff, *Barbarian Sentiments: How the American Century Ends* 25 (Hill & Wang, 1989).

[21] See David P. Currie, *Positive and Negative Constitutional Rights*, 53 U Chi L Rev 864 (1986), which includes discussion of instances in which the U.S. Supreme Court has found "duties that can in some sense be described as positive" in negatively phrased provisions of the Constitution. Id at 872-80.

[22] *Jackson v City of Joliet*, 715 F2d 1200, 1203 (7th Cir 1983).

[23] See, for example, *Lindsey v Normet*, 405 US 56, 74 (1972) (no constitutional right to housing); *San Antonio Independent School District v Rodriguez*, 411 US 1, 30-31 (1973) (no constitutional right to education). The Court in this period did, however, extend procedural due process protection to certain forms of "new property." See, for example, *Goldberg v Kelly*, 397 US 254 (1970) (welfare entitlements); *Mathews v Eldridge*, 424 US 319 (1976) (social security disability benefits).

[24] 489 US 189, 195 (1989).

mented traditional negative liberties with certain affirmative social and economic rights or obligations. The idea of government underlying the "positive rights" in European constitutions has a complex history. In part, it represents a transposition to the modern state of the feudal notion that an overlord owed certain protection to his dependents in exchange for their service and loyalty. More proximately, it reflects the programs of the major European political parties—one large group animated by Christian social thought, and another by socialist or social democratic principles. As Casper has observed, it was only natural that peoples accustomed to the notion of a state with affirmative responsibilities would carry that idea forward when they added bills of rights to their constitutions.[25]

C. International Human Rights

In view of the long-standing American rights tradition, and the recent history of expansive judicial protection of a broad spectrum of individual and minority rights, the third aspect of American distinctiveness may at first glance seem puzzling. I refer to the dubious distinction of the United States as the only liberal democracy that has not ratified a number of important human rights instruments, notably the two United Nations Covenants on Civil and Political Rights, and on Economic, Social and Cultural Rights.[26] This reticence, no doubt, is due in large part to our prudent unwillingness to submit to the jurisdiction of international organizations dominated by critics of the United States. But, particularly where economic and social rights are concerned, our reluctance is also attributable to our prevailing ideas about which sorts of needs, goods, interests, and values should be characterized as fundamental rights. Another likely reason is that the American civil litigation system is not well-equipped to handle the potential consequences of characterizing a new set of interests as fundamental rights.[27]

II. Welfare Rights and Welfare States

The reaction of many Americans to the foregoing contrasts might be that we have little to learn from other nations about wel-

---

[25] Casper, 1989 S Ct Rev at 331 (cited in note 17).

[26] Alfred de Zayas, *The Potential for the United States Joining the Covenant Family*, 20 Ga J Intl & Comp L 299 (1990); Lillich, 20 Ga J Intl & Comp L 279 (cited in note 15).

[27] See notes 50-51 and accompanying text.

fare, and even less about rights. Other Americans, especially reformers who do not regard this American distinctiveness as a
badge of honor, might be drawn in the opposite direction, toward
viewing the rights or welfare arrangements in other countries as
promising models for the United States to follow. Such reform-
minded persons might ask: How have constitutional welfare rights
worked out in practice? Do the "experiments" of other nations
shed any light on what might have happened here had the Supreme Court in the late 1960s and early 1970s found a basis for
welfare rights in the Fourteenth Amendment?[28] Though I will conclude that those questions lead almost to a dead end, it is instructive to examine why they do not open an especially fruitful line of
inquiry.

As it happens, the contrast between the means of implementation of the American welfare system and other welfarist systems is
less sharp than it initially appears. Though many countries have
included welfare rights or obligations in their constitutions, no
democratic country has placed social and economic rights on precisely the same legal footing as the familiar civil and political liberties. In most cases, the drafters have formulated the former somewhat differently than the latter.[29] In some countries, for example,
the constitutional welfare language is so cryptic as to be meaningless without extensive legislative specification.[30] More commonly,
the constitutions do specifically enumerate various social and economic rights, but present them merely as aspirational political
principles or goals to guide the organs of government as they carry
out their respective functions. For example, the Swedish Instrument of Government, in a section entitled "The Basic Principles of
the Constitution," provides:

> Art. 2 . . . . The personal, economic and cultural welfare of the
> individual shall be fundamental aims of the activities of the

---

[28] See, for example, Frank I. Michelman, *The Supreme Court 1968 Term—Foreword:
On Protecting the Poor Through the Fourteenth Amendment*, 83 Harv L Rev 7 (1969).

[29] "[T]here are two categories of fundamental rights: immutable and absolute rights
that exist whatever the epoch or the reigning ideology; and other rights, known as economic
and social rights, that 'carry a certain coefficient of contingency and relativity' and whose
recognition is a function of the state of society and its evolution." Favoreu, *La Protection
des Droits Economiques* at 701 (cited in note 5).

[30] For example, the German republic is a "social" state. German Basic Law of 1949, Art
20. The treaty of German reunification, however, obliges the legislature to consider adding a
list of affirmative "goals of the state" to the traditional political and civil rights presently
enumerated in the Basic Law. Fred L. Morrison, *Constitutional Mergers and Acquisitions:
The Federal Republic of Germany*, 8 Const Comm 65, 70 (1991).

community. In particular, it shall be incumbent on the community to secure the right to work, to housing and to education and to promote social care and security as well as a favorable living environment.[31]

Continental lawyers call such rights "programmatic" to emphasize that they are not directly enforceable individual rights, but await implementation through legislative or executive action, and through budgetary appropriations. Programmatic rights figure prominently in the constitutions of the Nordic countries, as well as in the French, Greek, Italian and Spanish constitutions.

The most interesting case in some ways is Japan, which accepted the American model of judicial review in 1947. In Japan, the catalog of constitutional rights (thanks to the New Dealers in the post-war occupational government) includes much of Franklin Roosevelt's "Second Bill of Rights,"[32] some of which are set forth in terms that are not, on their face, programmatic.[33] There is a right to decent minimum subsistence in Article 25, a right to receive an education in Article 26, and a right to work in Article 27.[34] In the drafting process, Article 25 was changed from a purely

---

[31] Gisbert H. Flanz, *Sweden*, in Blaustein and Flanz, eds, 17 *Constitutions* at 9-11 (cited in note 18).

[32] The "Second Bill of Rights," which Roosevelt urged in his 1944 State of the Union message, included the following:

  The right to a useful and remunerative job in the industries or shops or farms or mines of the Nation;

  The right to earn enough to provide adequate food and clothing and recreation;

  The right of every family to a decent home;

  The right to adequate medical care and the opportunity to achieve and enjoy good health;

  The right to adequate protection from the economic fears of old age, sickness, accident, and unemployment;

  The right to a good education.

See Cass R. Sunstein, *Constitutionalism After the New Deal*, 101 Harv L Rev 421, 423 (1987) (quoting Roosevelt's "Second Bill of Rights"). See also Cass R. Sunstein, *After the Rights Revolution: Reconceiving the Regulatory State* 21-22 (Harvard, 1990).

[33] See Akira Osuka, *Welfare Rights*, 53 L & Contemp Probs 13 (1990). See also Nobushige Ukai, *The Significance of the Reception of American Constitutional Institutions and Ideas in Japan*, in Lawrence Ward Beer, ed, *Constitutionalism in Asia: Asian Views of the American Influence* 114-27 (California, 1979).

[34] Property as such is not among the rights protected. It supposedly was excluded in order to conform the Japanese procedural guarantees to the American Due Process Clause as it stood *de facto* after the U.S. Supreme Court accepted "the necessity of direct state intervention in social and economic processes." Osuka, 53 L & Contemp Probs at 15-16 (cited in note 33). According to Osuka, the Japanese Constitution "substantially incorporate[d] the fruits of the New Deal." Id at 16. The Japanese Constitution of 1947 is set forth in Hiroshi Itoh and Lawrence Ward Beer, eds, *The Constitutional Case Law of Japan: Selected Supreme Court Decisions, 1961-70* 256-69 (Washington, 1978).

programmatic provision ("In all spheres of life, the State shall use its endeavors for the promotion and extension of social welfare and security, and of public health"), to a proclamation beginning with unvarnished American-style rights language ("All people shall have the right to maintain the minimum standards of wholesome and cultured living.").[35]

The adoption of the 1947 Constitution was quickly followed, however, by a Japanese Supreme Court decision holding that the right to a minimum standard of decent living in Article 25 was programmatic.[36] The government's constitutional welfare obligations, according to that decision, "must, in the main, be carried out by the enactment and enforcement of social legislation . . . . [The] state does not bear such an obligation concretely and materially toward the people as individuals."[37] In the years that followed, the Japanese Supreme Court has maintained the view that the welfare rights in the Constitution are not judicially enforceable individual rights. In a leading case, *Asahi v Japan*, decided in 1967, the Court held:

> [Article 25(1)] merely proclaims that it is the duty of the state to administer national policy in such a manner as to enable all the people to enjoy at least the minimum standards of wholesome and cultured living, and it does not grant the people as individuals any concrete rights. A concrete right is secured only through the provisions of the Livelihood Protection Law enacted to realize the objectives prescribed in the provisions of the Constitution.[38]

The *Asahi* decision went on to say that government officials would have to determine the minimum standard of living, subject to review for excess or abuse of power.[39] In Japan, then, as in the countries where constitutional welfare rights are explicitly programmatic, and as in countries like our own without any constitutional

---

[35] The original programmatic draft proposal was retained as Article 25(2), preceded by the right to a minimum standard of living in Article 25(1). Osuka, 53 L & Contemp Probs at 15 (cited in note 33).

[36] Id at 17.

[37] Id at 21.

[38] *Asahi v Japan*, translated and reprinted in Itoh and Beer, eds, *The Constitutional Case Law of Japan* 130, 134 (cited in note 34) (citation omitted).

[39] Id at 135.

welfare rights at all, the welfare state has been constructed through ordinary political processes.[40]

At this point, we might wonder whether the formal differences between the United States and other welfare states have any significance at all. After all, we too have a "program"—the New Deal statutes of the 1930s and 1940s, supplemented by the Great Society statutes of the 1960s—the cornerstones of our welfare state. Specifically, we have both aspiration and implementation in the Social Security Act of 1935, whose preamble declares that the statute is:

> [t]o provide for the general welfare by establishing a system of Federal old-age benefits, and by enabling the several States to make more adequate provision for aged persons, blind persons, dependent and crippled children, maternal and child welfare, public health, and the administration of their unemployment compensation laws . . . .[41]

Similarly, the Housing Act of 1949 calls for "the realization as soon as feasible of the goal of a decent home and a suitable living environment for every American family . . . ."[42]

Should we conclude, then, that the provisions of modern constitutions which commit the state to affirmatively protecting certain economic and social rights have little or no practical consequence? That conclusion seems too strong, if only because such rights at least endow statutes implementing the constitutional "program" with a strong presumption of constitutionality.[43] Moreover, the constitutional status of social and economic rights seems likely to have synergistically reinforced welfare commitments by influencing the terms, the categories, and the tone of public, judicial, and legislative deliberation about rights and welfare.[44] In

---

[40] Shortly after adopting the 1947 Constitution, Japan supplemented its pre-war social legislation with a series of important statutes in the areas of unemployment relief, social security, and child welfare. Osuka, 53 L & Contemp Probs at 16 n 5 (cited in note 33).

[41] Preamble, Social Security Act, 49 Stat 620 (1935), codified at 42 USC §§ 301 et seq (1988).

[42] Housing Act of 1949, 63 Stat 413 (1949), codified at 42 USC §§ 1441 et seq (1988).

[43] See Osuka, 53 L & Contemp Probs at 17-18 (cited in note 33).

[44] For an example of how the constitutional principle of the social welfare state has affected the interpretation of the equality principle in Germany, see the German Constitutional Court decision which held that medical schools could not impose numerical limits on admissions unless they had class size restraints. Numerus Clausus *Case I*, 33 BVerfGE 303 (1972), excerpted in Kommers, *Constitutional Jurisprudence* at 295-302 (cited in note 4). The Court explicitly stated,

> Any constitutional obligation [of the legislature] that may exist does not include the duty to supply a desired place of education at any time to any applicant.

countries with an already well-established welfare tradition, constitutional welfare commitments may well have strengthened that tradition, just as our Bill of Rights both emerged from and buttressed the Anglo-American rights tradition.

Nevertheless, there does not appear to be any strict correlation between the strength of constitutional welfare language and the generosity of welfare states, as measured by the proportion of national expenditures devoted to health, housing, social security, and social assistance.[45] For example, the United Kingdom, with no constitutional welfare rights, devotes proportionately more of its resources to social expenditures than its richer "neighbor" Denmark, where rights to work, education, and social assistance are constitutionally guaranteed. And analogous social expenditures consume considerably more of the budget of the Federal Republic of Germany, whose constitution merely announces that it is a "social" state, than they do in Sweden or Italy, whose constitutions spell out welfare rights in some detail.[46]

If there is a relationship between the constitutional status of welfare rights and the type and strength of a society's welfare commitment, it is only a loose relationship of consanguinity, with both

---

Id at 300 (bracketed text in excerpt). Of the constitutional right to education, the Court also said,

> [We] need not decide whether . . . an individual citizen can use this constitutional mandate as the basis for an enforceable claim [against the state] to create opportunities for higher study.

Id (bracketed text in excerpt).

[45] Percentages of central government expenditure devoted in 1988 to health, housing, social security, and welfare in selected countries with "high-income economies" are as follows:

Federal Republic of Germany	67.6%
Sweden	55.3
Norway	46.8
Italy	45.8
United Kingdom	44.5
United States	44.0
Canada	43.2
Ireland	42.7
Denmark	42.4

World Development Report 1990 198-99, Table 11 (Central Government Expenditure) (Oxford, 1990).

[46] Id. One cannot fit the United States readily into such comparisons because of the unique structure of our welfare state. But sophisticated analyses consistently rate us poorly, especially in assisting child-raising families. See Alfred J. Kahn and Sheila B. Kamerman, *Income Transfers for Families with Children: An Eight-Country Study* 182-95 (Temple, 1983); Samuel H. Preston, *Children and the Elderly in the U.S.*, 251 Scientific Amer 44 (Dec 1984); Timothy M. Smeeding and Barbara Boyd Torrey, *Poor Children in Rich Countries*, 242 Science 873 (Nov 1988).

the constitution and the welfare system influenced by such factors
as the homogeneity or diversity of the population; the degree to
which mistrust of government has figured in the country's political
history; the vitality of political parties; the health of the legislative
process; and the intensity of individualism in the culture. Such
speculation leads only to the sort of conclusions that make sociol-
ogy so unsatisfying to many people. It is difficult to become excited
about the idea that a host of mutually conditioning factors, of
which the constitutional status of welfare rights may be both cause
and consequence, determine in numerous ways the shape of a given
country's welfare state: its basic commitments, the priorities
among those commitments, the spirit in which it is administered,
the degree of support and approval it wins from taxpayers, and the
extent to which it disables or empowers those who resort to it.

III. WHAT IF . . . ?

Still, a reform-minded American might consider the inconclu-
siveness of the foregoing analysis a source of encouragement. If the
experience of other liberal democracies is any guide, the reformer
might contend, according constitutional status to social and economic rights at least does not seem to cause any harm. At the margins, it may well exert a benign influence on the legislative process
and on public deliberation by broadening the range of officially
recognized social concerns, heightening their visibility, and under-
scoring their legitimacy. What a pity, the argument would go, that
we have not bolstered the legal status of social and economic
rights, either by recognizing them in our Constitution, as proposed
to the Supreme Court in the 1960s and 1970s, or by ratifying
the United Nations Covenant on Economic, Social and Cultural
Rights, as the Carter administration advocated in the 1970s.

It would be risky, in my view, however, to draw those infer-
ences from the foreign experience, for reasons that reside, not in
the foreign experience, but in distinctive American attitudes toward rights. Americans, for better or worse, take rights very seriously. It is not just the term, but the very idea of "programmatic"
rights that is unfamiliar and uncongenial to us. It is thus almost
inconceivable that constitutional welfare rights, had they appeared
in the United States, would have been regarded by the public or
treated by the legal community as purely aspirational. An American, hearing of a "right" that merely represents a goal or ideal, is
apt to react as Mark Twain did when he learned that a preacher
was condemning the Devil without giving the Devil the opportunity to confront the witnesses against him. "[It] is irregular," he

said. "It is un-English; it is un-American; it is *French*."⁴⁷ Most Americans, like Holmes and Llewellyn, believe that a right-holder should be able to call upon the courts to "smite" anyone who interferes with that right.⁴⁸ Furthermore, we take for granted that behind the courts' orders to respect that right are sheriffs, marshals, and the National Guard, if necessary.

As soon as we begin to imagine constitutional welfare rights that are other than programmatic, however, we start down a road that no other democratic country has travelled. That does not mean that we cannot make an educated guess about what consequences would be likely to follow if we made such a trip: recent history suggests that the most likely consequence of according constitutional status to social and economic rights would be something that has not occurred in the other liberal democracies—namely, a great increase in federal litigation.⁴⁹

The crucial question for this symposium about that potential increase in federal litigation—a question whose answer is far from clear—is how private damage actions would affect the structure and performance of the welfare state. Some argue that such litigation would prod government agencies into action, that it would make them more responsive to the needs of the citizens. But it is at least equally plausible that the costs of defending such litigation, plus the occasional high damage award in Section 1983 actions, would prod financially strapped local providers in the other direction, toward cutting back services or eliminating some programs altogether. Unfortunately, there is little empirical data to evaluate the utility of private damage actions in promoting improved social services.

Still, comparing the United States to other countries does illuminate the problem. It demonstrates that we Americans place an unusual degree of reliance on our tort system (both ordinary personal injury litigation and constitutional tort actions) to perform certain social tasks that other advanced industrial nations handle with a more diversified range of techniques—for example, direct

---

⁴⁷ Mark Twain, *Concerning the Jews*, in 22 *The Writings of Mark Twain: Literary Essays* 263, 265 (Harper & Brothers, 1899).

⁴⁸ Oliver Wendell Holmes, Jr., *The Path of the Law*, 10 Harv L Rev 457, 460-61 (1897); Karl Llewellyn, *The Bramble Bush* 85 (Oceana, 1960).

⁴⁹ For example, since the 1960s, Section 1983 has been the second most heavily litigated section of the United States Code. Peter H. Schuck, *Suing Government: Citizen Remedies for Official Wrongs* 199 (Yale, 1983).

health and safety regulation and social insurance.[50] That reliance, in turn, suggests some further questions: Is our tort system well-suited for all the jobs we presently ask it to do? Do our substantive tort law and our civil litigation system adequately assure timely, fair, and cost-efficient disposition of legitimate claims, while effectively discouraging frivolous ones? If a major reason for court-centered reform efforts in the United States has been "legislative paralysis,"[51] can American legislatures ever be induced to take an active role in improving public services in the areas of health, education, and welfare?

IV. The Utility of Cross-National Comparisons

It may seem to follow from the discussion thus far that, contrary to what I asserted at the outset, Americans have little to gain from consulting other nations' experiences with rights and welfare. Certainly anyone who expects comparative studies to yield specific models for domestic law reform[52] is bound to be disappointed, for it is fairly clear that no other country has blazed a trail for the United States to follow. Nevertheless, the experiences of other countries may help us to find our own path by heightening our awareness of indigenous resources that we are inclined to overlook or underrate, because, as Braudel put it, we know them too well.

Beginning in the mid-1970s, economics became a constraint for all advanced welfare states. Even the Nordic countries (whose citizens are as proud of their famous cradle-to-grave welfare systems as we are of our Bill of Rights) began to sense that they had reached the limits of high taxation and direct public sector provision of services. In that climate, policymakers abroad have gazed with interest at our relatively greater capacity for governmental and non-governmental organizations to cooperate in the areas of health, education, and welfare, and at our ability, through our sort of federalism, to innovate and experiment with diverse approaches to stubborn social problems.

In some cases, tentative efforts at imitation have followed. In the area of industrial relations, for example, some countries have begun to experiment with American-style laws encouraging collec-

---

[50] Basil S. Markesinis, *Litigation-Mania in England, Germany and the USA: Are We So Very Different?*, 49 Cambridge L J 233, 243-44 (1990).

[51] Id at 242.

[52] For a critique of the use of comparative law as a source of "models," see Rodolfo Sacco, *Legal Formants: A Dynamic Approach to Comparative Law*, 39 Am J Comp L 1 (1991) (Installment I of II).

tive bargaining rather than the direct state regulation of the terms and conditions of employment that has been traditional in continental Europe.[53] Our innovative labor legislation of the 1930s—which has practically fallen into desuetude in the United States—has been seen in France and Germany as the prototype of "reflexive law" (legal norms that aim at facilitating and structuring private ordering, rather than imposing top-down state regulation).[54] And policymakers abroad have also begun to consider whether some types of social services can be delivered more efficiently and humanely by intermediate associations—churches, unions, community groups, and so on—than by the government. Our voluntary sector, shambles though it may appear to us, is still more vibrant than its counterparts in nations where excessive centralization has nearly extinguished non-governmental initiatives in the areas of health, education, and welfare.[55]

Ironically, these American institutions and experiences are attracting interest abroad just when they are showing the effects of long neglect at home. The United States represents a rare working example, albeit an imperfect one, of what European writers call the principle of "subsidiarity": the notion that no social task should be allocated to a body larger than the smallest one that can effectively do the job.[56] The legal apparatus that promotes and facilitates the subsidiarity principle includes federalism, reflexive legal norms that foster private ordering, and programs that use the mediating structures of civil society—such as churches and workplace associations—to help deliver social services.

These aspects of American law are attracting increased attention because every country in the democratic world is experiencing a tension between the two ideals that are linked together in the deceptively bland title of this symposium—a regime of rights and a welfare state. Every country is grappling with a set of problems that are in a general way similar: how to provide needed social aid without undermining personal responsibility; how to achieve the

---

[53] See Mary Ann Glendon, *French Labor Law Reform 1982-83: The Struggle for Collective Bargaining*, 32 Am J Comp L 449, 485-91 (1984).

[54] "Reflexive law" is an expression used by some legal sociologists to designate an alternative to direct regulation, in which legal norms shape procedures to coordinate interaction among social subsystems, rather than prescribe outcomes. See Gunther Teubner, *Substantive and Reflexive Elements in Modern Law*, 17 L & Society Rev 239, 276 (1983).

[55] For a comparison of non-governmental service organizations in the Netherlands, England, Israel, and the United States, see Ralph M. Kramer, *Voluntary Agencies in the Welfare State* (California, 1981).

[56] Markus Heintzen, *Subsidiaritätsprinzip und Europäische Gemeinschaft*, 46 Juristenzeitung 317 (1991).

optimal mix of markets and central planning in a mixed economy; and how to preserve a just balance among individual freedom, equality, and social solidarity under constantly changing circumstances. The problem of "the Bill of Rights in the Welfare State" is nothing less than the great dilemma of how to hold together the two halves of the divided soul of liberalism—our love of individual liberty and our sense of a community for which we accept a common responsibility.

Below the surface of that dilemma lies a more serious one. Neither a strong commitment to individual and minority rights, nor even a modest welfare commitment like the American one, can long be sustained without the active support of a citizenry that is willing to respect the rights of others; that is prepared to accept some responsibility for the poorest and most vulnerable members of society; and that is prepared to accept responsibility, so far as possible, for themselves and for their dependents. We should make no mistake about the fact that liberal democratic welfare states around the world are now demanding certain kinds of excellence in their citizens to a nearly unprecedented degree. They are asking men and women to practice certain virtues that, even under the best of conditions, are not easy to acquire—respect for the dignity and worth of one's fellow human beings, self-restraint, self-reliance, and compassion.

The questions that seldom get asked, however, are these: Where do such qualities come from? Where do people acquire an internalized willingness to view others with genuine regard for their dignity and concern for their well-being, rather than as objects, means, or obstacles? These qualities do not arise spontaneously in *Homo sapiens*. Nor can governments instill them by fear and force. Perhaps there are alternative seedbeds of civic virtue besides families, neighborhoods, religious groups, and other communities of memory and mutual aid. If there are, however, history provides scant evidence of them. It is hard to avoid the conclusion that both our welfare state and our experiment in democratic government rest upon habits and practices formed within fragile social structures—structures being asked to bear great weight just when they are not in peak condition. The question then becomes: What, if anything, can the government do to create and maintain (or at least to avoid undermining or destroying) social conditions that foster the peculiar combination of qualities required to sustain our commitments to the rule of law, individual freedom, and a compassionate welfare state?

CONCLUSION

In a large, heterogeneous nation such as the United States, this question about the underpinnings of civic virtue is particularly urgent. It has been constantly repeated since Tocqueville said in the 1830s that America was especially well-endowed with moral and cultural resources—with vital local governments, and with a variety of associations that stood between citizens and the state.[57] As with our natural resources, however, we have taken our social resources for granted, consuming inherited capital at a faster rate than we are replenishing it. Indeed, like an athlete who develops the muscles in his upper body but lets his legs grow weak, we have nurtured our strong rights tradition while neglecting the social foundation upon which that tradition rests.

We Americans, with our great emphasis in recent years on certain personal and civil rights, have too easily overlooked the fact that all rights depend on conserving the social resources that induce people to accept and respect the rights of others. Perhaps it is time, therefore, to take a fresh look at our constitutional framework, and to recall not only that the Bill of Rights is part of a larger constitutional structure, but that its own structure includes more than a catalog of negatively formulated political and civil liberties. As Akhil Reed Amar has pointed out, scholars, litigators, and judges who concentrated single-mindedly in the 1960s and 1970s on judicial protection of individual and minority rights permitted other important parts of our constitutional tradition to fall into obscurity.[58] As it happens, those parts of the tradition that have been in the shadows—federalism, the legislative branch, and the ideal of government by the people—have an important bearing on maintaining the social capital upon which all rights ultimately depend.

And so, by a long and circuitous route, a cross-national approach to rights and the welfare state points back toward the American Constitution and toward the "Madisonian understanding that individual liberty and strong local institutions need not be at cross-purposes with one another."[59] If America's endangered social environments do indeed hold the key to maintaining simultaneously a liberal regime of rights and a compassionate welfare state, then we must start thinking about how both rights and welfare, as

---

[57] Alexis de Tocqueville, *Democracy in America* 126-33 (Oxford, 1953).

[58] Akhil Reed Amar, *The Bill of Rights as a Constitution*, 100 Yale L J 1131, 1133-37 (1991).

[59] Id at 1136.

currently conceived, affect those social environments. Reflecting upon our own tradition, moreover, should give us pause before indulging the disdain for politics that underlies so much current thinking about legal and social policy. One of the most important lessons of 1789 the world learned anew in 1989: that politics is not only a way to advance self-interest, but to transcend it. That transformative potential of the art through which we order our lives in the polity is our best hope for living up to our rights ideals and our welfare aspirations in the coming years.

AFTERWORD

The Role of a Bill of Rights

David A. Strauss†

One of the happiest facts about the two hundredth anniversary of the Bill of Rights is that it occurs when, for many people in the world, the question whether to adopt a bill of rights is alive for the first time. What will they be adopting, if they adopt a bill of rights? In this Afterword I want to suggest an answer to that question, based on the American experience with the Bill of Rights generally and, in particular, with controversies of the kind reflected in the articles in this issue.

My suggestion is that there are three different conceptions of the Bill of Rights. Each conception sees the Bill of Rights as serving a different purpose. Each rests on certain normative and institutional premises. Each gives rise to a characteristic form of argument. None of these three conceptions, I will argue, is obviously wrong.

Many controversies that appear to concern the proper interpretation of a provision of the Bill of Rights, including many of the debates in this issue, are in fact contests between or among these different conceptions of the Bill of Rights. Disputes of this kind cannot be resolved until one conception of the Bill of Rights can be justified over another. Many confusions, illegitimate arguments, and unwarranted displays of defensiveness derive from the failure to realize that what is at stake in controversies about the Bill of Rights is often differing conceptions of the Bill of Rights.

In Sections I, II, and III of this essay, I describe the three conceptions. The first conception views the Bill of Rights as a code: a

---

† Professor of Law, The University of Chicago. I am grateful to Elena Kagan, Lawrence Lessig, Geoffrey Stone, and Cass Sunstein for comments on an earlier draft.

list of relatively specific requirements and prohibitions. The second treats the Bill of Rights as a means of correcting some of the systematic failures of representative government. The third views the Bill of Rights as a charter of fundamental human rights that should not be invaded in any society. In Section IV, I will conclude by describing five fallacies that, I believe, often occur in arguments about the Bill of Rights. These fallacies result from adopting one or another conception without realizing that it is just one possible conception, and without justifying it in preference to the other conceptions.

I do not mean to suggest that everyone must adopt one or another conception. Each conception may be true to some degree. But whichever conception or combination of conceptions one adopts must be justified. One cannot simply assume that an approach derived from one or another conception is the only correct way to interpret the Bill of Rights.

I also do not mean to endorse any controversial theory of interpretation. I do, however, necessarily reject a theory of interpretation that perhaps has some adherents. That is the view that the correct interpretation of the Bill of Rights is entirely determined by the text alone, by history, by precedent, or by some similar source of authority, and that arguments about justice or social welfare can play no role in its interpretation. Of course, text and history play a role, but they do not dictate one conception and foreclose all the others. To some degree, the choice among the competing conceptions must be made in light of the considerations I discuss below.

I. The Bill of Rights As a Code

A.

What would be most striking about the Bill of Rights to a stranger to our culture who was reading it for the first time? One plausible answer is something that played almost no role in the articles presented at this symposium: the detailed code of protections for criminal defendants. The Sixth Amendment is entirely a catalogue of such protections. The Fifth Amendment is also, except for the Just Compensation Clause.[1] The Eighth Amendment

---

[1] For an account of why the Just Compensation Clause is included, incongruously, with a list of protections of criminal defendants, see Akhil Reed Amar, *The Bill of Rights As a Constitution*, 100 Yale L J 1131, 1181-82 (1991). The Due Process Clause of the Fifth Amendment, of course, applies to civil as well as criminal proceedings.

applies only to criminal punishments. The Fourth Amendment applies principally to criminal investigations and arrests. Since the Second and Third Amendments have little practical significance, the Seventh Amendment does not apply to the states, and the Ninth and Tenth Amendments are often not regarded as part of the Bill of Rights, specific protections for criminal defendants are arguably the dominant feature of the Bill of Rights.

A celebration of the one hundred and seventy-fifth anniversary of the Bill of Rights would have paid a great deal of attention to this aspect of the document. For three decades, culminating in the 1960s, the Supreme Court reformed state criminal procedure, principally on the authority of the specific guarantees of the Fourth, Fifth, Sixth, and Eighth Amendments.[2] The Court used two complementary doctrinal tools in pursuing this agenda: incorporation and literalism. Incorporation, of course, is the view that the Due Process Clause of the Fourteenth Amendment applies the guarantees of the first eight amendments to the states. The most famous version of incorporation, Justice Black's, held that the Fourteenth Amendment applies each of those guarantees, but nothing more, to the states, in exactly the way that the original Bill of Rights applies to the federal government. Literalism insists that the words of the first eight amendments impose relatively clear requirements that must be followed. Justice Black reviled what he called the "natural law due process formula" under which government action could be upheld so long as it satisfied a test of "fundamental fairness" or consistency with "ordered liberty."[3]

In using the Bill of Rights in this way, the Court was following in a great tradition of law reform. The Court was using the Bill of Rights as a code—a list of specific, relatively determinate prohibitions and requirements. The criminal law reform movement of the late eighteenth century and early nineteenth century was also a codification movement. Jeremy Bentham, perhaps the most prominent reformer in England, was outspoken in his condemnation of the common law, which he viewed as the enemy of reform. Only a code—a catalogue of specific rules—could bring about changes in

---

[2] Before 1960, the Court relied principally on the Due Process Clause of the Fourteenth Amendment alone. See, for example, *Chambers v Florida*, 309 US 227 (1940); and *Powell v Alabama*, 287 US 45 (1932). Beginning in 1961, the Court began to apply the specific guarantees of the Bill of Rights to the states through the Due Process Clause. See the cases cited in *Duncan v Louisiana*, 391 US 145, 148 & nn 4-12 (1968).

[3] For especially clear statements of Justice Black's position on both issues, see *Duncan*, 391 US at 162 (Black concurring); *Adamson v California*, 332 US 46, 68 (1947) (Black dissenting).

criminal law. Justice Black's animadversions against the "natural
law due process formula" echoed Bentham's ridicule of natural
rights and the common law.[4]

Both Bentham and Black understood that a code can be a reformer's ally, and an open-ended natural law or fundamental fairness approach can be a reformer's enemy. If you are trying to uproot practices that have existed for many years but that you think
are corrupt or harmful, a "fundamental fairness" standard will seldom do the job. Committed reformers will agree that those practices are unfair. But a large-scale reform effort will not succeed unless it is also implemented by lower-level officials—bureaucrats, or
judges of lower courts—who will do their jobs in good faith but
who are not necessarily committed to the reform effort.

Such lower-level officials will tend to identify "fairness" with
existing practices. If, however, they are responsible for enforcing a
more determinate norm, they are more likely to decide that their
duty requires them to uproot an established practice. It will be difficult for a person who has worked within a system in which, say,
prosecutors have been allowed to comment on an accused's failure
to testify at trial, to conclude that such a system is fundamentally
unfair. It will be easier for such a person to conclude that the system violates the specific prohibition against compelled self-incrimination. That is not because the language deductively requires that
result; of course it does not. But it is easier for a person to justify
that result, to herself and others, if the specific norm rather than a
more general principle is in force. And a specific norm makes it
easier for a person to disclaim responsibility for the decision by
blaming it on the text, or the framers, or the codifiers.

This is also true outside criminal law as well. An Eastern European official who is trying to uproot a tradition of state control
over an economy and to establish a market is likely to find that
specific limitations on officials' authority are more effective than
general injunctions to "use price mechanisms" or "promote private
ownership." Max Weber associated the rise of capitalism with
codes and rule-governed bureaucracies,[5] and while this association
did not invariably hold, the reason for it is clear: entrenched patterns of privilege that prevent markets from developing will yield
more readily to rule-governed forms of political organization than

---

[4] See, for example, H.L.A. Hart, ed, Jeremy Bentham, *Of Laws in General* 152-95
(London, 1970).

[5] See Max Rheinstein, ed, Max Weber, *Law in Economy and Society* 350-56 (Harvard,
1954).

to a regime in which lower-level officials are controlled by less determinate norms.

One use of a bill of rights, then, is to serve as a code that facilitates reform—a specific list of requirements or prohibitions to help break up traditional practices that are in need of change.

B.

This conception of the Bill of Rights carries with it certain presuppositions. First notice, however, one thing that it does not presuppose: Nothing in this understanding of the Bill of Rights requires any form of judicial supremacy. A code—that is, a relatively specific catalogue of requirements and prohibitions—can be adopted by a legislature as a tool of reform. Bentham and other codifiers urged their codes on Parliament. Far from being initiators of reform, judges were the problem: the reluctant, tradition-bound officials who needed the sharp edges of a code, rather than the more gentle prodding of an open-ended norm, if they were to effect reform.

A code can be addressed to legislatures, too. International human rights treaties are an example. A treaty requiring nations to protect a specific catalogue of human rights is easier to enforce than a general rule requiring respect for humanity. Violations of specific rights can be identified and condemned with greater ease and greater effect, and without the need to argue over whether the practice violates an open-ended norm. The Supreme Court's use of the Bill of Rights to reform American criminal procedure was just a particular instance of a code-driven reform effort led by a court. The connection between the use of the code and the role of the Court was contingent.

This conception of a bill of rights does presuppose some state of affairs that needs reform badly enough to justify the costs inflicted by a code. A code, like any set of rules, is a crude device. It will be over- and under-inclusive. Some practices that will be found to violate, for example, the Double Jeopardy Clause or the Self-Incrimination Clause, might be practices that, everything considered, should be maintained. Conversely, some unjust practices might not violate any specific provision of the Bill of Rights; ideally they should be invalidated, but under the "code" conception of the Bill of Rights they will survive.

It makes no sense to incur these costs of over- and under-inclusiveness unless there is a potential gain. If, for example, there are entrenched practices that will yield to strict rules but not to more open-ended norms, the price might be justified.

C.

This conception of the Bill of Rights has two characteristic modes of argument, which I will call formalism and exclusivity. By formalism I mean three things: a heavy reliance on the precise language of the text; a pretense that the text resolves more issues than it actually does; and an effort to shift responsibility for a decision away from the actual decisionmaker and to some other party, such as the Framers. Justice Black's opinions are famous for displaying these traits. By exclusivity I mean the insistence that the catalogue of rights is exhaustive; that no other rights besides those enumerated in the code exist. This, of course, was one of Justice Black's central themes.

Formalism and exclusivity are necessary to this conception because otherwise the Bill of Rights would not serve the functions of a code: it would not provide the clarity needed for reform. A code forces officials to judge a traditional practice, which they might be inclined to uphold, in light of relatively specific language. If the officials can escape the language, they are more likely to follow their tendency to uphold the traditional practice, and the reform mission will fail.

They can escape the language by deemphasizing its importance, for example by saying that the specific guarantees of the Bill of Rights inform but do not determine the proper interpretation of the Fourteenth Amendment. Or they might escape the language by capitalizing on its indeterminacy, for example by saying that the words of the Self-Incrimination Clause do not, by virtue of their meaning alone, preclude the government from commenting on a defendant's failure to testify.

One might ask why, if the words of a constitutional provision do not *actually* require that a traditional practice be overthrown, judges who are disposed to accept the practice will feel that the words compel them to overthrow it. The answer, I believe, is that formalism is an attractive creed to people who have the power to make decisions. Formalism makes difficult decisions easier, in at least two ways. First, a formalist decisionmaker generally doesn't have to think as hard; she only has to work with the words of the authoritative text, instead of with complex and (obviously) inconclusive arguments about policy or fairness. Second, a formalist decisionmaker can more readily assign responsibility for the decision elsewhere. Because formalism is so attractive, a legislature, supreme court, or chief executive who promulgates a code and sets about creating a formalist legal culture can expect to have some success in inducing officials to act like formalists, even when that means that they will take part in uprooting a practice that they themselves do not consider unfair.

Exclusivity—we enforce the Bill of Rights; nothing less, but nothing more—functions in a more indirect way, by enhancing the credibility of the reformers. It allows them to appear restrained and principled. Like formalism, it helps assign responsibility elsewhere. Justice Black's position is again the paradigm. He criticized the Court for overreaching when, as in *Griswold v Connecticut*,[6] it enforced rights not clearly specified in the Bill of Rights. This allowed him to convey the message that he was willing to be bound by the same restraints he imposed on the states and on the other branches of the federal government. Self-denial of this form gives credibility to the claim that the reformers' efforts are not simply their own acts of will.

D.

The problems with the formalistic conception of the Bill of Rights are well known. The language, even of the most specific provisions, is not determinate; the words alone resolve few controversial cases. There are notorious problems in relying on the Framers' intentions as a way of making the language more determinate.[7] The argument for exclusivity is dubious, in light of, among other things: the Ninth Amendment; the indeterminacy of many of the specific guarantees in the Bill of Rights (a wide range of invasions of personal autonomy, for example, can plausibly be characterized as unreasonable seizures of the person); and the fact that the only language that literally applies to the states is the open-ended terms of Section 1 of the Fourteenth Amendment.

Perhaps the more difficult task is not to explain why the code conception need not be accepted as the only correct view, but rather to explain how anyone could ever accept it as the correct view. Perhaps the formalistic view of the Bill of Rights as a code should simply be rejected outright as obviously wrong and disingenuous. But I would like to describe, without endorsing, an argument that in some circumstances it would be defensible to adopt this conception of the Bill of Rights.

---

[6] 381 US 479 (1965).

[7] See, for example, Paul Brest, *The Misconceived Quest for the Original Understanding*, 60 BU L Rev 204 (1980); Ronald Dworkin, *The Forum of Principle*, 56 NYU L Rev 469, 476-500 (1981).

Suppose you were a Supreme Court Justice at a time when, you believed, many states' criminal justice systems were badly in need of reform. On their face the states' procedural rules were reasonable, even enlightened. For example, they permitted criminal defendants to be compelled to testify, but only before a judge, in open court, with counsel present; they permitted trials before a judge in some complex cases, even when the defendant requested a jury; in the interests of "nonadversary" justice, they provided for appointment of counsel only when there was a special need; and they permitted some witnesses to give evidence without cross-examination. But you were convinced that these reasonable-sounding procedures masked abuses—in particular the frequent conviction of innocent defendants and racial discrimination—that were widespread but hard to prove in any specific case.

Although the particulars are different, this is arguably the situation that the Supreme Court faced between 1930 and 1970. In effect, Justice Black's response was: We do not wish either to condemn or to praise these procedures. That is not our role. Our role is to enforce the Constitution. But the words of the Bill of Rights simply prohibit each of these practices. We therefore cannot allow them to continue.

By contrast, a completely candid Court might say the following. Whether these procedures violate the specific provisions of the Constitution is by no means an open-and-shut question. One could interpret the Sixth Amendment right to counsel not to require the appointment of counsel in any case, but only to ensure that the defendant may have counsel that she herself retains. (Indeed, that was probably the Framers' understanding.) It would be more of a stretch, but one could interpret the self-incrimination and jury trial rights to apply only in cases of potential abuse. The Confrontation Clause might be interpreted to allow a trial court to dispense with cross-examination in favor of some other reasonably effective way of testing a witness's credibility. In any event, the only provisions that literally apply to the states are those of the Fourteenth Amendment, and on their face, the state procedures do not violate "due process of law," if that is interpreted to require only fundamental fairness. Nonetheless, the candid Court would say, we believe that these practices have led to serious abuses, and our interpretation of the Bill of Rights is informed by that belief. We accordingly hold that they are unconstitutional.

To the extent the Court's rhetoric matters, there is not much doubt which of these approaches is more likely to succeed. The first approach, Justice Black's, appeals to a widespread allegiance to the language of the Bill of Rights; it assigns a fully plausible, even obvious, meaning to its terms; and it does not appear to be passing moral judgment on the states. The second approach accuses state officials of reprehensible conduct, does not rely on specific language, and explicitly invokes the Court's conception of fairness. If you believed that the states' procedures needed reform, there is not much doubt which strategy is better calculated to achieve your aims.

Even if the formalist approach would be more effective, however, it might still be unacceptably disingenuous.[8] Ordinarily one would want to say that deceptive and manipulative rhetoric is justified only in the most extreme circumstances.[9] But in defense of the formalist approach, one might say that a judicial opinion is, and is understood to be, a public document, issued in part to accomplish certain effects. It is not expected to be a completely candid account of the judges' actual reasons for their decision.

For example, a court might set aside an agency action because it is convinced that the agency was influenced by improper political considerations, without saying so explicitly. It might set aside a state referendum because it believed the voters acted out of racial prejudice, without explicitly saying that. The most important decision of this century, *Brown v Board of Education*,[10] is, notoriously, not fully candid in this sense. A fully candid opinion would have said (as the most compelling subsequent defense of the decision said[11]) that segregation as practiced in the South in 1954 was an odious system of racial oppression that could not possibly be squared with the constitutional requirement of equal protection. But it is difficult to fault the Court for not writing such an opinion. For similar reasons, it is difficult to fault the Court for not spelling out all of the reasons it became convinced that state criminal justice systems needed to be reformed.

---

[8] I refer to the formalist approach, rather than to Justice Black, because it is not clear that Justice Black intended to use his rhetoric in a manipulative way. That may have been a side effect of a formalist orientation that Justice Black adopted for other reasons.

[9] See Lee C. Bollinger, *The Tolerant Society: Freedom of Speech and Extremist Speech in America* 76-103 (Oxford, 1986), for a similar account and criticism of the use of formalist rhetoric in interpreting the First Amendment. Bollinger suggests that defenders of free speech, including judges, speak as if the dictates and foundations of the First Amendment were much clearer than they actually are; and that they do so because they fear that any admission of uncertainty will encourage the ever-present forces of mass intolerance. Bollinger comments on the "elitism" of this approach to the First Amendment. Id at 101.

[10] 347 US 483 (1954).

[11] Charles L. Black, Jr., *The Lawfulness of the Segregation Decisions*, 69 Yale L J 421, 428 (1960).

There is, however, a difference between not fully spelling out all of one's reasons for reaching a conclusion and stating supposed reasons that are not true—such as (in most cases), "the Framers decided this question for us," or "the text requires this result." The defense of the use of the Bill of Rights as a code is that it accomplished important objectives that otherwise might not have been achieved. The problem with this conception of the Bill of Rights is that it raises the question of the extent to which manipulatively false rhetoric is permissible in public life. That is a difficult question; it is possible that this approach oversteps the line.

II. THE BILL OF RIGHTS AS A STRUCTURAL CORRECTIVE

A second conception of the Bill of Rights treats it as a way of correcting certain structural deficiencies in representative government. This conception differs sharply from the view that treats the Bill of Rights as a code. It does not necessarily rely on specific language; it has different presuppositions and modes of argument; and, unlike the code approach, it does imply a form of judicial supremacy.

A.

The central idea of this conception is that representative government does some things badly, or at least cannot be trusted to do them well. The purpose of the Bill of Rights is to make up for these deficiencies of representative government.

The most conspicuous example of this conception is a well-known understanding of the Free Speech Clause of the First Amendment: that the purpose of this guarantee is to ensure the proper functioning of representative government.[12] Left to their own devices, officials will tend to suppress speech that is critical of them, thus preventing democratic accountability. The principal purpose of the guarantee of free speech is to keep the channels of communication open so that representative government can continue to operate. This understanding of freedom of speech is probably the most widely accepted view of the First Amendment today. It is, for example, the view that underlies *New York Times v Sulli-*

---

[12] The best-known example of this approach is Alexander Meiklejohn, *Free Speech and Its Relation to Self-Government* (Harper, 1948). See also Cass R. Sunstein, *Free Speech Now*, in this volume, 255, 300-14.

van,[13] arguably the most important free speech decision of the last thirty years.

In an important sense, however, this understanding does not see the First Amendment as establishing a *right* to free speech at all. This reflects the defining characteristic of the structural conception of the Bill of Rights. The structural approach does not regard the First Amendment as establishing rights in the sense that this approach is concerned with the condition of the system of expression as a whole, not the fate of any identifiable individual. So long as the system is working properly—so long as channels for criticizing government officials remain open—the fate of any particular individual is immaterial. Under the structural conception, individuals' legal rights are entirely instrumental: the only justification for allowing an individual to assert First Amendment "rights" is that there is no other satisfactory way of maintaining the system-wide quantity and quality of expression that we want.

In other words, in principle the structural view of the First Amendment would allow any individual's speech to be suppressed so long as the system of free expression as a whole was functioning properly. If, for example, the President's decision to veto a civil rights bill had been thoroughly criticized in literally thousands of well-publicized statements, there would be no harm in suppressing the speech of a single individual with a small audience, all of whom had heard the same arguments many times before. That particular speech would be surplusage because it would not provide any benefit to the system of democratic accountability. The leading proponent of this view made the point explicitly: "What is essential is not that everyone shall speak, but that everything worth saying shall be said."[14]

In practice, of course, there are dispositive institutional reasons not to allow a free speech claim to be defeated on this basis. Courts cannot be trusted to decide when the system as a whole is functioning well or when the speech in question is truly redundant. My point is not that, under the structural approach, we ought to allow the suppression of speech in these circumstances. It is only a point about the nature of the justification that this approach offers for protecting speech.

This view of freedom of speech contrasts with what I believe is the universal understanding of freedom of religion. Religious free-

---

[13] 376 US 254 (1964).

[14] Meiklejohn, *Free Speech and Its Relation to Self-Government* at 25 (cited in note 12).

dom is not instrumental in the way that, under the structural approach, free speech is. Punishing a person because of her religious beliefs is unacceptable in principle, not because of institutional concerns, but because it infringes on an individual right no matter what the condition of the "system" (whatever the relevant system is). There are many non-structural justifications for free speech, of course. But the structural argument—that free speech is necessary to keep democracy functioning as it should—places freedom of speech on a different foundation from freedom of religion.

The structural conception of the Bill of Rights is the same approach generalized beyond freedom of speech. According to this conception, the Bill of Rights does not provide a code that will spur reform, nor does it protect (other than instrumentally) individual rights. Instead, it protects against certain systematic weaknesses of representative government. This idea is associated with the *Carolene Products* footnote, which envisions more active judicial review both of "legislation which restricts those political processes which can ordinarily be expected to bring about repeal of undesirable legislation" and of "statutes directed at particular . . . minorities [because] prejudice against discrete and insular minorities may . . . tend[] seriously to curtail the operation of those political processes ordinarily to be relied upon to protect them."[15]

In addition to the Free Speech Clause (and of course the Equal Protection Clause), many Bill of Rights' protections for criminal defendants can be understood in this way. The Cruel and Unusual Punishment Clause[16] protects convicted offenders, a small and politically powerless group, against a vengeful society. The jury trial right[17] ensures, among other things, a form of popular sovereignty over decisions that, because of their particularity, the legislature cannot control. The Fourth Amendment's Warrant Clause and ban on unreasonable searches and seizures help control decisions by low-level officials that are not visible enough for elected bodies to control.[18]

Today perhaps the most significant structural interpretation of the Bill of Rights involves the Just Compensation Clause. Structural arguments, generally associated with public choice theory, are

---

[15] *United States v Carolene Products Co.*, 304 US 144, 153 n 4 (1938). For a leading statement of this generalized approach, see John Hart Ely, *Democracy and Distrust: A Theory of Judicial Review* (Harvard, 1980).

[16] US Const, Amend VIII.

[17] US Const, Amend VI.

[18] See Ely, *Democracy and Distrust* 96-99, 172-73 (cited in note 15).

increasingly offered as reasons for courts to expand the Just Compensation Clause, and there are signs that those arguments are becoming increasingly influential.

The public choice structural argument is, roughly, that when a representative body regulates or redistributes property, it systematically tends to benefit well-organized interest groups at the expense of more diffuse groups, to the detriment of society as a whole. If the Just Compensation Clause were applied to a wider range of government actions than it now covers, the government would be precluded from adopting some or all redistributive measures and would be forced to internalize the costs of regulatory actions. This, it is said, would reduce the distorting effects of interest group power.[19] This argument—my concern is not whether it is correct—parallels the *New York Times v Sullivan* approach to freedom of speech; both reflect a structural conception of a provision of the Bill of Rights.

The structural view is not the only possible understanding of the Just Compensation Clause. One might see it as protecting individual rights non-instrumentally. That is, quite apart from any arguments about the propensities of representative government, it is an unacceptable invasion of my liberty for the government to seize my car or my house without compensation. This understanding of the Just Compensation Clause belongs to the third conception. It does not justify as sweeping an interpretation of the Clause as the structural view; it does not preclude regulatory and redistributive actions wholesale. Rather, it just forbids actions of a particularly intrusive kind, those likely to inflict serious psychic or material injury. Arguably the Just Compensation Clause is already interpreted to prohibit this kind of government action.

The structural argument, by contrast, would expand the Just Compensation Clause to reach government actions that cannot plausibly be described as affronting human rights in the same way as a seizure of one's personal possessions. (Not every structural understanding of the Just Compensation Clause would call for such an expansion, but the influential public choice structural argument now being made in many circles does.) For example, much of what

---

[19] Richard A. Epstein, *Property, Speech, and the Politics of Distrust*, in this volume, 41, is an example of the argument for interpreting the Just Compensation Clause in this way. The public choice argument about the defects of representative government is summarized in Einer Elhauge, *Does Interest Group Theory Justify More Intrusive Judicial Review?*, 101 Yale L J 31, 35-43 (1991), which, however, questions whether that argument, even if correct, justifies an expanded judicial role.

is offensive about the classic seizure of an individual's property is
the surprise and sense of insecurity it engenders. But regulation
routinely occurs in volatile business settings in which it does not
have these effects. If a person is fully prepared to see the market
cause the value of her investment to fluctuate by thirty percent,
government regulation reducing its value by, say, one percent, is
unwelcome but cannot be compared, in the effect it has on the individual, to the uncompensated seizure of an individual's possessions. The argument against such regulation is structural: given the
propensities of representative government (the argument goes)
there is an unacceptable risk that the regulation will diminish
overall well-being. It is not an argument based on the effects the
regulation has on identifiable individuals.

B.

The structural conception of the Bill of Rights has its own
presuppositions. They operate whether the structural conception is
applied to a particular provision, or to no provision in particular—a legitimate thing to do, under this conception, as I will argue
below.

The most significant presupposition is judicial supremacy. Unlike the other conceptions, the structural conception of the Bill of
Rights necessarily presumes that courts will be the primary enforc-
ers. The whole point of a bill of rights, according to this conception, is to withdraw issues from the legislature. Recall that this was
not true of the formalistic conception of the Bill of Rights as a
code, and as I will argue shortly, it is not true of the third conception, which treats the Bill of Rights as a charter of fundamental
individual liberties. Under each of those conceptions, it would
make sense to have a bill of rights without the institution of judicial review. A bill of rights might be addressed solely to a sovereign
legislature: the English Magna Carta, Petition of Right, and Bill of
Rights were all addressed to the sovereign King or Queen in Parliament; some colonies and states had constitutions without judicial review; and international declarations of human rights are addressed to sovereign governments and not generally enforced by
courts. But under the structural conception, the purpose of a bill
of rights is to authorize courts to correct the legislature's failings.
It would, according to this conception, be otiose to have a bill of
rights without judicial review. The connection between judicial review and a bill of rights, so natural to Americans, is a necessary
connection only for the structural conception.

The other crucial presupposition is a relatively complete theory of how a well-functioning legislative process would work. You cannot draw any conclusions about how much speech is needed to protect representative government unless you know what representative government consists of and how it should function. Even more obviously, you cannot say which groups need judicial protection because they lack sufficient power, and which "interest groups" have too much power, unless you have a theory about how the legislative process should operate.

This point is significant because the underlying theory is often left implicit. The *Carolene Products* formulation "discrete and insular minorities," for example, begs many questions about which groups need special protection in a democratic system. Many theories about "rent seeking" in the political process seem simply to assume, without justification, that the only legitimate function of the political process is to correct market failures. A particular structural conception cannot be justified unless the underlying theory of the democratic process is also justified.

C.

The principal mode of argument under the structural conception is one of comparative institutional competence. A court should invalidate a statute if that statute is within a class of measures that are likely to be the product of some legislative dysfunction, and if the courts are likely to correct the legislative error. In every case, under this conception, that is the primary issue.

Under the structural conception the words of the document are incidental, and formalist arguments should play no role. This is perhaps not obvious, because many advocates of the structural conception also invoke the words of the document. The *Carolene Products* footnote, for example, suggested that active judicial review would be appropriate, not only where the political process might not function well, but also "when legislation appears on its face to be within a specific prohibition of the Constitution, such as those of the first ten amendments."[20]

The structural conception, however—taken by itself, not in combination with another conception—does not justify this kind of resort to the specific language of the document. It calls for active judicial review of those issues, but only those issues, that the legislative process will systematically handle badly, and the judicial

---

[20] *Carolene Products*, 304 US at 153 n 4.

process will systematically handle better. As I suggested earlier, a plausible claim can be made that many of the provisions of the Bill of Rights concern such issues. The Framers of the Constitution and the Bill of Rights may even have had such systemic dysfunctions in mind. But the justification for judicial intervention remains the structural argument, not the text. If the text is to be cited as authoritative in itself, some other justification will be needed.[21]

Of course, as I said at the outset, it might be possible to hold a view that combined structural and formalist elements. One might say, for example, that the text is authoritative but that where it is ambiguous it should be interpreted according to structural arguments.[22] One would then have to justify the use of those two conceptions in combination. The view that the text is binding might be justified by arguments about authority or precedent. But structural arguments alone—that is, arguments about institutional competence—do not by themselves justify the reliance on text.

III. The Bill of Rights As a Charter of Fundamental Human Rights

A.

The third conception of the Bill of Rights is probably closest to the popular image. It treats the Bill of Rights as a charter of fundamental human rights—those rights that an individual should have against the state in any society.

In one sense this conception is the easiest to justify. Everyone agrees in the abstract that there are human rights that no society should abridge. And there is nearly universal agreement on many of those rights: religious toleration, a general right to dissent, freedom from arbitrary punishment, and freedom from slavery and oppressive racial or ethnic discrimination. Every society should have, somewhere, a conception of these rights—either written down in a bill of rights, or informally understood in the culture. It is natural to view the Bill of Rights as our society's recognition of these basic human rights.

---

[21] See Charles L. Black, Jr., *Structure and Relationship in Constitutional Law* 11-12 (Ox Bow Press, 1985).

[22] Ely, *Democracy and Distrust* (cited in note 15), takes this approach at least to a degree.

This conception of the Bill of Rights has some overt advocates.[23] But the list of its advocates does not begin to convey how central this conception is in history and in current practice. A claim that a government practice is morally wrong is always a powerful argument in a controversy over any provision of the Bill of Rights. If you persuade a judge that a certain practice would be condemned if, for example, another country engaged in it, you are well on your way to convincing the judge to interpret some provision of the Constitution to forbid that practice.

In controversies about the Bill of Rights—for example, a case, not controlled by precedent, involving the First Amendment, the Fourth Amendment, or the Due Process Clause—the principal dispute often concerns not the text or the history of the particular provision (both of which are often indeterminate or otherwise unhelpful) but whether the challenged government action is, all things considered, a morally unacceptable way to treat individuals. The litigants will use moral terms like "fair," "reasonable," or "justified on balance," and the judges will think in (or react in) those same terms. Does this form of government involvement with religion endanger religious liberty in a way that seems unfair to some group? Does permitting this restriction on speech open the door to government abuse of political opponents? Does this police investigative practice interfere with citizens' legitimate interests in privacy and security? Is this a fair way to adjudicate this class of disputes, given the various interests at stake? Is this form of punishment barbarous? All of these questions reflect a conception of the Bill of Rights under which its purpose is to protect fundamental human rights.

Like the structural conception, this view of the Bill of Rights fits uneasily with its language. Many of the rights explicitly guaranteed by the Bill of Rights are fundamental in the sense that no civilized society would deny them. But some rights that virtually everyone would agree are fundamental in this sense are not explicitly enumerated in the Bill of Rights. Freedom from chattel slavery and from oppressive racial discrimination had to await the Thirteenth and Fourteenth Amendments. The right to bodily integrity, even in the barest sense of a right not to be beaten up by the police, is not obviously guaranteed by language anywhere in the Bill

---

[23] See, for example, Ronald Dworkin, *Unenumerated Rights: Whether and How* Roe *Should Be Overruled*, in this volume, 381; Michael Perry, *The Constitution, the Courts, and Human Rights* (Oxford, 1982).

of Rights.[24] In my view, a greater right to bodily integrity, of the kind anti-abortion laws violate, is also fundamental and is not obviously described in the text of the Bill of Rights either. (The abortion question is truly difficult, but only because the interest in fetal life is at stake.) A right to privacy in the sense of keeping certain private information from the government is in the same category.[25] We would not regard a society as just (or maybe as even a society) if it provided no protection against private violence; but that right, according to the Supreme Court, is not in the Constitution at all.[26] There are many other possibilities. And, of course, there is the problem that the text of the Bill of Rights itself applies only to the federal government, not the states.

Finally, not all of the rights enumerated in the Bill of Rights are fundamental in the sense that no civilized society would deny them. The states may dispense with grand jury indictments and civil juries, and that is not a violation of fundamental human rights. There are just societies in the world that do not observe the privilege against self-incrimination or some of the aspects of an adversary criminal justice system prescribed in the Sixth Amendment. There are also just and tolerant societies with established churches.

It might be argued that conditions peculiar to our society make, say, established churches and nonadversary criminal proce-

---

[24] Three provisions of the Bill of Rights arguably protect this right: the Fourth Amendment's prohibition against unreasonable searches and seizures "of persons, houses, papers, and effects"; the Due Process Clause of the Fifth Amendment; and the Cruel and Unusual Punishment Clause of the Eighth Amendment.

The Fourth Amendment, however, seems to refer simply to detention, not to battery. That is the ordinary meaning of "seizure," and the parallelism suggests that the Amendment applies only to actions of a kind that could also be taken against houses, papers, and effects—none of which can be subject to a battery. The most obvious meaning of "liberty" in the Due Process Clause is again freedom from physical restraint, especially since that Clause contemplates that "liberty" can be taken away if due process is provided, and no process justifies police brutality. The narrow definition currently given to "punishment" in the Cruel and Unusual Punishment Clause, see, for example, *Bell v Wolfish*, 441 US 520, 537-39 (1979), would exclude many acts of police brutality.

Of course, any of these provisions can be interpreted to prohibit police brutality without stretching their language beyond recognition. But if that is the test—whether the language would be stretched beyond recognition—then there are few rights that anyone would advocate that cannot be fit within some provision of the Bill of Rights.

[25] Everyone would agree, I believe, that no reasonably just society would permit the government unlimited power to monitor its citizens' private conversations. In *Katz v United States*, 389 US 347 (1967), the Court found this right in the Fourth Amendment. But as Justice Black's dissent showed, this outcome is not by any means obvious from the language of that Amendment. See id at 364-74 (Black dissenting). See also *Whalen v Roe*, 429 US 589 (1977); and *Roberts v United States Jaycees*, 468 US 609 (1984).

[26] *DeShaney v Winnebago County Department of Social Services*, 489 US 189 (1989).

dures unacceptable here, even if they might be benign elsewhere. But even if this argument is accepted, the fundamental rights conception of the Bill of Rights has powerful implications: it suggests that certain provisions are to be interpreted less generously than others.

It seems entirely plausible, for example, that religious establishments in this country (unlike, I suppose, the current Church of England) would seriously violate religious freedom. Even so, under this conception of the Bill of Rights, the Establishment Clause need not be interpreted with the same sympathy and scope as the Free Exercise Clause. The Free Exercise Clause secures a fundamental human right and should be interpreted generously. In contrast, the Establishment Clause (according to this view) should be interpreted narrowly, to forbid only those forms of government recognition of religion that really do endanger religious liberty. There might be structural justifications for giving a more sweeping reading to the Establishment Clause. For example, the Court at one time suggested that the special danger posed by religiously divisive political controversies was a reason for restricting the power of the government to aid religion.[27] And there might be formalist justifications as well, for example if one thought (again plausibly) that there are common forms of government aid to religion that in fact violate religious liberty but are not widely perceived that way.[28] But to the extent that one adopts the fundamental rights conception, one cannot simply say that the Establishment Clause (or the Self-Incrimination Clause, or the Contracts Clause) is as much a part of the Constitution as the Free Exercise Clause (or the Cruel and Unusual Punishment Clause, or the Free Speech Clause) and should be interpreted as generously.

B.

The fundamental rights conception, unlike the structural conception, does not presuppose judicial supremacy. Even a society without judicial review could profitably adopt a bill of rights: it would be used in political controversies as a means of persuading the legislature. As I said before, there are many examples of human rights charters adopted without a system of judicial review, ranging from the English Magna Carta, Petition of Right, and Bill

---

[27] This was the notion of "political entanglement." See Michael W. McConnell, *Religious Freedom at a Crossroads*, in this volume, 115, for criticism of this notion.

[28] See, for example, Mary E. Becker, *The Politics of Women's Wrongs and the Bill of "Rights": A Bicentennial Perspective*, in this volume, 453.

of Rights, to the constitutions of some colonies and states, to international declarations of human rights today.

The fundamental rights conception does have one important, and superficially controversial, presupposition: it presupposes some form of moral objectivity. That is, it presupposes that in a wide range of cases, there are right and wrong answers to moral questions. Otherwise it would not be possible to say that certain rights are fundamental, and that all societies should protect them.

The presupposition of moral objectivity is important not so much because it is doubtful as because many lawyers reflexively resist it. In fact, the opposite position—that two contradictory moral judgments might each be right—is difficult to make sense of, much less to justify. Some form of moral objectivism is almost surely correct. But the notion that judges who rely on moral arguments are "imposing their own values" is a familiar one. This notion does reflect a legitimate concern about institutional competence. That is the real concern with the fundamental rights conception, not the very dubious view that there is in principle no right or wrong in moral matters.

If it is to be implemented, the fundamental rights conception of the Bill of Rights must defend certain presuppositions about institutional competence. For example, even if moral judgments are, in principle right or wrong, it does not follow that judges are more likely to get them right if they make up their own minds than if they defer to a popularly elected body.

In fact, the questions of institutional competence raised by this conception are very difficult. There are serious problems with leaving the difficult moral questions raised by a bill of rights to *any* of the institutions that might possibly decide them. Courts can be arbitrary and willful, and have various kinds of class biases; legislatures are subject to popular passion, prejudice, and misjudgment, as well as the dysfunctions identified by public choice theory; and individuals are self-interested and sometimes irrational.[29] Undoubtedly different institutions are best suited to determine the scope of different rights, but in any event some difficult judgments about institutional competence must be made before the human rights conception can be implemented.

---

[29] Two examples of positions that leave difficult moral judgments about fundamental rights to individuals are the "pro-choice" position in abortion and the view that private charity should be responsible for all redistributions of wealth.

C.

The characteristic modes of argument of the fundamental rights conception follow from these presuppositions. The principal argument will be, at bottom, about whether a particular government practice is morally right or wrong. Interestingly, the rhetoric usually avoids explicit moral language; it never uses the term "moral" and often shies away from words like "unjust." Instead the rhetoric uses the terms of the Constitution—freedom of religion, freedom of speech, and so on—or, if necessary, technical-sounding terms like "unreasonable burden" and similar "balancing" language.

It might be objected that of course the courts and advocates use the terms of the Constitution; that is what they are supposed to be interpreting. But according to the fundamental rights conception, the correct way to interpret the terms of the Constitution is to recognize that it protects fundamental human rights. This conception is supported by existing practices: as I suggested earlier, in practice, in a wide range of difficult constitutional cases, it is generally accepted that the best legal argument is often an argument about fairness or decency—that is, a moral argument. In fact, the reluctance to use overtly moral language reflects the reflexive subjectivism I criticized, as well as a legitimate concern—related to the formalist conception—that a decision justified in terms of the text will be more readily accepted than one justified in explicitly moral language.

The other mode of argument under the fundamental rights conception ought to be institutional competence. Sometimes the institutional questions are settled by precedent or some comparable source, just as questions about the content of rights can be settled by such sources. In most systems there is no point in arguing about whether the courts or the legislature should decide whether a particular measure abridges religious freedom; that question was settled long ago, by deliberate act or, more likely, by culture. But often questions about institutional competence will be central—for example, in deciding the extent to which the courts will oversee police practices; or the way courts will attempt to control government actions that are impermissibly motivated; or the appropriateness of so-called "affirmative" rights to government aid (such as subsistence, or the right to be free from private violence). Even under the fundamental rights conception, it is a non sequitur to say that because it is morally wrong for the government to act in a certain way, the courts should prohibit it from doing so.

IV. CONCLUSION: FIVE FALLACIES IN INTERPRETING THE BILL OF
RIGHTS

I have suggested that there is no single, obviously correct conception of the role of a bill of rights. Instead, our history and current controversies reflect three competing conceptions, each with different presuppositions and modes of argument, and of course with different implications for how the Bill of Rights should be interpreted.

As I said at the outset, one need not choose one of these conceptions; they can be coherently combined in various ways. What is important is not to invoke arguments without justifying the conception from which those arguments are derived. As a conclusion, I will suggest five common fallacies that, I believe, result from this error: using arguments from a conception that has not yet been justified.

A. Where Is It in the Text?

Many of those who make this argument think that the lack of explicit textual support is an unanswerable criticism. Some of those against whom it is made think it is not a criticism at all, because the text is (for various reasons) indeterminate. Others resort to the view that the text is only one among many factors to consider, a view that gives the impression of being irresolute and unsatisfactory.[30]

In fact, this argument can be a legitimate one only if some antecedent conception is justified. For example, this argument would be sound if the formalist conception—that the Bill of Rights is a code—were shown to be the only correct conception. If you can demonstrate that the Bill of Rights (or any comparable charter) should, at this time and place, be used only as a code, then you are entitled to demand a textual source for any right. One might arrive at the same place through a structural argument, for example by showing that allowing judges to go beyond the explicit text creates too much of a danger that they will abuse their power. But that will be a difficult argument to make; it will require empirical and

---

[30] It might also be said that in any debate about the interpretation of the Bill of Rights, what is "in the text" is precisely the point in dispute. In a sense, that is correct: any argument about the Bill of Rights is a claim about how the text of the Bill of Rights should be interpreted. The argument I refer to here is the claim that rights not *explicitly* guaranteed in the text should not be recognized. If the notion that some guarantees are "explicit" is meaningless (I do not believe that it is), see Dworkin, in this volume, 381 (cited in note 23) then this argument is all the more fallacious.

normative premises and a way of addressing the obvious indeterminacy of the Bill of Rights.

The most prominent example of this argument today, of course, is the one made against *Roe v Wade*.[31] From one angle this argument is very puzzling, because it is not that difficult to come up with a plausible textual source for the right involved in *Roe*. More important, the issue of the moral status of fetal life is much more serious, presents a much more difficult question for the proponents of *Roe* to answer, and better reflects what the opponents of *Roe* are (I suspect) really concerned about. The reason much of the debate over abortion has been about the existence vel non of the right, I believe, is because the formalist view took such a strong hold during the Warren Court period. A structural or fundamental rights view would present the abortion issue in a much more useful way.

B. All Constitutional Provisions Are Equal

Justice Frankfurter and others made this argument in response to Justice Black's view, essentially adopted by the Court, that First Amendment rights occupy a "preferred position" that justifies more active judicial review (compared to property rights, for example). The argument is made today by what may be an emerging movement in favor of reviving constitutional protections for property. (It is not obvious how to measure which rights receive "more" protection; but for present purposes I assume that it can be done.) Why is it, proponents of this view ask, that the Just Compensation Clause (or the Contracts Clause) is interpreted so grudgingly, while the Free Speech Clause is interpreted so generously?

Ironically, in view of its use against Justice Black, the argument that all constitutional provisions are equal derives from the formalist view of the Bill of Rights as a code. For example, if you are trying to reform entrenched aspects of state criminal justice systems, you do not want to say that the Confrontation Clause can be interpreted flexibly to accommodate the interest in protecting victims of child abuse from cross-examination, but the Self-Incrimination Clause *cannot* be interpreted flexibly to accommodate the interest in obtaining confessions.

But unless you have sufficient reasons for using the Bill of Rights as a code, or can justify some other conception of the Bill of

---

[31] 410 US 113 (1973).

Rights that dictates that all provisions are "equal" in some sense, this argument is a non sequitur. Under the structural view, there is no reason to treat all provisions alike. Some provisions identify areas where the courts are superior to legislatures; others do not. Similarly, under the fundamental rights conception not all provisions should be interpreted with the same degree of generosity. As I have argued, some provisions of the Bill of Rights protect rights that are fundamental in any society; others do not. The notion that all constitutional provisions are equal sounds very appealing but is actually quite difficult to justify.

C.   The Judicial Nirvana Fallacy

This is the view that either ignores institutional competence arguments or uses them selectively, in a way that overstates the capacity of courts. It takes two forms. The first adopts the fundamental rights conception without recognizing its institutional presuppositions. You cannot justify active judicial enforcement of the Bill of Rights just by showing that there are moral rights and wrongs and that provisions of the Bill of Rights can plausibly be interpreted to constitutionalize various moral judgments. One must also explain why it is better on balance for the courts to make the necessary judgments.

The other form of the fallacy identifies defects in the legislative process as a basis for more active judicial review. The problem here is a one-sided application of the structural conception, which requires a *comparative* judgment of institutional competence. Even if legislatures do certain things badly, there is no guarantee that courts will do them better. Any argument for more active judicial review—for example, the public choice-based argument for more vigorous judicial enforcement of property rights—must address the competence of courts as well as legislatures.[32]

D.   The Fallacy of Misappropriated Moral Force

This fallacy takes advantage of the fact that many provisions of the Bill of Rights secure fundamental human rights to support an argument that is actually based on a different conception. It is the opposite of guilt by association: a provision of the Bill of Rights is treated as protecting a valuable right because other provisions, or other applications of that provision, protect valuable rights. There are several possible examples.

---

[32] See Elhauge, 101 Yale L J 31 (cited in note 19).

Consider, first, one common treatment of the Self-Incrimination Clause, which celebrates it as a foundation of liberty. It may be desirable, all things considered, to forbid compelled self-incrimination. But there are just societies, and decent systems of criminal justice, in which defendants are required to give testimony (under, of course, carefully controlled conditions).

Many of those who celebrate the Self-Incrimination Clause do so not because it is a fundamental human right but because they want to enforce it for other reasons. For example, the Warren Court's decision in *Miranda v Arizona*[33] can be seen as using the Self-Incrimination Clause in a formalistic, code-like way, to try to control abusive practices in police interrogation. Historically custodial interrogation had been analyzed under the Due Process Clause. That approach focused attention on the abusiveness of the interrogation and, to some degree, on the likelihood that the interrogation could have produced a false confession. *Miranda* shifted the focus to whether the suspect had been "compelled . . . to be a witness against himself," an approach that produces a different emphasis. The text did not compel this treatment of custodial interrogation, but the *Miranda* Court evidently believed that it was needed to combat unacceptable police practices.[34] It helps, in using the Clause in this way, to take advantage of the fact that other provisions of the Bill of Rights—and for that matter, certain applications of the Self-Incrimination Clause—do protect against violations of human rights. But doing so gives the Clause an aura of moral significance that it does not fully deserve.

Another example of an argument that misappropriates moral force involves the Just Compensation Clause. Some protection for private property is surely a fundamental human right: a government with unlimited power to take property from its citizens would be tyrannical. As I outlined earlier, however, some arguments for protecting property rights, based on public choice theories, would go far beyond the level needed to secure fundamental human rights. Those structural arguments invoke the Just Compensation Clause and the idea of property rights as a bulwark against tyranny, thus trying to take advantage of the moral force of those notions. In fact, however, the expanded public choice conception of property rights must be justified in structural terms. It is an illegitimate appropriation of moral force for the public choice

---

[33] 384 US 436 (1966).

[34] For a discussion of these points, see Stephen J. Schulhofer, *Reconsidering* Miranda, 54 U Chi L Rev 435 (1987).

conception of property rights to take advantage of the morally powerful connotations of the idea that every decent state guarantees some right of property.

E. Unreflective Moral Subjectivism

I addressed this fallacy in discussing the fundamental rights conception of the Bill of Rights. This fallacy consists of denying the authority of courts ever to consider moral issues, instead of discussing whether courts are institutionally competent to do so. The fallacy is reflected in the common claim that when courts invoke the fundamental rights conception—when they go "beyond the plain language," or, in some versions, when they go beyond structural justifications for judicial review—they are necessarily just "imposing their own values."

The fallacy lies in assuming that it is impossible to reason about moral judgments and to arrive at answers that are right or wrong. As I said earlier, moral subjectivism is in fact difficult to defend. Indeed, few of those who make the "judges' own values" argument are really moral subjectivists. They would not say, for example, that it is meaningless to make moral arguments to legislators or administrators, or that when parents or teachers or public figures purport to make moral arguments to children they are just "imposing their own values" instead of making claims that we can decide are right or wrong by reasoning about them.

The "judges' own values" argument does reflect a real concern, but one that raises complex and difficult issues. Plausibly stated, the argument can take one or more of four forms: (1) judges are more likely to decide a certain category of moral issues wrongly than legislatures are; (2) whether or not judges are more likely to make the wrong decision, the decisions will be wrong in a worse way (for example, the judges' errors will reflect some form of class bias, while legislatures' errors will be more randomly distributed); (3) although judges' decisions may be right, they will have adverse effects because society has not exercised its own capacities to decide;[35] or (4) even if judges' decisions are more likely to be right, democractic decisionmaking has instrinsic moral value that outweighs the risk of error. Each of these claims is plausible; each is surely right sometimes; but each must be justified. The simple,

---

[35] For example, the decision may be less likely to take hold than one arrived at through democratic means, or the society's capacities to decide certain kinds of issues may atrophy because it relies too much on judges to decide them.

rhetorically effective invocation of the danger of the "judge's own values" is not an adequate way to deal with these issues.

The Bill of Rights is a powerful symbol in our society, and the idea of a bill of rights is an increasingly powerful symbol in the world. But symbols, of course, do not interpret themselves, and the Bill of Rights will not be anything in particular until we decide what to make of it. In our history, and in current controversies, the Bill of Rights has been at least three different things. We should not underestimate the difficulty of deciding what we want it to be in the future.

INDEX